AN ARID EDEN

AN ARID EDEN

A Personal Account of Conservation in the Kaokoveld

Garth Owen-Smith

Jonathan Ball Publishers
Johannesburg & Cape Town

To improve the future we must first understand the present,
and to really understand the present we must know the past.

Published in trade paperback in 2010 by
JONATHAN BALL PUBLISHERS (PTY) LTD
PO Box 33977
Jeppestown
2043

ISBN 978-1-86842-363-7

Edited by Frances Perryer
Cover design by MR Design, Cape Town
Text design by Triple M Design, Johannesburg
Set in 10.5/14 pt Minion Pro
Printed and bound by Imago Printers

CONTENTS

This book is dedicated to Tuareg and Kyle,
who paid the price for their father's obsession.
And to the people of the Kaokoveld,
who showed that Africans do care about wildlife,
and led the way for one of the continent's most successful
conservation programmes.

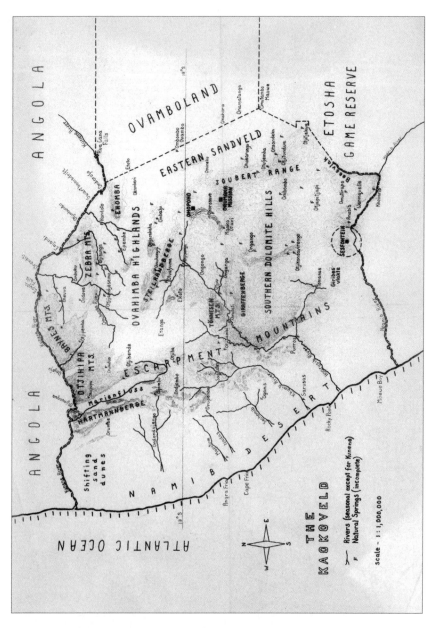

A hand-drawn map of the Kaokoveld territory as it was in the 1960s before the Odendaal Commission's 'homelands' policy was implemented.

PREFACE

Until the late twentieth century the Kaokoveld was one of the least known parts of Southern Africa. Isolated by the Skeleton Coast, rugged mountain ranges, and a strictly enforced entry permit system, it was romanticised as a place where wildlife abounded and the local tribes were still unaffected by the modern world. Although this was mostly true before 1970, since then the region's residents and its natural resources have undergone dramatic changes, which resulted in the collapse of the pastoral economy and almost led to the extermination of its big game.

As one of the few people left that knew the Kaokoveld before and after the disastrous events of the 1970s and early 1980s, and having also been involved in the efforts to stop the poaching, I felt a responsibility to record what happened and why – especially in the forgotten years before Namibia's independence. This is, therefore, my personal account of an African conservation success story, and a tribute to the men and women, black and white, who in a big or small way contributed to it.

I have mostly used my own experiences, as a participant or bystander, supplemented by reports written at the time, magazine articles and press cuttings. But they alone cannot tell the whole story, and inevitably there will be omissions and different perspectives on what is recorded here. A major short-coming is my coverage of the southern Kaokoveld, which is because I did not work there in the 1960s and was only marginally involved in this part of the region from 1982 to date. To those who feel that their roles are not adequately represented I offer my apologies, and hope that they will one day write their accounts of the events not in these pages, thereby making the record more complete.

History can be boring if it consists only of what happened, when and where. To make the book more interesting and useful I have also discussed *how* things were done, and given my interpretation of *why* they happened. To really understand what took place in the Kaokoveld it is necessary to know the political context that we worked in. For this reason chapters on my life away from the region between 1971 and 1981 have been included. Apart from giving continuity to the story, and a background to how nature conservation was then practised, they touch on the two defining features of this period in Southern African history: racial discrimination and the liberation struggles it spawned.

A second reason for writing the book is to document what I have learnt over 40 years about the region's wildlife and people, as well as the management of its rangelands. It has been written in layman's terms so that non-academics will be able to understand how the Kaokoveld ecosystem functioned before and after the introduction of European ways of managing livestock. To this end, chapter 11 includes a brief 'lecture' on ecology that will help those who did not study this vital subject at school or university.

Thirdly, although the book is not about Namibia's world-renowned com-munity-based natural resource management programme, which is still evolv-ing and now includes many different players, it *is* about the foundation laid that enabled it to take place. However, the last three chapters on the post-independence period do briefly cover how the rights and responsibilities over wildlife were devolved to local communities, the programme's achievements, as well as the opportunities and challenges it still faces.

Lastly, it is the story of an exciting and fulfilling life, and of the people I have had the privilege of knowing or working with. Some of them are excep-tional men and women in their own right whose stories should, but prob-ably never will be told. Changing the way conservation was being practised was not easy and there were many people who did not agree with the new approach. But right and wrong are just points of view and each one of us is a product of our times, our life experiences and the people we learned from. I was lucky to have had great mentors – my parents, who taught their children to treat everyone with respect no matter what their colour or creed, Dougie Horton, Hugh Goyns, Neil Alcock, Nolly Zaloumis and Allan Savory.

I started writing this book over 20 years ago, when my early life in the Kaokoveld was still fresh in my memory. At that time we were going through a difficult period, and I felt that the area and our work needed publicity. Although I was not able to find a publisher, whenever there were a few free days I wrote a little more – at an average of one chapter a year until it is now finally time to stop. But the story is ongoing, and the next chapters must be written by the new generation of role players.

A problem with writing about the past in Africa is that the names of places, and even of some countries, have since changed. A good example is the Kaokoveld itself, which was derived from the Herero name for the very mountainous north-west of Namibia, *oKaoko*, with the *Dorsland* Trekkers who passed through it in the late nineteenth century adding the geographic term *veld*. In 1970 the region was divided into the ethnic homelands of Kaokoland and Damaraland by the South African government, and it is now the western part of independent Namibia's Kunene Region. In this book I have used the names that places were known by at the time being written about.

Although all the events covered in this book are real, it is not an academic study. However, a considerable amount of information has been obtained from the printed works of other people, and for those who want to know more about the region there is a bibliography of books and articles in journals and magazines that they may find interesting.

I owe a special debt of gratitude to Chris Brown, Brian Jones and Chris Weaver, and our Zimbabwean colleagues, Brian Child and Ivan Bond (who died tragically in early 2010), all of whom also recognised the discriminatory way that nature conservation was being practised and played major roles in implementing community-based natural resource management in Southern Africa. But most of all to my partner in life and work over the last 26 years, Margie Jacobsohn: together we achieved quite a lot, much of which I did not believe was possible before we first met. Lastly, to past and present members of the IRDNC team – our extended family – who turned theory into reality.

I would also like to thank Jeremy Boraine for agreeing to publish this book, and Francine Blum and Kevin Shenton for making it happen. But especially Frances Perryer for her patient and good-humoured editing of this part-time writer.

ABBREVIATIONS AND ACRONYMS

ACE	African Conservation Education Project
ADMADE	Administrative Management Design for Game Management Areas
AERSG	African Elephant and Rhino Specialist Group
ANC	African National Congress
BAD	Department of Bantu Administration and Development
BSAP	British South Africa Police
CAMPFIRE	Communal Areas Management Programme for Indigenous Resources
CAP	Church Agricultural Projects
CBNRM	community-based natural resource management
CDM	Consolidated Diamond Mines
CGG	community game guard
CHS	Conservancy Hunting Safaris
CITES	Convention on International Trade in Endangered Species
DAS	Desert Adventure Safaris
DED	German Development Service
DRFN	Desert Research Foundation of Namibia

DNC	Department of Nature Conservation
DRA	Damara Representative Authority
DTA	Democratic Turnhalle Alliance
EED	German Evangelical Development Services
EIA	environmental impact assessment
EWT	Endangered Wildlife Trust
FAPLA	armed wing of MPLA
FENATA	Federation of Namibian Tourism Associations
GPS	global positioning system
HACSIS	human–animal conflict self-insurance scheme
ICEIDA	Icelandic International Development Agency
IRDNC	Integrated Rural Development and Nature Conservation
IUCN	International Union for Conservation of Nature
KfW	German Development Bank
KCS	Kunene Conservancy Safaris
LAC	Legal Assistance Centre
LIFE	Living in a Finite Environment
LIRDP	Luangwa Integrated Resource Development Project
MCA	Millennium Challenge Account
MET	Ministry of Environment and Tourism
MOU	memorandum of understanding
MWCT	Ministry of Wildlife, Conservation and Tourism
NACOBTA	Namibian Community-Based Tourism Association
NACSO	Namibian Association of CBNRM Support Organisations
NDT	Namibia Development Trust
NGO	Non-governmental organisation
NNDF	Nyae Nyae Development Foundation
NORAD	Norwegian Overseas Agency for Development
NPB	Natal Parks Board
NWT	Namibia Wildlife Trust
PTES	People's Trust for Endangered Species
PTO	permission to occupy
PV	protected village
RDCs	Rural District Councils
RISE	Rural Institute for Social Empowerment
RPG	rocket-propelled grenade
SADF	South African Defence Force
SAVE	Foundation to Save African Endangered Wildlife

SDG	short-duration grazing
SPAN	Strengthening the Protected Area Network Project
SRT	Save the Rhino Trust
SWAPO	South West Africa People's Organisation
TED	Technology, Entertainment and Design
TFCA	transfrontier conservation areas
TTL	Tribal Trust Land
UNTAG	UN Transitional Assistance Group
WESSA	Wildlife and Environment Society of Southern Africa
WSN	Wilderness Safaris Namibia
WWF	World Wide Fund for Nature
ZANLA	Zimbabwe African National Liberation Army
ZIPRA	Zimbabwe People's Revolutionary Army

CHAPTER ONE

BASALT MOUNTAINS

In north-west Namibia there is a region of red basalt ranges. It is a land-scape of rock: sheer cliff faces, endless scree slopes and stone-choked valleys. Westward, towards the cold Atlantic coast, the mountains flatten out and are separated by broad gravel plains, littered with the debris of ancient lava flows.

It is a place where rain seldom falls, and in most years the earth's hard sur-face lies barren and exposed to the baking sun and searing desert winds. The region is stark and hostile, but in the early morning and late afternoon light, when the basalt rocks turn to the colour of rust, and the distant mountains to soft shades of purple and blue, it can also be breathtakingly beautiful.

In spite of its aridity the basalt region supports a remarkable variety of hardy, drought-resistant plants. The stony pediments and less precipitous slopes are dotted with swollen-stemmed succulents, stunted trees and dwarf shrubs that in lean years wither to desiccated tufts of brittle, apparently life-less twigs. Many of the species here are endemic, occurring only in the deserts of Namibia and south-western Angola. Amongst them is one of the world's botanical wonders: *Welwitschia mirabilis*, a prehistoric cone-bearing plant consisting of just two giant, tentacle-like leaves growing from a gnarled and contorted woody stump.

Eastward, where the rainfall is slightly higher, the basalt ranges rise to over 1 500 metres above sea level. Here mopane bushes dominate the valleys, growing taller along the banks of rocky channels that drain the hill slopes. Although they flow only after heavy storms, these watercourses converge into dry riverbeds that traverse the gravel plains, creating arteries of life-supporting vegetation deep into the Namib desert. In a few places where the underground water-table is close to the surface there are also groves of graceful euclea trees and leathery-leafed salvadora bushes that provide shady refuges from the tropical sun.

When heavy rain does fall, the basalt region undergoes a dramatic transformation. From the shallow soil between the stones long-dormant seeds of annual grasses and forbs germinate and within weeks paint the valleys emerald green, in striking contrast to the red-brown scree on the hill slopes. The brief availability of moisture in the soil also enables the woody plants to produce new leaves and blossom. And with this abundance of fresh growth, insect populations explode, rodents and seed-eating birds multiply exponentially, and all the desert animals grow fat on the bounty of a benevolent season.

But the feast soon ends. Within months the green carpet of grass is bleached to pale yellow by the sun and dehydrating winds that in winter sweep down from the interior plateau. As the land dries out once more the ephemeral plants and insects die, but not before producing countless seeds and eggs to ensure that new generations of each species will appear when thunderstorms once more roll across the desert.

In spite of the very arid climate the basalt ranges are well endowed with small springs that provide drinking water for a remarkable array of large mammals. And because the volcanic soils are exceptionally fertile the grass that grows in the good seasons is cured into standing hay, thus retaining its nutrient value in subsequent years when little or no effective rain falls. This carry-over of high-quality grazing is crucial to Hartmann's mountain zebra, the only exclusive grazer permanently inhabiting the region, and together with its ability to migrate large distances and climb the steepest slopes, enables it to survive the frequent droughts.

Like zebra, gemsbok and springbok also congregate in large numbers to feed on the green grass that grows wherever heavy showers have occurred. However, when it dries out both species can switch to browsing the leaves of the desert shrubs, which combined with their low drinking requirements allows them to penetrate deeper and remain longer in the true Namib, one of the driest habitats on earth.

Because they are exclusively browsers, kudu and giraffe prefer the more wooded areas further inland, but after good rains in the pre-Namib – the belt of plains and rocky ranges along the edge of the desert – kudu move westwards to exploit the flush of new growth there. Giraffe also follow the larger watercourses that traverse the basalt region far into the desert, and small groups may be seen striding sedately across the virtually barren gravel plains between them.

The herbivores that occur here in turn support a full spectrum of large predators, with prides of lions hunting the hills and riverbeds, cheetah coursing their prey on the gravel flats and leopard stalking the rocky gullies and more rugged mountain slopes. Packs of spotted hyena clean up behind the big cats, but also run down their own prey when the opportunity arises, while jackals are ubiquitous. Man has long been a predator here too – in the past as a hunter-gatherer killing game for animal protein and fat, but in more recent times with a commercial incentive as well.

Most remarkably, elephants also inhabit the basalt ranges, finding sufficient sustenance in the bark and leaves of the sparse desert trees and shrubs to maintain themselves. On their wanderings in search of food and water the pachyderms have worn a network of paths through the region, some of which go over the highest mountain passes. During the cool dry season a few herds also move down the larger riverbeds deep into the desert, quenching their thirst at remote springs whose whereabouts has been passed down through the generations.

In the 1960s the north-west contained Namibia's biggest population of black rhino, but in little more than a decade the sky-rocketing black market price for their horns brought the species to the brink of extinction here and throughout most of Africa.

* * *

My story will start here, in the heart of the basalt ranges, one afternoon in March 1983. It was a dry year and although the wet season was nearing its end only a few light showers had so far fallen. Earlier in the day some promising cumulus clouds made a foray over the mountains, but they were soon driven back by a stiff breeze from the west and were now lying low on the eastern horizon. Before the wind picked up the day had been very hot: over 40 degrees in the shade and much higher in the sun. At such times life seemed suspended. Nothing moved and the only sound was the faint ringing in one's ears.

By four o'clock the west wind that routed the clouds had tempered the quivering midday heat, and as the air cooled the stony desert came back to life. Along the watercourses tree leaves fluttered and the occasional call of a bird punctuated the silence. On an open hillside a small group of springbok that had been resting in the sun stood up, stretched and started walking to where they knew the sparse grazing was better.

As the springbok fanned out and moved slowly down the slope they passed close to a black rhino cow quietly feeding on the long rubbery stems of a euphorbia bush. Standing by her side was a three-month-old calf – a small, hornless replica of its ponderous, prehistoric-looking mother. Hearing the faint shuffle of the springbok hooves on the hard ground, the cow swung round to face them, her large round ears unerringly picking up the direction of every dislodged pebble. A few of the nearer springbok skittered nervously away, well aware that black rhino have a low tolerance for anything coming too close to them. When the springbok moved on the cow stared belligerently after them for some time before turning back to chew on the succulent euphorbia stems. As she ate the calf lay down on the ground next to her and went to sleep.

On a ridge overlooking the valley two men squatted on the ground, talking low-voiced to one another. For most of the day they had been following the tracks of the cow and calf – no easy task over the rocky terrain. Now for the first time they could see them. Before going any closer, however, they carefully discussed the situation. The wind was in their favour, but although rhino have very poor eyesight their hearing is exceptionally acute. Carefully they made their way down the slope, getting to within 50 metres before one of them raised the .303 rifle he was carrying, aimed just behind her shoulder and squeezed the trigger.

Shocked by the impact of the bullet the cow squealed in fear and rage, spraying crimson foam over the euphorbia's branches and onto the stony ground. Now terrified by the smell of her own blood she charged across the rocks into another euphorbia, and with a mighty swing of her massive head demolished half of it before lurching on, seeking something else on which to vent her fury. But the bullet had shredded a lung and punctured her heart, and with the blood pressure to her brain dropping she staggered on for only a few more steps before collapsing. Woken by the cow's squeals and headlong flight, the calf had scrambled to its feet and run after her, stopping next to her lifeless body and looking around in bewilderment for the source of the danger.

Once they were certain that the cow was dead the two men walked towards her. When they were about 30 metres away the calf could make out their strange upright shapes, and instinctively knowing that they were dangerous it charged at them. In a reflex action one of the men picked up a stone and threw it at their diminutive attacker, hitting the calf on the nose and stopping it in its tracks. A second stone struck it on the shoulder. Although its instinct was to stay with its mother, confused by her not moving and overcome by fear the calf ran away.

'Why did you not shoot it?' the unarmed man asked.

'It was better not to risk the sound of another shot. The people from nature conservation sometimes come into this area now. We also don't have bullets to waste on a rhino that has no horns to sell. Let the hyenas kill it.'

The two men went quickly to work, propping the cow's head up on a stone and hacking her horns off with a machete. They took nothing else, but before leaving they cut branches from nearby bushes and covered the carcass. When they were satisfied that it would not easily be seen, even from the air, they picked up the horns and left.

The men had reason to be very pleased with their day's work. This was not the first rhino they had killed, and for reasons they did not understand or care about, the man they sold the horns to would take as many as they could supply. For something so useless he also paid them well enough – R200 for an average-sized pair and R300 if they were very large. It was more than a month's wages if you worked for the government, and a labourer would have to work even longer to earn that much on one of the white farms. If you did not talk too much about what you were doing in the bush, hunting rhino was a good way of getting money to buy cattle to replace the ones that died in the drought, buy school uniforms for your children or clothes for your wife.

While the men hurried back to their camp the rhino calf wandered aimlessly across the rocky landscape. Nearby a jackal yapped and then howled mournfully. In the distance another answered. By now the sun was hovering low over the horizon, and as its last rays lit up the mountain slopes they turned the basalt rocks to the colour of blood.

CHAPTER TWO

DUST AND STONES

Although March is one of the hottest months in Damaraland the nights are usually quite cool, and in the early hours of the morning I found a blanket insufficient and crawled into my sleeping bag. Now warm, but not exactly comfortable on the rocky ground, I lay on my back looking up at the brilliant display of pre-dawn stars and contemplated the day ahead.

It would probably not be very different to yesterday, or the day before – or many others my companion, Karl-Peter Erb, and I had spent recently. We had come here to carry out anti-poaching patrols on the farms purchased by the South African government in the 1960s to create a homeland for the Damara people. It was basalt country. Horizon-to-horizon rocks. Loose, treacherous, ankle-twisting rocks that made sure we walked with our eyes glued to the ground and paid little attention to the stark desert scenery around us. Regular foot-patrols here meant that you wore out a pair of veldskoen in less than six months.

Peter and I worked for the Namibia Wildlife Trust (NWT), a non-governmental organisation set up in 1982 to help the nature conservation authorities bring poaching in the country's north-west under control. Previously this rugged mountainous region was known as the Kaokoveld, and was part of the largest conservation area in the world: Game Reserve No 2, proclaimed in 1907 by the German colonial government. But on the recommendation of the Odendaal Commission it was de-proclaimed in 1970, and together with over 200 previously white-owned farms had been divided into Kaokoland and Damaraland, tribal 'homelands' where the Damara and Herero-speaking residents could 'exercise their right of self-determination'.

Prior to its de-proclamation the region had been inhabited by large populations of elephant and black rhino, as well as an exceptional variety of other big game animals, but little of this magnificent national heritage still survived. Elephant now numbered just a few hundred, while all other species had been decimated by the dual effects of illegal hunting and a devastating drought that ended the year before. Our greatest concern was for the black rhino. From the information we had so far gathered it was clear that the basalt ranges of western Damaraland contained the last viable population in Namibia, outside of the Etosha National Park – and that their numbers could be as low as 40! It did not require a crystal ball to see that time was running out for them, and for most of the Kaokoveld's other wildlife.

Between the government and the NWT we were only able to put a total of eight men into the field, with just three four-wheel-drive vehicles, to cover an area of over 20 000 km² in which rhino were still known to occur. And as most of the region had no roads, if we hoped to have any impact on the situation, getting out on foot was the only way. But just reaching the place to start a patrol could mean a hard day's driving – sometimes two – from our respective bases at Khorixas and Wêreldsend.

Although the commercial trade in ivory and rhino horn was being controlled by outsiders, we suspected that most of the poaching was now being done by the local people – men who were skilled in bush craft and knew the country we patrolled much better than we did. Moreover, after a hunting excursion they could return to their villages, and become just another one of the friendly cattle herders we regularly passed on the side of the road. Both literally and figuratively, it was not a level playing field.

Nevertheless, we had achieved some success. While doing an aerial game survey Slang Viljoen, an elephant researcher, and Colin Britz, a field officer with a diamond mining company carrying out exploration in the area, had seen a number of elephant and rhino carcasses on the eastern edge of the basalts. They reported them to the Senior Nature Conservator, Chris Eyre, who followed up on the ground. After a long investigation, Chris had finally arrested six Herero men who were now awaiting trial. A few months before, Chris had also been able to convict a local resident for being in possession of six elephant tusks.

The previous October, Peter Erb and I had come across the carcass of a two-year-old rhino calf in the basalt ranges, about 30 km from our base camp. A male lion had been feeding on it and there was plenty of hyena spoor around, but I was sure that it was too big to have been killed by either the lion or hyenas – unless it had already been injured. Suspecting that it might have been wounded by poachers, we had thoroughly searched the surrounding area, and about two weeks later Peter had found the fairly fresh remains of an adult rhino cow near a small spring about 10 km away. The skull was missing and the carcass covered with brushwood. A blood trail was still visible leading to the place it had been shot, where we picked up two used cartridges. But that was all the evidence we had, and the case was abandoned. Over the following months Peter and I found four more rhino carcasses in the area, all of which had been poached, and another two that might have been.

To give us a better chance of catching the poachers I had worked out a pa-trolling system whereby we left our base camp late in the afternoon, reach-ing the area we planned to cover after dark. At first light the next morning we would walk in a wide circle looking for the tracks of humans or don-keys, returning about midday to where we had left our vehicle. After having something to eat and a rest, we would then drive to the next foot patrol starting point – again arriving after sunset. We concentrated on the basalt ranges because they still had the greatest number of rhino, and we knew that poachers were now operating there.

This was our third night out from our base at Wêreldsend, and from my bed on the rocky ground I noted that Venus, the bush alarm clock, was now well above the horizon and the sky in the east was gradually getting lighter. Nearby a chorus of jackals shattered the silence. It was time to get up.

Crouching next to the remains of our previous night's fire I scratched among the embers until I found a few that were still glowing. After placing a handful of dry twigs on them I went for a pee and then washed my face in a nearby spring. When I returned, grey smoke was billowing from the twigs, and with a gentle blow they burst into flame. A few larger pieces of wood brought the fire to a bright blaze. After balancing our bent and blackened kettle over it, I found a suitable rock to sit on and waited for the water to boil. A few minutes later Peter, who had been sleeping nearby, joined me. When we had made ourselves a cup of tea he asked which way I planned to patrol. North-west, I replied, onto Palm, one of the farms that had been purchased by the government to create Damaraland.

'That's pretty rough country,' Peter said softly, perhaps thinking about all the more pleasant places he could be at that moment. I knew he was not complaining, just mentally preparing himself for another hard day's walk-ing. He was, after all, only 21, and this was his first job after leaving school and a failed year at a university in South Africa. The NWT paid him the princely sum of R250 a month, and since starting work a little over a year before, he had spent much of his time doing foot patrols.

I didn't blame him for being less than enthusiastic about another day of scrambling over Damaraland's basalt rocks. There was very little to inspire one. Whole days had gone by without us seeing a single live animal, al-though carcasses were common enough. In fact, the basalt ranges were lit-tered with the bleached bones of game that had died in the drought or been poached – in most cases it was now impossible to tell which.

By the time we had drunk a second cup of tea, rolled up our sleeping bags and started walking, all but the brightest stars had faded, and the still unseen sun painted delicate highlights onto a band of fluffy clouds along the eastern horizon. The morning air was crisp but I knew that in a few hours the temperature would be heading towards 40 degrees in the shade, and where we were planning to patrol there would not be many shady places.

By nine o' clock we had covered about six kilometres. The sun was now well up and drops of perspiration were already starting to trickle down the sides of our faces. So far the largest animal we had seen was a hare that had dashed out from under a bush a couple of metres from our feet. It looked like it was going to be another day of sun, sweat and stones, with very little to show for our efforts.

We walked on in silence, each of us lost in our own thoughts, when sud-denly, less than 30 metres ahead of us, we saw a small rhino calf. Peter and I instantly came to the same conclusion: where there is a baby rhino there has to be a mother rhino nearby, and without saying a word we both rapidly put a safe distance between ourselves and the little pachyderm. When this had been accomplished we stopped to catch our breath and take a more circumspect look at the situation.

We had instinctively run to high ground, and because the vegetation around the calf was just scrubby bushes less than two metres high we could clearly see that there was no rhino cow around. However, the calf was not alone. Three jackals were trotting alongside it, and as we watched one of them latched onto its ear and tugged viciously. While the calf shook its head and squealed, a second jackal slipped in closer and started savagely tearing at its groin. Although they were unlikely to pull the calf down and kill it, it would only be a matter of time before a hyena heard the commotion and came to investigate.

After making sure that the calf's mother was definitely not in the area, Peter and I moved in closer. When we did so the jackals slunk off, their heads held low. About 50 metres from us they looked back peevishly. There was little doubt that the moment we left they would return to harass the little rhino again. However, as the calf was unaware of our presence we were able to follow as it wandered along, periodically making soft mewing sounds and then standing still as if listening.

Because it was only a few months old, and rhino cows always stay very close to their offspring, we were sure that its mother had to be dead. Its only hope was for us to get it back to our base camp. Once there we could radio nature conservation and they would have to decide what to do with it. But there was a small problem. The calf weighed about 100 kilograms, and Peter and I could not catch and carry it back to the Land Rover on our own. One of us had to walk back to our overnight campsite and then drive the 70 km to Wêreldsend and get help. Peter volunteered. I would stay close to the calf and keep the jackals at bay.

'When you reach camp put a radio call through to Chris Eyre,' I told Peter. 'Just tell him that we have a major problem and it involves a rhino. He should come immediately. If you can't get hold of Chris for any reason contact Rudi Loutit in the Skeleton Coast Park. Give him the same message.'

Without hesitation Peter set off. While we were talking the calf had moved some distance away, but was still visible standing under a small mopane. The jackals were nowhere to be seen, but I had no doubt that they were still in the vicinity. The prospect of rhino veal, even it was just the scraps they could steal from the hyenas, would ensure that they stayed around. When the calf lay down I cautiously approached to within about 60 metres, and as I did not expect Peter to return for at least six hours, I also found a little shade to sit in. Nearby one of the jackals howled. For them and me it was going to be a long hot day.

While the calf slept I thought about the future of the wildlife in this part of Namibia. Did we really have any hope of stopping the poaching? How could a handful of us effectively patrol so vast an area? Since the de-proclamation of Game Reserve No 2 the region had become a hunting ground for all and sundry: at best, we might still be able to save some of the more common species, but with black-market ivory and rhino horn prices so high, the Kaokoveld's desert-dwelling elephant and black rhino seemed doomed to extinction.

Until recently, conservation in the country's ethnic homelands had been administered directly from Pretoria. When I had discussed the poaching situation in the Kaokoveld with South West Africa's then Director of Nature Conservation, Bernabe de la Bat, he had told me there was nothing he could do about it. Without actually saying so, he hinted that people very high up in the government were involved in the ivory and rhino horn trade, and as a civil servant his hands were tied. He saw his main responsibility to be keeping the country's national parks safe, and he had organised the translocation of black rhino and other endangered species in the homelands to Etosha National Park for safekeeping. One day, he told me, it might be possible to take some of them back to the areas they had come from.

By 1981, when control over nature conservation was transferred to Windhoek, the armed liberation struggle of the South West Africa People's Organisation (SWAPO) had spread to Kaokoland, and the whole northwest was also in the grip of the worst drought in living memory. By then De la Bat had been promoted to a higher post within the country's administration and the new acting director, Polla Swart, did not appear to regard the declining wildlife numbers in the Kaokoveld as a priority. Stoffel Rocher, the Chief Nature Conservator, was even less concerned about what was happening there, and asked why I was so worried about the game in 'Kaffirland', which to him was just 'dust and stones'.

That might be the way he and his colleagues saw it, but I had known the Kaokoveld before the poaching and drought had decimated its wildlife – when humans and elephants shared the same waterholes and herds of springbok and zebra grazed side by side with cattle, goats and sheep. At that time I believed the region's spectacular scenery and desert-adapted big game could in future make it one of Southern Africa's major tourist attractions. After it was de-proclaimed, assurances had been given that its wildlife would still be protected, but nothing was done, and over the following decade the slaughter began in earnest. What little now remained was at the mercy of anyone with access to a firearm.

But to me the Kaokoveld was more than just a potential tourist destination. It was also an example to other parts of Africa of the way people and
big game could live together on the same land, and from my first visit I had
fallen under its spell. How had it all gone so terribly wrong?

CHAPTER THREE

AN ARID EDEN

In most of our lives there are turning points – chance encounters or events that irrevocably change the direction in which we had previously been going. In August 1967, at the age of 23, I happened to visit the Kaokoveld. The trip was not planned or even previously contemplated. The opportunity simply arose, and seeking a break away from the small mining town I was working in, I took it.

At the time I knew nothing about this remote north-western region of South West Africa. I set off on that fateful trip in a holiday mood, looking forward to a cleansing of the spirit, much needed after spending eight soul-destroying hours a day in dark and dripping cockroach-infested tunnels deep within the bowels of the earth. However, when I returned a few days later I had found the place where I wanted to spend the rest of my life.

Mining was not my chosen career. After leaving school and completing nine months' compulsory military service, I had worked as a forester on the misty highlands of Zululand. It was a good life – on horseback out in the open air – and for the first few years I had revelled in it. But the forests I worked in were of alien species, pine, wattle and eucalypts that were planted in tidy rows and kept free of all local competitors. The only indigenous trees and animals on our estates were fugitives, depending for their survival on isolated patches of land that were too steep or rocky to be planted to commercially valuable exotics. Before the end of my third year, the initial exhilaration had waned and I yearned for wider and wilder horizons.

I had grown up in Natal, but by the 1960s the province's fertile rolling hills, like the war-loving Zulu people who inhabited them, had long since been tamed. Sugarcane fields and timber plantations had replaced virtually all of the high grasslands, thorn savannas and natural forests that previously supported one of the most diverse and productive ecosystems in Africa. All that was left of pre-colonial Natal was a few small game and nature reserves, pocket-handkerchief sanctuaries that bore witness to what had once been.

At first I tried to get a job as a ranger with the Natal Parks Board, the provincial authority charged with managing its game reserves, but I was advised to obtain a Bachelor of Science degree and then apply again. I had already failed my first year at university, however, and my parents had made it clear that any second attempt was going to be at my own expense. It was also quite obvious that I was not going to save the amount of money needed to pay for three years of study working in forestry – or in Natal, for that matter.

As part of my military service I was based in Walvis Bay, and the little I had seen of South West Africa was enough to make it my first choice in which to seek adventure, fortune, or perhaps both. The country had giant game reserves and huge tracts of land designated as tribal homelands or diamond mining areas. Unfortunately, apart from Etosha and the Namib Park, they were closed to the general public. Nevertheless, stories had circulated of the country's many mines and thriving fishing industry, as well as construction companies operating in remote areas, that were all seeking people willing to work under tough conditions, far from the city lights.

In late 1966 I resigned from my forestry post and headed for the sprawling ex-German colony, but soon discovered that the tales of numerous vacancies and extravagant wages were exaggerated. The highest paying job I got offered was as a shaft onsetter on the Tsumeb copper and lead mine in the north-east of the country. Working 1 000 metres underground was the exact opposite of the kind of life I was seeking, but the money was quite good, so until something better came up I took it.

It was while working here that the opportunity to visit the Kaokoveld arose. As it was designated a 'Native Reserve', accessible by permit only, I had paid little attention to it while travelling through the country looking for work. However, a colleague on the mine, Spike Bradfield, mentioned that his sister was married to a government official based in Opuwo, its administrative centre, and that he was allowed 12 entry permits a year for family and friends. Spike was planning to visit her over our next shift-change long weekend and he invited Keith Gray, a school friend, and me to join him. The chance to visit one of the least known parts of Southern Africa was too good to miss.

Spike's brother-in-law, Robbie Roberts, was the Assistant 'Bantu Affairs' Commissioner for the Kaokoveld, at the time one of only eight white government officials in a territory the size of Belgium. Apart from Opuwo, the only other 'white settlement' was Orumana, a Dutch Reformed mission station that provided religious and medical services to the region's approximately 12 000 local inhabitants. Spike's sister, Eleanor, had previously been the nursing sister at the mission, but after marrying Robbie she had opened a small government clinic in Opuwo.

During our short stay in the Kaokoveld we were taken to a number of nearby places of interest and saw quite a bit of game, as well as elephant tracks within 10 km of Opuwo. But it was the local people that fascinated me most. On the flats around the dusty frontier settlement, Herero herdsmen and their missionary-dressed womenfolk gathered under the umbrella-thorn trees patiently waiting to see the Commissioner, buy supplies from the small shop, or simply hear the latest news. Even more amazing were the skin-clad, red-ochred Himba nomads who drifted regally into the village to exchange goats or sheep for maize meal, or perhaps just to see what was going on in the white man's outpost. It was the old Africa I had read about in books by the continent's early European explorers, and the images I took back to Tsumeb haunted me every day I subsequently went underground.

On the morning we departed Eleanor rashly told me I would be welcome to visit them again. I lasted less than a month before radioing Opuwo, and when Robbie arranged for a permit to be left at the Otjovasandu gate I wrote 'final shift' behind my name in the mine's daily register, and went down the shaft for the last time. Two days later I packed my few belongings into the little pickup truck I owned and headed back to the Kaokoveld.

My sudden arrival in Opuwo was badly timed. Robbie was snowed under with paperwork and unable to leave his office. However, he kindly arranged for me to accompany Jod van der Merwe, the Kaokoveld's superintendent of roads, on an inspection tour he was making to Sesfontein in the south of the territory, returning on the western route via Purros and Orupembe. Although the place names then meant nothing to me, the trip made such a deep impression that as I write this book more than 30 years later, I can still remember virtually every part of it.

By the time Jod's four-wheel-drive Ford F250 truck had been packed with camping gear and food for the expected three days that we would be away, the sun had been up for an hour and its rays were already remarkably warm. It was early October, the hot dry season in the Kaokoveld. The short, early rains would soon begin, but until that happened, midday temperatures could soar into the forties. Among South West Africa's white inhabitants October was known as suicide month.

We headed southwest from Opuwo, through countryside that consisted of dry, broken ranges, their slopes covered with stunted trees and bushes, most of which were now leafless. Beneath their skeletal canopy a bare, stone-strewn substrate had been exposed by severe soil erosion. The landscape was hard, achingly arid and intoxicatingly wild.

Jod drove fast and said little as the Ford rattled and bounced over the rocks and into the ruts that constituted a road in the Kaokoveld. However, he did periodically point out things of interest and gave me an economical description of them. The first village we passed was Okorosave, a Herero settlement of sturdy dung-plastered and thatched houses. Long-horned, multi-coloured cattle were being driven out to graze by teenage boys accompanied by rangy, but not thin dogs. Jod explained that although the Herero grew some maize during the rainy season, they lived mainly on milk and meat. In terms of their livestock they were very wealthy, he added, and it was beneath their dignity to work for us whites. As a result, both of his assistants who accompanied us were from the neighbouring Ovambo tribal area.

Fifteen kilometres further on we came to another, much larger Herero settlement called Kaoko Otavi. In the middle of this village we drove over a narrow furrow that conducted water from an artesian spring a few hundred metres away. Jod pointed out a line of wild fig trees that grew near its eye and mentioned that the ruins of a 'Dorsland Trekker' church were under the trees, but he did not stop or elaborate further.

Just beyond Kaoko Otavi we turned south at a fork in the road, and after travelling through well-wooded hills for another hour entered a deep gorge, flanked by sheer limestone cliffs. In places the track here was no more than a jumble of stones and diff-cracking solid rock banks that had been hand-hacked down a steep slope into a dry river bed. Soon after exiting from the gorge we came to another strong spring, called by the tongue-twisting name of Otjikondavirongo, where Jod decided to stop in the shade of a large syca-more fig that overhung a series of crystal-clear pools. While he got out a ther-mos flask of coffee and his men handed down folding chairs and a table from the back of the truck, a group of Himba women and young girls appeared from the surrounding bush and sat on the ground a few metres from us. Jod and his assistants greeted them in Otjiherero and they gave a ritualised reply in high-pitched, singing voices. This done, the women said no more, apparently having only come to look at the vehicle and watch the strange ways of white men.

Our audience wore their traditional dress of calf-skin skirts, while the older women also had tightly spiralled copper armbands, iron anklets and a cone-shaped white shell that hung from a necklace between their naked breasts. On their heads was a rosette-shaped leather cap and their hair, which had been lengthened, hung in pencil-thin braids that draped down to their shoulders. The younger girls had all but a central strip of their hair shaved, which ended in twin plaits hanging over their foreheads. Both the women's and girls' bodies were liberally smeared with bright red ochre that glistened in the sunlight. To me they appeared exquisitely in tune with the wild grandeur of the surrounding mountains.

While Jod sat in the shade and took a well-earned rest from the difficult driving, I followed the small stream to see how far it ran. The banks were covered in cattle, goat and sheep spoor, but to my surprise there were also numerous elephant droppings. As I walked further I also disturbed a small herd of impala that bounded gracefully away, but showed no signs of panic. Following one of the paths that radiated into the bush from the water I saw the tracks of kudu and zebra.

Amazed by the fact that people, their livestock and big game were sharing the same drinking place, I hurried back to tell Jod, but he was unimpressed. Most of the springs in the Kaokoveld had plenty of game around them, including elephant, he told me. Didn't the people hunt, I asked, but Jod just said that the Himba had more than enough livestock, so they did not need to eat wild animals.

We drove on in silence, Jod no doubt thinking about how to improve the rugged roads in this part of the Kaokoveld, while I contemplated what he had just told me. It was certainly very different to the situation in South Africa, where the wildlife had long since been exterminated in areas of human habitation. On our forestry estates we overseers had spent a great deal of time protecting the few bushbuck, reedbuck and duiker on them from our Zulu labourers, who were inveterate hunters and snarers.

The country through which we travelled became progressively drier and more mountainous, but although the landscape around us seemed parched and desolate we passed a number of recently inhabited Himba stock posts. Small groups of springbok were also regularly encountered and high on a steep hill slope Jod pointed out a herd of mountain zebra. By now it was close to midday and the sunlight reflected blindingly off the bare rocks, making it difficult to keep my eyes open.

'Sesfontein,' Jod said, jolting me awake.

We had crested yet another dry stone-strewn ridge, and below us the mountains had drawn back dramatically, creating a natural amphitheatre encircling a broad alluvial plain that was covered, not by stunted desert bushes, but by tall and graceful acacia trees. Jod stopped on a high point overlooking the valley and pointed out some of the landmarks.

Immediately in front of us was a shiny corrugated iron roof with a red cross painted on it. This was the government clinic, he informed me, manned by a male nurse named Nel, the only white man living in Sesfontein. Once a month, Nel was visited by a doctor from the Oshakati State Hospital, over 300 km away in Ovamboland. However, during the rainy season all the access roads to Sesfontein could become impassable and then his only link with the outside world was by two-way radio. At such times critically ill patients had to be airlifted out.

On the slopes and on the edge of the plain there were also a number of enormous sycamore fig trees, their roots apparently getting water from the artesian springs that gave Sesfontein its name. Partly hidden by the branches of a particularly large wild fig were the roofless, crumbling walls of an old military fort that was built, Jod told me, by the German colonial government just after the turn of the century. On the flat ground behind the ruins was a grove of tall date palms amongst fields of golden wheat.

After a brief stop at the clinic to talk to Nel we drove on to the ruined fort where Jod planned to have lunch. The track we followed passed through the ripe, wind-rippled wheat fields, above which the long fronds of the date palms creaked and rustled in the breeze. The people living here, many of whom were an offshoot of the light-skinned Nama tribe that inhabited the south of the country, had already begun their harvest, and we passed groups of their womenfolk wearing ankle-length patchwork dresses, sitting in the shade and wind-winnowing the freshly scythed grain.

Jod parked under a particularly large sycamore fig that overhung what remained of the fort, and as we offloaded our chairs and lunch, semi-naked, apricot-coloured children watched us shyly from their perches on the rubble. A few metres away a stream of clear water flowed in a furrow down from one of the springs, and ran past the fort to the date palms and wheatfields. The ground for a metre on either side of the furrow was an emerald green carpet of closely cropped sedge, and when we arrived the croppers, a disreputable looking bunch of goats, were hard at their work, only stopping momentarily to see if there was anything worth cadging from us. Overhead, hundreds of birds created a cacophony of sound as they fluttered among the branches and shuttled to and from the water in the furrow. A scene more different to the drought-racked country we had just passed through would have been hard to imagine.

By the time we left Sesfontein the sun was well past its zenith, and although the sky was still clear, the mid-afternoon heat was tempered by a cool breeze blowing strongly from the west. We drove into the wind, parallel to the unseen bed of the Hoanib, the seasonally flowing river responsible for carving out the spectacular Sesfontein basin. The tracks – for there were many, all going in the same direction – meandered haphazardly between acacia trees that gave the surrounding landscape a park-like appearance. However, beneath the trees the earth was bare, and where the soil surface had been broken, fine, powdery silt blew restlessly over the ground. The Ford churned through deep ruts that had been dug by previous vehicles, sending up great clouds of dust that liberally covered our camping gear and the two men on the back with what looked and felt like talcum powder.

After about 10 km we turned away from the Hoanib and headed north up a broad valley, flanked by rugged black mountains. Acacias were now scarce, their places taken by butterfly-leafed mopane trees that grew quite tall on the deep alluvial soils of the valley but shrank to gnarled dwarves on the slopes of the ranges. Just after leaving Sesfontein I had noticed the first elephant spoor, and soon their plate-sized footprints and fresh dung littered the ground under most of the bigger trees.

When we had climbed out of the Hoanib valley Jod stopped briefly. Looking back from where we had come, the view was breathtaking. Chain after chain of jagged desert mountains extended to the southern and western horizons. Somehow the Hoanib River had cut a channel through them to the Atlantic Ocean 100 km away. Jod told me he had once driven down the bed of the Hoanib to where the course of the river was blocked by massive sand dunes a few kilometres from the coast. There were no people living there, he said, 'just hundreds of elephants'.

Away from the Hoanib valley the landscape opened out into arid hill country in which game was quite plentiful. They were all desert-adapted species: springbok, gemsbok, ostrich and a few small herds of mountain zebra. Whenever less wary individuals stood within easy rifle range the men on the back shouted excitedly to Jod: 'Shoot, Baas, shoot. We are dying of meat hunger.' But Jod paid no attention to their pleas.

On a straight section of road, eight ostriches paced the Ford, running parallel to us, about 50 metres away. Jod pressed his foot down on the accelerator and the speedometer needle crept up to 60 and then 70 km/h. This was too much for the ostriches, but instead of breaking away the lead bird inexplicably decided to cut across in front of the truck, with the others following closely behind. Jod braked and the first six ostriches passed comfortably in front of us, but the seventh made it with only a few metres to spare. The last bird, now panic-struck, was clearly not going to make it. For a split second it looked like a collision was inevitable, but with a flurry of feathers and a nifty, although somewhat ungainly bit of footwork, it changed course and just managed to slip past the back of the truck before high-stepping it in earnest for the horizon. Roars of laughter came from the back and even Jod smiled quietly to himself.

About 30 km out of Sesfontein we crossed a large watercourse fringed by mopane and leadwood trees. The coarse white sand was criss-crossed with elephant tracks

'The Ganumub River,' Jod said, passing me a 1:250 000 topographic map that he kept on the dashboard. In bold type across the area were the words KAOKOVELD RESERVE, as well as GAME RESERVE NO 2. To the south of the Hoanib River the area was designated ETOSHA GAME PARK. I was confused, but Jod explained that the Kaokoveld was both a native reserve and a game reserve. In 1907, the German government had proclaimed most of their colony's north-west as Game Reserve No 2. It included what later, under the South African administration, became the Etosha Game Park, which extended for another 250 km south of the Hoanib to the Uchab River. Combined, Etosha and the Kaokoveld then formed the largest conservation area in the world.

'How is poaching controlled in such a large area?' I asked.

'The Bantu Affairs Commissioner is in charge of everything that happens in the Kaokoveld,' Jod replied. 'He decides what can be hunted. We resident officials take out a monthly pot licence that allows us to shoot one kudu or two springbok. The local people are also allowed to hunt for meat as well as protect their livestock from predators.'

'But who makes sure everyone sticks to the rules?'

At this question, Jod smiled wryly. 'Nobody, but if anybody shoots too much the word will soon get around.'

I wondered how strictly the definition of 'too much' was interpreted.

Soon after the Ganumub River, the road crossed a vast treeless plain. The deep sandy soil here supported an excellent sward of perennial grass. It was by far the best grazing I had seen since leaving Opuwo and I asked Jod why there were no cattle here.

'No water,' he said, but then added: 'The government has sunk a borehole near the Ganumub River. There will be plenty of livestock around after we put a windmill up there.'

At the northern end of the plain the track re-entered the mountains. The sun was by now quite low on the horizon, and as we drove on their steep bare slopes drew in closer, casting long shadows across the valley floor. Our road frequently crossed over or followed another large dry watercourse where signs of elephant were again much in evidence – but the great beasts themselves remained out of sight.

At one riverbed crossing, as Jod was slowly manoeuvring the Ford through a thicket, he suddenly jammed on the brakes, unclipped one of the rifles from its rack against the dashboard and climbed out. I joined him as he walked back a few metres along the track.

'Fresh lion spoor,' he said, pointing out large pug-marks in the sand.

Jod cocked his rifle and followed the clear tracks into the riverine bush. I walked a few metres behind, noting that the spoor of many other animals was visible along the path we followed. Easy to recognise were those of elephant, zebra and gemsbok, but to my amazement there were also the unmistakable three-toed tracks of a rhinoceros. I knew that rhino occurred in the Kaokoveld, but here, deep in the Namib Desert, was the last place I expected them to be.

About 200 metres from where Jod had stopped we came to a number of holes in the riverbed that had clearly been dug by elephants. At the bottom of them the sand was damp and in some a few centimetres of water was still visible. It was not much, but from the amount of spoor around the waterholes it was obvious that many animals had drunk there. Beside me, Jod was quietly surveying the surrounding bush. We were in the shadow of the mountains and the light was gloomy. Apart from the rustle of the wind in the trees there was no sound. After a few moments he broke the silence.

'This is getting a bit dangerous,' he said in little more than a whisper.

Until then I had been so spellbound by the atmosphere of the place that I had just followed Jod, without giving any thought to this aspect of our situation. I now became aware that, even in the clearing around the waterholes, visibility was less than 10 metres. I also noted that some of the elephant dung at our feet was still soft and damp. The air smelled musty and it crossed my mind that there could be hidden creatures watching us at that very moment. The back of my neck started tingling and the palms of my hands felt clammy. The truck now seemed very far away.

Jod was obviously having similar thoughts, for without saying any more he started walking back on the same path we had come along. Five minutes later we were standing next to the Ford. Although I hadn't previously noticed it, the wind had become very cold and I found myself shivering.

We drove on and after a few kilometres the mountains ended abruptly. Once again the scenery had changed dramatically. Stretching out in front of us were broad, open plains, while in the distance, over 20 km away, a spine of high, rugged peaks was silhouetted against the setting sun. In front of us the soft evening light had turned a sparse mane of dry grass to gold, giving the whole valley a warm, almost surreal radiance. Jod touched my shoulder and pointed out a long line of gemsbok walking in single file across the desert plains.

Once we were out of the mountains the road got smoother and Jod drove faster. The Hoarusib River, where he had planned to camp for the night, soon appeared as a dark ribbon of trees across the sandy flats between the ranges. In front of us springbok pronked and raced away from the speeding truck. Ignoring the renewed bloodthirsty shouts from the back, Jod drove past them, but when a single ram stood nonchalantly less than 100 metres away, he braked hard and stopped. While the springbok gazed inquisitively at us, Jod unclipped the lighter of the two rifles, climbed out and leaning over the bonnet of the Ford fired a single shot. The ram leaped into the air and dashed off for about 50 metres before doing a spectacular somersault and crashing to the ground.

The instant Jod had fired the men on the back had jumped off and within minutes the limp body of the springbok – minus intestines and testicles – had been unceremoniously hoisted onto the truck. With fresh blood now spattered over the Ford's tailgate we sped on towards the Hoarusib River. Just before reaching it, Jod turned off the track and drove across the smooth sand flats to the site of an abandoned Himba village. Led by one of his assistants, we walked to a pile of white stones on the edge of a circle of derelict huts. Next to it, hung on a pole, were the bleached skulls of long-horned oxen.

'The old headman of Purros is buried here,' Jod explained. 'Everyone who comes to Purros puts a stone on his grave. According to local tradition, if you don't do it you will have bad luck.'

Jod's two assistants knelt down near the stones and prayed loudly to the deceased headman before placing their stones on the grave. Whether he acknowledged the power of the Himba's spirit or not, Jod was taking no chances. Picking up a piece of white quartz, he added it to the pile. So did I.

The Hoarusib River at Purros was magnificent. Where the road crossed its white, sandy bed it was over 100 metres wide. When heavy rain fell inland and it came down in full flood it would be an awesome sight. Jod informed me that a number of vehicles had been swept away while attempting to cross the Hoarusib when it was running. Some of them had never been seen again.

Growing in and along the winding riverbed were large winter thorn trees, while fringing its course was a belt of well-developed riparian woodland. Jod stopped under a camel thorn tree, and while he supervised the setting up of our camp I took up his suggestion of walking downriver to the strong spring that gave Purros its name. As I set off Jod warned me to be careful. Purros, he told me, was the place of elephants.

I soon realised that his parting comment was not in jest. Wherever I looked, elephant dung littered the ground; in some places it would have been difficult to walk without stepping on the huge footprints that meandered between the tall trees.

At first I followed the course of the Hoarusib, conscious of the protection its steep banks would afford should the need arise. However, after a few hundred metres the river made a sweeping S-bend and as it was already late, I decided to leave the relative safety of the open sandy bed and take a short cut through the woodland. The sun had already set and beneath the trees the light was poor and visibility restricted. I was already regretting my decision when there was a rustling in the undergrowth and then a terrifying racket. My pulse-rate rocketed and adrenaline surged through my bloodstream as a francolin broke cover and, with a whirr of stubby wings, flew into the safety of a tree. With my heartbeat still in overdrive I now literally tip-toed over the soft layer of leaf litter towards the gap in the rocky hills that Jod had pointed out as the spring's source.

I soon found myself on the riverbank again, and just ahead a patch of sedges clearly indicated where underground water rose to the surface. Relaxing now that I was out of the woodland I had just started scrambling down the steep bank towards the spring when I happened to glance upstream – and froze.

Less than 50 metres away four huge bull elephants were striding purposefully down the riverbed straight towards me. My legs refused to move and, with my heart once more pounding like a drum, I stood transfixed. Seconds later the bulls had walked sedately past me, completely oblivious to my presence.

Once they reached the spring the elephants lowered their trunks into the stream and with great dignity sucked up long trunkfuls of water. Behind them the black silhouetted ranges contrasted with a dust-laden sky that turned to pale pink and then to carmine. The timeless scene in front of me seemed dreamlike in its serenity and I found uncontrollable tears welling up in my eyes. What an unbelievable day it had been. The Kaokoveld, a place I hardly knew existed two months before, had turned out to be more amazing than I could possibly have imagined. Surely there was no other part of Southern Africa that had such spectacular landscapes and big game animals. But to me the Kaokoveld was more than that. Here the local people were still practising a way of life that was in harmony with the natural world, something modern societies had drifted away from in the quest for material wealth and techno-logical progress. Surely there were lessons to be learned from them?

As I followed the middle of the wide Hoarusib riverbed back to camp my mind was in turmoil. I had found the place I was looking for, but what chance did I have of getting a job in this arid Eden when my only experience was in forestry?

CHAPTER FOUR

THE WHITE MAN'S GAME

I stayed with Robbie and Eleanor Roberts for six weeks, and in this time accompanied Robbie, Jod van der Merwe and other officials to different parts of the Kaokoveld. Although they were just carrying out their official duties, I found each trip an unforgettable adventure into an Africa I had previously only dreamed about. The vastness of the Territory meant that most of our days were spent driving four-wheel-drive vehicles over rugged tracks through wild and often spectacular scenery. In the evening camp was made wherever we happened to be, dinner prepared on an open fire, and we all slept out under the stars.

Once these modern Afrikaner frontiersmen left Opuwo, home comforts were dispensed with and life was reduced to the basics: a canvas tarpaulin on which they rolled out their bedding, a few folding chairs and large metal trunks which seemed to store everything else they needed. When not accompanied by their wives they lived on a simple diet of meat, maize meal, coffee and homemade *boerebeskuit* – much as their forefathers had done.

The meat we ate came from sheep and goats bartered from the local Herero and Himba stock owners, or game hunted on apparently elastic pot licences. In fact what and when game was shot seemed to be determined by need and what occurred in the area, and not by any rules set in Opuwo or Windhoek. Jod once summed up the general attitude of the white residents of the Kaokoveld to hunting: 'It doesn't matter how much a person shoots, as long as nothing is wasted.' Considering the small number of officials living in the territory and the relative abundance of wildlife, this laissez-faire approach to conservation was hard to argue against.

By the end of November the rainy season had begun. I had also considerably overstayed Robbie and Eleanor's generous hospitality, and so before the track out of Opuwo became impassable for my two-wheel-drive vehicle, I set off back to Tsumeb and 'civilisation'. Along the way I thought about my future. The first priority was to find a job, but I now knew that I needed more than just employment. After having experienced life in one of Southern Africa's last remaining wildernesses, going back to working underground or any similarly mindless occupation was no longer an option.

While in Opuwo, I had got to know the Kaokoveld's livestock inspector, Tom Sopper, and his wife Maizie. Tom had previously held a similar position in Botswana's veterinary department and around the campfire he had enthralled me with tales of that country's vast open spaces and great herds of big game. The Soppers had left Botswana when it became independent in 1966 because Tom saw no future for himself as a white official in a black-governed country. He was not optimistic about my chances of getting a job there, but just seeing the Kalahari Desert and the Okavango Swamps would make visiting Botswana worthwhile. I was also keen to experience what life was like in a black-governed country. However, to get almost anywhere in Botswana you needed a four-wheel-drive vehicle.

Before reaching Tsumeb, I came up with the solution. While on a trip with Robbie we had seen the tracks of a bicycle near Swartbooisdrift on the Kunene River. Although we never found the cyclist I reasoned that if he could ride a bicycle in the Kaokoveld I could surely cycle through Botswana. After all, if the going got tough I just had to get off the bike and push. It would be a slow, hard way of seeing the country, but I had plenty of time and was in pretty good physical shape. Riding a bike would also be cheap – a not insignificant factor, as the bars in Tsumeb had seen more of my monthly salary than its banks. And if I did not find suitable employment in Botswana, then I would simply cycle on to Rhodesia.

On my first day back I purchased the best bicycle available in Tsumeb: a Carlton racing bike with ten-speed gears. After a practice run of about 150 km, I packed my rucksack with a sleeping bag, waterproof groundsheet, a change of clothes and a windbreaker, two water-bottles, a camera and a bicycle puncture repair kit, swung into the saddle and pedalled off down the main road to Windhoek. On the tar cycling was a pleasure, but 50 km east of Windhoek the paved road ended. From here to Buitepos, on the Botswana border, the surface was hard gravel and very corrugated. Nevertheless, I made good progress and reached the little customs and immigration office in high spirits. On the SWA side the white immigration officer merely raised his eyebrows when I said I was riding a bicycle, but the Botswana border officials were clearly unused to seeing white cyclists.

'So you are going to ride a bicycle all the way to Ghanzi,' one of them said. 'Maybe you won't even get half-way before the lions will have eaten you. The next time we go along that road we will look out for vultures.'

A little disconcerted, and with an audience of laughing men behind me, I got back into the saddle and set off down a road that rapidly deteriorated into a sandy, two-spoor track. My folly in purchasing a racing bicycle, with its narrow rims and tyres, was now all too apparent and I soon found myself pushing the bike as much as I rode it. The day had also been extremely hot and although great thunderclouds were building up to the north, the December sun still shone down mercilessly. Fortunately, it was only a few kilometres to Charleshill, a trading store and not much else, situated on a slight rise overlooking flat, scrub-covered plains that stretched uninterrupted to the northeastern horizon – the direction I was planning to go.

At the Charleshill store I bought a warm Coke and sat down under a tree to assess the situation. My idea of riding any kind of bicycle across the Kalahari now seemed seriously flawed. Ghanzi, the only village in this part of Botswana, was 200 km away. If the road had a reasonably hard surface it should take me less than four days, but if it was as sandy as around Charleshill there might well be vultures circling over the plains in a few days' time. My greatest concern was whether there was any water along the way. The store-owner, a Mr Sharpe, was most helpful and offered to give me a lift to Kalkfontein, another trading store he owned, about 70 km along the road to Ghanzi. I gratefully accepted.

By the time we reached Kalkfontein it was almost sunset, so the Sharpe family kindly offered me a bed for the night. After dinner I joined my hosts on the verandah of their rustic home. They had no electricity and by the light of a flickering paraffin lamp and the occasional flash of distant lightening, we listened to gramophone records played on a battery-operated turntable. With the haunting voices of a Cossack choir singing Russian folksongs – somehow in harmony with the vast, sparsely inhabited Kalahari Desert that surrounded us – I told the Sharpes of my hope to find employment in Botswana.

I could forget about getting a government job, Mr Sharpe told me bluntly, and there were very few other work opportunities for a white man in Botswana. My best bet would be in Maun, where a relatively large expatriate community lived, but riding there on a bicycle would definitely not be possible. I might get to Ghanzi – the road was not too bad and there were cattle posts along the way, but from there on it was thick sand, with long, waterless stretches. By the time I went to bed I was thoroughly disheartened.

In the morning I wandered down to the spring that gave this dot on the map its name and watched as local herdsmen brought their thin cattle in from the bush to drink. By nine o'clock, clouds of fine, hoof-churned dust hung in the still air, filtering the sunlight and giving the scene a hazy, almost surreal atmosphere. The cattle-owners I greeted spoke little English and even less Afrikaans, but when I tried Fanagalo, the pidgin Zulu spoken on the South African gold mines, a group of older men who in their youth had done their time underground gathered around me. I asked them how life had changed for them since Botswana's independence, but it was soon apparent that events in the distant capital caused very small ripples in Kalkfontein and we changed the subject to cattle, droughts and the road to Ghanzi. They assured me that the immigration officials were not joking about the lions in the area.

I set off in the afternoon as great cumulus clouds sailed in from the north-east, making the temperature bearable, although no rain fell. The track was sand interspersed with hard banks of calcrete and I was able to ride, albeit very slowly, for about 20 km before making camp under a large camel thorn tree. I was now completely alone, deep in the Kalahari, and my accommodation for the night had a 360 degree view of the flat, featureless bush. But at that moment there was no place in the world that I would rather have been. Ahead of me lay a journey of discovery, as much about myself as the continent I was born on. The winds of change were sweeping down from the north and I knew that we South African whites had to radically alter the way we interacted with our black countrymen, or return to our roots in a cold, grey Europe that most of us had never even visited.

Before dawn I was back in the saddle again and made good progress for a few hours before soft sand and the devastating heat made every extra kilometre covered an achievement. I battled on, stopping at cattle posts to gulp down litres of water and rest for a few minutes. I saw no vehicles until around midday a battered old Land Rover, overloaded with black men, drove past on their way to Ghanzi. Through the dust they waved and shouted good-humoured encouragement, but did not stop. For the rest of the day I was completely alone, with no wild animals in sight apart from a large monitor lizard and a few fleeting glimpses of steenbok.

In the afternoon clouds formed overhead and this time grey veils of rain swept across the plains, but by sunset they had dispersed. Just before nightfall I reached a windmill attached to a half-full cement reservoir. After a luxurious swim in its slimy green water I made a quick meal of rice and soup, lay on top of my sleeping bag and drifted into blissful sleep under a now clear, star-spangled Kalahari night sky.

On the third day a government vehicle came from behind and pulled up next to me. The driver was the local police commissioner, an expatriate Scotsman, and alongside him sat his Motswana understudy. I must have looked quite a sight to them: dirty, dishevelled and soaked with sweat, but riding on one of the best of British racing bikes. Apparently the border officials had informed them of the 'mad white man' riding a bicycle through the Kalahari. After a few questions about where I came from and my motives for coming to Botswana, they seemed convinced that I was harmless and offered to give me a lift to Ghanzi, still nearly 50 km away. I accepted.

On our way, the police commissioner also strongly advised me against trying to ride to Maun. To attempt it would be grossly irresponsible, and would give him the unpleasant task of going out to fetch my corpse. He suggested that I catch the bus which departed once a week from D'kar, a trading store 40 km north of Ghanzi. By the time we arrived the commissioner had obviously decided that I was not as disreputable as I had at first appeared and he invited me to stay with him and his wife until the next bus to Maun left in four days' time.

That evening, as we sipped ice-cold gin and tonics, my host gave me some historical background to this part of Botswana. The Ghanzi district had been settled by Afrikaner farmers who trekked here from the Transvaal and under the Cape administration of Cecil Rhodes obtained freehold title to their farms, something not allowed anywhere else in Botswana. Isolated from their kith and kin in South Africa by the Kalahari Desert, the little community had retained many of their nineteenth-century ways and the district was now an anachronism: a virtual Boer Republic inside an independent black African state.

Ghanzi was not an exciting place in which to spend four days. However the police commissioner invited me to accompany him on a trip to investigate some minor infringement of the law by labourers on one of the white-owned farms. After collecting the evidence needed he drove on, perhaps for my benefit, past the last cattle fences across the wide open plains. Here, far from any signs of human habitation, we came across three Bushmen, a man and two women, wearing only bead-decorated leather aprons. Both women had a skin carry-bag over their shoulders, while the man carried a small bow and a quiver of arrows. Their only visible link with the twentieth century was a plastic water container.

We stopped and the commissioner's assistant called out a greeting to which they hesitantly replied. The Bushmen were not unfriendly, but I noted that they kept their distance from the vehicle and appeared nervous, like shy antelope, poised ready for flight at the slightest hint of danger. After a brief conversation we drove on and when I looked back a few moments later, they were only just visible in the long grass, walking towards a destination beyond the horizon, for a purpose that only they knew.

Like the Ghanzi Afrikaners, the Kalahari Bushmen seemed to be misfits in newly independent Botswana. The dominant socio-economy of the various Tswana-speaking tribes that governed the country was cattle farming, and the little light-skinned hunter-gatherers lived uneasily alongside them. Many had resorted to taking employment on the Ghanzi farms, selling their exceptional bushcraft and tracking skills for meagre cash wages. They were clearly looked down on by both white and black stockowners, and tolerated only as long as they were usefully employed. Living free, where a lack of water precluded livestock, they were perceived as potential cattle thieves or a primitive minority that was an embarrassment to the new political order.

On the trip we also saw no large wild animals and I asked the commissioner what had happened to the big herds of game for which the Kalahari was historically renowned. The white farmers had done a lot of hunting, he told me, but the biggest killer had been the veterinary fences that now cut across their migration routes. When we returned to Ghanzi he gave me a copy of a report on Botswana's Bushmen written by an Australian anthropologist, George Silberbauer, to read. Apart from being a fascinating account of the hunter-gatherers' way of life and present plight, it also documented the mass mortality of over 60 000 wildebeest and other migratory game along the 'Kuki' Cordon Fence built a few years earlier. The purpose of the fence had been to restrict livestock and wildlife movements, thereby preventing the spread of foot-and-mouth disease.

'That bloody fence has killed more game in the past three years than all the hunters over the past 50,' the commissioner told me. 'Mark my words. Cattle ranching will mean the end of Botswana's big game herds – and with them will go the Kalahari Bushmen.'

I set off for D'kar on the afternoon before the bus to Maun was due to leave. It was full moon and, because of the great heat during the day, I planned to ride late into the night. In fact the track turned out to be so sandy that it was impossible to stay in the saddle for more than a few hundred metres at a time. After a couple of hours I gave up trying to ride and pushed the bike through the night, arriving at D'kar early the following morning.

The bus was scheduled to leave at eight and arrive in Maun that evening. However, in true African tradition, after loading a full complement of passengers, their various bags and cardboard boxes, many fowls and even a few goats that were tied onto the roof – alongside my bicycle – we finally departed after eleven. On route, the bus's engine also continually overheated, forcing the driver to stop frequently to allow it to cool down. It was after sunset when we reached Sihitwa, a predominantly Herero settlement on the edge of Lake Ngami, and here the bus driver decided to call it a day. By this time, I too had had enough. Anything, even pushing a bicycle, was preferable to the D'kar–Maun express. I de-bussed.

Next morning I cycled across the hard clay soil around Sihitwa to see the fabled lake, which in 1849 David Livingstone had been the first European to visit. I had read the great explorer's account of Lake Ngami and was expecting to find a substantial sheet of deep water with tall trees along the shoreline. In fact, after cycling and finally walking across seemingly endless mud flats I eventually found a stretch of shallow water that was less than a kilometre in width and only a few kilometres long. The lake, which was clearly shrinking, was now mostly under a metre deep and the warm water had the colour and consistency of pea soup.

Although its size was disappointing, because of its concentrated fertility the bird-life on and around Lake Ngami was amazing. Literally thousands of wild geese, duck, teal and countless pelicans, storks, ibises and herons floated on, or circled in enormous flocks over the dying oasis. The mud flats were also littered with the bleached skeletons of giant barbel and, although I never saw any, the local herdsmen warned me that crocodiles still inhabited the deeper waters.

I spent two nights camped on the shores of Lake Ngami before cycling the last 80 km to Maun. The going was comparatively easy, but when a Land Rover stopped and the driver offered me a lift I gratefully accepted. My benefactor was Mark Kyriocus, a professional hunter whose father owned

stores in Ngamiland. Beyond Maun was the southern edge of the Okavango
Delta, a vast wilderness of meandering waterways, papyrus swamps and
sandy islands of higher ground covered with palms and tall trees. It was one
of the finest remaining wildlife areas in Africa, much of it only accessible by
boat. Mark dropped me at Riley's Hotel on the banks of the Tamalakane River,
which drained the bottom end of the delta. With permission from the owner,
Ronnie Kays, I leant my bike against one of the large leadwood trees in front
of the hotel and camped there for the following 10 days.

By 1967 Ngamiland, which encompassed the whole of north-west
Botswana, was fast becoming one of the trophy-hunting meccas of Africa.
Maun was the gateway to big game country and Riley's, the only hotel in
town, was the drinking place of the hunting fraternity. From late morning
until midnight the pub and open-air courtyard buzzed with loud but generally good-natured arguments about rifle calibres, the most effective killing
shots and common malfunctions of various four-wheel-drive vehicles. I had
arrived a few days before Christmas and the town's white, largely expatriate
male residents were at their rowdiest. These sunburned and often alcohol-
battered men were Africa's cowboys; macho outdoorsmen who rode in open
Land Rovers and gunned down elephant, buffalo and lion – but, as I soon
learned, only in the hunting season. Summer was for duck-shooting and tiger
fishing, interspersed with frequent bouts of serious drinking.

During my stay in Maun I accompanied some of the town's less illustrious
characters into the swamps, joining in the merry slaughter of an apparently
inexhaustible supply of feathered and scaly denizens of the surrounding bush
and waterways. Botswana had fairly strict game laws – enacted by the previous British colonial administration – but with a few exceptions these seemed
to apply only to warm-blooded, furry creatures. My companions were also
quick to inform me that bird shooting was not really hunting, but merely
'off-season sport to keep one's eye in and provide a reason for staying out of
the pub'. I also noted that there were no Batswana professional hunters and
virtually no black people frequenting Riley's. Although the country was now
independent, this was clearly still the white man's game.

Trophy hunting was obviously a lucrative business and the out-of-doors
lifestyle appealed to my sense of adventure. While working as a forester I
had done a fair bit of hunting, but the largest animal I had shot there was a
bushbuck. During my stay in the Kaokoveld with Robbie and Eleanor, I had
accompanied a Windhoek official, Hine Swart, on a moonlit elephant hunt.
We had spent the night on the platform of a windmill tower, intending to

shoot one of a group of elephants that had been damaging water installations in the area. When the elephants came to drink my companion had picked out a bull on the far side of the reservoir and shot it between the eyes with his .458 rifle. The elephant had collapsed immediately, while the rest of the herd ran shrieking into the bush. But from here on my one and only elephant hunt became an embarrassing farce.

Hine and I quickly climbed down the tower and hurried around the reservoir, eager to admire our trophy. But just as we got to it the elephant staggered to its feet, causing us to rush back up the windmill tower just in time to fire a few shots in its direction as it disappeared into the night.

The next day we tracked the wounded animal down and killed it, taking a further four shots before it finally fell over. On inspecting the carcass we discovered that in the excitement of the moment, Hine had forgotten to take into account the fact that he was firing from above the elephant's head. The result was that the bullet had missed the brain, passing down through its palate and smashing the lower jaw. It also seemed likely that one of my shots at the departing elephant had grazed its foot! When Robbie heard about my contribution to the hunt, he suggested that perhaps, at the exact moment I fired, the elephant had been scratching its ear with its foot! The final humiliation was the discovery that our 'bull' was in fact a large cow.

In spite of having nothing to boast about with regard to previous hunting experience, whenever a suitable opportunity arose I inquired about the possibility of getting a job. As no trophy hunting was taking place at that time of the year, I was advised to come back to Maun around March, when the safari outfitters started preparing for the next hunting season. It was possible that one of them might be looking for a camp caretaker. The starting salary would be little more than pocket money, but if one of them decided that I was made of 'the right stuff', they might take me on as an apprentice.

During my short stay in Maun I had the privilege of meeting two men who certainly qualified as being made of the right stuff. Harry Selby had started big game hunting as a teenager in Kenya and later became a partner in the best known hunting safari outfitters in Africa: Kerr, Downey and Selby. In the 1950s he had been Robert Ruark's professional hunter on the famous author's first Kenya safari, and Ruark had used him as a model for the hero in his best-selling novel, *Something of Value*. Harry Selby epitomised the popular image of what a 'white hunter' should be; debonair, fearless and an English gentleman to the core. Although I was just a youngster on a bicycle, he found the time to discuss trophy hunting with me.

Humans had always preyed on wild animals, he told me, and the challenge of the chase was deeply embedded in our genes. Because of this he believed that when given the opportunity most men enjoyed hunting, particularly when it involved potentially dangerous game. Shooting the biggest trophy was just a means of satisfying the natural competitiveness of our species.

The way Selby saw things, trophy hunting was an integral part of wildlife conservation. As an example, he told me that in the vast concession areas that Kerr, Downey and Selby controlled in Botswana, his staff were the only effective deterrent to the local people poaching. Professional hunters had to be conservationists, he emphasised, because they needed the game to survive so that they could stay in business. His final point was that trophy hunting gave big game an economic value which, in a country like Botswana, was essential to prevent species that threatened people's lives or livelihoods from being exterminated.

Bobby Wilmot was a professional hunter of a different kind. His father, Cronje Wilmot, had been one of the first whites to work in northern Botswana, and Bobby was raised in the bush with a rifle in his hands. In the late 1940s he had pioneered crocodile hunting for their valuable skins, going out at night in a small boat and shooting them with the aid of a spotlight. The centre of his operations was Maun, and in a career spanning 20 years he was reputed to have killed more than 20 000 of these man-eating reptiles – a measure of his courage and skill. It was also an indication of just how many crocodiles had once inhabited the Okavango Delta.

I stayed two nights at Bobby Wilmot's 'Croc Camp' on the Tamalakane River, 20 km upstream from Maun. He had by then stopped hunting crocodiles and had just started a photographic safari operation – the first in the Okavango Delta. Bobby played down the dangers of hunting crocodiles at night and told me that he now regretted having killed so many. Although they had previously taken hundreds of cattle and quite a few people every year, he believed that crocodiles had an important role in the delta ecosystem and that their numbers should now be allowed to recover.

Tragically, six months after I met him, Bobby Wilmot was bitten by a black mamba while out walking alone in the Delta. He made it back to his bush camp and there tried to inject himself with antivenom. By that time, however, the snake's nerve poison was affecting his co-ordination, and when he tried to open the two life-saving glass ampoules both of them broke. Wilmot then instructed his assistant to drive him back to Maun, but died before reaching the hospital.

Another one of the more memorable characters I went out with during my stay in Maun was Kenny Kays, a sometime professional hunter whose brother, Ronnie, ran Riley's Hotel. Kenny was not a scholar but he was a keen observer of wildlife and could accurately and often hilariously mimic the behaviour of different species. A few days after Christmas he told me that he was planning to drive to Francistown, 500 km away, and near the Rhodesian border. As I had already decided to move on I jumped at the opportunity of a lift. Because Kenny found it difficult to leave a pub while it was still open, we only loaded my bike onto his short-wheelbase Land Rover late that night. The vehicle had long-range fuel tanks, and to ensure that we did not get thirsty along the way, we also loaded a dozen beers. Well tanked up, we then sped off into the night.

After a few hours of driving along the sandy bush track, Kenny started feeling sleepy and suggested I take over the driving for a while. 'Put your foot across here on the accelerator and keep it flat,' he shouted above the roar of the peak-revving engine. I did so and without further ado, Kenny opened his door and climbed out of the cab, over the bonnet and, a few seconds later, back into the Land Rover on the passenger side. With me now driving, he made himself comfortable and was soon asleep. When my spell of driving was over I was expected to follow the same route to the passenger seat, while he kept the vehicle at peak revs. Kenny would not even stop when nature called. This had to be acrobatically accomplished out the door of the moving vehicle.

We arrived in Francistown at dawn and as we drove into the deserted Kays family home, Kenny remembered that he had left the door key on the bar counter in Maun. I suggested we break a window to get in but Kenny was appalled at the thought of facing his mother if he did so. Instead, he simply turned the vehicle around and headed back to Maun to fetch it. Seven hours later we were again at Riley's Hotel, where we picked up the key, bought some sandwiches and drank a few beers, filled up the Land Rover and drove back to Francistown. We arrived after dark, having driven 1 500 km over rough bush roads in less than 24 hours.

That night I stayed with Kenny, and the following day cycled on to Plumtree on the Rhodesian border. Although riding a bicycle had not proved a very practical way of getting around Botswana, with more than a little help I had been able to traverse the whole country and had seen some of its remoter parts. However, as Tom Sopper had predicted, I had been unable to find a job. My hopes now lay in Rhodesia, the British colony that two years previously had unilaterally declared its independence.

After passing through customs and immigration at Plumtree, I rode on to Bulawayo, where I spent a few days with relatives before heading south-east, via Shabani, to Fort Victoria. My destination was Rhodesia's lowveld, where a school friend, Ray Weight, had worked on a sugar mill construction site in 1962. On his return to Natal he had described the area as a bushveld paradise, teeming with big game. As agricultural developments were still taking place in this part of Rhodesia, it seemed like a good place to start looking for a job.

Back on tarred roads, cycling was a pleasure and I took my time, stopping at places of interest along the way. The friendliness of the people, both black and white, added considerably to my enjoyment of the trip. Among the pale-skinned Rhodesians, this was undoubtedly due to the isolation they felt after having sanctions imposed on them by the rest of the world. All visitors from other countries were warmly welcomed, but in my case their inherent English admiration for persons undertaking unusual enterprises caused their hospitality to know no bounds. Soon after my arrival at a country pub for a drink someone would invariably notice my rucksack, or see my bike standing outside against a tree, and ask me where I came from. When I told them that I had ridden from South West Africa on a bicycle, I would pay for no further drinks and would often be taken back to their farms for the night, or shown the sights of the area.

From Fort Victoria I headed south to Chiredzi, in the centre of the lowveld, where Ray had been based. One of the local sugar company managers passed me riding into town, so when I turned up at the company headquarters that afternoon I was given a VIP welcome and invited to stay in his home. The following morning I accompanied my host to work and was introduced to the company's senior management, who arranged for me to be taken on a guided tour of the mill and the newly cleared sugar and cotton fields. That evening I was invited to the company's private club to have a few beers with the local residents.

The lowveld was pioneer country; virgin bushveld was being bulldozed out and brought under the plough, and the men who lived here were tough, hard-drinking and self-assured. In their eyes, Rhodesia was God's own country and their mission – to make the land productive – was part of His plan. After a rapid succession of lagers had been drunk all round, I brought up the subject of wildlife in the area. I had driven for the whole day, including visiting places quite far from town, but had seen no signs of any big game. This was contrary to the impression I had been given by my school friend, I told them, who had worked in Cheredzi just six years before.

He had not been exaggerating, the burly Rhodesians around the bar assured me, but since then many thousands of wild animals had been killed to

reduce the threat they posed to the newly established crops. On the neighbouring cattle ranches, large-scale game harvesting had also been carried out.
Some of the men around me had taken part in these cropping operations and
I was regaled with light-hearted banter about their exploits at the time. At this
point a grizzled old man, who had been sitting quietly at the end of the bar,
thumped the counter with his fist and said angrily: 'What you blokes are talking about wasn't harvesting. It was bloody slaughter and on a diabolical scale.'

One of my companions turned to him good-naturedly and said, 'Aw, come
on, Jack. You can't let sentiment stand in the way of progress.'

Before leaving Chiredzi I was taken to Chipinda Pools, a game sanctuary
on a beautiful stretch of the Lundi River. It was a magical place where the wild
inhabitants of the area had not yet been disturbed. There were signs of elephant and buffalo all along the Lundi's forested banks, while in the long pools,
schools of hippo lazed contentedly. My hosts informed me that a considerable area along the Mozambique border, between the Lundi and Nuanetsi
rivers, was in the process of being set aside as a new national park. Future
Rhodesians would at least inherit some of their lowveld in its pristine state.

Although it was already mid-January, very little rain had so far fallen in the
area and the cattle ranching country I had passed through around Chiredzi
was achingly dry. Every afternoon great thunderheads were now building
up and before I got back to Fort Victoria the season's first heavy downpour
occurred. Caught on the road, I was soon soaked to the skin and decided to
seek shelter at a nearby farmhouse. The rancher and his wife immediately
offered me the use of their rather luxurious guest cottage and invited me to
join them for dinner. After an excellent meal we talked at length about South
West Africa and my trip so far. Finally, our conversation turned to the wildlife
situation in the area.

There was still quite a bit of game on the lowveld ranches, my host told me,
but the big herds of wildebeest and zebra had gone. The farm fences had restricted their movements and periodic droughts had then killed them off. He
was not concerned about the demise of these two species, as they competed
with cattle for grazing. However, he assured me that impala and kudu were
still plentiful and that most farmers had some giraffe, eland and sable on their
land. Although lions had occurred in the area during his father's time, they
had now been exterminated. Elephants also occasionally visited the district
but usually did not stay long.

'There would be a lot more game on our ranches if the munts didn't do so
much poaching,' my host said in conclusion. He owned over 10 000 acres, he

told me, and on such a large ranch it was impossible to stop the local people
from coming onto it and setting snares. Apparently, because of the drought,
snaring had become particularly bad in recent years. What made matters
worse, he added, was that when they were able to catch a poacher, the sentences were so light that they were hardly a deterrent. 'A few months as guests
of the government, a roof over their heads and three meals a day – for many
of them gaol is a picnic compared to life in the Tribal Trust Lands.'

His wife took a much harder line. She felt that the only way to stop the
poaching would be to shoot a few of the culprits. 'That would make the rest of
them think twice before coming onto our land and stealing our game.'

I asked my host what he thought about the recent game-culling operations around Chiredzi. 'Unfortunate, but necessary,' he replied: 'We have got
to open up this country for modern farming so that we can grow enough to
feed the starving masses in the Tribal Trust Lands.'

I was amazed that my hosts seemed completely unaware of the contradictions in what they were saying. In the name of progress, game could be
slaughtered in vast numbers on what had once been tribal land, but if hungry
black people snared a few wild animals to feed their families on a white farm,
it was a crime which, according to the lady of the house, warranted the death
penalty. Was it just racism or really a matter of ownership? Since the British
South Africa Company had pioneered the route to Salisbury and put down
the subsequent Ndebele and Shona 'uprisings', the land and everything on
it was governed by laws drawn up solely by white Rhodesians. On freehold
farms, for the relatively small cost of a licence, landowners could hunt most
species. But as snaring had been made illegal, the residents of the communal
areas, who had no title deeds and did not own firearms, had lost access to a
previously valuable resource.

A few kilometres before Fort Victoria, I turned southwards and cycled
down to what was then known as the Zimbabwe Ruins. Leaving my bicycle at
the nearby hotel, I walked across the manicured lawns and neatly cleared veld
to the massive stone fortresses and temples that were built long before any
white people had come to Southern Africa. The distance between the luxury
hotel and the remnants of this once mighty indigenous civilisation was only
about 500 metres – but it passed through a time-span of at least 500 years.

That night I stayed in the nearby campsite and by the light of a full moon,
climbed over the fence to walk again through the ruins. Without the day-
time tourists, the silence was now broken only by the sound of crickets and
the persistent calls of nightjars. Stippled moonlight filtered onto the towering

stone walls and into the open courtyards, but along the narrow passageways and in the dark recesses I felt the eerie presence of ancient spirits silently observing my intrusion into their ancient domain.

According to Rhodesian government propaganda at the time, Great Zimbabwe had been built by Arab gold and ivory traders, while some of the more romantic white Rhodesians even claimed that it had connections to the Phoenicians, or the legendary Christian kingdom of Prester John. Any suggestion of it having been indigenous architecture was scornfully dismissed: 'Look around you,' the white barman at the hotel said sarcastically: 'If Zimbabwe was built by Africans, where are these skilled stonemasons today?'

From Great Zimbabwe I cycled on to Kyle Dam, one of the water sources for the irrigation projects I had visited in the lowveld. The area surrounding the lake had been proclaimed as a national park and restocked with game, turning it into a popular recreation area. However, the only black faces to be seen here were the room and ablution block cleaners. I wondered if it was just the cost and means of getting to game reserves that deterred native Rhodesians from visiting them, or had they been so alienated from wildlife that they had now completely turned their backs on it?

After spending a few days camping in the park I returned to Fort Victoria and headed eastward along the road to Birchenough Bridge over the Sabi River. The country I cycled through alternated between white ranches and Tribal Trust Land, solely reserved for the use of Rhodesia's rural black population. The grazing on the ranches was not good, but the tribal lands had been completely devastated by the drought. Nevertheless the black farmers I passed on the roadside were invariably friendly and I was greeted with cheerful waves and much laughter from the children as I rode by. Around them the maize in their fields was stunted or dead and there was a low-level stench of decomposing livestock carcasses. It was impossible not to be impressed by their ability to carry on with their daily lives with such fortitude and apparent good humour.

From Birchenough Bridge the road climbed steeply up onto Rhodesia's predominantly white-owned eastern highlands and it took me a day and a half to cover the 100-odd km to Melsetter, an attractive village set amongst pine and wattle plantations. My destination was the Chimanimani National Park, a mountain sanctuary that straddled the international border with Mozambique. As the road from Melsetter onwards was gravel I decided to leave my bike at the local hotel and walk the 15 km to the park boundary. Before I had reached the foot of the mountains, however, a group of school teachers in a VW minibus stopped and offered me a lift. They were also on route to Chimanimani, where they planned to spend a few days in the park's mountain hut, and invited me to join them.

After the steamy heat of the low country I had come through, the cool misty climate of the Chimanimani Mountains was a most welcome change. While the school teachers fished for trout or looked for birds I climbed the nearby peaks or just basked in the heady atmosphere of the park. In the evening, as we cooked and ate our dinner, we shared the highlights of our day.

The teachers, all of them keen birdwatchers, often spent hours haggling over the identification of the different species they had seen. *Roberts' Birds of Southern Africa* was their bible, which went everywhere with them during the day. During the evening discussions they frequently referred to it, and I noticed that some of them even went to sleep with it lying conveniently next to their beds – presumably so that they could identify any strange birds that might appear in their dreams.

By the third evening I was tired of talking about birds and broached the subject of wildlife in Rhodesia's lowveld. They all agreed that game numbers had decreased drastically in recent years, but although they claimed to be conservationists the question of who was to blame and what could be done about it seemed to be of little concern to them. There were enough people worrying about the big and hairy wild animals, I was told; their interest was only in birds. But, I countered, Rhodesia's birds were not being slaughtered in their thousands to make way for new irrigation projects or cattle ranching.

The four birdmen looked at me condescendingly and their spokesman replied in the tone of voice he no doubt reserved for his most feeble-minded pupils. 'When you have learned a bit about ecology, you will realise that habitat destruction caused by man's short-sighted agricultural practices can affect birds just as much as large mammals. In fact, declining bird populations, or changes in their distribution, are often the first indication that something is wrong in an ecosystem.'

I said little more for the rest of the evening and the following day climbed the highest peak in the Chimanimani range. To the east, the mountains fell away precipitously to the flat sandy plains of Mozambique. Less than 250 km from where I stood was the Indian Ocean. I had almost traversed the subcontinent, but had still not found a job. Nevertheless, the trip had been infinitely worthwhile. The remote outposts I had visited and the broad spectrum of people spoken to had exposed me to many aspects of nature conservation I had not previously considered.

Before leaving Natal I would have confidently stated that the greatest threat facing Southern Africa's wildlife was poaching. But was this really the case? I had also believed that most conservationists came from the ranks of English-speaking whites, while the sub-continent's native people were the greatest killers. I had now come to realise that conservation issues were much more complicated. In fact, apportioning the blame for declining wildlife numbers varied according to the prejudices of the person asked, and double standards seemed to be the order of the day.

From Melsetter it was undulating highlands all the way to Umtali on Rhodesia's border with Mozambique. While there I briefly considered riding down to the Indian Ocean port of Beira, but the chances of getting a suitable job in a Portuguese-speaking country were virtually zero. Instead I pedalled on to Salisbury, Rhodesia's capital city. Here, as I had found since entering Britain's rebel colony, the people I spoke to were invariably friendly and helpful, but the answer to my enquiries about employment opportunities was always negative. Trade sanctions had depressed the country's economy and unemployment rates were high. Understandably, in both the government and private sector, the policy was to offer any available jobs to Rhodesian citizens.

Before heading back to South Africa I decided to visit Kariba Dam to see what was then the largest man-made lake in the world, and also to explore the game-rich Zambezi valley. After cycling north from Salisbury I left my bike at Makuti, where the tarred road ended, and walked the 80-odd km down the escarpment to the dam wall. Because it was a tsetse fly area, this part of the valley was uninhabited by humans and the verdant, well-wooded hill slopes had an exciting primeval aura about them. No longer having a sense of urgency, I frequently left the contoured motorway and wandered deep into the forest.

Where the canopy was dense, the light under the trees was dappled and soft, and as I walked further from the road, the undergrowth would rustle mysteriously as small, unseen creatures scurried out of my way. However, the larger denizens of the area were shy, and apart from fleeting glimpses of impala I was aware of their presence only from the spoor that criss-crossed the damp red earth. Twice I was lucky enough to see elephants – a single bull slowly working his way along a steep path up the escarpment, and a small cow herd that I was able to approach to within 60 metres before they detected my presence and, trumpeting in anger, shuffled off into the gloom. Before sunrise one morning, as I lay in my sleeping bag, I heard a lion roar. Alone, with no protection but the trees around me, the deep reverberating sound inspired simultaneous feelings of primordial awe and cold clammy fear.

At the small village that had sprung up near Kariba's dam wall I met a group of young soldiers. Presuming that I had arrived by vehicle, they advised me not to go too far from the outskirts of the village. Wild animals were not the danger, they said, but 'terrorists' who had recently infiltrated the valley from Zambia. The first group of guerrillas had crossed into Rhodesia in 1966, and more recent incursions were known to have taken place in the Kariba area. The army and special units of the police were at that time on follow-up operations to capture or kill the insurgents. When I told the soldiers that I had walked down from Makuti, the lieutenant in charge decided that, for my own good, I needed a lecture on African politics.

According to him, the majority of the 'terrs' were just gullible youngsters who had been conned into taking up arms against the Rhodesian government by 'commie agitators and bleeding-heart liberals'. Missionaries were also to blame, apparently for teaching black kids that they were the equals of whites. 'Before the do-gooders of the world started putting fancy ideas into their heads, the blacks in this country were quite happy to accept the white man as their boss. They knew their place. Now they are being given weapons and told to overthrow the government.'

'Unfortunately,' one of the other soldiers added with a stone-faced smile, 'somewhere along the way to Salisbury the young freedom fighters bump into a security force patrol and get blown away. That's how much all this equality bullshit has helped them.'

After my lecture I promised the lieutenant that I would stay close to town. I also agreed to take a lift back to Makuti with a supply truck that was leaving in a few days' time. Disappointed at not being able to explore the area myself, I asked some of the local residents about the wildlife situation in the Zambezi valley. There was still plenty of big game around, I was told, 'in spite of the tsetse-fly control operations'. In order to prevent the spread of nagana, a deadly livestock disease carried by tsetse-flies, Rhodesia's veterinary services annually killed thousands of head of game to create a wildlife-free corridor between the Zambezi valley and the white-owned ranches above the escarpment. This scorched-earth policy was also justified as 'the price of progress'.

It was time for me to leave Rhodesia, a beautiful country of contrasts and contradictions that I would need time to come to terms with. I cycled via Salisbury and Bulawayo and then turned southwards to Beit Bridge and on to Johannesburg. Most of my journey was through well-managed and visibly productive farms, whose owners were tough, sun-burned men of settler stock. Both in the countryside and in the towns along the way I continued to be treated with great hospitality, and by the time I crossed the border into South Africa, I had been welcomed into the homes of many kind and generous Rhodesian families. This had given me numerous opportunities to discuss conservation as well as the political predicament that the country had found itself in after UDI.

In general the people I spoke to made light of the guerrilla incursions and were confident that their security forces would have no difficulty containing the situation. International trade sanctions were perceived to be a much greater threat and most of them were particularly angered by what they saw as Britain's double standards in recognising Zambia and Malawi's independence but not theirs. The fact that Rhodesia had been self-governing since 1923 and that they had 'stood by Great Britain in two World Wars' made the pill even more bitter. White Rhodesians took justifiable pride in their exceptional war service record for the Allied cause and saw it as confirmation of their courage and determination – a warning to the rest of the world that they would not easily bow down to international pressure.

In the years ahead the Rhodesians' remarkable ingenuity and the support they received from South Africa would overcome the economic sanctions. But the internal security threat, which seemed so insignificant in early 1968, would steadily grow into a whirlwind that swept across virtually every part of the country and finally brought the white government to its knees. The laughing, good-natured black Rhodesians I had met on my trip would show, within a decade, that their patience and humour did indeed have limits, and their numbers were overwhelming.

The last 100 km to Johannesburg were by far the most dangerous of my trip. It poured with rain and on the busy highways of South Africa the speeding cars and big trucks paid little attention to bicycles. After a few close shaves I decided to load my bike onto a train and travel in comfort down to Durban. I had been on the road for nearly three months. It had been an eventful and eye-opening trip, but I was still unemployed.

While in Natal I visited the provincial headquarters of the Department of Bantu Administration and Development (BAD) to inquire about the possibility of getting a job in one of South West Africa's northern tribal areas. They suggested that with my forestry background I should apply for an agricultural supervisor post, and advised me to write to their Pretoria head office. As I knew there was no agricultural post in the Kaokoveld, on the application form I gave my choice of station as Rundu. While working in Tsumeb I had once had the opportunity to fly up to this small town on the banks of the Okavango River, which was the administrative centre for the vast, sparsely populated Kavango Territory.

Instead of just sitting around waiting for a response to my application, I took a job as an operator on the Shell and BP petrol refinery near the Durban Airport. Two months later, when I had almost given up hope, I received a reply from BAD. It simply stated that there were no posts available in the Kavango Territory, but that a new agricultural supervisor position had just been created in the Kaokoveld. If I was interested in this post I should fill in and return the application forms they had enclosed. Hardly believing my good fortune, I sent the completed forms back the next day, but waited on tenterhooks for another month before receiving confirmation of my appointment and instructions to report for duty in Opuwo on 1 August 1968.

CHAPTER FIVE

WORKING FOR BAD

In 1968 the outside world knew virtually nothing about South West Africa's northern tribal areas – Caprivi, Kavango, Ovamboland and Kaokoveld. The reason was that soon after taking over the administration of the country the South African authorities had drawn a line from east to west across the map. South of this 'Red Line' was the police zone, where whites could own property and were under the laws of the government in Pretoria. North of the Red Line was land reserved for the exclusive use of the indigenous people – and here, excepting for cases of murder, rape or treason, customary law prevailed, administered by traditional leaders in their respective areas. Before the inhabitants could leave, or persons not on official business enter the tribal zone, permits had to be obtained from the local commissioner, and after the National Party came to power they were seldom granted.

South West Africa was initially annexed by Germany in 1885 during Europe's infamous 'scramble for Africa'. However, upon the outbreak of the First World War the Supreme Allied Command asked South Africa to invade the Territory, and in July 1915 the vastly outnumbered German colonial forces surrendered. A military government was installed to maintain order in the country until June 1919, when by the Treaty of Versailles, Pretoria was given control over South West Africa. In 1921 this was confirmed as a C Mandate under the Covenant of the recently formed League of Nations.

In the idealistic terms of the post-First World War period, a C Mandate was seen as a 'sacred trust' to promote the wellbeing and development of the indigenous people. However, the mandate also granted South Africa the right to administer her acquired territory 'under the laws of the mandatory power'. In effect, this authorised Pretoria to introduce its already established policy of creating 'native reserves' – putting South West Africa on the road to racial segregation.

In 1922 the Kaokoveld was proclaimed as a reserve for Chiefs Oorlog Thom, Muhona Katiti and Kasupi, the three leaders of the Herero-speaking people who inhabited the region at that time. It was included in the Outjo District, to be administered jointly by the resident magistrate there and the Native Commissioner in Ovamboland, but because of its remoteness and lack of roads the Territory was in fact seldom visited by either of them.

The 'Prohibited Areas Proclamation' of 1928 declared the Kaokoveld a game reserve – known, with the contiguous Etosha Game Park, as Game Reserve No 2, and covering a total area of 37 000 square miles. In 1939 it became a separate magisterial district, which was proclaimed as a native reserve in 1947. The boundaries of the Kaokoveld Native Reserve were the Atlantic Ocean to the west; in the north the Kunene River border with Angola; east, the Ovamboland Native Reserve, and south, the western extension of the Etosha Game Park.

The first South African officials to actually reside in the Kaokoveld were Sergeant Hildebrand and Constables Coghill and Adams, who in 1926 were based at Swartbooisdrift on the Kunene River. Their main responsibility was to stop poaching and control cattle movements to and from Angola. This police post was abandoned in 1939, when one of the policemen died of malaria and the traditional leaders in the Territory agreed to the stationing of a Native Commissioner in the Kaokoveld.

Establishing a permanent government presence in the Kaokoveld was not a simple matter for the South African authorities. While the Territory was administered from Ovamboland, one of the tribal chiefs, Oorlog Thom, had used his well-armed Herero and Himba followers to entrench himself as the most powerful ruler north of Sesfontein. The Native Commissioner at the time, 'Cocky' Hahn, was on good terms with Oorlog and had seen no reason to upset the local status quo. However, by 1936 the 73-year-old Herero chief's health had deteriorated to such an extent that Hahn requested permission from the Council of Headmen set up to hear serious cases and manage the Kaokoveld's affairs, to station a Native Commissioner in the Territory. But like Oorlog Thom before them, they strongly opposed the presence of a permanent European administrator within the Territory.

When Oorlog Thom died in 1937 a new factor added urgency to the South African government's need for a base within the Kaokoveld. The rapidly expanding aviation industry was in the process of developing a passenger and postal service to Luanda, and from there on to Europe along the western side of the continent. To achieve this, a refuelling station was needed north of Windhoek, but within the borders of South West Africa. As large tracts of the Kaokoveld were then still very sparsely populated, an uninhabited plain on the eastern side of the Territory was identified as being suitable for an aircraft landing field, and although there was no natural water in the area the problem was solved by the drilling of a borehole.

All that remained was to get the Council of Headmen to sanction the use of the area as both an airport and the station for a Native Commissioner. After tough negotiations the traditional leaders eventually agreed to the request, but insisted that no further land would be given to the government. To emphasise this they named the place they had granted to the whites *Opuwo*, which translated into English means 'no more'.

In 1939 Mr AM Barnard took up residence as the first Native Commissioner in Opuwo. However, the outbreak of the Second World War a few months later caused the proposed flights to Europe via the Kaokoveld to be postponed. And by the time the war ended, advances in aircraft design had considerably increased the range they could fly before needing to refuel, making a stopover in Opuwo unnecessary. In 1943 Commissioner Barnard was replaced by Mr B Wessels, and in 1949 Ben van Zyl took over the post.

Although a Dutch Reformed mission station and clinic were also established at Orumana in 1954, the missionaries were merely tolerated by the traditional Herero and Himba and very few conversions to Christianity were made. When I arrived 14 years later even the pupils attending the school they started were mainly orphans, or children of black government employees. The Territory's wealthy pastoralists were quite comfortable with their old ways and saw little need for the white man's religion or book learning.

*   *   *

On the afternoon of 31 July 1968 I arrived in Opuwo to take up my post as the Kaokoveld's agricultural supervisor, but I found the little town virtually deserted. Fortunately, Commissioner Van Zyl's wife, *Tannie* Babes, directed me to a group of acacia trees on the western end of the plain where her husband was holding a meeting with the Territory's Council of Headmen. Most of the other white government officials based in Opuwo were seated alongside him.

Ben van Zyl invited me to join the meeting and formally introduced the latest addition to the Kaokoveld's civil service to the gathering. I noticed a few of the older men nod sagely, but most of them paid little attention. They had not requested my services and had, no doubt, already seen too many white government officials coming to work in the Territory.

At the time the Kaokoveld's Council of Headmen comprised 25 Herero and Himba traditional leaders, plus the Topnaar Nama chief from Sesfontein. Each of them was also entitled to bring advisers to such meetings, which meant that if important issues were to be discussed as many as 100 headmen and their councillors might attend – although not necessarily all at same time. In fact, during that afternoon's session there was a constant coming and going of people and seldom were there more than 30 men actually sitting and listening to the proceedings.

The Council 'Chambers' were demarcated by a circle of stones with two gaps, referred to as *omivero* (doors), through which everyone leaving or re-entering the meeting passed. Van Zyl informed me that stepping over the stones was regarded as an offence, punishable by a fine of a goat or sheep. We white officials were equally subject to this rule, but could pay our fines in cash, which contributed to the Territory's Tribal Trust Fund.

After the meeting ended I learned that Robbie and Eleanor Roberts had left the Kaokoveld a few months previously. As there were no unoccupied houses it had been arranged for me to stay in the servants' quarters at the home of Burger Baard, the government official responsible for erecting and maintaining water installations in the Territory. With typical Afrikaner hospitality Burger and his wife, Frikkie, immediately made me feel part of their family, and I ended up staying with the Baards for nearly a year.

In his forties, bearded and sunburned to the colour of dark oak, Burger Baard took it upon himself to teach the 'five-thumbed *Engelsman*' he had been landed with how to live in the bush and get back home safely. I was in good hands. Born into a *bywoner* (sharecropper) family and brought up on a sheep farm in the south of South West Africa, Burger had not been an enthusiastic scholar and had left school with only a standard six. But he qualified *cum laude* in the 'school of life', was an outstanding bush mechanic and general handyman, and for what I really needed to know proved to be an excellent tutor.

Before joining BAD Burger had been working for the Department of Nature Conservation in the Etosha Game Park, but apparently left under a cloud. A lion had been found dead with a .22 bullet in it and he was the prime suspect. To kill a full-grown lion with such a low-calibre firearm would have been a remarkable feat, but Burger remained tight-lipped about the incident, saying only that there was more to the matter than met the eye. Once he did hint vaguely about having to cover up for a very prominent official, but would not say whether it was over the shooting of the lion or not. I never did find out whether he had, in fact, pulled the trigger.

While staying with Burger I accompanied him on a number of visits to Etosha, where we stayed with Peter Stark, the Park warden at that time. In his youth, Peter had been a notorious poacher, who was credited with outwitting its nature conservators on numerous occasions. One of the many stories about him that Burger told me was that he had once shot a large male lion on an open plain, but before he could escape with his trophy a nature conservation vehicle had come onto the scene. The only place to hide was to lie down behind the carcass, and when the driver stopped to look at the 'sleeping' lion Peter had lifted its head, so that it appeared to have just woken up. Satisfied that the lion was 'alive and well', the official had driven on his way.

The fact that Peter's illegal hunting exploits were well known made them an even greater embarrassment to the Park authorities. Finally, they decided that the only solution was to offer him a job as one of Etosha's nature conservators and challenge him to protect its wildlife as well as he had poached it. Peter accepted and soon rose up through the ranks to become the warden, and one of South West Africa's greatest conservationists.

* * *

The morning after my arrival in Opuwo, Commissioner Van Zyl briefed me on my duties. The agriculture section within BAD had decided to embark on a major livestock-marketing programme in the Kaokoveld, to reduce its cattle, goat and sheep numbers and prevent overgrazing of the Territory's rangelands. However, before any cloven-hoofed animals could be sold south of the Red Line they first needed to be inspected by veterinary officials, blood samples taken and then kept in isolation for a specified period to ensure that they were not carrying any contagious diseases. For this purpose a huge quarantine camp for cattle was in the process of being built at Omatambo Maue, in the corner between the Kaokoveld, Ovamboland and the Etosha Game Park. My first task was to complete a much smaller enclosure for goats and sheep at Otjitjekua, the southern entry point into the Territory.

As the fencing team under its experienced Herero foreman, Grootman, had already started work, Van Zyl felt there was no need for me to visit the site immediately. Instead he asked me to transport maize meal to Chief Simon //Havachab in Sesfontein, which would be a good opportunity for me to inspect the irrigated gardens there, as well as those at Warmquelle, a settlement 25 km further to the southeast, both of which would now fall under me.

That afternoon the Commissioner assigned me an ancient Chevrolet four-wheel-drive truck. It was clearly well past its sell-by date, but he assured me that a new vehicle had been ordered for my post and was expected to arrive before the end of the year. In fact, I only received my new truck in June the following year. Nevertheless, although I did not appreciate it at the time, just keeping the old Chev on the road provided me with many valuable lessons in basic mechanics. The agricultural section in the Kaokoveld also had a three-ton lorry in reasonable condition and a tractor that served as Grootman's official transport.

That evening a young Herero arrived at the Baards' home and announced his wish to be my translator. He spoke good Afrikaans, wore a clean T-shirt and had a very engaging smile. I was also impressed by his forthrightness and self-confidence, and so asked him to accompany me on my trip to Sesfontein. If all went well I would give him the job. Elias Tjondu immediately proved to be a great asset and soon became my right-hand man, remaining with me for the whole time I was in the Kaokoveld. A few months later I retired one of the older men in Grootman's gang and employed him as my cook and camp caretaker. Daniel Gavazepi was dour and pessimistic, the perfect foil for Elias's youthful exuberance.

The route we took to Sesfontein was the same one that Jod van der Merwe had followed when I accompanied him the year before. As I was in no hurry, this time I stopped at Kaoko Otavi to see the ruins of the 'Thirstland Trekker' church that Jod had mentioned on my trip with him. A side road took us to the eye of a strong spring, near which were the broken walls of a rectangular building made from limestone blocks cut out of the surrounding calcrete. It was all that remained here of one of the more remarkable chapters in the nineteenth-century Cape Dutch diaspora.

The reason why a group of Boers had trekked from the western Transvaal across the virtually waterless Kalahari to what became South West Africa is not clear. When questioned about it many years later, one of the participants could only say that: 'A drifting spirit was in our hearts. We just sold our farms and set out to find a new home.'

The first party had set off in 1875. It comprised 10 families in 16 wagons, under the leadership of GJL van der Merwe. With the assistance of the BaMangwato chief, Khama, the trekkers successfully crossed the Kalahari Desert to Lake Ngami and then headed south-west to Rietfontein, a strong spring under the jurisdiction of the Oorlam leader, Andries Lambert of Gobabis. Although they suffered considerable hardship along the way, all the wagons arrived safely. But Chief Lambert did not want a large group of Afrikaners living in his territory and only gave permission for them to rest there for a few years before moving on.

In 1977 a second party of Boers, comprising about 200 wagons, 700 people and 8 000 head of cattle, left the Transvaal. This time, convinced that such a large group could not cross the Kalahari, the BaMangwato chief did not give his support. Nevertheless, under their leader, Jan Greyling, who had been a hunter in the area, the trekkers pressed on and were able to prove Khama wrong, but at great cost. As they struggled through the deep sand between the widely scattered waterholes their livestock sometimes went for up to four days without drinking, and the people were rationed to a few spoonfuls of muddy water per day. After two months of great suffering, the trekkers finally managed to get most of their wagons to Lake Ngami. They would not have done so if it had not been for the help of the first party, still at Rietfontein, who sent fresh oxen to replace the hundreds that had died of thirst or been lost along the way.

At Lake Ngami they split up, with those under Greyling not wishing to face the prospect of another desert crossing to Rietfontein, and deciding instead to stay close to the Okavango River. But on this route they faced two even more deadly dangers, mosquitoes and tsetse flies that swarmed in the low-lying area along its banks. Men, women and children went down with malaria, while the livestock died in their hundreds of nagana. With the food supplies they brought from the Transvaal exhausted and most of the menfolk too weak with fever to hunt, those who did not die of malaria soon faced starvation. In a heartrending letter one of the women wrote: 'Fever is raging. Our cattle and sheep are almost all dead. The worst is the sore famine. God save us from this wilderness of hunger and sorrow.'

A Swedish hunter and trader, Axel Eriksson, met the trekkers on the banks of the Okavango, and through a Cape Town newspaper appealed on their behalf for help in the form of food, medicines and clothes. But their real saviour was a coloured ex-medical assistant from the Cape, William Worthington Jordan, who nursed the sick back to health and led the survivors to higher ground around Grootfontein, where the other two parties of trekkers were outspanned. Although the land was good here, their negotiations with the local chiefs were again unsuccessful and they decided to move on.

From Grootfontein they went west, following the southern edge of the Etosha salt pan to another large spring, which they also named Rietfontein. The area was only inhabited by Hei//um Bushmen, but the shallow calcareous soil was unsuitable for growing crops. While resting here they learned that Eriksson's newspaper appeal had been successful and that two schooners had been dispatched up the South West African coast with nearly £6 000 worth of provisions and other necessities for them. Hoping to find a suitable harbour for offloading these much-needed supplies, Gert Alberts led a small mounted party down the valley of the Hoarusib River to the sea, becoming the first white men to traverse the Kaokoveld from east to west. But the place they chose for the landing, Rocky Point, proved unsafe and the schooners returned to Walvis Bay, forcing the Boers to send their wagons on a long overland journey to collect the supplies donated by the people of Cape Town.

On his way through the Kaokoveld Alberts had noted its many springs, the majority of which were uninhabited because cattle raiding by Topnaar and Swartbooi Nama had driven most of the Herero-speaking pastoralists across the Kunene River. In 1879 the Thirstland Trekkers moved to Otjitundua and Kaoko Otavi, but although some maize could be irrigated from the strong springs there, the area as a whole was too arid for crop farming.

Another likely reason for their decision not to settle in the Kaokoveld was the possibility of South West Africa being annexed by Great Britain. The area around Walvis Bay had just become a British possession and while visiting the port to collect their donated supplies, the Boers had met a representative of the Cape Parliament who was lobbying for Britain to extend her sovereignty inland. William Coates-Palgrave saw the Trekkers as a stabilising factor in the region and hoped that they would stay in the Kaokoveld, but by the time they returned with their provisions the Boers had received a more inviting offer. Axel Eriksson had used his good offices with the Portuguese administrators in southern Angola to secure them permission to settle on the fertile Humpata plateau. In August 1880, now rested and re-provisioned, 57 families with 61 wagons, 120 horses, 3 000 cattle and about the same number of goats and sheep, forded the Kunene River on the last stage of a journey that had taken them over 2 500 km from their Transvaal homes.

Back in south-western Africa, Will Jordan still hoped the Trekkers would come back and set up a Boer Republic on the broad savannas to the south-east of the Etosha Pan, and had negotiated on their behalf with the Ondonga chief, Kambonde. But his plans were delayed by disagreement between Kambonde and Maherero, the Herero chief in Okahandja, over who owned the area. During this dispute, Kambonde asked Maherero where the borders of his territory were, and is reputed to have received the legendary reply: 'Wherever Herero cattle have grazed is Herero land.' Before ownership of the area could be settled, Will Jordan was murdered by Kambonde's nephew, Nehale.

In 1928, after almost 50 years in Angola, the Thirstland Trekkers returned to South West Africa. Although they had got on well with the local Portuguese officials, and played a major role in helping them extend their authority into the south of the colony, the fact that Roman Catholicism was the only official religion was hard for the strongly Protestant Boers to accept. At the invitation of the new South African administration in Windhoek, they once more inspanned their wagons and gathered at Swartbooisdrift on the Kunene River. Many graves had been left in Angola, but they were going back to their own people, who shared their religious and social beliefs. After crossing into SWA they were transported by government lorries to farms allocated to them in the Grootfontein and Gobabis districts. Ironically, it was the same land they had requested and been refused by Chiefs Lamberts, Maherero and Kambonde half a century before.

* * *

We drove on towards Sesfontein, stopping for the night at a small spring next to the road about 15 km south of Kaoko Otavi. There was no sign of human habitation nearby, and as it appeared to be well used by wild animals I laid out my sleeping bag between the buttress roots of a sycamore fig about 30 metres from the water. Before we had finished eating there were already soft noises coming from the surrounding bush, so I turned in early – not to sleep, but to lie and wait for the game I hoped would come to drink.

Elias, who chose to sleep on the back of the truck, also went to bed early and an hour after the sun set all was quiet in our camp. Gradually the faint rustles, shuffles and clicking of hooves on rock came closer. But the truck was parked too close to the spring, and the unidentified creatures that approached saw it and clattered off into the night. As there was very little moonlight, all I could see was ghostly clouds of dust, but just sleeping again on the Kaokoveld's hard ground was exciting enough for me.

In the morning Elias inspected the tracks around the spring and found that quite a few zebra and impala had drunk after I went to sleep. He also pointed out the spoor of a hyena that came within five metres of where I had been lying. It would not be the last time he would have doubts about the common sense of his employer-to-be.

After packing up our camp and driving on we came upon a fresh kudu carcass lying next to the road. In its flank was an arrow, which I suspected had been poisoned. Remembering what Jod had told me about the Herero not needing to hunt, I asked Elias who he thought was responsible.

'This arrow belongs to an *omuTjimba*,' he replied. 'They have no cattle. That's why they must hunt wild animals.'

Elias explained that the Tjimba were just poor Herero who had lost all their cattle in wars with the Nama people. Later, after Daniel had joined us, he admitted that his own family were, in fact, Tjimba, but claimed that this derogatory term no longer applied to him because he had recently acquired two cows, both of which had calves. Daniel, who came from a wealthy family, did not accept Elias's self-proclaimed rise in social status, and insisted that he would need to own many more cattle before he could call himself a real Herero.

We reached Sesfontein by midday, and as Chief Simon could only see me the next morning I spent the afternoon inspecting the irrigated wheat fields beneath the date palms, and talking to their owners. The majority of the individual plots belonged to Topnaar Namas, but they were not the first people to inhabit this oasis on the edge of the desert.

The earliest inhabitants of the area would have been small nomadic bands of hunter-gatherers. When the government ethnologist, NJ van Warmelo, visited Sesfontein in the late 1940s he found that there were still a few Bushmen there, who according to the only man he interviewed called themselves Kubun, and spoke a language without clicks. Van Warmelo's informant told him that they had previously lived in the Namib and on the coast, 'eating what veldkos they can get and fish found along the shore'. However, most of them had taken Damara wives and now stayed around Sesfontein, where they were given food handouts by the Nama.

Traditionally the Damara had been hunter-gatherers, and had probably once lived throughout the Kaokoveld. Their dark skins caused some anthropologists to believe their origins were in west-central Africa, but this was impossible to verify because they had since adopted the language of the Nama. In spite of being the largest ethnic group in Sesfontein, the Damara were subjugated by the pastoralists, in whose fields they now worked for little more than their subsistence. In the past they were not allowed to keep livestock, I was told, but many families did now own small flocks of goats and some of them even a few cattle.

When Herero-speaking pastoralists came into the Kaokoveld they would also have used the many springs around Sesfontein to water their herds and flocks, although the low rainfall probably ensured that they remained only until the sweet grazing on the highly alkaline plains was depleted. Nevertheless, their greater organisation and iron weapons would have enabled them to dominate the hunter-gathers while they were in residence.

The last ethnic group to come on the scene were the Topnaar Nama, who migrated here from the lower Kuiseb River around the middle of the nineteenth century. With the firearms they had acquired from the early white traders in Walvis Bay they were able to drive out both the Herero and the Damara and claim Sesfontein as their stronghold. From there, together with mounted bands of Swartbooi Nama who settled around Fransfontein a few years later, they set about plundering the pastoralists' livestock throughout the Kaokoveld.

On foot and with only spears to defend themselves, the widely dispersed Herero could offer little resistence, and emboldened by their success Swartbooi Nama began raiding further afield, including crossing the Kunene River into Angola, where they twice besieged the small port of Moçâmedes. However, in 1892 one of their raiding parties made the fatal mistake of stealing cattle from the Thirstland Trekkers who had settled on the Humpata Plateau. Quickly organising a mounted commando, the Boers were able to catch up with the stock-thieves before they crossed back into the Kaokoveld, and after taking them by surprise killed nine of the 17 raiders. Two Boers also died in the battle, but all the cattle were recovered.

Although they carried out no more raids into Angola, the Nama remained the most powerful force in the region until the Swartboois in Fransfontein rose up against the German colonial government in 1898. The rebellion was brutally crushed, and to keep order in this remote part of their territory a fort was built at Sesfontein and manned by a garrison of mounted troops. But by then the great rinderpest epidemic that swept through Southern Africa had decimated the Namas' herds, and shattered their pastoral economy.

Destitute without cattle and prevented from raiding their neighbours, the Topnaar chief, Jan /Unuweb, brought an evangelist from the Rhenish Mission in Fransfontein, Nicodemus Kido, to teach his people how to irrigate wheat, maize and other crops from the strong springs in the area. In 1941 Nicodemus's son, Benjamin, became chief of Sesfontein, but when he died six years later the leadership reverted to the original Topnaar patriline with the appointment of Simon //Havachab. Under him were four Nama headmen, one of whom was resident at the nearby settlement of Warmquelle. For the first time, Simon also chose two prominent Damaras, Levi Ganuseb and Elias Amchab, as well as two Herero leaders, Uerimunga Kasaona and Hivetira Karutjaiva, to serve on his council.

When the rinderpest epidemic ended the people living around Sesfontein rebuilt their cattle herds, which soon overgrazed the fragile grasslands growing on the alkaline plains in the Hoanib basin, and by 1968 it had been reduced to a dustbowl. As a result, at the time of my visit irrigated crops were still the mainstay of the local economy.

*   *   *

On the morning after my arrival Simon //Havachab and two of his councillors came to my camp under the fig trees near the old German fort. The Topnaar chief was by then deep in his sixties; small and fine-featured, but with the aura of a man whose forefathers had once struck terror into the hearts of all who lived in the region. Simon still ruled Sesfontein with an iron fist, apparently having his Herero and Damara subjects flogged for infringements of the local laws. When there was work to be done in the fields a bell would be rung each morning and all the able-bodied men had to report for duty, which lasted until he decided enough had been done for the day.

After my bags of maize meal had been offloaded, we sat in the shade and discussed the situation in this remote corner of old Africa. The irrigation system that Nicodemus Kido had laid out still worked smoothly, but after 70 years of cultivation the soil on which the crops were grown was exhausted and the recent harvests had been poor. Simon also told me that at the remote cattle-posts hyena and African wild dogs were causing considerable livestock losses. Growing trees in the high rainfall areas of Natal had provided nothing to prepare me for these issues, and with no useful advice to offer I could only promise to report these problems to the Commissioner on my return to Opuwo. For me, working as an agricultural official in the Kaokoveld was going to require a steep learning curve.

That afternoon Elias and I drove in a south-easterly direction across the dusty plains to Warmquelle, where there were more artesian springs that fell under the jurisdiction of Chief Simon //Havachab. After passing through a gap that the Hoanib River had cut through a spectacular limestone mountain range, we reached a small settlement at the foot of a low ridge where, as at Sesfontein, wheat and maize fields were being furrow irrigated by the people living there. From the strongest of the springs there was also a broken stone aqueduct that led to a reservoir made from the same material – all that remained of an attempt to introduce European farming methods into the region during the German colonial period.

Reich Chancellor Otto von Bismarck, the driving force behind Germany's acquisition of colonies, had been a frugal man, who believed that they should be developed mainly with capital derived from the private sector and not the state. In line with this policy, in 1902 the largely uninhabited north-west of the country was leased to the Kaokoveld Land and Mining Company, which appointed Carl Schlettwein to be its local representative. His instructions were to prospect for minerals, as well as divide the Territory into farms for sale to immigrants. However, two years later war had broken out with the Herero and Nama in the centre and south of the colony. With no settlers interested in buying a Kaokoveld farm while hostilities continued, Schlettwein moved to Warmquelle, where he planned to breed horses for the colonial forces. When this scheme failed he began irrigating crops from the abundant spring water here, building a system of aqueducts and a large overnight storage dam.

By 1907 the Herero and Nama had been defeated and large numbers of settlers did start coming into South West Africa. In 1910 alone there were over 50 applications for land in the Kaokoveld, but the Company held out for higher prices and none were approved until 1912. By this time the *Bizerkshauptmann* in Outjo, under whose authority the area fell, was deeply frustrated. After ten years no exploitable minerals had been found and no development had taken place, resulting in the Company not even being able to pay the land taxes due to the Colonial government. Five years later, when South Africa nullified the Company's concession, only four farms had been surveyed and sold, and they were never occupied.

Half a century later I found Warmquelle inhabited mainly by Damara people, who had given up their nomadic way of life to work in the fields of the Nama. As they owned few livestock most of them still gathered veld foods from the surrounding area, one of the most important being the seeds of grass and herbs that had been collected and stored underground by harvester ants. They were also renowned honey collectors, with individual families 'owning' wild beehives whose whereabouts they kept secret.

My informant was Markus Hartley, a Herero descendant of an Englishman who hunted in south-western Africa during the late nineteenth century. Markus was employed by the government to stop the movement of livestock across the Red Line, so the next morning I drove with him to the southern border of the Kaokoveld, where the Hoanib exited from a spectacular gorge through limestone ranges. Along the way we saw quite a few springbok and ostrich, as well many elephant tracks, and as the boundary was not fenced Markus told me that lion, cheetah and wild dog also moved freely across it, killing their cattle, goats and sheep. However, he said, if any livestock strayed into the Park they were shot by nature conservation officials.

Surely the game coming into the Kaokoveld suffered the same fate at the hands of the local people, I said, but Markus assured me that the Herero and Nama only killed predators. However, he did concede that the Damara still hunted with bows and arrows, as well as snares, sometimes even inside the Park. 'They have no cattle and must eat meat sometimes. It is the way of their forefathers, but they only kill what they need and there are many wild animals in Etosha.'

The government officials I accompanied the previous year had used a similar excuse for exceeding their pot licences, and as the Damara had lost their land to the Herero, Nama and Europeans it was hard to begrudge them hunting.

*   *   *

The following day we returned to Opuwo and the rest of the month was spent with Grootman's team working on the quarantine camp at Otjitjekua. In early September the Department of BAD's chief agricultural officer, Nico Smit, visited me there. He was a lean, fit man in his late thirties, who unlike most of the government officials in Opuwo was well educated and spoke good English. Around the campfire that night he told me why livestock marketing was necessary, and what my responsibilities as an agricultural official were.

When it was designated as a native reserve there were relatively few cattle, goats and sheep in the Kaokoveld. But since then their numbers had rapidly increased and serious overgrazing was now taking place around most of the water-points. One of the reasons for the high cattle population was that traditionally the Herero and Himba only slaughtered them at funerals and other ceremonial occasions, but Smit believed that if a market was available many families would be prepared to sell their surplus oxen – as was now happening in Herero areas south of the Red Line.

However, this was not a simple matter. Cloven-hoofed animals could only be moved across the Red Line if they were guaranteed to be free of foot-and-mouth disease and, in the case of cattle, also bovine pleuro-pneumonia. Consequently, before any animals could be bought by the government, veterinary officials had to inspect them, as well as take blood samples from all the cattle in areas where they came from. On top of this, those purchased would have to stand quarantine – for three months in the case of cattle and three weeks for small-stock. These rules were laid down in international agreements with the countries that imported animal products from South West Africa, and any contraventions could mean a ban on all meat or skin exports from the country.

Apart from building the quarantine camp at Otjitjekua, my role was to get permission from the stockowners for veterinary officials to inspect and take blood samples, which the Kaokovelders had never allowed in the past. In fact, Smit said, in most areas stock inspectors were not even allowed to enter cattle kraals to count their animals. This was a major hurdle, and as the Herero and Himba attached less value to goats and sheep, Ben van Zyl had recommended we start by buying small-stock. Once they got used to the marketing procedures they would more likely agree to cattle being inspected.

When Grootman's team completed their work at Otjitjekua they had to start building dip tanks in places where headmen had given permission. This would enable Tom Sopper's men to first treat all the small-stock in the area for mange, to ensure that they did not infect the quarantine camp with this contagious skin disease. A further duty of mine was to maintain the fence between the Kaokoveld and Ovamboland that prevented livestock from moving between them.

Back in Opuwo I discussed the proposed livestock sales with Ben van Zyl, who suggested we start buying from the Himba in the north of the Territory. Little rain had fallen there, which meant that milk would be in short supply. He hoped that this would encourage people to sell their animals in order to supplement their diets by purchasing maize meal. As a first step he suggested I speak to Headman Johannes Ruyter at Oruhona, who would give me the best advice on how to proceed further.

Johannes Ruyter turned out to be a portly but dignified man in his fifties, who was dressed in western clothes and to my surprise spoke perfect Afrikaans. After I had explained the purpose of my visit and been brought a cup of sweet tea by one of his daughters, we sat under his shade porch and talked about the weather, livestock and the proposed selling thereof.

He personally welcomed the government's plan to buy goats and sheep, and understood the veterinary requirements that had to be adhered to before it could happen. But inspecting livestock was a sensitive matter, he told me, and recommended I first speak to Munimuhoro Kapika, the wealthiest and most influential Himba headman in the Kaokoveld. If he agreed to the selling of small-stock, none of the other headmen in the north would stop their people from doing so. After thanking him for his advice and requesting his support in the future, Elias and I drove on and made camp where the road crossed a large riverbed below the imposing Omuhonga Mountain.

Before dark I took a walk through the well-developed woodlands on the riverbank and discovered that the Department of Nature Conservation's game capture team had also camped just a few hundred metres away. The officers in charge, Peter Flanagan and John Dixon, invited me for a beer and explained that they were there to capture black-faced impala, a local subspecies of this otherwise common antelope, which only occurred in the Kaokoveld and neighbouring parts of Angola. Because it was believed that their numbers were declining, the impala they caught would be translocated to Etosha National Park to ensure the survival of the subspecies within South West Africa.

They had already caught over 70 impala, which were being held in a quarantine pen before they could be moved to Etosha. It was clear that some of them were not well, and they admitted that a few had already died of injuries they sustained during their capture. With no immobilising drugs yet available, the method used was to blind the impala with a spotlight at night, and then jump off the vehicle and catch each animal by hand. I later learned that fewer than half the impala caught in this operation reached their destination alive.

The following morning we arrived at Omuramba, about 30 km south of the Epupa Falls on the Kunene River, where Munimuhoro Kapika was then living. When Elias explained the purpose of our visit to one of his councillors we were told that the headman was sleeping, and that we should come back when it got cooler. We returned at about four o'clock and were led to a cleared area under a tree where the meeting would take place. Seated there were a group of mostly elderly men, who greeted us cordially and asked where we had come from and what news we had heard along the way. Elias answered their questions on my behalf, but when he mentioned the game capture camp I became the focus of their attention: Why were white people catching impala? Where were they taking them, and who had given them permission to catch wild animals in their area?

I could only repeat what Flanagan and Dixon told me, but they were clearly not happy with my answers, particularly when I tried to explain the reasons for the impala being taken to Etosha. They had always lived together with wild animals, they told me, and if their numbers were now decreasing, it was because of white government officials killing them, not the Himba. I was not in a position to contradict them.

By Kaokoveld standards Munimuhoro was fabulously rich, and although no one had actually counted them, he was reputed to own over 4 000 oxen and at least that many breeding cows and calves. Consequently, I expected such a renowned Himba leader to have a regal presence, but when he finally made his appearance the headman turned out to be so fat that he could hardly walk, and was led to our meeting tree by a young boy. He was also suffering from a severe case of opthalmia, and yellow pus exuded from both his eyes. As soon as he had seated himself Munimuhoro asked what gifts I had brought for him. I had none – a bad start to my relationship with the Territory's most powerful Himba headman.

While I explained the government's plans to buy goats and sheep, and the necessary veterinary requirements, Munimuhoro's councillors listened carefully and asked for clarification on a number of points. However, the old headman soon nodded off to sleep, and when I finished speaking had to be tapped on the shoulder and told that I was waiting for his reply. He then grandly informed me that he would consider the matter overnight, and that I should come back in the morning for an answer. When I did so, he added, I must make sure that I brought him a present.

Next day, armed with a little sugar and tea, we returned to the headman's onganda, where he informed us that because his people were hungry he had no objection to them selling goats and sheep. However, in each area the local headman would have to decide whether or not to allow the stock to be inspected and dipped. Before leaving, Munimuhoro instructed me to also tell the government that he needed more boreholes and dams in his area as there was not sufficient water for his cattle. He had started to ask for something else when one of his advisers suggested he had already requested enough for this occasion.

As Munimuhoro had no objection, the road was now open for me to visit the other important Himba leaders and get permission for the building of dip tanks. But although I was always given a polite hearing, many of them clearly had reservations about allowing outsiders to look inside the mouths of their animals for gum blisters, the most obvious symptom of foot-and-mouth disease. They first wanted to hear about the government's plans from the Commissioner, a man they knew and trusted, and not from a newcomer whom they did not know. When I reported my findings back to Van Zyl he decided to call a meeting of the Kaokoveld's Council of Headmen to discuss the matter.

On the appointed day a group of Himba headmen, including Munimuhoro and Johannes Ruyter, as well as many of the other leaders from the central and southern parts of the Territory, gathered under the trees on the Opuwo flats. The Herero delegates were immaculately dressed in formal western clothes, the Tjimba in a more tattered version of the same, while the Himba wore only traditional loincloths, in some cases covered by army jackets or greatcoats. Although they all shared a common ancestry and spoke the same language, the groups sat separately. Johannes Ruyter, looking out of place in a collar and tie, took his seat among the Himba.

Van Zyl started by telling the gathering that it was now time for the people of the Kaokoveld to start selling their livestock to markets in the towns south of the Red Line. In response most of the western clothes-wearers at the meeting nodded in approval. But, he said, for this to happen all the animals sold would first have to stand quarantine. This also seemed acceptable to the headmen present. He then went on to say that before any livestock could be purchased all the animals in the area had to be inspected to ensure that they were not carrying foot-and-mouth disease. When he explained how this would be done, by veterinary officials looking into their mouths, there was an increase in attentiveness: even those of the older Himba headmen who had been sleeping became suddenly alert.

A heated discussion then followed and Van Zyl could only continue when the meeting had once more settled down. He concluded by saying that at this stage the government was only planning to buy goats and sheep, and just from the north. All that was required from the Council of Headmen was their permission to start inspecting the small-stock belonging to those Himba who wished to sell. Once again the air buzzed with lively debate about the issue, and when after an hour it seemed no nearer to reaching a consensus, the proceedings were adjourned until later that afternoon.

At four o'clock, the meeting re-convened and Van Zyl asked whether they had come to a decision. A number of headmen, as well as some smartly attired younger councillors, stood up to give their views. Although every speaker put a slightly different angle on the issue, there was general agreement that each headman would be left to decide whether or not to allow the small-stock in their areas to be inspected. However, it was also made very clear that the approval of the Council applied only to goats and sheep. In effect, it was the same message that Munimuhoro had given me, but this time the Commissioner himself had spoken, and everyone had heard.

By early October the quarantine camp at Otjitjekua had been finished and Grootman's team was able to concentrate on building the small-stock dipping tanks. As each one was completed Tom Sopper and his new assistant, Kallie van Zyl, dipped and inspected the local goats and sheep, finding no signs of foot-and-mouth disease. The final part of our preparations for the marketing programme was the welding together of a double-decker cage to be fitted on the three-ton lorry, which would be used to transport the purchased small-stock to the quarantine camp. This was to be done in Opuwo by Burger Baard.

As Grootman's team required little supervision I was able to spend much of the next two months getting to know the Kaokoveld, its people and wild-life. As I was also eligible for a pot licence, I had brought my double-barrel shotgun with me and soon after arriving in the Kaokoveld purchased a 30.06 rifle. With my Herero staff regarding life as not worth living without a regular supply of meat, many afternoons were spent hunting, and like most of my colleagues I soon lapsed into shooting what was needed, and not necessarily what was legally allowed. It was the lifestyle I had been looking for when I left Natal, and although my salary with BAD was only half what I earned on Tsumeb Mine, I had everything I wanted – and it all fitted onto the back of my official truck.

* * *

By late December the small-stock inspections had gone so well that Tom and Kallie van Zyl decided to go with their wives on a fishing trip to the Skeleton

Coast over Christmas, and invited me to join them. Ben van Zyl had built a
wooden shack at Rocky Point for officials stationed in Opuwo to use on such
occasions, but as he and the Commissioner General, Dr Marti Olivier, would
be staying there, we went to Angra Fria, 100 km further north. It was where
possibly the loneliest weathermen in the world had lived a few years earlier.

Ernst Karlova was one of the Kaokoveld's legendary characters. As a teenager he had left South West Africa to train as a pilot in Germany and served
in the *Luftwaffe* during the Second World War. On his return he settled in
Swakopmund and in the early 1960s, when a consortium of South African
companies planned to build a harbour on the Skeleton Coast, he was asked
to man a meteorological station at Angra Fria. Using wood from shipwrecks
that had washed onto the beach and panels of hardboard, he built a house
near a large salt pan 5 km inland, and for two years radioed information on
the weather conditions to the port authorities in Walvis Bay.

To reach Angra Fria we drove via Orupembe and then down the Munutum
River, which disappeared into the coastal dunes about 20 km from the sea.
Tom led the way, followed by Kallie in his vehicle, while I brought up the rear.
I was able to keep up with them until a fierce sand storm obliterated the view
ahead and I lost their tracks. Fighting rising panic, I ploughed on through the
deep sand, following the setting sun until I reached the gravel flats near the
coast. Here I was able to find their tracks, and followed them to Karlova's now
weather-beaten home.

A few kilometres away, on 29 November 1942 a mixed passenger and cargo
liner, the *Dunedin Star*, had come too close to the shore and ripped its hull
open on a reef. Fearing that the vessel would sink the captain had run her
aground, and then ferried the passengers and 42 members of the crew ashore
by motorised lifeboat. By then a number of ships in the vicinity had heard the
mayday call and three days later the first of them arrived on the scene and
took the remaining crew members on board. But the rough seas prevented
them from rescuing the survivors on the beach – including eight women and
three small children.

A second ship that came to the stricken vessel's assistance attempted to
float rafts of provisions onshore, but strong currents washed them all up the
coast and none were found. When a shortage of coal forced the last rescue
vessel to sail away, an overland expedition of eight trucks, led by police captain WJB Smith, was dispatched from Windhoek, over 1 000 km away, the last
300 km through trackless desert.

In order to get food and water to the people stranded on the beach a

Ventura bomber took off from Walvis Bay, but the tubes of water it dropped all burst on hitting the ground. Hoping to at least pick up the women and children, the pilot, Captain Immens Naude, then landed nearby, but the aircraft became bogged in the sand and could not take off again. To further unnerve the castaways, while looking for firewood in the remains of a wrecked wooden ship, they found five headless human skeletons!

At the mouth of the Khumib River, 80 km to the south, another drama was unfolding. One of the ships that came to assist in the rescue, the *Sir Charles Elliot*, drifted off course in the high seas and also ran aground. A lifeboat was lowered, but it overturned and one of the crewmen drowned. Although the others on board managed to swim ashore, one of them, Mathias Khoraseb, died of exhaustion on the beach.

In the meantime, the overland convoy had been making painstaking progress through the Kaokoveld. The greatest problem was the many sandy riverbeds that had to be crossed, which necessitated deflating all the trucks' tires and re-inflating them with the single pump they had brought with them. Finally, seven days after leaving Windhoek, and ten days since the *Dunedin Star* ran aground, they reached Rocky Point, where they first rescued the surviving crew members of the *Sir Charles Elliot*. They then headed on up the coast to Angra Fria.

By now the seas had calmed sufficiently to allow the *Nerine* to come close inshore and rescue 26 of the *Dunedin Star* passengers and crew. Three days later the overland expedition got within a few kilometres of Angra Fria, where they again bogged down in sand. Smith and the medical doctor accompanying the expedition then walked the final stage of their epic journey. It had taken 11 days for the overland party to cover the 1 000 kilometres, a large part of it blazing their own trail through the Kaokoveld. Although some of those stranded on the beach were hospitalised, all of them survived.

But the saga had not ended. In January Capt. Naude returned to Angra Fria to salvage his aircraft. After taking four days to get it out of the sand and to a suitable runway, he took off with two crewmen, but less than an hour into the flight one of the Ventura's engines seized and the plane crashed into the sea. Although all three men were able to float on part of the plane's fuselage to shore, they too were now stranded on the Skeleton Coast, and no one would have known where to look for them. Their only hope was to get back to Sarusas spring in the Khumib River before the vehicles that took them to Angra Fria passed by. In spite of their minor injuries, they managed to walk the 50 km up the coast just in time.

When we visited the place where the *Dunedin Star* had been wrecked, we found two large fuel tanks and some Second World War gas masks washed up on the beach. Nearby, we also saw what remained of the flimsy shelters built by the castaways to protect themselves from the blisteringly hot days and bitterly cold nights on the coast. For us, the sun shone bleakly once the morning fog had lifted, but a south-wester soon started blowing off the sea, and when it got too cold we returned to the shelter of Karlova's makeshift home. As we huddled around our driftwood fire, with the fog once more rolling in off the sea, I thought about the many other shipwrecked sailors who had managed to reach this desolate shore, but for whom there had been no hope of rescue.

We stayed at Angra Fria for three more days, doing a little fishing, but mostly just exploring this fascinating stretch of coastline. Sun-basking Cape fur seals were plentiful along the beach and in places the sand was criss-crossed with the tracks of brown hyena and jackal. Both species also came to visit us at night, clearly visible in the moonlight. On our way back to Opuwo we found the dehydrated remains of four lions, and I wondered if they had died naturally in the dunes, or been shot inland and dumped here. Soon their skeletons would be covered by the shifting sand, along with countless others that lie buried on the Kaokoveld's desert coast.

CHAPTER SIX

THE CLASH OF CULTURES

On the day after New Year, Tom, Kallie, Burger and I started the final preparations for buying small-stock in the Kaokoveld. We were sailing in uncharted waters. In the past the Himba had used their cattle, goats and sheep to pay for the services of traditional herbalists and diviners, or exchanged them for food, weapons, beads and shells with neighbouring tribes. More recently, government officials had bought animals for slaughter, giving the owners maize meal and tobacco in return. But the magnitude of our planned purchases, the compulsory pre-sale inspections and dipping, as well as the fact that we would be paying a fixed amount of money that was based on the animals' live weight, made our operation unique in the Kaokoveld's history.

To bridge the Himba into the modern cash economy, Ben van Zyl had suggested that we have bags of maize meal available for purchase at each of the villages where we planned to buy small-stock. As very little rain had as yet fallen in the region, he felt that the actual sight of them would provide an extra incentive for the stockowners to offer their sheep and goats for sale.

Grootman's team had built the first dip tank at Oruhona, where we planned to begin purchasing. My reason for starting there was that Johannes Ruyter understood our new marketing procedures, and as he was highly respected, a successful sale at Oruhona should mean plain sailing in the other headmen's areas.

Once we had set the date for the first small-stock sale, Ben van Zyl notified the senior BAD animal husbandry officer in Windhoek, Hine Brand, and the State Veterinarian in Kamanjab, Dr Ian Scheepers, both of whom intended to be present at this historic occasion. On the day before, we all gathered in Opuwo to discuss the details and plan the logistics. Hine Brand also informed us that the live-weight price for both sheep and goats had been fixed at 4c a pound – the best that could be offered under the uncertain circumstances that prevailed. He explained that the government would have to cover all transport costs, both to the quarantine camp and then a further 120 km on to Kamanjab, the nearest town south of the Red Line. It would also be responsible for any losses that might occur during transport, or in the quarantine camp, and because the animals were expected to be in poor condition, these might be considerable.

According to Hine, the only butcher in Kamanjab, Paul Robberts, had driven a hard bargain. A short, rotund Afrikaner who had been born in Angola of Thirstland Trekker stock, he was known throughout the area as a man who was quick to use his fists and proud of his racism. The price he was prepared to pay for 'Kaffir goats' was 6c a pound, delivered to his farm just outside of the town. As the next possible market was in Outjo, 160 km further away, the government had no option but to accept his offer.

Ben van Zyl was very concerned about the amount we were planning to pay. A quick calculation showed that it would be significantly less, when compared to the price of a bag of maize meal, than what was paid by officials when buying small-stock. But Hine was university trained and his figures were based on a profit and loss analysis. Our casual transactions involved no risks or transport costs, and therefore could not be used for comparison. If the Himba wanted to become commercial farmers, then they must learn the hard facts of modern business right from the start.

All of us could clearly understand his reasoning, but would the stockowners? Although I was too junior to contradict him, I also thought that it was us BAD officials who wanted the local people to market their livestock. We were the ones who believed that the Territory was overgrazed, a concept that was well known to every European farmer, but was not in the vocabulary of the Himba I had spoken to. Without the benefit of rain-gauges and previous records, their only measure of the season's rainfall was how much grass actually grew. Consequently, if the grazing was poorer than in past years, to them it simply meant that less rain had fallen.

Having too many cattle, goats or sheep was also not an idea they easily accepted. Apart from their utilitarian value, a man's herds and flocks were his wealth, from which he gained his status in the community. Exchanging your livestock for what you needed was perfectly acceptable, but deliberately reducing their numbers to improve the grazing was not part of the Himba worldview.

The following morning I loaded 20 bags of meal onto the three-ton lorry and drove to Oruhona, where we made a temporary campsite under a shady tree and prepared ourselves for the first small-stock sale. The lorry was parked nearby, with its side flaps down so that the bags of maize meal were clearly visible. I then hung the scale from a stout branch a few metres away and set up a folding table on which piles of bank notes were placed. All that was missing was the sheep and goats we were supposed to purchase.

While Daniel made us tea, Elias and Tom's assistants went off to find out where the stock-owners and their flocks were. Three cups of tea later, there was still no sign of any small-stock, so we had lunch. At two o'clock Elias reported back. Some heavy showers had fallen in the hills to the south and most of the livestock had been taken there to exploit the flush of new growth in that area. Messages had been sent out and the first stockowners were expected to arrive soon. Daniel put the kettle back on and we sat back and waited.

At about four o'clock a single Himba man arrived with two sheep and three goats. After an exchange of greetings, each animal was placed in a sack and hung on the scale. The weight was called out to Hine Brand, who recorded it in his notebook. By the time the last goat had been weighed, a small group of men and women had gathered to watch the show. All the local people, like the goats and sheep after being released from the sack, seemed rather bemused by the proceedings.

When Hine had calculated the combined weight he converted it into a cash value, and through Tom's translator informed the owner of the price we would pay him. Spectators, government officials and our assistants now all looked expectantly at the Himba stockman. He looked blankly back at us. The translator spoke to him again, but he still seemed mystified. Thinking that the sight of the money would help to clarify the issue I counted out the number of bank notes his animals were worth and grandly put them in front of him. He now looked at the money, shook his head vigorously and let out a stream of to us unintelligible but obviously uncomplimentary comments in Otjiherero, at the same time gesticulating towards the back of the lorry. Tom's assistant roared with laughter and then translated what he had said.

'This Himba man says we can take all the tree leaves we have brought with us back to Windhoek. He only wants to know how many bags of meal we will give him for his animals.'

I quickly worked it out and informed him that, altogether, his animals were worth three bags of meal, with one rand and ten cents over. As my words were being translated the man looked me straight in the eye and I saw his expression change from defiance to disbelief. For a few seconds I thought he was going to cancel the sale, but the sight of the maize meal must have been too much for him. Saying no more, he turned around and walked off to where the lorry was parked. I sent the interpreter after him with his change and watched as he turned, saw what was being offered, spat dramatically on the ground, but took the money anyway. I wondered what he would do with it.

No more small-stock were brought for sale that afternoon or the following morning, and at two o'clock on the second day we broke camp and moved on to the next buying point. Here there were quite a few prospective sellers, but after much haggling over the price only three goats were purchased and two bags of meal sold. The next day Hine Brand and Dr Scheepers returned to their stations and I drove back to Opuwo to discuss the situation with the Commissioner. It was obvious that the low price we were paying was the main problem and Van Zyl agreed to try and get my superiors to raise it. Until an answer had been received I postponed all further small-stock sales. A week later I was informed that 4c a pound was the maximum that could be offered and that I should continue trying to purchase as many animals as possible at that price.

By the end of February, after two more weeks of buying, we had a total of only 37 head of small-stock in the quarantine camp. The rainy season had now begun in earnest and, as the Himba cattle fattened and milk became plentiful in the villages again, maize meal was no longer needed by the herdsmen. The result was that at many purchasing points no sheep or goats were offered for sale at all. To add to our problems, long sections of the tracks we followed had turned to muddy quagmires and the lorry repeatedly got bogged down. With heavy rain now falling almost every day, the previously dry river beds that drained the northern Kaokoveld were also frequently turned to raging torrents that kept us waiting for hours, and sometimes days, before they subsided and we could safely cross. As there was now a real danger of getting stuck in one of them and the vehicle being swept away before we could dig it out, I decided that the few animals we were buying did not justify the effort or the risk. After getting Nico Smit's permission, the first livestock marketing project in the Kaokoveld was called off.

*   *   *

When I returned to Opuwo, there was a very different problem to attend to. Foot-and-mouth disease had broken out in neighbouring Ovamboland and the Commissioner informed me that the Kaokoveld's eastern boundary fence was in urgent need of repair. During the dry season, the 10 labourers strategically placed along this 200 km fenceline had been able to maintain it in a reasonable condition. However, with the onset of the rains large numbers of elephants had moved into the border area, and were apparently wreaking havoc on the fence.

Although foot-and-mouth disease was seldom fatal to livestock, the seeping blisters that formed in the mouth and between the segments of the hoof were so debilitating that it caused severe weight loss in the infected animals. Because it spread so quickly, the loss to the farmers where an outbreak occurred could be considerable. A few years previously, foot-and-mouth had broken out in Great Britain and over half a million cattle, sheep, goats and pigs had been slaughtered before it was eradicated.

North of the Red Line in South West Africa, foot-and-mouth disease was regarded as endemic and the measures taken to control an outbreak were less drastic. Nevertheless, the situation in Ovamboland was taken very seriously, and ensuring that it did not spread to the Kaokoveld was vitally important. If foot-and-mouth were to break out here, Commissioner Van Zyl told me, it would put an end to all future plans to market livestock from the Territory.

Over dinner that night, Burger Baard told me that it was not livestock that the veterinary officials were planning to kill to prevent the outbreak spreading to the Kaokoveld, but the elephants that were damaging the fence separating the two tribal territories. Apparently there was no shortage of willing big game hunters among the ranks of the local government officials. However, the Commissioner had insisted on getting more detailed information on the situation along the fenceline before deciding what action to take.

As the border fence was my responsibility, the following morning Ben van Zyl instructed me to send Grootman's team and their tractor out to assist with the repair work as soon as possible. He also asked me to drive along its

entire length, from the Kunene River to the small-stock quarantine camp at
Otjitjekua, and report back to him on its condition. Finally, he wanted an assessment of the numbers of elephant in the vicinity of the fence. Grootman
and I left that afternoon.

The eastern border area was very different to the rest of the Kaokoveld.
Once one had climbed up the rocky escarpment out of the Kunene valley,
the country here was flat sandveld underlain with calcrete – very similar to
the Kalahari around Ghanzi, through which I had tried to cycle in 1967. In
the far south-eastern corner, where the Omatambo Maue cattle quarantine
camp was nearing completion, grass- and scrub-covered dunes had formed.
Here the sand was so deep that even the camel thorn trees that were virtually
synonymous with the Kalahari were only a few metres tall.

Along the entire length of the eastern border fenceline, there was only one
permanent spring, Ombombo Ovambo, where I knew many elephants drank
during the dry season. When I visited the spring now, I found no sign of
elephant having drunk, but the reason was soon apparent. Numerous clay
depressions that studded the sandveld had been filled with rainwater, and
the muddy perimeters of most of these natural pans were churned up by the
huge footprints of the pachyderms. There were certainly large numbers of
elephants in the area but, because they were now dispersed over a vast tract of
land, making an assessment of their numbers would not be easy.

My task was made considerably more difficult by the wet conditions. While
driving along the track that followed the fenceline we were continually having
to dig the old Chev out of the sticky black mud. And because of the numerous
clay pans, going off the road for any distance was just looking for trouble. A
visiting official from Windhoek had got so badly stuck in one of the pans that
he left his vehicle there until the mud dried out a month later.

I stayed in the Ovamboland border area for 10 days. During that time,
while just driving along the boundary fenceline, I had seen over 80 elephants
and estimated the actual population there at the time was at least double that
number. The men who were based along the border told me that the elephants
came into the sandveld every rainy season. In previous years they had simply repaired the fence breaks they caused as best they could until the pans
dried up and the elephants returned to Ombombo Ovambo and springs in
the Joubert range, about 30 km to the west. They could not understand why
we were now making such a fuss about what was a regular occurrence. They
knew that elephants could not carry foot-and-mouth disease and assured me
that there were no livestock living near the fence.

Be that as it may, the vets had declared a crisis and were now calling for blood – and I had to make a report on the situation. The big question was, how many elephants would have to be shot to drive them out of a wet-season grazing area they had undoubtedly used for thousands of years?

I concluded that the problem would not be solved by shooting a few elephants near the fence. Either we shot most of them or none at all. Ben van Zyl supported my findings and would not hear of large numbers of the Kaokoveld elephants being killed. Tom Sopper – who, as the senior veterinary official in the Territory, would be responsible for any foot-and-mouth outbreak – also agreed with me that shooting a few elephants would be unlikely to stop the fence from being damaged. Our unanimous decision was to leave the elephants in peace. Fortunately, the inoculation campaign in Ovamboland quickly brought the foot-and-mouth under control, and no cases were recorded in the Kaokoveld.

By this time, Tom Sopper, his wife Maizie and I had become close friends. Not only were Tom's and my duties in veterinary services and agriculture closely linked, but we all shared a deep love of the bush and everything in it. Like the other officials, we hunted our share of game for the pot – including, in my case, a periodic zebra for Grootman's gang while they were in the field. Nevertheless, we saw wild animals as an asset to the Kaokoveld beyond their value as a source of meat. Ben van Zyl and Burger Baard also clearly shared this point of view, but some of my other colleagues seemed to regard game and hunting as synonymous. To them, the opportunity to hunt big game had been one of the main reasons that they had requested a posting to South West Africa's northern homelands.

Tom and I were also the only two government officials in the Kaokoveld whose home language was English. After 1948, when the National Party had come to power, the Afrikanerisation of the civil service had been a high priority to Pretoria. By the 1960s, membership of the Broederbond had become a prerequisite for attaining a high post in government. My application for employment had undoubtedly been screened for compatibility with Nationalist policies, but not having been overtly political in my youth, I had obviously passed the test for a junior civil servant. However my honeymoon with the anonymous securocrats in Windhoek was soon to end.

In April Ben van Zyl resigned from his post as Commissioner in order to go farming in the Omaruru district. For most of the previous 20 years Ben and Babes had been the face of the South African government to the local inhabitants of the Kaokoveld, as well as the few privileged outsiders who had been able to breach the red tape and obtain permits to visit the Territory. I had enjoyed working under Ben. Although he and Babes were old-school Afrikaners in much of their thinking, their stewardship of the Kaokoveld's post-war years was tempered by a deep love of the Territory and a genuine respect for the traditional culture of its indigenous people. In turn, they were generally held in high regard by all who worked for or with them.

Just before they left, a farewell party was held in Opuwo. As was customary on such occasions, large quantities of alcohol were consumed while we officials discussed the latest local and national events. By the latter part of the evening the main topic was politics. In 1966 SWAPO had launched its armed struggle to liberate Namibia from South African rule, and the first group of freedom fighters had been captured or killed at Omgulumbashe, in Ovamboland. There were also rumours of SWAPO insurgents having infiltrated into the Kaokoveld. However, like most of the Rhodesians I had met on my bicycle safari the previous year, my colleagues were contemptuous of their black countrymen's fighting abilities. In their eyes, the country's most dangerous enemies were white liberals – personified by the Progressive Party's sole representative in the South African parliament, Helen Suzman.

My parents had been founder members of the Progressive Party and I had been brought up to have great respect for Helen Suzman's courageous stand against apartheid. Made bold by my own not inconsiderable intake of beer, I objected to their vitriolic character assassination of her, and throwing caution to the wind, I launched into a gallant defence of right-wing Afrikanerdom's public enemy number one. For good measure I added that the National Party's policy of separate development would never succeed, and that sooner or later black South Africans would have to be brought into the country's government. Given the fact that a number of senior officials were at the party this was not wise, but we had all been quite inebriated and I soon forgot about the incident. Later, I would learn that some of those present had not taken my statements so lightly, and a security file had subsequently been opened on me.

Ben van Zyl's post was filled by Mr TJB van Niekerk, an elderly Afrikaner who had served BAD for most of his working life in Zululand. Whether he had chosen to spend his last few years before retirement in the Kaokoveld, or had been sent to this remote corner of SWA as punishment because of his regular overindulgence in the fermented fruits of the vine, was a well-debated subject among the residents of Opuwo. He was certainly an eccentric who hailed from a time when Bantu Affairs Commissioners had ruled the tribal areas under them as their kingdoms.

Within a few weeks of arriving, Van Niekerk informed us that no vehicles were allowed to drive off the road on the flats in front of the town, because it caused dust to be blown into the white residential area. As the flats were a short cut to the 'location', few people took any notice of his instruction until one Saturday afternoon, when sitting in full view on his residency verandah, Van Niekerk fired off about 10 rounds from his rifle at a transgressing vehicle. We all presumed that he had aimed to miss the fast-moving truck, but the fact that he was already on the day's second bottle of brandy ensured that Van Niekerk's future decrees were taken much more seriously.

In mid-1969 a post office was opened in Opuwo. The first postmaster, Jimmy de Kock, and another BAD administration officer, Nico van der Merwe, arrived at about the same time, increasing the number of white officials in the Kaokoveld to eleven. To accommodate them, new prefabricated houses were built and the postmaster and I moved into one of them. I had enjoyed staying with the Baard family, but sharing a house with Jimmy, who was often away, gave me the freedom to invite my own guests to join me for a cup of tea, or a beer in the evening.

While working as a forester in Zululand, I frequently had discussions with the estate's black foremen in my home, and it had certainly contributed to good working relations in the field. It seemed natural to do the same with the Kaokoveld's headmen when they came to Opuwo. However, I soon learned that in the SWA civil service apartheid was applied to the letter of the law, and not even the traditional leaders were exempt. One day, after Commissioner Van Niekerk had seen me having a beer with Johannes Ruyter on my verandah, he called me into his office and warned me that providing alcohol to non-whites was illegal, and that inviting them into my house was against government policy. I agreed to only serve soft drinks in future, but would not back down on inviting headmen, as well as other black colleagues, into my home. This too, I would later learn, was 'reported to Windhoek'.

On one of his visits Johannes Ruyter told me his life story. He was the son of Chief Oorlog Thom's daughter, Blandina, while his father, Thomas Ruyter, had gone with the Thirstland Trekkers to Angola, where Johannes had grown up. After leaving school he worked for a medical doctor, and in his youth accompanied his employer on a trip to Portugal. When in his thirties Johannes moved into the Kaokoveld, where he settled down and took a number of Himba wives.

Having grown up speaking Afrikaans, his command of the language was flawless, and he assured me he also spoke fluent Portuguese. A gentleman in every sense of the word, it was ironic that he was not socially accepted by my colleagues, some of whom came from 'poor white' backgrounds and had low levels of education. However, he seemed to bear no grudges and possessed a great sense of humour, which enabled him to chuckle at the frequent slights he experienced at the hands of much lesser men. In a different situation he would probably have been seen as an 'Uncle Tom', but in the Kaokoveld during the 1960s there was no other way for an educated black man to survive.

In the talks we had, both in Opuwo and at his home, Johannes Ruyter led me into the fascinating world of the Himba and Herero, thereby preventing me from making too many blunders during my interactions with the Territory's still traditional inhabitants. A more academic source of information on the history and culture of the diverse ethnic groups in the Kaokoveld was Johan Malan, who had replaced Robbie Roberts as the assistant Bantu Affairs Commissioner in Opuwo. Johan had grown up in a missionary family, and was then studying the religious system of the Himba for a doctorate in social anthropology. Although we came from very different backgrounds we soon became good friends.

Johan told me all the Herero-speaking people were part of a western off-shoot of Bantu agro-pastoralists that migrated into Southern Africa around the sixteenth century. Many of them settled on the fertile Cuvelai and Kunene floodplains to the east of the Ruacana Falls, where they grew millet, maize and sorghum, as well as keeping cattle, and now formed the eight closely related tribes making up the Ovambo nation. Those who chose a semi-nomadic pastoralist lifestyle skirted the already well-populated floodplains and spread out across south-western Africa's high, semi-arid plateau.

The group that migrated east of Ovamboland into present day Botswana became known as the Mbanderu. There they clashed with the BaTawana, the most westward of the Tswana-speaking people, who had migrated into Southern Africa at about the same time. Because the latter lived primarily from growing crops, an accommodation was reached, with the Mbanderu occupying the dry savannas west of Lake Ngami and the Tawana cultivating the more fertile land along the southern edge of the Okavango Delta.

For the Herero pastoralists who moved through the Kaokoveld onto the central highlands of South West Africa, there was no possibility of a compromise with the resident Nama. As both depended on the widely scattered springs here for the survival of their herds and flocks conflict was inevitable, and because the Herero were physically stronger and possessed iron weapons, they initially gained the upper hand. However, this situation would be turned around by a series of events that began far from the battlefields of south-western Africa.

In the eighteenth century the expanding Dutch settlement at the Cape had pushed the local Nama people northwards towards the banks of the Orange River. Here they were joined by fugitive slaves and other renegades from the colony's harsh penal system, who formed lawless bands that plundered live-stock from both the Dutch and their Nama neighbours. During their contact with the white settlers, the refugees had adopted many aspects of European culture, including the Afrikaans language, and became known as the Oorlams. They had also acquired guns and horses, which enabled them to become the dominant force on the Cape Colony's northern frontier.

The most powerful Oorlam leader was Jager Afrikaner, and in 1830 the chieftainess of the Rooinasie, a Nama tribe living along the upper Fish River, asked for his help against the encroaching Bantu pastoralists. Jonker Afrikaner, his second son, went to assist them, defeating the Herero in three successive battles and pushing them north to the Swakop River. In return for his help Jonker was given land around present-day Rehoboth, but in 1840 he and his followers moved to Ai-gams, a hot spring in the Auas mountains, which he named Windhoek. From this base he began plundering the Herero and Nama alike, and also attacked the Ovambo in their northern stronghold, taking 20 000 head of cattle from them. By the time of Jonker's death in 1861 he had become the tyrant ruler of most of the country between the Orange and Kunene Rivers.

Jonker Afrikaner was succeeded by his son, Christian, who was killed two years later in a battle with the Herero at Otjimbingue on the Swakop River, which the Oorlams lost. The following year, assisted by the Swartbooi Nama and European traders – who supplied them with guns and in some cases fought by their side – the Herero decisively defeated the Afrikaners. Nevertheless, sporadic fighting between the Oorlams under their new leader, Jan Jonker, and the most powerful Herero chief, Maherero, continued for an-other six years before peace finally settled over South West Africa's central plateau.

In 1880 war broke out again, this time with the Herero on the offensive. Hundreds of unprepared Afrikaners were slain and Windhoek was sacked. But the Oorlams counter-attacked and it was now the turn of the Herero to sustain heavy casualties. The European missionaries who were in the re-gion tried to bring the warring leaders together, but to no avail, and in 1882 Maherero stated unequivocally that: 'There can be no talk of peace while the old Nama leaders are alive and Jan Jonker Afrikaner must go back to the land he came from.' It would take the arrival of the Germans, providing a common enemy for Herero, Oorlams and Nama alike, before a lasting peace between the pastoralists could be achieved.

Because they had supported the Herero against the Afrikaners, the Swartbooi Nama base in Rehoboth had been sacked in 1863. Their then chief, Abraham Swartbooi, who had found himself on different sides at different times in the Herero–Oorlam conflict, decided to seek a way of escaping from the interminable bloodshed. Through the mediation of a missionary, Hugo Hahn, he asked Chief Maherero for permission to take his people to a safe place in the north of the country. This was granted and the Swartboois settled around Fransfontein, in the south-eastern Kaokoveld. However, as the Rooinasie chieftainess is reputed to have said after giving Jonker Afrikaner a place to live, 'it was the equivalent of putting a lion into the cattle kraal'.

Abraham Swartbooi died shortly after arriving in Fransfontein, and was succeeded by Petrus Swartbooi, a man who had not yet had his fill of warfare, particularly if the spoils of battle were the large herds of cattle owned by the Kaokoveld Herero. Together with the Topnaars at Sesfontein, the Swartboois embarked on a campaign of terror, attacking and plundering the dispersed pastoralist settlements throughout the region. Unable to offer any resistance to the guns of the raiding horsemen, most of them fled across the Kunene into Portuguese territory with what possessions they could carry. Those that did not were faced with the choice of either hiding in the remoter mountains of the region, where they hunted and gathered to survive, or becoming vassals of the new ruling elite in the Kaokoveld.

Once in Angola the destitute Herero refugees asked their relatives, the Ngambue people, with whom they shared many key aspects of their culture, for a place to settle, as well as livestock to live from. Their requests were granted and the refuge seekers were given the name *ovaHimba*, derived from the verb *okuhimba*, which roughly translated means 'to request'. However, three decades later the fortunes of the Himba would be dramatically changed by a remarkable man – who happened to be Johannes Ruyter's maternal grandfather.

In 1863, during the Afrikaner attack on Otjimbingue, Kaitundu, the niece of a prominent Herero lineage head, gave birth to a son. The child's father was Tom, a Tswana man who was employed by Charles John Andersson, the most famous nineteenth-century European hunter and explorer in south-western Africa. Because it had been born during the height of the battle the baby was given the name Vita, the Herero word for war. Soon after the birth Kaitundu died and the child was raised by her mother, Kahitondereka, who moved to Omaruru where her brother, Manasse Tjiseseta, became the chief in 1884.

When Andersson died in 1867, Tom 'Bechuana' as he was known, started working for one of his partners, Frederick Green, and four years later accompanied him and Axel Eriksson on a hunting expedition through Ovamboland to southern Angola. Although he was then only eight years old, Vita went with his father on the trip, and when Green and Eriksson returned to South West Africa, Tom obtained permission from the Portuguese authorities to stay on the well-watered Humpata plateau, making his home on the banks of the Neves River. In 1880, seeking more white settlers to stabilise this undeveloped part of southern Angola, the district governor also gave the Thirstland Trekkers permission to settle in the area. Tom developed good relations with the Boers, and the young Vita was strongly influenced by them, preferring to be known by the Afrikaans translation of his name: *Oorlog*.

As a headstrong youth, maternally related to one of the most powerful Herero families, Oorlog soon became a leader of the Himba refugees who lived alongside the Ngambue in between Neves and the upper Kunene River. At first he and his followers were just small-scale cattle thieves who raided their neighbours, but in 1885 Oorlog was asked to fight on the side of the colonial forces against the Nkhumbi, who had refused to accept Portuguese authority over them.

The situation had been given urgency by the Conference of European Colonial Powers in Berlin earlier in the year, at which it was agreed that before a colony's borders would be recognised, the colonising country had to prove its effective control over all the land it claimed. As the small Portuguese garrison stationed in southern Angola was too weak to meet this requirement, the commander of the fort at Humbe recruited local volunteers to bolster his own troops. With 38 Thirstland Trekkers and 44 Himba under Oorlog Thom, the Nkhumbi were defeated. Over the next three decades the young man from Omururu and his Kaokoveld refugees would be called on to serve the colonial authorities against the Kwamatui, the Kavare and the Kwanyama, whose royal village was finally captured in 1915. By then their numbers had been increased by the addition of more refugees, this time from the 1904 Herero war against the colonial government in South West Africa.

War between the German colonisers and the Herero inhabitants of the country's central plateau had been inevitable. Initially the stationing of a small number of mounted troops on a hill overlooking Windhoek in 1990 had brought a measure of stability to the war-torn region. But with the *Schutztruppe* came traders who brought tempting European goods and alcohol with which to barter for cattle from the Herero's large herds, and land on which to graze them. In the eyes of the shop-owners, these grazing areas had been 'bought' and now belonged to them, but there was no concept of selling land in Herero culture. In this misunderstanding was the seed of one of the most bloody conflicts in Africa's colonial history.

A second factor that undoubtedly contributed to the Herero uprising was the rinderpest outbreak that swept through South West Africa in 1897, decimating both the country's livestock and wild ungulates. Before the rinderpest, the area acquired by the colonists would have been insignificant when compared to the vast amount of grazing land available on the plateau. But without their cattle, goats and sheep, many of the pastoralists were left destitute and turned for food to the traders, who as payment marked out more farms. Soon much of the land previously occupied by the Herero had been 'sold', further alienating them from their ancestral grazing grounds.

As the Herero rebuilt their herds the loss of land and springs became a crisis, and in January 1904 Samuel Maherero, the son of the Okahandja chief, Maherero, secretly gave the order for all Herero leaders to take up arms against the Germans, 'but not to interfere with the missionaries, English, Basters, Damaras, Namas and Boers'. They were also instructed not to kill any women or children. In just two days 123 of the settlers were murdered.

It was a devastating blow to German pride. Theodore Leutwein, the moderate governor of the colony, was accused of having been too lenient with the Herero, and was replaced as military commander by General Lothar von Trotha, and over the following six months Berlin poured more troops into the country. Outgunned, the Herero army retreated to the Waterberg plateau, where they were decisively defeated by the Germans in August 1904. The surviving men, women and children were driven into the Kalahari, and many more of them died of thirst before reaching safety among their Mbanderu relatives in the British Protectorate of Bechuanaland. In October von Trotha issued a proclamation stating that the Herero were no longer welcome in the German colony, and had to leave it or be shot. Although it was rescinded three months later, the total number of Herero throughout the whole country was reduced from an estimated 80 000 to less than 20 000.

Even before the war, news had reached the Herero living in Omaruru and Okahandja of Oorlog Thom's exploits in Angola, including the fact that, in gratitude for his services, the Portuguese had recognised him as chief of the area from the Kunene River westwards. Consequently, after the battle of Waterberg a number of them walked overland through Ovamboland to join him at Chevia, his new home 150 km east of Neves. They would provide a valuable addition to his military forces, further entrenching his power in the region.

Oorlog had always planned to return one day to Omaruru, the place of his birth, but the plight of the Herero under the Germans after 1904 stopped him from doing so. However, when South African forces took over in 1915 he was granted permission by Major Manning, the head of the military administration set up in the Territory, to settle with his followers in the Kaokoveld. The defeat of the Germans was not Oorlog's only reason for wanting to leave Angola. He had recently undertaken a number of unauthorised raids on neighbouring tribes and driven away large numbers of their cattle. The Portuguese authorities regarded them as having been stolen and requested his presence in their southern capital, Sa da Bandeira, to explain his actions. When he declined their invitation they made an unsuccessful attempt to arrest him, after which he crossed the Kunene River.

Once safely in the Kaokoveld, Oorlog made his home at the Otjiyanyasemo hot springs, while his Himba followers settled on the high plateau west of the Zebra Mountains. The Herero that had joined him after the German-Herero war occupied the strong springs at Okorosave, Kaoko Otavi and Oruandjai, south-west of present-day Opuwo. Oorlog never went back to Omaruru, living the rest of his life in the Kaokoveld, where the new South African administration regarded him as the senior chief of the Territory. He died near Ongandjera in Ovamboland, on his way back home after being discharged from hospital in Windhoek. He was then 74 years old.

Oorlog was not the first of the refugees in Angola to return. A group of Himba under headman Muhona Katiti had already crossed the Kunene and settled in the north-east of the Territory. Together with Kasupi, whose Tjimba followers never left the Kaokoveld, they were the three chiefs recognised by the South African government when it was given authority over the country at the end of the First World War. Half a century later the total population of the then Kaokoveld Territory was still only about 13 000, which apart from the Nama and Damara inhabitants of Sesfontein and Warmquelle, included a number of more recent immigrants.

The largest group were Herero pastoralists who had been moved from their home areas in south-eastern Kaokoveld in 1928 to create a cattle-free zone between the native reserve and the area around Kamanjab, which was being opened up for white farmers. There were also families belonging to related southern Angolan tribes that lived amongst the Himba, the most prominent of which were the Hakaona and Zemba, who were renowned diviners and herbalists, services they provided to the pastoralists in return for livestock. Another scattered group with unknown ethnic origins were the Thwa iron-smiths, who made spears and knives for the Himba and Herero. Lastly, in the rugged ranges flanking the Kunene River west of the Epupa Falls were small numbers of 'Mountain Tjimba', a mysterious tribe of hunter-gatherers not re-lated to the Herero.

*   *   *

In May, Wolfgang Mentzel, my immediate superior in BAD's division of agri-culture, came to the Kaokoveld for the first time since I had been appointed. After he had spent a few days inspecting the dip-tanks that Grootman's gang had built, he informed me that small-stock purchasing would no longer be a priority. Instead I was to go ahead with preparations for the buying of cattle. My first job would be to build holding crushes in the areas where individual headmen had indicated their willingness to allow inspections of their herds and blood sampling.

However, before any cattle crushes could be built, permission had first to be obtained from the Kaokoveld's Council of Headmen, and a meeting was duly arranged by Commissioner Van Niekerk. Based on our experiences during the aborted small-stock marketing campaign, I was not optimistic about our getting the headmen's support, but even I was not prepared for their heated and acrimonious opposition to the inspection of any cattle in the Kaokoveld. At this meeting there was no nodding off to sleep by the older participants. Cattle and everything concerning them was very serious business, and even some wizened old patriarchs gave impassioned speeches, denouncing the mere suggestion that their herds should suffer the indignity of having gov-ernment officials look into their mouths and take their blood.

Our plan appeared to be going nowhere, but as the meeting proceeded, I noticed that two of the Herero headmen, Keefas Muzuma and Joel Tjiahura, from the southeast of the Territory, were cautiously arguing for the sale of large-stock. I also noted that Johannes Ruyter, who had played such an active role when the Council of Headmen had discussed small-stock marketing, was now uncharacteristically quiet.

After a break for lunch, the meeting was reconvened, but there had been no change of heart on the part of the Kaokoveld's traditional leaders. Soon the debate degenerated into the hurling of abuse and threats – not at the Commissioner or myself, but at the two pro-sale headmen and their few supporters. Van Niekerk, who had only been in the Territory for a few weeks, eventually gave up trying to keep order and the meeting broke up in chaos. The following morning the headmen and their councillors returned to their homes. Although no formal decision had been taken, those against the inspections were clearly in the majority.

Until the Council of Headmen was prepared to allow inspections, the plan to build cattle crushes would have to be shelved. By now most of the pans along the Ovamboland border had dried up, causing the elephant herds to return to the permanent springs and thereby relieving the pressure on the boundary fence. With no more pressing work issues I took the opportunity to further acquaint myself with the Kaokoveld's human and other inhabitants.

While travelling in the north-east of the Territory, I called in to visit the renowned 'black Van der Merwe family' on the slopes of Ehomba, a massive quartzite mountain that rose above the plains south of Swartbooisdrift. The oldest surviving member of the family at the time was *Ouma* Ragel, the half-sister of Chief Oorlog Thom. Born in 1889, she was the daughter of Tom Bechuana and his second wife, Katryn, a Tswana woman who had accompanied the Thirstland Trekkers to Angola. Ragel's late husband, Jan Slagveld, was the grandson of a Zulu child, reputed to have been the nephew of King Dingane, who had been found on a battlefield in Natal. Called Slagveld, the boy had been raised by a Boer family who later moved to the western Transvaal. His son, Klein Ruiter, had worked for the leader of the first Thirstland Trek, GJL van der Merwe, and went with him to the Humpata highlands. In 1912, Klein Ruiter's second son, Jan Slagveld van der Merwe, and Ragel Thom married, living at Neves and Ombulo before moving to the Kaokoveld in 1943.

At the time of my visit, Ragel's eldest son, Ruyter, was the head of the clan, while two of her other sons, Krisjan and Oorlog, worked as stock inspectors for Tom Sopper. Her second son, Tom, took over as foreman of my team when Grootman retired. Although most of Ragel's children and grandchildren married local Himba women, they all spoke perfect Afrikaans and were devout Christians. Around their spectacular mountain home they grew a variety of fruit and vegetables and even ground their own coffee from trees they had planted. I subsequently visited Ehomba on a number of occasions, and each time it was like going back in time, to when courtesy and hospitality were simply taken for granted, and hard physical work was the natural order of each day.

The black Van der Merwes, who in many ways lived like the Thirstland Trekker families Ragel and Jan Slagveld had worked for in their youth, added just one more variation to the remarkable array of ethnic groups in the Kaokoveld. As fascinating as each was, my main interest was in the dominant semi-nomadic Herero-speaking pastoralists. To find out more about their way of life, and why they were so reluctant to have their livestock inspected, I again turned to Johannes Ruyter and Johan Malan, who helped me to understand the intricacies of a social and religious system that had its roots buried deep in old Africa.

To emphasise the importance of cattle to the Himba and Herero, Johannes told me that there were many different words just describing their various colour patterns and horn shapes. He added that they never needed to count their animals because each of them – and their bloodline, going back many generations – was individually known. In fact, counting one's livestock was regarded as boastful and an invitation for the ancestors to visit some catastrophe on the family, which was the reason why the government stock inspectors were stopped from doing so.

In fact, cattle belong to the lineage, and not to a person, and each generation is merely their custodian on behalf of previous and still unborn members. The present lineage head is charged with ensuring that the ceremonies and taboos laid down by his ancestors are respected and adhered to. Contact with his deceased father and grandfather is maintained through a holy fire (*okuruwo*), which is situated in a conspicuous hearth between the main hut and the entrance to the cattle enclosure inside the *onganda*. The holy fire is kept smouldering during the day, and at night it is taken into the hut of the lineage head's senior wife, who is responsible for ensuring that it does not go out. Should this happen for whatever reason, a goat has to be ritually slaughtered to request forgiveness from the ancestors. The *okuruwo* can then be relit, but only with sacred fire-making sticks (*ozondume*), which on a lineage head's death are passed on to a surviving younger brother or son.

The Himba believe in God, called *Ondjambi-Karunga* or *Mukuru*, but can only have contact with Him through the spirits of their deceased forefathers (*oviruru*) who have the power to influence Him on their behalf. The *okuruwo* is the focal point of religious activities, and during ceremonies the smouldering coals are blown into flames and more wood added, to attract the ancestral spirits' attention and invite them to be present. On a daily basis, the *okuruwo* is also the place where the family head must taste the first pail of milk, to cleanse it (*makere*) before members not born into his patri-line may drink the produce of his herd. It is also where all major decisions are made, enabling the forefathers to take part in the discussions 'by influencing the thinking of the people present'.

Although the head of the patri-lineage is responsible for all religious functions within the extended family, the Himba and Herero, like only six other ethnic groups, have a double descent system. This means that at birth every child inherits both the patri-clan (*oruzo*, pl. *otuzo*) of his or her father, and the matri-clan (*eanda*, pl. *omaanda*) of the mother. But whereas a woman changes her patri-clan to that of her husband on getting married, her matri-clan never changes, and is inherited by her children. Members of a person's matri-clan are thus regarded as a person's true relatives (*omihoko*, sing. *omuhoko*) and form the basis of their relationships throughout their life. Because all the members of a matri-clan are regarded as being related, marriage between them is not permitted.

The primary role of the matri-lineage, of which there are only seven distinct clans, in contrast to over 20 patri-clans, is the division of material possessions when a family head dies. However, because a man's children do not belong to the same matri-clan as him, it is his oldest sister's firstborn son that inherits his livestock. In this way, cattle wealth is regularly dispersed throughout the society, with no single family being able to accumulate excessively large herds for more than one generation.

To make the Kaokoveld pastoralists' social system even more complicated, not all of a man's herd belongs to his matri-clan. As the religious head of the extended family he has the right to designate certain animals of specified colour variations as holy cattle, known as *ozondume hupa*; 'sacred firesticks that are alive'. These cattle cannot be estranged from the sacred fire and are inherited patri-lineally by a younger brother or eldest son. Furthermore, because they are given considerable religious significance, neither their milk or meat, nor the animals themselves may be handled by people of a different patri-clan. When Johannes told me this it explained why there was such strong opposition from most of the Kaokovelders to veterinary officials inspecting and taking blood samples from their cattle.

I was fascinated by what Johannes told me about the complex spiritual relationship the Himba and Herero had with their cattle – so different to the purely functional one a white farmer had with his stock. But trying to understand it was heavy going, and seeing my furrowed brow he lightened the atmosphere by telling me that the nicest thing he could say to one of his wives was that she looked like a 'fat cow'. Roaring with laughter, he added that this Herero compliment might not go down too well with white women!

*   *   *

Considering the hostility of the Koaokoveld headmen towards inspections and blood sampling, it seemed unlikely that marketing of cattle from the Territory would take place in the near future. But in late July, Tom passed on a message from Nico Smit that I was to start building cattle crushes at Ombombo and Otjondeka, the main villages of Keefas Muzuma and Joel Tjiahura. Apparently both headmen had agreed to their stock being inspected, in spite of fierce opposition from the other Kaokoveld leaders. I immediately sent Grootman's gang to Otjondeka, and by mid-August the cattle crush was completed there and they moved on to Ombombo.

While we were putting the finishing touches to the Ombombo crush, Dr Scheepers and Senior Stock Inspector Boet Weekly mouthed and took blood samples from over 1 000 head of cattle in Joel's area. The following evening the veterinary team joined me in my camp at Ombombo. They were elated. The first cattle inspections in the Kaokoveld had taken place without any serious hitches. It was a major breakthrough.

The following morning we all went to the Ombombo crush, to check whether everything was ready for the second round of inspections. The first cattle had already arrived and their owners were gathered in small groups under the nearby trees. They talked loudly among themselves but there was clearly tension underlying their nonchalance. The decision to defy the Council of Headmen could not have been taken lightly, and the possible reaction of their ancestors must have weighed heavily on their minds. At about ten o'clock Headman Muzuma came up to where we were sitting, and after greeting us politely, he gave Boet's assistants instructions to start driving the cattle into the holding pen. He then walked away and joined a group of Herero men 20 metres from us. The inspection could now begin.

As they had never been confined before, the Herero cattle were very nervous as Boet's men and some local helpers drove them into the crush. A huge ox was first to squeeze between the parallel poles and bolt for the opening at the other end. Elias and one of Grootman's men quickly jammed three short poles across the exit. Seeing its escape route blocked, the now terrified ox tried to jump over the side of the crush. It almost made it, but one back leg went between the side poles and it crashed down outside the crush with its foot firmly trapped. It took us 15 minutes to free the pitifully bellowing ox and then convince another group of now highly excited animals to enter the crush. By this time the mood of the Herero stock-owners was electric.

At last we were ready to begin. While Dr Scheepers prepared his equipment, Boet moved along the now tightly packed crush, opening the mouth of each wide-eyed beast to look for the gum blisters that would show the animal was actively suffering from foot-and-mouth disease. The audience under the trees intently watched the proceedings. As Boet neared the end of the crush, Dr Scheepers went up to the first beast, a scalpel in one hand and a sample bottle in the other. Behind him some of the stock-owners edged forward. Now no one spoke.

The first animal's tail was lifted and with a deft stroke of the scalpel, Dr Scheepers sliced through the large vein on its underside. A stream of crimson blood spurted from the cut and was caught in the sample bottle. Every Herero's eyes were transfixed on the vet as he then ineffectually tried to stem the flow of blood from the ox's tail. I looked around me just in time to see an old man collapse onto the ground in what appeared to be a dead faint. Near me another man started wailing as if it was his own blood that was spattering onto the dusty earth. His companion rushed towards the crush shouting at the veterinary officials and had to be forcibly restrained. Under the trees the blood letting was being heatedly discussed by the stock-owners. I looked across at Keefas Muzuma. Near him a tight knot of elders argued vociferously, but the headman seemed unmoved by the emotional outburst of his people. He was looking straight ahead, the expression on his face inscrutable. I wondered if he was saying a silent prayer.

When the uproar died down, the mouthing and blood collecting continued without further incident, and by the following afternoon nearly 1 000 head of Ombombo cattle had been inspected. It was certainly not all of them, but the veterinary officers accepted it as a representative sample – enough to test and then pass judgement on the health of the area's large-stock. The next day, Dr Scheepers and Boet Weekly returned to Kamanjab and I drove down to Warmquelle, where Keefas had asked for another crush to be built, so that his followers in that vicinity might also be inspected at a later date.

Warmquelle fell under the authority of Simon //Havachab, so after making camp under the wild fig trees near the spring, Elias and I drove on to Sesfontein to see the old Topnaar chief. I told him about Keefas Muzuma's request for a cattle crush, but Simon would not give permission for it to be built at Warmqelle. His reason for opposing it had nothing to do with ancestor spirits: Warmquelle had always been a Damara area and he felt that the Herero were now trying to take it over. Any cattle crush built in his ward should be at Sesfontein. If Keefas's people wanted their cattle inspected then they would have to trek them the 25 km between the two settlements. Simon pointed out a site under a large acacia tree near the road just south of the fort where we built a crush, but it was never used.

While at Sesfontein I received a message from Markus Hartley, the 'policeman' at Warmquelle, that many cattle had been illegally taken into the Etosha Game Park. When I visited Markus, he told me that the foreman in charge of the herds was Joshua Kangombe, but that many of the animals actually belonged to Headman Keefas Muzuma. I immediately sent a messenger to ask the herdsmen responsible for the cattle to come and see me. A few hours later, a very hostile group of about ten Herero men arrived in my camp under the wild fig trees near the main Warmquelle spring. Joshua Kangombe was among them.

After I had greeted them, some of the Herero launched into a tirade about government regulations preventing them from entering the park. The areas that they came from had received no rain this season, they claimed, and if they remained there all their cattle would die of starvation. To calm the situation down, I invited Joshua and some of the older men to join me for a cup of tea. By the time Elias had boiled the water and handed each of them a well-sugared cup, tempers had cooled and we were able to discuss the situation rationally.

I was well aware that the combination of relatively poor rains and high livestock numbers had resulted in much of the southern Kaokoveld being denuded of grass. Their predicament was understandable but, I told them, I did not have the authority to allow their cattle to graze within the game reserve. All that I could do was inform my superiors of the situation and wait for their response. In the meantime, they must restrict their livestock to areas near the border, and as soon as rain fell take them back into the Kaokoveld. Joshua politely thanked me for listening to their problem and promised to do as I requested. It was the start of a long friendship between Joshua Kangombe and myself, that many years later would be crucial to nature conservation in the region.

* * *

No sign of foot-and-mouth disease was found in any of the cattle inspected at Otjondeka and Ombombo, but the blood samples would take another month to analyse. If they were also found to be free of lungsickness antibodies then we could start buying stock from these two areas in early November. As I was by now due for leave, I decided to take it in October so that I would be back in the Kaokoveld in time for the historic first cattle sale. On my way back from leave I called in at the BAD's Windhoek office and learned from Hine Brand that the blood samples had tested negative, and that the date set for the first cattle sale was 5 November. It would be at Otjondeka in Headman Joel Tjiahura's area.

Another piece of information Hine gave me was that the price the government would be paying for the purchased cattle was 5c a pound liveweight – only a cent more than we had offered the Himba for their small-stock. I suspected there would be problems, but Hine was again adamant that the Herero would have to accept realistic market prices. He had done the calculations, taking into account the three months' quarantine and higher transport costs to Windhoek, as well as all the risks the government would have to take. As it was the end of the dry season, he believed the Herero were likely to bring many old animals for sale, which might die in the quarantine camp. The market price three months ahead was unpredictable. Finally he did admit that the price was low, but if all went well this time, it could be increased at later stock sales.

On the set date, Nico Smit, Commissioner Van Niekerk, Dr Hubert Schneider, the new State Vet in Kamanjab, Boet Weekly, Elias and I gathered at Otjondeka. Headmen Joel Tjiahura and Keefas Muzuma were also present, along with their councillors and a large number of stock-owners, as well as local spectators. Undoubtedly many other Kaokovelders, in different parts of the Territory, would take a keen interest in the events of the day.

By 10 o'clock about 15 oxen, mostly young and in remarkably good condition, had been brought for sale. The first two animals were driven through the crush onto the portable scale and weighed. After a brief calculation, Nico Smit informed their owners of the price the government was prepared to pay for them. There was a murmur from the men who crowded around him to hear the verdict of the scale, but they said nothing and walked off to discuss the matter with the two headmen. Soon a large group had gathered under the trees where Keefas and Joel were seated. I realised we were not going to get a quick answer and asked Elias to put a kettle on the fire and make coffee.

As we government officials sat around the fire, my superiors chatted lightheartedly about mundane matters. Nico Smit clearly understood the ecological implications for the Kaokoveld if cattle were not marketed, but was he aware of what was at stake for the two Herero headmen and their followers? In the six months Van Niekerk had been in Opuwo he had seldom left his office, and seemed to have little interest in the people he was appointed to administer. Dr Schneider had only recently replaced Dr Scheepers and could not be expected to know the undercurrents that influenced the stock-owners' decisions. Only Ben van Zyl would have understood the courageous path that Keefas and Joel had taken, and had the authority to influence the day's events. I nervously tried to raise the issue of the holy cattle and the conflict the cattle inspections had caused, but my colleagues were not interested. From their casual conversation, it seemed as though they were quite confident that the Herero would accept their offer.

After about an hour a young man came and said that the headmen wished to speak to us, and we all returned to the scale. Through an interpreter, Keefas spoke on behalf of the 30 or so men who had gathered around to hear what was said.

'We Kaokovelders are people of the bush and, because of this, the whites think that we are backward and ignorant. But unlike the Himba who know nothing of selling livestock, we Herero have relatives who live in other parts of South West Africa. These relatives visit us and we visit them. I have myself been to Okakarara and while there attended auctions at which whites came from Windhoek to buy Herero cattle. With my own eyes I have seen up to 11c a pound being paid for fat oxen at such auctions. This is a good price, but we know that the cattle the government have come to buy from us today must be kept in quarantine for a long time, and then taken to distant places before they are sold. Because of this we cannot expect the government to pay us the same price that is paid in Okakarara. The white chief has offered us 5c a pound but we cannot accept this. We ask the government to pay us 7c a pound. If we agree on this price today, Headman Joel and I will tell our people to bring their best oxen for sale.'

Two men from completely different cultural backgrounds now held in their hands the future of livestock marketing in the Kaokoveld. I was sure that if Nico Smit was prepared to meet Keefas Muzuma half-way, the sale of cattle would go ahead. But with all the conflict that our marketing project had caused, it was now not just a matter of economics. Face would also have to be saved.

Nico Smit did not consider the matter long before replying. He was sorry, but the price had been carefully worked out and could not be changed. After considering Smit's words for a few moments, Keefas said that if the government was not prepared to increase the price, then no cattle would be sold at Otjondeka or at Ombombo. The Chief BAD Agricultural Officer and the Herero headman looked at each other in silence for a few seconds before Keefas turned on his heel and walked away. Joel Tjiahura and the other stockowners followed him. For the sake of one cent a pound a year's work had come to nothing.

The repercussions of our failure to initiate a livestock marketing programme in the Kaokoveld were far greater than any one of us could have foreseen. If Keefas and Joel's followers had started earning cash for their cattle, it is likely that other Herero leaders would have joined the rebel headmen and also allowed their livestock to be inspected and sold. As it turned out, the conservative traditional leaders in the Territory consolidated their power, while the independent actions of Keefas and Joel over cattle inspections further alienated them. At the time of writing the rift between the two groups had not been completely healed, and still sometimes bedevils co-operation and progress in the region.

No more attempts were made to buy cattle in the Kaokoveld, and the huge quarantine camp at Omutambo Maue became a white elephant. In the years ahead livestock numbers continued to increase, until finally the rangelands could no longer withstand the grazing pressure. The consequences were disastrous, not only for the pastoralists, but also for the wildlife in the region.

CHAPTER SEVEN

A WILD LIFE

In September 1968, when Nico Smit came to Opuwo to inform me of my duties and discuss the marketing of livestock across the Red Line, he mentioned that nature conservation was a function of the local agricultural official. He did not elaborate, possibly because he did not regard it as an important part of my work, but I took this responsibility very seriously.

The Kaokoveld's remoteness and the severe restrictions placed on access meant that there was very little literature available on the region's natural history. The only comprehensive survey of the Territory's wildlife had been carried out by Captain Guy Shortridge, the curator of the Grahamstown museum, who travelled through the Kaokoveld by ox-cart in the late 1920s. His two-volume report, *The Mammals of South West Africa*, contained population estimates for all of its big game animals, but as it was now 40 years old I decided to update his survey.

The Otjitjekua quarantine camp – the completion of which had been my first task in the Kaokoveld – was situated on the northern border of the Etosha Game Park, and game moved freely between the two areas. After our day's work, when Grootman's gang returned to the camp to rest and prepare their evening meal, I wandered through the surrounding low mopane bushveld making notes on everything I saw. The springbok, kudu and occasional harte-beest I encountered were quite wary, but just being on foot in their domain made each walk an exhilarating experience.

On most days, Elias or some of the more energetic members of Grootman's team accompanied me. Their senses were much more in tune with the bush, and as we walked they pointed out many signs of wild creatures that I, with my book-learned knowledge, would have completely overlooked. The pug-marks of a leopard showed that it had walked around our camp one night, while on another occasion we followed the spoor of a cheetah to where it had killed a springbok, but after eating part of it had been driven off by a pair of hyenas. The whole drama was clearly written in the sand, and just needed someone to interpret it. My colleagues' skills also had a practical value. After finding the track of a puff adder we followed it to where it was lying, wonder-fully camouflaged among the dead leaves. On my own I might have stood on the snake.

Walking through the bush with my keen-eyed Herero companions was the equivalent of reading the local newspaper. Our visual wildlife sightings were the eye-catching photographs that illustrated the news of the day, but the most interesting information was to be found in the fine print that – once one learned to read it – gave the real story of what was happening in the area. Gradually, under their expert tutorship, I also learned to identify the spoor of many unseen animals that were actually quite common around Otjitjekua.

Some tracks I did not need any help identifying. The main road between Opuwo and Otjitjekua went past the large Herero settlement of Otuzemba, and crossing it here were well-used game trails on which the fresh footprints of many elephants were clearly visible. Deciding to investigate, I followed Elias's directions to a spring in a calcrete outcrop from which clear water ran down a gentle slope to small maize and tobacco fields. When we arrived, cat-tle and goats were milling around the water, while Herero women in their long missionary dresses tended their crops and chatted gaily to one another. It was a typical rural African scene, excepting for the fact that the whole area was strewn with elephant dung.

Through Elias I asked the women about the elephants, and they told us that large numbers of them drank at the spring every night. As a key part of my planned survey of the Kaokoveld's wildlife was to estimate the numbers of elephant in the Territory, what better way would there be to do this than to sit near a waterhole on a moonlit night and count them? As it turned out, over the next full moon period I was on the Ovamboland border, close to another natural spring, Ombombo Ovambo. Here there were no villages or livestock in the vicinity, but from the amount of spoor and dung around the water it was clear that many elephants and other game drank there. It was the ideal place to carry out my first 24-hour game count.

Making camp in a copse of trees about 500 metres downwind of the spring, I walked to the water at first light the next morning and found a concealed area, with a clear view of the surroundings in which to sit. Although large numbers of birds, ranging from quelea finches to lappet-faced vultures, visited the water during the morning, the only mammals that came to drink were a few small herds of springbok. The afternoon was even less successful. No animals at all came near the water, and just an occasional flock of birds relieved the monotony of my sweltering vigil.

At about six o'clock I walked back to camp for a hasty supper and returned to the spring half an hour before the sun set. To compensate for the reduced vision at night I moved in closer to the water and made myself comfortable under a small mopane bush about 40 metres from the large pool where the game drank. It did not provide much cover, but I reasoned that the dappled moonlight filtering through its leaves would break up my outline and make me invisible – as long as I did not move.

All was quiet until sunset, when a single jackal trotted down to drink cautiously for a few moments before melting back into the bush. In the fading twilight, small flights of double-banded sandgrouse winged to and from the water, making their characteristic twittering calls. After the last sandgrouse left, nothing moved around the spring and with darkness came silence, eerie in its intensity.

As the last light faded from the western sky an almost perfectly round, salmon-tinted moon rose majestically over the stark silhouettes of the nearby trees. Gradually the glassy smooth surface of the pool became visible again. It was deathly quiet and I seemed to be the only living creature in the area. Or was I? According to the border guards who repaired the fence along the border, there were still lion in this part of the Kaokoveld. Could a pride have chosen tonight to ambush game at this, the only waterhole in the area? With their far superior night sight, was I being watched at that very moment?

In the bush to my right something moved a stone. The hair rose on the back of my neck and my hands were clammy on the binoculars, as I carefully scanned the direction of the sound. I saw nothing, but could now definitely hear a large animal moving over the rocky ground. My heart pounded in my ears as I searched the shadowy scrub for some indication of what was approaching. Then, through the binoculars' magnified image I saw a small movement and magically a zebra took shape before my eyes. Its stripes had blended so perfectly with the background of leafless mopane bushes that I had not seen it until it had taken a step forward. Soon I made out five more striped forms moving hesitantly towards the water.

I was so engrossed in the zebras' painstaking progress that I did not turn my attention back to the spring for some minutes. When I did, an elephant bull was standing at the water's edge. In spite of the rocky ground, his coming to the water had been so silent that I had completely missed it. The elephant drank for a few minutes and then left the spring as quietly as he had come.

By now the zebra herd had reached the water, and as I watched them splashing and squabbling amongst themselves another elephant – or possibly the first one returning – walked just as soundlessly to the spring and started sucking up long trunkfuls of water. After drinking for a few minutes he stood at the water's edge, perhaps contemplating his reflection in the still surface of the pool.

The first group of zebra left, but now other herds were gathering in the surrounding bush, from where a few braver individuals made nervous attempts to approach the spring. However, before reaching the water one would take fright and all of them would dash back to the safety of the tree-line. After much nodding of heads and calling to each other, another zebra would pluck up the courage to walk cautiously forward. I had often watched wild animals drinking during the day, but in the silvery moonlight the scene was spellbinding.

I spent some time watching the zebras' antics through my binoculars before casually glancing back to see what the elephant was doing. But he was no longer at the pool. He had obviously drunk enough and was now leaving the spring along a path taking him straight towards me! My first thought was to run, but the elephant was already so close that he would have to see me and undoubtedly give chase. My mind raced like the engine of a car that has slipped into neutral. There was no place to hide and my few seconds of indecision now meant that it was definitely too late to have any chance of escape. As he walked the last few paces towards me I sat transfixed, like a mouse in front of a snake, my mind just vaguely comprehending that I was in very real danger of being killed.

Less than 20 metres from where I was sitting the path veered away, and the bull walked past me, so close his huge body blocked out the moon. A few seconds later he had disappeared into the trees, and the only sound was the pounding of my heart. As my pulse rate gradually subsided I was overcome by an uncontrollable fit of shaking. I was alive – in fact more than alive. The adrenaline rush I had just experienced jolted my system like some mind-bending drug – and it would prove just as addictive.

Using all my willpower, I managed to stay at the spring for another hour, but my heartbeat now surged with every unidentified sound I heard. At 10 o'clock – after another 30 zebra but no more elephants had drunk – I walked back to camp. Around the fire I told Daniel and Elias of the night's events, but they were not impressed. After lecturing me about the stupidity of going to a waterhole at night, they went to bed. But I was too excited to sleep. As I sipped a cup of tea and gazed into the dancing flames, I felt euphoric. I knew it had been dangerous to sit in such an exposed place, but watching game drink in the moonlight had opened up a whole new world to me: wild Africa at night.

It was December before I had a chance to do a moonlight game count at Otuzemba. On our way there we were delayed and the sun was already setting as we reached my pre-selected campsite, some distance downwind of the waterhole. By the time we had laid out camp and eaten a hurried dinner it was already dark, so I decided to wait until the moon rose before setting off. At the last moment Elias, who had previously said he saw no sense whatsoever in the exercise, decided to accompany me. Daniel would remain in camp to keep the fire going and make sure that Tshaka, my bull terrier, did not follow us.

With the moon still hanging low over the horizon, we carefully picked our way through the dense trees to the spring. I led the way, with Elias lagging a few metres behind – perhaps now having second thoughts about his decision to accompany me on such a foolhardy mission. A hundred metres from the water, without any warning, the silence was suddenly shattered by a series of ferocious snorts. I swung around in time to see Elias nimbly shooting up the only climbable tree in the immediate vicinity. As it was not big enough to hold both of us, I dived under a nearby bush, severely skinning my shin in the process.

Silence.

Not daring to make a sound, I lay wondering what kind of animal could have made such a terrifying noise, and equally importantly, where was it? Surely Elias could see what was going on. Why didn't he say something?

Minutes passed. My shin ached. Leaves and other debris had got under my shirt and I could feel a creature of unknown identity or disposition crawling over my stomach. To get more comfortable I moved slightly, and immediately there was another explosion of sound. However, to my relief it was soon apparent that whatever we had walked into was now departing. After a few moments I extricated myself from the bush, and while Elias climbed down from his precarious perch I shook a large beetle out from under my shirt.

'What was it?' I whispered.

'Rhino. A cow and calf,' Elias replied, the whites of his eyes gleaming in the moonlight. 'They were standing close to you, so I couldn't say anything.'

By the time we reached the spring there were at least 20 zebra at the water, and many more milling around, waiting for a turn to drink. Finding a safe seat on a rocky ledge, we settled down to watch the action in front of us. The various herd stallions strutted or galloped across the open area around the water, kicking and biting at each other, while desperately trying to keep their mares in order. Dust billowed in the moonlight and the night air was rent by the zebras' shrill *kwe-ha-ha* calls.

Soon after we arrived two magnificent kudu bulls strode elegantly through the throng of zebra to the spring. A few minutes later a group of kudu cows appeared on the edge of the tree line, and after cautiously assessing the situation, delicately walked down to drink. More zebra came out of the bush and those that had already quenched their thirst departed back to their grazing grounds.

About an hour after we arrived 12 elephants, including two small calves, shuffled out of the bushes and walked purposefully to the spring. Before they finished drinking, a larger herd of elephants joined them. While they drank the zebra moved away from the water, forming a virtually solid mass of mingling stripes around the waterhole. The now bright moonlight gave the scene a dreamlike aura, but the action in front of us was real and Elias and I were sitting almost in the middle of it. I looked across at my companion. He seemed engrossed in what was taking place in front of us, but we came from very different backgrounds and I had no way of knowing what was really going through his mind.

By midnight, as no more elephant had come to the spring, and as most of the zebra had drifted away, we walked back to camp. It had been an amazing night that taught me more about the big game in the Otuzemba area than I had previously learned from all the daylight drives to and from Otjitjekua. Although Elias said he had found the experience very interesting, he declined all my future invitations to join me on night counts at other Kaokoveld springs. From his perspective, the dangers far outweighed the benefits. But I was hooked, and whenever my work brought me close to a water-hole over the full moon period I would camp nearby and watch the evening's performance

The many more moonlit nights I spent sitting at Kaokoveld springs were always exciting. By day herdsmen leisurely watered their livestock or sat idly in the shade, while women came and went with pails of water or tended their small irrigated plots. But when the sun set ownership of the spring reverted to the wild animals of the area. Man was then an intruder, and visiting them at night meant one had to tread warily or risk injury and possibly death. At any moment the bark of a startled kudu, a rustle in the undergrowth, or just the click of a dislodged stone would send my adrenaline levels soaring. I was also constantly aware that the more dangerous denizens of the bush would not signal their presence, ensuring that when I walked to the water or back, all of my senses were on red alert. Fortunately, the Territory's rugged terrain ensured that near most of the springs there were rock outcrops from which one could record their nocturnal visitors in safety.

Sometimes I had the opportunity to observe the same spring for two or even three consecutive nights, and noted that the numbers of the different species that came to the water varied considerably. The obvious conclusion was that most of the wild animals inhabiting this arid part of South West Africa, including rhino and elephant, did not need to drink every day – contrary to what most biologists then believed.

As my work entailed travelling throughout the whole Kaokoveld, including its remotest areas, from these moonlight counts, spoor observations and the information supplied by local people, I could build up a picture of the distribution of the larger mammals, and estimate their populations. Where possible I also recorded important interactions between the pastoralists and the wildlife living around them, as well as their attitudes towards it.

*　*　*

In the German colonial era the great mountain ranges in the north of the Kaokoveld were never surveyed, and the area appeared as *terra incognita* on the maps of the period. However, in 1911 a 19-year-old Scot, Maudslay Baynes, came to South West Africa seeking adventure, and seeing this blank space decided to hike down the Kunene River, which cut through the heart of it. Without informing anyone, and taking no companions, Baynes set off from Eriksonn's Drift in southern Angola, and reached the coast 500 km and 93 days later.

The modest Baynes told few people of his epic journey, which had passed through some of the most rugged country in southern Africa. In fact, it might never have been recorded if he had not shared the same train compartment on his way back to Walvis Bay with Dr Kuntz, the German geologist and cartographer, who together with Georg Hartmann had surveyed the rest of the Kaokoveld. The young Scot mentioned his trip down the Kunene, and when he cleared customs at Swakopmund his luggage was briefly confiscated so that the sceptical Kuntz could examine his notes. A few years later Baynes was astonished to see, on the latest German map of their colony, his name written across the spectacular mountain range that he had been the first European to penetrate.

In January 1969, while visiting Himba headmen in preparation for the purchasing of small-stock, I decided to undertake a trip into the Baynes Mountains, down a road that followed a narrow valley dissecting the range to reach the Kunene at a place called Otjimborombonga. Tom Sopper had told me that he and Kallie van Zyl regularly used this very rugged route to pay the border guards stationed along the river here, but few of the other white officials ever ventured into the area.

From the Otjiyanyasemu hot springs, Elias, Daniel and I drove westward to Etengua, where a hardly visible track turned off northwards, passing through well-wooded hill country to Otjipemba, a small Himba settlement characterised by massive baobabs. When we stopped under one of them for lunch we were surrounded by lean-muscled, spear-carrying mountain men who had made no compromises whatsoever with the twentieth century. But their menacing attitude soon changed when Daniel offered them some of the potent Sesfontein tobacco – a commodity much sought after in the remoter parts of the Kaokoveld – which we carried with us for just such occasions.

Once their pipes were alight the Otjipemba men chatted amicably with us about the affairs of the valley. Elias had introduced me as the government's agricultural official, but this made no impact on them at all. Only later, when in the course of the conversation he mentioned that I sat near waterholes at night to count elephants, did they start taking an interest in their young white visitor. But they were still not impressed, only curious.

'Why did I count elephants?' a powerfully built man in his thirties asked. 'Did they belong to me?' If so, he would be grateful if I would remove all the elephants from around Otjipemba, as they were troublesome creatures that killed people.

Another man demanded that I take 'my rhinos' away as well. According to him, rhino were numerous in the area and were very aggressive. To make his point he assured us that just the day before he had been chased by a rhino that got so close to him it 'blew saliva all over his back' before he managed to climb up a tree. The rest of the Himba around our vehicle found the account of his near escape very amusing, and suggested the reason he had been so careless as to walk into a rhino had something to do with the fact that he had recently been brewing honey beer.

Obviously pleased to have a stranger to talk to, the Himba continued their light-hearted banter with Elias translating. I was fascinated. These were men who had grown up in this wild and rugged region, and had spent all of their lives in close contact with the big game animals I knew only from books or brief visits to game reserves. Through Elias I asked them about what wildlife inhabited the area, and was impressed by how much they knew of the different species' behaviour and where they occurred. Before moving on, Elias and I went with them to the nearby spring, where the abundance of elephant and rhino dung confirmed their presence in considerable numbers. Unfortunately it was new moon and I had to decline their invitation to sit at the spring and 'count my animals'.

As we drove deeper into the mountains, bare rock faces towered up on both sides of the track. In places the road descended incredibly steep and stony slopes, repeatedly crossing the boulder-strewn dry watercourse that led us down to the Kunene. Had I not known that Tom and Kallie used the route, I would have seriously doubted the Chev's ability to climb back out of the valley. After covering only 16 km in the final two hours of driving, we reached the banks of Southern Africa's least known major waterway, at one of its most inaccessible spots.

That night we camped on the banks of the Kunene, under the large lead-wood trees that had given Otjimborombonga its Herero name. In the evening we were visited by the two border guards stationed at this remote outpost to prevent livestock from illegally entering the Territory from Angola. Like most of the veterinary staff in the Kaokoveld they were not local men, and welcomed the chance to talk to people who brought news from a world beyond the mountains.

After Elias and Daniel had updated them on recent events, they told us that their two counterparts at Onjezu, another guard post 15 km downstream, had been absent from their posts for more than two weeks. It was just the excuse I needed to explore the area, and I immediately decided to investigate the matter. The guards thought it was an excellent idea too, but there was a problem: there was no road to Onjezu, only a donkey path. Then we would walk, I answered, and asked them to organise us donkeys to carry our bags and bedding. Daniel, who regarded himself as too old for such excursions, would stay and look after the vehicle.

At sunrise the next morning our guides led us along a steep path that hugged the slopes of the deep gorge the Kunene entered west of Otjimborombonga. The scenery was awesome. Below us the constricted river surged between sheer cliffs rising over 50 metres straight out of the water. All around the horizon comprised only desolate and forbidding mountains. It was here that Johannes Ruyter had told me there were 'real Tjimba', who still lived by hunting and gathering and were unrelated to the Bantu-speaking pastoralists.

Johan knew of this tribe from a paper published in 1965 by anthropologists MacCalman and Grobbelaar, who claimed to have made contact with Tjimba groups that still used stone implements. Apart from this one scientific manuscript, virtually nothing else was known of them. In this vast mountain wilderness it was easy to believe that new anthropological and biological discoveries might still be made.

As we neared Onjezu the ranges opened up to form a large valley through which a now tranquil Kunene meandered, its blue-green waters fringed by tall trees. Spurred on by the tantalising vista of shade, we walked faster, but the path first turned away from the river before winding slowly down to a dry watercourse. Four hours from where we had left the truck, we reached the banks of the Kunene and flopped down onto the cool white sand in the shade of a winter thorn tree. I was tempted to dive into the river, but the border guard who had accompanied us assured me that Onjezu had the largest crocodiles along the whole length of the Kunene.

That afternoon the two AWOL guards turned up. They had been attending a funeral at a village about 30 km to the south, and had not thought to inform their colleagues at Otjimborombonga. They offered no apologies and were surprised that I had come to look for them. Even when I pointed out that they had been missing from their posts for two weeks they still seemed not to know what all the fuss was about. From the other mourners they had received regular news about everything that happened in the valley, and they assured me it would have been impossible for any livestock to come across the river without them knowing about it. Clearly we lived in different worlds and different time zones.

Elias chose to join the guards in their camp for the night, leaving Tshaka and me alone on the banks of the river. The evening was very warm, so after a simple dinner of rice and soup I lay on the sand watching a rainstorm

over Angola. Long after dark, lightning flashes still periodically silhouetted the higher mountain peaks, and distant rumbles of thunder competed
with the sounds of the Kunene's restless waters cascading over a nearby
rapid. As Tom and Kallie dropped the Onjezu guards' wages and rations at
Otjimborombonga, I knew that I was one of very few whites to have visited
this beautiful valley.

On our way to Onjezu the blistering heat of the rocks we walked on had
badly burned the pads on Tshaka's paws. Carrying a 25 kg bull terrier on our
shoulders over the precipitous path back to Otjimborombonga would not be
easy, but Elias came up with a solution. After putting him into a mealie meal
bag with just his head sticking out, we tied it onto the back of one of the donkeys. Fortunately, Tshaka accepted this indignity with the stoic fortitude of
his breed. As he bumped along the rocky contour path he looked around at
the passing scenery with an expression of resigned boredom. But whenever
Elias or I came near, his battered and scarred face split into the inimitable bull
terrier grin, and a muffled thumping from the depths of the sack indicated
that his tail was wagging.

A few weeks after the trip to Otjimborombonga I had the opportunity of
going to Purros, retracing the route that Jod van der Merwe and I had followed on my visit to the Kaokoveld in October 1967. After briefly stopping
at Sesfontein, we drove on via Ganumub and Tomakas, where windmills had
recently been erected, but as yet no cattle had moved in. Wildlife was still
plentiful here, and as it was seen against the backdrop of stark desert mountains, I was sure that this part of the Kaokoveld could one day become a major
tourist attraction. The fact that it supported populations of elephant, rhino
and giraffe deep within the desert made it unique.

After we had set up our camp on the banks of the Hoarusib, Elias and I
went looking for a springbok to provide us with meat for the next few days.
Finding a suitable ram did not take long, but in spite of it being within easy
range my first shot missed completely. Hardly disturbed by the high-velocity
bullet whizzing past it, the ram just trotted off a few metres and then offered
me another perfect target. To my embarrassment, the second shot also went
wide. This time the springbok got the message and bounded off across the
plains. Cursing the rifle and the nationals of the country where it was manu-
factured, I started walking towards another group of springbok visible in the
distance.

Before I had gone very far Elias called out to me: 'Muhona won't shoot a
springbok here until we have been to greet old Kapuhe.'

At first I didn't have a clue what he was talking about. But then I remembered the ritual Jod van der Merwe and his assistants had performed when I first visited Purros. To humour Elias we walked back to camp, picked up the rest of the party and drove to the old Himba's grave. When we got there Daniel placed a little tobacco next to the remains of the sacred fireplace and prayed out loud to his spirit, introducing me and requesting Kapuhe to take care of us while we were in Purros. When he finished, each of us placed a white quartz stone on the mound that marked where he had been buried, and in the now-fading light drove back towards camp. Along the way Elias pointed out a single springbok ram standing over 200 metres away. It would be my last chance that night, so I took a long shot. The bullet smashed through the ram's spine and it dropped dead on the spot. Neither Elias nor I said a word as we loaded its limp body onto the truck, but Kapuhe's grave became a mandatory stop on all my future visits to Purros.

Early the following morning we drove southwards across the Gomatum River and up a broad tributary with only scattered desert trees along its course. When we returned to camp a few hours later we had seen three black rhino, a small group of giraffe, a cheetah female with two cubs, and numerous gemsbok, springbok and ostrich. It would have been a good morning's drive in any of Southern Africa's game reserves. From their excited discussions about the game we saw, my assistants had also clearly enjoyed the excursion, but they could not have known how much money international tourists would have been prepared to pay for such an experience.

* * *

By March I was getting to know what and where wildlife occurred in the Kaokoveld, but their numbers were much harder to assess. In Opuwo, whenever my colleagues estimated the populations of species it usually generated a lively discussion, and one of the major disagreements was about how many zebra there were. The local police commander, Sergeant Laufs, claimed that the total number of Burchell's zebra and Hartmann's mountain zebra was over 50 000, while to the other extreme, Eugene Joubert, a wildlife researcher studying black rhino in the region, believed that together there were only about 1 000. With zebra skins fetching high prices at the time, I was not surprised that Sergeant Laufs had also recommended that their numbers be reduced, 'to prevent them from competing with the people's livestock for grazing'. As managing the Territory's rangelands was my responsibility, not that of the police, I took it upon myself to come up with a more realistic estimate of the zebra population.

In April, Johan Malan returned from a trip to the west, having seen hundreds of zebra along the way, and over 1 500 springbok and many gemsbok on the plains around Orupembe in the pre-Namib. With our small-stock buying project now abandoned, and the fence along the Ovamboland border once more in good condition, I took the opportunity to visit the area, as well as the Marienfluss, which I had heard much about, but not yet seen.

We travelled via Kaoko Otavi, on the first night reaching Otjiu, where we made camp amongst tall vegetable-ivory palms that grew along the banks of the upper Hoarusib River. Johan had told me that he had seen the greatest numbers of zebra in this valley, but so far we had seen none. That evening some of the local Himba joined us around our fire, and I asked them about the wild animals in the area. After listing the different species that occurred around Otjiu, they confirmed that there had been many zebra here, but that they had now gone. Where to, I asked?

'We do not herd the zebra like our cattle,' an old man answered, 'so how can I say where they have gone? Like rain clouds they come and go according to the season. When they are with us we are happy, and when they go away our hearts miss them. That is all I can tell you.'

I then asked whether the zebra were not a problem because they ate so much of their grazing, but he simply replied that it was their way to eat grass, and they did not wish them to starve. 'Wild animals are God's cattle,' one of the other men said, 'and the grass is for them too.'

That night, as I lay in my sleeping bag listening to a hyena whoop close to the nearby village, I thought about our European way of seeing everything around us in terms of whether it was an asset or a problem. In South Africa, Rhodesia and Botswana the white farmers and veterinarians had exterminated enormous numbers of wild animals in the name of progress and profit. But had it really been necessary? The Kaokoveld livestock lived in close proximity to big game, and the local people seemed to accept it as the natural order of things.

The following afternoon we camped at Sanitatas spring. Good rain had fallen here and grass grew high up the rocky slopes of the surrounding mountains. Although we had now entered the pre-Namib, we saw plenty of both Burchell's and mountain zebra. Suspecting that they might be the same ones that a month earlier had been at Otjiu, that night I sat on a knoll overlooking

the water until well after midnight hoping to get an estimate of their numbers. But none came to drink. 'It has rained well this year,' Elias told me in the
morning. 'Zebra will not drink from a spring if there are still rainwater pools.'

We broke camp at sunrise and drove on towards Orupembe. After the last
rocky ridge the landscape opened up to reveal broad grass-covered plains
stretching from the tree-lined course of the Khumib River to distant red basalt ranges. A month earlier, on my way back from Purros, this area had been
bare ground littered with stones, lifeless save for the presence of a few herds
of gemsbok and springbok. Now it was a lime-green sea of annual grasses on
which many family groups of mountain zebra grazed. As we drove through
the Khumib five giraffe craned their necks to watch us pass by.

At the Orupembe windmill I turned south-west along the track to Rocky
Point, where Johan had reported seeing such a large number of springbok on
his trip. Here the desert grasses were only a few inches high and still bright
green, which made the plains shimmer in the early morning light. After about
30 km I turned around, by which time we had seen more than 1 000 springbok, 120 gemsbok and 65 ostriches, but no zebra. I presumed the grass here
was still too short for them.

After returning to Orupembe we headed north through the basalt ranges
onto a large sandy plain where I counted over 600 Burchell's and 70 mountain zebra, although the actual number could have been much higher. On
our way back, less than a week later, we did not see a single zebra here. This
time we had a Himba hitchhiker on the back of the truck, who took us to the
rainwater pan where they had been drinking, which was now just churned-
up mud. Clearly the zebra had migrated into the pre-Namib because of the
good rain it had received. But where did they come from, and where had
they gone?

Instead of taking the short route to the Marienfuss I drove via Otjiha
spring, around which there was much zebra dung, and then climbed up the
escarpment back onto the highlands. This was some of the most rugged country in the Kaokoveld and I wanted to see what wildlife lived there. We saw
only two herds of mountain zebra and a pair of klipspringer, but the Himba
herdsmen we spoke to along the way told us that zebra, kudu and impala were
plentiful. Rhino also occurred here, as well as elephants, but what they really
wanted to talk about were 'the animals with claws'. Leopards took a heavy
toll on their small-stock and calves, while spotted hyena maimed and even
killed adult cattle. When they took their livestock down into the pre-Namib,
cheetah caused them the greatest losses, but since the issuing of poison by the

early commissioners, lions now occurred only around Sanitatas and in the Marienfluss.

Unlike their attitude to other wildlife, the Himba were not pragmatic about living with predators. The offending animals were hunted down with dogs and killed with knobkerries and spears, or firearms by those who owned them. A few people had also obtained gin traps from Portuguese traders along the Kunene River, but poison was regarded as the most effective way of killing lions, leopards and hyena. In the past they had used the dried sap of toxic local plants, but apparently it was difficult and dangerous to prepare. Strychnine was much better, they assured me, and asked me to bring some with me on our next visit to the area.

Once on the highlands we drove via Otjitanda to Otjihende, and made camp in a sandy riverbed on the far north-western edge of the Kaokoveld plateau. Around us were small granite koppies, and on an evening walk I saw two small herds of impala and plenty of kudu spoor. A troop of baboons also clambered over the rocks ahead of me, barking at my intrusion into their domain. That night a leopard sawed in the nearby hills. The altitude here was 1 200 metres, and the night was quite cold. To the north the western extension of the Baynes Mountains, known as the Otjihipas, rose to over 1 900 metres above sea level.

The next morning we drove down the notorious Van Zyl's Pass into the Marienfluss, nearly 1 000 metres below Otjihende. In some places the track comprised just jagged rocks and the last kilometre was very steep, but I had become used to driving the old Chev over the Kaokoveld's pick-and-shovel-made roads, and apart from the steep slopes I found it no worse than the track to Otjimborombonga.

At the foot of the pass we found many cattle, and as there were no springs marked on my map here I asked one of the herdsmen where they got water. After a short walk up the dry riverbed he showed us a large cavern that had been filled during storms by the run-off cascading down off the steep surrounding slopes. There was clearly enough water for their livestock to drink from it for many months, and our guide told us that there were many smaller rock pools in the mountains. When these dried up they dug pits in the riverbeds, sometimes many metres deep, from which water was bailed into log troughs for their livestock to drink from.

We left Eorandara in the mid-afternoon and drove out into another world. Behind us was an unbroken wall of near-vertically folded gneiss and schist ranges that formed the eastern side of the valley, while in the distance were the bald red granite slopes of the Hartmann Mountains. Between them was a grass-covered sandy plain that stretched for 70 km from north to south. At its northern end the Marienfluss was less than 10 km across, and here the highest peaks of the Otjihipas towered up to 1 500 metres above the valley floor.

The area had received exceptionally good rain, and as we sped along a now smooth track through the wind-rippled grass, springbok pronked playfully ahead of us, while further away Elias and Daniel pointed out herds of gemsbok, mountain zebra and flocks of ostrich. With the abundance of food available, countless finch-larks and other seed-eating birds flew up in front of the truck, and when I stopped to enjoy the scenery they filled the air around us. It was easy to see why Georg Hartmann, the man appointed by the Kaokoveld Land and Mining Company to survey their new acquisition, was so enchanted by the Marienfluss that he named it after the mother of Jesus.

We camped at Otjinungua on the banks of the Kunene. The next morning I walked upstream to the river's exit from the Otjihipa Mountains, climbing high up the rocky slopes to where I could see into the awesome canyon it had cut through them. To the west, just 80 km away, was the Atlantic Ocean. Less than a year before I had been working on a petrol refinery near Durban, and now by amazing luck I was being paid to explore the wildest and remotest part of Southern Africa.

By the time we got back to Opuwo we had seen over 1 500 zebra, having travelled through just a small part of the Kaokoveld. Eugene Joubert's estimate of their numbers was clearly far too low. Nevertheless, I believed that Sergeant Laufs's figure of 50 000 was also unrealistic, and that he was probably unaware of how mobile both species were. When I had got to know the Kaokoveld better my own conservative population estimate was about 5 000 Burchell's and 1 200 mountain zebra. As there were over 120 000 cattle in the Territory at the time, they could not have made a major contribution to the overgrazing in the region.

* * *

In June my mother, brother Norman, and a school friend, Ray Weight, came to visit me. Just after they arrived Commissioner Van Niekerk instructed me to prepare a campsite and helicopter landing pad on the 'Beesvlakte' for a group of VIP visitors, including the Administrator General, who were on a 'fact finding' mission to the Kaokoveld. As the Beesvlakte was a series of alkaline plains between dolomite hills in the far south of the Territory bordering on the Etosha Game Park, I was happy to oblige.

After clearing a site in a grove of umbrella thorn trees close to Omuramba, a borehole the government had drilled to enable Herero stockowners to utilise the sweet grazing here, we drove over the dusty flats to the Park boundary. Along the way we saw springbok, gemsbok and Burchell's zebra, some of them grazing amongst the herds of cattle. Although the area was strewn with elephant dung, the pachyderms kept out of sight in the wooded drainage lines that crisscrossed the plains. We also found the fresh spoor of a pride of lions, but they too seemed to know that they were on the wrong side of the border, and kept a low profile in the thicker bush.

With no reason to hurry back to Opuwo, I decided to return via the western route, stopping briefly at Warmquelle and Sesfontein to see if any urgent assistance was needed in the irrigated gardens there, and then drove on to Purros. After we had all put a stone on Kapuhe's grave, I shot a springbok and hung it in a tree to cool overnight, about 20 metres from where we camped. When we woke the next morning it was gone, and the tracks going to and from it clearly showed that two large male lions had pulled the carcass down and carried it off. As we had been sleeping on a tarpaulin under the stars, Ray asked the question that was on all of our minds: What would have happened if there had not been a springbok conveniently hanging in a tree for them?

In the final week of my guests' visit I again received instructions from Commissioner Van Niekerk, this time to go to the Marienfluss and look for three boreholes that had been drilled there some years before. As Ben van Zyl had been against opening up the valley for cattle grazing, they had never been equipped, but now that he was no longer in charge the agricultural officials in Windhoek clearly planned to reverse this decision. My task was to bring back the serial numbers that had been stamped on their metal casings, so that the water delivery potential of each borehole could be obtained from the written records.

With the help of the local Himba from Eorandara we quickly located one of them at the southern end of the valley, but they knew of no other boreholes that had been drilled in the Marienfluss. However, our guides told us that two more had been drilled and not equipped further west, so the next morning we went in search of them. The first was located 10 km from the 'red drum', a marker used to indicate the turnoff into the Marienfluss, which became such a prominent feature that the place was given this name on the topographic map of the area.

While looking for the second hole west of the Hartmann Mountains we found the plains covered with quite fresh vehicle tracks. As this part of the Kaokoveld was very seldom visited by officials from Opuwo, out of curiosity I followed them until we came to a large, recently abandoned campsite. Nearby, wires had been stretched between two trees, and as a few small pieces of dried meat still hung from them, I had no doubt about what they had been used for. To confirm that it was a hunting camp, a little distance away we found the rotting skins, heads and feet of a large number of gemsbok and springbok. From the tracks, Elias also established that there had been two large trucks, precluding the possibility of it belonging to Kaokoveld-based officials. As nobody else was permitted to hunt in the Territory it had to be poachers, so we immediately returned to Opuwo, where I informed Sergeant Laufs.

After I had given him a full report of what we had found, and the location of the camp, he looked me sternly in the eye and said that it belonged to 'the Honourable Minister of Water Affairs, Mr SP Botha'. He added that cabinet ministers had the right to hunt in the Territory, but nevertheless told me that if I or anybody else in my family said one word about it to anyone 'I would be transferred out of the Kaokoveld immediately'.

A few days later I took my guests back to Windhoek and along the way asked the veterinary official at the Otjovasandu checkpoint, Jaap Meyer, who always diligently searched our vehicles for any animal products, why he had allowed the minister's biltong to pass through the Red Line. Jaap was well aware that the trip had been a hunting expedition, but had been told that a cabinet minister's vehicles could not be searched.

The possibility of game shot in the western part of the Kaokoveld carrying foot-and-mouth disease would be very remote, but were politicians really allowed to hunt in what was then a proclaimed game reserve? When I later discussed the matter with Tom Sopper he just shrugged his shoulders and told me that every winter cabinet ministers and senior government officials came to hunt in the Territory. The previous year the Minister of Transport, Ben Schoeman, had set up his camp at Orupembe, where he had killed plenty of game, including a rhino. I was naive to believe that the camp I had prepared for the Administrator General on the Beesvlakte, a hunter's paradise, was for a 'fact-finding mission'.

For a while I considered exposing the SP Botha case to the press, but we had taken no photographs, and without evidence to back up the story, would we be believed? With so few people having even heard of the Kaokoveld, did anybody care about cabinet ministers hunting there? I also had no doubt that

Sergeant Laufs's threat had not been idly made. In the end I did what all good civil servants do when confronted with a difficult decision: nothing.

*   *   *

My next assignment from Commissioner Van Niekerk was to accompany an elderly couple who had somehow been granted a permit to collect plants in the Kaokoveld for the Botanical Research Institute in Pretoria. As it was considered dangerous for two old people to travel alone in the Territory I was to stay with them wherever they went. However, I soon learned that my wards were by no means typical 60-year-olds, and certainly did not need nursemaiding.

Hugh and Dorothy Goyns were born in Scotland, but after the Second World War came to South Africa, where Hugh managed an engineering company. After retiring in 1959, at the age of 53, they undertook annual expeditions to remote parts of Africa. When not on safari, Hugh directed the Witwatersrand Retirement Council, which was devoted to preparing corporate executives for life after they left the helms of their businesses. This was often a very traumatic experience, Hugh told me, from which some men never recovered. However, the Goynses believed that life really began at 60 and they were busy proving it.

The focus area for their plant collecting was the Baynes Mountains, and I suggested that a trip to Otjimborombonga on the Kunene River would be a good place to begin. Having just started learning the names of the commoner plants in the region, I saw the trip as an excellent opportunity to learn the correct way of pressing botanical specimens and getting them identified. In fact, the three weeks I spent with Hugh and Dorothy Goyns would change my life.

After turning off the main track at Etengua we made frequent stops, during which Hugh and I scrambled up the rocky hill-slopes collecting plants, while Dorothy stayed near the vehicles and produced watercolour paintings of the rugged mountain scenery. We made camp at Otjimborombonga and while sitting around the campfire that night I told my companions about my hike to Onjezu a few months before, describing the great heat and precipitous slopes along the way. To my surprise, Hugh informed me that it was exactly the sort of place he wanted to collect plants in – and Dorothy took it for granted that she would be coming along too!

Even though I assured him that it would be easy to arrange, Hugh scorned the use of donkeys to carry their not inconsiderable equipment as well as food for the few days that we would be away from our vehicles. Everything would be carried on our own backs, including a bulky plant press that Hugh insisted should be strapped on top of his rucksack. As he was only just over five feet tall, it made the whole load nearly as high as him. But it was five feet of superbly toned muscle, without an ounce of fat, on a body that a man half his age would have been proud of.

We left Otjimborombonga before dawn, and in spite of walking slowly in deference to my companions' age reached Onjezu by midday. Although it was nowhere near as hot as on my first trip I was quite tired by the time we put our rucksacks down and sat in the shade of the winter thorn trees on the riverbank. Dorothy, who had kept a few metres behind Hugh and me, looked almost as fresh as when we had started walking!

After spending the afternoon collecting plant specimens we camped under the winter thorns, far enough from the water's edge not to attract the attention of the Kunene River's carnivorous denizens. During the night I shone my torch over the pool in front of us and three pairs of fiery red eyes reflected back across the water. One of the crocodiles seemed particularly large.

The next morning we walked downriver to where the Kunene entered another steep-sided gorge, collecting and pressing many more plants along the way. At midday we stopped in the shade of a small winter thorn that clung desperately to the river's rocky bank and ate a handful of nuts and raisins – the frugal fare that Hugh and Dorothy mainly subsisted on. Ahead of us the Kunene seemed to have been swallowed by towering ranges that once more closed in on its now fast-flowing waters.

Maudslay Baynes had left the river's banks here, following contour paths away from its course until he reached the Marienfluss valley. The only men known to have actually traversed this gorge through the Otjihipa Mountains were Willem van Riet and Gordon Rowe, who canoed down the entire length of the Kunene in 1964/5. I had read an account of their epic trip in the journal of the South African Wildlife Society, in which they described high cliffs rising straight out of the water, huge rapids and frequent attacks by crocodiles. In the mood of the moment Hugh and I talked about one day following in Maudslay Baynes's footsteps down the Kunene, from Eriksson's Drift to its mouth. It would be an amazing journey along one of the wildest and least known rivers in the world.

After returning to Otjimborombonga we drove back to Etengua and then turned west, descending Van Zyl's Pass into the Marienfluss. At Otjinungua we met up with a party of VIP officials who had not come to hunt, but to look at the Kaokoveld's tourism potential. Amongst them was Bernabe de la Bat, the Director of SWA's Department of Nature Conservation. Johan Malan was acting as their guide and he invited us to join them for a braaivleis that evening. As both Hugh and Dorothy were vegetarians they turned down the invitation, but having lived for more than a week on a diet of fruit and vegetables, my mouth watered just at the thought of a juicy steak. So after setting up camp near Okapupa spring, at the foot of the highest peaks in the Otjihipa range, I drove back to where the VIPs were camped. As most of them were Afrikaners I knew there would be no shortage of meat on the fire.

When I arrived De la Bat and his companions were discussing the dilemma facing nature conservation in the Kaokoveld. Everyone agreed that the spectacular western parts of the region had high tourism potential, but there were also political agendas to be considered. The United Nations had recently declared South Africa's occupation of South West Africa to be illegal, and that the country should fall under their direct control. Although Pretoria had not accepted this decision, the government was under pressure to show it was acting fairly with regard to all of its inhabitants. Six years earlier, a Commission had been set up, and it recommended that the western part of Etosha be deproclaimed and the Kaokoveld lose its game reserve status. Apparently, De la Bat had argued against the plan, but as one of the VIPs in the party pointed out, wildlife did not have the vote.

Later that evening one of the nature conservation officials accompanying the party, Robbie Hawthorne, told me he had information that ivory and rhino horn were being smuggled out of the Kaokoveld, and asked me to keep my ears open. Having never found any rhino or elephant carcasses on any of my trips, I thought it unlikely that serious poaching was taking place in the Territory, but it was huge and I had only covered a tiny fraction of it.

At first light the next morning Hugh and I set off to climb the highest peak in the Otjihipa Mountains. This time Dorothy decided not to join us. She would spend the day painting and keep the home fires burning in case we got back after dark. Perhaps it was just her polite way of taking the pressure off me to stay ahead of her.

It was a glorious, clear morning and at first we made good progress up one of the dry watercourses that scarred the sides of the mountain, but as we climbed higher the going became more difficult. I now learned that apart from being a font of knowledge on botany, anthropology, archaeology and healthy eating habits, Hugh was also an experienced mountaineer. As he had

brought basic rock climbing gear with him, we tried our hands at some relatively easy cliff faces, as an alternative to scrambling up scree slopes on which
a dislodged stone seemed as though it could start a major landslide. However,
we soon found that the ancient marine sediments of the Otjihipa range were
so fractured and rotten that the hand- and footholds were very unsafe. After
a few heart-stopping moments Hugh decided that in this remote part of the
Kaokoveld it was just not worth the risk of falling.

By eleven o'clock we were two-thirds of the way to the top. By now the temperature was deep in the thirties, and we called a halt under a rock overhang,
a few metres above a small, dry watercourse. After a few mouthfuls of water,
I had just started to peel an orange when I looked up and saw a large male
leopard making his way down the gully, right in front of us. He was so deeply
engrossed in the olfactory information on the ground that he was clearly unaware of our presence. I nudged Hugh and we both froze, watching spellbound as he passed below us, less than 10 metres away! Only when he had
crossed to the far side of the watercourse did the leopard see us. In an instant
his body flattened, every muscle rippling with pent-up power. For an instant I
thought he was sure to attack us, but instead he just disappeared. One second
he was there: sleek, fierce and awe-inspiring. The next his superbly camouflaged coat had simply melted into the scrubby bushes. We were not even sure
in which direction he had gone.

At two-thirty we reached the top. The view was mind-blowing. Most of the
Marienfluss was obscured by intervening peaks so that wherever one looked
there were folded mountains stretching uninterrupted to a distant, haze-
blurred horizon. The Kunene River, less than 5 km away horizontally, and
over 1.5 km below us, was completely invisible in a narrow canyon, the course
of which we could only guess. In the distance, more than 30 km from where
we stood, was the Onjezu valley – just distinguishable by a slight dent in an
otherwise endless sea of wild mountains.

While we savoured our conquest, Hugh talked again about walking down
the Kunene. But as Maudslay Baynes had taken 93 days I saw little chance of
my being able to do so in the near future. My interest was in the gorge it had
cut through the mountains between Onjezu and the Marienfluss. Was it possible to follow the river through it on foot, and what wildlife occurred deep
within these virtually unexplored ranges?

With no time to linger on the top, after about 20 minutes' rest we started
the descent, reaching camp at nine o'clock by the light of a single fading torch.
Dorothy had a blazing fire and a hot cup of thick soup waiting for us. It had

been another memorable day with the 60-years-young couple, who in less than two weeks had taught me how to squeeze every ounce of living out of each day.

From the Marienfluss I led Hugh and Dorothy down to the Skeleton Coast at Angra Fria, in order to see the place where the *Dunedin Star* had been wrecked. We spent the night in Ernst Karlova's shack, very grateful for its creaking hardboard walls to protect us from the cold wind that howled across the desert until well after sunset. Late that night the wind dropped, and huddled around a small fire we listened on my transistor radio to a live broadcast as Neil Armstrong, in a far distant but not dissimilar landscape, took 'one small step for man; one giant leap for mankind'.

Two days later we were back in Opuwo. During our few weeks together Hugh and Dorothy had taught me so much about so many different things, while they in turn had come to realise what a remarkable place the Kaokoveld was. Hugh and I had also shared many wild dreams about future expeditions, and we promised to keep in contact.

* * *

The chance to walk through the Kunene gorge arose sooner than I anticipated. At the end of August Kallie van Zyl mentioned that he would be going to Otjimborombonga on 3 September, to pay salaries and deliver rations there. That evening, when my housemate, Jimmy de Kock, told me that he and some friends would be at Otjinungua four days later, I decided the opportunity was too good to miss. However, to avoid any possible opposition to my plan I told no one but Kallie about it, and simply said to Jimmy that I might see him at Otjinungua on the 7th.

At about four o'clock on the afternoon of the 3rd, Kallie dropped me on the ridge overlooking Otjimborombonga. After taking a long drink of water I shouldered my rucksack and before I could have any second thoughts, headed westward along the now familiar path to Onjezu. As I walked, dassies scampered over the steep slopes, chattering indignantly to each other about the unwelcome intrusion into their domain. For a while a pair of black eagles soared effortlessly overhead, and as the sun slowly set behind the Angolan ranges three klipspringers bounced as if on pogo-sticks ahead of me. I reached Onjezu in twilight and was startled by nine black-faced impala bounding gracefully from a patch of tamarisk. After spreading my sleeping bag on the sand beneath the winter thorns I shone my torch over the river, but this time there were no red eyes reflected in its beam. I had no doubt that my presence had been noted, however, and resisted the temptation to wash, or even fill my water bottle in the dark.

To avoid walking in the midday heat I set off the next morning before sunrise, and well before noon had passed the point where Hugh Goyns and I turned back. Although it was still early September the heat in the Kunene's deep valley was devastating and I only started walking again at four o'clock, hoping to make a point that my topographic map showed to be only 4 km away by sunset. But I had underestimated the ruggedness of the river's banks and soon found myself having to climb high up the steep slope as a series of deep ravines slashed the mountainside here. In some places it took me half an hour to reach a point that, horizontally, was only a few hundred metres away. By the time I picked my way down to a small beach near the place I had planned to camp, it was already dark. Flicking my torch over the slow-moving river, I saw the brightly glowing eyes of a very large crocodile. I again went to sleep unwashed and covered in sweat.

The following morning I boulder-hopped along the bank, determined to stay close to the water's edge. But the going became progressively harder and I soon found myself having to make quite difficult traverses across smooth, near-vertical rock faces. By eight o'clock it was no longer possible to stay near the river and I was forced to climb straight upwards. Fifty metres above the deep, restless water the slope eased. Adrenaline was coursing through my veins and I found that, although the sun's rays had not yet penetrated this deep into the gorge, and it was still relatively cool, sweat was trickling down my face.

For the next few kilometres I was periodically able to scramble down to the Kunene for a drink and, if there was fast-flowing water, a quick swim. By that afternoon, however, the banks on both sides had become sheer cliffs, polished smooth by annual floods that here, where the river was often less than 30 metres wide, had raised the water level by over 10 metres. It was more than 24 hours before I could again reach the river and I was forced to sleep that night on the slopes, my foot against a tree stump to stop me from sliding. Although I had seen a number of impala and kudu near Onjezu as well as a few rhino dung middens, the only game in the gorge itself was klipspringers, baboons and leopards, whose spoor I often saw near the river. I did not see any crocodiles along this stretch of the Kunene, but there were very few places that they could come out of the water.

With a deadline to reach Otjinungua, and no idea of how difficult the going ahead would be, I started walking again at first light. Most of the morning was spent climbing up and down the steep scree slopes as I searched for
ways to cross the gaping ravines that seemed to get bigger and deeper the
further I went into the gorge. At one point I found myself over 500 metres
above the river before concluding that I would have to climb virtually to
the top of the mountains in order to get through a huge, boulder-strewn
gash that virtually split the Otjihipa range from the river to its highest
peak. Making a rash decision, I tried to climb down a near vertical face,
but slipped and fell about 3 metres. I was not hurt but it served as a chilling
warning. There would be no rescue helicopter to airlift me out if I broke
a leg. Fortunately, further down the slope I found an easier place to get
down into the ravine, and followed it to the Kunene without further mishap.
Finding a pool that was protected by boulders, I rewarded myself with a
most enjoyable swim.

Getting out on the other side was equally difficult and again I was forced
to climb high above the river to a ridge from which sheer cliffs fell vertically
down to the still, deep waters of the Kunene, at least 300 metres below. Here
I was greeted by a gust of cool wind from the coast, and in the far distance I
could make out the outline of the Hartmann range. In the now fading light I
once more scrambled and slid down to the riverbank, reaching a small beach
just as it got dark. In my torchlight, the very fresh tracks of a leopard were
clearly visible on the soft, white sand. With my enthusiasm somewhat dampened, I carefully made my way through the riparian vegetation to the water
and nearly stood on a three meter crocodile. Our surprise was equal, but its
reflexes were far superior. With a scurry and a splash the croc plunged into
the water while I could only stand and gape. A few minutes later it returned
to the shallows and, with head and shoulders well out of the water, watched
me as I prepared my evening meal.

The last few kilometres to Otjinungua were relatively easy and I walked
into Jimmy de Kock's camp just before noon – three days and 20 hours after
setting off from Otjimborombonga. He and his party had already packed up
and were just about to leave, but Jimmy found a cold beer in his coolbox for
me. It went down very well.

Having experienced first hand the Kunene's spectacular gorge through the
Otjihipa Mountains, I wanted to learn more about this little-known river, and
the best way to do so was actually on it, in a canoe. While on leave in October
I bought myself the same model fibreglass kayak that was used by Gordon

Rowe and Willem van Riet on their trips down the Kunene and Okavango Rivers. I also acquired a companion.

While working in Tsumeb I had got to know Rosalie Morant, and at the end of my 'bicycle safari' had briefly stayed with her and her mother in Johannesburg. During my leave I got to know her better, and just before going back to Opuwo took a chance and asked her to come with me. To my surprise she agreed, resigning from her job with the municipality and setting off into the unknown with a starry-eyed conservation missionary with very dubious prospects.

When the cattle sale at Otjondeka failed I again had no urgent work to attend to. My bosses in Windhoek had gone back to their drawing boards, and while they weighed up their options on how to reduce the Territory's livestock numbers, Tom Sopper asked me to start building cattle crushes on the Kunene River. They would enable Veterinary Services to inspect and take blood samples from any cattle that, legally or illegally, crossed the river from Angola. It suited me perfectly, as I could take my canoe along with me and in my free time practise shooting the Kunene's many rapids.

While improving my canoeing skills I got to know the many creatures that lived along the river: rock-resting darters and cormorants, goliath and grey herons patrolling the shallows, hovering pied kingfishers and giant kingfishers that surveyed the water from overhanging branches. Flocks of honking Egyptian geese were common, while black duck hid in the more secluded channels, and numerous smaller bank birds brightened my river days with their beauty and cheerful song. Most of the species that occurred on the Kunene were old companions whose presence I hardly noticed, but others were rare and seldom seen – exciting new records for my notebook.

I also learned on which islands the Kunene's few surviving hippo grazed, and where they sought refuge during the daylight hours. For good reasons the hippo resented my intrusion into their hideaways, and if by accident or design I came too close they were unfailingly aggressive. In contrast the otters I occasionally saw were always friendly, providing some of my most magical moments on the river. Once a pair of these sleek, subtle creatures played tag around my canoe, but mostly they would just swim up close and stare inquisitively at the strange new creature on the water.

Along this part of the Kunene crocodiles did not often expose themselves. I knew they were there from their unmistakable tracks on hidden sandbanks and from thin profiles on the surface of the water that slowly sank as I approached. But although they were seldom seen, they were a constant and omnipresent threat that I could never quite forget.

Building the cattle crushes along the Kunene gave me plenty of spare time, enabling me to canoe virtually all the river from Ruacana to Epupa. I estimated that between 10 and 15 hippo still survived here, and as the local people told me that none occurred below Epupa, it was the same number Shortridge had found in the Kunene 40 years earlier. Apart from just below the Ruacana Falls, I only encountered them where there were islands in the river on which they did not face competition for grazing from the Himba cattle, and the narrow channels between them provided safe refuges during the day.

While building a cattle-crush at Epupa Falls I also had another close encounter with a leopard. The border guard here had caught one in a gin trap and requested my help to shoot it. It was not the first time I had been asked by local people to do so, but on this occasion the trap had been tied to a log that was too small, and the sheep-killer had taken off with the trap still attached to its foot. Elias and I returned to the site with the guard and easily followed the clear drag-mark up a sandy watercourse, which ended at the foot of a small mopane tree that it had obviously climbed into. From about 20 metres away we carefully studied the few branches, but saw nothing, and I presumed that it must have jumped down and gone on. It hadn't. I had taken only a few more steps when there was a deep guttural growl and a large male leopard sprang from the foliage and came straight for us.

My two companions immediately took off with a very angry spotted cat in hot pursuit, and as it went past, less than 10 metres from me, I aimed behind its shoulder and pulled the trigger. The only effect was to turn the leopard's attention towards me. And having bought cheap ammunition, which expanded in the chamber and prevented the cartridge case from being ejected until it had cooled, I could only hold the rifle up in front of me in an attempt to fend it off. But just as the leopard was about to spring it seemed to trip and fell at my feet, stone dead. The bullet had passed through its heart.

In December Rosalie went back to Johannesburg to start training as a nursing sister, and in order for her to attend Christmas Midnight Mass we drove to Windhoek via the Catholic Mission Station at Ombalantu in Ovamboland. After having supper under the trees nearby, we waited until just before the service began before joining the many local black Christians in the tightly packed church. The Mass was conducted in Latin by an elaborately robed white priest, and together with the harmonious voices of the choir and congregation created a soul-lifting blend of old European ritual and African exuberance. By the time we left the church I was deeply moved. In spite of the dark cloud of apartheid spreading over South West Africa, here blacks and whites were still able to rejoice together in celebration of the Christ child's birth. Surely there was still hope that a violent racial confrontation could be averted?

*   *   *

The sixties, the decade that was to define a generation, had drawn to a close. They had been tumultuous years of burning activism and bloody revolution, of state repression and shocking assassinations – of Sharpeville, the Congo, Biafra and Vietnam. The decade had seen the building of the Berlin Wall, which divided a nation and polarised the world, and the Cuban missile crisis, which brought it to the brink of a nuclear holocaust. In the sixties the United States passed the Bill of Rights, finally making all its citizens equal before the law; China 're-educated' its intellectuals and burnt its cultural heritage; Japan rose from the ashes of Hiroshima and Nagasaki to challenge centuries of European economic dominance, and Israel occupied the West Bank and Gaza, creating flash points that would smoulder into the next millennium.

But in spite of this it had been a time of hope, when two Kennedy brothers inspired the world with their idealism and Martin Luther King had a dream, when millions of young people in America and Europe rejected the materialistic values of their parents and imagined a new Age of Aquarius that would outlaw war, address poverty and conserve our planet's precious natural resources.

During the sixties man had used his technological ingenuity to put an astronaut on the moon, and make a contraceptive pill that would liberate women from their own fertility, thereby forever changing the relationship between the sexes. But he had also used it to defoliate vast tracts of rainforest with 'Agent Orange,' and incinerate whole villages with napalm.

In Southern Africa the decade saw Dr Chris Barnard perform the world's first human heart transplant, while Hendrik Verwoerd and John Vorster used political scalpels to dissect South Africa and transplant its 'surplus people'. It was a time when a few courageous men and women stood up for the rights of the country's black and brown majority, while the government trampled on them, and most white South Africans just stood by. In 1963 Nelson Mandela was convicted of treason and sentenced to life imprisonment, taking with him the hopes of all who opposed apartheid, and igniting liberation struggles across the sub-continent.

Many of the momentous events of the decade were to become the milestones and millstones that moulded our future. But the sixties had ended. The seventies would be different.

CHAPTER EIGHT

A NEW DECADE

Before 1960 South West Africa was a geographic location rather than a country, a forgotten mandate granted by a defunct organisation, administered as a virtual fifth province by South Africa. Until then, opposition to the way Pretoria ran the Territory had been passive – petitions to the United Nations by the Herero paramount chief, Hosea Kutako, and the Reverend Michael Scott. The National Party had ignored this internal dissent and continued to implement its apartheid policies – segregating the country's population not only racially, but also according to their tribal affiliation.

The situation changed in 1959, when police fired upon protesters against the forced removal of Windhoek's non-white residents to the newly created township of Katutura, killing 11 people. Internationally this official brutality drew attention to the country's mandated status, while internally it led to the formation of indigenous political parties, with a number of black politicians going into exile. In the following year the Ovamboland People's Organisation, originally set up to oppose the contract labour system operating in the northern tribal areas, was reconstituted as the South West African People's Organisation (SWAPO), the country's first national liberation movement.

In 1962 the Chairman of the UN Special Commission for SWA was sent on a fact-finding mission to the country, but his report was ambiguous and controversial. In the same year the International Court of Justice decided that it did have the right to hear the case brought by Liberia and Ethiopia against South Africa over its implementation of the mandate. To counter these developments Prime Minister Verwoerd appointed FH Odendaal to chair a Commission of Inquiry into SWA Affairs, with the object of 'further promoting the material and moral welfare and social progress of the inhabitants of SWA, and more particularly its non-white inhabitants'.

In May 1963 a new player entered the fray. The Organisation of African Unity (OAU) was formed by the 32 new sovereign states on the continent, and in the first Article of its Charter called for the eradication of all forms of colonialism. Frustrated by a lack of progress on the diplomatic front, and with the full support of the OAU, SWAPO also started recruiting young men and sending them for military training in Egypt.

In 1966 the first group of armed SWAPO guerrillas entered the country, and in October that year fought a pitched battle with South African security forces at Ongulumbashe in Ovamboland. All of them were either killed or captured, but the struggle for South West Africa's independence had now gained a new dimension. Although the SWAPO leadership were naïve to think that they could take on the might of the South African army with conventional military tactics, there were other ways of winning a war against superior forces.

By the end of the 1960s Pretoria's apartheid legislation was being applied to all government institutions throughout South West Africa, while in the police zone most commercial establishments also had separate entrances, counters and even queues for black and white customers. North of the Red Line the situation was more complex. Here the traditional leaders still had considerable autonomy – although the government often tried to manipulate them and even deposed non-compliant chiefs if they felt it was necessary 'to maintain law and order'. But the great majority of people living here were not significantly affected by the humiliating racial policies introduced in the rest of the country. The 1970s would change this.

While I was in the Kaokoveld the little information about discriminatory laws and oppressive practices, or the opposition to them, filtering into the Territory caused only minor ripples among a few school-educated Herero. All the other inhabitants still perceived the South African government in terms of the actions or inactions of one man: the Bantu Affairs Commissioner (BAC).

As the most senior government official, as well as the resident magistrate, the BAC had the power to influence virtually everything that happened in the

Territories he administered. Not surprisingly, commissioners who held their posts for many years often regarded the areas under their authority as personal fiefdoms, in which they ruled supreme over the local inhabitants. Dave Marais, the long-time Commissioner in Rundu, was only half-jokingly called 'the King of the Kavango'. In the Caprivi Strip Major French Trollip, the BAC from the late 1930s to mid-1950s, became so attached to the region that when he was finally transferred he refused to leave, and had to be evicted from his post. For more than two decades, until 1943, Cocky Hahn was synonymous with the affairs of Ovamboland.

The Van Zyl years in the Kaokoveld, from 1949 to 1969, were characterised by the maintenance of the status quo. During this period the tribal residents had continued to practise their ancient traditions unhindered and unnoticed by the outside world. When I arrived in the Territory, although government officials and the local people lived separate lives, the day-to-day relationship between them was still generally good. However, it started deteriorating under Van Zyl's successor, Van Niekerk, and got even worse when Beesie Jooste took over in 1970. As a man who had been moulded by the hard-line Nationalist policies of South Africa, he had no tolerance for 'liberal' English-speakers, and I soon found myself in conflict with him. Jooste also brought his own Assistant Commissioner, Dirk Keet, and he and I knocked heads from the start.

In 1969 Johan Malan got permission from the Territory's Council of Headmen to build a house at Okanguati, 100 km north of Opuwo, in the heart of Himba country. Here he still acted as the local Assistant Commissioner, but was relieved of most of his administrative duties, enabling him to concentrate more on his PhD research. We remained good friends, and whenever I was in the vicinity I called in to see him and his wife Wilma, in their new home on the tree-lined banks of the Omuhonga River.

By early 1970 Jod van der Merwe, Kallie van Zyl and Burger Baard had all either resigned or been transferred out of the Territory. This meant that, of the government officials who had been in Opuwo when I arrived just 18 months before, only Tom Sopper, Sergeant Laufs and Constable Louis Lombard still remained. But the most important change was the replacement of the Commissioner General, Dr Marti Olivier, with Jannie de Wet – a born 'South Wester' from Outjo, one of the most right-wing farming districts in the country. Based at Ondangua in Ovamboland, the Commissioner General had the final responsibility for implementing Pretoria's separate development policies in all of the homelands in South West Africa.

The major changes taking place in the Kaokoveld did not only involve BAD staff. In 1970 construction started on a new white residential area, the first stage of a major development programme recommended by the Odendaal Commission. It would eventually include a hospital, primary and secondary schools, a commercial wholesaler, a government office complex, and houses for black employees and contract workers. Also under construction was an all-weather road from Kamanjab to Opuwo and the Ruacana Falls, where a large hydro-electric power scheme was being built.

The dusty little outpost I had first visited in 1967 was becoming a town that for better and worse would be firmly linked to the rest of the country. Inevitably these developments signalled the end of an era in the Kaokoveld. But at the time the residents of the region, and in particular the Himba, were still blissfully unaware of what was planned, and could not have comprehended how much it would affect their future lives.

*   *   *

When the older generation of government officials left, the atmosphere in Opuwo changed. My new colleagues had not come to the Kaokoveld because they were attracted to the wide-open spaces, or enjoyed working with its still traditional people. Most of them were bureaucrats, who had landed in Opuwo on their way up the civil service promotion ladder. The Territory's big game may have been a factor in their requesting transfers here, but if so it was not because of any wish they had to conserve it.

An incident in early 1970 clearly illustrated that things in the Kaokoveld were different. A newly appointed black clerk had an accident while driving a government vehicle. No one was seriously injured, but it was suspected that he had been under the influence of alcohol, and the case was investigated by the police. As one of the passengers in the cab was my lorry driver, Oskar Kazondu, he was called in for questioning and held in custody for three days. After his release he told me that he had been beaten and given electric shocks to his testicles in an attempt to make him sign a statement saying that the clerk was drunk while driving. The detail with which he described what had been done to him left me in little doubt that he was telling the truth.

Appalled by his story, particularly as he had just been a witness in the case, I confronted the young policeman involved. He did not take kindly to being questioned about his actions, and told me to 'stick to agricultural affairs and the police would carry out their duties as they saw fit'. I would not have hesitated to take the matter to Ben van Zyl, but now that Beesie Jooste was Commissioner I knew it would be a waste of time.

One aspect of the Territory that had not changed was the overgrazed state of its rangelands, particularly around the permanent water-points. The 1970 rainy season was well below average, and though the highlands turned green as the trees and bushes came into leaf, in most places the grass beneath them only grew a few centimetres before it wilted and died. It was going to be a very long dry season.

On a visit to the BAD headquarters in Windhoek I asked whether there were any plans for future livestock marketing, but my superiors seemed to have lost interest in the Territory's problems. To men with science degrees or diplomas, the social and religious reasons for the Himba and Herero not wanting to have their cattle inspected carried little weight. The Kaokovelders had been given their chance, was the general consensus, and they were now concentrating their efforts in homelands where the people were more co-operative. I could understand their position, but if the overgrazing in the region was not solved both its livestock and wildlife would always be threatened.

With marketing now no longer an option the only alternative was to introduce better grazing management. As this was a field I had no previous experience in I borrowed books on the subject, and asked some of the older agricultural officers for their advice. The best they could offer was to drill more boreholes, thereby opening up new areas for grazing, but as Nico Smit had said on his first visit, it would only be buying time until cattle numbers could be reduced

Tapping the underground water table had long been the favoured solution to overgrazing problems in Southern Africa, and in tribal areas it was also a way for the government to win the support of the local people. However, in the long term it had usually resulted in livestock numbers increasing even further and just extended the area of degradation. Nevertheless, I drove back to Opuwo with instructions to look for ungrazed areas where new water-points could be developed. In effect it meant that my superiors had given their blessing to my exploring the Kaokoveld.

I started in the north, where Munimuhoro Kapika asked me for more bore-holes every time I visited him. The old headman had moved to Ombuku, his rainy season residence on the banks of the Omuhonga River, and in the shade of a huge winter thorn tree we sat and discussed cattle, water and grass. The place he wanted a borehole was in a large valley east of the Baynes Mountains.

It still had good grazing, but the only water was a spring near the highest point of the range, too far away for livestock to reach. I agreed to visit the area to make my own assessment of the situation, and he assigned me one of his councillors, Katjira Muniombara, to act as my guide.

We left the next morning, driving cross-country for as far as possible before walking along a well-used footpath that led up the mountains to the spring. Although I estimated Katjira to be at least 50 years old he set a cracking pace, which he kept up for four hours before stopping to take a short break. When I commented on his fitness he assured me that all Himba men, unless sick or very old, were capable of walking from sunrise to sunset without a rest. When he was younger he had often walked from Okanguati to Opuwo in a single day. From the map I had brought with me I estimated that the shortest distance between the two places was about 80 km!

After a cup of tea and an hour's rest – an indulgence Katjira endured patiently – we started walking again. As we climbed higher up the slopes, dark-bellied clouds built up and rain-squalls were soon sweeping across the valley below us. By four o'clock it was obvious that we were in for a thorough soaking, and our guide signalled a halt. He and Elias then collected a large pile of wood, and with an ancient flint lighter and some old elephant dung he found nearby, Katjira had a blazing fire going just as the first raindrops started to fall.

I had already learned that the Himba were masters in the art of travelling light and our guide was no exception. While Elias and I carried rucksacks, Katjira had only a stout stick over his shoulder from which hung a skin bag containing all his requirements for the journey. After taking a hand-carved pipe from it, he tucked the bag into a hole in a nearby mopane tree and sat down next to the fire. By the time Elias and I had removed our shirts and shoes, stashed our gear and joined Katjira, the heavens had opened up and streams of muddy water were running all around us.

As the rain pelted down Katjira kept the fire going by feeding it logs from the pile collected before the storm broke. He also managed to keep his pipe burning by cupping his hand over the bowl. While we squatted close to the hissing and spluttering flames to keep warm, our guide told us an amazing story about the hazards of being a Himba in the white man's world.

Although the Kunene formed the international border with Angola, Katjira told me that the Himba frequently crossed it to visit relatives on the other side. They also went across to trade oxen, leopard skins and even ivory with the Portuguese shop-owners along this part of the river. However, once livestock had been taken across the Kunene, SWA's veterinary regulations prohibited them from being brought back, which gave the traders a distinct advantage in the transaction. But where else could the Himba get the things they needed – 'especially the white man's strong water', he said with a twinkle in his eye.

Katjira re-lit his pipe with a glowing ember from the fire, and after puffing for a few moments went on: 'A man had to be very careful when trading with the Portuguese because they were as smart as jackals. When you arrived at their shop they would offer you a bottle of sweet wine before discussing business. This was the dangerous time, and if you did not keep your wits about you, you would be fooled by the trader's generosity and pass out on the ground. The next morning he would kick you awake and give you a cooking pot, a thin blanket and a case of cheap wine, saying that the previous night you had agreed to this price for your fattest ox. The beast would already be in his kraal and you would have to go back to your wife and explain why you had come back home with so little in your hands. Of course, she would be very cross and tell you how stupid you are, or maybe even accuse you of giving some of the things you received to another woman.'

After a short break to refill his pipe, Katjira carried on with his story. When he was young he was tricked in this way and decided to take the case to the Portuguese police. After laying his complaint he returned with a police officer to the trading store. As it had been a long hot journey the shop owner naturally invited the policeman in for refreshments, while Katjira sat outside and waited. A few hours later they came out on very friendly terms, and to his astonishment Katjira was told by the policeman that the shop-owner had accused him of theft and that he was under arrest!

Back at the police station, Katjira said that he was put into a cell with sharp spikes sticking out of the walls, which was then filled with water to the level of his chin. He was kept in it for the whole night, unable to even lean against the walls and rest. The following morning he was taken out of the cell, 'his skin as pale as a white man's', and brought before the station commander, who now asked him if he still wanted to lay a charge against the trading store owner. Realising the folly of his actions he withdrew his complaint. Once he had done so the theft charges against him were also forgotten and he was released – but now with nothing at all to show for the oxen he had brought across the river.

Elias, who became very angry while translating, asked Katjira where he now sold his cattle. To the same trader, he replied, but he had learned never to drink any alcohol before concluding the deal. 'It is better to do business with a man whose tricks you know than to go to someone else and be caught by some new deception,' he added with worldly wisdom. Elias, who was from a younger generation, did not accept this and after I went to bed that night they argued until late about the matter.

When the storm had passed, we dressed and walked the last few kilometres to the spring. There were no Himba in the vicinity, but from the dung around the water it was obvious that many elephants, as well as other game, drank there. That night we camped at the spring, and the following morning I climbed to a rounded knoll which, according to my map, was 2 070 metres above sea level – the highest point in the Kaokoveld. Far to the east were the strangely striped peaks of the Zebra Mountains, while northwards I could see across the Kunene to unnamed ranges deep in Angola. Elias and Katjira had not come with me. Climbing to the tops of mountains was a European obsession not shared by the Kaokovelders, for whom spectacular views were just a part of their everyday life.

Around the campfire that evening Katjira was again talkative. He confirmed the presence of 'mountain Tjimba' in the Baynes and Otjihipa ranges, but said I would not recognise them. Although in the past they only wore wild animal skins, most of them now dressed like the Himba, for whom they worked as cattle herders. But they had not yet learned how to keep their own livestock, he said, and if they were given a goat it was killed and eaten the same day.

I asked what they lived on when they were not working for the Himba, and Katjira replied that they ate anything they could find: 'roots and berries, worms and even snakes!' Honey was their most prized food, with each man having his own hives. 'Bees are their cattle,' he said, 'and when an omuTjimba gets married he gives his wife's family honey from his hives to show them that their daughter is marrying a wealthy man.' This last bit of his story had both him and Elias laughing until the tears rolled down their cheeks.

From Katjira I also learned more about Himba traditional livestock management strategies. To conserve the grazing around springs their cattle were moved away from them during the rainy season. This was the responsibility of the younger men and their wives, who would spend many months in makeshift stock posts wherever there was rainwater. At this time of the year only a few milking cows were kept around the main villages to provide for the older people who could no longer move far.

Another way of reducing grazing pressure around larger settlements was the practice of wealthy stockowners loaning poor families some of their livestock to live from. Acquired goats and sheep could be used for household meat, and even oxen slaughtered on ceremonial occasions with the owner's permission. If they were well looked after, some of the progeny of the loaned animals became the property of the caretaker family, enabling them to start their own flocks and herds. These and other examples further emphasised how much the Himba and Herero social and religious systems were interwoven with their livestock management practices. Before we could address the overgrazing problem, I would need to know more about them.

The next day we followed one of the larger watercourses back to the vehicle, finding most of the area to be under-utilised, with generally good grazing. Back at Ombuku I informed Munimuhoro that I would write a report recommending two new boreholes there. The old headman thanked me, but was clearly sceptical about seeing them drilled in the near future. He was right, and his people would have to get through the present drought without the white man's technology – as they had survived many others in the past.

*   *   *

Although it brought hardship to the people, the poor rainy season did give me the opportunity of observing how the pastoralists coped with the situation. As with most droughts, a few areas did receive adequate rainfall, and large numbers of cattle from the neighbouring areas came together to share the grazing there. The general rule was that the first man to bring his stock to a water-point had priority rights over it, but under these conditions all later arrivals were also accommodated. To prevent disputes arising between the herdsmen, the elders from the different lineages regularly came together to decide on each stockowner's grazing area.

A key management strategy in droughts was to set up temporary stockposts far from the water-points, and only take their cattle to drink every second day. On the alternate days they would be herded in the opposite direction, thereby considerably increasing the area that could be grazed around each spring or borehole. To my colleagues in BAD who had studied animal husbandry this was seen as putting unnecessary stress on the cattle, and to them developing more artificial water-points was a better solution. But in a drought it was the lack of grazing, not water, that was the problem, and I believed that our focus should be on what was best for the grass – and not the cattle.

In fact, the large-framed and long-legged indigenous Sanga cattle were very well adapted to surviving droughts. Unlike the imported breeds found on the country's white farms that drank every day, natural selection under these harsh conditions enabled them to drink less frequently and walk greater distances from water. My superiors had learned this to their cost a few years earlier, when they attempted to improve the quality of Kaokoveld cattle by in-troducing Afrikaner bulls bred for South African conditions. When I arrived in Opuwo only two of them were still alive, and the local people told me that after walking the long distance between water and the grazing grounds 'they had no energy left for any cows that might be on heat'.

Another factor that made the Himba and Herero cattle better able to sur-vive the region's droughts was their ability to browse the foliage of many trees and shrubs, as well as the protein-rich pods of acacias and other legumes. Even the tannin-rich leaves of the mopane, once they had dried and fallen to the ground, were eaten, helping them to maintain relatively good condition in areas where there appeared to be no grass at all.

But if the pastoralist's livestock and their grazing management practices were so well adapted to the region's arid climate, why were there now large areas of bare ground around virtually every water-point? Was it the result of too many cattle, goats and sheep, as my superiors believed, or had it always been like this in dry years?

To answer this question I often asked older men if the grazing had changed since they were young. In many cases their eyes would go misty as they re-called a time when the rains were much better, and the grass grew so tall that while their cattle were out grazing 'only their horns were visible'. They also told me that many of the grasses that had been very common in the past were now only found on steep hill-slopes, or far from any water. Although I suspected that time had erased their memories of previous droughts, the consistency of their replies convinced me that the Kaokoveld's rangelands had deteriorated, and the biggest change was the disappearance of perennial grasses and their replacement with annual species.

By June I had a good idea of the situation on the plateau, but knew nothing about what was happening in the west. To rectify this I decided to undertake an-other trip through the pre-Namib. As the Sesfontein gardens now fell under the agricultural official based in Khorixas, the administrative centre of the 'Damara Homeland' recommended by the Odendaal Commission, I took a shortcut from Otjikondavirongo to the just-erected windmill at Ganumub. On the way I noticed many vultures, and on investigation found that they were feeding on the remains of four gemsbok, all of which had had their legs removed.

There were no people living nearby, but at Ganamub I found the *onganda* of Isak Uararavi, a Herero lineage head from Sesfontein. Knowing that not much happened in an area without the local people being aware of it, I asked Isak about the gemsbok carcasses. He told me he had visited the camp of the official who was repairing their windmill, and had seen a large amount of meat hanging up to dry. From the man's workers he also learned that a total of nine gemsbok had been killed. To shoot so many animals could hardly be called hunting for the pot, but as the official had since returned to Opuwo, I decided to continue the trip and report the matter to the Commissioner when I got back.

Purros was very different from my previous visit. This time there were at least 600 head of cattle and large flocks of goats and sheep grazing near the banks of the Hoarusib. From the herdsmen I learned that they had come downriver from Omutati, more than 80 km away. The cattle had clearly been there for some time and it was now hard to find a single blade of grass on the sandy plains. There was also very little game in the vicinity, and no fresh sign of elephants.

North of Purros a few showers had fallen and large numbers of springbok and gemsbok had gathered on the short grass, but at Orupembe there were again large herds of cattle and the plains around the windmill were heavily grazed. At the 'Red Drum' I turned left to the Hartmann valley. The previous year our trip up this most westerly route to the Kunene had been interrupted by finding Minister SP Botha's hunting camp. This time I planned to go all the way.

The road ended in a dune field a few kilometres south of the river, but after following a faint track to the top of a sandy promontory we were rewarded by a 360 degree view of one of the most spectacular desert wildernesses in Africa. On the SWA side of the border ivory-coloured dunes tumbled down to the Kunene's azure waters 200 metres below, but no sand had crossed the river and the mountains in Angola were steel-grey, and seemed as barren and lifeless as the surface of the moon.

On our return journey we camped at Sanitatas. This time the spring was well used, with elephant dung littering the many game paths that radiated out from the water into the surrounding basalt hills. It was a few days before full moon, so that night I made myself comfortable on a rocky ridge overlooking the waterhole and waited for the show to begin. I was not disappointed. By the time I slipped back to camp over 50 elephant, eight rhino and seemingly endless streams of zebra had come to drink. The sound effects were equally impressive. Apart from the continuous clatter of hooves on rock, there were frequent whinnies, squeals, trumpeting and throaty elephant rumbles, while in the grey shadows behind me a pack of hyenas regularly whooped to each other. The finale was a chorus of lions that started roaring just before I went to bed, and continued periodically throughout the night.

Before returning to Opuwo I decided to shoot a zebra for the building team. In the early morning the area around Sanitatas appeared to be deserted, but about an hour after sunrise Elias pointed out a small group of Burchell's zebra on a far hill slope, moving slowly down a path towards us. Not wanting to hunt in the immediate vicinity of the spring I decided to intercept them before they reached the water.

Following a gully I was able to approach within 200 metres, and from there crawled on my hands and knees across scrub-covered flats, stopping every time one of them looked in my direction. When I was close enough to be confident of a clean, heart shot, I carefully moved into a sitting position. But just as I raised my rifle I heard a deep-throated grunt, and turning to see what it was looked straight into the big golden eyes of a lioness crouching less than 20 metres away. She seemed as astonished to see me as I was her, and for a few heart-stopping seconds we both froze, each expecting the other to make the first move. Then she stood up, growled again in annoyance, and with a flick of her tail, stalked off into the bushes. Scrambling to my feet, I was just in time to see another three lions also slinking away into the scrub. We had obviously been stalking the same zebras – which were now galloping over the horizon, *kwe-ha-ing* to each other about their lucky escape.

When I got back to Opuwo I reported the nine gemsbok killed at Ganumub to the Commissioner, and gave him the name of the official Isak Uaravi told me was responsible. But Jooste was clearly not interested. It was just hearsay and he had much more important things to attend to. When I spoke to the official concerned he admitted being in the area at the time, but said he had shot only two gemsbok, and if I saw more they must have been killed by the Herero I spoke to. Without the Commissioner's support there was nothing more to be done about the case. But I knew it was very unlikely that local people would kill so many animals, and they would also have taken the whole carcass – not just the most favoured parts for making biltong.

* * *

By the end of July I had been in the Kaokoveld for almost two years, and was now well known to most of its inhabitants, who seemed intrigued by a white man who caught snakes, counted wild animals at night and walked alone in the mountains. As was the custom among rural Africans, each of us officials was given a name, which in my case was *Ondwezu ongombo,* the goat ram, apparently because of my beard and rock climbing habits. It could have been worse, one of my colleagues was known as *Ombinda korambi,* the thin pig!

The easygoing relationship I had developed with the local people certainly helped my work and made life more pleasant, but it also resulted in them sometimes bringing problems to me, a junior official, instead of taking them to the Commissioner. As Beesie Jooste already regarded me as being insubordinate, because I seldom reported on my activities to him, our relationship had steadily deteriorated. On top of this, he and the hard-line Nationalists in Opuwo saw me as a *Kaffir-boetie* – a black man's little brother.

A few days after I reported the gemsbok killing at Ganamub to Jooste he called me into his office and accused me of 'just driving around and not doing any work'. As he was not a man I could discuss things with, I wrote a report on all my activities since the livestock marketing had been called off. Apart from looking for potential borehole sites, as requested by my superiors in Windhoek, I had used my time to learn more about the local people's livestock management strategies, which I regarded as essential if we were to address the overgrazing in the Territory.

In August Nico Smit asked me to investigate a complaint from the nature conservator at Otjovasandu that large numbers of Herero cattle were again grazing in Etosha. They had apparently entered from the Beesvlakte and dispersed to a number of springs deep inside the Park. Elias and I left the following day, taking with us Phineas Mutuezu, recently returned from a one-year diploma course in agriculture I had arranged for him as a young school leaver. At Omuramba we picked up two local men who knew where the cattle were, and drove across the unfenced boundary into the Park.

The sun was setting by the time we reached the first waterhole our guides led us to. It did not have much water and although there was plenty of fresh cattle dung around it, the people and livestock had left. As it was too late to follow them we made camp near the spring. Soon after dark a pride of lions started roaring from very near by, and at regular intervals during the night I heard the muted voices of our guides as they added more wood to the fire. I felt quite safe, but knew it would have been a very different situation if I had not been sleeping next to a vehicle with a rifle by my side.

Within ten minutes of leaving camp the next morning we found the lions lying under a tree next to a zebra kill. As they slunk off into the bush the two men from the Beesvlakte shouted at me to shoot them quickly, before they got away. I reminded them that we were in a game reserve, where wild animals were not allowed to be killed. But they were unrepentant: 'Lions are not animals,' they insisted. 'They are the devil's children and should be killed wherever they are.'

An hour or so later we came to another spring where we found a group of men watering large numbers of cattle. After ascertaining to whom the live-stock belonged and estimating their numbers we drove on. Over the next two days we followed the guides' directions to four more stock-posts, the last one in the Khovarib Schlucht, an awe-inspiring canyon the Hoanib River had cut though limestone mountains.

For much of the way a strong stream of water ran in the bed of the Hoanib, and soon after entering the gorge we met five elephant bulls returning from their morning drink. As this part of Etosha had never been open to the public and vehicles were still a novelty to them, they all swung around to face us, their ears spread wide. Behind them, against a background of towering cliff faces, a long line of cattle trudged through the dust on their way to the spring. It was a scene that captured the essence of the Kaokoveld, where people and wildlife lived together in one of the most spectacular parts of Southern Africa.

By now I had established that there were at least 3 000 cattle in the Park, and that they belonged to Headmen Keefas Muzuma and Joel Tjiahura and their followers. In charge of the cattle in the Khovarib Schlucht was Keefas's senior councillor, Joshua Kangombe, whom I had met the year before under similar circumstances. At the time he had promised to return to the Kaokoveld as soon as rain fell there, and had done so.

'So you're back in the game reserve,' I said after we had discussed the pleas-antries that African etiquette required.

'That is true,' Joshua replied. 'But as you know, there was no rain this year. A man cannot just sit and watch his cattle die.'

'You should have asked permission before going into the Park,' I told him.

'Perhaps, but we have still not heard the white chief's reply to our last re-quest for grazing in the game reserve,' he politely reminded me. 'How many cattle would have died before permission was granted this time?'

By now we were surrounded by many of the other stockowners, and their attitude was much more aggressive. If the 'big heads' in Windhoek wanted them to leave the game reserve, they shouted at me, then the government must 'bring their rifles' because they would not leave peacefully. Fortunately, Joshua calmed them down and we were able to discuss their predicament rationally, and look for less drastic solutions.

The following day some of the senior men took me to two places where boreholes had already been drilled on the Beesvlakte near the Kaokoveld–Etosha border, but had not yet been equipped. Because there was no natural water in the area the grazing around them was still in fair condition and developing them was clearly the best short-term course of action. Before leaving I told Joshua that they could remain where they were, as long as they undertook not to hunt any wild animals – not even lions. He smiled and promised that 'even the lions will be safe' – but I wondered whether he, or any headman, had enough authority over their followers to stop them killing predators.

On my way back I visited Headman Joel Tjiahura to discuss the situation, and he provided me with some interesting historical information. Apparently, both he and Keefas Muzuma were born at springs in what was now the Etosha Game Park. However, in 1928 their families had been resettled in the virtually uninhabited south-eastern Kaokoveld, in order to create a cattle-free zone between the pastoralists and white farmers who were being settled in the Kamanjab District. According to Joel, their people had initially refused to move, and were prepared to take up arms to resist, and it was only Commissioner Cocky Hahn's diplomacy that had averted bloodshed.

Johan Malan gave me more information about the two maverick headmen. Being wealthy stockowners, when they arrived in the Kaokoveld they had automatically assumed leadership positions over the resident Tjimba-Herero who had lost their cattle to the Nama raiders. But they and their followers had never been fully accepted, and were still referred to as the *Ovandamuranda*, 'the people from Damaraland'. Our failed cattle-marketing project had once more ignited these old resentments against Keefas and Joel, which resulted in the formation of two rival factions in the Territory, known simply as the 'Small Group' – composed of the *Ovandamuranda* and some of Oorlog Thom's Herero followers – and the 'Big Group' consisting of all the rest of the Territory's indigenous inhabitants.

After speaking to Joel I wrote a report on what I had found to Nico Smit. In it I stated that serious drought conditions prevailed in the areas where the cattle in the park came from, and asked for the two boreholes on the southern Beesvlakte to be equipped with windmills as soon as possible. Until this was done, or rain fell, I requested that the two headmen, Keefas Muzuma and Joel Tjiahura, be granted emergency grazing in the Park.

Both boreholes were later developed, but as the Odendaal Commission had recommended that this part of Etosha be de-proclaimed, the stockowners who entered the Park were never evicted. Keefas Muzuma subsequently moved his home village from Ombombo to Otjokavare, a strong spring near the new western boundary of Etosha. Most of Joel Tjiahura's followers also stayed where I had found them in the Park, but he kept his home at Otjitjekua, the old entrance gate into the Kaokoveld.

*   *   *

By September all the water-dependent wildlife was concentrated around the Territory's permanent springs, so at full moon I camped at Otuzemba, to find out what game was now drinking there. During the night more than 60 elephants and at least 250 Burchell's zebra, as well as kudu and impala, came to the waterhole where I sat. From the sounds I heard coming from the second spring here, less than a kilometre away, just as many animals could have drunk there.

Having stayed up until very late I only awoke after the sun had risen, and was embarrassed to find that two local Herero men were already sitting with Elias and Phineas at our fire. They had been sent by their headman, Werimba Rutjani, to ask me a question: 'Did I think it was right for a man to kill six wild animals in one day?'

Werimba and I had met on a number of occasions before, and I knew that the reason why the game was so plentiful around Otuzemba was because he did not allow any hunting in his area. Consequently, according to our visitors, he was very angry because a few days previously 'Muhona Jan' had shot six kudu in the vicinity. Even though he gave the unwanted meat and skins to the local people, the headman was not placated, and had sent our morning visitors to inform me of the matter.

At his onganda, Werimba confirmed the story and showed me the skins of the animals killed. As I knew who 'Muhona Jan' was, and this time had witnesses and evidence that he had killed the kudu, I drove straight to Opuwo and reported the matter to Commissioner Jooste. He listened impassively to what I told him and then simply said that he would 'speak to' the official involved. As it was a gross abuse of our pot licences, I argued that action should be taken to prevent further hunting excesses. But Jooste just became annoyed and reminded me that he would decide what measures to take in such cases, not a junior agricultural official.

That evening I told Elias what the Commissioner had said, but he was not at all surprised: 'How can he charge *Muhona* Jan when his family and friends do the same thing when they come to visit?' Elias, like everyone else living in the 'location', knew of these hunting excursions from the men they took along to do the skinning and slaughtering of the animals they shot. A few days later I confronted the man accused by Headman Rutjani, but from his surprised reaction it was obvious that the Commissioner had not spoken to him about his hunting at Otuzemba.

* * *

After learning the correct way to press plant specimens from Hugh Goyns, I had started my own collection of the Kaokoveld's trees, shrubs and grasses, which were identified by Willie Giess, the government botanist in Windhoek. As very few people had previously collected here my specimens were given priority attention, and whenever I visited the State herbarium Willie always made time to discuss the vegetation of the region. But although his knowledge of South West Africa's flora was unsurpassed, he was a taxonomist, and I wanted to know more about how the perennial grasses were affected by being grazed, and what actually caused them to die out.

The answers to my questions lay in the field of ecology, which looked at inter-relationships between plants, animals and their physical environment. And as it was one of the subjects that my brother Norman had studied for his doctorate on the white rhino in Umfolozi Game Reserve, I was very pleased when he came to visit me again in October – this time with two university friends, Willie Davy and Paul Shorn.

By now I knew that a key factor enabling the Territory's wild grazers to live in the Kaokoveld's harsh and drought-prone environment was their mobility, which allowed them to opportunistically exploit the seasonally variable local conditions. Apart from dispersing away from permanent water-points during the wet season, zebra, gemsbok and springbok also migrated down into the pre-Namib whenever good rains fell there.

The pastoralists managed their livestock in a similar way, using the larger watercourses as routes through the rugged mountain ranges. On the plateau I had already hiked down the Omuhonga and Otjitanga rivers through the Zebra Mountains to the Kunene, and was now keen to follow the Hoarusib's course through the escarpment to Purros, a distance of about 80 km as the crow flies, and closer to 100 km along the winding course of the river. It would be much more pleasant, and safer, to have company along the way.

As I had not visited the Marienfluss on my inspection tour of the west, I also wanted to walk along the Kunene from the Hartmann valley to Otjinungua. After good rain in the pre-Namib I knew that Himba from Otjitanda brought their cattle down the escarpment to graze here, and I wanted to see what wildlife occurred along the river's lower course through the desert.

The day after Norman and his friends arrived we headed west, reaching Omutati, where the Hoarusib enters the escarpment ranges, at about five o'clock. When we had off-loaded our backpacks, Elias drove on to Purros to wait for us. As the Chev disappeared into the distance, Willie Davy perused the 1:250 000 topographic map that would locate our position during the hike. After a few moments he pointed out that there were no springs marked along our way and asked a very pertinent question: where would we get water? In response I suggested that he should have thought of that before Elias left, and then added flippantly: 'But don't worry, we'll find water somewhere.'

The full impact of what we were about to undertake now seemed to hit my companions. Our route would take us through one of the most rugged parts of the region. Walking 80-plus kilometres down a dry riverbed was a long way to walk in the October heat. Without water it would be impossible.

But I was not being as reckless as I had made out to my companions. On previous hikes along other large riverbeds I had found that wherever they cut through mountain ranges their underground flow was periodically forced to the surface by transverse bands of hard rock, creating springs that seeped up from the sand and briefly flowed on the surface. Although I did not know this part of the Hoarusib, it was the biggest seasonal river in the Kaokoveld. There also had to be water along the way because the Himba used this route to take their cattle to Purros. How far apart the springs were we would soon find out.

In silence we shouldered our rucksacks and started walking into the wild mountains that soon closed in around us. We had only gone a short distance when our reveries were interrupted by a herd of elephants, including small calves, walking up the river towards us. Luckily, the Hoarusib had steep rocky banks here, and Willie and Paul shot up them like rock rabbits while Norman and I followed at a more dignified pace. The elephants stopped about 100 metres ahead of us and congregated at the foot of a 10-metre cliff. With the wind in our favour, we were able to carefully make our way to a safe place above them and watch as they played and sloshed mud on themselves in a series of shallow pools. We had found water – albeit now rather muddied – and elephants within a few kilometres of setting off.

By the time the herd had finished their evening ablutions and wandered away it was getting dark, and for safety we decided to camp on a wide ledge above the riverbed. We had not got very far that afternoon, but it had been an auspicious start and as we sat around a small fire drinking cups of soup, even Willie managed to smile.

At dawn we were on our way again and within the first hour saw small herds of gemsbok and mountain zebra. By nine o'clock it was hot, and by ten the sun beat down mercilessly from an unblemished blue sky. The spectacular folded ranges through which we walked had been only lightly touched by the skin-sandalled footprints of the hardy Himba herdsmen. We were intruders here, brief visitors from a world that had now yielded to modern man's relentless urge to control nature and mould it to his own needs. If one of us were to get injured, our only link with the outside world was my truck and its two-way radio, still more than 70 km away.

By 12 o'clock it was too hot to continue and we rested under a spreading acacia tree, idly chatting and brewing numerous cups of tea to quench our thirst. At four o'clock we set off again and walked till sunset. This time our camp was on a large sandbank, next to a sparkling, sedge-fringed spring. So far we had found water more or less whenever we needed it. The others were clearly relieved about this, and although I kept up the pretence of being unconcerned, so was I.

That night I slept soundly and was startled when, at about midnight, Norman touched my shoulder and said: 'There's a rhino at the spring.' Realising that this meant it was less than 30 metres away I slid silently out of my sleeping bag, and after carefully waking Willie and Paul we all crept to the base of a steep incline, up which we could escape if necessary. The rhino, completely unaware of us, stayed at the water for about 20 minutes before going on its way. When it had gone we fetched our hastily abandoned sleeping bags and moved camp – by unanimous decision – to this less comfortable, but much safer position.

With the availability of water no longer a major concern, we relaxed our pace and enjoyed the privilege of being in this vast mountain wilderness. Although we periodically encountered more elephants, the breeze that blew from about midday onwards came up the valley towards us, so we were always able to see or hear them before they became aware of our presence. The favourable wind also gave us many opportunities to watch their undisturbed behaviour.

At this time of year the seedpods of the winter thorn trees started dropping, and they were much sought after by the elephants. When all the pods on the ground had been picked up and eaten, the larger bulls would put their foreheads against the trunk of a tree and give it a hard push, causing more ripe pods to rain down around them. Another favoured food was mopane bark, which they stripped off young branches by pulling them between their molar teeth. A wide range of other riparian trees and shrubs were also browsed as the elephants slowly moved along the riverbed. But in the midday heat they just stood around and rested in the shade, gently flapping their ears to pass air over the network of large blood vessels on the back of them.

Once we had walked past a herd they would inevitably get our wind. Their trunks would rise like periscopes and the cows would round up their calves and shuffle off, clearly annoyed by our obnoxious scent. Sometimes a few of them would trumpet in disgust, as they had every right to. The rugged ranges were still a haven from the man-dominated world around them. But for how much longer would they remain a sanctuary?

During our lunchtime break on the third day we were all resting in the shade when a deep, rasping grunt shook us out of our midday torpor. I had heard the sound before and immediately knew what it was. Shouting for the others to follow me I scrambled up a nearby sandbank just in time to see a large black-maned lion loping away through the undergrowth. Willie and Paul were too late to see our uninvited visitor, but when we went to the spot where the sound had come from, and saw the huge pug-marks in the sand, there was no dispute about what had interrupted our siesta. The tracks also showed that in fact two lions had been walking up the riverbed, and only become aware of us when they were less than 20 metres from where we lay.

'Fortunately they weren't hungry,' Willie quipped half-heartedly as it sank in how close the lions had been to us. Perhaps, but I knew that their response might have been very different if they had found us all sleeping. To relieve our tension a cup of tea was called for and quickly made. But no one slept for the rest of the afternoon break.

That night we camped near a particularly impressive peak, called by the Himba *Karonda namanga* ('it can't be climbed with a spear'), because two hands were needed. As Purros was now less than 40 km away, we decided to take a day off and see if we could get to the top. Leaving camp before dawn, we were on the summit by noon, and as it was between the valleys of both the Hoarusib and Khumib rivers, the view was breathtaking. Five hundred metres below us their tree-lined courses dissected the now barren desert plains, and in the distance I could just make out Purros through the midday haze.

We were back on the banks of the Hoarusib by five and the rest of the afternoon was spent relaxing, talking, and drinking many cups of tea. Now that we had seen the end of our hike the anxiety of the first few days was forgotten and replaced by a feeling of exhilaration. We had taken on the unknown, a challenge denied to most young people in our modern age.

'If every teenager had the opportunity to go on an adventure like this,' Willie said emotionally, 'then drugs and alcohol would not be such a problem in the world. Standing on top of that mountain I was flying as high as any cat on LSD – and there's no big let-down afterwards, no overdosing, and you can't get addicted.' I only disagreed with his last point; after more than two years spent exploring the Kaokoveld's remotest areas, I was addicted.

Next day we came across the largest herd of elephants we had seen – over 20 of them, including many calves. As they were feeding leisurely in the riverbed we were able to stay on the downwind bank and pass by without disturbing them. However, a few kilometres later we encountered another group of eight elephants with what appeared to be a just-born calf, standing far out on the plains. Intrigued by what they were doing in such an exposed place, we stopped and watched them through binoculars.

It seemed as though they were picking up single blades of dry annual grass, so I decided to go a little closer to confirm this. But at that moment a change in wind direction sent a gust of air from us towards the elephants. Seconds later they all raised their trunks, and then set off for the protective cover of the Hoarusib's riparian vegetation, the cow with the tiny calf lagging in the rear. All of this was predictable, but the elephants' behaviour once they reached the riverbed sent a chill down my spine. Trumpeting in fury and tearing up large bushes, they cut a zigzag path through the woodland, clearly searching for the source of the dreaded human smell. We were left in no doubt that they had murder on their minds and very rapidly made ourselves scarce.

At 11 o'clock on the sixth day we walked into my old campsite at Purros and were greeted by a smiling Elias, and a just-as-broadly grinning Tshaka. The kettle was already on the fire and as soon as we had thrown off our rucksacks and sat down, my good man handed us each a cup of tea. We had made it, undaunted and unscathed. Water had not been a problem anywhere along the way, so it was easy to see why the Himba chose this route to the pre-Namib.

Although we had passed a number of abandoned stock-posts, we had seen no people or livestock. Even the Himba I had seen on my last visit had departed to unknown pastures, and the beautiful Purros Valley once more belonged to the wild animals.

On the hike we had counted over 80 elephants and although we had only seen one rhino there was plenty of their spoor and dung around all the springs in the mountains. Mountain zebra, gemsbok, springbok and ostrich occurred in the less rugged areas, but we had found no sign of giraffe, a species not uncommon along the other dry riverbeds that traversed the pre-Namib.

Next morning we drove up the Hartmann valley, stopping where a high sand-dune formed a barrier just south of the Kunene's deeply incised valley. As the sun had just passed its zenith and it was still blisteringly hot, we parked on its lower slopes and waited for a cool breeze to start blowing from the west.

At five o'clock, after watching Elias drive safely back to the main track, we started walking north across the burning sands towards an unseen Kunene River. Around us the landscape was so desolate it was difficult to believe that one of the largest waterways in Southern Africa lay just ahead. I had been here before, but my companions' faith in me was again sorely tested as we trudged through the soft sand until we crested the last dune and looked down on the Kunene's green waters shimmering far below us.

With a combination of relief and excitement we jogged down the steep slope, reaching the river as a fiery sun hovered just above the silhouetted mountains of Angola. Here, near the Kunene's banks, I was amazed to find many large rhino dung middens. But after our walk across the dunes all of us were keen to quench our thirst, and only briefly stopped to look at them before pushing our way through the dense riparian vegetation to the river.

We had gone just a few metres when a succession of snorts and a loud crashing of branches informed us that one of the dung depositors was still in occupation – and it was not pleased about being disturbed. For a few seconds we weren't sure which way it was going, or coming – and just froze in our tracks. Then not one, but two rhino burst from the bushes about 20 metres away and trotted out across the sand flats, their heads held high and their tails curled over their rumps in anger.

It took us less than two days to reach Otjinungua, a distance of about 30 km. At times we had to climb quite high up steep rocky slopes that came right to the water's edge, but nowhere was the going anywhere near as difficult as in the gorge to the east of the Marienfluss. There was also more vegetation on the river banks here, providing a relatively lush habitat to support the many wild animals that concentrated here during the dry season.

In October the Kunene's water and thin band of trees, shrubs and reeds was clearly a magnet to the creatures living in this desolate part of the Kaokoveld, as well as the Iona National Park in Angola, on the other side. Although we encountered no more rhino, we did see 26 elephant and many mountain zebra, gemsbok and springbok. On the slopes of the ranges we also saw large troops of baboons and occasional klipspringers, while steenbok and vervet monkeys frequented the vegetation along the banks. From the frequency of their spoor, these smaller animals supported a healthy leopard population, and on both nights we heard lions roaring on the Angolan side. We saw few crocodiles, but some very big tracks on the beaches ensured that swimming was in well-protected pools only.

At Otjinungua there were large numbers of Himba cattle and for about 10 km from the river the plains had been grazed down to bare red sand. A similar situation prevailed around Okapupa, where more livestock were drinking from a spring at the foot of the Otjihipa Mountains. With no permanent water in the valley itself, the rest of the Marienfluss could not be grazed by cattle, and was still a sea of golden perennial grass. But if the boreholes were equipped most of the plain would become accessible, and as we drove back to Opuwo I had lots to think about and discuss with Norman.

The day after Norman and his friends left, Commissioner Jooste called me into his office and handed me a telegram. It came from the Chief Bantu Affairs Commissioner and simply stated that I had been transferred to Nkandla in KwaZulu. I was to report for duty there on the first of November – just nine days away! In a state of shock I asked Jooste the reason for my transfer, but he told me he was not prepared to discuss the matter. Now angry, I demanded some explanation and we soon got into a heated argument. At one point, he threatened to tell me 'the real reason' for my transfer, but then thought better of it and ordered me to leave his office. Two years later I would find out what it was that he had nearly said.

Little more than a month later I received a letter from Tom Sopper informing me that Jooste's son had appeared in the Ondangua magistrate's court, charged with transporting the carcasses of 17 springbok and one kudu between the Kaokoveld and Ovamboland without a permit. He had been found guilty and paid a fine of R50. According to Tom, the only reason he had been prosecuted at all was because he had fallen out with the local veterinary official in Ondangua. But he had not been charged with illegally hunting the animals, as he claimed to have been given the carcasses by friends in the Kaokoveld!

CHAPTER NINE

THE KAOKOVELD CONTROVERSY

On the appointed day I arrived in Nkandla, a small village on Zululand's misty highlands, high above the Tugela River and quite close to where I had begun my forestry career six years earlier. I was back where I had started, with little more money than when I had left South Africa. But what I had learned and experienced in the Kaokoveld had made me independent and self-assured – and quite arrogant.

My new job as shift foreman at a flax decorticating factory could hardly have been more different from my post in the Kaokoveld. Clearly I was being punished by my superiors in either Windhoek or Opuwo for something that I had or had not done. There was certainly no love lost between myself and Beesie Jooste, but did he have the authority to have me summarily transferred out of the Territory?

Under different circumstances I might have served out my time in Nkandla, but my heart was now in the Kaokoveld and I decided it was time to have another go at getting a university degree. If I was frugal, the money I had saved would be enough to pay for one year's study. Depending on whether I passed or not, the future would then have to look after itself. In December I resigned from BAD and registered for a BSc at the Pietermaritzburg campus of the University of Natal.

It was not my first time there. After leaving school I started a degree in agriculture – part of a family plan to groom me for taking over my uncle Dougie Horton's prestigious dairy farm in the province's midlands. But like many others I was unable to resist the freedom and extra-curricular diversions that university life offered. Studying was low on my list of priorities, behind rugby, cricket, mountain climbing, snooker and pub-crawling – not necessarily in that order. By the end of the year I had been invited to the Natal under-20 rugby trials, played above-average snooker, knew intimately most of the alcohol-serving establishments in Pietermaritzburg – and had failed hopelessly.

Over the next year I freewheeled along, my life focused on playing sport, having fun and diligently avoiding any form of responsibility. I reached the bottom of the hill during my compulsory military service when I spent three sobering and soul-searching weeks on 'Spike Jones' Farm', the army's detention barracks for its hard-core offenders. The inmates here learned little agriculture, but it was an education on a side of life that very few middle-class South Africans were exposed to. Being reduced to the bottom rung of society, albeit for just a few weeks, was also an experience I did not wish to repeat.

In 1964 I started work as a learner forester with the Natal Tanning Extract Company. My parents breathed a sigh of relief. Managing a timber and wattle-bark estate would be good training before joining Uncle Dougie on the farm. But working in Zululand's misty forests just opened my eyes to the possibility of a career in places without fences or cultivated fields. Going to South West Africa and then spending nearly two and a half years in the Kaokoveld had finally precluded any possibility of my settling down to dairy farming in Natal. I now knew what I wanted to do with my life, and although I had been transferred out of the Territory, I hoped that a university degree would be my ticket to return one day.

The subject that I was most interested in learning more about was ecology. At the University of Wisconsin, where Norman had done the theoretical part of his doctorate, it was now an integral part of zoology and botany courses, and had become a buzz-word among the 1960s generation of conservationists in the United States. Ecology was where answers to the Kaokoveld's overgrazing problems would be found, and it had also spawned the exciting new fields of animal behaviour and wildlife management, which I hoped to study after graduating.

However, back at Natal University I soon discovered that little had changed in the nine years since my first failed attempt to get a degree. The environ-

LEFT: Camping out 'wherever we found ourselves in the late afternoon.' With Robbie Roberts in November 1967.

BELOW AND BOTTOM: Flash floods are a major hazard when driving in the Kaokoveld during the rainy season. Robbie's vehicle stuck in a flooding river, and getting it out with help from the local people.

Headman Johannes Ruyter, who with Johan Malan taught me about the social and religious systems of the Kaokoveld's pastoralists. *(Namibian Archives)*

Nico Smit, the Chief Agricultural Officer who I worked under in both the Kaokoveld and later in KwaZulu. *(Creina Bond)*

Elias Tjondu, my translator and assistant in the Kaokoveld, with a leopard that was trapped by the local people near the Epupa Falls, and which I then shot.

Allan Savory, revolutionary range ecologist, politician in opposition to Ian Smith during the liberation war in Rhodesia and founder of the tracking unit that would become the Selous Scouts.

GOS with KwaZulu Cabinet Ministers (*from left*) Mr A.W. Nxumalo (Education), Mr J.C. Mtethwa (Justice) and Chief O.S. Sitole (Agriculture), during the first meeting to discuss game ranching with Zulu politicians and traditional leaders on Sungulwane Game Ranch in 1976. (*Creina Bond*)

Participants at the Umgeni Valley meeting in February 1976 – the first time office bearers of the Wildlife Society discussed environmental education with Zulu leaders. *Back from left*: Sibusiso Nyembezi, Bongani Bophela, Nolly Zaloumis, David Hatton, Liz Hatton, Mrs M. Nyembezi, GOS, Douglas Y. Zimu, Otty Nxumalo. *Front*: Sibusiso Bengu, Simeon Gcumisa and Don Richards. (*Keith Cooper*)

Herero women in the traditional dress they adopted from the early missionaries in South West Africa.

A Himba woman in traditional dress, circa 1969.

Hakaona (*left*) and Zemba (*right*) women in their 'traditional' dress. The hairstyle of the Hakaona women includes rolled up Coke and Windhoek lager cans.

A 1973 photograph of two Himba men with a 'Mountain Tjimba' man (*centre*), who was working for them as a stock herder. Although the Tjimba have adopted the language and dress of the Himba they are not ethnically related. (*Johan Malan*)

Theofilas //Havachab, the last Topnaar chief in Sesfontein. In the nineteenth century the Topnaars and Swartboois of Fransfontein terrorised the Herero-speaking pastoralists in the Kaokoveld, forcing some of them to seek refuge in Angola where they were given the name Himba. (*Mitch Reardon*)

Chief Keefas Muzuma, who in 1969 broke ranks with the other Kaokoveld pastoralists over the selling of cattle. He later became the most powerful Herero traditional leader in southern Kaokoland, and was the first to try and stop his people from poaching. (*Mitch Reardon*)

Chief Justice//Garoeb, a strong supporter of conservation, who as head of the Damara Representative Authority during the 1980s created the Palmwag, Etendeka and Hobatere tourism concessions. (*The Namibian*)

TOP: The three-month-old rhino calf rescued after its mother was poached in March 1983, with June, Titus, Elias and Filimon.

CENTRE: After ten days she was taken to Etosha and raised by the Park's veterinarian, Ian Hofmeyr, whose wife Rea gave her the name Suzi Slippers. *(Rea Hofmeyr)*

BELOW: When Ian was killed in a vehicle accident two years later, Rea left Etosha and saw Suzi Slippers only once in the next seven years. On her second visit, the now full-grown rhino immediately recognised Rea and came up to greet her surrogate mother. *(Jen Bartlett)*

Early community game guards: Kamasitu Tjipombo (*left*), Naftali Taurob (*centre*) and Sakeus Kasaona (*right*), who became my tracker during the first rhino census in 1986. He then joined the Save the Rhino Trust and trained their trackers. (*Photos, left to right: Marc Durr; John Ledger; Colin Nott*)

Turning poachers into partners. Many of the community game guards had been 'hunters' in the past.
Back from left: Erens Mbomboro, Salmon Karutjaiva, Johannes 'Ganumub' Kasaona. *Front*: Piet Hizeraku, who was twice convicted for killing rhino and elephants, and Johannes Kasaona, who shot Suzi Slippers' mother. (*Colin Nott*)

LEFT: Dr John Ledger, who took over as director of the Endangered Wildlife Trust from Clive Walker in 1986, standing next to a large *Pachypodium lealii,* one of the many endemic plants in the Kaokoveld.

RIGHT: Government field workers in the 1980s. *From left*, game ranger Duncan Gilchrist; pasture scientist Trevor Nott; Ruth Gilchrist; and lion researcher Flip Stander.

Senior Nature Conservator Tommy Hall (*right*) delivering rations to community game guards in 1988. With him is Clive Algar, the Public Relations Officer for Rössing Uranium, which gave a lot of support to conservation in the region. *(John Ledger)*

Blythe Loutit, who formed the Namibia Wildlife Trust with Ina Britz in 1982, and five years later started the Save the Rhino Trust. *(John Ledger)*

Rudi Loutit with Damaraland game rangers in the Khorixas DNC office in 1988. Rudi would later head Namibia's rhino custodianship programme on freehold farms. *(John Ledger)*

Save the Rhino Trust trackers on a camel patrol into the more inaccessible parts of the rhino range in north-western Namibia.

1993 Goldman Environmental Prize winners. *Clockwise from top:* Juan Mayr (South America), John Sinclair (Australasia), Sviatoslav Igorevich Zabelin (Europe), Dai Ching (Asia), GOS and Margaret Jacobsohn (Africa). Missing is JoAnn Tall (North America).

Key players in Margie's team during the Epupa Hydro-electric scheme EIA: Muatjimbike Mutambo (*left*) and Shorty Kasaona.

Epupa in April when the river is full. If the planned dam had been built 10 km below the falls they would have been 100 metres under water, and the lake would have extended to Enyandi, 60 km upstream. *(Chris Weaver)*

LEFT: SWAPO's first Minister of the Environment and Tourism, Nico Bessinger, who had a vision to make nature conservation relevant to everyone in Namibia. CENTRE AND RIGHT: The 'dream team' of Chris Brown and Brian Jones, architects of the MET's community-based natural resource management policy. (*The Namibian*)

By 2010 there were 59 registered conservancies on communal land in Namibia, covering an area of over 13 million hectares, in which more than 225 000 people lived. Conservancies cover 16.1 per cent of Namibia's land surface. (*David Sandison*)

Kunene Region's Governor Simson Tjongarero on a visit to Wêreldsend in 2004, with some of IRDNC's conservancy support staff. *From left:* Anton Esterhuizen, Margie, Bennie Roman, Sandy Tjaronda, John Kasaona, Lina Kaisuma, the governor's driver and his assistant, Governor Tjongarero, GOS and Wandi Tsanes. *(Colin Nott)*

IRDNC staff discussing plant resources with Himba women in the Marienfluss.
From left: Anna Davis, Australian volunteer Pam McGrath, Margie, Lina Kaisuma and Aino Paavo.

The first headman to appoint community game guards, Joshua Kangombe, standing next to a truckload of meat delivered by MET during the 1991 game harvest.

Filimon /Nuab rhino monitoring. Protecting the north-west's elephant and rhino is now a joint effort between the government, NGOs and the local communities, which has to date proved very successful. *(David Sandison)*

Human–wildlife conflict is an ongoing challenge facing communal area conservancies. Apart from elephants drinking large amounts of water meant for cattle, the (*top right*) photo shows what they can do to a windmill if for whatever reason it stops pumping. *(Mark Holker)*

Another major problem is the loss of riparian vegetation along the region's larger rivers. The photo shows the winding, well-wooded course of the Hoarusib at Purros in 1969.

The same place today; a broad sandy bed with only one of the trees (second from left in top photograph) still standing. *(Russell Vinjevold)*

In spite of the shortcomings of the still inexperienced conservancy committees, devolving rights and responsibilities to local communities has proved very successful in protecting the Kaokoveld's big game. Hartmann's zebra (*left*) now number over 15 000 and the future of the desert-living elephants has been secured. (*Photo of desert elephants: Colin Nott*)

In recognition of this the MET has translocated species that were wiped out in the 1970s back into areas where they previously occurred. In this photo a conservancy chairman and some of his staff, together with IRDNC's Richard Fryer (*second from left*), pose next to the first black rhino they received in 2010. (*Tina Vinjevold*)

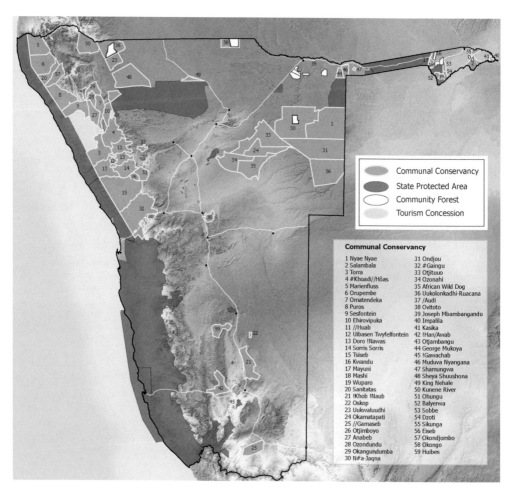

Communal Conservancy

1 Nyae Nyae	31 Ondjou
2 Salambala	32 #Gaingu
3 Torra	33 Otjituuo
4 #Khoadi//Hôas	34 Ozonahi
5 Marienfluss	35 African Wild Dog
6 Orupembe	36 Uukolonkadhi-Ruacana
7 Omatendeka	37 /Audi
8 Puros	38 Ovitoto
9 Sesfontein	39 Joseph Mbambangandu
10 Ehirovipuka	40 Impalila
11 //Huab	41 Kasika
12 Uibasen Twyfelfontein	42 !Han/Awab
13 Doro !Nawas	43 Otjambangu
14 Sorris Sorris	44 George Mukoya
15 Tsiseb	45 !Gawachab
16 Kwandu	46 Muduva Nyangana
17 Mayuni	47 Shamungwa
18 Mashi	48 Sheya Shuushona
19 Wuparo	49 King Nehale
20 Sanitatas	50 Kunene River
21 !Khob !Naub	51 Ohungu
22 Oskop	52 Balyerwa
23 Uukwaluudhi	53 Sobbe
24 Okamatapati	54 Dzoti
25 //Gamaseb	55 Sikunga
26 Otjimboyo	56 Eiseb
27 Anabeb	57 Okondjombo
28 Ozondundu	58 Okongo
29 Okangundumba	59 Huibes
30 N#a-Jaqna	

Legend:
- Communal Conservancy
- State Protected Area
- Community Forest
- Tourism Concession

Map of Namibia in 2010 showing the 59 registered communal area conservancies, the community forests, tourism concessions on communal land and national parks. Another 15–20 communities are in the process of developing conservancies and more community forests are also expected to be registered.
(Map by Helge Denker, Namibian Association of CBNRM Support Organisations)

mental revolution had not yet reached South Africa, and biology undergrad-
uates were still just taught zoology, botany, physics and chemistry as discrete
subjects – as if the real world was compartmentalised in this way. Most of
the faces of the faculty staff were also familiar. Greyer and perhaps wiser,
but the same museum-minded men with their aura of leather-bound books,
musty old bones and specimens preserved in formaldehyde. Although I was
probably not the best judge, it seemed to me that even their lectures had not
changed, and that if I had taken any notes worth keeping in 1962, I could have
used them again in 1971. Even our afternoon 'practicals' still consisted of dissecting toads and white rats, or peering blurry-eyed down a microscope at the
tissues and cells of garden plants!

Before the end of the first quarter I knew that I was not going to find what
I was looking for at Natal University. But what were the alternatives? Needing
to talk to someone about my predicament, I drove up to the Transvaal over
a long weekend and visited Hugh and Dorothy Goyns in their Benoni home.
They were sympathetic, but their advice was for me to hang in and complete
my degree. Although Hugh was a trained engineer, after retiring he had become involved in a range of fields for which he had no formal qualifications,
and knew from personal experience how difficult it was to be taken seriously
by the professionals if you did not have a certificate to prove your competence.

While in Benoni I also updated Hugh and Dorothy on the latest happenings in the Kaokoveld, including the events leading up to my transfer out
of it. No doubt trying to lift my spirits, Hugh suggested I write a paper on
the Territory. He was helping to convene the biannual congress of the South
African Association for the Advancement of Science, to be held on Natal
University's Durban campus in July, and could arrange for me to present it in
the student section of the conference.

On returning to university I made an appointment to see one of the younger,
more enlightened members of the Zoology Faculty, Dr Gordon McLean, to
get an overview of the undergraduate course. He understood my impatience,
but did his best to convince me that it was important to get a good grounding
in classical biology, even though it seemed irrelevant at the time. This was all
well and good, I said, but when *would* we start studying ecology? In the third
year, Dr McLean replied. He would himself be presenting a six-week course
on bird behaviour and ecology!

Over the Easter recess I again joined Hugh and Dorothy, this time on a
trip to the Magaliesberg Mountains, north of Pretoria. After a day of rock-
climbing, we made camp next to a small stream, and in this wild place – so

close to two of Africa's largest cities – I told Hugh that I had finally made up
my mind to leave university. I was already 27, and could no longer afford to
waste three years of my life learning 'Stone Age biology'.

As Hugh was in his sixties and was at the time studying botany, anthropology and archaeology, he just smiled at my youthful arrogance and asked what,
if I was not going to get a degree, *did* I have in mind? By then I had given it a
lot more thought, and told him that I believed I could get a more practically
useful education by attaching myself to experts who were actually working in
the fields of ecology and range management, not just teaching it. In this way I
would be doing an apprenticeship rather than a theoretical degree, and could
also select what I wanted to learn, and from whom, instead of just passively
accepting what an out-of-date education system decided was relevant.

Although Hugh wouldn't commit himself to actually supporting my idea,
he did promise to help in whatever way he could. But before we parted he
gave me a warning: 'Those who choose to take the unconventional road in
life go against the stream of people following the normal way. You won't find
it easy to get through the throng, and don't expect anyone to step out of their
way for you.' In the years to come, I would have many occasions to remember
his words.

On my return to Natal my mother gave me the latest edition of *African
Wildlife*, the Wildlife Society's magazine, which included a supplement by
Ken Tinley entitled 'Etosha and the Kaokoveld'. The author had been Etosha's
resident biologist in the mid-1960s and from there had undertaken a num-
ber of trips into the Kaokoveld. As he had left the Park before my visits to
Okaukuejo with Burger Baard we never met, but I had heard a lot about him
and knew he was regarded as one of the top ecologists in Southern Africa.
When the government had announced it was implementing the Odendaal
Commission's recommendations to de-proclaim the Kaokoveld and parts of
Etosha, the Society had commissioned him to draw up an alternative plan
'based on the intrinsic ecological potential and capabilities of the different
land types'.

Tinley's case against the Odendaal Plan rested primarily on the fact that
the western Kaokoveld was one of the richest areas of endemic flora and
fauna in Southern Africa. He also believed that, for the people's own benefit,
and for conservation of the sensitive desert habitats, man's farming activities should be confined to areas that received more than 100 mm of rainfall.
Ideally, Tinley recommended that all permanent human settlement should be
restricted to above the 200 mm rainfall isohyet, and that the far-western areas

be reserved for wildlife 'which had evolved specifically for survival in a desert land'. He also stated that wild herbivores were opportunistic and moved to take advantage of changing conditions in their habitat. 'In this way the sensitive substrate is maintained in a good state, but movement is the key factor for the survival of the animal, and the substrate it depends on.'

After further discussing the endemic flora and fauna, scenic masterpieces and human ecology of the region, Tinley made 11 suggestions 'to preserve the unique natural features of Etosha and the Kaokoveld and to provide better living sites for man'. They were:

1. The establishment of a Kaokoveld National Park in the Hoarusib, Hoanib and Uniab river basins with a narrow national park enclave to link it with the Etosha National Park. The enclave would also serve as a stock-free zone for veterinary requirements. The Kaokoveld National Park should be bounded on the south by the Koichab River and in the north by the divide between the Hoarusib and Khumib rivers. The watershed of the Hoanib and Uniab should form the eastern boundary where it joins the 19 degree latitude enclave to Etosha.

2. The establishment of a Kunene National Park to include the Marienfluss Valley, Epupa Falls and the adjoining Namib desert. It is probable that the Water Affairs Department will require an unoccupied water conservation zone along the Kunene River. This zone should form part of the Kunene National Park.

3. If the country between the suggested Kaokoveld and Kunene National Parks is not required for harbour developments, mining or communications between the coast (Cape Fria and Rocky Point) and the interior or as a coast extension of the Himba Herero homeland then these Parks should be linked as one.

4. A narrow triangle of land should be added to the north-east of Etosha National Park to enclose the whole of the Andoni plains and the migratory routes of the ungulates within the Etosha sanctuary area. The sector presently within the Ovamboland boundary is too small to be of any value as a separately administered park area.

5. Farmland should be bought out for inclusion in the Etosha and Kaokoveld National Parks (i) to include the headwater catchments of the Hoanib and Uniab rivers, and (ii) to include the

first line of hill ranges on the southern edge of Etosha.

6. Extension of the present Himba–Herero homeland to include the present western Etosha National Park mostly north of the 19 degree latitude and west of the Okahakana drainage. In the Kaokoveld the Himba and Herero should be confined to the country east of the 100 mm isohyet.

7. The Nama people at Sesfontein and in the adjacent country should be moved to the same homeland area as the Fransfontein area.

8. Farmland should be bought out to increase the size of the Fransfontein Nama Reserve to include the country between the Huab and Ugab rivers.

9. The magnificent old German fort at Sesfontein in its mountain setting should be rebuilt, as was done at Namutoni. The road from Otjovasandu to Sesfontein and Purros to the coast should be made an all-weather road (without harming the scenery) for tourism and nature conservation research and administration.

10. If the powerlines from the Ruacana hydro-electric scheme are not planned to follow the national road between Ruacana, Ondangua and Tsumeb, bypassing the Etosha National Park, they should pass through the narrowest part of the Etosha Park following the national road between Kamanjab and Ruacana. Powerlines etc should be kept out of national parks.

11. If the above primary ecological requirements for man can be fulfilled, it would be of value in time to include part of the Otavi mountain range within the Etosha National Park (i.e. NW of Otavi town).

The Wildlife Society had submitted Ken Tinley's counter-proposals to the office of the Prime Minister in late 1969. A year later they received a reply stating that: 'Your recommendations cannot be accepted with a view to the drastic deviating nature thereof and also viewed against the background of all the relevant considerations and Government decisions which emanated from the Report of the Odendaal Commission.'

The Society was further advised that: 'The Government is responsible for the balance of all elements to be taken into consideration and it should be realised that the interests of the natives – the more so because they themselves have made strong representations to the Government about it – could not be subordinated to nature conservation.'

However, in a press statement the Department of Bantu Administration and Development did commit itself to: 'at a time convenient to both parties, negotiate with the natives concerned in regard to the establishment of a game park in their homeland. In the meantime, conservation of fauna and flora will be carried out in accordance with existing SWA legislation and, if necessary, special steps will also be taken.'

The Tinley supplement in *African Wildlife* had addressed most of the major issues and echoed much of my own thinking about threats to the Kaokoveld's wildlife posed by the Odendaal Commission Plan. But there were aspects of his report with which I did not agree. Tinley had proposed a link between the Etosha Game Park and the Skeleton Coast because he believed elephant and other game annually migrated from around the Etosha salt pan to the western Kaokoveld, and had included a map showing the migration routes. But during my residence in the Kaokoveld I had seen no evidence of any large-scale migration between these two areas, and believed that the game movements in the region were more local – concentrating around permanent springs during the dry months and dispersing into the surrounding area when the wet season began. Zebra, gemsbok and springbok certainly did move westwards into the desert after good rains there, but I did not believe they came from as far as the Etosha Pan.

However, the main issue I disagreed with was the translocation of people that Tinley's Kaokoveld and Kunene National Parks would entail. Although I also believed the pre-Namib would be more valuable as a game reserve than as a homeland for indigenous people, I was not surprised that his proposed boundaries were unacceptable to the government. They would require three of the Territory's most influential headmen, Keefas Muzuma, Munimuhoro Kapika and Simon //Havachab, to move from their home areas. Although the National Party had shown no qualms about moving whole communities in South Africa to enforce their separate development ideology, South West Africa was only a mandated Territory. From personal experience I knew that the affected people would resist, and did not think the government would invite international criticism by forcibly removing them.

Ken Tinley was clearly more qualified than me to oppose the Odendaal Commission Plan, but whereas he had lived in Etosha and just visited the Kaokoveld, I had spent two and a half years in the Territory and had got to know its people and wildlife much better. In April I contacted Hugh Goyns and asked him to book a slot for me at the Advancement of Science Congress (S_2A_3).

The first step in preparing my paper was to read all the literature I could find on the Kaokoveld. To do this I moved to Johannesburg, renting a room just a short walk from the centre of Hillbrow, a suburb of high-rise flats that was then the most densely populated place on the African continent. Apart from wishing to experience a 'concrete jungle', at the time it was the only place in South Africa where whites and blacks openly mixed, and had become one of the main centres of protest against apartheid. A third reason for choosing to live here was because it was close to the Johannesburg General Hospital, where Rosalie was undergoing her nursing training.

For the next two months I spent my days at the Witwatersrand University's Africana Library and at night, whenever she was not on duty, Rosalie showed me a very different kind of 'wild life'. It was her home ground and she expertly guided me through the suburb's late-night crowded streets, sidestepping its many hapless and hopeless inhabitants, and introducing me to a world of underground musicians and comedians who were courageously confronting the gross inequities of South African society.

While on the Wits campus I learned that a group of local students were also planning to give a paper on Etosha and the Kaokoveld at the S_2A_3 Congress, and we arranged to meet at the university cafeteria. However, it was soon apparent that only one of the trendy, longhaired young men had any first-hand knowledge of the area – and even he had just made a single holiday trip to Etosha. Their disagreement with the Odendaal Commission Plan came almost entirely from the *African Wildlife* supplement, and the primary motivation for their presenting a paper seemed to be the oppor-tunity it afforded to attack the government. I held no brief for the National Party, but did point out that in this case it was Tinley who proposed the translocation of people, and government that opposed it. But the irony of the situation was lost on these privileged sons of South Africa's white elite, and I soon found myself in a fruitless argument, characterised more by political rhetoric and ecological jargon than by any meaningful exchange of ideas. We parted with the Wits students thinking I was a government stooge, while I concluded that they had little contribution to make in any rational debate on the subject.

To better understand why the Odendaal Commission had recommended that the Kaokoveld and western Etosha be de-proclaimed, I obtained a copy of the full report from the Government Printer in Pretoria. The first point I noted was that its conclusions had been drawn up before the assassination of Prime Minister Verwoerd. Consequently, their plan for South West Africa broadly followed the master plan he had devised as the solution to the racial 'problem' in South Africa: the creation of independent homelands for each of the country's nine ethnic groups. But one of many flaws in South Africa's separate development policy was that the country's whites, who made up just 20 per cent of the population, owned 87 per cent of the land. In the mandated territory, it was clearly necessary to find a way of more equally dividing the land.

As only so many white farms could be expropriated without seriously eroding the National Party's support in SWA, de-proclaiming the Kaokoveld and western Etosha provided the politically expedient option. The Park's northern border had also been re-aligned southwards to increase the size of a proposed Ovambo homeland, and an area north of the Hoanib River was added to the Kaokoveld, now re-named Kaokoland. The remainder of the vast wilderness west of Otjovasandu, together with the existing Otjihorongo, Okombahe and Fransfontein native reserves as well as over 200 white-owned farms, had been expropriated to become a new tribal homeland for the Damara people. Only a thin strip along the coast would be retained by the central government, ostensibly as a national park, but also undoubtedly to prevent the northern ethnic homelands from having independent access to the sea.

Seen in this light, for any alternative plan to be acceptable to the government, its deviation from the Odendaal recommendations should be minor, and the land retained as game reserve kept to the absolute minimum. For this reason I proposed that only the ecologically sensitive pre-Namib, with its spectacular scenery and desert-adapted wildlife, should have formal conservation status. Although the neighbouring escarpment ranges were an important habitat for many large mammals during dry years, they were so rugged and sparsely inhabited that they formed a natural buffer zone between the highlands, where the people's interests should prevail, and a wildlife sanctuary in the west.

In my S_2A_3 paper I simply recommended that the Odendaal Commission's coastal park should be extended eastwards to the escarpment, a distance that varied between 40 and 55 km. The game reserve would also exclude Sesfontein and all other permanently inhabited areas apart from Orupembe and Onyuva, where about 150 Himba and Tjimba had settled in the vicinity of boreholes drilled there by the government. I further proposed that these few families could be encouraged to move inland by developing new water-points for them on the neighbouring plateau.

My case for retaining the pre-Namib as a game reserve was based on the ecological uniqueness of big game such as elephant and rhino living in a desert, as well as the likelihood of severe damage being done to this sensitive habitat if it were permanently grazed by large numbers of livestock. I also felt that if conserved, the western Kaokoveld had the potential to become a tourist attraction that rivalled the world-renowned wildlife sanctuaries in East Africa, thereby becoming a major economic asset to the country as a whole.

Although only a few people lived permanently in the pre-Namib, the Herero and Himba regarded the whole Kaokoveld as belonging to them, and a game reserve here would only succeed if it had their support. Therefore, in my paper I stated that: 'Conservation education is essential and local participation should be encouraged at all levels. Furthermore, as they would be giving up land they rightfully regard as their own, they should directly benefit from any income that is generated in the region through tourism.'

I concluded by saying: 'The past twenty years have already much changed the Kaokoveld. Today, the inhospitable coastline and rugged mountain ranges no longer afford sanctuary to the wildlife of the region and what is preserved of this irreplaceable heritage now depends entirely on us – the present generation of South Africans and our elected representatives. We must accept the final responsibility.'

The paper preceding mine in the auditorium allocated to student participants was by the Wits University group I had met in Johannesburg. It was poorly prepared and clearly showed they had little knowledge of what was at stake in northern South West Africa. Consequently, when I gave my presentation, based on first-hand experience of the Kaokoveld and backed up by slides of the scenery and desert-adapted wildlife, it was well received by the tightly packed audience. I was particularly encouraged by the many questions asked at the end of the talk, and by the number of people who later approached me to discuss the situation in the region.

One of them was Brian Huntley, a more diligent fellow student during my first year at Natal University, who had just been appointed as the chief ecologist for Angola. His responsibilities would include an array of wildlife sanctuaries proclaimed by the Portuguese authorities in their huge and climatically diverse colony, but he told me he was especially interested in the Iona National Park, which was adjacent to the Kaokoveld. Brian was about to leave for Luanda to take up his new post and we agreed to keep in touch.

Ken Tinley was also at the Congress, although he had gone to a concurrent presentation in another auditorium. However, he later apologised for missing my paper, and we had a friendly talk about the Kaokoveld and Gorongoza National Park in Mozambique, where he was now based. However, the most valuable contact I made at the congress was Dr Nolly Zaloumis, the chairman of the Natal Branch of the Wildlife Society. He complimented me on my balanced approach to the situation, and said he fully supported my recommendation that the local people should participate in and benefit from any game reserve created in the Kaokoveld. In fact, he believed that unless black Africans became involved in conservation there was no hope of wildlife being protected anywhere on the continent. He added that he had been trying to get the Society to start a conservation education project among the Zulu people in Natal, and asked me whether I was interested in taking on such a job if it became available. I was flattered but told him my real interest was in the Kaokoveld, which I hoped to get back to one day.

Later I would learn that my paper was not highly rated by all South African wildlife enthusiasts. Many of them did not appreciate my contradicting the man who had pioneered an ecological approach to land use planning, and believed that I had just confused the issue by proposing a second alternative to the Odendaal Plan. There was some merit in this point of view, but in spite of Tinley's recommendations being ecologically sound, the government had already rejected them. I also suspected that in some cases my critics' demand for 'ecological principles' to be applied was just a smokescreen for putting the protection of wildlife before the interests of the local people.

The most controversial part of my paper was undoubtedly the exclusion of the game migration corridor between Etosha and the pre-Namib. One prominent conservationist I spoke to saw this as sacrificing a prime wildlife area for the sake of 'primitive natives who would soon destroy it with their backward farming practices'. Even my proposal to involve the Territory's residents in any game reserve created on their land, and give them a share of the income generated from it, usually fell on deaf ears. Black people had no interest in protecting wildlife, I was told, and therefore did not deserve to get any benefits from tourism. There was no point in arguing. The Kaokovelders had been convicted without a trial, but I hoped that one day I would have the opportunity to prove them wrong.

At the Congress Dr Zaloumis told me that he would recommend my paper for publication in *African Wildlife*, and asked me to contact its editor, Creina Bond. On my way to the Transvaal a few weeks later I visited Creina in the home she and her husband, Neil Alcock, had made on the Maria Ratchitz Mission in northern Natal. From this rustic retreat Creina had turned the

Wildlife Society's staid natural history journal into a dynamic, glossy magazine that contained high quality, controversial articles on contemporary conservation issues, and had just won the first of many national awards.

Neil was a man with a past that kept the local security police on their toes. He had been a founder member of the banned Liberal Party in South Africa, and was still a close friend of the internationally famous and locally infamous author, Alan Paton. At Neil and Creina's wedding, the best man had been a young Zulu chief named Gatsha Buthelezi, who had recently taken the political reins of the country's second most populous ethnic group. At the time, Chief Buthelezi's refusal to accept Bantustan status for the Zulu people's land was frustrating the South African government's plans to further partition the country into semi-independent homelands.

Under the name of Church Agricultural Project, Neil had taken over the management of the Mission's overpopulated and degraded lands, convincing the resident stockowners to combine their cattle into a single herd and start rotational grazing. In less than 10 years, using a short-duration grazing system developed by the Howell family in the eastern Free State, he had turned previously bare and eroded ground into perennial grasslands that were the equal of those on the neighbouring white-owned farms. I was impressed by what I saw, but fencing the land into small camps was not possible in the vast woodlands and savannas of the Kaokoveld.

That evening Creina showed me a number of articles that had appeared in the local and international press on the government's plans to implement the Odendaal Commission recommendations. Without exception they criticised the de-proclaiming of western Etosha, and many also questioned the logic of adding semi-desert areas to the Kaoko and Damara homelands. It was heartening to see such a high level of interest in the Kaokoveld controversy, but I found that the media debate was clearly handicapped by all the authors' lack of basic knowledge about the region, its people and wildlife. Creina fully agreed with me. But apart from myself, she asked, who else was in a position to provide the detailed, up-to-date information that was needed? I had to admit that she was right.

*   *   *

Having now finally abandoned my idea of getting a university degree, I moved into my mother's home in Hillcrest, a country village overlooking the

Umgeni River's 'Valley of a Thousand Hills' about 30 km inland from Durban. It proved to be the perfect environment in which to work on a manuscript entitled: 'The Kaokoveld: An Ecological Base for Future Development Planning'.

After a general introduction to the area I summarised the Territory's European administration and then gave a short historical and cultural overview of the indigenous people living there. This was followed by a condensed geography of the Kaokoveld and a more detailed description of the eight ecological sub-regions I divided it into, describing their physical features, availability of water, dominant vegetation, as well as the human settlement and land use.

The second part was a survey of the larger mammals in the Kaokoveld. It was compiled from various sources: my own live sightings and spoor observations during two and a half years of driving, hiking and canoeing in virtually every part of the Territory, as well as the information I got from other officials and the relatively few written historical records. To this I added the wealth of local knowledge I had gleaned from the Kaokoveld's Himba and Herero residents while walking with them, or just sitting around many campfires and talking about the wild world they lived in.

The survey covered 40 mammals, ranging from elephant down to the different species of mongoose inhabiting the Territory, but I focused mainly on the big game animals that would be threatened by de-proclamation. For most of them I was able to give their distribution and estimated numbers, as well as any ecological information I had gathered, including behavioural adaptations to the arid environment and interactions with the human residents of the region.

Part three began by discussing the major developments now taking place in the region, as well as those planned for the near future, and the long-term effects they were likely to have on the Kaokoveld's people and wildlife. These included a move away from tribal customs and traditions, and the fact that with a higher standard of living and education the residents would be less likely to accept the economic losses caused by predators and elephant. The emergence of a cattle-less, and therefore protein hungry, working class in the indigenous population would threaten the survival of the larger wild ungulates. However, I saw the most immediate danger to the wildlife being 'the influx of European officials and construction workers, with the subsequent rise in poaching'.

I concluded this section by stating: 'an informed assessment of the changing Kaokoveld scene leads to the conclusion that the gradual disappearance of

most of the large mammals in the Territory is inevitable under the proposals
recommended by the Odendaal Commission. But is the destruction of wildlife the unavoidable price of progress?'

I then divided the Territory along the escarpment mountains into the interior plateau, where the average annual rainfall varied from 400 to 150 mm,
and the pre-Namib, where it was less than 100 mm. On the highlands I noted
that the absence of many tropical stock diseases mitigated the arid climate
and made it very suitable for livestock. However, I added that 'the present
considerable overstocking in many areas has already resulted in the virtual
elimination of perennial grasses in much of the region and to prevent further
degeneration, the present uncontrolled growth of the native herds must be
checked by exporting to markets in the south. Only when this has been accomplished should the better distribution of livestock be attempted by the
opening up of undeveloped tracts with new boreholes.'

Improved cattle management around the existing water-points should
also be undertaken by resting some severely overgrazed areas. But overall
I believed that: 'with judicious management, the present per capita land
availability on the interior plateau (approx. 300 ha) is sufficient to ensure a
good livelihood to all Kaokovelders, even by the existing standards of animal husbandry.'

With regard to the pre-Namib I stated that: 'Traditionally, the Herero and
Himba did not permanently reside west of the escarpment and only used the
arid grasslands here in periodic dry years. However, the expanding herds on
the highlands have recently caused an overflow of about twenty families into
the pre-Namib, most of whom have settled in the vicinity of the boreholes at
Orupembe and Onjuva. Continuous grazing in these areas has already led to
a degeneration of the grass cover and the exposure of the soil to erosion.'

As an example, I noted that during the 1970 drought, people from the
western plateau had migrated with their cattle down into the pre-Namib and
in just three months had devastated the grazing in the Marienfluss, upper
Khumib and Purros areas. I then used the situation around Sesfontein and
Warmquelle as a warning, stating that: 'Sustained heavy grazing on these alkaline plains has reduced the whole area to a dustbowl, and in 1970 the people
here would undoubtedly have suffered severe livestock losses had they not
been granted emergency grazing in the Etosha Game Park.'

My next point was the scientific importance of the Kaokoveld. Apart from
the numerous endemic species of plant and lesser animal life noted by Tinley,
the pre-Namib also supported viable populations of elephant, black rhino,

giraffe, lion and cheetah. How these large mammal species were able to survive in this very arid environment was of great scientific importance and I believed the loss to science 'would be inestimable should they pass from the scene before a proper study could be made of their ecology'.

I then discussed the importance of wild land to modern man, stating that: 'In the western world the increasing pressures of urban living were creating an awareness of the essential value of wilderness to the human environment, and South Africa cannot afford to disregard this trend. Many of the country's game reserves are now showing signs of overcrowding, and the quality of experience derived by visitors to them is decreasing as traffic congestion increases. Wild land is also becoming a national resource of considerable importance, both for our own cultural and recreational needs, but also as a tourist attraction and source of foreign exchange.'

I ended my manuscript with 13 conclusions:

1. Although considerable numbers of elephant, zebra, kudu, impala and springbok still survive on the Kaokoveld plateau, a realistic assessment of the position on these fertile highlands, dictates that the requirements of the human population must take precedence in any conflict of interest – even if it means the disappearance of much of the local fauna.

2. The large-scale introduction of livestock (or any other agricultural practice) into the sub-desert region must, in the long term, lead to a degeneration of habitat and an inevitable expansion of the Namib desert.

3. Over the years the game populations of the western Kaokoveld have balanced themselves according to the carrying capacity of the region, and are unlikely to cause a downgrading of the environment.

4. The stark mountains and tawny plains of the west offer spectacular panoramas of arid scenery, and with the added lure of big game, the region could rival the world-renowned tourist Meccas in east and central Africa.

5. In the context of South West Africa's rapidly expanding tourist industry, a game reserve in the western Kaokoveld has vast potential as a tourist attraction. In time this potential can be turned into an economic asset to the country as a whole, but particularly to the people of the neighbouring homelands.

6. The Skeleton Coast Park, as proposed by the Odendaal Commission, consists of barren desert and as such is unable to support any large mammal life. Even the few migrant springbok and gemsbok encountered on or near the coast appear to depend on areas outside the twenty mile limit, for much of the year.

7. As no evidence was found of any large-scale game migrations between the Etosha Game Park and the western Kaokoveld, there is insufficient justification for a corridor across valuable ranchland to link these two regions.

8. Although the escarpment mountains are used by many of the sub-desert game animals, they need not necessarily be included in the game reserve. The ruggedness of this range generally prohibits agricultural development, making it into a natural buffer zone between the inhabited highlands and a western wilderness.

9. The Herero and Himba people have in the past seldom used the western sub-desert region, but they regard the whole Kaokoveld as belonging to them and the need for a sympathetic understanding for their traditions and future requirements cannot be too heavily stressed. In the final analysis, it will only be with their co-operation that the viability of any game reserve in the Kaokoveld can be ensured.

10. Conservation education is essential, and local participation should be encouraged at all levels. In future a considerable portion of any revenue derived from tourism should be channelled directly to the existing tribal trust funds and when established, to the homeland treasuries.

11. In occasional years of severe drought, the grasslands of the sub-desert could probably be grazed by the Himba cattle with little or no detrimental effects. As protected and conserved emergency grazing, these areas will be of infinitely greater long-term value to the people of the Kaokoveld.

12. The approximately 150 Himba now resident near Orupembe do not seriously threaten the wildlife, and need not immediately be moved. In the future, however, these people could be persuaded to return to the more fertile highlands by the development of boreholes in previously waterless areas of the western plateau.

13. As the situation in the western areas of the new Damara home-

land is essentially similar to that in the Kaokoveld, it should be possible to extend a game reserve southward along the sub-desert to the Ugab River, thus linking it with the existing Brandberg Nature Reserve.

In December Kaymac Industries, the company my mother worked for, kindly printed 100 copies of my manuscript for distribution to appropriate government departments, universities, non-governmental organisations, public libraries and leading conservationists. With sponsorship from the Wildlife Society, I was able to include black and white photographs and bind it in a glossy colour cover. It was not a scientific masterpiece, but the information it contained was up-to-date, relevant – and, because few people could claim to know the Kaokoveld as well as I did, it was the most accurate available.

*   *   *

I also used my year in Natal to start putting into practice my plan of getting a practical education in ecology. My first mentor was my brother Norman, who was completing his research on the behaviour and ecology of the white rhino in the Umfolozi Game Reserve. His home was a caravan at Madlozi – the place of spirits – on the edge of the first proclaimed wilderness area established in Southern Africa.

A hundred years earlier the land between the White and Black Umfolozi rivers had been the hunting preserve of the Zulu kings. But when their sovereignty was broken in 1879, more avaricious white hunters had virtually wiped out the once plentiful big game here. Finally, in a last-ditch effort to save the southern white rhino – which was by then teetering on the brink of extinction – the Natal colonial authorities had proclaimed the area as a game reserve.

Thanks to the pioneering work of the province's early game rangers, the white rhino made a remarkable recovery – from fewer than 50 animals at the turn of the century to a total of over 1 500 in 1970 – and they were now threatening to overgraze the reserve. Under the supervision of Prof Tom Emlen, Norman's doctoral thesis was meant to come up with recommendations for the species' future management.

With Norman's help I was able to fast-track my education into the realm of ecology, and with every visit learned more about the natural processes that, in spite of man's short-sighted interventions, still governed our world. When not out walking in the Umfolozi wilderness I read the books he had acquired in America, some of which were not available in South Africa, giving me a head start on my peers at Natal University.

Among them was Rachel Carson's *Silent Spring*, Raymond Dassman's *A Different Kind of Country* and Peter Nash's *Wilderness and the American Mind*, which were then at the cutting edge of the field. From Norman I also got a copy of the 1968 *East African Agricultural and Forestry Journal* covering the proceedings of a Symposium on Wildlife Management and Land Use. In it was a paper by SA ole Saibull on how local pastoralists were being integrated into the Ngorongoro Conservation Area in Tanzania. Equally valuable was a paper by David Western on the Amboseli National Park in Kenya, where Maasai and wildlife co-existed in a way similar to the Himba and Herero in the Kaokoveld. In it, Western proposed that the pastoralists should get direct benefits from the Park!

As Norman owned a canoe, on one of my visits we paddled down the Black Umfolozi River, drifting close to buffalo and other game that stared curiously at us, oblivious to the fact that the strange objects on the water were in fact the most dangerous species on earth. On a number of occasions we floated over huge crocodiles that saw us coming and only sank beneath the surface when we were less than 20 metres from them. Remembering Van Riet and Rowe's account of how the Kunene's crocodiles had attacked their canoes I was expecting at any second to be upended into the muddy water – from where there would be no comeback. But Umfolozi's crocs obviously had enough game to eat, and did not see us as an attractive meal.

I sometimes joined my mother and her Danish friends, Nina and Fleming Marcher, on weekend trips to other Natal game reserves, as well as visiting the many battlefields that were so much a part of the province's turbulent and blood-soaked history. We took with us written accounts of the stirring events that had taken place at each site, bringing to life the heroism, follies and skulduggery of the participants. Occasionally I thought of the lectures I was missing, but had no doubt that I had chosen a better way.

As the government took a year to respond to Tinley's alternative proposals, and was unlikely to give my manuscript more favoured treatment, it was time to move on. In January 1972 I used what remained of the money I had saved for my university fees to buy a return ticket on an Italian passenger liner bound for Australia. My reason for choosing the huge southern continent was that much of it was climatically similar to South West Africa. In its arid areas livestock production was also the primary form of land use, so it seemed to me a good place to look for answers to the Kaokoveld's range management problems.

A few weeks before I left I heard that Eugene Joubert, who had recently been promoted to senior wildlife biologist in Windhoek, was also drawing up an alternative to de-proclaiming the Kaokoveld and western Etosha. Unlike Tinley's and my proposals, his would have official blessing and be submitted directly to the Prime Minister's Scientific Advisory Council.

Eugene's recommendations for land apportionment were similar to mine, with the game reserve's boundary along the escarpment, and did not include a corridor linking Etosha to the Skeleton Coast Park. But he proposed that the Kunene valley west of the Ruacana Falls should also be proclaimed. However, unlike Tinley, he believed that the Himba living there need not be moved, as they were 'an additional tourist attraction'. Nevertheless, to prevent further immigration into the area he proposed that 'controls should be exercised and cattle numbers limited'.

With information he had access to as a senior civil servant, Eugene justified his case for the pre-Namib being kept as a game reserve with official statistics on mining, farming and tourism. The most telling was that white farmers in comparable rainfall zones in the country's south had been unable to make a living on their huge properties, in spite of receiving considerable technical support and subsidies from the SWA Administration. He also quoted a recent study showing that 10 000 ha farms in the southern pre-Namib had an average net income of R3 000 per year, whereas he calculated that just one tourist rest-camp at 50 per cent occupancy would earn R174 000 annually for the Administration.

Eugene also pointed out that tourism revenue in South West Africa grew by 33 per cent between 1970 and 1971, and that the numbers of tourists entering the country had increased by over 500 per cent since 1963, the year that the Odendaal Plan had been published. This explained why the Commission had devoted only one paragraph to tourism in its entire 300 page report. But although one could understand the Odendaal Commission's lack of foresight, there was no excuse for South Africa's present political leaders ignoring the future tourist potential of the Kaokoveld and western Etosha.

The government had now received three sets of alternative proposals for land distribution in north-western SWA to consider. Although each one differed with regard to the actual boundaries of the area to be conserved, all of us agreed that the agriculturally marginal, but ecologically unique pre-Namib should be a sanctuary for wildlife.

CHAPTER TEN

LOOKING FOR ANSWERS

After a cold and rough passage across the Southern Ocean the *Achille Lauro* docked in Melbourne. I disembarked with only a rucksack of clothes, my fibreglass canoe and the address of Ken Gilmour, a distant relative of Hugh Goyns's secretary. I arranged for my canoe to be stored on the docks and then caught the recommended bus to its endpoint. From there I started walking, putting out a thumb to any passing vehicle that looked like a possible ride.

A few minutes along the road a middle-aged woman pulled over and offered me a lift. I gratefully accepted, and as she manoeuvred her old car through the suburban streets we started talking. Quickly noting from my accent that I was not Australian, she asked me where I came from. South Africa, I replied, and to my amazement she stopped the car and told me to get out, saying only that she did not give lifts to racists! I walked the rest of the way to Keilor, with plenty of time to think about my country's pariah status in the world.

Having spent most of my working life in remote rural areas I had not been exposed to the more noticeable aspects of the government's segregation policies. Nevertheless, I believed that they were immoral and would not solve South Africa's complicated race issue. But I also knew that anti-apartheid activists could be detained for up to 180 days, banned, or placed under five-year house arrest. My personal freedom was too important to be put at risk, so to ease my conscience I simply treated everyone I met on merit, regardless of their skin colour. During the 1960s in Zululand and the Kaokoveld this policy had served me well, enabling me to forge good relationships with the black people I worked with. But when I returned from South West Africa I found that a different atmosphere prevailed, particularly in the urban areas.

In many ways the early 1970s were the pinnacle of the apartheid era. After the National Party had recovered from the shock of Hendrik Verwoerd's assassination, his ideological successors set about implementing his plan to racially segregate the country with missionary zeal. But whereas Verwoerd may have believed that separation was the only way for the ethnically diverse inhabitants of South Africa to co-exist, the new leadership, under 'Jolly John' Vorster, used the creation of Bantustans as a means to divide and rule.

With their large majority in parliament they had first rammed through brutal security legislation to crush any internal dissent. And as a dismayed world looked on, this was followed by the banishment of all non-whites whose labour was not needed in the towns to distant homelands, while a plethora of racist laws were passed that dehumanised black and mixed race South Africans, and made virtually all social contact across the colour-line illegal. Public buildings, banks and most shops were segregated and 'whites only' signs blossomed everywhere, including on beaches, buses and even park benches. To ensure that the blacks stayed permanently in their place an inferior 'Bantu education system' that had been developed by Verwoerd was also forced on the country's non-white school children.

Living in Johannesburg had opened my eyes to some of the government's more ruthless discriminatory policies, but it was three personal experiences – two minor and one of national importance – that made me realise just how evil apartheid was.

In my mother's Hillcrest home she had another free lodger – a very talented black artist named Duke Ketye, whom I became friendly with. In August he was invited by the Bantu Investment Corporation to exhibit his work at an upmarket art gallery in Pretoria, and as I was going to the Transvaal at the same time I gave him a lift.

On the day of the exhibition I went to see how his work was being received, and found the white guests raving about his charcoal sketches and wooden sculptures. However, Duke was nowhere to be seen and none of the elegantly dressed Pretoria art-lovers were even aware he was in the city. Eventually I found him sitting in a back room having a cup of tea in a tin mug with the cleaner of the building. Dismayed, I asked Duke why he was not making the most of his celebrity status, but he just shrugged his shoulders and told me that no one had invited him into the gallery!

That evening I took Duke to his hometown, Soweto, where we celebrated his exhibition's success in 'township style'. By midnight, I was far too drunk to drive back to white Johannesburg, so one of Duke's friends kindly invited me to spend the night in his home. My host even offered his own bed, and if I had accepted would have been prepared to sleep on the floor in the sitting room! The situation was ridiculous and symbolic of the warped society we South Africans lived in. Because Duke was black, he had been paid no attention by the whites who organised his exhibition, while I, who had really just been his 'taxi driver', was given the status of an honoured guest by his black friends. It was also sobering to think that if the police had found me staying overnight in Soweto I would have faced serious criminal charges!

On a trip to Pretoria I attended two days' proceedings in the Transvaal Supreme Court, where the Anglican Dean of the Province, the Reverend Gonville ffrench-Beytach, was on trial for conspiring to commit acts of terrorism. Although the State's case – based mainly on conversations between him and an undercover agent who had faked friendship with him – was often farcical, the crime he was charged with potentially carried the death penalty. In spite of the evidence being torn to shreds by the Dean's eloquent defence council, Sidney Kentridge, the rather unworldly cleric was found guilty and sentenced to five years in jail. On appeal the verdict was later overturned, but what kind of country would bring such a clearly honourable man to trial on such a serious charge in the first place?

The third incident took place while I was walking in a park in the centre of Johannesburg. A black man in his twenties came running towards me, chased by the police, and I presumed it was because of some crime he had just committed. Since I had been a rugby winger of some note, the fleeing suspect had little chance of getting past me. But when I handed him over to the panting and overweight white police constables, they immediately gave him a few clouts for the exertion he had caused them, and then asked for his pass to be in the city. As he didn't have one, he was handcuffed and bundled into a nearby police van. Appalled by my part in his capture, I remonstrated with the two policemen, who now threatened to arrest me 'for trying to prevent them from carrying out their duty!' At that moment I knew that we were all accomplices to apartheid. It was time for me to get out of South Africa.

* * *

When I reached Ken Gilmour's address in the suburb of Keilor I was given a more typical Aussie welcome. Ken and his wife kindly offered me accommodation, and for the next few weeks I used their home as a base from which to make contact with some of Melbourne's prominent conservationists. Here again Australian hospitality came to the fore. At the Victoria State's Department of Fisheries and Wildlife I was referred to Bob Warneke, a senior biologist who was studying the Cape fur seal – the same species that occurs along Africa's south-western shores. Bob and his assistant, Fred Bourn, were about to spend a week in his study area, a tiny island just off the Victoria coastline, and he invited me to join them.

Seal Rock was exactly what its name said: a narrow sliver of rock jutting from the cold, rough sea between Australia and Tasmania, that was the breeding ground of 5 000 seals. As was the case in South West Africa, the local fishing industry accused them of eating too many commercially valuable fish, and had requested the State authorities to reduce the numbers. Although Bob's research showed that the seals fed mainly on squid and other crustaceans, the fishermen were unconvinced. I wondered how they would feel about the more than a million seals on South West Africa's coast.

When not helping my hosts to observe, measure or take samples from the seals, I read up on Australia's strange marsupial fauna, or just walked around the little island sanctuary. Nearly every metre of flat ground was covered with tightly packed nursery groups of sleek and shiny black pups, through which the returning cows had to search for their offspring. The combined calls of sea birds and the bleats of thousands of hungry young seals were deafening – a far cry from the silence and vast open spaces of the Kaokoveld.

On our return Bob and his vivacious wife, Jill, invited me to stay in their home and over the next month I accompanied Fred and other researchers to many different parts of Victoria, learning about the State's natural history and how its wildlife reserves were run. Here the life of a Park ranger was very different to that of his counterpart in Southern Africa, and seemed to consist mainly of attending to the needs of visitors – including cleaning the toilets!

In April I caught a boat to Tasmania, spending a few days hiking in a cold, rain-sodden Craddle Mountain National Park, and even getting caught out in an early snowstorm. From there I trekked through Tasmania's vast central wilderness to Lake Pedder, a picturesque sheet of deep-blue water with pink sandy beaches that was about to be 'drowned' by a hydro-electric scheme. Although its remoteness meant that few people had visited the lake, it was regarded as a natural wonder, comparable only to Lake Baikal in Russia, and the dam was being contested by local and national conservationists.

As my real interest lay in the arid outback, in May I salvaged my canoe from the docks and Jill Warneke gave me a lift to Echuca on the Murray River. My plan was to canoe all the way to its mouth in Adelaide, but Australia's longest waterway was not at all like the fast-flowing Kunene, and over its last 1 000 km to the sea fell only 200 metres. This meant there was virtually no current, and when the wind blew from the front the canoe actually drifted upstream! Adding to my disappointment was that its course wound across the plains in a steep-sided channel, and when I scrambled up the banks the scenery was invariably just wheat-fields or scrubby savanna, grazed by exotic breeds of cattle and millions of sheep. It was canoeing of very low quality, with my only reward being good birdwatching and two memorable sightings of duck-billed platypus.

After four days on the Murray, I decided that Australia's rivers were not made for muscle-powered crafts. Abandoning my canoe on the bank, I hitch-hiked the rest of the way to Adelaide. Here I looked up friends from my days in Tsumeb, Nigel and Muffin Rowlands. Nigel was in charge of a base-metal exploration project in the South Australian outback, and he offered me a temporary job as a field assistant. As I was by now running very low on funds, I gratefully accepted.

Our base camp was near Quorn, a dusty and dilapidated small town north of Port Augusta, itself a rather nondescript harbour on the eastern side of the 'Great Australian Bight'. The area we worked in was mostly flat, and even the nearby Flinder's Range, prominently marked on the map, would hardly have warranted a name in South West Africa. Nevertheless, it was relatively wild country, inhabited by many red kangaroos, as well as feral goats, donkeys, horses, camels, foxes, cats and rabbits. It also had an interesting history.

From the older residents of Quorn I learned that in the late nineteenth century British settlers had taken up farms here in order to grow wheat. For the first few years all had gone well and they harvested good crops, but then the rains failed. With the hope that the next season would be better, the farmers continued planting wheat for another decade, hanging on grimly as their properties gradually turned into dustbowls. Eventually they realised that what they had taken for 'average rainfall' when they first arrived had actually been an exceptionally wet period, and what they later took for a drought was the region's normal rainfall.

It was a classic case of man's over-expectations from the land, but it did not end there. As most of the wheat growers were forced to leave their farms, those who still had the resources to continue bought up their neighbours' land and turned to sheep farming. Again all went well for a while, but once again they had overestimated the region's natural potential and stocked too heavily. Finally, just before the Second World War, this part of Australia was struck by a real drought and as their sheep died of starvation around them, most of the remaining farmers were finally forced to give up their long struggle against the elements. Many just packed what they could carry and walked away, hoping to find jobs in the towns. Most of them never returned.

In the area we were prospecting in there were a number of such abandoned homesteads, and under bluegum trees that had been planted around the houses, old horse-drawn farm implements were still to be found. In some cases there was also vintage furniture in the rooms, and in one of the kitchens I found a 1938 calendar on the wall. It was an eerie scene: apart from the thick layer of dust over everything the room was exactly as it had been left by the departing family, 34 years previously. There were certainly lessons here for anyone wishing to manage land in dry climates, but the Quorn farmers' solution had just been to call it quits and walk away.

By July I had made enough money to move on, and hitch-hiked my way via Coober Pedy, famed for its opals and underground homes, to Alice Springs in the heart of Australia's 'red centre'. Bob Warnecke had given me the name of a biologist living here, Laurie Corbett, who was doing research on dingoes – the once-domestic dogs brought to Australia by Aboriginal people over 30 000 years ago. After I had introduced myself, Laurie kindly invited me to join him and his colleagues on a trip to the Great Simpson Desert, where he and his colleagues were working at the time.

Apart from the obvious similarities due to the low rainfall, the arid landscapes here were much more like the Kalahari than the Namib. In fact, the only thing I found impressive about Australia's deserts was their enormous size. Although the vegetation was structurally similar, with many families and genera shared between the two continents, when it came to animals, even drawing ecological parallels was difficult. At a push one might say the many species of kangaroos and wallabies filled the same niche as Africa's antelope, but there were no Australian equivalents of elephant, rhino and giraffe, or African equivalents of koala bears, wombats, numbats and bandicoots.

Australia's marsupials were also not easy to see in the wild, which together with the continent's huge size accounted for the remarkable fact that some of them had been described after the finding of just a single specimen. In a few cases a species was only known from the bones found in owl pellets! Australian scientists were also not even sure if some animals still existed. The best example of this was the Tasmanian wolf, or thylacine, which had last been reliably recorded in 1935, although most biologists that I spoke to believed a small population of this marsupial predator still survived in the vast Tasmanian wilderness.

Laurie was carrying out research on the dingo for two main reasons. They and other introduced species were regarded as the primary cause of many native marsupials becoming extinct – and like jackals in southern Africa, dingo were sheep killers. Consequently, in the sheep farming areas landowners hunted, trapped or poisoned them whenever the opportunity arose, with the result that they were now generally scarce and very secretive there. However, in the predominantly cattle ranching centre of Australia they were less persecuted, and thus easier to study.

Where we camped was state land too dry for ranching, but further north the rainfall was higher and I asked my companions about the range management practices there. In the Northern Territory some properties were over a million acres in size, they told me, and because they had 'more land than they could use' and abundant artesian water, few farmers saw the need to apply rotational grazing. To erect internal fences was also expensive, and unlike the situation on freehold land in South West Africa, it was neither subsidised nor encouraged by the government. The livestock simply walked to where the rain had last fallen. A 'natural' system, but cattle were not indigenous, and had not evolved with the Australian grasslands.

I spent two weeks with Laurie Corbett and his colleagues, learning a lot about Australia's desert ecosystems, as well as the main land management issues and the Aussie way of dealing with them. As in Southern Africa, farmers were a powerful political lobby, and the Federal and State governments had gone to considerable length and expense to placate their concerns. A dingo-proof fence had been erected virtually across the continent to keep the predators from coming into the sheep farming area of the southeast. Poison was also freely available to stock-owners, although a campaign by conservation-

ists had led to the banning of 10/80, a highly toxic and persistent organophos-
phate that also killed bird and animal scavengers.

The main concern about the use of 10/80 and other poisons was the decline in numbers of Australia's only large inland raptor, the wedge-tail eagle,
which was accused of taking lambs and killed by many farmers. According to
Laurie, the outback landowners also complained about kangaroos competing
with their cattle or sheep for grazing, and enormous numbers of them were
shot annually. In some cases, their tails were sold as pet food, but more often
the carcasses were just left in the bush to rot. I was in no position to point a
finger. The mass slaughter of game to reduce competition for grazing or control the spread of livestock diseases on white-owned farms had been government policy since the first colonists arrived in Southern Africa.

However, in Australia the greatest competitors for grazing were not kangaroos, but rabbits that were introduced from Europe in the previous century.
In the wetter farming areas the flea-transmitted disease, myxomatosis, had
been introduced to control the plague. Here in the drier parts of the continent, where there were no fleas, rabbits were still exceedingly common and
most evenings Laurie and his colleagues shot two or three of them for our
dinner. They were very tasty, and although a pest to the white livestock owners, must have been a boon to the Aboriginal people.

Coober Pedy and Alice Springs were the first places that I actually saw
'full-blooded' Australian Aboriginals. Most of the fairly large community in
Alice Springs lived in 'humpies' along a dry riverbed on the edge of the town,
and as none of them seemed to be doing anything I asked how they made a
living. Some worked as 'jackaroos' on cattle stations, I was told, but most of
them didn't bother. Why should they? Every adult Aboriginal in Australia
was given a monthly welfare allowance of A$250 from the Federal govern-
ment, which at the time was more than enough to feed and clothe them and
their families. Much of the money was in fact spent on alcohol, my informant
added. From the inebriated state of many of the Aboriginals I saw, I had no
reason to doubt this.

While here I met David Hulette and his wife, who worked at Docker River,
an Aboriginal welfare station about 300 km west of the world-renowned tourist attraction, Ayers Rock. David invited me to be their guest on the station,
'to see how the local Pitjindjara tribe lived when not in the white man's towns'.
I gratefully accepted and ended up staying with the Hulettes for six weeks.

By 1972 there were no longer any Aboriginals living traditionally as nomadic hunter-gatherers, David told me, although many families from Docker

River and other remote settlements did periodically 'go walkabout' for a few months in the rainy season. However, when the waterholes dried up and the bush-food became scarce the government allowances, instant shop-foods and tap water lured them back to the welfare stations. At Docker River the government provided schooling for the children and some adult training, but few of them ever seriously sought employment away from the settlement. There was no incentive to, and as David explained, if a man did start earning a salary his relatives and friends would soon pitch up on his doorstep to share in the spoils of his 'good fortune'.

While staying with the Hulettes I spent time at Ayers Rock, where the Docker River staff ran a tourist shop. Here, along with groceries and other western fare, crafts made at the settlement were sold. The huge sandstone inselberg that attracted the tourists to this very remote part of central Australia was a place of great religious significance to the surrounding Aboriginal tribes, who called it Uluru. In the past they had made long pilgrimages to pay homage to their ancestral spirits here, and painted mythical creatures and symbols on the walls of its caves and overhangs. While I was there many thousands of visitors came to Uluru to photograph, or just marvel at this natural wonder, but I never saw an Aboriginal near it. Their spirits had proved powerless in the face of the white colonists, who had taken their land and claimed everything on it. Perhaps they no longer saw any reason to pay them homage.

With everything they valued lost, Australia's original people seemed to have been demoralised and overcome by a deep sense of despair. At Docker River the descendants of the nomadic hunter-gatherers who had once been the masters of an entire continent, now huddled around their makeshift shacks and murmured unsmilingly to each other in their strange language, or just sat staring beyond the bustle of the settlement in unfathomable silence. In the towns, where they were forced to interact with a dominant and unfriendly white society, they sought solace from the pain of their ancestral memories in cheap bottles of wine. There was no apartheid legislation in Australia, but was this paternalistic welfare system much better – or did it just soothe the consciences of the country's liberal city-dwellers?

In late August I hitched a lift on a road-train to Tennant Creek, little more than a fork in the dusty highway between Alice Springs and Darwin, then turned east across the Atherton Plateau to Mount Isa, in the heart of Queensland's cattle country. I had hoped to learn something about range management here, but my discussions with ranchers only confirmed what the dingo researchers had told me. The continent was so vast that landowners saw no need to do anything more than provide water for their cattle, and then leave them to find their own preferred grazing. Twice a year the station manager and his jackaroos rounded up all the stock, branded the calves and sent the selected steers to market. As Australia was virtually free of tick-borne diseases it wasn't even necessary to dip the cattle. Although many ranchers admitted that there was overgrazing, especially around water-points, this could be solved by simply drilling more boreholes – or a good rainy season the following year.

By now I was losing interest in Australia's arid land ecology. Unlike the white colonists in Southern Africa, their counterparts here had introduced cattle and sheep onto a continent without comparable indigenous species, or competing pastoralists. Therefore there was just not the same pressure on the land, and no reason to apply any system of range management. Rain usually fell somewhere on their huge stations, but if it didn't then they could always fall back on the government to 'see them right' until the next season. It was an enviable position to be in, but it meant that there was little I could learn in Australia that would be useful in the Kaokoveld.

East of the Great Dividing Range the rainfall increased dramatically, and near Cairns I found myself in sugar cane fields reminiscent of the Natal coast where I had spent my childhood. The object of my visit to this part of Australia was to see the Great Barrier Reef, but soon after arriving in Cairns I found that this was not as easy to do as I had expected. Coral reefs stretched for 2 000 km along Australia's north-eastern coastline, but nowhere were they less than 40 km offshore. Within the constraints of my dwindling finances the only way of getting out to one of them was to join a tourist cruise to Green Island, which included a day's snorkelling on a nearby reef. It was not the way I would have chosen to experience the Great Barrier Reef, but the few hours I did spend in this amazing coral wonderland was one of my most indelible impressions of the continent.

In February 1972 my S_2A_3 paper had been published in the *South African Journal of Science* and in June *African Wildlife* carried Creina's shortened version of it. By October my full Kaokoveld manuscript had also been with the relevant government authorities and conservationists for nine months. It was time to find out what reaction there had been to it.

Now in a hurry to get home, I hitch-hiked from Cairns down the east coast, stopping for only a few days in Sydney to see the city, and reached Melbourne in early October. After saying farewell to Bob and Jill Warneke, and thanking them for all their help, I boarded another Flotta Lauro liner and two weeks later docked in Cape Town. I had not learned much about range management in Australia, but my time 'down under' had not been wasted. The biologists I met and briefly worked with taught me much about the continent's ecology and strange marsupial fauna. The many political discussions I had with usually critical and often self-righteous Australians had also broadened my mind, and helped me to see my own country's racial problems from a new perspective.

Equally valuable was being able to buy and read two books that had been banned in South Africa: *The Struggle for Mozambique* by Eduardo Mondlane, and *A Long Walk to Freedom*, a compendium of Nelson Mandela's speeches. Both men made eloquent and moving cases justifying the armed struggle against Portuguese colonial rule and apartheid. But at the time Mandela was serving a life sentence on Robben Island for treason, and Mondlane had been assassinated. I did not have the courage to follow their revolutionary road, but there had to be other ways of making Southern Africa a better place for all of its inhabitants to live in.

*　　*　　*

Upon arriving back in South Africa my first priority was to acquire a four-wheel-drive vehicle. With help from Norman I bought a battered, ex-police Land Rover on a government auction, and set off for SWA. In Windhoek I stayed with Johan Malan, who had obtained his doctorate and was now working as an anthropologist at the State Museum. That night he brought me up to date with what had happened since I had left the Kaokoveld two years previously.

Beesie Jooste was still Commissioner in Opuwo, and as the Territory, now known as Kaokoland, was no longer a game reserve, hunting by government officials had increased. Tom Sopper was still in the Territory, but he kept a low profile and just got on with his veterinary duties. Nobody was prepared to speak out against any excesses, particularly as the Commissioner General, Jannie de Wet, was rumoured to be one of the main offenders.

My successor as agricultural supervisor had also made no progress on the livestock marketing front. Nevertheless, in spite of poor rains the previous season the resourceful strategies of the pastoralists had so far prevented any major livestock losses from occurring. Finally Johan told me that my manuscript and articles on the Kaokoveld had not been well received by local BAD

officials, with Jannie de Wet being particularly incensed about my public criticism of the government's policies.

I was now even keener to get back, and Johan offered me a way of doing so.
As part of his work for the museum he planned to write a paper for its journal,
Cimbebasia, on the ethno-botany of Kaokoland. But although his previous research on the Himba made him eminently suited to covering the ethnological
side of the study, he had only a rudimentary knowledge of the region's plants.
However, jointly we could produce a really authoritative manuscript on the
subject. Johan was ready to start immediately after New Year, and undertook
to arrange for me to get a technical assistant's post at the museum, as well as
the permits to carry out the necessary fieldwork.

With a few weeks to spare I revisited Botswana, exploring parts of its
wildlife-rich north-west that had been inaccessible to me on a bicycle. Over
Christmas I joined my mother, who was camping with Flemming and Nina
Marcher at Serondela in Chobe National Park, where we had elephant, lion
and buffalo walking to water within a few metres of us. On the return journey
I drove via the Mababe depression, where the first good rains had turned a
recently burned area into a vast expanse of short green grass, on which thousands of zebra, wildebeest, tsessebe and buffalo grazed. After having spent a
great deal of time searching for Australia's elusive marsupials, it felt very good
to be amongst Africa's much more visible big game animals again.

Back in Windhoek, Johan had bad news. My applications for both a technical assistant's post at the museum and an entry permit into the Kaokoveld had
been turned down. The reason given to Johan was that I was a 'security risk'
and could not be employed in government service, nor was I allowed to enter
any of the ethnic homelands in South West Africa!

Although I was shocked, it explained why my application for a post in one
of the forestry department's wilderness areas, for which I was certainly qualified, had been turned down. I also remembered my argument with Beesie
Jooste, when he informed of me of my transfer to Zululand. Was this what
he meant when he threatened to tell me 'the real reason' for it? Or had the
decision to ban me from government service only been taken after I publicly
criticised the Odendaal Plan? Whichever was the case, if the powers that be
wanted to get me out of the Kaokoveld, labelling me a security risk was the
best way to do it. For all misconduct charges, I would have to be advised of the
complaint, and given a hearing. But an official believed to be a threat to state
security was neither informed, nor given the opportunity to defend himself.

Johan was in as much of a dilemma as I was. Without my participation his planned ethno-botanical research project would be seriously compromised. Fortunately, he was a prominent (albeit enlightened) member of the National Party and promised to try and get the decision overturned. Two weeks later he had pulled enough strings to get me a temporary post with the museum, until the end of March, and two permits to enter Kaokoland under his supervision. It was the best he could do, and he apologised for the fact that, although we would be co-authors of the paper, my salary would only be a fraction of his. But I would have accepted no pay at all just to get back into the Territory.

Late in January we drove to Opuwo for our first field trip, and on our arrival reported in to the Commissioner's office. When Beesie Jooste looked up from his desk and saw me standing in front of him, I thought he was going to have a heart attack. Without even returning my greeting, he ushered Johan into an adjoining room. A few minutes later, grim-faced and still not speaking to me, he stamped my permit and we walked out. Jooste's consternation at seeing me back in the Kaokoveld made my return – although it was just for a few weeks – even more pleasurable.

Once the word had got around that Johan and I were back in Opuwo, many of our previous colleagues and workers came to greet us, and from them I received a very different welcome. Apparently, a rumour had spread that I had been killed in a vehicle accident and as we later travelled around, many local people came to see for themselves 'that I was still alive'. Everyone seemed to be genuinely pleased to see us, but nobody had a good word to say about the Commissioner. I also heard many disturbing stories of hunting excesses by government officials and their visiting friends.

The news I got about Elias Tjondu, my old assistant, was also not good. A year after my leaving he had been fired for being 'too white' – an expression used to describe blacks who acted in a manner above their station in life. Clearly the easygoing relationship that Elias had got used to while working for me had not been appreciated by my successor. I had hoped to see him, but was informed that he had left the Territory, apparently seeking a job south of the Red Line.

After picking up Johan's previous assistant, Kasita Mburura, to act as our translator, we set off for Swartbooisdrift on the Kunene River. Over the next two weeks we travelled throughout the interior highlands, stopping periodically to collect samples of as many different plant species as we could find in the area. Usually we took local people along with us, but if none were available the specimens were brought to the nearest village, where a group of men and women were gathered together to discuss each one in turn. Almost without fail our Himba or Herero informants recognised the tree, shrub, forb or grass from which the sample had been taken, and in most cases they could tell us what its leaves, fruit, or bark were used for.

On our second trip in February we visited the western Kaokoveld, thereby covering most of its main vegetation types. Apart from the Himba and Herero's exceptional knowledge of the plants around them, we also found that nearly all of them were used by the pastoralists in some way or other. This was not surprising to our informants, as one of them explained: 'The white man's shops are new to us, so the plants around us were the shops of our parents. Each one of them is valuable, even those that we no longer use. In the past, when the Nama stole our cattle, we would have died if we had not known how to live from the bush. That is why we still teach our children about how each plant can be used.'

One old Himba we asked about a particular tree could not tell us anything that they used it for. 'So it has no value,' Johan said, and Kasita translated. He did not say that, our informant replied. 'Then what value does it have?' Johan asked again, and in all seriousness the old man answered: 'The birds sit on its branches.' Johan and I laughed, but the joke was really on us and our human-centric definition of the word *valuable*.

Although the Himba and Herero still relied on a wide range of plants to provide for their everyday needs, some were clearly more useful than others. The most important was undoubtedly the ubiquitous mopane, or *omutati*, which provided hard, durable wood for the construction of huts and shade shelters, as well as livestock enclosures. The pliable bark stripped from young stems was also the best binding material, while its thornless, leafy branches were used as a clean surface on which to place the meat of slaughtered animals. The tannin-rich leaves were also chewed and placed on open wounds as poultices to stop bleeding and prevent infection.

However, it was the role played by the mopane in religious ceremonies and social rituals that gave it special significance to the Herero-speaking pastoralists. Only its wood could be used for the sacred fire, and a pile of branches was always kept stacked next to it. A lineage head could also seek the assistance of his ancestors by stirring a small bowl of water containing its leaves.

An important social ceremony in which mopane was used was the removal of a child's four lower incisors just before puberty. The actual knocking out of the teeth was done by placing a sharpened sliver of its very hard wood against each tooth, and tapping with a heavy object until it became loose enough to remove with the fingers. When all four teeth had been extracted in this way they were given to the child, who was required to wrap them in a mopane leaf and throw them in the direction of his or her birthplace. At the end of the ceremony the child's torn gums were attended to by heating a mopane leaf against a glowing coal, and then using it to press the wound shut, a process that was regularly repeated over the following days.

Another common tree in the Kaokoveld that is used in social rituals was *Terminalia prunioides*, called *omuhama* in Otjiherero. When a young girl first menstruated, a branch of this tree, preferably with its characteristic wine-red pods still attached, was wound around the central pole of the ceremonial shelter in which she was required to stay until the end of her period. This important rite of passage into womanhood was so closely linked to this tree that a girl's first menstruation was called *wateka* (to break) *omuhama*. The bark was also chewed and the sap swallowed as a remedy for coughs, sore throats and stomach cramps.

Some of the relationships between Herero-speaking Kaokovelders and the plants around them were unexpected. A creeper usually found in rocky areas, *Cyphostemma ruacanensis*, was called 'the mother of women' and men were not allowed to pick or injure it in any way. However, we were told that young men did often deliberately break off a piece of the plant to initiate a game in which the woman had to chase the culprit and punish him – all accompanied by much mirth and merrymaking by participants and bystanders alike.

Unfortunately, our two field trips were handicapped by the lateness of 1973's rains, which meant that many annual forbs had not germinated and were thus not included in our study. In the short time available we were also not able to get any specialist information from professional herbalists or diviners, and only covered those medicinal plants that were in everyday use. Nevertheless, we had recorded 192 plant species that the pastoralists regarded as valuable. Their uses were then classified into 25 categories that ranged from food, medicines and cosmetics, through religious and cultural uses, for the making of household utensils and field equipment, to poisons, tanning agents, artwork and toys. Ninety-seven of the species collected were regarded as important food for their livestock.

While in the Kaokoveld I also tried to update myself on what was happening to the wildlife in the Territory, and when we camped at Ombombo Ovambo over a full moon period I used the opportunity to see what, and how much, game came to drink there. As both Johan and Kasita declined my invitation to join me, I walked alone to the spring just as the sun was setting. The exceptionally dry conditions had created a very different situation to my previous moonlight counts here, and when I reached the waterhole, now much reduced in size, it was already surrounded by about 20 elephants. By the time I went to bed at midnight, I estimated that at least another 100 had come to drink. With so many elephants together there was almost continuous growling, squealing and trumpeting as they jostled and sometimes fought over a place at the water's edge.

The following morning, Kasita and I walked to the spring, now churned to the consistency of liquid mud, and found a single bull elephant standing in the middle of the pool sucking the cleanest water off the surface with its trunk. An old Himba shepherd had also just arrived with his flock of goats and sheep, and as we watched he started talking to the elephant, which stood quietly, as if listening to what he was saying. When he finished speaking the elephant slowly left the waterhole and walked off into the bush. I asked Kasita what the old man had said. 'He just told the elephant that his goats and sheep were also thirsty,' Kasita replied, 'and that it was now time for it to leave so that they too could drink.'

During the many years that I was unable to come back to the Kaokoveld, this scene of two old gentlemen courteously resolving their dispute over drinking rights became one of my most abiding memories of the harmony that existed between the local people and wildlife in this remarkable region.

We returned from our second field trip in late February and I straight away began writing up the *Cimbebasia* paper. Apart from the list of plants and their uses, I wrote a section on 'The Impact of Man on the Habitat' which included the effects of livestock grazing on both the semi-arid highland savannas and the arid pre-Namib grasslands. In its opening paragraph I stated: 'Most African habitats have evolved under the impact of grazing and browsing animals and the indigenous vegetation is as much in balance with their presence as it is with the prevailing climatic and edaphic conditions. Kaokoland is no exception. Indeed, the accounts of early travellers indicate the region was, relative to its harsh climate, exceptionally well endowed with wild ungulates, both in variety and abundance.'

Large numbers of cattle came back into the Kaokoveld after 1915. Since then more efficient methods of predator control, the development of many artificial water-points and some veterinary services had enabled them to increase to around 160 000, as well as about 125 000 small-stock. To explain the impact they have had on the grass I quoted from a publication by the American ecologists, Dasman, Milton and Freeman:

> Most plants produce a surplus of vegetative growth and seed, part of which can be used by animals. However, each plant must maintain a metabolic reserve – a minimum amount of leafage to permit it to store food for its own survival, or set seed for its own reproduction. In other words, they can tolerate some degree of use, and their response will vary according to the intensity and timing of that use.
>
> Perennial range plants have three periods when they are most vulnerable to grazing pressure: Firstly, at the start of the growing season when the plant is dependent on reserves of nutrients stored in the roots. Grazing on newly sprouted leaves prevents the plant from establishing enough photosynthetic surface to manufacture the food material it requires, so that when the stored reserves are exhausted the plant dies. Secondly, when it is developing and maturing a seed crop, and thirdly towards the end of a growing period when reserves are being stored for the next year's growth. (p. 38)

My paper continued:

> Light nomadic grazing by either wild or domestic animals will therefore have no effect on the plant population because, during the critical growing and seeding period herbivores are scattered over the whole region. Concentrations in the vicinity of the watering points occur only in the dry season, when the plants are dormant and consequently most resistant to intensive grazing.
>
> In areas of high animal density with limited seasonal movement, heavy grazing pressure is extended well into the growing season. This is intensified in years when the early rains are light and scattered – a frequent occurrence in semi-arid regions… The end result is the eradication of perennial plants and their replacement with annual species, which have a very short growing period and are not affected by any amount of grazing after the seeds have matured.
>
> Today most rangeland on the highlands is dominated by annual species – *Aristida effuse, Schmidtia kalahariense* and *Eragrostis* spp. – which appear for a few months only during and just after the rainy season. The much healthier state of those pastures where a

lack of permanent water prevents intensive exploitation leaves little doubt that the elimination of perennial species can be directly attributed to overgrazing by cattle and not to any climatic or edaphic factors. This is substantiated by the accounts of old people who claim that tall perennial grass once grew in many areas now only seasonally covered with a sparse sword of annuals.

Apart from the decreased fodder production, this also results in a considerable reduction in plant cover during the critical period preceding the first rains, with a consequent increased rate of water runoff and soil erosion… The red-brown colour of the flooding seasonal rivers, as well as the frequent dry season dust storms graphically testifies to the volume of topsoil being lost annually.

In April, although nowhere near finished writing up the ethno-botany paper, I was again without a salary. From Pieter Mostert, a friend working for the Department of Nature Conservation, I learned that one of the research technicians in Etosha planned to resign. The opportunity was too good to miss, but worried about my 'security risk' label I first decided to discuss the post with Peter Stark. When I had visited him in Okaukuejo with Burger Baard he had encouraged me to apply for a job in the Park. At the time I was happy to stay in the Kaokoveld, but now I needed his help.

Pieter had since been promoted to a more senior post in the DNC's Windhoek headquarters. Looking very uncomfortable behind a desk, he assured me that he had neither sought nor wanted his new position. When we discussed my prospects of being employed, Pieter told me that outside the homelands nature conservation fell under the SWA Administration, not Pretoria, and recommended that I speak to the director. He promised to put in a good word for me.

I had first met Bernabe de la Bat in the Marienfluss, while escorting Hugh and Dorothy Goyns, and he had been included on the list of people my full report on the Kaokoveld had been sent to. When I told him about my being labelled a 'security risk' he smiled and assured me he was well aware of the reason for my transfer: 'You posed a threat to the senior officials' hunting expeditions, so they had to get you out.' He then advised me to fill in an application form and he would 'see what he could do'.

With the post only becoming available in July, I decided to spend the time visiting Iona National Park. Although it was ecologically similar to the Kaokoveld, I knew there were no pastoralists living west of the escarpment, and I wanted to see how its arid grasslands responded to being grazed only by wild ungulates. However, there was a small problem. While working for the museum I had earned a very low salary and had no money to pay for the trip.

The solution was my mother. As I knew she would be interested in visiting Angola I offered her a simple deal: if she paid for the petrol I would provide the vehicle, and we could share all other expenses. Without hesitation she agreed, and in order for her to have company while I was away from camp I suggested she invite a companion. Initially her brother, Dougie Horton, planned to join us, but at the last minute he could not make it and she brought a friend she had got to know while living in Salisbury.

June Ade turned out to be a divorcee in her early thirties, who grew up in Rhodesia and after leaving school trained as a nursing sister in Nairobi. There she had married a Swedish professional hunter, Jan Rugsten, and lived with him in Kenya, the Central African Republic and Tunisia. They had a daughter who was brain damaged at birth, and when she and Jan got divorced June returned home with her to Salisbury, where she was now working as a dental nurse.

We got off to a bad start. To save money we spent our first night in my Windhoek home – a riverbed just beyond the rubbish dump in the hills to the east of the town. Embarrassed by my humble abode, I paid her little attention and spent most of my time discussing the planned trip with my mother. Annoyed by my bad manners, June responded by arguing about everything that I did say to her. By the second day I was sorry that my mother had brought a friend, while she no doubt regretted having to spend her annual leave with such an anti-social and stony-broke bush-bum. But we were stuck with each other for the rest of the trip.

After visiting Gobabeb Desert Research Station and spending a night in the foggy dunes along the coast we headed north, camping near the Brandberg, South West Africa's highest mountain. Good rains had fallen here, turning the central Namib into a sea of golden grass, on which many herds of spring-bok and gemsbok grazed. From there we spent a few days in Etosha with Pieter Mostert's friend, Rob Reid, who confirmed that he had submitted his resignation. No doubt impressed by the scenery and wildlife, June relaxed and we actually started enjoying each other's company.

From Etosha we crossed the palm-studded Ovamboland plains to the Angola border, making our first stop on the banks of the Kunene where it formed a broad floodplain with many channels and backwaters that were alive with waterfowl. Although I suspected that a few crocodiles might also be lurking in the deeper pools, as the day was very hot I chose a fast-running section and dived in. June had no hesitation in joining me, possibly because she was not aware of the danger, but more likely just showing me that anything I did she could do too.

After driving via Sa da Bandeira and the port of Moçâmedes, we spent two weeks exploring Iona. While I collected plants and made notes on its animal life, my mother pottered around camp and June sketched the rugged mountain scenery and the Himba who lived in the east of the Park. As the warden, Carlos Magalaise, had loaned us one of his staff to act as our guide and interpreter, whenever we came across the pastoralists I stopped and talked to them. But they had an uneasy relationship with the authorities, and were clearly suspicious of my motives for asking them about their livestock management practices.

One night over the full moon we sat at a spring in the mountains. It was a magical experience, with the deep silence of the ranges around us only broken by hooves clattering on rock, as family groups of mountain zebra and kudu cautiously made their way down the steep slopes to the water. The highlight was four black rhino that drank just a few metres from the ledge we were sitting on. They were the only rhino we saw on the trip, but their tracks and dung were common throughout the escarpment ranges.

In the second week we went west into the pre-Namib, where the deep sandy plains that were the equivalent of the Marienfluss had received very little rain. Nevertheless, although the perennial grass tufts were grazed down to ground level by the very high population of gemsbok here, they were still closely spaced and very much alive. It was the evidence I needed for the final section, 'The Impact of Man on the Habitat', of my *Cimbebasia* paper.

After we had returned to Windhoek and my mother and June had caught their flight home, Eugene Joubert told me that the research technician's post in Etosha had been given to a recent university graduate. Was it a matter of the less experienced but more academically qualified man getting the job, or was my 'security risk' label the real reason? The only senior DNC official I knew well enough to give me the answer was Peter Stark. But while we were in Angola he had resigned and joined the South African Defence Force to start a mounted infantry regiment, and had left the country.

My first letter from June brought even worse news. She had returned to find that her younger brother, Brian, had been paralysed in a vehicle accident while on military service in the Zambezi valley. Knowing that she was very close to him, and as the museum was no longer paying me a salary, I flew to Salisbury to finish my part of the *Cimbebasia* paper there.

* * *

With government service no longer an option, and with no other suitable employment prospects in South West Africa, I unsuccessfully applied for a number of jobs in Rhodesia. But my heart was still in the Kaokoveld, so after a few months of moping around June's flat I decided to return to Natal, where I hoped to raise enough money for a longer stay in Iona National Park. As we had become very close, June resigned from her job and came with me.

The first person I visited was Nolly Zaloumis, but he was not optimistic about getting support from the province's conservationists. Natalians were very parochial, he told me, and for most of them Angola might just as well have been on another continent. The Kaokoveld and Etosha were also no longer an issue. The Odendaal Commission's recommendations had been implemented and the controversy was over.

During our discussions Nolly reminded me of his hopes of starting a conservation education programme for black South Africans. Since we met at the S_2A_3 Congress, a lecturer at the Zulu Teacher Training College in Eshowe, Lynn Hurry, had organised weekend excursions for his students, but had since been transferred to Pretoria. The Natal Branch of the Wildlife Society now had the funds for a full-time person to develop the project further. But I was set on going to Iona, and again said no.

After two months camping on the lounge floor of my sister Linda's flat and spending most of my weekends canoeing Natal's flooding rivers, I had only raised R600. Nevertheless, I was confident that once we got to Angola something would turn up to keep us going – after all, we only needed money for petrol and very basic food supplies. I was used to living cheaply, and June knew what she was letting herself in for when she decided to join up with me. But she now had a good reason for seeing our planned trip to Iona a little differently – she was pregnant!

In February I loaded my old Land Rover with basic camping gear and we set off for Angola. We did not get very far. On the way up Van Reenen's Pass a main shaft in the Land Rover's gearbox sheared and we were only just able to limp into Pretoria. After putting up a tent in the Fountains campsite for

June to live in, I spent the next week helping one of Norman's friends strip the gearbox in his backyard and replace the shaft and bearings. By the time the spare parts and his labour had been paid for, even I could see that we did not have enough money to get to Iona, let alone live there.

Once the Land Rover was back on the road I visited Hugh and Dorothy Goyns, who told me that they were planning to walk down the Angolan bank of the Kunene River in June. Was I interested in joining them? It was the trip that we had talked about while standing on the highest point of the Otjihipa Mountains five years before, and now it was my only chance of getting back to Iona. With our baby due in mid-July I would be back just in time for its arrival.

I also called in at BAD's headquarters and spoke to Dr Hamburger, the Director of Animal Husbandry, whom I had briefly met in Opuwo. He had read my Kaokoveld manuscript, and to my surprise complimented me on its balanced approach to the controversy. He especially supported my recommendation that conservation education should be carried out among the local people. Dr Hamburger then told me that the government was planning to re-proclaim the western Kaokoveld on very similar lines to those I proposed, and that his Directorate was already in the process of appointing nature conservators for the northern homelands of SWA. After telling him why I believed I had been transferred out of the Kaokoveld, I asked to be considered for one of the new posts. He was non-committal, but did say we should keep in touch.

As I was not optimistic about BAD appointing me I accepted the post that Nolly had offered me with the Wildlife Society, on condition that I could take the month of June off. The funds available for the project were limited and my salary would be very low, with no housing provided, so Nolly was hardly in a position to say no. I also asked for permission to visit similar education projects in Botswana and Rhodesia, to get ideas on what activities we might undertake. As we would be using our own vehicle, Nolly again had no objection.

While in Rhodesia I got a message that Dr Hamburger wanted me to call in at the BAD offices on my way back. I did so and was introduced to their newly appointed Chief Nature Conservation Officer, Hannes de Beer. He told me all the posts in SWA's homelands had been filled, but they were about to start a nature conservation diploma course for black students at the Cwaka Agricultural College in Zululand. The course was meant to begin in early August, but they had not yet found a suitable person to present it. As I was interested in conservation education and had good field experience, they offered me the post. I would be responsible for leading the course, giving lectures on ecology and nature conservation, and organising field excursions.

That night June and I discussed Dr Hamburger's unexpected offer. A month before I had been unemployed and living largely on June's savings. Now I had to choose between two of the most challenging conservation positions in the country. Both were long overdue and crucial to the long-term future of wildlife in South Africa. Working for the Wildlife Society would give me more freedom, but the BAD post would break the government ban on employing me, and also offered the possibility of a transfer back to the Kaokoveld at some later time. The next morning I informed Dr Hamburger that I would accept the Cwaka post if they allowed me time off in June. Walking down the Kunene with Hugh and Dorothy Goyns had become something I wanted to do more than anything else in the world.

It had been a chaotic month, but more was to come. In 1964 I had completed my compulsory military service, and had thereafter been required to do two further camps over the following 10 years. These I had done, but the law was subsequently amended to three camps in 10 years. Although I was well aware of this, I had not informed the Defence Force of my changing address, and had managed to stay just ahead of the military police until now. But with less than six months to go before the 10 years was up they had tracked me down. When I contacted my commanding officer and told him about my tight schedule he was not at all sympathetic. If I did not attend this camp in Walvis Bay I would be charged with desertion!

Before leaving I discussed the new situation with Hugh and Dorothy, and we decided they should pick me up in Windhoek when my camp ended in late June. We also reduced the trip's length to just walking from the Marienfluss to the sea, which could be done in 10 days, plus the travelling time to and from Iona. It would give me just two weeks before the Cwaka students arrived at the beginning of August, but as I was happy to work at night to prepare my lecture notes I did not see this as a problem. However, I had not taken into account that babies have their own time schedules.

After a frustrating three weeks spent digging trench latrines and preparing a farcical military show for SWA's top brass and their wives, Hugh, Dorothy and I headed for Iona. With no time to spare, we checked in at the Park's headquarters and drove straight to 'the rapids', the only track to the Kunene between Otjimborombonga and the mouth. Here we buried enough food to cover our last few days, and then went on to Foz du Kunene pump station, to arrange a lift back at the end of our hike. This done, we drove cross-country to the closest point a vehicle could get to Otjinungua on the Angolan side – about 20 km away – and left Hugh's Land Rover under a tree. From here we would be on foot, without any backup, but we needed none.

We reached the river at nightfall and made camp on a sandy beach. To the east, black mountains towered menacingly above us, their jagged outline silhouetted against an indigo sky. The air was still and the night silent except for the sound of water flowing over unseen rapids. As I knew crocodiles lurked in the river here, we were careful as we filled our water-bottles and drank deep draughts of the Kunene's clear water. I gazed across at the opposite bank, but nothing could be seen or heard of the small veterinary guard post there.

That night we sat around our little fire until late. I was exhilarated, not only because I was within a stone's throw of the Kaokoveld, but also because I was again in the company of the two people who had been such a powerful influence in my life. We talked mainly about the future of the area. I had recently learned that the Department of Water Affairs had plans to build a series of dams along the Kunene, between Ruacana and the sea. They were to provide hydro-electric power and water for irrigation, but dams here would destroy the wild atmosphere of this magnificent river.

In the developed world wilderness was becoming an accepted form of land use, and in the USA legislation had been passed to protect large tracts of wild land in its pristine state. But did it have a legitimate place in Africa, where the burgeoning human population was spreading inexorably into the remaining uninhabited areas? If present trends continued, all but the continent's deserts would be needed for food production, and most of its great rivers harnessed to power industrial development. So was wild land a luxury that only had value to wealthy whites, whose basic living requirements were well satisfied? And was conserving nature relevant to young blacks whose aspirations the continent's natural resources would be hard pressed to meet?

Hugh pointed out that, contrary to what most conservationists predicted, many African countries had actually increased the number of their national parks after independence. This might be so, but what would happen 30 years down the road, when their human populations had more than doubled? Would a liberated generation of black Southern Africans value the Kunene River and western Kaokoveld as they were now, or would they prefer to see its course through the gorge dammed, and crops irrigated on the sandy plains of the Marienfluss? As members of the privileged class we could not answer these questions, but for me they were no longer academic. In a month's time

I would be teaching the first young blacks to choose nature conservation as a career.

After putting a last piece of wood onto the fire we concluded that none of us, including the present white and black politicians, could predict the attitudes of future generations towards our natural environment. Consequently, while we still had the choice of conserving or despoiling what little wild land remained, it was our responsibility to ensure that at least some of it stayed undeveloped, so that the option to keep it in this state would still be open to our children.

The following day we walked a few kilometres into the Kunene's spectacular gorge through the Otjihipa Mountains. It did not take long for me to realise that the time I had spent out of the Kaokoveld had taken its toll on my fitness, and I was glad that we had not started our hike at Epupa Falls as originally planned. Hugh and Dorothy seemed to come to the same conclusion, so with a wistful glance upriver we turned around and headed west along the last 100 km of the Kunene's course to the sea.

After walking for only a few hours our feeling of isolation from the modern world was shattered by the deafening clatter of a helicopter flying upstream towards us. However, just before it reached us the pilot turned southwards, away from the river and onto the Marienfluss. Climbing up a rocky ridge, I could clearly see a tented camp, presumably belonging to the SADF, where the helicopter landed. Unconsciously we increased our pace and soon passed the encampment without its occupants having seen us.

For the rest of the day we were alone with the river and soon forgot about the security forces' intrusive presence into the wilderness. But the next morning, an hour after sunrise, we again heard the helicopter's aggravating racket as it flew downriver. This time we just stood beneath a large winter thorn tree and let it go overhead before continuing our walk. An hour later it came back, and in the course of the day flew over us another four times. On each occasion we just moved under a tree or rock overhang until it passed. I presumed it was patrolling the river to make sure no SWAPO guerrillas infiltrated the Kaokoveld from this part of Angola. But I was wrong.

The next morning we discovered the real reason why the helicopter had flown over us so many times the previous day. On the bank of the Kunene was the fresh carcass of an elephant bull. A chainsaw had been used to cut through the skull to remove its tusks. All four feet had also been sawn off and a piece of skin cut from its flank. On closer examination I found a number of bullet holes in the carcass, at least one of which was fired from directly overhead.

There were also boot prints from the site to a rocky ledge where the helicopter had landed. After taking photographs we walked on in silence – profoundly shocked by what we had seen.

But it was not all. About 6 km further west we found the clear imprints of a helicopter's wheels in the soft sand. Nearby in the dense vegetation were more boot prints, and close to the riverbank a pool of dried blood indicated where a large animal had been killed. Around the site was the fresh spoor of at least one lion. I also picked up four empty 7,62 cartridge cases of South African military origin. It was clear that one or more lions had been shot there, and a drag mark to the place where the helicopter landed showed that at least one carcass had been loaded onto it. We found no more hunting sites on the Angolan bank of the Kunene, but there was no way of knowing if anything had been killed on the SWA side.

With our spirits somewhat dampened, we carried on walking downstream. The helicopter passed over twice more, but showed no sign of having seen us. As an anti-insurgency patrol they were clearly ineffective, and I concluded that killing elephants or any other big game they found had to be the main reason for making so many flights the day before. But if so, were those on board just rogue elements in the security forces, or were such blatant hunting excursions sanctioned by the top military brass and BAD officials? And if helicopters were being used to kill elephants in this remote part of the region, how many would be left by the time the western Kaokoveld was proclaimed?

Nine days after leaving Hugh's Land Rover we reached the Kunene mouth. No living elephants were encountered along the way, but the spoor of a few bulls was seen to within 20 km of the coast. There was also no sign of lions, and in contrast to the large amount of spoor and dung we had seen on the SWA side in 1970, this time we recorded only one rhino track.

The French-speaking crew at the pump station kindly gave us a lift to where Hugh's Land Rover was parked, but on our way out we found the Park's headquarters empty. In April a bloodless coup had overthrown the Caetano government in Lisbon, and as major changes were now taking place in Portugal's colonies, all the senior officials had been called to Luanda.

From Moçâmedes I posted a letter to Brian Huntley, the chief ecologist for Angola's parks, giving him details of the poached elephant we had found on the banks of the Kunene. Not wanting to risk sending the cartridge cases by post, I kept them, but promised to send him prints of all the photographs I had taken at the site. I also offered to come to Luanda for any court case that might result from the incident. I ended by saying: 'The South African security forces will probably be patrolling this border for many years to come. If they get away with this, it will be the end of the lion, elephant and rhino there.'

Three weeks later I received a reply from Brian which included the following: 'Many thanks indeed for the excellent elephant poaching information. I went straight to the SA Consul General and threatened all hell unless immediate action was taken. He panicked due to the current extremely strained SA–Angola situation and sent off radio messages immediately. I also spoke to a good friend, JCI Director, who is a personal friend of the ex-Minister of Police and who is very interested in Iona, and he promised to launch an attack through his very high contacts. So it is clear that someone is going to catch a pretty thorough investigation and no doubt the case will put the wind up all police and army personnel along our frontier.'

I also considered giving my information and photographs to the press, but knew it would dash any hope I had of getting back to the Kaokoveld. Brian's letter also convinced me that action would be taken against the guilty parties. Perhaps it was, but much bigger things were happening on the sub-continent. Eighteen months later the new government in Portugal withdrew its troops from Angola and granted the colony independence. Within days war broke out between the three liberation armies – bringing death and destruction to the country, and dooming its elephants and other big game. Together with South West Africa's own independence war, it would also have a devastating impact on wildlife in all of the country's northern homelands.

Three days before I arrived back in Natal, June gave birth to our son. It was not a good start to our relationship, particularly as he had not been in a hurry to enter the world, and she had a very difficult labour. I was also unprepared for the wizened little creature she showed me, and was at first convinced we had produced a cretin. But as his legs straightened and the wrinkles smoothed out he became recognisably human. I had not planned to have a family, but Tuareg and later his brother, Kyle, would add immeasurable pleasure to the unconventional life I had chosen.

CHAPTER ELEVEN

A STITCH IN TIME

Involving black South Africans in nature conservation was not an entirely new idea. Since the 1950s a few far-sighted individuals had urged wildlife enthusiasts to reach out to all sections of the country's population. In 1961 Colonel Jack Vincent, the Director of the Natal Parks Board (NPB), had stated that without the education of blacks there could be no hope for wildlife conservation. Two years later his Board announced it was to build a special rest camp for non-whites just outside the Umfolozi Game Reserve. However, Colonel Vincent retired a few years later, and the new camp, Masimba, would only be opened in 1977!

In 1963, after the Natal Branch of the Wildlife Society presented an evening of conservation films to a packed hall in Edenvale, Pietermaritzburg's black township, the first African Wildlife Society was launched. The new society started off enthusiastically, but they needed help. Simply arranging or getting to regular meetings was not easy under the dual yoke of poverty and apartheid, and a lack of funds and transport made it almost impossible for the members to visit game or nature reserves. It also soon became apparent that, although many Natal Branch members gave lip-service to the idea of blacks being involved in conservation, only a dedicated few were prepared to help, and without support the African Wildlife Society floundered and died.

In 1967 BAD created a game reserve for the exclusive use of non-white South Africans. Manyeleti adjoined the Kruger National Park and had good game viewing, but for the great majority of black South Africans it might just as well have been situated on the moon. Nevertheless, in spite of the financial and logistical difficulties they faced getting there, the number of visitors to Manyeleti grew from 1 325 to over 17 000 in just three years.

The sparks that had been caused by a far-sighted few did finally ignite a small fire. In May 1971, Chief Gatsha Buthelezi, chairman of the KwaZulu Executive Council, was invited to attend a conference organised by Game Conservation International in San Antonio, Texas. The Chief's interest in wildlife had already been fostered during visits to the Umfolozi and Hluhluwe game reserves that were organised by Ian Player, Hugh Dent and Nick Steele, and on his return he was interviewed by Creina Bond. His thoughts on conservation in Zululand were published in the September issue of *African Wildlife*:

> Most of my people have never seen a game reserve. In fact, for many of them the game reserves are a source of bitterness. ... Whichever way you look at it, wildlife is for Whites in the eyes of most Africans. ... If Africans are going to change their attitude, Whites are going to have to spend a lot of money on education. ... We need films and subsidised tours of the parks for our teachers and schoolchildren. ... Even now we hear white and black voices advocating the de-proclamation of our reserves. ... Do not blame us – blame yourselves.

Chief Buthelezi's challenge had been taken up by Nolly Zaloumis. In 1972 the Wildlife Society's Natal Branch gave support to Lynn Hurry's field courses for black trainee teachers, enabling him to extend them from one day to a whole weekend, as well as to run similar activities for students at other educational institutions in Zululand. They were enthusiastically received, and when Lynn was transferred to Pretoria the Society employed me to continue and expand his work. Although I had now re-joined BAD, when I accepted the Cwaka post I promised Nolly that we would also keep their environmental awareness project going until someone was found to take my place.

I had accepted the Cwaka post because I believed it would have a greater im-pact on wildlife conservation in the country as a whole. But I was under no illusions about the government's belated attempt to involve blacks being a move away from apartheid. In fact, the decision to start training non-white nature conservators was directly in line with the National Party's policy of separate development.

As the ethnic homelands in South Africa were meant to become independent 'mini-states' all of them needed to develop their own civil service, including a section to manage natural resources. The first step had been to establish a nature conservation division in BAD, from which one of its all-white officers would be stationed in each homeland to protect any wildlife that still occurred there. However, in future they would be replaced by staff appointed from the local ethnic group. For this to happen, young blacks would need to be trained for these positions.

Although the venue chosen for the course was in Zululand, students would be enrolled from all the homelands in South Africa. The entry qualification was a Standard Eight school certificate and 18 months at one of the country's black agricultural colleges. At Cwaka College they would then do a year specialising in nature conservation theory, followed by six months' full-time fieldwork before receiving their diplomas. Apart from the subjects I was to teach, the students would also be given short courses on zoology, botany, law enforcement, animal diseases, basic mechanics and government administration, all presented by staff already at the college.

During my initial discussions with Dr Hamburger and Claude Hardwick, the Director of Forestry in KwaZulu, under whom the fledgling division of nature conservation fell, I was assured that what they envisaged was a very practical course. To facilitate this, a part of Cwaka College's extensive grounds would be game fenced and appropriate species of wildlife introduced. I would also have the use of Ndumu and Kosi Bay Game Reserves for field excursions, and before leaving Pretoria I was given permission to start the course with a two-week trip to these reserves as an introduction to nature conservation in the province.

The historic first intake of black nature conservation students comprised five Zulu-speakers from Cwaka College itself, and two young men from each of six other homelands in South Africa. The day after their arrival we set off for Ndumu, a small but beautiful piece of pristine Zululand between the Pongola and Usutu rivers, on the border with Mozambique. Accompanying me on this orientation trip was Simeon Gcumisa, a senior lecturer at Cwaka who would help me facilitate the course and also give the zoology and botany lectures. About my own age, Simeon was a budding poet and writer who had a deep love of nature, and we soon became friends.

Although it fell within the borders of the proposed KwaZulu homeland, Ndumu was still administered by the Natal Parks Board, and according to their policy blacks could neither stay at the tourist rest camp, nor overnight in the very basic research camp where I was given accommodation. This meant that Simeon and the students had to leave the reserve every evening and return the following morning as soon as the gates opened. Fortunately, the ranger in charge, Gilbert Schutte, gave us his full support and bent the regulations as far as he could, the first of many NPB field staff who went out of their way to show their black countrymen what nature conservation actually entailed.

Gilbert arranged a full and exciting programme for the students, during which we travelled either by vehicle, boat, or on foot to all parts of the reserve. He also gave permission for us to camp – accompanied by two Zulu game guards – next to one of Ndumu's beautiful natural pans, enabling the would-be rangers to observe hippo and crocodile at night from a distance that was a little too close for comfort. As none of them had any experience of dangerous big game, it gave me the opportunity to see how they reacted to the situation, as well as giving them the chance to decide whether they really did want a career in nature conservation. Although I had no doubt that most of them had been terrified, when they emerged from their tents the next morning, bleary-eyed from lack of sleep, all of them chose to continue the course.

While we were in Ndumu, KwaZulu's Minister of Agriculture, Chief Owen Sithole, officially opened the Cwaka course. In his address to the students and VIP guests he stated his belief that if we allowed the wild animals to become extinct, then man himself would soon follow them to extinction. We were all then given a guided tour through the reserve that ended at its world-renowned crocodile breeding station. After the students had watched in awe as its larger inmates were fed huge chunks of meat, each of them was given the chance to hold a newly hatched baby croc, while Tony Pooley, then the leading authority on these man-eating reptiles, explained their vital role in the ecosystem.

From Ndumu we undertook a four-day, 80 km hike across the Makathini flats, from the Pongola River to Kosi Bay on the northern Zululand coast. Our route took us through the Sihangwana forest, where Natal's last elephants survived, but although we saw fresh tracks and plenty of droppings, they remained out of sight – perhaps luckily, as they had a reputation for being very aggressive. Even without angry elephants, the hike was an endurance-testing experience for the group, not least for Simeon, who had spent most of his previous teaching career in the classroom.

At Kosi Bay, Ranger Herman Bentley showed us many interesting features of this unique estuarine system, as well as Thongaland's famous turtle nesting beaches. In two weeks we had covered a cross-section of Zululand's major natural ecosystems – savanna, rivers and pans, swamp-forest, estuary and coast, while from our Natal Parks Board hosts the students gained an insight into what their future work could entail.

* * *

The field excursion had been a great success, but for me the real test would be teaching in a classroom. After accepting the Cwaka post, I had visited the Pretoria Technical College, which had just started a nature conservation diploma course for white students. There I spoke to Andrew Lawry, who had previously studied cheetah in Etosha National Park, and from him I obtained copies of its ecology lecture notes. However, although they contained many valuable ideas on what to include in the Cwaka curriculum, I found them to be very technical and more like a mini-degree aimed at training research assistants rather than nature conservators.

Apart from only having a Standard 8 certificate, the young men I would be teaching had done their schooling in South Africa's inferior 'Bantu education' system. And as most of them came from impoverished townships or rural areas, they would also have had very little exposure to the environmental concepts that their Pretoria counterparts had grown up with. To address this, instead of starting with the theory of nature conservation, I decided to use the first semester to teach 'field biology', a term from the textbook Norman had recommended I use, *Ecology and Field Biology,* by Robert Leo Smith. It would include a range of basic information about the natural world – from the climate and soils, to how animals and plants were adapted to the habitats they lived in.

This created the first problem. I did not want the students to just accept what I told them in the 'talk and chalk' method of their schooling, but to really understand how adaptations occurred. To do this they first needed to know Charles Darwin's theory of evolution by natural selection. However, under the National Party's policy of 'Christian National Education' this was not allowed to be taught in South Africa.

While walking down the Kunene River I had come up with a way to get around this prohibition. Instead of giving them a formal lecture on their first day in the classroom, I would just tell the students the fascinating story of Charles Darwin's life, starting from when he was a young man, more or less the same age as them. They would not be required to take any notes, but just listen and think about what they could learn from it.

In 1831, with help from his father, a renowned physician, young Charles was appointed as the naturalist on board the HMS *Beagle,* which left England on a round-the-world trip. The ship made long stopovers on the east coast of South America, which gave him the opportunity to explore the jungles, grass-lands and mountains in the continent's hinterland. While on these trips he collected numerous specimens and filled many notebooks with wide-ranging natural history observations. Of particular interest to him were the fossilised bones of extinct creatures that had been unearthed there, which although dif-ferent to the living wild animals he encountered on his travels, shared many similarities with them.

The *Beagle* next visited the Galapagos Islands, situated 600 km off the west coast of South America, where most of the specimens Darwin collected were new to science. To his surprise he found that here every island had its own distinct species of plants and animals. But even more remarkable was that most of the terrestrial birds living on these tiny slivers of land in the middle of the Pacific Ocean were different kinds of finch, each with its own physical and behavioural adaptations to the various feeding opportunities available. Why were only finch-like birds so dominant here, he asked himself, while on the mainland many bird families filled the same feeding niches? The most likely explanation was that after the volcanic eruptions that created the Galapagos Islands, finches were the only seed-eaters that had managed to cross the sea and colonise them. But what had then enabled the original birds to change into the many species of finch that now inhabited the islands?

Upon his return to England five years and many adventures later, Darwin pondered these and numerous other unexplained observations, all of which suggested that plants and animals were continually changing. He was not the only biologist at the time to recognise this, but none of them had come up with a natural mechanism that caused these changes to happen.

The answer to this question came from the monk Gregor Mendel, who had spent much of his life artificially fertilising garden peas. His meticulous experiments had showed that the physical characteristics of individual plants, such as their size or flower colour, were passed from one generation to the next, and could be predicted according to the characteristics of its male and female parents. This was already well known to farmers, who for centuries had been selectively breeding domestic plants and animals to make them stronger or more productive.

Although Mendel established the principles by which individual variation within a species was passed on, his work did not explain why the physical characteristics of wild species changed, or why the changes always seemed to be in a direction that was favourable to survival. This came from a paper that Darwin read by Thomas Malthus, entitled *An Essay on the Principle of Population*. Malthus had studied the population dynamics of fruit flies and other insects, and had written:

> Through the animal and vegetable kingdoms, nature has scattered the seeds of life abroad with the most profuse and liberal hand. She has been comparatively sparing in the room and the nourishment necessary to rear them. The germs of existence contained in this spot of earth, with ample food, and ample room to expand in, would fill millions of worlds in a few thousand years. Necessity, that imperious all-pervading law of nature, restrains them within prescribed bounds. The race of plants and the race of animals all shrink under this great restrictive law. And the race of man cannot, by any efforts of reason, escape from it. Among plants and animals its effects are waste of seed, sickness and premature death. Among mankind, misery and vice. (p. 5)

This was the simple solution that had eluded scientists up till then: if in nature many more of a plant's seeds, or an animal's offspring, died than survived, it was logical that those with favourable variations would be most likely to reach adulthood and reproduce. And as Mendel had shown, these life-promoting characteristics would be passed on to subsequent generations, until every individual within the population had them. However, if the population became geographically separated, each section of it would change in response to a different set of environmental conditions, and over numerous generations they would diverge into distinct species.

Darwin's theory was the first scientifically credible explanation of how the first primitive marine organisms had evolved into the enormous diversity of life on earth today. However, as he knew that it was contrary to the teaching of the Christian churches in Europe and America, he did not publish his book, *On the Origin of Species by Means of Natural Selection* until 1859 – more than 20 years after returning from his voyage on the *Beagle*. In fact, he only did so when he learned that another British naturalist, Alfred Wallace, had come up with a virtually identical explanation of how plants and animals evolved.

Not wanting to contradict the religious beliefs of the students, I ended the story by saying that evolution was just a theory, which they could accept or not. I then told them that there were three valuable lessons they could learn from Darwin's life: you should take every opportunity you get to travel to new places; learn from others no matter how mundane their field of study, and don't procrastinate or you may be pipped at the post by someone else.

A few days later I was summoned to the office of the college principal, Mr Bezuidenhout. After dismissing my argument that a working knowledge of natural selection was essential to the understanding of ecology, he gave me a stern lecture about upholding the college's Christian principles. While he was in charge, he told me, Darwin's 'blasphemous theory' would never be taught at Cwaka, and I must remove it from the syllabus. It was an inauspicious start to my teaching career.

The next challenge was to bring ecology – which Natal University students only learned in the third year of a zoology degree – down from its scientific pedestal and make it into a commonsense subject that anyone could understand. To do this my plan was to teach the Cwaka students the way I had taught myself – by spending much of the time in the field, and encouraging them to constantly ask *why* the plant and animal communities around them were the way they were, and *how* they had come to be that way. But first they needed to learn the basic ecological principles and processes that govern the way the natural world worked. For those readers who have not studied this vital subject, they are summarised here to aid understanding of some of the more technical issues in the latter part of this book.

To start with, the students needed to be aware of the physical requirements that make life on earth possible; energy, water and chemical nutrients, as well as how they become available to the plants and animals in the ecosystem. Energy exists in many different forms, but only sunlight that has been fixed and transformed into chemical energy in the green leaves of plants during photosynthesis, can be used by living organisms. Plants are, therefore, the *producers* of energy, which then moves up the *food chain* to herbivores (*consumers*) and carnivores (*secondary consumers*). Of course in nature energy does not flow in a straight line through these *trophic levels,* but spreads out across a vast, intricate web of organisms that consume others, or are themselves consumed.

A critical fact here is that the amount of chemical energy that passes from one trophic level to the next does not remain the same. As each transfer occurs up to 90 per cent of it is transformed into heat energy, most of which is lost into the atmosphere. Therefore, because of the diminishing amount of chemical energy available as it passes through an ecosystem, there must always be a much greater *biomass* of plants than herbivores, and far fewer predators than prey – a principle known as the *ecological pyramid*.

When an animal or plant dies, the chemical energy remaining in its body is consumed by scavengers and detritus-feeding organisms (*decomposers*), and heat is also given off (the reason why compost heaps are warm). In today's ecosystems the amount of energy left after decomposition is negligible, but at an earlier period in the earth's history the prolific growth of plants on land and in the sea exceeded the capacity of the organisms of decay to break them down. Their still energy-rich remains were later covered by geological deposition and have become the fossil fuels that now drive our modern civilisation.

From a land manager's perspective the amount of chemical energy produced by plants from sunlight is vitally important because it determines the potential *productivity* of the ecosystem, and thus how many wild or domestic animals it can support. However, photosynthetic activity only takes place when plants are actively growing, and to do so they also need water, the second basic requirement of life.

Water forms the major part of all living plant and animal bodies, as well as being the medium in which all of their metabolic processes take place. Without it there can be no life, but unlike energy, which is constantly being radiated to the earth from the sun, the amount of water in the world is finite. Furthermore, over 95 per cent of it is either too salty to drink, locked up in the polar ice-caps, or stored deep underground. The remaining 5 per cent that can be used by terrestrial organisms occurs in four forms: water vapour in the atmosphere, surface water in rivers and lakes, soil moisture, and that which is in the bodies of plants and animals. These sources of water are not in a fixed state, but are constantly moving in a continuous cycle that potentially spans the entire planet.

The amount of moisture in the atmosphere is primarily dependent on solar energy – in this case the heat needed to vaporise water from the oceans, lakes and soil surface. Plants also take in ground water through their roots and give it off into the atmosphere during transpiration. At a local level the water that is available for plant growth is the difference between how much rain falls, and the combined amount that runs off into rivers or is lost to evaporation, which is called the *water balance*. Therefore, although we have no control over the rainfall, if our land management practices increase the rate of runoff and soil surface evaporation, the energy production potential of the ecosystem will be significantly decreased.

The third basic requirement of life is a wide range of chemical elements and compounds that are needed by plants and animals to grow, and which are weathered from rocks or obtained from the atmosphere. Carbon, one of the main building materials of all living organisms, is taken from the carbon dioxide in the air during photosynthesis, and with water makes the carbohydrate compounds in which solar energy is fixed, while also releasing free oxygen molecules. When organisms respire or when dead plant material is burned, the carbon combines with oxygen molecules and returns to the atmosphere, thereby completing a cycle that has maintained the oxygen to carbon dioxide balance in the air more or less stable for millions of years.

However, this was not always the case. Initially the Earth had a predominantly carbon dioxide atmosphere in which respiring animals and fires could not occur. Over hundreds of millions of years the oxygen released during the photosynthetic activity of plant plankton in the oceans and later of primordial forests on land created the atmospheric conditions that prevailed before humans started burning fossil fuels. But the extra carbon dioxide produced by the combustion of fossil fuels can no longer be balanced by the Earth's present vegetation, which is causing an increase in the CO_2 level in the atmosphere. The resulting 'greenhouse effect' reduces the amount of solar radiation reflected back into space, causing a rise in average temperatures throughout the world.

Nitrogen, essential for the conversion of carbohydrate molecules into proteins, is primarily derived from the atmosphere during electrical storms, from where it is then carried to the earth in raindrops. However, in this form it can only be used by blue-green algae in the oceans, and bacteria that occur in nodules on the roots of legumes. In nature all other plants get nitrogen from nitrite and nitrate compounds that are the by-products of organic material decomposing.

The many other chemical nutrients needed by plants and animals come from rocks in the earth's crust. Although most of them occur in abundance globally, some essential elements or compounds may be locally in short supply. Once they have been dissolved in soil moisture, they can also be transported deep underground to where they cannot be reached by shallow rooted plants, a process that is called *leaching*. In areas of low soil fertility they may also be scarce because large amounts have been locked up in the woody parts of trees and shrubs.

At ecosystem level nutrients are continuously imported or exported during the different phases of the water cycle. Soil erosion will also cause chemical loss, but if not too excessive will be balanced by new mineral salts being weathered from rocks under the ground. Modern agriculture can play a major role in depleting soil nutrients because the crops are no longer consumed locally, thus requiring the use of natural or artificial fertilisers to replace those that have been taken out of the system.

However, as chemical elements are not diminished during respiration or destroyed by combustion, an ecosystem's productivity can be boosted by their passing through the different trophic levels and then being returned to the soil during decomposition. Vital minerals locked up in dead plant material can be even more rapidly brought back into circulation in the ash after a fire – the reason why slash and burn agriculture is practised on low-nutrient soils by pre-industrial societies.

Although natural ecosystems are so complex that no square metre of land has identical physical and biotic components, and so dynamic that they are never exactly the same today as they were yesterday, or will be tomorrow, the changes that occur are not haphazard. In fact, their structure and functioning is governed by a relatively small number of natural laws and processes, the understanding of which makes the interactions between living organisms, and between them and their physical environment, broadly predictable.

The most basic is the concept of *limiting factors*, which was first proposed by Justus von Liebig in 1840. His research analysed the relationship between plants and the soil, reaching the simple – but for its day revolutionary – conclusion that crops in the field 'diminish or increase in exact proportion to the amount of the mineral substances conveyed to them in manure'. Furthermore, if one vital nutrient is present in minimal quantities, even if everything else a plant needs is available in abundance, its growth will also be minimal.

Some minerals may also occur in too high quantities (salt, for example), making them a limiting factor. This does not only apply to chemical nutrients. The amount of many other environmental factors, such as water and sunlight, or the frequency of defoliation, can all affect a plant's performance, and even cause its death if it is below or exceeds the species' *range of tolerance*. The same principle applies to animals, although in their case the limiting factors will be different. But as with plants, it may be just one of them that will determine their success or failure in a given habitat.

Different factors can also act together to either negate or increase their detrimental effect on an organism. For example, low soil moisture may only reduce a plant's performance if it is exposed to high temperatures, while a large number of predators will only cause a prey species to be exterminated if it is forced, by a lack of suitable food or water, to enter a habitat in which it is more vulnerable to predation.

Although limiting factors in relation to a species' range of tolerance are the main determinants of their distribution, another ecological principle is involved. Competition between individuals within a population (*intra-specific competition*) is one of the pillars on which the theory of evolution by natural selection is based, while competition between different species (*inter-specific competition*) is also constantly occurring in ecosystems. However, in his textbook Robert Leo Smith states that: 'Few concepts have had such an impact on ecological and evolutionary thinking; yet basically the nature of inter-specific competition and its effects on the species involved is one of the least known and most controversial fields of ecology.'

Smith goes on to describe how in the nineteenth century two scientists, Volterra and Lotka, independently came up with mathematical formulas to show that if two species lived together and utilised identical food resources, only one would survive. Since then these formulas have been tested in experiments using laboratory-kept organisms with short life-cycles, which enabled observations over many generations. The results showed that the species whose ranges of tolerance for all the potential limiting factors most closely matched the laboratory conditions would survive, while the other would inevitably die out. This became known as the *competitive exclusion principle*.

In spite of it not having been proved outside the laboratory, ecologists assume that the same broad principles apply in natural ecosystems. Thus two similar plants or animals can inhabit the same area if all of their living requirements are available in abundance, but if one or more factors become limiting the species best adapted to the prevailing environmental conditions will out-compete the other, and in time become the only one occurring there.

Although it is controversial in some academic circles, for land managers the most important ecological process is *succession*. Botanists in the early part of the twentieth century were the first to recognise that by simply growing in a particular place plants alter the *micro-habitat* around them. For example, when hardy species colonise bare ground their leaves provide shade, which reduces the soil surface temperature and, thereby, the rate of moisture loss to evaporation. Consequently, their mere presence has created more favourable conditions, enabling less robust species to germinate. The new arrivals will in turn further modify the micro-habitat, allowing a range of other plants to colonise the area.

They also found that the changes occurring in natural ecosystems were not random, but followed a broadly predictable direction from small *pioneer* plants in simple associations, towards larger species and more complex communities. The early botanists just looked at the changes taking place in the vegetation, but because new *ecological niches* will also be created for consumer and decomposer species to inhabit and exploit, the animal and micro-organism component of the ecosystem will also develop in parallel with the plants.

Ecological succession will continue until the biotic community reaches the highest and most complex state that can be supported by the soil type and climatic conditions in the area. Although these *climax* ecosystems are very stable, because they are dominated by large, slow-growing woody plants, with large amounts of nutrients locked up in their trunks, their productivity is relatively low. In contrast, ecosystems kept at a *sub-climax* stage by frequent fires, regular flooding or human activities consist of faster-growing species that rapidly re-cycle the available soil nutrients and have a high rate of solar energy fixing. However, because sub-climax ecosystems are naturally unstable, if they are not well managed ecological regression can take place back to a less diverse and less productive biotic community – a process called *desertification*. Nature conservation, then, is by definition maintaining the ecosystem's biodiversity and productivity.

* * *

It did not take me long to learn that Cwaka was one of the many anomalies created by the South African government's policy of separate development. Although it was situated in the designated Zulu homeland, and the staff was either employed by, or seconded to the KwaZulu Ministry of Agriculture under Chief Owen Sithole, our accommodation and all the college facilities were still racially segregated. But most remarkable to me was the level of racism still openly displayed by some of my white colleagues.

The most outspoken of Cwaka's staff was the State Veterinarian based at the College, Dr Nesser, who boasted that he had never shaken the hand of a black man. Nor would he ever do so, he assured me, not even that of Chief

Gatsha Buthelezi, the head of KwaZulu's Executive Council, who we all in fact worked for. With great pride he also told me how he had once stormed out of his family home when his mother tried to introduce him to a coloured guest. I asked him if he could not see how his behaviour must have embarrassed her, but he was unrepentant and I could only wonder why such a bigoted man had chosen to teach at a Zulu agricultural college.

However, in some respects Cwaka was typical of all government institutions throughout the world. At ten o'clock and three-thirty all work stopped, while we officials gathered to drink a morning and afternoon cup of tea or coffee. But because Pretoria's policies still held sway at the college, the black and white staff drank their refreshments from identical crockery, sitting on similar chairs, but in separate tearooms only 20 metres apart, across an immaculately maintained lawn. It was just another ludicrous situation that had become part of living in South Africa, and I gave it little thought until a few weeks after my reprimand for teaching the theory of evolution, when I again landed in trouble with the college's custodians of National Party policy.

We had just started fencing the college's game camp, a practical exercise that I carried out with the students and one of the black lecturers. On a hot afternoon I misjudged the time, and when my colleague and I arrived at our separate facilities, thirsty and in real need of a cuppa, all the other members of staff had already returned to their workplaces. Fortunately, in the white tea room there was still half a pot of tea, but across the way I noticed that he was not so lucky, and without thinking invited him to join me. He gingerly sat down, clearly nervous of being in a white preserve, while I did my best to make light of the matter. However, before our cups were empty Dr Nesser walked past, and although he said nothing it was enough to send the young man scuttling back to his own side of the lawn. The whole episode would have been amusing if it had not been so humiliating for my colleague.

It also resulted in my being summoned for another fire and brimstone lecture in Mr Bezuidenhout's office. This time, to my surprise I found most of the other white members of staff already seated there, and some of them joined in the thorough dressing down I received for contravening the laws of the college and country. As I had been caught in the act of undermining white authority, respect and security, there was little I could say in my defence, and before being allowed to leave the principal's office I promised not to commit such a scandalous offence again.

On Wednesday afternoons it was also a tradition at Cwaka to invite guest speakers to address the students and staff in the College hall. Quite soon after the tearoom incident the weekly lecture was presented by a social anthropology professor from the nearby University of Zululand. His talk was on cross-cultural relationships, and he emphasised the importance of both racial groups making an effort to learn each other's social customs. In this way, he told the audience, misunderstandings and much of the consequent friction could be reduced. I was impressed, especially because he was Afrikaans-speaking.

At the end of his lecture our guest was invited to the white common room for coffee and a social get-together with the pale section of the staff. After some general discussion about events of the day, I decided to personally thank the professor for a very stimulating talk. My colleagues said nothing so I plunged in and asked whether he did not think that better understanding would be promoted if Cwaka's white and black staff at least spent our tea breaks together.

The silence from my colleagues was deafening, but the professor thought it was an excellent idea, and proceeded to inform us that the university had not two, but three tearooms. One for whites; one for blacks and a third for those who wished to venture across the colour-line and actually drink tea together! This was too much for the more doctrinaire staff members and they sprang to the defence of Dr Verwoerd's creed of racial separation. Dr Nesser went so far as to call the university's solution a dangerous 'liberal practice' and a 'slippery slope'. It would never happen at Cwaka, he assured the professor. Here the line had been drawn and they would hold it.

In the heated argument that followed our learned visitor defended his case admirably, and I said no more. In fact, as the talk in our staff room was normally about rugby, motor cars or hunting expeditions, I was quite pleased with myself for having initiated a serious and relevant discussion, exactly what I thought the weekly guest lecture programme was all about. But I was wrong.

The following morning I was again called before Cwaka's all-white disciplinary committee. This time I was accused of 'embarrassing the College' by raising a sensitive topic in front of a guest, and the stern faces in front of me showed that they were not joking. But by now I had had enough and totally rejected their charge and refused to apologise. Taken aback by my outburst, they could only threaten undisclosed action if I persisted with my 'disloyal and subversive' behaviour.

*   *   *

When I started lecturing at Cwaka, there had been no housing available and June and I lived in a small room at the back of a friend's house in Empangeni. It was far from comfortable, especially now that we had a baby, but initially it had suited me. To cut travelling costs I bought a motorcycle, and rode the 20 km to and from the college each day. After two months, however, Dr Nesser offered to give up his government house on the campus so that we could move into it. He was a bachelor and did not need so much room, but it was still a kind gesture that showed me he was actually quite a decent fellow – as long as your skin was white. From my side, it would have been churlish not to accept his offer and deny June the chance of raising our son in a real home. It also meant that, for the first time, we could store our combined belongings in a room instead of in my old Land Rover.

Having our own house had other advantages, one of which was being able to invite guests around for a drink or dinner. At Cwaka the only whites June and I got to know well were an introverted German couple who lived on the campus but did little socialising. However, I had made a number of black friends, the closest of whom was Simeon Gcumisa.

Simeon had been teaching at Cwaka for some years and was well respected, even by the white staff. Apart from lecturing he was also in charge of the college hostel, but although married with a small baby daughter, he did not have his wife with him on campus. Soon after moving into our new home I suggested that he join June and me for dinner a few days later. We had lots to discuss informally and it would be a change from his normal diet of hostel food.

In a small community news travels fast. By the next day Mr Bezuidenhout already knew about my invitation to Simeon, and once more I found myself being summoned to his office. This time he was alone.

'Is it true that you have invited Mr Gcumisa to dinner?' he asked.

I confirmed that it was, but told him that the dinner had been arranged for after working hours in my private home. Therefore, I could not see how the college administration had anything to say over the matter. But Mr Bezuidenhout reminded me that the house I lived in belonged to the State, and was not my private property. So he did have a say over who was invited into it, and asked me to please withdraw the invitation. I did not accept his argument and insisted that he first show me a college regulation that stated I could not invite black guests into our home. Alternatively, he should give me a written instruction to that effect. I then left his office.

The next day Mr Bezuidenhout told me that he had discussed the matter with Nico Smit, the Director of Agriculture in KwaZulu, and that Simeon and

I must drive down to Pietermaritzburg in a government vehicle that after-noon and report to him. If we did not reach BAD's headquarters before five o'clock, we were to phone Mr Smit from along the way to arrange a meeting place. This we did, but when I called his secretary gave me the message that he did not want to see us, and that we should go back to the College. The follow-ing evening Simeon, June and I had a very pleasant dinner together, staying up until midnight discussing the strange place and times we lived in.

*   *   *

In October I took the students on a short excursion to Durban, where we first visited the museum to see the province's larger mammals at much closer quarters than was possible in the wild. Although they were only mounted specimens, it did give them the opportunity to study the physical adaptations that each animal had made to survive in the ecological niche it occupied.

We spent the next morning at the Fitzsimons Snake Park, seeing the wide range of both harmless and dangerous species that inhabited Southern Africa, and their reaction to humans, in this case an employee who walked fearlessly amongst them. Our final destination was the Aquarium and Oceanographic Research Institute, where they observed the array of marine creatures that inhabited the oceans off our shores. I had planned to take them for a swim that afternoon, but there were no nearby beaches where blacks were allowed. In the end this didn't matter, because after seeing the sharks, rays and giant turtles that morning, only the two Transkei students were prepared to go any-where near the sea.

As was the case on the trip to Ndumu and Kosi Bay, I was impressed by the students' interest in everything they saw and heard. This was particularly gratifying because at the beginning of the course I had asked each of them to tell me what wildlife they had previously seen, and why they wanted to have a career in nature conservation. Those that came from rural backgrounds had all encountered small animals while herding livestock, but apart from two Zulu students who lived near Umfolozi Game Reserve, none of them had actually seen any big game before.

The reasons they gave for choosing to specialise in nature conservation were even more depressing. The most common was that they had seen wild-life film shows at their school or college, while a few of them admitted that they had hoped to study one of the more popular majors, but did not get high enough marks to be accepted. Two students claimed to have been coerced into doing the Cwaka course by their previous lecturers, and one young man simply said that he had once kept a rabbit as a pet and that he now liked animals.

Initially I was quite downcast by their answers, which were unlikely to provide them with sufficient motivation to succeed in the difficult career they had chosen. But what else could I have realistically expected? My own interest in wildlife had been sparked by a grandfather who read us children *Jock of the Bushveld,* and was then nurtured by annual family visits to the Kruger National Park. But in our segregated society game reserves were exclusively for whites, like beaches, city parks and virtually all other places of recreation.

When I was young nature conservation to me was brave, suntanned game rangers who had dedicated their lives to protect wild animals from poachers; but from a rural black child's perspective it was more likely to mean uniformed men who kicked over cooking pots to see what meat was in them, or arrested a family member for snaring. If the Cwaka students stayed the course they would be the ones wearing the uniforms, and they would not find these perceptions easy to change. When Creina Bond wrote an article in *African Wildlife* about the new diploma course for blacks she titled it 'A Stitch in Time.' But was there still time to reverse 75 years of 'whites only' nature conservation policies in the minds of the majority of South Africans?

*   *   *

As the end of the year loomed the Cwaka students had spent all but three weeks in the classroom. To rectify this I planned to spend much more time in the field during the second semester, starting with another excursion to Ndumu and Kosi Bay as soon as the students returned from their Christmas holidays. The last hurdle before this was the end of year exams.

Academically the courses I presented might not have been up to university standards, and were not meant to provide the answers to all the problems the students might face in their future careers. But they did give them a basic understanding of the way that ecosystems functioned, which would at least enable them to ask themselves and others the right questions. However, what I most wanted to achieve was to instil in these first black nature conservators that protecting the land and everything on it was important for all South Africans.

The exam results were much as I expected. Those who had done their schooling in English got through easily, while those who did not would need a lot more attention in the second semester. Nevertheless, I was satisfied with my first six months of teaching and looked forward to putting theory into practice when they returned to the college in the new year. But in late November Nico Smit dropped a bombshell. My planned trip to Ndumu and Kosi Bay had been cancelled. The reason he gave was a disagreement with the Natal Parks Board over accommodation for the students. Although I assured him that we were all prepared to sleep in tents outside the reserve, his decision had been made on principle and it was final.

Looking back I can see that in the big picture Nico Smit's stand was right, but at the time I was devastated by the thought of not being able to take the students into the field. I had never seen myself as a classroom teacher, and had looked forward to getting away from the college and its petty apartheid policies. For six months June and I had worked late most nights preparing lecture notes, as well as running weekend environmental education courses for the Wildlife Society. It was a schedule we could not maintain. Out of frustration I threatened to resign if the Ndumu and Kosi Bay field trip did not go ahead.

Leaving Cwaka would ruin any chance I might have had of BAD transferring me back to the Kaokoveld, but the reputation I had gained as a liberal, or worse, had no doubt already burnt that bridge. Teaching at the college gave us financial security, a nice home and beautiful surroundings in which to bring up our son, while if I joined the Wildlife Society full-time I knew that there would be no housing for the first few months. But at least I would be working with like-minded people, and the Zululand zone members would surely rally round to help us. When there was no response to my ultimatum I resigned and left Cwaka at the end of the year.

CHAPTER TWELVE

WHEN IT IS LATE AFTERNOON

The first conservation education projects in Africa were the Wildlife Clubs of Kenya and Chongololo Clubs in Zambia. Both were sponsored by NGOs that believed a new urbanised generation of the continent's youth needed to learn more about their natural environment. In the early 1970s the Rhodesian government also started Mushandike School in the Bush, the brainchild of Dave Rushworth, a senior ranger in the Department of National Parks and Wildlife and a teacher in the Ministry of Education. As I had no experience in this new field, when I first joined the Wildlife Society in February 1974, Nolly Zaloumis agreed to June and me spending a week at Mushandike, as well as visiting any other relevant projects along our way.

We drove via Gaborone in Botswana, where both government and expatriate aid workers had plenty of ideas, all of them in the planning or early implementation stage. Some radio programmes had been produced and a few school groups taken on excursions to nearby game reserves by the Botswana Society and African Wildlife Foundation, but that was all.

In Rhodesia we stopped near Que Que at the Mlezu Technical Training Institute, which taught its black students a wide range of conventional and unconventional agricultural activities, all of which were interlinked. Kitchen waste was fed to ducks that in turn fertilised the water in a series of highly productive fish dams. Guinea fowl and wildlife were encouraged onto the property, and all were cropped to increase the overall productivity of the land. The man behind the college's holistic farming practices was Fritz Meyer, who told us that he was also looking for ways to harvest the protein-rich reproductive stage of termites.

I was impressed by the idea of a farm being managed as an ecosystem, and as Fritz applied the same philosophy on his own cattle ranch, he invited us to come and see how he had integrated game into his livestock management practices. On a drive around his property we saw impala, kudu, and a sizable herd of eland. As they were all primarily browsers, Fritz explained that they did not compete with his cattle, and by cropping them he had considerably increased the productivity of his ranch.

I was also very interested in the grazing system he used, which entailed large herds of cattle staying for a very short time in the multiple paddocks the ranch was divided into. Neil Alcock had followed the same short-duration grazing system to rehabilitate the degraded grasslands on Maria Ratschitz Mission in the Natal midlands, but here it was being practised on semi-arid savanna not unlike the Kaokoveld highlands.

In Rhodesia short-duration grazing (SDG) was being promoted by Allan Savory, an ecological consultant who was also the country's only independent member of parliament. At a local farmers' day we attended with Fritz the next day, I met two government conservation and extension officers who told me there was a great deal of opposition to the 'Savory system' from the agricultural research scientists. Nevertheless, they knew of many cattle ranchers who were using SDG with considerable success, and it had also been introduced into some Tribal Trust Lands near Fort Victoria. A major attraction for the residents was that it did not require cattle numbers to be reduced. In fact, Savory advocated stocking rates should be *increased* to rehabilitate overgrazed rangeland!

In early 1974 the name Allan Savory was very much in the Rhodesian news. The all-white parliamentary elections were about to take place, and under the banner of the Rhodesia Party he and a number of other progressive-thinking countrymen were providing the only challenge to the Ian Smith government. When we reached Salisbury June and I went to one of Savory's well-attended public meetings, where for the first time I heard a Southern African politician realistically address the issues facing the sub-continent, and not just playing on the white community's fears about their future.

Unfortunately, most of the country's electorate did not share my opinion. A few months later the Rhodesia Party was trounced at the polls, with Savory losing his seat. A major reason for their defeat was his recommendation that detained African nationalist leaders should be released so that a round table conference on the country's future could be held. The State-controlled press and TV denounced it as 'encouraging the terrorists', and quoted Ian Smith as saying that just suggesting it was 'irresponsible and evil'. Rhodesia's whites had closed ranks and minds behind the man who promised them that 'blacks would not rule the country for a thousand years'. But within a year, with some prodding from Pretoria, the Rhodesian Front government would do exactly what Savory had proposed.

After speaking to a number of prominent conservationists in Salisbury we headed south to Mushandike National Park, arriving just as a group of 50 Standard 5 girls from Bulawayo began their week-long visit. The activities they were given comprised a blend of theoretical lectures that included many practical examples and demonstrations interspersed with sometimes exciting and always fun outdoor excursions. By the time they returned to their school the 11-year-olds would have had an experience to remember, and also learned a great deal about Rhodesia's natural environment. The organisers of the course proudly informed us that from the following year 'every Standard 5 child in the country would spend a week at Mushandike as part of their school curriculum'. Of course they meant every *white* child in the country, but it was still a remarkable programme that had no equal in Southern Africa.

Although South Africa was far behind Rhodesia in environmental education, it did have one programme that was a world leader. In 1963 Natal Parks Board rangers Ian Player, Jim Feely and Hugh Dent had started the Wilderness Leadership School. Although its philosophy of preserving large tracts of land in a pristine state was likely to have limited appeal to black South Africans, the School had taken thousands of young people into wild country, and I wanted to learn how they put their conservation message across.

Before leaving Cwaka I had arranged for some of its black lecturers to take part in a four-day Wilderness Leadership School course. At the last minute, however, the College refused to give them time off and I turned to Neil Alcock and Creina Bond to find alternative participants at very short notice. Visiting Neil and Creina at their mission station home also gave me the opportunity of getting their ideas on how I should proceed with what had now been named the African Conservation Education Project, or ACE for short. Creina was very enthusiastic about the Natal Branch of the Society's new initiative, but

Neil had doubts about its all-white membership's commitment to any conservation education programme that would have real relevance to blacks.

'They don't have the faintest idea of the African's real conservation needs,' he told me bluntly as we ate a traditional Zulu meal of *uputu* and *amasi* in their converted wine-cellar home. 'And if they did,' he added with a wry smile, 'you can bet your life they would not be spending money promoting it.'

In spite of his cynicism Neil was very helpful. His advice was also based on a lifetime of working closely with rural Zulus, and was worth far more than the grand ideas June and I had heard expounded from plush offices and elegant homes in Botswana and Rhodesia. To have any impact, Neil believed that what we advocated on our courses would have to be politically acceptable and economically realistic to our audience. 'Wilderness is a wonderful and worthy concept to you and me,' he said, 'but what does it mean to people who don't have enough land to make a living on? You have to talk about the things that *they* understand, and are relevant to *their* daily lives.'

As our guinea pigs Neil chose four of his young Church Agricultural Project (CAP) demonstrators, and I drove with them to the Wilderness Leadership School headquarters near Durban, where the course would begin. Our trail leader was Jim Feely, the philosophical father of the wilderness concept in South Africa that Ian Player would later turn into an international movement. With him would be John Tinley, the brother of the man who had drawn up the Wildlife Society's alternative to the Odendaal Commission's plan. I could not have hoped for two better guides.

After a stop at Twinstreams farm near Mtunzini, where its owner, Ian Garland, gave us an introductory lecture, we spent two days each in the Umfolozi and Lake St Lucia wildernesses. For me it was a fascinating experience, hiking through some of Natal's most pristine areas with two of the province's most experienced conservationists. To Jim wilderness was a religion, and the few virgin tracts of Zululand that still remained were sacred places, where man had to discard his machines and walk softly in the footsteps of his ancestors. In them he saw jaded city-dwellers finding refuge from the noise and disorder of their everyday life, rekindling the spirituality that had been extinguished along their road to material wealth. Both of our guides believed that these tiny islands of untamed land would one day be modern man's salvation.

Most of our campfire discussions went over the heads of the poorly educated young men from CAP, and they retired early each night to rest in preparation for another day of walking with madmen. On one of the few occasions that we were able to draw them into our conversation they readily agreed that it was a good thing to observe wild animals, in all their 'ferocity and beauty'. But what they failed to understand was why we approached them on foot and not from the safety of a motor vehicle. Their lives were filled with enough excitement and danger without inviting more by stalking close to rhino, buffalo or hippo. They also saw nature as an adversary whose capricious assaults often laid waste to a man's best laid plans, and could cause him great hardship. Jim was disappointed in their general response to the course, but I found it a valuable reality check.

On our return to Durban I visited the Wildlife Society's offices and discussed the ACE Project with Keith Cooper, the National Conservation Director, and John Fowlkes, who had recently been appointed as Natal Branch Manager. Both of them were fully behind the Project, but were concerned about how to raise the money needed to keep it going.

'Whether you like it or not, publicity is essential,' John told me. 'We must do things that catch the public eye – high-profile activities that will be picked up by the press, or can be published in *African Wildlife* magazine. If people are not continually hearing about what ACE is doing, our funding for it will dry up.'

*   *   *

While at Cwaka, June and I had run a number of weekend excursions, similar to those previously organised by Lynn Hurry and the Wildlife Society's Zululand zone members. The participants, usually between 12 and 15 in number, were taken to one of Zululand's game ranches, where they camped for two nights, viewing game by vehicle or on foot, and listening to lectures on various conservation topics given by myself, as well as invited guest speakers. In most cases we also got the ranch owner to join us for a while and explain why he was farming with game and not cattle. Although they were informal and largely dependent on what each game ranch had to offer, the response from the young Zulus who participated was excellent, and we decided to continue with them once the schools re-opened in the new year.

As the Society's funds designated to the ACE Project did not cover housing for us, I had hoped that one of the Zululand Zone members would be able to help out temporarily with a vacant room or cottage on their farm. However, none appeared to be available and we lived from the back of my Land Rover until Ian Scott-Barnes kindly allowed us to put up a tent on his game ranch. It was more than adequate for me, but having only a canvas roof and a cold water tap made life quite difficult for June, particularly as she had the added responsibility of looking after our now crawling baby son.

Game farming was still in its infancy, and Scott-Barnes's Nyala Game Ranch had been the first property in Natal to remove all of its cattle and be entirely re-stocked with wild animals. The theory behind this new enterprise came from two American Fulbright scholars, Raymond Dasmann and Archie Mossman, who had carried out their research on cattle ranches in Rhodesia's lowveld. By farming with a wide variety of indigenous species that utilised different parts of the habitat and had a natural resistance to diseases and parasites they believed that more meat could be produced per hectare, at a lower cost, than with cattle. It was a good message to put across to the reputedly 'meat-hungry' Zulu participants of our ACE courses.

In spite of the very basic facilities, Nyala Game Ranch proved adequate for our needs until mid-March, when a cyclone hit Zululand and it received one of the highest monthly rainfall figures on record. Roads and bridges were swept away and the world around our tent turned into a swamp. As we were all constantly wet, Tuareg came down with a persistent case of bronchitis, and if my Land Rover had not also chosen this time to break down, I suspect that June would have taken her son and gone back to Rhodesia.

The situation was saved by Quentin and Annette Mann, two strong supporters of the project, who arrived one day and took us back to their home to dry out. While there I used the opportunity to phone Nolly Zaloumis and ask whether the Society would in any way be able to assist with better accommodation. The best they could do was increase my salary to nearly what it had been at Cwaka College – but there we had also been given a free house.

Eventually the rain ended, and with the sun once more shining, the luxuriant Zululand bush produced its finest autumn show. All around us young impala, zebra and wildebeest frolicked in the long grass, and even the baby Owen-Smith started smiling again. We had not joined the Wildlife Society for the money anyway.

By May, when the schools stopped extra-curricular activities because of the mid-term exams, we had held 14 courses, including those run while at Cwaka. Most of them were for high-school pupils, but weekend excursions had also been held for students from the University of Zululand and Eshowe Teacher's Training College. In most cases we were given permission to pick the participants up at 10 o'clock on Friday morning and return with them on Sunday evening, which because of the large distances involved usually meant that we only arrived home late that night. The rest of my week was spent organising venues and guest speakers, visiting schools to arrange courses and show films on wildlife. It was a full week, with little time for relaxation, but we were our own bosses and believed that we were making a worthwhile contribution to nature conservation in South Africa.

The young men and women on our courses were the privileged few, who in spite of the odds that apartheid stacked against them had made it through to a secondary education. But the cost had not just been financial. The majority of them had never herded cattle or goats in their youth, nor had their elders told them stories about how their forefathers once lived with wild animals. In fact, most of them were born and raised in the crowded townships around South Africa's cities, and unlike the CAP demonstrators they were eager to learn and hungry for excitement.

I also found their aesthetic appreciation of nature to be no different to that of the white children we had also run courses for. Neil might have been right about the very basic conservation needs of rural Zulus, but these young urbanised black men and women were a new breed of South Africans, whose world view was closer to that of Europeans than that of their own parents. They were clearly an important target for the ACE Project, but with our limited resources what was the best way to get our conservation message through to them in the short time they were with us?

Judged by the joyous singing of the participants on their way home, the courses appeared to be a success, but would a single weekend on a game ranch have a lasting effect? For the more politicised students it could take a day just to break down the suspicion and distrust created by our racially segregated society. If the ACE Project was to have any chance of real success I needed more time with them, to find out what was going on inside their heads.

On the positive side, ACE had been given good publicity in the English and Zulu press. It had also received some substantial donations from individuals and companies, including the loan of a Volkswagen minibus by Avis Rent-a-Car. We now had sufficient resources to run a small 'feel-good' project, but although this would have been enough for most Society members, I wanted ACE to achieve tangible results, and hopefully be an incentive for other organisations in South Africa to start similar programmes.

On returning to school every participant had been asked to write an account of their experiences, telling us what they found to be most interesting. To encourage them to put real effort into their feedback, I had promised to hold a longer field excursion in the winter vacation for participants chosen by the quality of their essays, as well as their interest shown during the course. More than half of them submitted essays, many with moving accounts of what they learned and how the weekend had affected them:

- Let me confess that the birds, the grass, the trees and wild animals were as useful as a pair of old boots to me. Modern life and its wonders built a barrier between nature and me. For 16 years I walked with my eyes closed. My eyes are open today.
- Standing on guard one night I heard the wind singing softly among the branches. I spent an hour with nature entertaining me. Before that we had been two strangers walking side by side, not having been introduced.
- The trip for me was like a journey to our ancestors. I had not thought there could be such a place.
- Excitement fills to capacity my capillaries. All that beauty cannot be defined by words.
- The days at Nyala Game Ranch were the happiest, mind-opening and most informative in my life.
- Will the coming generations spit on our graves for the way we have used the land?

When Avis donated us a new minibus I came up with a plan to fulfil the Society's need for publicity and enable me to spend more time with the best of the participants. We would make the promised holiday excursion into a really high-profile event by taking them on a 'Zulu safari' to Botswana and Rhodesia. In Botswana they would be able to see how an independent African country was conserving its wildlife, while Rhodesia was a leader in many conservation fields, but unlike South Africa had no segregation policy in its parks and resorts.

Avis Rent-a-Car's managing director, Noel de Villiers, agreed to our using their vehicle on the safari, as well as for a preliminary trip to organise the itinerary. Society members Quentin and Annette Mann and Joan Kuyper offered their minibuses, and Arthur Konigkramer, editor of the Zulu language newspaper *Ilanga* also decided to join us with his private Land Rover. With my personal vehicle this would enable us to select 15 students and eight teachers who, together with the five drivers, the Mann's twin sons and Tuareg, would make a grand total of 31. Nolly gave his blessing to our recce trip, but final approval for the safari would have to come from the Natal Branch of the Wildlife Society at their next monthly meeting.

On the recce we got great support from everyone we spoke to, enabling us to draw up an itinerary that included talks by Botswana's Director of Wildlife, the BaTawana Tribal Council that had first established Moremi Game Reserve, park wardens, professional hunters, wildlife researchers and even veterinarians. We would be visiting six national parks or game reserves, the Victoria Falls, Great Zimbabwe, a crocodile farm and an eland domestication project. A day would also be spent at Mushandike and Mlezu, as well as two of the short-duration grazing schemes in Rhodesia's Tribal Trust Lands.

June and I arrived back very excited, but when I contacted Nolly he told me that the Natal Branch Committee had turned down the trip! They did not think it justified the expense, and were not happy about my having gone so far with arrangements before getting their approval. It was no doubt their way of reminding me, and perhaps Nolly, that I worked for them.

Until then the Branch committee had shown little interest in what we did, but as Nolly always backed our activities, I had run the project as I saw fit. Consequently, the rejection of our Zulu safari – particularly as it was the high-profile event John Fowlkes had requested – took me by surprise. But my greatest concern was that, as time was short, we had already chosen and informed the students, as well as made arrangements with the people we would be meeting along the way.

After talking to the Manns, Arthur Konigkramer and Joan Kuyper, we decided to try and raise the funds for the trip ourselves. Each of us contributed money to buy food on route, the headmasters of schools the participants came from contributed bedding, cooking pots, eating utensils and whatever provisions they could, and the managing director of Kaymac Industries, Ken MacKenzie, donated R800 for petrol. As we had either been offered free accommodation or would be camping along the way, the trip would cost the Society nothing but my time, so Nolly agreed to us going.

We set off on the day after schools broke up, spending our first freezing night in a patch of blue gum trees just south of Pretoria. It soon became apparent that most of the teachers and students were not used to roughing it, and there was much muttering about having 'given up sheets and beds for a tent on the hard, cold ground'. Not being able to bath or at least have a full body wash the next morning brought more grumbling. Our soft modern lifestyle had taken its toll on the descendants of the tribe whose bravery and endurance were legendary in Southern Africa.

Camping at a dam near Gaborone the next night was just as cold, but this time it was on foreign soil – a first for almost everyone in the group – and there were no more complaints. However, King Shaka must have turned in his grave when a cow walked innocently through the camp, causing two of the lady teachers to scuttle into their tents. Less than a week later, they would both redeem themselves by walking on foot for three hours through 'lion-infested' Moremi Game Reserve.

In Gaborone our group was welcomed by Botswana's Director of Wildlife, Mr Matenge, who told us that his government regarded wildlife conservation as one of its most important national responsibilities. We then visited a number of local environmental education projects before moving on via the Makgadikgadi and Nxai Pans to Maun, where we were given various talks on tourism and trophy hunting, before spending two nights in Moremi Game Reserve.

As it was established and at that time managed by the BaTawana Tribal Council, Moremi was an excellent example of local people conserving wildlife. After a talk by the reserve warden some of the students accompanied him to shoot an impala for our dinner, providing us with a good lesson on the difference between preservation and conservation. Although a few of the women were unhappy about such a beautiful animal being killed, once it had been roasted on the fire everyone approved of their first taste of venison. On the following day part of our group had a close encounter with a pride of 16 lions, and everyone saw plenty of big game.

At Savuti, in Chobe National Park, we got our first close-up view of elephants – very close up! Four large bulls came into the camp and walked nonchalantly between the tents, while their occupants scattered and took refuge in vehicles or the ablution block. A few of the braver tourists and students hid behind bushes and took photographs, until one of the elephants became irritated by all the attention it was receiving. After flapping its ears to show its annoyance it charged, causing people to pop out of the undergrowth like rabbits and hightail it for the showers. Fortunately, it was not serious and stopped after a few metres, appearing to have rather enjoyed the chaos it had caused.

The track from Maun to Kasane was deep sand, and although on our recce trip I had got the Avis minibus through without getting stuck, the less experienced off-road drivers frequently got bogged down. The result was that both vehicles and owners took strain, for which we would soon pay. Just before Victoria Falls the Mann's vehicle burnt out its clutch and just managed to limp into the little tourist town. But worse was to come; sand got into the engine of Joan Kuyper's old minibus and it seized, leaving us no option but to rail it back to Natal. At this point the Manns informed us that they wanted to go straight down the main road back to Natal. Taking 30 people on a low-budget camping trip had been no easy matter and when Arthur decided that he had also had enough it looked like our Zulu safari was over.

While the Manns' minibus had its clutch plate replaced, June and I took the group to see the Falls. Here the obvious wonder felt by the Zulu teachers and students lifted my spirits, and by the time we had visited a crocodile farm and done an evening cruise on the Zambezi, I had a solution to propose: if we all stayed together as far as Great Zimbabwe, and the two leaving vehicles then took most of the camping equipment with them, I would ask the extension officers organising our visit to the TTL grazing schemes if they could provide us with transport. From there some of the group could catch a train back to Zululand. By the next morning everything had been arranged. We were on our way again.

At Great Zimbabwe I decided to again visit the stone ruins at night, and most of the group joined me. Walking by the light of a half-moon along the narrow passageways into the ancient temple that once had been the heart of a vibrant African empire was a very moving experience. Before leaving one of the teachers led us in a prayer for the peaceful coming together of blacks and whites on the sub-continent, and when he had finished we all sang 'Nkosi Sikelel' iAfrica'. I was glad it was too dark for anyone to see the tears in my eyes.

For me, our next few days were the most valuable of the trip. Overgrazing was something that everyone who lived in or had visited a 'native reserve' knew about. It was perhaps the biggest conservation problem in the sub-continent, one for which nobody in South Africa had yet come up with an effective solution. But here in the Gutu and Chibi TTLs we were introduced to communal farmers who had used short-duration grazing to achieve remarkable results. On their land perennial grasses flourished, or were clearly recovering, while in the neighbouring areas there were only annuals, and large tracts of bare ground. As we walked through the veld our guides also pointed out the tracks of guinea fowl, francolin, hares and duiker – wild creatures that were coming back because of the permanent grass cover.

Both of the SDG schemes were under the authority of individual chiefs who had convinced their followers to combine their cattle and rotate them through paddocks divided by simple fences, in many places just strands of

wire strung from tree to tree. But what impressed me most was the enthusiasm of the local Tribal Councils as they took us around their grazing lands,
and the obvious pride they felt in what had been achieved.

After providing us with an excellent traditional Karanga lunch, our Chibi
hosts confided that they had been 'terrified' when they were told that a group
of Zulus was coming to visit them. According to local legend Zulus were all
fearsome giants over two metres high, and when our group arrived and they
saw that none of them was very tall they had been quite disappointed. How
were they going to tell the people in their home villages that Zulus were just
ordinary people like themselves?

Before parting ways we camped next to the Tokwe River. It was a cool
and sparkling evening, reminiscent of many that I had spent on the banks
of similar dry riverbeds in the Kaokoveld. Now that politics had stopped me
from returning to the ethnic homelands of South West Africa, the lowveld of
Rhodesia seemed like a good alternative place to work.

When we got back to Natal I was told that Joan Kuyper had asked the
Wildlife Society to pay for her vehicle repairs and the cost of railing it back
from Victoria Falls. As they had not authorised the trip many of the Branch
Committee members felt that June and I should be held responsible. Having
used our own money to pay the students' rail fares home, as well as our share
of the trip's expenses, we were hardly in a position to do so. Fortunately Nolly
was able to convince them that as the trip had been made in the Society's
name and had promoted the objectives of the ACE Project, it should cover
these unforeseen expenses. I was very grateful to Nolly, but it did not improve
my relationship with the committee.

*   *   *

Before leaving on the trip June used some of the money she had saved for
her daughter Kerry's education, and paid the deposit on a one-roomed flat in
Mtunzini, a small village on the coast. It faced onto a golf course and looked
down over the mangrove-fringed estuary of the Umlalazi River. It was not the
wilds of Africa, but would certainly make our life more comfortable.

An advantage of living in Mtunzini was that Ian Garland, who had been
one of the main supporters of Lynn Hurry's field excursions, lived on a farm
just outside the village. An expert on indigenous trees, Ian had planted an
arboretum of coastal forest species and built an environmental resource

centre under their shady canopy, which was used as a stopover on Wilderness Leadership School courses.

In August a group of Society members interested in environmental education held a meeting at the centre on Ian's farm. They decided that a sub-committee should be appointed to guide ACE's future activities – no doubt to stop me coming up with any more hare-brained ideas. Its first meeting was scheduled for late October, and I was asked to prepare an annual report on the Project's achievements to date as well as a work plan for the following year.

By then we had run 22 weekend courses, of which 16 had been for Zulu high schools, colleges and the university, two for coloured schools, one for an Indian school in Durban and three for whites – including an excursion for some of the Wildlife Society members' own children. A total of over 300 pupils, students, teachers and lecturers had taken part. Added to this we had held many wildlife film shows, with audiences of up to 500, and manned a conservation education stand at the Zululand Agricultural Show. I had also been interviewed on the English, Zulu and external services of the SABC, while June had written an article on our Zulu safari for *African Wildlife*.

It looked impressive for our first year, but what had we really achieved? Lynn Hurry had the advantage of being with his teacher trainees for the whole period of their diploma, and his weekend visits to game ranches were simply an opportunity for them to experience in the field what he had taught them in the classroom. Apart from our trip to Botswana and Rhodesia, the time I had with each course participant was just one weekend – hardly enough to turn them into future environmentally conscious citizens.

I was also worried about the numbers. During the year we had taken out less than 10 per cent of the matric students, and according to government statistics at the time only about 10 per cent of Zulu children who went to school – and many did not – actually reached matric. In my report I concluded that 'for all our Don Quixote like efforts we need to face the fact that the only organisation with the resources to implement an effective environmental awareness programme is the KwaZulu government's education department. Therefore a more realistic role for the Wildlife Society would be to encourage and assist them to take on this responsibility.'

How this could be done came from the biology teachers we took to Botswana and Rhodesia, who told me that a section on ecology and nature conservation was now included in the matric syllabus. But as they had not been taught the subject at school or college, most of them left it to last, or advised their pupils to learn it parrot-fashion from the textbook. I proposed that in the following

WHEN IT IS LATE AFTERNOON

year the ACE Project offer a field-based, in-service training course in ecology and nature conservation to the KwaZulu Education Department. This would both improve the quality of the teachers' lessons and indirectly reach all high school biology students.

I also recommended that the participants attending our in-service training courses be encouraged to start wildlife clubs in their schools. In this way their pupils could be given extended exposure to conservation, and not just the two days we had so far provided. Lastly, I asked the Natal Branch to consider appointing a Zulu-speaking assistant for me, to help me provide support to any school wildlife clubs that formed.

My recommendations were not only accepted by the sub-committee, but the Natal Branch increased my salary and decided to pay June R60 a month for her 'secretarial services'. This enabled us to rent a larger flat, take a week's holiday on the Transkei coast, and for the first time have money to spare. Although it was not enough to undertake another expedition to Angola, it was sufficient for an air ticket to Windhoek.

My reason was that in May BAD's Deputy Minister had 'approved in principle the establishment of a conservation area covering 34 000 square kilometres for the peoples of the Kaokoland and Damaraland Homelands'. A month later Dr Anton Rupert, Chairman of the South African Nature Foundation, issued a public statement on behalf of Prime Minister John Vorster to the effect that the government would soon be proclaiming the new game reserve. Dr Rupert added that a master plan for conservation and tourism in the two ethnic homelands had also been commissioned, and would be carried out by the University of Pretoria.

It was the news that I had been waiting four years for. But what did 'for the peoples of the Kaokoland and Damaraland homelands' really mean? Had it been negotiated, as promised in 1970, and if so who had been present at the negotiations? Was it white government officials deciding on their behalf, or were the traditional leaders involved? If so, knowing the major divisions between the Herero and Himba headmen, did they all support the proposed conservation area and its boundaries – as well as the Damara leaders? Even if they had all agreed, what benefits would go to them? No one in Natal could answer these questions.

On my arrival in Windhoek I contacted Inge Peters, the SWA Wildlife Society's secretary. After hearing the reason for my visit she arranged a meeting with the branch chairman and some of its prominent members, but they had no other information than what was stated by Dr Rupert. In our discussion I expressed the opinion that the Park would not succeed unless the local people were fully informed and involved in its implementation. I added that there was also a need for conservation education amongst black South West Africans, and in this field the Society could play a crucial role.

They told me they had already started a project for white school children from Windhoek, and that they might consider including some 'Bantu' pupils as well – although funds were limited, as were voluntary workers to run the courses. Much more was needed, I said, including getting support from the country's black political leaders for the new Kaokoveld game reserve. 'But that would mean standing on the government's toes,' one of them said. 'That is just what needs to be done,' I replied.

The Wildlife Society members I spoke to were all German-speaking captains of business and industry, who saw nature conservation from a scientific perspective. To them politics, or anything to do with their black countrymen, should be left in the hands of the government. Although Angola was on the brink of independence, and Rhodesia and South West Africa were fighting liberation wars, they had still not thought of involving blacks in conservation or encouraging them to join their snow-white Society! In the end all I was able to achieve was a promise that they would send free copies of *African Wildlife* and their local *Roan News* to the homeland leaders and other 'moderate Bantus'. I had little confidence that even this would be done.

While in SWA I also spoke to Piet de Villiers, the nature conservator BAD had appointed for Kaokoland. He and his family were living in Windhoek, but he assured me that it was not of his own choosing. He also told me that senior government officials were still using the homeland as their private hunting grounds, and his investigations of suspected illegal hunting cases were being obstructed. I returned to South Africa frustrated and disturbed by what I had heard, but at least the western Kaokoveld was about to be proclaimed.

*   *   *

Back in Natal I set about getting the support of the KwaZulu government for our proposed in-service teacher training course. During the year June and I had got to know a number of prominent people in its education department, including the principal of the elite KwaDlangezwa High School, Dr Sibusiso Bengu. An eloquent, soft-spoken man, he obtained his PhD from the University of Geneva, and his thesis had been published under the title:

Chasing Gods Not Our Own. After we had run a course for his pupils he became a strong supporter of ACE, and invited June and me to dinner at his home near Mtunzini.

At the time Dr Bengu was Secretary General of the Inkatha Cultural Liberation Movement, and had written its founding charter. He explained that Inkatha had been created to promote the Zulu language and values, in an attempt to stop them from losing their cultural identity along the road to modernisation. I could certainly relate to this goal, but knew that the conservative Society members would have reservations about my having contact with any kind of 'liberation movement'.

Dr Bengu supported my plan to work with in-service teachers and promised to discuss it with KwaZulu's Minister of Education, Mr Nxumalo, a personal friend of his. A few weeks later he told me that the Minister had accepted the idea in principle, but that the department's director, Mr Steyn, would also need to approve it. I reported this to the ACE sub-committee members, and as Ian Garland knew Mr Steyn, he undertook to get his support.

Over the Christmas holidays I visited Neil and Creina Alcock, who had recently moved from Maria Ratschitz Mission to Mdukatshani, an abused 'labour farm' adjoining the Msinga Reserve in the Thukela valley. It was one of the poorest and most violent parts of Natal, a place where young Zulus regularly killed each other in faction fights – rural gang warfare motivated by cattle theft and clan conflicts. The police had little control here, only visiting the district after battles had occurred to collect the bodies. Neil had moved to Mdukatshani – which meant 'where the grass has been lost' – so that he could put his social and land-management philosophies to the ultimate test. If they could improve the lot of Msinga's neglected inhabitants, then they could be successfully applied to any other communal area in the country.

In their new stone and local wood home, perched on a cliff above the Thukela River, overlooking Zululand's 'frontier district', Neil and I talked late into the night. Their first year at Mdukatshani had not been easy, and the lives of some staff members had been threatened. The clear message from the local gangs was to go back to where they had come from. A few of them had.

'A white skin is still good protection around here,' Neil joked. 'They haven't threatened Creina or me yet. But wait until we start being seen as part of the community. Then things might be different.'

One issue we discussed was in whose hands the environmental destiny of South Africa really lay. Was it the academics that made government policy, or was it the rural farmers whose stock actually overgrazed the land, who grew crops on steep hill-slopes and hunted the wildlife? Although Neil could see the value in teaching ecology at schools, he believed it was the traditional leaders who should be our highest priority. As he was having a meeting with local indunas and their councillors at Mdukatshani in a few days' time, he invited me to talk to them about nature conservation.

On the appointed day I joined the gathering in the shade of a large tree near the Alcocks' house, where Neil introduced me to the stern-faced men. For much of the previous night I had lain awake thinking about what to say. While in the Kaokoveld I had often discussed livestock marketing with Herero and Himba traditional leaders, but not wildlife conservation. In the end I just scribbled down a few notes and hoped for guidance from Neil once the meeting started. But he gave me none. As I rambled on, fishing for issues that would elicit some sort of response, I noticed a few older indunas were nodding their heads. Soon many of them were clearly asleep in their chairs. At least the younger men had the courtesy to hear me out, but from the stand-ard of the questions they asked at the end of my talk, it was obvious that they too were not very interested in what I had to say.

When they had all politely shaken my hand and gone back to more impor-tant activities, Neil was characteristically to the point: 'The trouble is that you do not understand these people's lives any more than they do yours. Without common ground people cannot communicate.' The Msinga indunas might not have learned much from me that day, but I had been taught a valuable lesson.

That night Neil and Creina told me of their idea to bring a group of influen-tial Zulu chiefs and indunas together to discuss conservation, and they asked if I was prepared to organise the venue and programme. The theme would be the economic value of wildlife. 'To poor people that's a good starting point,' Neil said. 'If we can show them that wild animals could one day fill their bel-lies or pay their children's school fees they might then listen to all the other reasons for conserving nature.'

As Creina attended the Natal Branch meetings in her capacity as the edi-tor of *African Wildlife*, she was well aware of the criticism that had been lev-elled at me 'for getting too involved in politics'. Therefore, she suggested that the meeting should not be held under the banner of the ACE project, but that CAP publicly take the lead. Neil was already regarded as a left-wing lib-eral – a rank higher than me in Natal terminology, but he did not work for the Society, and Creina's 'editorial discretion' provided her with the freedom to delve into controversial subjects with political leaders.

The venue I chose was the Butler family's Sungulwane Game Ranch near

Mkhuzi. I knew they would not be concerned by any political fallout, and their youngest son, Roger, was a fluent Zulu linguist who would be an ideal host and raconteur. As we envisaged a whole weekend, I arranged a morning visit to Ubizane Ranch for talks on trophy hunting and wildlife capture, and in the afternoon to go to the Bester Brother's game meat butchery – to see and taste the end product of game ranching. The manager of Southern Sun's Zululand Safari Lodge, just outside the Hluhluwe Game Reserve, also offered to provide the whole group with lunch and show them around their up-market 40-bed tourist establishment.

While I was putting the programme together Neil and Creina contacted Nico Smit, who gave the meeting his full support and agreed to select and officially invite the appropriate chiefs and their councillors. They would come mainly from areas where wildlife still occurred or could be re-introduced, and therefore had the potential to make a significant contribution to the local economy. He also invited the KwaZulu Ministers of Agriculture, Education and Justice, and promised to attend himself.

All three cabinet ministers, ten chiefs and their councillors, as well as over 20 members of KwaZulu's Legislative Assembly arrived at Sungulwane on Friday afternoon – together with an overloaded truck full of uninvited guests from the corridor between Hluhluwe and Umfolozi Game Reserves. The latter group had come to complain about bush pigs destroying their crops and lions killing their cattle. On top of that, they added, they had recently dug the grave of a family member who was shot while poaching, and demanded to know from us whether a wild animal's life was worth more than that of a human being.

Many of the chiefs had heard similar complaints before and sympathised with the demonstrators. Predators, hippos and even elephants on the Mozambique border caused considerable livestock and crop losses to the people living alongside Natal's game reserves. One of them summed up the prevailing situation by saying: 'Even if we protect our wildlife – we get nothing from it.' Everybody knew the truth of his words.

Fortunately the cabinet ministers were on hand to calm the situation down, but there were many more tense moments and tough questions over the next two days. It was the first time that such senior delegations of black leaders had got together to discuss conservation and they had a lot to get off their chests. At one point a government official told the group that when white farms full of game were handed over to KwaZulu it was all killed: 'Black people destroyed what could have been a valuable resource.'

'I remember,' replied one of the older chiefs, 'when the plains of my country were full of game. Then the whites said that the tsetse fly must be killed. This fly could only live on game, we were told, so they sent for whites from all over South Africa to kill the game on my plains and there was a terrible slaughter. There were hunting parties everywhere, trampling on our fields, shooting, shooting, shooting. Now, when it is late afternoon, you say we must put back the animals that were killed.'

But when we got past the jibes and sparring, when everyone had had their fill of roasted game meat – the first time that most of the black guests had legally eaten it – we all got down to talking about the business of game farming. The value of wildlife was an eye-opener to most of the chiefs. On Ubizane Ranch, professional hunter Gary Kelly told the group that the trophy fee for a nyala was R200, and it was worth even more if caught and sold alive, while Brian Thring showed how wild animals were captured with a dart gun. Roger Butler explained the economics and management of Sungulwane Ranch and at the Bester Brother's venison butchery everyone tasted and the VIPs took home huge polonies made from game meat. Going into a hotel normally reserved for whites only was another first for the traditional leaders.

There were also game drives, on which the excited chiefs and councillors marvelled at species that some of them had never seen before. Everything was interesting to them: wildebeest, zebra, giraffe, impala and warthog – even jackals and hares. A lucky few also saw a group of white rhino. The question on many lips was – how did one acquire wild animals?

The workshop was a great success. Both sides had given their points of view, heard the other's problems and, hopefully, reached a better understanding for working together in the future. In the closing speeches KwaZulu's Minister of Agriculture, Owen Sithole, said he hoped that this would be the first of many such meetings, and so did his director, Nico Smit. Other traditional leaders were equally grateful for our brief coming together. One of them was Chief Tembe. A few years later the Tembe Elephant Reserve was proclaimed between Ndumu and Kosi Bay.

*   *   *

In January I addressed a gathering of KwaZulu's headmasters at Ulundi, the capital of KwaZulu, and they gave their full support to our ecology and nature conservation in-service training proposal. A few weeks later Dr Bengu and

Keith Cooper arranged a weekend at Umgeni Valley Game Ranch for senior Wildlife Society members and a group of prominent Zulu educationalists, to also acquaint them with the ACE programme's objectives and activities.

It turned out to be a remarkable gathering. Apart from June and myself, the Wildlife Society was represented by Nolly Zaloumis, Keith Cooper and Dave Hatton, an ex-NPB ranger who was the public relations officer for BP, a major sponsor of the ACE Project. On the KwaZulu side, Dr Bengu would later become Minister of Education in South Africa's first democratic government, Professor Nyembezi, then a prominent academic, would be appointed as KwaZulu-Natal's Director of Education, and Otty Nxumalo served as the province's Director General from 1994 to 2000. Although Keith had previously had some contact with the Transkei government, it was the first time that the Society had discussed conservation issues with such an eminent group of Zulu leaders – and the sky did not fall!

In February the KwaZulu government gave the in-service teacher training courses official recognition. The education department would select the participants and pay their rail fares to and from Mtunzini. In March the first group of 10 teachers arrived, and after an introductory lecture from Ian Garland we spent the next three days visiting marine, forest and savanna ecosystems in the vicinity, using worksheets to study the ecological principles and processes that governed the way they functioned. The teachers then moved to Ubizane Game Ranch to learn about the economic value of wildlife, and on the last day visited the Hluhluwe game reserve.

A few months earlier I had requested permission for the teachers to stay a night in Hluhluwe, but this had been refused by the Natal Parks Board. At the time, non-white visitors were not permitted to enter areas under the Board's control, and just allowing them through the entrance gate was seen as a major concession. Nevertheless, once they were inside the reserve Warden Keith Micklejohn and his rangers went out of their way to make the teachers' visit as informative as possible.

The course had not been easy. Apartheid policies had caused deep-seated hostility towards whites, and teachers were one of the most politicised groups in Zulu society. On their first night camping some of the participants told us that they did not accept having to 'sleep on the ground like peasants' – even though I was sleeping under the stars beside them. As they had simply been instructed to attend the course they were also unsure of why they had been sent 'into the bush', and were very suspicious of our motives for teaching them about conservation.

The next morning Ian Garland's exceptional knowledge of indigenous trees, their Zulu names and traditional uses helped to reduce the tension, while the beauty of the wild places we visited – which most of them had not previously known existed – seemed to make their thin mattresses a little softer. Around the campfire that night, one of the participants confided that he had been teaching about ferns and mosses for many years, but until then had never actually seen one. Another told us that even though ecology was now part of the syllabus, because he knew nothing about it he had just told his class to pray that not many questions on it came up in their exams. The others laughed, but most of them admitted that they had the same problem.

Seeing wildlife in its natural habitat in Ubizane and Hluhluwe provided even more exciting experiences and some of the teachers told me that for the first time they saw game reserves as part of South Africa's priceless heritage. By the end of the week the atmosphere was relaxed, and our discussions ranged across a broad range of topics, from animal behaviour to the racist laws that prevented blacks from visiting many of the places we had been to. But there were no polemics; walking through nature and camping together had brought us closer, and opened our minds to issues beyond the politics of our divided country. When we parted we no longer spoke as whites or blacks, but as South Africans who shared a beautiful land, and needed to keep it so.

*　*　*

One of the recommendations that came out of the Umgeni Valley meeting was that the sub-committee directing the ACE Project should be more racially representative. The members chosen were Nolly Zaloumis as chairman, Dr Sibusiso Bengu, Ian Garland, Dave Hatton and Simeon Gcumisa, who had recently been promoted to vice-principal of Cwaka College. Getting this committee accepted by the Natal Branch of the Society was a major breakthrough, for which Nolly and Keith deserved all the credit.

With more funds being donated to ACE it was also agreed that the Society should appoint the Zulu-speaking person I had requested. After the meeting I asked Simeon if he knew any suitable candidates, and to my surprise he said he would like to apply for the job. His appointment as vice-principal of Cwaka had only been a token, he told me, which gave him more responsibilities but still very little say over the college's internal policies. I warned him about the difficulties and insecurity of working for an NGO, but he applied anyway and was appointed at the beginning of April.

ACE was not the only environmental education project the Natal Branch was now running. It had also purchased the Umgeni Valley Game Ranch, where a parallel initiative, aimed mainly at white school children, was being run by Don Richards, a teacher and ex-Wilderness Leadership School Trails Officer. The property was situated at the foot of the Howick Falls on the Umgeni River, and in October the previous year Nolly had asked me to run a course there for the pupils of the Adam's Mission High School in Southern Natal. It had gone very well, and when the two teachers accompanying them requested we take another group the following year I agreed, even though I planned to move away from such courses.

A few days after Simeon started work for the Society, he and I motored down to Umgeni Valley to run the second Adam's Mission course. The 15 bright-eyed and excited pupils arrived in the late morning, and after a quick lunch we set off on foot down into the valley. It was a sunny day and by the time we reached our camping site, we were all hot and sweaty. As the previous group had swum in a nearby pool in the Umgeni River, I decided to do the same before going on a game viewing hike later in the afternoon.

The rainy season had just ended and I found the pool to be considerably larger, with a relatively strong current flowing through it. After warning those that were not good swimmers to remain in the shallows, I dived into the bracing cold water and swam to a flat rock from where I had a clear view of everyone in the water. Most of the boys plunged in behind me while the girls and the accompanying teacher rested or paddled in a side stream. Simeon, who was not a swimmer, settled down under a tree. It was his first course with me and he was observing how I ran things. In future he would take over the responsibility for the school wildlife clubs, and would then have to run similar courses on his own.

I was very pleased to have Simeon working with me. I had known him for nearly two years, and from the start we had enjoyed each other's company. ACE now also had a committee that I had confidence in overseeing our activities. The most pressing issue was accommodation. June was happy in our flat next to the golf course, but I needed wild animals around me. Although they were predominantly English-speaking, I had also learned that the residents of Mtunzini were quite conservative and suspected that they would not take too kindly to our having regular black visitors. But the biggest problem was where Simeon stayed. South Africa's race laws did not allow him to live in

Mtunzini and it would even be illegal for him to spend a night in our flat. He had applied for a house in Ngwelezane, the township near Empangeni, but it was 20 km away, and the ACE Project had only one vehicle.

The solution I came up with was for both of our families to move into an old double-storey house on Ubizane Ranch. Brian Thring and his wife, Doreen, had no objections to us sharing it, but he first needed permission from the ranch owner, Peter Herbert, before we could move in. Simeon was happy with my plan but June, who had just produced our second son, was non-committal – a sure sign that she did not support me. While sitting on the rock I tried to think of a way of getting her to see the sense in my idea.

My thoughts were broken by hearing voices asking where one of the boys, Linda Magubane, was. Immediately concerned, I told everyone to get out of the pool and look around – perhaps he had walked off into the bush. But some of them had seen him in the water just a few minutes before. 'Then he might have swum across the pool and got out on the other bank,' I said, trying to control my rising feeling of alarm. But, one of them replied, Linda can't swim …

An icy feeling ran down my spine and I dived in, swimming underwater to all parts of the five by ten-metre pool. I felt nothing. While the others combed the surrounding bushes, I continued searching underwater until I was shaking uncontrollably with cold and shock. But there was no sign of Linda. He had drowned right in front of us and been swept downstream. His body was found by the police six days later, five km from where we were swimming.

By the time I gave up looking it was too late to walk out of the valley, so we returned to our campsite. From the teacher I learned that Linda was the only child of a single mother. He was 16 years old and in Standard 9. After the others had gone to bed, Simeon and I sat staring into the fire. We did not talk much. What was there to say? A mother had trusted me to look after her only son and he had drowned.

The following day we packed up and left early. I stayed to show the police where the accident had happened, while Simeon accompanied the teacher and pupils back to Adam's Mission, to inform the headmaster and Linda's family. On the Sunday I also drove to the school and spoke to the staff. I did not see Linda's mother – that would have been more than I could bear. In the afternoon I went to see Nolly Zaloumis at his home and gave him the details of what had happened and then drove on to Mthunzini. When I arrived, June had already heard about the accident. She came out and when she put her arms around me I burst into tears and cried uncontrollably until there were no more tears left inside me.

Simeon attended the funeral on behalf of the Society. When he returned we visited all the in-service training course venues and I introduced him to the various people who were assisting us. We also went through each of the activities that the teachers would be doing. While at Ubizana, Brian Thring told me that Peter Herbert had agreed to our staying in the old house and would charge us only a nominal rent.

When we got back to Mtunzini, I phoned Dave Hatton and informed him that Simeon and I planned to move to Ubizane after the next in-service training course. Dave was not happy with the idea and reminded me that under South Africa's apartheid laws it was illegal for our two families to live in the same house. Because of this, he added, the sub-committee would not give us permission to do so. I again went through all the practical reasons for the move and argued that, as the house was deep in the bush and on private property, nobody need even know that we were staying together. But Dave was unmoved. Now annoyed by his conservative attitude and still emotional after the Umgeni Valley tragedy, I told him that if the Society planned to stop us from moving, I would resign. Dave replied that they would then be forced to accept my resignation, and put the phone down.

Nolly Zaloumis was my last resort. After telling him about my conversation with Dave, I requested his support for our proposed move to Ubizana. But Nolly was also unsympathetic and told me that, as chairman of the sub-committee, he agreed with what Dave had told me. I lost my temper: when we were living in a tent on Nyala Game Ranch and Tuareg was continually sick, the Society didn't give a damn! In spite of promises that were made they had still not given us a cent towards our Mtunzini flat. But now they were telling us where we may or may not live.

But no one was listening. The line had gone dead. Nolly had not even had the courtesy to hear me out. Now I really lost control and exploded to June, who had been listening to my side of the conversation – but she agreed with Nolly and Dave. That was the last straw. I stormed out of the flat and walked onto the golf course. Did nobody understand that if we meekly accepted the government's racist laws the ACE programme was dead? I was the one that had to win over black, very politically aware teachers and students to our conservation cause. Did they think that was easy in the sick society we lived in? They all complimented me on the successes we had achieved, but these had only been possible because we were seen to be challenging the apartheid system, and not bowing down to it.

A little calmer, I returned to the flat to discuss the situation more rationally with June. But she had taken the children and gone. In a cold fury, I packed my rucksack, left a signed cheque for the rent and another for the few rands that remained in my account, and then walked to the main road. I needed to get away. South West Africa's open spaces beckoned – it was where I belonged. The second car that came past picked me up and took me all the way to Johannesburg. Two days later I was in Windhoek. From there I got a lift to Gobabeb, the desert research station where Pieter Mostert was now working. I did not tell anyone where I had gone.

On 16 June 1976, three weeks after I left Mtunzini, thousands of school children in Soweto, Johannesburg's sprawling black township, marched to Orlando Stadium to protest against 50 per cent of their syllabus being taught in Afrikaans. They were blocked by the police, who when stones were thrown at them fired teargas and some live rounds. A 14-year-old boy was killed and others injured. During that afternoon and evening the West Rand Administration Board's offices, beer-halls and vehicles were attacked and burnt. A WRAB official was beaten to death and a number of other white bystanders injured, while more school children were shot by security forces. Over the next few days the destruction escalated and the death toll rose.

At Gobabeb, we listened on Pieter's transistor radio as one of the most dramatic events in South Africa's history unfolded. I eventually came to my senses when we heard one night that the violence had spread to other parts of the country, including Zululand University's campus, only 20 km from Mtunzini. I had to get back.

Before reaching Durban I phoned Nolly Zaloumis, who invited me to come to his home in Kloof. Quite legitimately, the Natal Branch Committee had been furious about my having just walked off the job, and had accepted my verbal resignation to Dave Hatton. Nolly, who knew the difficulties I worked under, was more sympathetic. At my request, he agreed to convene a sub-committee meeting, so that I could put my side of the story. I then hitchhiked to Mtunzini to see my wife.

My sudden and complete disappearance had obviously been very distressing for June. However, with her characteristic fortitude she had controlled her personal feelings and helped Simeon and Ian Garland run the in-service training course I had missed. In appreciation for this, and to help her cope financially, the Society had increased her salary from R60 to R120 a month – a gesture that was sincerely appreciated. Everyone else had acted admirably. I was the only villain in the piece.

A few weeks later the ACE sub-committee came together to decide on my fate. I was given a fair chance to state my case, but there was really very little I could say in my defence. No matter how much stress I had been under, it was totally unacceptable for me to have just disappeared, and inexcusable to have abandoned Simeon just before the start of his first in-service training course. I knew that the Natal Branch Committee would not just accept their black sheep back into the fold. I had handed them my head on a plate, and the members who disagreed with the way I was running the project would at the very least demand their pound of flesh.

June and I were excluded from the sub-committee's deliberations, but I later heard that both Simeon and Dr Bengu had argued for my reinstatement, and with Nolly's deciding vote in my favour, I was offered another chance. But there was a price to pay. In the future I would have to work directly under Ian Garland's supervision and my salary would be cut substantially.

Going back to the dire financial straits we had lived under at the start of the project was a difficult pill to swallow. But most of all I knew that I could not run somebody else's ACE Project, so I turned down their offer. However, Simeon remained with the Wildlife Society, and with the help of Ian Garland and other members would take over 400 teachers on the in-service training course I had drawn up, earning himself the name of 'Mister Conservation' in KwaZulu.

After the meeting June returned to Rhodesia, while I visited the Alcocks at Mdukatshani. Here Neil told me that things were still pretty hot in the valley, and he was not talking about the weather. He could certainly use another white skin around to help out at the remoter cattle posts. It was unusual for Neil to specify a person's race, but he explained that only a European could get a licence from the police to carry a gun – and a firearm was needed to stay healthy in this part of the Thukela valley. I knew that working with Neil and Creina would be an inspirational experience, but the only accommodation was a traditional Zulu hut. My marriage to June was in tatters and I did not think it could survive the tensions that the security situation and living in a dung hut would bring.

In 1983 Neil Alcock was taking participants back from a meeting to discuss a truce between Msinga's warring factions when their vehicle was ambushed. Five Zulus were killed and Neil was fatally wounded. He died on the roadside before help arrived.

* * *

While at Mdukatshani I received a message that Ian Player wanted me to come and see him. At the Wilderness Leadership School office near Durban, Ian told me that they had been given a grant to start trails for black South Africans, and asked if I would I be interested in running them. The offer was flattering – at least Ian recognised what ACE had achieved. I accepted, and after organising a flat on the beach at Amanzimtoti – where I knew June would be happy – set off for Salisbury to pick up my family.

But along the way I had second thoughts. I would be going back to a similar situation to that while working for the Wildlife Society. Apart from the Alcocks and very few others, conservationists in Natal seemed terrified of challenging the racist policies prescribed by Pretoria. I also needed to live in the bush again.

In the late afternoon I reached Rutenga in the Rhodesian lowveld, where I was stopped at a police checkpoint. There had been some 'terrorist' activity in the area and they advised me to spend the night at the local club. The little railway junction town was not far from the TTLs we had visited on our Zulu safari the year before, and over a few beers I talked about Allan Savory's grazing system with the local cattle ranchers sitting around the bar. Although they knew little about what was happening in the TTLs, they told me that the biggest landowner in the lowveld, Liebigs Rhodesia, which marketed its beef products under the Fray Bentos label, had hired Allan Savory as its range management consultant. They added that the company had advertised for a section manager on its nearby Towla Ranch.

The next morning I went to see Mike Gawler, the overall manager of Liebigs' giant 550 000 ha property, and told him of my previous experience. Fortunately, I had copies of the various papers and articles I had written with me. He was clearly interested and suggested I come back in a few weeks' time, when Allan Savory himself would be visiting the ranch. Mike would not be there, but he arranged for us to meet on Wanezi section, which was run by his brother Bob.

The chance of working with the man who had been rocking both Rhodesia's range management and political boats seemed almost too good to be true. However, there was the country's security situation to consider. The liberation forces had made major inroads into the north and east of Rhodesia, and the white farmers there were living under virtual siege. I also knew that a group of motor cyclists had been gunned down by guerrillas on the main road between the South African border and Rutenga. But on the positive side, the American Secretary of State, Henry Kissinger, had finally got Ian Smith to admit that black rule was inevitable and agree to working towards an interim multiracial government in the country. Rhodesia was also June's home.

CHAPTER THIRTEEN

A RHODESIAN RANCH

In October 1976 June, our two boys and I drove down to Wanezi for our meeting with Bob Gawler and Allan Savory. After leaving Tuareg and Kyle with Bob's wife Denise, we flew in Allan's private aircraft to Sovalele – the northernmost section of Liebig's Ranch – to meet Alex Barclay, its manager and a strong supporter of short-duration grazing.

By any standards Liebig's Ranch was enormous, but because new blocks of land had been added over the years it had an odd shape, with some sections protruding deep into the neighbouring Tribal Trust Lands. Soon after leaving Wanezi we crossed the boundary between freehold and communal area and were immediately flying over another world. The ranch seemed empty; endless open woodlands with only occasional roads and fence-lines to show it was inhabited at all. In contrast, the tribal land was a patchwork of ox-ploughed fields and traditional homesteads. Here grazing was scarce and trees restricted to the banks of watercourses or around the bases of massive granite domes that crouched impartially on both the white and black man's land. I remembered the TTLs I had cycled through in the 1968 drought. The inhabitants had been cheerful and friendly then. But there was a war on now.

After less than ten minutes we crossed a fence and were back on the ranch.

Allan flew directly over the Makukwe section manager's house, which was situated on top of one of the bald outcrops and commanded a magnificent view over the surrounding countryside. Nearby were more large granite koppies and, in the east, a high conical mountain. 'That's Vinga,' Bob said. 'It marks the eastern tip of Makukwe, where it juts in between the Belingwe and Maranda TTLs.'

The bright red roof of Makukwe house was all that was visible between the *Sterculia*, *Brachystegia* and *Commiphora* trees that had somehow found enough soil to anchor them onto the bare rock. The *Brachystegias* had recently come into new leaf and some still had their crimson and gold spring colours. June was impressed and told Allan and Bob that she would be very happy to live on a place like Makukwe. The section manager was Bob's brother-in-law, but as he was spending most of his time on military call-up it was being caretaken by a young South African bachelor.

Alex Barclay, Sovalele's manager, was a burly Rhodesian-born man in his mid-thirties who had grown up ranching cattle. After picking us up at the section's airstrip, he drove back to the homestead where we had tea with his wife on the veranda of their spacious company house. Jean had come to Rhodesia as a 'sunshine girl' – the local term for newly trained nurses in Britain who had signed up for contracts in the colonies. The Barclays had three children, the youngest a year older than Tuareg. They were a relaxed and friendly couple, obviously enjoying living on the Ranch, and both June and I got on well with them from the start.

After tea we drove out to a dipping tank, where we talked with Alex about cattle. He was cross-breeding Brahmins with Herefords on Sovalele, one of 11 sections on the ranch, all of them using Savory's short-duration grazing system. On Sovalele alone there were over 12 000 head of cattle, divided into mobs of between 500 and 700 animals of the same age and sex. Each mob had its own cell, consisting of a central water point with eight paddocks radiating out from it. All the cattle in a cell were kept in the same paddock for a period of between three and seven days, depending on the growth rate of the grass, before being moved into the next paddock. They would thus have moved right around the cell in four to eight weeks, with each paddock having been heavily grazed and then rested to allow the perennial grasses to recover. The idea was simple, but according to Alex and Allan, very successful. Some of the cells were carrying twice the government recommended stocking level and yet the cattle had maintained their condition.

This might be so, I said, but how were the perennial grasses coping with the heavy grazing?

'You should have seen this part of the ranch five years ago, when we started using short-duration grazing.' Allan said. 'Then you had to walk a long way to find any perennial grasses at all.'

Alex agreed. In the early 1970s the Rhodesian lowveld had just come out of a severe drought, in which many ranchers had lost large numbers of their cattle. Much of Liebig's Ranch had then been bare ground, and over large tracts the soil surface was so hard that even annual grasses had difficulty germinating. At that time it was not easy for Allan to convince the ranch management to invest in the fencing necessary to implement his unconventional grazing method. But within two years the profits Liebig made from the increased number of cattle they were marketing had more than covered the extra costs.

That afternoon we flew back to Wanezi via the Towla headquarters, where we spoke to Mike Gawler. Allan felt that I should work directly under him as the Ranch's 'resident ecologist', assisting the other section managers with the management of their SDG cells. However, everyone agreed that I should first get a good background in practical cattle management by working with Alex Barclay on Sovalele for a few months and then running my own section before becoming involved full-time with range management. A few days later I drove to Durban and personally informed Ian Player that I would not be taking the Wilderness Leadership School position he had offered me. I also arranged for our few items of furniture to be transported to Rhodesia.

On my return from South Africa we moved straight to Sovalele, where we learned from Alex that the security situation on the Ranch had deteriorated in the few weeks since we flew over it with Allan and Bob. Just prior to our arrival the caretaker manager of Makukwe section, Alan Norrington, had bumped into a group of guerrillas near Vinga Mountain. They had opened fire on him and one of his foremen riding on the back of the truck had been fatally wounded. Alan himself had received a bullet through the hand, but managed to swerve off the road and escape. There had also been a number of ambushes in Maranda TTL, where a white and a black member of the security forces had been killed.

The increased guerrilla activity in the area was attributed to the withdrawal of Portuguese forces and the independence of Mozambique the previous year. Its long border with Rhodesia now provided a launching pad for incursions by Robert Mugabe's Zimbabwe African National Liberation Army (ZANLA) into the eastern and southern parts of the country. There were also reports of Joshua Nkomo's Zimbabwe People's Revolutionary Army (ZIPRA) having infiltrated the south-west from bases in Botswana and Zambia. The beautiful Rhodesian lowveld was not the peaceful haven it seemed.

* * *

Alex Barclay was regarded as being one of the best stockmen in the lowveld, and he soon set about teaching me the finer points of commercial cattle ranching. On Sovalele there were over 20 mobs of cattle, all of which had to be dipped weekly in summer and every second week in winter, to kill the disease-carrying ticks that infested this part of Rhodesia. For every five mobs there was a 'dipping gang' of 20 or more labourers under a foreman. Each week day the gangs went out before dawn to round up the relevant mob, ensuring that all the cattle were brought to the dip tank.

Alex rose early and before breakfast usually visited at least one of the dip tanks to count the mob and check for any injuries or signs of sickness among them. It was also an opportunity to discuss any problems with the mob fore-man or his workers. The same procedure was followed at other cells for the rest of the morning, while afternoons were reserved for returning to places where there were issues that needed addressing, or just doing the rounds of any other work that might be in progress on the section. It was a long day, by the end of which we had usually counted and inspected between two and three thousand head of cattle. Alex had been following a similar routine for much of his working life and still clearly loved it. 'When you are working with animals, no two days are the same,' he told me, and I was sure he would have a lot in common with the Himba and Herero pastoralists in the Kaokoveld.

The Rhodesian lowveld, unlike the arid parts of South West Africa, was infested with ticks. Missing dipping for just one week in summer exposed the cattle to the two most common stock diseases in the area: heartwater and anaplasmosis, or 'gall sickness', while outbreaks of East Coast Fever (theile-riosis) also occasionally occurred. For non tick-borne diseases there was a strict programme of inoculations, carried out at specific times each year. To ensure that the stockowners adhered to these disease control measures, every ranch was periodically visited by government stock inspectors. When I told Alex about the problems we experienced in just getting the Kaokovelders to allow cattle inspections and blood sampling, he found it amazing that large numbers of their livestock did not die every year.

One problem Liebig did share with the residents of the Kaokoveld was predators. Although lions only rarely visited the ranch, both leopard and cheetah were widespread and on some sections took a significant toll of the calves each year. However, the species that caused the greatest damage was spotted hyena, which on some sections killed and maimed stock on a weekly basis. In summer, the problem was compounded by the fact that even small wounds became infected by screwworm, fly larvae that ate away the flesh until they were gaping maggot-infested holes that could lead to a beast having to be put down. But, Alex told me, in the last few years Sovalele had lost more livestock to snares set for game by poachers from the neighbouring TTLs than to all the predators combined. That the ranch's own labourers were also involved was suspected but could seldom be proved. Within a year all of these losses would be insignificant in comparison to the number of cattle stolen.

Although I was working hard and learning a great deal, with no serious responsibilities I was soon able to relax and enjoy my family for the first time since Tuareg was born. On Sundays this meant accompanying the Barclays to the Sandawana Emerald Mine, situated on the north-eastern corner of Sovalele, where we played tennis or just lazed around the swimming pool. On Christmas Day, most of the mine's white staff joined us for a picnic lunch on top of one of the section's large granite koppies. Below us the wooded savanna stretched benignly to a hazy horizon, where a low range of hills indicated the border between Liebig's Ranch and the Belingwe TTL. As we lounged in the shade and ate a luxurious lunch, no one gave much thought to what was happening across the boundary fence. Only missionaries, government officials and now the security forces regularly went into the TTLs, and each side's residents knew very little about how the other lived.

A few weeks after New Year, however, a priest travelling to Sandawana Mine along the gravel road running just inside the border with Belingwe was shocked out of his reveries by a volley of bullets that ripped into the sedan car he was driving. Although he was not injured, one of the bullets put a hole in his carburettor and the vehicle spluttered to a halt a few hundred metres down the road. By his own account he climbed out of the vehicle and walked away in full view of his attackers. At first they fired a few shots in his direction, but their aim was poor and the shooting soon stopped. He carried on walking until he reached Sandawana about two hours later. When he recounted the details of the incident to the mine staff, he told them that after his car came to a standstill, he had deliberately not taken cover – to demonstrate to the guerrillas his contempt for their 'despicable attack on a man of the church'.

The police investigation concluded that it had not been a planned ambush. Probably the guerrillas had been crossing the road when they heard the vehicle approaching, and on the spur of the moment had opened fire on it. Nevertheless, it was our main route to West Nicholson, the nearest town, and if they were crossing the road, they had to be either coming onto or leaving Sovalele Section. It was the second time in three months that vehicles had been fired at on Liebig's Ranch.

Alan Norrington emigrated to Australia after his ambush on Makukwe. This was not his war. Why should he risk his life on a lonely outpost more than 25 km from his nearest white neighbours? Bob Gawler's brother-in-law also informed the Ranch management that he intended staying in the army for at least another year. This meant Makukwe was without a manager, and I was offered the position. We moved in early February, excited by the prospect of running our own section. My experience on Sovalele had shown me that a great deal could be done to upgrade the lives of the black workers on the Ranch, thereby hopefully improving the relationship between section managers and their staff. From the moment she first saw it, June had also fallen in love with Makukwe's homestead, and had plans to start her own clinic there. Although the security situation was no longer good, and Makukwe was very isolated, we believed that together we could make a difference. We had come to Rhodesia to play our part in the great changes that lay ahead. This was our opportunity.

I started working on Makukwe in high spirits. While I spent the first week getting to know the section's senior employees and inspecting its 5 000 Brahman–Afrikander cross cattle in eight SDG cells, June started arranging the necessary paperwork to dispense drugs at her clinic, as well as improving the previous two bachelor managers' very basic attempts at a garden.

Our new home could hardly have been in a more spectacular place. The granite koppie on which it was situated had sheer rock faces on all but the western side, making it into a natural fortress – a not insignificant asset in the troubled times we were living in. The house itself faced south, and from a small patch of lawn between the boulders we had a magnificent view over Maranda TTL, the border of which was less than 3 km away. Halfway down the western slope was an attractive thatched office and below that, on the wooded flats at the base of the koppie, the staff compound, workshops and store rooms. It was the classic colonial layout: the white boss on the hill and the black workers out of sight amongst the trees below. But it was beautiful, and for June and me the first real home that we had lived in as a family.

Our euphoria lasted just one week. Early on the second Monday morning I walked down to my office and found it a smouldering pile of ashes. Only the brick walls and iron window frames remained – nothing else had survived the inferno generated by the thatched roof and shelves of books and files containing the section's records. In the compound, a storeroom had also been burned to the ground and an attempt had been made to set the diesel fuel tanks alight. A few of the labourers were sitting around but they claimed to have gone to their homes in the TTL over the weekend and knew nothing of the night's events. Although I suspected some of them must have been in the vicinity, there was little I could say as I had also not been awakened by the fires.

I radioed the Ranch headquarters and at about 12 o'clock the West Nicholson police and Bruce Cook, Liebig's security officer at Towla headquarters, arrived to inspect the damage. Before leaving they pointed out the tracks of two men who had apparently been kneeling just off the path between our house and the office. 'They were no doubt planning to shoot you if you had come down to investigate,' one of the policemen said. 'You're lucky you slept so soundly.'

That night, after we had put the boys to bed, June and I sat until late discussing the situation. The police had taken four hours to get to Makukwe in daylight. What if the house had been attacked at night? Our nearest white neighbours, Arthur and Maeve Hawkesworth on Majingwe section, were more than 25 km away. Could we reasonably expect our black staff to come to our assistance? Was living on Makukwe and working with Allan Savory worth the risk to ourselves and our sons? We eventually went to bed without making a decision.

February is a glorious time of the year in the Rhodesian lowveld. When we awoke, sunlight was already streaming through the bedroom window. Outside, a shroud of thick mist covered the plains and swirled delicately through the tall trees at the base of our koppie. We were on an island, and in the distance other granite domes floated serenely on a snow-white sea. At that moment Maranda TTL and all it represented did not exist. Could we give up so easily? I had met all the senior staff on the section and they seemed like good men to work with. Perhaps, if we were given a chance, we could make Makukwe a place of racial harmony, in spite of the growing conflict around us.

The following weeks were spent securing our homestead by adding an electric alarm system to the security fence and building a natural stone wall in front of the kitchen, which was on the vulnerable western side of the koppie. I also joined the British South Africa Police (BSAP) reserve, and was issued with an FN automatic rifle to replace the Second World War Sten gun provided by the Ranch. As their contribution to our safety, Liebig organised us a 'brightlight' – the Rhodesian security codeword for men too old for military call-up, but who had volunteered for duty on the remoter farms. Their role was to protect wives and children while their husbands were away during the day, as well as to provide extra firepower should the homestead be attacked at night. The brightlight assigned to Makukwe was deep in his sixties and very rightwing in his attitude to our black staff. After two weeks June and I decided he was more of a liability than an asset and dispensed with his services. We would try and make Makukwe safe our own way.

In March the police loaned us a radio that gave us direct contact with the BSAP base in Maranda, which in an emergency could come to our assistance faster than West Nicholson. It turned out to be a mixed blessing, because we could now hear the news of what was happening in the area – and it was not good. Since the beginning of the year there had been an average of at least one vehicle ambush, homestead attack, or landmine detonation a week in the Nuanetsi district, and Maranda TTL was getting a reputation as one of the 'hottest' places in the country. Two policemen were killed and a number of others injured when their vehicle was ambushed while crossing the Nuanetsi River about 20 km from Makukwe. A few weeks later, three young white soldiers died in a hail of bullets when their patrol unexpectedly walked into a guerrilla base at the foot of one of the granite koppies we could clearly see from our lounge window. By the end of April, two more policemen had been killed in Maranda, bringing the total security force death toll here to nine. Only five 'terrs' had been killed in the TTL during the same period.

The highest number of civilian casualties had occurred in the Mateke Hills – a group of freehold ranches situated due south of Liebig's, across the Beit Bridge–Fort Victoria road. Six farmers had been killed there in the space of two months, mainly in vehicle ambushes using rocket-propelled grenades (RPGs) that could be carried by a man and fired from the shoulder. By the end of April, the frequency of incidents reported over the Nuanetsi police radio had increased to one every second day.

On Liebig's the other section managers were also reporting a great deal of labour intimidation. A number of the Ranch's 'police boys' had disappeared and were presumed to have been murdered. In one case a man known for his harsh methods of interrogation was rumoured to have had his eyes gouged out by the guerrillas before being led from village to village in the TTL, as an example of what happened to lackeys of the whites. One of my own staff assured me that he had personally seen the man crawling on his hands and knees, his eye sockets filled with maggots, a few days before he died. Across the Ranch all the remaining 'police boys' resigned or were assigned to other tasks.

*   *   *

Having decided to stay on Makukwe, we saw our first priority as being to improve the living and working conditions of the staff. To find out what the main problems on the section were, I arranged for the labourers of each work activity to choose a representative who would sit with me on a committee that met weekly to discuss any issues affecting the smooth running of the section. Initially, there was a great deal of suspicion regarding my motives for setting it up, so to promote better trust I invited all the members to dinner in our home – the first time that most of them had ever been inside a white man's house. From then on the atmosphere in our meetings improved considerably, and I was soon much better informed about what was really happening in the workplace, as well as the surrounding area.

The two main staff complaints were poor housing and wages. I was myself appalled at the dilapidated state of Makukwe's compound, but there was no budget to undertake improvements during the present financial year. However, the committee came up with a simple solution. If some of the workers' wives could come onto the section to cut the abundant thatch grass in our paddocks, half of what they collected could be used for re-thatching the compound and the other half taken back to their homes in the TTL, where thatch grass was now hard to find. For a small daily wage, other local women would be prepared to collect cattle dung and re-plaster the compound huts, which could then be painted with a cheap whitewash. I was also able to find some insecticide with which we de-loused the interior of all the houses.

The low wage problem was more difficult to solve. With densely populated tribal areas neighbouring the Ranch, labour was plentiful and there had been no need for Liebig to pay salaries above a basic survival level. On Makukwe, many mature married men were earning little more than enough to buy a bag of maize meal a month, and, although each employee did receive a weekly food ration, it was only meant to feed one person. It was the worst face of capitalism, and it meant that the liberation armies' political commissars were finding fertile ground in the Rhodesian lowveld.

Because the Company had wage limits laid down for each employment category, all I could do was review all salaries and push as many as possible to the top of their scales. It was not much, but the fact that I had shown concern for their problems seemed to be genuinely appreciated. However, my white colleagues were less than enthusiastic about my 'benevolent staff policies' and some of them complained that Makukwe's salaries were the highest on the Ranch. Mike Gawler discussed the matter with me, but at the end of our meeting I was not sure if he had agreed with me or censured me for acting without his approval. I also asked him about an additional budget to rebuild Makukwe's compound. Once again he was non-committal and just promised to 'see what he could do'.

Mike had a tough job. The Ranch had 11 sections and a total of over 2 000 employees. Because of the deteriorating security situation, just protecting the white staff and their families required major additional expenditures, and the costs of running the Ranch were soaring. Although often indecisive, he clearly wanted to do the right thing regarding the black workers' welfare, but often seemed to be influenced by the more conservative section managers, who saw conceding to a labourer's complaints as a sign of weakness. In fact, most of my counterparts believed that the best way to keep their sections functioning efficiently was to show their black employees 'who was the boss'. Winning the war that was rapidly intensifying around us was seen in the same light.

In April June opened the Makukwe clinic, which was situated just outside our security fence. By now it had become too dangerous for most government officials to work in Maranda and all the State clinics there had been closed. The result was that she soon found herself inundated with patients from far beyond the borders of the Ranch. As they got to know and trust her, many of the women she treated talked about their lives in the TTL, giving her a different perspective of what was happening across our boundary fence to that we heard on the police radio.

Soon some of my senior staff also started taking me into their confidence, especially the section's clerk, Eliot Thoma, who had become my right-hand man. Like many other Makukwe employees, his home was in Maranda and on most weekends he walked back to the TTL to be with his family. On Monday mornings he too would brief me on the latest happenings there – the local version. Apparently, both ZANLA and ZIPRA operated in Maranda, but as most of the people were Shona-speaking, Mugabe's ZANLA enjoyed the greatest support. According to Eliot, Nkomo's ZIPRA, which drew its members mainly from the Ndebele, had only a tenuous foothold in the west of the

TTL. As there was considerable animosity between the two guerrilla armies, any contact between them usually ended in a shooting match.

From our house on the hill we often heard 'contacts' in Maranda, and one evening we sat and drank tea on our front lawn and listened to a running battle that lasted for more than half an hour. When we radioed the police to ask what was going on, they assured us that no security forces were involved. The next morning they reported that a patrol had been to the site and confirmed that it had been a 'punch-up' between ZANLA and ZIPRA. Although many spent cartridges were found, and we had heard at least 15 explosions, there was no sign of any casualties. The police were not very complimentary about the guerrillas' marksmanship. We were just grateful that they had used up so much ammunition on each other and not on targets closer to our home.

In spite of their base in Maranda, the police could offer little protection to the local inhabitants, and the liberation forces had become the de facto authority in the area. When units of the Rhodesian army moved in for a few weeks they regained control of the TTL during daylight, but the nights always belonged to the guerrillas. Under cover of darkness they called meetings of the residents and convened 'people's courts' where revolutionary justice was meted out to those who still resisted the *chimurenga* call. Apparently, some white farmers had also been tried 'in absentia', with their own black staff being called as witnesses, to decide whether they were 'enemies of the people'. In this way the guerrillas could rely on local support to carry out the sentences they passed.

As my discussions with the staff became more relaxed, it was obvious to me that Eliot was having frequent contact with ZANLA, the liberation army with whom his sympathies clearly lay. I never questioned him directly about these contacts, as I knew that deliberate non-attendance of meetings by a man of his status would have risked his being branded as a 'sell-out', the punishment for which was usually death.

Philip Burarai, Makukwe's builder, was a dark horse. Highly intelligent and a skilled tradesman, it seemed strange that he was working on Liebig's for a pittance when he could get employment in town at a much higher salary. Although our relationship was good, Philip never said much about his background, or where his political allegiances lay. As he was Shona-speaking, I presumed he supported Mugabe's ZANU Party and I suspected he might have been involved in political activities he now wished to hide.

Pasani, the grey-haired old Ndebele who installed and maintained the water pipes to the SDG cells, was a supporter of Joshua Nkomo's ZAPU Party, and he did have a past. In 1972 he had been jailed for organising opposition to the Pearce Commission, which the British government had sent to test black support for the granting of independence under a proposed Rhodesian Front constitution. Probably because of my friendship with Eliot and Philip, Pasani said little to me about events in Maranda. But he spoke much more openly to June, who had been able to give him considerable relief during his frequent bouts of asthma. It had been a ZIPRA camp the army had blundered into and lost three soldiers, he told her, adding quite a detailed description of what had happened. I wondered if he had known about the camp beforehand – perhaps even visited it?

Some of the information that June and I were getting put us in a difficult situation. We supported neither the Rhodesian security forces nor the liberation armies, and were trying to remain neutral until the armed conflict ended and a negotiated settlement was put in place. I had rationalised my joining the police reserve because it would prevent my being called up for military service – compulsory for non-Rhodesians after two years' residence in the country. Fortunately, reservists who lived on remote farms were not required to do anything more than remain at home and provide information on what was going on around them. That was our dilemma. We did not feel we could betray the trust of the people who gave us information by passing it on to the police, but people were now being killed just a few kilometres from our home. As yet, we had only been given the local version of an incident after it had taken place, and it was probable that our informants did not know beforehand. Absolute secrecy was obviously the key to the guerrillas' success ... unless they needed local participation.

In May, things changed. Pasani told June that ZIPRA was planning to kill Arthur Swales, the section manager of Jopempi section on the south side of Maranda. We drove to Towla and told Mike Gawler, without giving away the informant's name. He listened patiently, but as June had no details of when or how, seemed to think she was just getting a bit hysterical. The war was quite understandably making all the wives a little jumpy, he told me when we were alone, but did promise to warn Arthur. Nothing happened on Jopempi – no doubt confirming Mike's suspicions about June's state of mind.

When I took over Makukwe, the section's biggest problem was TTL livestock being deliberately grazed on our side of the border. In many paddocks adjoining Maranda I had found nearly as many of our neighbours' cattle as our own. The grass they ate was not the issue, although they were disrupting our rotational grazing system. Much more serious was the fact that livestock dipping was no longer taking place in the TTL and they therefore posed a very real threat of transmitting tick-borne diseases to the Ranch cattle. After discussing the problem with the staff committee, we decided to invite the neighbouring stockowners to a meeting on our common boundary. Not all of them came, but the discussions were cordial and a week later there were no more Maranda cattle on Makukwe.

By May the greatest threat to Makukwe and Sovalele sections was stock theft. Up to 20 head of cattle at a time would simply disappear. When questioned by Alex or me, the cell workers usually had no explanation, although on a few occasions they claimed to have seen strange men in the paddocks, but thinking they might be guerrillas, had run away. As they could hardly be expected to intercept potentially armed men, we could only stress the importance of our being informed as soon as possible. On the few occasions when we did receive information in time, Alex and I had tried to track down the stolen cattle. But the thieves always headed straight for the nearest TTL, and following them across the Ranch border was just inviting an ambush.

All cases of stock theft were also reported to the police, but short-staffed and under pressure due to the deteriorating security situation, they seldom had the time or manpower to assist. Consequently, as the stealing of cattle escalated across the lowveld, the ranchers were encouraged to employ their own anti-stock theft units. Liebig responded by appointing Gary Scott, an Australian who had fought in Vietnam before serving five years in the Rhodesian Light Infantry. He gathered together some of the Ranch's ex-'police boys' and formed them into a quasi-military force that could respond to both stock theft and any other security-related incident that might occur. Because the northern sections were experiencing the most problems, Gary and his unit were based on Sovalele, in the homestead that we had lived in.

Gary operated in the way he had, no doubt, learned while wearing a military uniform. Whenever he came onto the section I received complaints from staff that they had been manhandled, and in one case severely beaten up. This put me in a quandary. The investigation methods used by the stock-theft unit were breaking down the good staff relations I was trying to build up, but the rate at which Makukwe was losing cattle gave me little room to complain. I explained the situation to the staff committee, and we agreed that the best solution was for me to accompany Gary every time he followed up a case on the section.

The following Sunday two cell workers came to our house and informed me that eight head of cattle had just been stolen from one of the paddocks, and that they were being taken in a northerly direction. After calling Gary and arranging to meet him on the section boundary, the informants and I then tracked the thieves to where the fence had been cut in rocky country and the cattle taken into Belingwe TTL. The Makukwe men would go no further, and as none of the stock-theft unit had been sober, Gary had come with Alex and one of Sovalele's senior workers. Leaving our vehicles, the four of us crossed the fence and followed the still-fresh spoor into the TTL on foot.

Although their tracks were easy to follow, the thieves were moving fast and we soon found ourselves in uninhabited wooded hills deep within 'enemy territory'. Gary was clearly nervous without his askaris, but Alex and I had lost too many cattle in recent months to let any chance of recovering some of them slip through our fingers. After about 5 km the country opened out. In front of us there were scattered homesteads with local cattle grazing around them, making it very difficult to differentiate between their tracks and those of the stolen animals. Alex called a halt. We had got so close, but with the sun now low on the horizon all of us agreed it would be foolish to continue. Tense and frustrated, we turned around and walked fast back to the vehicles.

We reached the fence-line after sunset and because we were quite close to Sovalele homestead, I decided to use the opportunity to pick up our post. As Alex and Gary drove off into the gathering darkness, I radioed June to tell her I would be late, and then followed after them. Soon after crossing Makukwe's border I heard a series of single shots ring out up ahead, and a few minutes later found their stationary Land Rover with all three men standing next to it. Four dead cattle were lying on the road. In the vehicle headlights I could see they were long-horned and multi-coloured – clearly they did not belong to Liebig. Alex's assistant was shaking his head and repeating over and over: 'You should not have done that, Mr Gary. You should not have done that.'

Gary Scott seemed elated. 'That will show the bastards that they can't steal our cattle and get away with it,' he said triumphantly, and suggested to Alex's man that he cut a haunch off one of them and take it home to his wife.

'No, Mr Gary,' he replied. 'They are not my cattle. If I take some of the meat I will be stealing from an innocent man.' The way he emphasised the word innocent made me suspect that he knew whose cattle they were, but I did not ask him.

Killing somebody else's livestock, even if they were trespassing on your property, was a serious crime in the Rhodesian law books. But the police were virtually under siege and no longer responding to the white ranchers' stock-theft cases. What chance did a black cattle owner have if he took his complaint to them? The local people would just chalk it up as another injustice committed against them by us whites. I was very glad that Gary had not killed the cattle on Makukwe.

Even under the present trying circumstances, it was also not Liebig's policy to shoot TTL cattle on the Ranch – but I knew that Alex was unlikely to report the incident. Law and order had become the latest casualty of the liberation struggle. All that now remained to prevent the situation descending into total chaos was the strength of our consciences.

Managing 5 000 head of cattle on over 30 000 hectares of war-torn Rhodesian bushveld had so focused my mind that I hardly had time to think about the Kaokoveld. However, in May I received a letter from Struik Publishers, asking me to write a chapter on the Territory for a coffee-table book on Namibia they were preparing with two well-known photographers, Peter Johnson and Anthony Bannister. Although I would not be paid much for my contribution, it did provide an unexpected opportunity for June and me to break away from the day-to-day problems on Makukwe. After requesting and being granted three weeks' leave, we drove to Gobabeb Research Station, in the middle of the Namib Desert, where I had once before sought refuge from stress.

Although I had complete confidence in Eliot and the committee running the section, I was concerned about how stock theft would be handled in my absence. We had started to get good reports from the cell workers, including where they thought stolen cattle were being taken, so before leaving I told Eliot to give any information he received to Bob Gawler on Wanezi. This should be done in person, I added, as our radios could be monitored by the guerrillas. I also asked Bob to take charge of any response that might be necessary, and not Gary Scott.

We arrived back from the Namib over a weekend, relaxed and ready for whatever Maranda had in store for us next. We did not have long to wait. Early on Monday morning Eliot asked to speak to me privately, and then proceeded to tell me a very disturbing story. A week after our departure one of the cell foreman told him that some of Makukwe's stolen cattle had been seen at a village in the TTL, only a few kilometres from the section boundary. As instructed, he had informed Bob Gawler and requested that any attempt to recover the cattle should be kept well away from Makukwe homestead, in order to keep the source of the information a secret.

But this had not been done. The following morning Gary Scott and his men arrived at the section office, and after talking to Eliot had demanded the use of my Land Rover. They then drove straight into the TTL in search of the stolen cattle. According to Eliot, the people in the suspected village heard the vehicles approaching and all but an old man had hidden themselves and the cattle in the bush. When Gary and his men found the village virtually deserted, they had beaten the old man so badly that his arm had been broken and then set all the huts on fire before leaving.

The following weekend, as Eliot was going to see his family he was stopped by one of his children, who warned him that there were guerrillas at his house waiting for him to arrive. Afraid to go home, he had returned to the section and had not been back to Maranda. He was clearly very distressed, and by this stage of his story tears were running down his cheeks. 'You whites have fire-arms and security fences around your homes,' he sobbed. 'We have nothing to protect us. I don't even know if my wife and children are still alive.'

I was at a loss for what to say and offered to arrange a police escort to take him back to his village. Eliot stopped crying and said bitterly. 'If I go to my home with the police I will be dead within a month.'

I was appalled by what Eliot told me and furious at Gary Scott's brutality. It seemed like he had deliberately implicated Eliot, but I could think of no plausible motive for his doing so. At the first opportunity, I discussed the matter with Bob, but got little sympathy. The Ranch had now bought into the philosophy of fighting fire with fire, and I was finding myself increasingly isolated from the rest of my colleagues.

At every spare moment during the rest of the week I worked on my Kaokoveld chapter in order to meet the publisher's deadline. On Saturday morning I looked for Eliot to discuss his going home, but heard that he had already left for Maranda. Early on Monday he was back in the office and just mentioned that all was well at home. I was relieved, but as he did not seem to want to talk about it, I said no more on the subject. Pressured by having to run the section and trying to finish the book chapter, I naïvely presumed that the guerrillas had forgotten about the incident.

When I saw him on Wednesday morning, Eliot told me that there was a problem on the Maranda boundary that he thought I should come and see for myself. With my mind still focused on the last edit of the book chapter we climbed into my Land Rover and headed down the road towards the TTL. Along the way Eliot broke the silence by saying that if we ever met 'the boys', as he always referred to the guerrillas, I should not shoot at them. I laughed and reminded him that we were in a war. They're armed and so am I; of course we'll shoot at each other. I musn't do that, he insisted, they know that you are a good man and they will not harm you. By now I was wondering what on earth Eliot was talking about.

It was still early morning and sunlight was streaming through the dense trees on the sides of the track. We crossed a dry river bed and I changed down into second gear to climb out on the other side. On top of the bank, we turned a corner and came face to face with a man kneeling in the middle of the road. He was aiming a rocket launcher straight at the front of the Land Rover. On his left another man was standing with an RPD machine gun and bandoliers of ammunition over his shoulders. Everywhere I looked there seemed to be more men pointing AK-47s at me. There was no escape. I stopped and for a split second looked at my FN rifle on its rack in front of me, but knew I would be dead before I could fire a single shot. None of the guerrillas moved and suddenly it dawned on me what Eliot had been trying to tell me. I climbed out of the Land Rover and stood unarmed next to the door. The man with the RPD lowered it and walked towards me. 'Don't be afraid,' he said in English. 'We just want to talk to you.'

Reassured that I was not going to resist, he shook my hand and introduced himself as the commander of the ZANLA forces in the area. A number of other guerrillas also came up and greeted me, courteously saying that they were pleased to meet me. I was too stunned to reply. The commander then asked me to follow him away from my vehicle into the bush. My veins were still surging with adrenaline but I was no longer afraid. Eliot had primed me well and the guerrillas had clearly made an effort to show that they meant me no harm.

After walking a few hundred metres we stopped next to a large termite mound and the commander indicated we should sit down. All but two of the other guerrillas then fanned out in a circle around us and either knelt or stood on guard. The leader of the group, a man of about 30 who spoke excellent English, then proceeded to tell me that my workers had told them that I was not a racist, and that I treated them well. For this reason he had asked Eliot to 'arrange our meeting'. He then assured me that ZANLA was not fighting against the whites, but only to overthrow the Smith government. After they had won the war they hoped that whites would remain in the country so that we could all work together to make Zimbabwe free and democratic. I mumbled something about sharing their ideals and he thanked me for saying so – undoubtedly well aware that there was little else I could say under the circumstances.

Once the ice had been broken the commander and one of the other men on the termite mound started asking me questions: Was I a Rhodesian? No, I was South African. Why had I come to Rhodesia? To work for the country now that Ian Smith had accepted majority rule. Was I a member of the security forces? I was in the police reserve. Who owned Liebig's Ranch? It was owned by an international company, but the local headquarters were in Bulawayo. Why did Liebig supply bully beef to the Rhodesian army? I could not answer that one. Why did the army sometimes stay at Bob Gawler's homestead? The army stays where it wants to. Bob does not have a choice. We are all in the same position, I added, but then remembered Eliot knew that after an army platoon had stayed at Makukwe, I had requested them not to do so again. Fortunately Eliot did not contradict me.

Their next question was more difficult: Did I think ZANLA forces were stealing our cattle? I thought for a moment and then answered that I did not know who was stealing them. They smiled at my tactful reply and then said emphatically that ZANLA did not steal cattle or anything else from the local people, or the whites. If they needed food, they were always given it willingly by the inhabitants of the area in which they operated. I was not in a position to dispute this and simply stated that stock theft was causing a lot of trouble on the Ranch and it was resulting in people being hurt unnecessarily. They agreed.

'ZANLA is also very unhappy with the cattle stealing,' the commander said. 'We are not involved, but are being blamed for it.' He then promised me they would do their best to stop the stock theft on Makukwe section. I thanked them for their offer of help.

Many more questions followed, some of which clearly showed how little the guerrillas knew of what was happening on the ranches. Perhaps this was not surprising, as there was so little social contact between the races in the lowveld. Whites and blacks worked together for most of the day, but that was all. At night and over the weekends each went back to their own worlds. Although there was no legislated apartheid in Rhodesia, in the rural areas the races were as segregated as in any farming district in South Africa, and just as ignorant of each other's problems or aspirations.

By now the atmosphere had become fairly relaxed and we even occasionally laughed at some of the misconceptions across the present battle lines. I was impressed by the men I spoke to and depressed at the thought that, under different circumstances, we could have been shooting at each other. However, the mood changed dramatically when one of the guards shouted something, and I too heard the sound of a vehicle in the distance. Everybody was instantly alert. Their tension pushed my heartbeat back into the red. It was not difficult to read the guerrillas' minds: had Eliot and I set up an ambush for them? I was jolted back to the reality of the situation. If our captors thought that they had been double-crossed, I knew what they were likely to do with us. As the commander shouted orders to his men, I desperately tried to think of whose vehicle it might be. Eliot, who was squatting alongside me, seemed to be as mystified and panic-stricken as I was. Then he visibly relaxed. It was our tractor taking labourers to one of the cattle dips, and would not come past us. He quickly explained the situation, and the guerrillas seemed as relieved as we were.

After a few more questions, the commander stated that he was satisfied with my answers. He added that he also knew about my wife's clinic and the valuable service she was performing for the people in the area. He then assured me that ZANLA would not attack us. However, he did have a small request to make. In African custom, friends always exchanged gifts. Would I be prepared to give his men something? What they really needed was new clothes – especially denim jeans or jackets, ZANLA's unofficial uniform. But anything was acceptable, he added, no matter how small it was. My mind raced. It was one thing to remain neutral in a war, but giving the guerrillas a gift would definitely be seen as taking their side, and if discovered I would certainly be charged with assisting the enemy. Deportation from Rhodesia would be the minimum sentence. The best answer I could give was that I would first have to ask my wife. He chuckled at this, but simply said that I should inform Eliot when *she* had given *her* answer.

When we got back to the Land Rover, some of the guerrillas had taken my FN rifle out of the vehicle and were passing it around, expressing amazement at how much it weighed. One of the men gave me his AK-47 to show me how light it was in comparison. The situation was bizarre. I was standing amongst about 15 so-called 'terrorists' with one of their automatic weapons, while they had mine, and we were humorously comparing their relative merits. Surely a negotiated settlement to the liberation struggle was possible?

Half an hour later I was back at our homestead, having breakfast with June and the boys as if nothing had happened. But something had happened, and it brought a dramatic new dimension to our life on Makukwe. Rhodesia's emergency laws stated that any contact with the guerrillas had to be reported to the security forces within 24 hours. If I did not do so, I could be sentenced to two years in jail!

I only told June about the incident that night, having needed time to come to terms in my own mind with what had happened. By then the high of the meeting had dissipated, and we had to face the implications of whatever we did. If I informed the police, what would happen to Eliot? And if I didn't, what would happen to me if one of the guerrillas I met was captured or killed and there was a record of the meeting in his notebook? The only person I felt I could discuss our predicament with was Allan Savory, who arrived on the ranch a few days later. He believed that although I did not initiate my contact with the guerrillas, the security forces had become so paranoid that in future I would be regarded as an enemy collaborator. As Allan had started what later became the clandestine Selous Scouts Regiment, I took his advice seriously, and in the end decided on a compromise; I would inform the Company management, but not the police.

The following week we drove to Bulawayo and I told Graham Ballard, Managing Director of Liebig Rhodesia, the whole story, including Gary Scott's botched raid into Maranda and the brutal interrogation methods that I believed were doing damage to the Company's reputation. June added that Jean Barclay had told her about 'torture' sessions that Gary conducted on Sovalele, sometimes using Alex, who spoke fluent Chikaranga, as a translator. As a British national Ballard was sympathetic, but urged us to inform Mike Gawler, which we later did, again explaining our reasons for not going to the police. He also assured us that he did not support what was happening on the Ranch and promised that he would immediately follow up on the Gary Scott issue. A week later, Gary was fired.

For the rest of July, things went very well on the section. We had only one case of stock theft and staff relations seemed to improve by the day. But in early August Jean Barclay radioed June to say she had heard gunfire close to their homestead. As Alex had not yet returned from a trip to Towla, she was alone in the house. June immediately tried to contact me, but I was away from my vehicle at one of the dips. By the time I got the message it was an hour later and three vehicles had already been sent out from Towla to investigate. Nevertheless, I immediately set off for Sovalele and met the Towla convoy on the road. About three kilometres from the homestead we found Alex's vehicle. The windscreen had been shattered and the driver's side raked by machine gun fire. Lying on the road 20 metres beyond the vehicle was Alex's body. He had been killed instantly by two bullets in the head and at least one in the chest.

A few minutes after we arrived on the scene, an agricultural extension officer who had been travelling in the vehicle with Alex emerged from the bush.

Amazingly, he had not been injured in the ambush and, realising that Alex was dead, had run away and hidden until we arrived.

After a simple but moving funeral, Alex was buried next to a large baobab tree on Sovalele, the section he had managed and loved for eight years. A few weeks later, Jean returned to England, taking her three children with her. June and I were devastated by Alex's death and the loss of our only real friends on the Ranch. Both of us had such a high regard for Alex that we had asked him to be Kyle's godfather. To me he had been a trusted colleague and mentor, with whom I had shared many pleasant and sometimes exciting experiences. Alex had also been one of the most respected cattlemen in the lowveld and although he had been a strong supporter of the Rhodesian government and a member of the Police Anti-Terrorist Unit, his practical experience and knowledge would have been an asset to a multiracial Zimbabwe.

For weeks after Alex was killed I found it difficult to function. Would the guerrillas have been so brazen as to carry out a daylight ambush so close to the Sovalele homestead if Gary Scott had still been based there and able to respond rapidly? Logic told me that the group that ambushed Alex probably came from Belingwe, the nearest TTL, but what if it had been the same men I had met on Makukwe only a month before? Alex's death did resolve one issue. We could no longer consider giving the guerrillas the gift they had requested, and I asked Eliot to pass the message on to them.

Liebig replaced Gary Scott with Neville Robinson, an ex-Selous Scout, and once again I started receiving reports from my staff about people being beaten up. In September two women who had been cutting thatch grass on the section came to June's clinic with severe back bruising. One of them was urinating blood. They claimed to have been in a paddock from which cattle were stolen, and when they denied having seen the thieves, were beaten with rifle butts. I again complained to the Ranch management, but this time received no support. 'Stolen cattle were costing Liebig tens of thousands of dollars a month and the problem could no longer be handled with kid gloves.' My case was also weakened by Makukwe once more losing cattle to stock-thieves.

One of my severest critics was our new neighbour, Pete Richards, who had taken over Majingwe section. Pete had previously been a professional soldier with Rhodesia's elite SAS parachute battalion. He was a tough man who had seen action both in and outside the country's borders. 'Your way won't work,' he told me in one of our frequent arguments. 'We're in a bloody war. The terrs don't pull their punches, so why should we? If you can't take it then go back to South Africa.' To Pete the most important thing was for the whites and moderate blacks to stand together against the 'terrorists' until a multiracial government could be put in place. He saw any softening of the Ranch's policies as playing into the enemy's hands.

In October Bruce Cook obtained information that some of Liebig's cattle were being kraaled at a village near Majingwe's border with Maranda. Since they might have come from Makukwe, and in solidarity with Pete Richards, I joined in the operation to recover them. On the night before, four section managers, as well as Bruce and his assistants, all gathered at Pete's homestead and early the next morning drove to the section's border. Here we left our vehicles and set off in an extended line into the TTL.

We walked for over two hours, by which time the sun was already quite high and the temperature climbing. When we arrived at the suspected village, however, there were no cattle or adult men to be seen – only women and children who stood around apprehensively looking at the armed strangers in their midst. I moved to the shade of a tree about 50 metres away and watched as Bruce and his men searched the huts, periodically taking one of the villagers aside for questioning.

It was another failed mission. On our way we had met a number of young herd-boys who fled in apparent terror when they saw us. They had no doubt informed the people in the area of our approach – giving them enough time to hide any stolen cattle. I had heard pub-talk that in similar circumstances children running away had been shot, to prevent them from alerting the guerrillas about the approach of security forces. When I expressed my disgust at such tactics I had been confronted with the unanswerable question: what would you do if you knew they were informing the enemy, and your life was at stake?

After about 20 minutes a middle-aged woman was singled out and interrogated by one of Bruce's assistants. Although I could not understand what was being said, he was clearly threatening her. After replying she spat on the ground. The man questioning her then raised his rifle and hit her across the shoulders. She staggered, but struggled to her feet again. Another blow hit her in the small of the back and this time she crumpled to the floor. I was incensed and ran up to the interrogator as he kicked her twice while she lay on the ground. Trying to control myself, I demanded to know why she was being beaten.

'Her son is a terrorist,' I was told. 'She says he is in Johannesburg, but she has no proof. We got information from one of these children that he is with the terrorists.'

'Even if it is true,' I said to Bruce, who had also moved in closer, 'probably half the mothers in Maranda have sons supporting the liberation armies.'

Before he could answer, one of the senior section managers, Don Munroe of Mazunga, stepped in and said that we had come to look for cattle, not terrorists, and ordered Bruce's men to leave the woman alone. She slowly got to her feet and stood defiantly in front of us. Although she said nothing, the blazing hatred in her eyes left me in no doubt what she felt. And if any of the children in our silent, unnoticed audience were hers, I knew where their sympathies would lie as soon as they were old enough to take up arms.

We returned to Majingwe hot, tired and empty-handed. Without the support of the local people we had little hope of achieving any real successes against the stock thieves. Although I had tried to stop the woman from being assaulted, I also knew that in the minds of the Maranda residents I would be seen as having taken part in the operation. I was being sucked inexorably into Rhodesia's conflict and was losing credibility on both sides. I also knew that I had made an enemy of Bruce Cook.

By the second half of 1977 stock theft had become a major problem across virtually the entire Rhodesian lowveld. The police had no hope of containing the situation, which was now costing the ranchers and the country considerable losses in revenue. Armed militias were being employed in many areas, and to assist them in their difficult task the government passed drastic new emergency legislation that gave landowners the right to shoot non-employees found on their properties. All that they were required to do afterwards was make a statement to the police about the incident.

Shortly after our unsuccessful operation to recover stock in Maranda, Bruce Cook and his assistants arrived at Makukwe homestead while I was out dipping cattle. He stopped in our driveway and called June to his truck, saying that he had some stock thieves and wanted her to see if she knew any of them. Expecting to find the accused men sitting in the back, she had strolled casually up to the vehicle and was horrified to find three corpses. When I arrived back Bruce had already left, but June was still very upset. His only explanation had been that they were seen in one of Makukwe's paddocks, and when he had called to them they had tried to run away. Eliot later confirmed that they were not Liebig's employees, but the fact that they were afraid of Bruce and his assistants was slim evidence on which to convict them of being stock-thieves – and execute them. I did not discuss the issue with Mike Gawler. Bruce had the country's emergency legislation behind him and my frequent complaints were only making me more unpopular with my white colleagues. As June pointed out, we had our small children's lives to consider – and one day we might need their assistance.

* * *

Rhodesia was now rapidly sliding into a full-scale civil war. With the change in the American administration, Henry Kissinger was no longer a player in the international community's search for a settlement with Mugabe and Nkomo, who had politically united under the banner of the Patriotic Front. Andrew Young, his replacement in the process, was popular with the liberation forces but deeply mistrusted by the country's whites, and the ball had now been passed on to the British. Rhodesia was their colony, so it was their responsibility to find a solution. A series of peace brokers were sent out to negotiate with Smith, but he seemed to be back-tracking on the commitments he had made to Kissinger the previous year. It was now majority rule only if the whites still retained control of the security forces and other key arms of government.

In August Ian Smith called another general election. The ostensible aim was to get a mandate from the country's white electorate to negotiate on the latest British and American settlement proposal. His opponents were the Rhodesian Action Party, formed by a group of breakaway right-wingers from the ruling Rhodesian Front, and the National Unifying Force, an alliance of moderate whites led by Allan Savory. Once again Smith's men won all 50 seats in the election.

Confident that his white countrymen were united behind him, and after seeking the South African government's support, Smith now rejected any settlement with the exiled Patriotic Front and set about seeking an accommodation with Bishop Abel Muzorewa and other compliant internal black leaders. It was a popular decision among my white colleagues on the Ranch, but in the short term it could only mean a further escalation of the war – and the end result would depend on who had the greatest support from Rhodesia's overwhelming black majority.

On Makukwe both stock theft and the encroachment of TTL cattle onto the section had once again increased. To make matters worse, the management committee was now reluctant to take any responsibility, and even my senior staff seemed more unwilling to discuss work-related events on the section, or in the surrounding area. The security situation also continued to deteriorate. On Shobi Section east of the Beit Bridge–Bulawayo road, Tom Crawford was ambushed by a group of guerrillas, but survived with minor injuries. He probably owed his life to Liebig's having recently armour-proofed all the section managers' Land Rovers with quarter-inch steel plates on the cab and bullet-proof windscreens. It was effective against standard 7.62 ammunition, but not against armour-piercing AK-47 rounds or rocket-propelled grenades.

The only ray of light was that June's clinic had gone from strength to strength. Not only was she treating more patients, some of whom came from up to 60 km away, but she had also made a breakthrough with regard to family planning. The subject was politically taboo, being seen as a plot by the whites to reduce the black population, but it was sorely needed in Rhodesia's rural areas. Since the introduction of modern medicine child mortality had dropped dramatically and eight or more children surviving per family was now the norm. One of Makukwe's retired foremen, known only as 'old Sambok', had 12 wives and over 60 children. My staff joked that on a number of occasions he had asked who a young boy or girl was, only to be told it was his own child!

The men on the section might not be prepared to discuss family planning, but in private sessions with June their wives certainly were, and they carried the main burden of raising the children. Once she had gained their trust, June actually found that many of the women she treated saw the advantages of smaller families, and unbeknown to their husbands requested depo provera injections, which kept them infertile for periods of up to six months. It was devious, but in the prevailing irrational political climate, we regarded it as a service to both the overburdened wives and the country as a whole.

After Alex had been killed, Ken Drummond, one of the youngest and most promising section managers on the Ranch, had been transferred to Sovalele. Still in his early twenties, he had gone straight from school into the army where he had been trained for killing and had, no doubt, done his share of it. The enemy were black terrorists and, like so many of his generation, his experiences had taught him that there was a thin line between 'terrs' and the black population as a whole.

Alex's death had been a great shock to all of us, and Ken had taken it particularly hard. He was convinced that some of Sovalele's black staff had collaborated in the ambush and decided to find out who they were. Without discussing it with anyone, he informed the section's entire labour force that they would not be paid at the end of the month unless they told him who the guilty persons were. No information was forthcoming and no one was paid.

By the end of the second month he had still been given no names and again refused to pay any salaries. At this stage, one of the workers rode on a bicycle to Towla and reported the matter to Richard Stringfield, the Ranch's assistant manager, who immediately radioed Ken and asked him to come into head-quarters and explain his actions.

Undoubtedly knowing that he was in trouble, Ken first went to Towla's la-bour compound and tracked down the man who had reported him to Richard. According to eye witnesses, in a fit of uncontrollable rage he knocked the man down and, with his heavy army boots, kicked him repeatedly in the head and body. Ken's Alsatian dog was also reputed to have savaged the man while he was lying on the ground. When he lost consciousness and could not be re-vived, Ken loaded him onto the back of his truck, but before he could be taken to hospital, the man died.

For me this incident was the last straw. Because of the security situation and his military record I seriously doubted whether Ken would be found guilty if the case even came to court. The moral sanctions under which civilised societies operated were breaking down and young men who under normal circumstances would be upright citizens had been turned into racists whose concept of right and wrong was now determined by the colour of their oppo-nent's skin. It was not the sort of environment I wanted my children raised in.

I had come to Rhodesia to get experience of Savory's short-duration graz-ing methods, and only after Ian Smith accepted majority rule. But Smith's idea of majority rule was very different from the rest of the world's, or mine, and the chances of there now being an orderly transition to a black government in Rhodesia seemed very slim indeed. I was also spending most of my time just holding Makukwe section together, and anything more than basic grazing management was out of the question. I was ready to resign.

Before doing so I expressed my frustrations to Mike Gawler and Allan Savory. They were sympathetic and suggested that I transfer to Ken Drummond's previous section, Lutope, in the far south of the Ranch. It was here that Allan had set up his 'advanced project', a wagon-wheel with 30 pad-docks in which the cattle moved every one or two days. The Ranch was also planning to introduce more in-service training for its black staff and Mike recommended that I be put in charge of this. Although Lutope section bor-dered Mtetengwe TTL, it had experienced very little stock theft and there had been no security problems. Their offer was too good to refuse.

CHAPTER FOURTEEN

ZIMBABWE RISING

The day after June and I moved to Lutope, Allan Savory flew down to brief me on my responsibilities with regard to the management of his 'Advanced Rotational Grazing Project'. We met on the section's airstrip and he suggested that we first take a flip over this part of the ranch, so that I would have a better perspective of its layout. Five minutes later we were in the air, flying 100 metres above the basalt country that made up most of the southernmost part of Liebig's massive property.

Lutope was not as attractive as Makukwe. This was real lowveld – table-flat with only a few low ridges and small hills to break the monotony of the landscape. On one of the hills, little more than a pimple on a vast panorama of tree and scrub covered plains, was our new home. On another rise about a kilometre away was the homestead of the adjoining section, Lamulas, which was managed by Max Stockhill. The only other feature of any significance to be seen was the tree-fringed course of the Bubye River that formed the eastern boundary of Lutope.

The Advanced Project was basically laid out like all the other short-duration grazing cells on the ranch, but instead of just eight wedge-shaped paddocks radiating out from a central water-point, in this case there were 30.

From the air, it looked like a great wagon wheel, with the fence-lines between the paddocks forming the spokes. The cattle spent only two days in each paddock, so that it still took them two months to rotate around the whole cell. The ultimate in short-duration grazing would be for them to move every day through 60 paddocks, Allan told me, but the Ranch management had balked at the cost of that much fencing.

So far Allan's advanced project had been remarkably successful. From its start in 1971 it had been stocked at three times the recommended government rate for the district, of one cattle unit per 10 hectares. In spite of this, the 350 breeding cows it carried on just 1 200 hectares had consistently outperformed the rest of the section. In fact, Allan said proudly, the pregnancy rate of 92 per cent that the Advanced Project cows had achieved the previous year was the highest on the ranch, and far above the average for the lowveld as a whole.

I asked Allan about the extra labour costs of rounding up the cattle every two days, but he assured me that there were none. The cows had quickly learnt the system and now automatically went into the next paddock. 'After two days 350 cows have quite an impact on 40 hectares of grazing,' he told me, 'so they can't wait to move into a paddock that has been rested for two months.' The whole cell was run by an old man and four youngsters, and if it wasn't for the odd cow that got a bit confused about what day it was, Allan thought that the old man could run it on his own.

That afternoon we drove out to inspect the Advanced Project on the ground. Although it was now late November no effective rain had yet fallen on Lutope and the veld was parched and dry. Nevertheless, all the cattle we saw were sleek and still quite fat, a tribute to the quality of the section's grazing. A major contributing factor was that its soils were predominantly basaltic clay, which was very fertile compared to the granite-derived sands that covered most of the northern sections of the ranch. Lutope's 'sweetveld' undoubtedly played a role in the remarkable calving percentages achieved by the Advanced Project, but I had to admit it could not alone explain how the cell had maintained such a high stocking rate.

Up to this point I had been impressed by all I had seen and heard from Allan about the increased production and easy management of cattle by using his SDG system. But when we reached the centre of the 'wagon wheel', I was surprised at how bare the ground was for the first few hundred metres from the water-point. To me, it looked like a severe case of overgrazing and I told Allan so. 'Heavily grazed, not overgrazed,' he replied. 'Don't make the mistake of measuring the condition of the grass by its height. That only reflects how much grazing it has recently been subjected to.'

Allan conceded that, because the paddocks were so narrow near the drinking trough, the frequent coming and going of cattle to and from water resulted in it becoming very trampled at the end of the dry season. However, he told me, this was not harmful. In fact, it was beneficial because it loosened the topsoil and also 'opened up' the grass tufts, which were still there, but invisible under the dust. To prove his point, he scuffed the surface a few metres from the gate into the drinking area and uncovered a number of tufts that had been eaten right down to ground level.

The correct way to gauge veld condition, Allan went on, was to measure its basal cover – what percentage of the ground was actually covered by perennial grass tufts. This was dependent on how closely they grew together, as well as how broad the tufts were. Heavy grazing, like the mowing of a lawn, caused perennial grasses to grow outwards and not upwards, increasing their diameter at ground level. Although the area might seem overgrazed to an inexperienced eye, he explained, the basal cover was very good and the veld would respond well when the rains came.

Allan and I then walked into one of the paddocks where I soon noted that not all of the grass tufts were broad – in fact, some were quite small, and I challenged him about the condition of the veld, based on his theory of basal cover being the best indicator. However, once again he had no problem explaining what was happening.

'When the Advanced Project was set up most of Liebig's Ranch was just bare ground. What you see are young plants, showing that the veld is still improving. Where there are only large tufts it is static, and if there are big gaps between old grass tufts, then some of them have died and the grazing is degenerating.'

All this made good sense, but I had also learned to judge veld condition by its species composition. As we walked along, I asked Allan which grasses he regarded as being the most valuable on Lutope Section.

'The first thing you must realise,' he answered, 'is that all grasses are highly nutritious while they are still growing – even the so-called unpalatable species. Of course, some grasses will be more favoured by cattle than others, which is generally dependent on how broad their leaves are. Try eating a green leaf yourself and you will have a rough guide as to how good it tastes to a cow.'

Allan saw no harm in improving species composition – although it was easier said than done – but from a practical ranching perspective it was more important to focus on keeping the grass tufts actively growing for as long as possible. This was the key to increasing the protein production of the veld and, thereby, the performance of the cattle using it. That was why SDG was so successful, he added; by heavily grazing a paddock it stimulated re-growth–for as long as there was still moisture in the soil to support it. However, frequent defoliation pushed a plant's metabolism into top gear, which if maintained depleted the nutrients stored in its roots, causing it to lose vigour and eventually die. Consequently, allowing the grass tufts a sufficient recovery period after they had been heavily grazed was one of the most critical parts of range management.

In the dry season, when perennial grasses were dormant, a different situation prevailed. At this time, Allan said, it was important to remember that the leaves and stems of tufted grasses were dead and could be totally removed without any detrimental effect to the plant. In fact, if not removed they would accumulate and reduce the amount of sunlight reaching the growth-points at the base of the tuft. This decreased productivity during the following year, and could also cause the plant to become moribund and eventually die. For this reason Allan rejected the conventional theory of leaving at least one third of the grazing in a paddock at the end of each year.

After we had walked to the back of the paddock, far from the water-point, Allan estimated that from the previous season's growth still on the tufts, there was enough grazing left to keep the cows in the cell going for a couple of months. By then the rains should have set in. But the lowveld was prone to droughts, and if no effective rain had fallen by then, there would literally be nothing left for them to eat. I was concerned by the lack of a safety margin, but Allan just chuckled and told me that the object of the Advanced Project was to push short-duration grazing to its limits.

'Obviously we can't hope to carry this amount of cattle through a drought, but if one occurred we would not reduce the stocking rate. The grazing in the cell must eventually collapse and I want to see what happens when it does, and also how quickly it recovers afterwards.'

Caught up in the enthusiasm Allan generated for range management, I offered to start monitoring the grass condition in the Advanced Project, and asked what system he recommended I use. But again, Allan showed his iconoclastic nature: 'The best way to measure the condition of veld is to track the performance of the animals eating it.' He replied. 'That is why we pregnancy test each breeding herd every year. If the number, and thereby the percentage of cows not in calf increases, then we will know that they are under nutritional stress.'

This might be so, but I questioned whether it would tell us if the grass sward was deteriorating in time to do something about it.

'With due respect to the pasture scientists,' Allan said simply, 'they do not yet know which grasses we should be managing for on lowveld ranches. For stability the climax species might be the best, but for beef production, sub-climax species could be much more valuable. Until we know more about the grasses we are farming, just walk through these paddocks as often as you can – but throw away the books and keep your mind open.'

Allan stayed with us that night, and over dinner I asked how he had developed his ideas about range management. He told me that as a young man he had worked as a wildlife biologist in the Zambezi valley. At that time, it supported huge numbers of buffalo, wildebeest, zebra and other grazing game that he found were not spread out randomly, but concentrated into herds, sometimes many thousands strong, that had to keep constantly on the move to find enough grazing. He also noted that, because prides of lions were constantly harassing the buffalo herds they remained tightly packed together, kicking up clouds of dust whenever they ran away from the predators. Although this churned up the soil surface the perennial grasses bounced back every year, creating – in terms of large mammal biomass – a remarkably productive ecosystem.

From these observations he had concluded that, because the grasslands and savannas of Africa had evolved together with its indigenous ungulates, they would have been well adapted to this type of grazing. His high-density, short-duration grazing system was simply duplicating with cattle the natural behaviour of the wild herbivores that inhabited Rhodesia before it was fenced off into individual ranches.

Using concentrations of cattle to soften the soil surface and create a suitable micro-habitat for perennial grasses to germinate, and then providing them with a recovery period to replenish their root reserves after heavy grazing seemed logical, but what made SDG so productive? To find this out I looked at it from the perspective of basic ecological processes, and again it passed with flying colours. Periodic defoliation kept the grasses actively growing for longer – which would increase the amount of solar energy that was fixed during photosynthesis. Maintaining a good basal cover also reduced rainwater runoff, as well as surface evaporation, thus improving the water balance and making more soil moisture available to plant roots each growing season.

The impact of SDG on the mineral cycle was more complex. A rapid turnover of nutrients – soil to plants and animals, and then back to the soil via dung and urine – would maximise the soil's potential productivity. But with more animals being sold, large amounts of the scarcer trace elements, such as phosphorus and calcium, would be transported out of the ecosystem. However, the Ranch compensated for this by providing the cattle with bone-meal on the basalt soils and a comprehensive mineral-supplementing lick on the less-fertile sandy soils in the northern parts of the ranch.

Although SDG was being applied on many commercial farms and in some communal areas, in academic circles it was still very controversial. Soon after starting work on Liebig's Ranch I had been invited to attend a symposium organised by the Grasslands Society of Rhodesia, where I was cornered by a number of rangeland scientists. They were fanatically opposed to Savory's grazing system and assured me that there was no research to back up his claim that SDG significantly outperformed the conventional grazing systems they were promoting on the country's commercial cattle ranches.

When I mentioned this to Allan he just shrugged his shoulders and told me that if the farmers he advised were not convinced that his methods worked they would not have spent thousands of dollars on the extra fencing needed. Small plot experiments did not prove anything, he said, and believed that the main reason SDG was not accepted by the orthodox agricultural establish-ment was because the concept had not come from within their own ranks. Paradigms were usually broken by people on the fringes of a field, he added, and those in the middle were the last to accept new ideas.

Nevertheless, Allan did not claim to have all the answers, and said he was continually learning about how grass and grazers interacted with each other – not from research carried out on experiments plots, but under real-life condi-tions on commercial farms. It was the kind of experience that I had rejected a university education to get, and Allan Savory, who was leading a revolution in range management, was the best man to get it from.

The following morning, after outlining my job description and explaining how the information from the Advanced Project and other SDG cells on the section needed to be recorded, Allan flew back to Salisbury. June and I were alone in our new home, but here on Lutope, we were not as isolated as we had been on Makukwe. That afternoon we walked across to visit our neighbours.

Max Stockhill was a large man, both in height and breadth. He had only recently joined Liebig's but, having grown up on a ranch in the south-eastern lowveld, cattle management was not new to him. His wife Elaine was also a born Rhodesian, with a passion for music. Their two elder children were at boarding school, while the youngest, a daughter, was being taught at home by her mother. We stayed for dinner, finding the Stockhills progressive in their attitude to race relations, but strong supporters of Ian Smith's government and its handling of the war.

*   *   *

A few months before my transfer a young black agricultural college gradu-ate had been appointed as my assistant on Makukwe, making the clerk's po-sition redundant. Consequently, Elliot Thoma asked to accompany me to Lutope, and Mike Gawler agreed on the grounds that he would help keep the Advanced Project records, as well as assist me when the black staff-training programme got off the ground. From my side I hoped that Eliot would be able to keep me informed about what was happening in the staff compound – and further afield.

Lutope was a larger section than Makukwe, carrying over 8 000 head of cattle in 12 SDG cells. To maintain the water-points and fences, as well as to round up the cattle for dipping, Lutope had a workforce of 180, most of whom came from Mtetengwe Tribal Trust Land, which shared a common border with the Ranch in the south-west. I soon found that, although they were not unfriendly, there was a general reserve amongst the section's black staff, which made me suspect they were not as untouched by the war as the Ranch management believed. A few weeks after our arrival, Elliot confirmed that there were ZANLA forces in the area. They were not from Maranda, was all he would say on the matter.

In mid-December the rains started. After a few days of almost unbearable heat the heavens opened and soaking downpours fell throughout the lowveld. The 'black cotton soils' on the section were quickly saturated, turning the low-lying areas into vleis of open water and many of Lutope's roads into impass-able quagmires.

Soon after the rains began I was amazed by the transformation that took place in the Advanced Project. The ground right up to the water-point gates was now an emerald carpet, as the perennial tufts previously hidden under the dust sprang back to life. If I still harboured doubts about the perennial grasses' ability to withstand the pressure of such a high stocking rate they were soon dispelled. Although the pasture scientists' SDG research plots had been inconclusive, the 'Savory system' certainly worked on Liebig's Ranch.

Over the next few weeks I regularly drove out to the Advanced Project, where by late January the majority of perennials were in seed, making it easy to identify them. The genera renowned for producing high-quality fodder, *Themeda, Panicum* and *Setaria,* all occurred in fair quantities, but the most abundant species were *Eragrostis rigidior* and *Urochloa mosambicensis,* which grassland scientists claimed favoured disturbed habitats, and only had moderate grazing potential. Nevertheless, the cows in the Advanced Project ate them like ice-cream, were soon as fat as pigs, and judging by their horny behaviour when the bulls were introduced, seemed set to maintain their record of virtually all of them getting in the family way.

For me the big question was – could short-duration grazing systems be applied in the Kaokoveld? Fencing in a communal area would obviously be a problem, but was it really necessary? Allan had told me about a farmer who marked out his SDG cells with white stones and used herdsmen to keep the cattle within the 'paddocks'. Another difficulty would be to get all the stock-owners using a particular water-point to combine their herds, but the communal farmers in the Chibi and Gutu TTLs had done so with visibly successful results. However, the greatest advantage of the Savory system was that it did not require cattle numbers to be reduced, which had made other attempts to rehabilitate overgrazed rangeland unacceptable to local people. In fact, as long as they did not continuously graze the same area, high cattle densities were needed for their hooves to keep the soil surface loose and promote perennial grass growth.

*   *   *

Just as June and I were starting to relax and enjoy living on Lutope we were again reminded that there was a war on. Tom Crawford, who had taken over Sovalele from Ken Drummond, was again ambushed by guerrillas, but again escaped without serious injury. A week later, while out walking in one of the section's SDG cells, I came across the shoe prints of about six men, and when I asked the man in charge who they were, he either could not, or would not tell me.

In late 1977, to stop local people from supplying food to the liberation forces, the Rhodesian government had started building protected villages (PVs) in TTLs that were known to have been infiltrated. A similar system was used with doubtful success by the Americans in Vietnam, but Smith's military men were losing control over many rural areas and were prepared to try anything in order to regain the initiative.

In February, the first protected villages were completed in Mtetengwe, and via Elliot and a few other members of staff I received regular reports on what was happening across Liebig's boundary fence. According to them domestic life had been completely disrupted. Everyone had to be inside the PV fence an hour before sunset and could only leave again, to tend fields and herd livestock, an hour after sunrise. Any transgressors could be shot on sight by the security forces operating in the TTL. Because of the curfew large numbers of livestock had gone astray, and because crops were left unattended during the critical early mornings and evenings, they were being ravaged by birds, bush pigs and porcupines as well as stray cattle.

My staff, most of whom had their homes in Mtetengwe, did not conceal their dislike of the PVs and they assured me that the majority of the TTL's residents were equally bitter about yet another burden the war had imposed on them. And if my informants reflected the general feeling of people in the TTLs then it was the Rhodesian government alone that was blamed for their livestock and crop losses, providing yet another grievance for ZANLA and ZIPRA's political commissars to exploit.

As I knew there were liberation forces operating in Mtetengwe, I wondered where they would get food now that the local people were confined behind barbed wire at night. It did not take long to find out. Before the end of the month I received a report that a police anti-terrorist unit had tracked a group of guerrillas onto the southern end of Lutope. We had not escaped the war by moving from Makukwe.

In March we drove to Bulawayo on a shopping trip. We booked in at the Holiday Inn, where as a member of the police reserve I qualified for a family room at a greatly reduced rate. That evening we strolled through the city's broad, tree-lined streets and found ourselves in what could have been another country.

It was not surprising that most town-living whites in Rhodesia firmly believed that they could stop the clock and maintain their colonial lifestyle. As yet, the urban centres had hardly been affected by the increasingly bloody struggle taking place on the remoter farms and communal lands. Although almost every adult white male was now regularly called up to do some form of counter-insurgency service, the townsmen went to war for six weeks and then came back home to where their families lived in safety. For them there was also an undeniable excitement and camaraderie in doing a stint in the bush, as long as your side had the fire-power and air support to ensure its superiority in any contact with the enemy.

The farmers living in guerrilla-infiltrated areas had a very different per-spective of the conflict. As the targets of ambushes and house attacks, they shared the danger and tension with their wives and children. By 1978 the white civilian death toll was also rising, and most residents of the operational zones had lost friends or loved ones. Many only stayed on their farms because leaving them would mean losing them, but very few still believed that a mili-tary solution was possible. Even the Rhodesian cabinet seemed to be coming round to this point of view, and Ian Smith had recently signed an agreement with three moderate black leaders, incorporating them into a transitional government that was meant to lead the country to majority rule.

As a South African with no farm to defend, my own position was much more ambiguous. Rhodesia was my wife's country and I had grown to love its lowveld, which in many ways was similar to the Kaokoveld. The knowledge and experience I was gaining while working under Allan Savory would also be invaluable if I ever got back into South West Africa's northern homelands. But living on the Ranch was not easy. Our vocal opposition to some of the worst excesses of our colleagues had also not made June and me popular, and most of the ranch's section managers now treated us with cool reserve.

On one occasion when we returned from town to the Ranch headquarters in the late evening no one offered us accommodation, even though it was foolhardy to drive on to Lutope in the dark. The attitude to our predicament was summed up by an only half-joking comment that as the terrorists were our friends, what were we afraid of? In the end we set off after midnight, reasoning that any guerrillas still walking around at that time would be too surprised by our approach to set up an ambush.

When we returned from Bulawayo we passed through the Ranch head-quarters early on a Saturday afternoon, but this time Mike Gawler stopped us. We could not go on to Lutope, he told us, because there was trouble on Lamulas. Max Stockhill had been besieged in his homestead by a large group of guerrillas.

In his office, Mike briefed me on what had happened. Late on Friday af-ternoon Smiley, Max's assistant, had informed him that ZANLA guerrillas had come into the staff compound and were demanding to see him. Initially Max had refused, but when they threatened to attack the house, he agreed to talk to them. At dusk he and Smiley had met the guerrilla commander at the homestead's security fence gate. He told him they wanted him to give them food, radio batteries and penicillin.

Max told Smiley to provide the guerrillas with as much maize meal as they needed. However, he was unable to give them any drugs because only June had a key to the clinic. There were also no radio batteries on the section, but he offered to go to Towla the following morning and purchase some for them. The commander agreed to this, but warned Max not to report their presence.

Early the next morning Max hid his wife and daughter in his vehicle and drove to Towla, where he informed the Ranch management of what had happened. The decision was taken to call in the security forces, and a plan was drawn up to attack the guerrillas in the Lamulas compound. In order not to arouse suspicion, Max returned home, but left Elaine and their daughter at Towla. Soon after June and I got back from Bulawayo an army lieutenant arrived at the Ranch's headquarters, but as heavy rain was falling the rest of his strike force were still struggling to get their heavy vehicles through on the muddy roads. When they did not arrive by that evening the operation was postponed until the following morning.

We spent the night on the floor of the Ranch clubhouse. The rain had now set in, and unable to sleep, I listened to the rolls of thunder and wondered how Max was coping alone in Lamulas homestead. It had taken a brave man to go back, knowing that if the guerrillas found out he had betrayed them they were likely to attack the house, or at least set an ambush for him if he tried to leave.

If it hadn't been for the seriousness of Max's plight, the events of the next day would have been a farce. When the army strike force finally arrived, the lieutenant decided that the roads were too wet for his heavy trucks to get to Lamulas, and that the ground attack they had planned with such bravado the previous afternoon would no longer be possible. The Rhodesian Air Force was contacted, but no helicopters were available to transport his men. His next plan was to bomb the guerrilla camp with Hunter jets, but it was a Sunday and the officer who kept the keys to the Beit Bridge armoury was missing, and it was more than an hour before he was found on the golf course.

At two o'clock Max radioed in to Towla and cryptically informed us that the guerrillas had moved out of the compound, but were still in the area. By now he would have handed over the radio batteries and they could have got a message about the arrival of military vehicles at the Ranch's headquarters. If so, they would suspect that Max had double-crossed them. However, the army lieutenant was not prepared to move until the roads had dried. Apart from the possibility of his vehicles getting bogged down, there was now also the chance of an ambush being set for them on their way to the section. The following morning was the earliest that they would go in, and because the guerrillas had dispersed I gained the impression that he was now losing interest in the whole operation. At four Max radioed Towla again. The edge in his voice left us in no doubt that he was very worried about spending another night alone on Lamulas.

In their discussions with Max, the guerrillas had been friendly – suggesting that their intentions towards us section managers was not hostile. They would also know that I was expected back at Lutope by that evening. After weighing up the risks involved I offered to go to Lamulas in my vehicle. As one of the soldiers in the group was Bob Gawler's brother in-law, he and two other men volunteered to accompany me. But having gung-ho soldiers with me would blow any chance of talking my way out of trouble – if I was given a chance to. I also still hoped to calm the situation down, so that I could get back to managing the Advanced Project. I decided to go in alone.

The trip proved uneventful and I updated Max on what was happening at Towla. But even if there was no military operation on Lamulas he did not believe the situation on our sections could be normalised. Max had been through a traumatic two days, and as the road appeared to be clear he decided to go straight back to the Ranch headquarters. I did not blame him for wanting to get out of the danger zone.

After Max left I drove across to Lutope homestead, letting myself in through the security gate and being enthusiastically greeted by Rucksha, our young Alsatian dog. Everything seemed quite normal. A few minutes later the gardener arrived and we made a pot of tea. As we drank it he told me that there were 'boys' in the area. It was dangerous and I should not stay. I pretended to be completely ignorant of the situation on Lamulas, but was very moved by the fact that he had come to warn me. As Eliot had gone back to his home in Maranda for the weekend, I gave the gardener a message for Smiley, asking him to come to my office on Lutope first thing in the morning.

When it got dark I moved out of the house – which had a very flammable thatch roof – and slept in the mortar shelter Ken Drummond had built in the front garden. I decided not to turn the security fence alarm system on, confident that Rucksha would wake me should anyone approach. Alongside me lay the FN automatic rifle that had become a permanent fixture of my life on the Ranch. The rain had cleared up and the air was cool and crystal clear, but I did not sleep much. Where were the guerrillas, and what would they do now that Max had left?

Soon after sunrise Smiley arrived and told me that the guerrillas, who numbered over 30, had moved their camp, but were still in the vicinity. I asked him what he thought I should do. Go back to Towla immediately, he replied, and asked to come with me. As he lived inside the compound, the drama of the past few days had no doubt been even more traumatic for him than for Max. I told him that I would pick him, his wife and child up at their house at exactly eight o'clock.

As I drove into the compound two unfamiliar men dressed in denim jeans – the unofficial uniform of ZANLA – got up from where they had been sitting and disappeared behind some buildings. Fortunately, Smiley and his family were ready and waiting for me. They jumped in and we sped out of the compound gate. An hour later we were in Towla. If I had harboured any hopes of not being implicated in the events on Lamulas, they had now been dashed. From the perspective of the liberation forces operating in this part of Rhodesia, I would in the future be seen as just another white farmer – perhaps even as an 'enemy of the people'.

Over the next few days Liebig's management discussed how to handle the situation on Lamulas and Lutope. In the end it was decided that, until the security forces had eliminated the guerrilla presence on the two southern sections, it would be too dangerous for us to return to our posts. Max accepted a position in the Ranch's stock-theft unit, and I was offered a transfer to the company's fruit farms on Rhodesia's Eastern Highlands. June, who had grown up in this part of the country, found the proposition attractive, but I had not joined Liebig's to grow apples.

Since leaving Natal I had used my spare time to work on a layman's guide to ecology, using the province's diverse habitats to illustrate how its key principles and processes functioned in the real world. The book was aimed at the youth of all races, in the hope that they might make a better job of managing the natural environment than their parents had. If I had to leave the Ranch I chose to rather spend my time in Natal finishing it, and asked the Company for two months' unpaid leave, which they readily granted. June decided to take a six-week family planning course in Salisbury while I was away.

If most people in Bulawayo knew little about the real situation that prevailed in the operational areas, then the good citizens of Natal knew even less about what was happening anywhere in Rhodesia. The latest news coming out of the country was that the security forces had attacked guerrilla bases in Mozambique and killed hundreds of people. Good old Smithy, was their attitude; he knows how to deal with terrorists. After a few frustrating attempts, I gave up trying to convince the province's 'English liberals' that, even though the raids on the Chimoio and Tembue camps had been successful in military terms, they would not stem the tide of black nationalism.

By the middle of May my ecology handbook was still far from finished, but my leave was over and I headed back to Rhodesia. On the way I stopped in Pretoria to see Ken Tinley, now running an ecological consultancy firm, and Willem van Riet, who with Professors Fritz Eloff and Hannes Botma, had been tasked with drawing up master-plans for conservation in Damaraland and Kaokoland. From them I learned that the much-heralded national park in the western parts of the Kaokoveld had not yet been established. In fact, during a recent visit to the region Willem had found evidence of rampant illegal hunting – particularly of elephant and rhino.

Back at Towla, Mike Gawler informed me that the security forces had had no success against the guerrillas in either Mtengwe TTL or the southern part of the Ranch. The decision whether or not to go back to Lutope would be mine. Until there was a political settlement that the majority of Rhodesia's blacks accepted, I believed that the removal of the guerrilla presence on the Ranch was just wishful thinking. Nevertheless, I saw no point in moving to the Eastern Highlands, and told Mike that I was prepared to go back to Lutope immediately. June and our two boys joined me at the end of the month.

If anything, the security situation in the area had deteriorated in our absence. A private rancher whose land bordered Lutope on the eastern side of the Bubye River had been murdered in April. Tom Crawford on Sovalele had also been ambushed for the third time. This time a rocket-propelled grenade had actually exploded against the front fender of his Land Rover, knocking off the wheel and crushing one of his feet between the firewall and control pedals. By amazing luck, the Ranch's newly acquired spotter aircraft had been flying in the area and had frightened his assailants off. Soon after we returned, the homestead on Shobi Section was attacked, but no one was injured.

Although Lutope had generally functioned well while I had been away, a number of water installations had broken down, many cell fences were in a bad state of repair and, ominously, more than 300 head of cattle were missing. In fact there was so much work to be done that, at least during the day, I was able to forget about the possibility of unwanted trespassers lurking somewhere on the section's 50 000 hectares.

When I left the ranch in March, Elliot Thoma had resigned and gone back to his home in Maranda, where he knew 'the boys'. Without an assistant section manager or clerk I promoted one of Lutope's senior foremen, Chilongo Muchapa, to be my personal adviser on staff and work matters. He was not very literate, but knew virtually everything about the section and I enjoyed his 'old school' company.

One morning, at about 10 o'clock, we came across an antbear in one of the black staff's maize fields. As it was very unusual to see these creatures in broad daylight I drove closer, but Chilongo, who was sitting alongside me, became hysterical and virtually crawled under the dashboard. When we had driven on, and the old Shangane had calmed down, he told me that according to their belief, a person who saw an antbear in the middle of the day would soon die. It was not what I needed to hear.

Early in June, Bruce Cook radioed me on Lutope to ask for help. He claimed to have information that there was a guerrilla base on the section and had been given the name of one of my employees who knew where it was. The man worked at one of the SDG cells, but Bruce believed that if his armed security unit went there and asked for him, he was likely to run away. However, the man would trust me, and if I accompanied them they could question him without it creating an incident. Having had experience of how trigger-happy Bruce and his askaris were when people ran away from them, I agreed to cooperate on condition that the man was not hurt. I was assured that he would be 'handled with kid gloves'.

Within the ranks of the Ranch's white staff, Bruce Cook and I were at opposite extremes and there was no love lost between us. Consequently, we drove in separate vehicles to the cell where the man to be questioned lived. Arriving first, I called him and he came forward to greet me. Just then Bruce's vehicle roared into the little compound and the black security men on the back leapt off, and after giving my employee a few cuffs bundled him onto their truck. I remonstrated with Bruce but he brushed me aside, saying only that for his assistants 'that was kid gloves!' I had been naïve to trust Bruce. The other workers standing around said nothing. We all knew that back at their base, the gloves would be taken off. I felt like a Judas.

July was the time for pregnancy testing the cows on the Ranch. There was a lot at stake – and not just for us section managers. Mature cows that hadn't calved the previous year and heifers put to the bull for the first time that were not found to be pregnant would be sent on a one-way journey to Liebig's bully beef factory in West Nicholson. The results would also determine how well each SDG cell had performed. A calving rate of 70 per cent was the Rhodesian lowveld average, but most of Liebig's tested in the middle to upper eighties. Less than this was regarded as poor management.

The man who had to put his hand up the nether regions of over 20 000 cows was a private veterinarian from Fort Victoria, Dr Japie Jackson. The whole operation was long and tedious, now made more difficult by the stringent security measures that had to be taken. Lutope was the last section to be tested and from here it was my responsibility to take Dr Jackson to the Lion and Elephant Hotel, on the main Beit Bridge to Fort Victoria Road, where he had left his private car.

In spite of the war and many management disruptions, Lutope's cows had not let us down. The overall average for all the SDG cells on the section was well above 80 per cent, but it was the Advanced Project results that I was most proud of. Of 343 cows tested, all but 18 were positive – giving them a pregnancy rate of just under 95 per cent, the highest ever achieved. I knew that Allan, who was planning another inspection tour in August, would be very pleased.

We finally finished on the section late on a Friday afternoon and Dr Jackson stayed the night with us on Lutope. He had been our first guest since returning to the ranch and June and I had really enjoyed talking to him. The following morning, throwing caution to the wind, we decided to all go to the Lion and Elephant to play tennis, and also indulge ourselves by having lunch at the hotel. As it was the end of the month, on the way back I would pay workers at two of the SDG cells along the way. It would be breaking one of the cardinal rules of living in a guerrilla-war zone – not letting anyone know beforehand where you were going – but everyone already knew that we had to take Dr Jackson back that day.

A morning of socialising proved to be just what June and I needed to relieve the constant tension we were living under. Reluctantly we left the hotel at three and arrived at the first SDG cell half an hour later. Although we found the men strangely subdued, I paid them and drove on – deciding at the last minute to follow a longer, but much more beautiful, route along the Bubye River to the next pay-out point. Here we found everyone to be very drunk and effusive in their expressed affection for June and me. As it was a Saturday afternoon, after giving them their salaries, I brushed the matter off and we drove home. Apart from the rather odd behaviour of the workers we had paid, it had been a most pleasant day and we promised ourselves to do it more often.

Early the next morning, Chilongo came to our house and informed me that the tractor that was meant to visit the same two SDG cells and drop off rations had not returned. Before I could go out and look for it, however, the tractor driver arrived on foot and handed me a note signed by the local

ZANLA commander. It was short and to the point, saying simply that 'the next time they would get me'. They also said they planned to kill Bruce Cook, whose name I was not at all pleased to be linked with. When I had finished reading it, the driver handed me an AK-47 armour-piercing bullet they had given him, presumably to show that they meant business. He then explained what had happened the previous evening.

While travelling between the two SDG cells his tractor had been stopped by about 15 well-armed guerrillas. They had forced him to jack-knife the tractor and its trailer across the road and had then taken up ambush positions behind a nearby rocky outcrop. When I had not turned up by about 10 that night, they burned the tractor and trailer and gave him the note and bullet to take back to me.

I was stunned. June and the boys had been in the vehicle with me. Although it was bullet-proofed, the guerrillas had shown me that they had armour-piercing rounds, and according to the tractor driver at least one rocket launcher. It was just by chance that we had taken a longer route between the two cells. Did I have the right to risk my children's lives in order to work with Allan Savory? Colonial Rhodesia was now in its death-throes, but with characteristic stubbornness the country's whites had decided to fight on to the bitter end. Many more people were going to die before they were forced to admit defeat. I did not want my family to be included in these grim statistics.

I went inside and told June what had happened, adding that it was no longer possible for her and the boys to continue living on Lutope. We decided that she should take a midwifery course in Salisbury. I would work a month's notice and then go to Natal and complete my ecology guidebook. I knew that she loved living on the Ranch and helping her country in its hour of need. Leaving would be a bitter pill for her, but there really was no option.

A few days after I had submitted my resignation Mike Gawler passed on a message that the police in Gwanda wanted me to come and see them before I left the Ranch. I did so and was introduced to Inspector 'Nobby' Clark from the Special Branch in Salisbury and two local officers. They started the interview by telling me that they knew all about my having made contact with guerrillas the previous year while working on Makukwe. The fact that I had not informed the police was a very serious offence, they said, for which I could go to jail.

I exploded, and with nothing to lose told them exactly what had happened: the stock theft, Gary Scott's botched raid and his breaking the old man's arm and then burning down the village. I ended by saying that I had not informed the police because I did not trust them or the army to protect my staff should there be a follow-up operation.

Inspector Clark listened patiently to what I had to say, and then told me that they were willing to overlook the matter if I was prepared to do something for them in return – make contact with this group of guerrillas again, and work with the police to set up a meeting with them.

After the establishment of the transitional government in March 1978, the new multiracial leadership of Rhodesia had brought about a number of important changes. In April, 460 political prisoners had been released, in May ZANU and ZAPU were unbanned, and in July the last vestiges of racial discrimination were finally removed in all public places, including the restrictions on blacks purchasing farms in white areas. While the politicians were busy trying to sell the new, re-named Zimbabwe-Rhodesia to the outside world, amnesties had been offered to members of all the liberation forces that were prepared to lay down their arms. To further this policy, attempts were being made to contact guerrilla groups in the field in order to explain the government's 'safe return' policy.

The first part of Inspector Clark's request did not prove too difficult. Via Elliot Thoma I was able to send a letter to the commander of the ZANLA forces in Maranda, and a week later received a reply. It was not encouraging. They were disappointed that I had not given them the gift they asked for at our first meeting, and also had reason to 'suspect my relationship with the security forces'. The tone of their letter was lukewarm, but it did say they were prepared to consider a meeting with me. As it was now the end of August, I decided to visit my family in Salisbury before following up this part of the assignment. However, when I returned to Gwanda a week later, Nobby Clark told me the amnesty offer had been withdrawn.

The reason was ZIPRA's shooting down of an Air Rhodesia Viscount with a SAM-7 missile just after it had taken off from Kariba Airport. Thirty passengers were killed in the crash and 10 of the 18 who survived were later gunned down by guerrillas who arrived on the scene. When interviewed by the BBC, Joshua Nkomo claimed his forces were responsible for bringing the aircraft down, but denied that they had killed any of the survivors. The resultant outrage amongst the Rhodesian public led to the cancellation of the amnesty programme. ZAPU and ZANU were once more banned and martial law declared in many rural areas.

Ian Smith, who had been wooing Nkomo to join the transitional government, stated that this 'barbaric act' had seriously prejudiced the whole situation and changed the course of the country. It did, but perhaps I was one of the few who benefited from this tragic event. Most of those who met with ZANLA guerrillas to negotiate their 'safe return' were brutally murdered.

There was no denying that a new mood now prevailed in Rhodesia. Muzorewa, Sithole and Chirau – referred to in the local media as the 'bickering black trio' – had promised to end the war within weeks of their sharing power in Salisbury. But it had not ended, and they were rapidly losing credibility in the eyes of the whites, many of whom now demanded a full-scale mobilisation and all-out war against the Patriotic Front. It was time for me to leave.

On the way to Natal, where I planned to continue work on my ecology textbook, I spent a night with my brother Norman in Pretoria. Over dinner he showed me a copy of a report to the IUCN's Species Survival Commission by Clive Walker, the Director of the Endangered Wildlife Trust, on a trip he had undertaken with Prof Eloff to the Kaokoveld. 'I think you might find it interesting,' Norman said.

In the report Walker stated that: 'The Kaokoland elephant, the true desert population, may now number less than 80. … The black rhino is in a far worse situation with, possibly, less than 12 to 15 animals in the whole of Kaokoland. The fact that we found the remains of three rhino and four elephants highlights the position as one for grave concern. In the case of the elephants, the tusks had been chopped out in three of the four animals examined. The other skull was missing.'

Walker also noted that in late 1977, restrictions on the public entering the northern homelands of SWA had been removed. But no nature conservator had been stationed in Kaokoland and the area still had no conservation status. In conclusion, he proposed a total ban on elephant, rhino and giraffe hunting 'regardless of who it is' and the immediate implementation of the Eloff recommendations, including an urgent study of the elephant and rhino by the University of Pretoria.

Clive Walker's report confirmed what Willem van Riet had told me in April; that the wildlife situation in the Kaokoveld was disastrous. On the spur of the moment, I cancelled my flight to Durban and flew to Windhoek instead.

*　*　*

Major political changes were taking place in South West Africa. In 1975 a constitutional conference had been convened in the old colonial gymnasium, still known as the Turnhalle. Although SWAPO did not participate, the initiative attracted support from factions of all the country's ethnic groups. A year later the delegates had reached consensus on a three-tier constitution providing for autonomous ethnic areas as well as a national government – each with clearly defined powers. A multiracial interim administration was also created to supervise elections and see the country through to independence, set for the end of 1978. Although a Western Contact Group, representing the governments of the USA, England, France, Germany and Canada, had rejected the Turnhalle Constitution because of its retention of ethnic homelands and exclusion of SWAPO, South Africa decided to go ahead with the internal elections.

In striking contrast to Salisbury, I found the atmosphere in Windhoek very upbeat. The country's black inhabitants were about to be given their first opportunity to vote for a national government. Without SWAPO or the South West Africa National Union (SWANU) taking part, the political scene was dominated by the Democratic Turnhalle Alliance (DTA), founded by Dirk Mudge and the assassinated Herero Chief Clemence Kapuuo. It comprised 10 ethnically based parties from all regions of the country, and the DTA's symbol – two fingers raised in a victory sign – now blossomed like flowers wherever one went in the capital.

The day after I arrived I was able to get an appointment with Bernabe de la Bat, the Director of SWA's Department of Nature Conservation. He was friendly and cheerful, but when I asked him about the situation in Kaokoveld, he lit another cigarette before answering. It was not good, he said, but game was still plentiful in the de-proclaimed, western parts of Etosha, now northern Damaraland. The biggest problem was that his department had no say over the homelands.

'They're still run from Pretoria by the Department of Plural Relations – your old colleagues from Bantu Administration and Development with a fancy new name. But things are changing in the country. There will soon be a new political dispensation: first and second tier governments – and the Administrator General assured me that nature conservation will be a first-tier function. That means that my department will then be responsible for protecting wildlife throughout the whole country. You know Kaokoland. I want you to come and join us so that, when we take over the homelands, I can station you there – hopefully soon after the elections take place in November.'

Before leaving South West Africa I visited Rudi Loutit at the mouth of the Uchab River, where he had been stationed as a nature conservator at the southern entrance to the Skeleton Coast Park. I had known Rudi since schooldays and we had bumped into each other periodically since then. His wife, Blythe, had been an artist for the Natal Parks Board, and we had also met while I was working for the Wildlife Society in KwaZulu. Sitting on the postage stamp lawn in front of their driftwood and salvaged flotsam home, Rudi gave me chapter and verse about the wildlife situation inland of the Skeleton Coast Park.

'The army, government officials, the local people and who knows who else have shot the shit out of everything in Kaokoland. Now it's starting to happen in Damaraland. If you've got four legs and a tail the only safe place these days is on the coast, but you know as well as I do that this park's just desert. Unless you eat sand, you can't make a living here. Blythe and I only started working at Uchabmond a few months ago but we've seen enough game being slaughtered to make your whiskers curl. When is it going to end? Who is going to do something about it?'

By this stage, Rudi was standing up and his questions were being fired at the heavens. My old friend hadn't changed. He and Blythe were nature conservators of the Natal school. People were the problem, and whenever he saw wildlife being killed illegally, his thoughts usually turned to homicide. According to Rudi, half the country's civil servants were a waste of oxygen for whom euthanasia would be too lenient.

After spending a week with Rudi and Blythe in their cold and windy desert home, I flew back to Salisbury and told June about what was happening in SWA's north-west, as well as De la Bat's offer of a job. She knew that there was no point in asking me to stay in Rhodesia. The Kaokoveld was where I had always wanted to be – and now it desperately needed people who cared about the future of its wildlife. However, she had already started her midwifery course and wanted to finish it. I agreed to stay in Salisbury until I heard that nature conservation in the homelands had been transferred to the SWA Administration.

The situation in Rhodesia had not improved. Even the head of the country's combined forces, General Peter Walls, had recently admitted that in some areas they had lost ground. In October the interim government announced that all black Rhodesians aged between 18 and 25 and who had three years of secondary education would also be called up for military duty. Virtually every able-bodied man in the country was now doing active service for one or other side in the war.

Although I had joined the police reserve while on the Ranch, because we were living in an operational area, I had only been called up for an induction course. Thereafter, my presence in our remote home was seen as more valuable than doing duty elsewhere. But now that I was living in the leafy suburbs of Salisbury, I started feeling guilty about just sitting on my butt writing. In early November I volunteered for a three-week call-up and was sent to the Mateke Hills, a white ranching area in Nuanetsi District, to the south-east of Liebig's Ranch.

The unit I was seconded to had its base on an unoccupied farm, appropriately called Battlefields. In March 1977 the owner, Ben Stander, had been seriously wounded and his only son killed when their vehicle was ambushed. A few months later, his nephew had both his legs blown off below the knee by a mortar bomb. The house had also been attacked many times, and its walls were broken and pockmarked by the impact of rocket-propelled grenades and numerous bullets. Although Stander still periodically visited the farm, his wife and their two daughters had moved to Salisbury. There was a limit to how much even a tough Afrikaner woman could take.

By November 1978, nine white ranchers or members of their families had been killed in the Mateke Hills, and of the 20 farms only five were still occupied by their owners. Our job as police reservists was to protect the abandoned properties and provide escorts for government officials working in the vicinity. In fact, we could do little more than protect the farm we lived on, and all civil activities had long since ceased in the district. But our presence did show the liberation forces that they did not yet have complete control of the area.

During my three weeks in the Mateke Hills, we visited the farms that still had resident owners, to give them moral if not physical support. One farm belonged to a wealthy horse breeder, Mr Du Plessis, who had literally turned his homestead into a fortress, from which he sallied out in a landmine and bullet-proofed vehicle to give instructions to his few remaining workers. On my first visit, I met Paul, a young South African trainee teacher who had volunteered to act as a 'brightlight' on remote Rhodesian farms during his summer vacation. He had just arrived and was waiting to be picked up by Van der Heever, the farmer he had been assigned to. It was Paul's first time in a war zone, and he seemed very excited about doing his bit to help South Africa's beleaguered northern neighbour.

Three days later, Van der Heever's farm was attacked and next morning I was part of the patrol sent out to investigate. Nobody had been injured –

apparently on either side – but there were mortar craters on the front lawn and, like the Battlefields homestead, windows were shattered and walls pockmarked by bullets. Still wide-eyed and breathless, Paul told us how he had experienced the attack.

About an hour before sunset Van der Heever had left the house to meet with his labourers in the compound, but had not returned. At dusk, while Paul was sitting reading in the lounge, 'all hell broke loose'. Not knowing from where the firing was coming he was lying flat on the floor when the kitchen door opened and Van der Heever calmly walked in, muttering about 'bloody kaffirs' not being able to shoot straight. He had then proceeded to pour two very stiff brandies, handed one to Paul, and sat down on the sofa. Every now and again Van der Heever got up to fire a few shots from one of the windows, 'to show them that we're still alive' and then went back to drinking his brandy. Before they finished the bottle the shooting had stopped – but they finished it anyway.

On one of our patrols, far from any homestead, we came across the wife of another bitter-end farmer, walking alone along the road, carrying only a suitcase. We stopped, and as I was the only one in our group who could speak Afrikaans, I asked her where she was going. To the Lion and Elephant Hotel, she replied, which was at least another 20 km away. Once loaded into our armoured vehicle, Mrs Boshoff told me her sad story. She and her husband had had a fight, and when he punched her she decided to leave him. Waiting until he went to one of the dip tanks, she packed a bag and walked out the front door. As the area was heavily infiltrated with ZANLA forces, we had to take her back to her husband – although she begged me not to, claiming to be more afraid of his temper than the possibility of meeting up with 'terrorists'.

A few days later, while driving on the same road, we were ambushed. At the time, I was accompanying Patrol Officer McGregor in an unprotected Land Rover, travelling behind an armour-proofed Puma truck that contained the rest of our group. As most of the initial firing, including two RPGs or rifle grenades, was directed at the Puma, we were able to stop and take cover before getting into the 'killing zone'. Crouching in the road verge, not even knowing where the bullets whistling overhead were coming from, I finally decided that I wanted no more part in this futile war that had already claimed over 20 000 lives.

When the firing stopped we regrouped a few hundred metres down the road. The Puma had only been struck by small-arms fire and no one in it had been injured. In a thorough search of the ambush area we found no bodies or even any blood, showing that our return fire had been equally ineffectual. For all the momentary noise and adrenaline, it was an insignificant incident on a little-used road in the vast Rhodesian lowveld – meaningless in the bigger picture of a liberation struggle that could only end one way. But if we had been travelling in front of the Puma the outcome for me and Patrol Officer McGregor might have been very different.

A few days before completing my three weeks in the Mateke hills, I heard over the police radio that Pete Richards had been ambushed and killed instantly by an RPG on Majingwe Section. While we were on Makukwe, he and his wife Margaret had been our nearest white neighbours. Although we often sparred over how to manage labour and the activities of the Rhodesian security forces, during our last few months on Liebig's June and I had often felt that they were our only remaining friends on the Ranch. We had no patrol that day, and as I listened to the unsuccessful follow-up operation I remembered Pete saying a few weeks before we left that perhaps my way was the best: 'We need the munts just as much as they need us, so I guess we better start learning to like each other.' Yes, I thought, that is what living in Southern Africa is all about. And if we did start respecting each other the region could be an example to the rest of the world. But why did it take a war and so many deaths before we realised it?

When I got back to Salisbury I phoned De la Bat to find out what was happening in South West Africa. According to him the elections had gone exceptionally well: 78 per cent of the eligible electorate had voted and the DTA had won a massive majority in the new parliament. The country was moving in the right direction, he told me, but it would take a few months before conservation in the homelands was transferred to Windhoek. He suggested I join the Department anyway, so that when the legislation changes occurred my posting to Kaokoland would just be an internal transfer. There was a regional services post open in the south of the country, based in Keetmanshoop.

This time I caught the train to Windhoek. As we pulled out of the station and moved slowly through Salisbury's industrial areas it passed close to the petrol storage depot that had been rocketed by ZANLA guerrillas a few days previously. As hundreds of firemen fought to bring the massive inferno under control, a pall of black smoke hung over the city. The war had reached the urban areas and everybody in the country was now affected. Rhodesia was burning and from its ashes Zimbabwe was rising.

CHAPTER FIFTEEN

SOUTH-WEST OF SOUTH WEST

I had forgotten that most government officials in Windhoek take long holidays over Christmas and New Year, and the country's civil service virtually closes down until late January. After a frustrating few weeks my application was finally processed, and I was appointed as a nature conservator in the Keetmanshoop regional service office. It was at the opposite end of the country from the Kaokoveld, but it also meant that I would be far from the areas where SWA's armed liberation struggle was now gaining momentum. After our experiences in Rhodesia I looked forward to living in a peaceful environment.

On my first day at work the Principal Nature Conservator for the south, Robbie Hawthorne, called me into his office. We had met before in the Marienfluss, when he accompanied Bernabe de la Bat and other top government officials on an inspection tour of the western Kaokoveld. Then I had told him I did not think elephant and rhino poaching was a problem in the Territory. I had been wrong, a fact he now took great pleasure in reminding me of, before giving me a breakdown of my duties. My area of responsibility would be the country's extreme south-west, which included the districts of Karasburg, Bethanie and Lüderitz, as well as Diamond Area No 1 – known locally as the Sperrgebiet.

'I think you'll enjoy working in the Sperrgebiet,' Robbie told me. 'Very few people have been allowed into it since the German times, so it's one of the most undisturbed parts of the country. You'll need a security clearance to get in of course, but that's my problem. Do you have a camera?'

'Yes, I do,' I answered, wondering what a camera had to do with the Diamond Area.

'I hope it can take close-up photographs. The Director tells me you're a botanist. He wants you to continue with the work Derek Clark – the man you've replaced – was doing on protected plants. Mainly succulents: some of them are very valuable and there's a lot of illegal trading going on. A camera with all the fancy lenses has been ordered, but we can only get it on next year's budget. The routine work around here is farm inspections. You might find it rather boring, but you'll just have to knuckle down to it. I hear you were in Rhodesia. What was the terrorist situation like in your area? I'd like to talk to you about it, but later, we've got work to discuss now.'

At this point Robbie picked up his telephone and put a call through to the General Manager of Consolidated Diamond Mines in Oranjemund, the little town on SWA's southern coast that was the centre of one of the biggest diamond mining operations in the world. Five minutes later he assured me that my permit to work in the Sperrgebiet was being organised.

'Contacts,' he said to me with a conspiratorial wink. 'That's what you've got to have in this game. Now, as I was saying about the camera. Derek Clark started a photo reference file on the succulent plants in this part of the country so that the rest of us conservators, who are not plant boffins, can recognise which ones are listed in the nature conservation ordinance as being protected. Eugene!'

Robbie had called at the top of his voice for one of my new colleagues even though he was sitting in an adjoining office. 'Bring me that file of Clark's photographs and make it snappy.'

'Clark was bloody good with a camera. I only use a miniature myself – for evidence. I can carry it in my pocket and slip it out without anyone noticing. It's very useful for our work. Good photographs can make all the difference in a poaching case.'

While Robbie spoke, Eugene Cronjé quietly entered the office, placed the requested photo file on the corner of the desk and left. Robbie paid no attention to him or the file, and went on talking.

'Another important part of your job is problem animals – mainly jackals, but there are still a few cheetah and leopard around. Caracals also kill a lot of sheep on some farms. Even dassies can be a problem where there are too many of them. They come down from the hills and eat everything around. Farmers here complain about anything on their properties that they can't eat or sell. We still have some poaching going on, mainly in the Diamond Area and on properties along the edge of it.'

He then gestured towards the plant file, and apologising for his lack of knowledge about succulents, suggested that I go through it in my own time. In his inimitably disjointed way he had given me the low-down on my new job, but his real interest lay in other matters: 'Were the terrorists in your area ZANLA or ZIPRA …?'

Robbie Hawthorne was one of the DNC's most experienced law enforcement officers, and always seemed to be involved in some sort of cloak and dagger assignment, either involving the illegal trade in game products, or counter-insurgency matters. However, as I got to know him better I suspected that his role in undercover operations was somewhat exaggerated. He had a very strong-willed wife and four daughters. Perhaps, the world of secrecy and intrigue he created around him was just a means of escaping from his female-dominated domestic life.

Apart from Eugene Cronjé, two other nature conservators, Rhett Hiseman and Johan le Roux, were based in Keetmanshoop. Each one of us was responsible for a part of the vast area controlled by the regional office. The south-western quarter that I had been made responsible for comprised more than 60 000 km^2 of arid mountains and desert, which I would soon learn was in parts as scenically spectacular as the Kaokoveld.

The Senior Nature Conservator under Robbie Hawthorn was Peter Lind, who had just been promoted and transferred from the Etosha National Park. Peter was in the classic game ranger mould: tall, broad-shouldered and ruggedly good-looking. Although a dedicated conservationist, he was also a hard-drinking extrovert whose company men enjoyed and many women found irresistible. Peter had set up home in the 'ghost-house', a derelict stone building that dated back to the early days of German rule, and from there organised some of the wildest parties that the very conservative residents of Keetmanshoop had seen.

The regional office also had two Nama-speaking general assistants, Albert Duncan and Dirk Neels. Both men had grown up in the south and worked many years for nature conservation, and as the rest of us were newcomers to the region, their local knowledge and experience were invaluable. Soon after my arrival a third general assistant, Frederik Eiseb, was also employed.

A diminutive Damara man with limited schooling, he would not have been my first choice from the applicants for the post. However, Peter explained that Albert and Dirk were far too capable to be used as labourers, which was what the office really needed, and Frederik fitted the position perfectly.

Before my first field trip Robbie called me into his office to give me a warning: 'You'll find that nature conservation is not rated very highly by most of the farmers around here. They are a pretty independent lot – mainly Afrikaners who came here after the First World War – and they believe they should be able to do what they like on their own farms. Most of them don't love Englishmen either. I'm OK because I'm Irish. They reckon we've been fighting the English longer than they have. Of course my family's from the north, loyalists you know. But they don't know the difference. You'll probably be given a tough time by some of them, but if anyone tries to chase you off his farm just give me a call. We've got the law behind us and can make life pretty difficult for them if we want to.'

Our 'big stick' was the Nature Conservation Ordinance of 1975, which gave us wide-ranging powers – in some respects even exceeding those of the police – to investigate suspected illegal hunting. On my first day Robbie had given me a copy of the thick, hard-backed document and sternly told me to read it. 'If you don't know the law, you can't enforce it – and that's our job.'

With regard to wildlife utilisation, however, SWA's nature conservation legislation was regarded as being the most progressive in Africa. It was the policy of the government to encourage bona fide landowners to see the game on their properties as a valuable economic resource. To this end, on farms that were 'adequately fenced' they were given the right to hunt springbok, gemsbok, kudu and warthog for their own use at any time of the year without restrictions. Furthermore, during the designated hunting season they could allow other persons to hunt these four species on their land and charge them a fee. Only for the selling of game meat was a permit required.

Landowners who had gone to the considerable expense of game-proof fencing their farm, or a camp on it of more than 1 000 ha, were given additional rights to undertake trophy hunting. But irrespective of its fences, the live capture of wild animals could only be carried out with permission from the Director of Nature Conservation – to ensure that those in charge of the operation were competent to do so.

To facilitate the use of wildlife a number of game-cropping companies had been registered that were given special permission to hunt at night. However, before a landowner was granted a night-harvesting permit, his farm first had to be inspected by a nature conservation officer – which was one of our major functions. The object of these inspections was to confirm that the property was adequately fenced, and also to estimate the number of animals that could be hunted on a sustainable basis.

Prior to the SWA nature conservation legislation changing from strict protection to promoting commercial utilisation, the game numbers on white-owned farms had been in steady decline. The 1975 Ordinance and its 1967 predecessor, which first opened the door to trophy hunting and wildlife harvesting, were credited with having turned this situation around. But the battle had not yet been won. The country's farmers had a long history of seeing game only as a nuisance that broke fences and competed for grazing with their cattle or sheep. The fact that, before 1967, they could be arrested for shooting a springbok on their own land had also not endeared them to nature conservation or the officials who enforced it.

On the other side, many conservationists were philosophically opposed to wild animals being brought into the marketplace and morally against all forms of hunting. Some of them were very vocal in their condemnation of the SWA authority's having given use-rights to the farmers, and any abuses of the new legislation played right into their hands. It was an interesting juxtaposition: landowners versus conservationists – with us, the officials who were tasked with applying the law, somewhere in the middle.

The first trip that I undertook with Albert Duncan in early February was not to carry out any formal farm inspections, but to start acquainting myself with the area I was responsible for, and the people who lived in it. We set off on a cloudless day, westwards along the main road to Lüderitz. There had been some rain the previous evening and the cool morning air was crystal clear. In the distance, more than 30 km away, were the Great Karas Mountains. Between them and the road was just a flat, sparsely bushed plain. The scenery was massive, stark and majestic. It felt good to be back in South West Africa.

I was in no hurry, so stopped frequently to collect and press plant specimens. A number of the grasses, shrubs and small trees that grew along the roadside were familiar old friends from the Kaokoveld, but many were new to me. In Keetmanshoop I had found the cupboard that contained the office herbarium to be almost empty, and had decided to rectify the situation. If our job was to inspect farms then it should be done professionally, and that meant at least knowing the names of the common plants that occurred on them.

Wherever I saw game from the road I called in at the nearest homestead, hoping to learn something about the local attitudes to wildlife. To break the ice, I first asked the rugged, sun-tanned farmers I met about their livestock and grazing management practices – explaining to them that I had recently come from a Rhodesian cattle ranch. At the time, most 'South Westers' were anxiously watching events in the ex-British colony, and were very interested in first-hand information about its deteriorating security situation. My being English-speaking was therefore overlooked and I was invariably treated with great hospitality.

The southwest of SWA was karakul sheep country, and the main economic activity was the sale of 'Persian lamb' pelts – the glossy-black skins of lambs slaughtered within 48 hours of birth. Nobody liked killing newborn lambs, I was assured, but in this harsh unpredictable climate, karakul farming had an important advantage over all other forms of animal husbandry; the ewes did not have to raise their offspring in order to produce a saleable product. In a region where the good years were droughts by normal standards, no other form of livestock could compete with the coal-coloured sheep, and when the price of the satiny lamb skins had been high they were referred to as South West Africa's 'black diamonds'.

But the prices obtained for Persian lamb pelts had fallen sharply. International anti-cruelty organisations and high-profile personalities such as Brigitte Bardot had successfully campaigned against the killing of baby seals and the whole fur-trade was now in decline. Although the farmers I spoke to felt threatened, they were not yet prepared to consider game ranching as a possible option. The general feeling was that there were still too many regula-tions controlling the use of wildlife: 'A farmer likes to decide for himself what and how many of his animals to market. We don't need youngsters in green jackets and epaulettes walking all over our farms and telling us how to run them.'

Nevertheless, I found a begrudging admission that the new conservation legislation was a considerable improvement, as one of them explained. 'Under the old laws, my father was supposed to get a permit from the local magistrate just to make a little biltong in the winter. Out of sheer cussedness, he refused to do so. We fed the damn springbok on our farm and he saw no reason to ask the government's permission to shoot one.' Looking me straight in the eye, he added: 'And it never stopped us always having game biltong in the house.'

The farmers' frustrations with the inspection and permit system that still applied were understandable. Eugene, Rhett and Johan were all under 25, with little, if any, practical experience of farming – and yet their reports could de-termine whether a permit to crop game was granted or not. However, most farmers did admit that there were many amongst them who had no scruples when it came to hunting, and conceded that there had to be some control. On one point they all agreed: now that game had a commercial value, its numbers on farmlands in the south had considerably increased.

While on a farm visit I heard that a second passenger aircraft had been shot down in Rhodesia, killing everybody on board. A few days later June phoned to tell me that Ted Whigg, who had taken over from Graham Ballard as managing director of Liebig's Rhodesia, as well as the manager of its meat canning factory in West Nicholson, Loris Zukini, had both been on the flight.

*   *   *

Three days after leaving Keetmanshoop, Albert and I reached the port of Lüderitz. The bay and surrounding desert had been the first part of SWA annexed by imperial Germany in 1882. Although strikingly beautiful when not shrouded in fog, there can be few more desolate and hostile coastlines in the world. That Adolf Lüderitz had been able to convince the 'Iron Chancellor' that it was a suitable acquisition for the Reich must rank as one of history's greatest feats of salesmanship. But although neither Lüderitz nor Bismarck lived to see it, the barren desert would prove to be more valuable than they could possibly have imagined.

The man credited with discovering the first diamond here was August Stauch, a permanent-way inspector on the railway line from the coast inland. But it was Zacharias Lewala, a coloured man from the Cape, who actually picked the gemstone up from the desert sands, and having previously worked on the Kimberly diamond fields, recognised it for what it was. He gave it to his white foreman, who in turn passed it on to Stauch.

Once it was confirmed as a diamond, and of very high quality, Stauch secretly set about pegging claims in the area where Lewala picked it up. At first, there was great scepticism about the railwayman's discovery. It was only when he started giving diamonds away 'in a most generous manner' that people took his claims seriously and diamond fever hit the German colony's southern port. By the end of the year, an average of 200 carats – representing over 1 000 diamonds – were being found a day and many new claims were granted both up and down the desert coast. Five years later, Stauch's Pomona mine alone would be averaging more than 50 000 carats a month.

At the beginning of the diamond rush, only two policemen had been stationed at Kolmanskop – the heart of the early diggings – to keep order amongst the fortune-seekers flocking into the area from all over the world. They could not hope to control the chaotic situation that was developing, and in September a huge tract of desert, from the Orange River northwards to the 26th degree of latitude and for 100 km inland, was proclaimed a prohibited area. At the time only four German companies had been granted the right to operate within it, but when diamonds were also discovered further to the north, a second 'diamond area' was proclaimed, that extended to the southern border of the British Territory around the harbour of Walvis Bay.

At the end of the First World War, Dr Lubbert, a lawyer and old friend of August Stauch, convinced him and the other German companies that the best way for them to avoid being expropriated was to merge all the South West African diamond-mining interests with a South African producer. The giant De Beers Company in Kimberly was the obvious choice, but to everyone's surprise Lubbert decided instead to go with a newly formed company, the Anglo-American Corporation. In 1920 the Consolidated Diamond Mines of SWA was formed. Stauch and the other Lüderitz diamond producers were paid £3.5 million pounds, half in cash and the rest as shares in CDM, as the new corporation was to become known.

*   *   *

As my security clearance to enter the Sperrgebiet had not yet arrived, Albert and I drove back inland to Aus, a one-hotel village that nestled amongst granite hills on the edge of the desert. We then turned south through sheep farming country to the Rosh Pinah zinc mine, owned by South Africa's iron and steel giant, ISCOR. It was situated in rugged schist and gneiss ranges that were renowned for the succulents growing on them, but the whole region was in the grip of a major drought and all but a few species of aloe had shrivelled to unidentifiable, sun-blackened stubble.

To salvage something from the trip, I called in to see the mine manager, Jan Botha, to discuss nature conservation in the vicinity of the little town. He told me that he had recently been appointed as an honorary nature conservator, and had always done his best to limit the amount of illegal hunting done by his employees. However, because of what was now happening in the Sperrgebiet he was no longer prepared to take action against them.

'Because of the drought there's no grazing in the Namib, and hundreds of gemsbok carcasses are lying along the border fence. I've sent reports to your head office, but they do nothing. Nature conservation is very close to my heart, but you don't just let animals starve to death. It's a waste, man, a scandalous waste.'

I used his phone to call Keetmanshoop and inform Robbie of the situation. He promised to see what could be done, and then passed on a message from the Chief Control Warden in Windhoek, Stoffel Rocher. I was to proceed immediately to a farm between Rosh Pinah and Aus and inform its owner, Mr Blaauw, that, according to an inspection carried out in November his farm, Grens, was not adequately fenced. Therefore, he had no rights to hunt or capture game on it until his fences complied with the Nature Conservation Ordinance stipulations.

Apparently Blaauw had applied for a permit to cull 30 gemsbok and 50 springbok on Grens and sell the meat, but as it bordered on the Diamond Area it was suspected that the animals had recently come onto the farm through breaks in his boundary fence. After inspecting Grens, I was to make recommendations on whether or not the permit should be granted. I had been working only a few weeks for the DNC and was already in the hot seat.

Hendrik Blaauw turned out to be a man in his forties, living in a modest homestead with long vistas across the plains to distant desert mountains. Over a cup of strong *boerekoffie* he told me that he owned a second farm, Arasab, situated about 15 km to the north-east, on which his wife was then staying. Together, they totalled nearly 40 000 hectares, but there was no grass left on Arasab, forcing him to move all his stock to Grens, where a few showers had recently fallen.

'One farm is not enough in this area, no matter how big it is. Arasab has not had rain for two years, and if I had not been able to take my stock to Grens they would have died. Having a second farm doubles your chances of getting rain, but it is still no guarantee. Most of my neighbours are working in Rosh Pinah, or grading the roads. They're now just part-time farmers – when they get a bit of rain on their farms they keep a few animals, but most of the time they depend on their salaries.'

In the afternoon Blaauw and I inspected his fenceline, which I found to be in good order. However, along the western boundary, there were four gates that led into the Diamond Area. All were shut, but there was nothing to stop him opening them. Along the fence-line were deeply worn paths, showing that game had been trying to migrate eastwards, as they did in the Kaokoveld during droughts. The few gemsbok we did see in the Sperrgebiet were in very poor condition, and some were just walking skeletons.

When I questioned Blaauw about the gates, he had plausible explanations for all of them. Nevertheless, I instructed him to wire three of them into the fence-line, which he agreed to do. The fourth was on a proclaimed track into the Sperrgebiet that CDM's security officers and the police sometimes used. It should then be kept permanently locked and only these two parties should have the keys, I told him. But he assured me that CDM had given permission for him to periodically go into the area just west of Grens, to check for locust breeding grounds.

While driving around Grens I counted over 250 gemsbok and estimated there could have been double that number. Blaauw did not deny that they had come in from the Sperrgebiet, but they were on Grens now and I had ordered the gates along the boundary to be closed. Even if we were able to get them back across the fence, and there was no practical way of doing so, under the present conditions there they were likely to die of starvation. The drought had also given Blaauw a legitimate reason to remove some of them, as they were now competing with his livestock for the sparse grazing on the farm. I recommended that his permit be approved, and any further requests to capture or cull up to 120 more gemsbok be viewed favourably.

Once I had received my CDM security clearance, which gave me unrestricted access to the whole Sperrgebiet outside of the actual mining areas, Albert Duncan, Johan le Roux and I were able to inspect the boundary fences of all the farms bordering it. We soon discovered that Hendrik Blaauw was by no means the only farmer to have acquired large numbers of gemsbok from the Diamond Area.

The worst case was Nieu Tsaus, adjoining Grens, where we found a 20 metre opening in the border fence and the tracks of many animals going through. I ordered the owner to close it, but estimated that over 400 gemsbok had already crossed onto the farm. Two months later the owner applied for a permit to capture and sell 80 gemsbok, and cull for sale a further 100. This time I carefully read through the legislation before making any recommendation, but it was clear that once the gap in the fence had been closed he was legally the owner of the gemsbok. Because of the lack of grazing on the farm his permit was also granted.

Over the following months we found a total of 28 gates along the Sperrgebiet border between Aus and Rosh Pinah – six on one farm alone. Many of them had been cunningly placed behind kopjes or sand dunes that could not be reached by vehicle. Some farmers had also used natural features or fence extensions to create funnels that allowed gemsbok to come onto their properties, but not to leave. Another tactic, used by one farmer after his gates had been ordered closed, was to lift the 'hanging mats' across watercourses, enabling the gemsbok to just walk under them.

In a report Albert and I wrote at the end of the year I estimated that, because of the drought in the Diamond Area, possibly as many as 3 000 gemsbok had crossed onto at least 11 border farms, and permits to capture or crop 1 044 gemsbok were issued. During the designated hunting season the landowners also had the right to sell game to biltong hunters and many more were, no doubt, used in this way. In conclusion we stated: 'That in 1979 large-scale irregularities and many illegalities occurred on farms along the Diamond Area boundary is beyond dispute ... and yet we were unable to make a single prosecution. Even though there may be some justification for the farmer's attitude towards this often blatant theft of State gemsbok – that we were allowing them to die in their thousands in the drought – the fact remains that as long as we continue to take no action, the farmers and other persons residing in the area will have no respect for nature conservation legislation.'

We recommended regular patrolling of the Diamond Area boundary and visits to the border farmers, but most importantly that a management policy for the southern Namib gemsbok was urgently needed. To this end I requested and was granted permission to carry out research on this virtually unknown population of what was then one of the least studied ungulates inhabiting the country. In fact the only previous research on gemsbok had been done on captive animals in Russia!

*   *   *

Early in May Robbie called all of us nature conservators into his office. 'The rainy season is over,' he said, 'which means the trigger-finger of every self-respecting biltong-lover has started itching, and those that don't have their own farms will be out to shoot a springbok, kudu or gemsbok anywhere they can find one.' He then gave us a lecture on law enforcement, based on his many years of outwitting and apprehending poachers. After planning the priority places for Rhett, Eugene and Johan to patrol, Robbie told me that my 'hotspot' was the Koichab Pan, a fossil riverbed north of the Aus–Lüderitz highway. It was unfenced State land with plenty of gemsbok on it. One of his many contacts had tipped him off that a lot of illegal hunting had taken place there the previous year, and the same could be expected in the coming winter.

Over the Ascension Day long weekend I drove to the Koichab Pan with Frederik Eiseb, our new general assistant. Heeding Robbie's warning that news of a nature conservator in the area 'gets around faster than a good-looking whore on a Saturday night', we left Keetmanshoop after dark and made camp alongside the track leading from Aus to the pan. At first light I hid my Toyota Landcruiser behind some granite boulders and we set up a lookout post on a hill from where a large tract of State land could be observed.

During the day nothing suspicious happened, but about an hour before sunset a white Ford truck with three men on the back came down the road from Aus. They drove past without seeing us and headed off across the plain towards the Pan. I watched through binoculars as they first stopped near a flock of ostriches – which ran off – and then started chasing a small herd of gemsbok. By now the vehicle was at least 10 km away, but I was able to clearly see one gemsbok falling down and being loaded onto the truck. The same procedure was followed with another gemsbok before it became too far and too dark for me to see any more.

As there was only one access route to the Pan, I decided to set up an ambush for them on their way back. Finding a place where it would be impossible for a vehicle to leave the track, I blocked the road with the Toyota and sent Frederik, who was not in uniform, 50 metres ahead and told him to signal the truck to slow down. I then concealed myself next to the road, took out the .38 revolver I had been issued and waited.

At about eight o'clock a vehicle approached. It was moving fast and only just managed to stop a few metres from the Toyota – right next to where I crouched. Before the driver knew what was happening I was standing at his window, ordering him and his two white companions to get out. Taken completely by surprise by my sudden appearance they complied, while the two black men on the back of the truck huddled against the cab, too frightened to move. Hidden under a sail were three gemsbok carcasses, and behind the front seat I found two rifles. While all this was happening I had no idea where Frederik was. I occasionally shouted in his direction to 'keep the men covered', but had heard no reply. Only when I had put their firearms in my vehicle and was ready to leave did he finally make an appearance, the whites of his wide eyes shining in the vehicle headlights. I wondered what the poachers thought when they saw that my only companion was an unarmed black man who was literally shaking with terror.

Ordering one of the whites to accompany me and the other two to follow in their vehicle, we then drove to the Aus police station where all three were charged with hunting game on administration property without a permit, and hunting game from a moving vehicle. At some stage along the way both black men had jumped off the truck and run away. The officer on duty, Sergeant Mostert, impounded the two rifles and the Ford truck until the court hearing, which he told me would take place the following week. Late that night Frederik and I made camp just out of town, amazed that it had all gone so smoothly.

On 9 May Mr Dana Oosthuizen, a road construction contractor, appeared before a circuit magistrate from Lüderitz. He pleaded guilty to the charges, claiming that it was his idea and that he alone had done the hunting. He was sentenced to a total fine of R1 200 or 15 months in jail. One rifle was confiscated, but the vehicle was returned. The case against the other two men, both salesmen from South Africa, was withdrawn, but I hoped that in future they would buy their biltong, not poach it.

* * *

Thanks to SWA's progressive nature conservation legislation, game biltong and venison was legally available in the country, and the frozen meat of springbok and gemsbok was being exported to South Africa and Europe. Much of it came from farms in the south, and to facilitate the efficient killing of large numbers of game, professional cropping teams had been licensed to hunt at night with the aid of a spotlight. After being skinned and degutted the carcasses were hung in refrigerated trucks until taken to the nearest market. Nature conservators were not required to be present at these game harvests, but out of interest I joined one of the teams for two nights. Out of over 250 springbok cropped, only seven were not killed with the first shot. This was a business, and hard economics ensured that high standards were maintained.

The live capture of game was much more strictly controlled, and on a number of occasions Robbie asked me to observe gemsbok being caught on farms. At the time different techniques were used, but all had relatively high mortality rates, both during the capture operation and from stress in the days that followed. The most primitive method was simply to chase a gemsbok in an open truck across the plains, and as it tired to firmly grab it by the base of one horn, while a man behind caught its tail and pulled the rump against the vehicle. At the same time the driver applied brakes and slowly brought truck and gemsbok to a standstill. Short pieces of hosepipe were then fitted over its rapier-like horns and a piece of cloth tied over its eyes. Most capture teams also administered a stiff tot of brandy to the captured animal as a 'tranquilliser'. If all went well, the blindfolded and slightly inebriated gemsbok was then quietly led onto the back of the transport vehicle.

On one operation I observed the farmer had specially trained dogs that he released from the pursuit vehicle when the chased animal showed signs of being exhausted. In this situation a gemsbok's natural response was to back up against a bush or boulder and face its attacker. After a few feints a good dog would then dart in and catch it by the nose or ear and hold it until the capture team arrived. Bad dogs could easily end up being skewered on the gemsbok's horns, and even the best of them were not allowed to catch more than five animals a day, after which they tended to get careless and also risked having short careers.

In 1979 the price paid for gemsbok carcasses ranged between R80 and R120, while live animals were sold for up to R250 – over two-thirds of my monthly salary at that time. Springbok and kudu fetched equally competitive prices. In spite of the restrictions on their use, wildlife had become a marketable resource, and the days of farmers allowing people to hunt illegally on their land had ended. On freehold land nature conservation was no longer a matter of catching poachers; it was now about assisting the owner to get the maximum benefit from his wildlife.

The SWA ordinance did still contain a few contradictions, one of them relating to a landowner's responsibility for eradicating jackals – a proclaimed 'problem animal'. If a neighbour complained about their numbers on a particular farm, its owner was given three months to take appropriate action. Thereafter, a nature conservator was sent to trap as many jackals as he could on his property, and for every jackal killed the farmer was given a fine.

In August I was sent to the farm of a Mr Oberholzer, a prominent cattle and sheep breeder in the Karasburg District, who had been accused of not controlling the jackals on his property. He had been given the prescribed written warning and three months later a Windhoek-based nature conservator had trapped a single jackal on his land, and had given him the required fine. The problem was that, although the amount was very small, Mr Oberholzer refused to pay it. My superiors were in a quandary and I was asked to try and sort the matter out.

Mr Oberholzer received me very cordially, and over lunch explained why he had chosen to stand on principle, 'even if it means going to jail'. His policy was to farm in an environmentally friendly way, and he believed that jackals played an important role by keeping down the numbers of mice and locusts – creatures that might otherwise reach plague proportions. He was quite prepared to admit that some individual jackals preyed on sheep, but as the Windhoek conservator had only been able to kill one in four days of trapping, it proved that their numbers were very low. Moreover, if all the jackals were removed from an area, caracals would take over their ecological niche – and the wily cats killed more sheep and were much harder to control.

I could not fault his reasoning. Fortunately, I was able to convince Robbie that taking action against Mr Oberholzer would not serve the interests of conservation and that, if the matter got into the press, we could end up with egg on our faces. The case was dropped.

Not all of the farmers I spoke to were as ecologically minded as Mr Oberholzer. In fact, few of them had even heard of ecology and saw farming as a matter of extracting as much as possible from the land before drought, floods, locusts, or some other natural disaster struck. There was some logic in this: SWA's south-west was a place of extremes, where the success of a man's endeavours often depended more on the benevolence of the seasons than on how well he managed his land and livestock. As a result, most of the region's farmers had a hard-nosed, pioneer attitude that gave no quarter to the predators on their properties.

A sheep farmer from Bethanie told me that he saw no reason for any other creature to be on his land. Every week he slaughtered a sheep and cut its tail fat into small blocks, into each of which he put a few grains of strychnine. He then drove around his farm, randomly throwing them out of the window to poison jackals and anything else that ate meat. Later in our discussion he asked me if I knew of a way to eradicate the harvester termites that were eating all the grass in camps he had set aside for reserve grazing – but refused to see the link between killing bat-eared foxes and other small predators and his termite problem.

*   *   *

By the middle of the year nature conservation had still not been transferred to the first-tier government, and as June was working night shifts and cramming for her final exams, our now five- and three-year-old sons came to live with me. It was a great pleasure having them, and even though I was spending most of my time in the field they both quickly adapted to a nomadic lifestyle. But single fatherhood did bring new responsibilities and a few minor mishaps.

From May to September the Keetmanshoop nature conservators did shifts at the Fish River Canyon, overseeing the hiking trail from the lookout point to Ai-Ais, a hot spring and tourist resort 80 km away. Part of our duty was also to keep the area clean, so while patrolling the canyon rim I gave the boys the task of retrieving any litter along the road and throwing it onto the back of the truck. It soon became a competition between them to see who could get to a can or bottle first, and in Tuareg's haste to climb out of the cab the back-swinging door hit him on the lip, opening a 10 mm-long cut right through to his gum.

As we were 300 km from the nearest hospital and it was already late afternoon, I was in a quandary. But then I remembered that the party of hikers that had climbed down into the Canyon that afternoon were medical folk from Cape Town. Carrying Kyle on my shoulders, I hurried Tuareg down the steep path to where I knew the doctors were camping. We arrived just as it got dark, and they told me that not only did they have one of South Africa's top plastic surgeons in their group, but he had also brought all his 'needles and threads' with him. By the light of a lamp at the bottom of the Fish River Canyon Tuareg received better treatment than he would have got in any local hospital!

June finally joined us in September and a few days later we drove to Warmbad, a small farming town in the far south. The area was renowned for the spectacular wild flowers that grew here when sufficient winter rain fell, and as she loved gardening I saw it as a good introduction to my new work place. I was not disappointed. After years of drought the heavy showers during the preceding months had produced a prolific display of annual daisies that on some farms covered the desert flats as far as the eye could see. But it was the succulents that I was most interested in.

Stretching from Lüderitz to the Little Karoo in South Africa is a crescent-shaped belt where the Cape winter rainfall and the predominantly summer rain that falls over the rest of the sub-continent overlap. Within it grow over 80 per cent of the world's species of succulents, ranging from giant tree aloes to tiny 'stone plants' that comprise just two bulbous leaves protruding less than a centimetre above the ground. All of them have disproportionately large and colourful flowers, which together with their unusual and often grotesque shapes make them highly sought after as ornamental plants. Because of their scarcity and restricted range, with some species occurring only on a few farms or a single range of hills, most of them are listed as protected in the SWA nature conservation ordinance. Nevertheless, a lucrative black market trade had developed which was very difficult to control.

Succulents are best adapted to regions where the rainfall is very low, but can fall at virtually any time of the year, thereby allowing the moisture in their swollen organs to be replenished regularly. But having moisture stored in the leaves or stems has one serious disadvantage; it makes the plants much sought after by herbivores inhabiting the area. Consequently, most of them have evolved strategies to prevent them from being browsed that include formidable thorns, toxic or very bitter sap, and growing in inaccessible places. The different species of *Lithops* are also camouflaged to make them indistinguishable from the stones around them. Perhaps the most remarkable adaptation belongs to the *Fenestrarias* which have fleshy, finger-like leaves with transparent 'windows' at the tip, allowing sunlight to reach their photosynthetic tissue even when they are covered with sand.

In October we visited Lüderitz to record the succulents that a few centimetres of rain had brought back to life around the picturesque little harbour town. From there we drove inland to Kaukausib, the only permanent spring in Diamond Area No 1, to see how many gemsbok were drinking from it in the dry season. With farmers along the Sperrgebiet border claiming to be saving these desert-adapted antelope by 'allowing' them to come onto their properties, I wanted to know if it was lack of water or grazing that caused them to go east.

Situated about 50 km from the coast, Kaukausib consisted of just a thin stream of water that rose from the desert sand, ran for a short distance and then disappeared back under it. With midday temperatures in the high thirties and no trees in the vicinity for shade, I rigged a tarpaulin from the roof of the truck to crouch under while we counted. It was a gruelling experience for all of us, but after three days and nights only 60 gemsbok had come to drink, in spite of our having seen over 1 000 of them in the surrounding area – suggesting that individual animals were going for at least two weeks without water!

On a later count in February, the hottest time of the year, only 150 gemsbok drank at Kaukasib in two days. No summer rain had yet fallen, and as the sparse growth from the winter showers had by then completely dried out, it showed that water was not the primary limiting factor in the southern Namib. How they conserved body fluids was described in a paper written on the captive Russian population. Instead of sweating, in the heat of the day, only blood going to the brain was cooled by passing it through a knot of capillaries in their sinuses, while the temperature in the rest of their body was able to rise up to 43 degrees without any harmful effect. The heat accumulated during the day was stored in muscle tissue and released at night to keep the animal warm.

I also carried out a plant utilisation study in places with very large numbers of gemsbok and was again surprised by the results. No stem succulents were eaten, and only a few leaf succulents – mainly *Zygophyllum* species – were lightly browsed. In fact, I found the Diamond Area gemsbok to be grazers by choice, only browsing when there was no grass of a suitable nutritional quality available. However, there was one important exception: *Grielum sinuatum*, a small carrot-like annual forb that geminated on soft sandy soil after winter rain. As it only occurred deep into the desert, the gemsbok trekked long distances to find and dig up its moisture-filled roots, leaving the area pock-marked with holes.

That gemsbok were very mobile was well known, but were their movements opportunistic, going wherever rain had recently fallen, or was there a regular seasonal migration? To find this out and get an estimate of their numbers I mapped all my sightings of gemsbok, as well as those of my colleagues. But the area was just too vast to be covered by vehicle, so early in 1980 I asked Robbie to request an aerial census of both Diamond Areas.

Gemsbok were by far the most common large mammal in the southern Namib, where they favoured the dune fields and open plains, but could climb high up hill-slopes to find grazing or just get the benefit of the cool winds that blew from the coast. On the harder substrates there were also many springbok and ostrich, with klipspringer inhabiting the rocky ridges and steenbok the few small watercourses traversing the desert. Other large mammals included troops of almost black baboons that seemed to survive without ever drinking, brown hyena, jackal, Cape and bat-eared fox, wildcat, aardwolf, honey badger and porcupine, all of which were sometimes found deep in the desert. Twice I saw cheetah, and leopard spoor was quite common in ranges near the Orange River. From the older border farmers I learned that African wild dogs had also once inhabited the region, the last pack having been killed in the 1940s.

With a CDM permit that allowed me to patrol the entire Sperrgebiet excepting the actual mining area, June and I visited many fascinating places: the great Bogenfels Arch on the rugged coastline; Wolf Bay where over 200 000 Cape fur seals bred each year; the long-abandoned diamond diggings at

Elizabethbücht and Pomona; the Roter Kamm, a huge sand-filled crater created by a meteorite strike, and the Aurus and Klinghardtberge, which together
formed a succulent-rich mountain range across the middle of Diamond Area
No 1. Apart from the few vehicle tracks made by CDM's security officers and
Anglo-American prospectors, it was an untouched wilderness that we were
very privileged to be able to explore.

During our time together June and I had lived an abnormal life, following
my obsession with a place she had never been to. But here we could just enjoy the desert with little thought for the world beyond the next sand dune or
rocky ridge. It was an idyllic escape from the racial conflicts now enveloping
much of the sub-continent, making it all too easy for me to forget why I had
come back to South West Africa.

In November Robbie gave me 'top secret' information that brought me back
to reality and put a new perspective on my pending transfer to Kaokoland.
SWAPO guerrillas had infiltrated the homeland, blowing up power-lines and
setting landmines on the main road to Kamanjab, which had caused a number of casualties. According to him, the security forces were taken completely
by surprise, with the senior SADF officer in Opuwo, Captain Jurie Lombaard,
having consistently reported that all was quiet on the liberation war's western
front. 'The arsehole spent all his time hunting and didn't have a clue about
what was going on right under his nose,' Robbie said in disgust.

As the Herero were the backbone of the ruling DTA Party, I had thought
that SWAPO was unlikely to gain much support in Kaokoland. But I had forgotten about the bitter conflict between the 'Big Group' and 'Small Group'
within the homeland, and wondered if it had played a role. Whether it did
or not, having guerrillas operating there, as well as the inevitable increase
in security forces to counter their offensive, was going to make stopping the
poaching even more difficult. I also did not relish the thought of taking my
family back into a war zone.

*   *   *

Another decade had drawn to a close. For me it had been a nomadic ten years,
during which I had worked in four countries and in many different fields –
or government, an NGO and the private sector. Having rejected a university
education, I nevertheless found myself carrying out ethno-botanical research
and teaching ecology – necessitating my own crash course in the subject. But

LEFT: The basalt region of western Damaraland: a vast rock-strewn landscape with just a few 4x4 tracks.
(Neil Jacobsohn)

BELOW: Black rhinos in the basalt ranges. When I returned to the Kaokoveld in 1982 this was the only viable population left in Namibia outside of Etosha National Park.

Opuwo in 1968. From this dusty little outpost, eight government officials administered the Kaokoveld, a territory the size of Belgium.

The ruins of the German Fort built in Sesfontein after the Swartbooi rebellion in 1898. Mounted *Schutztruppe* were stationed at this lonely post to keep order and stop elephant poaching by the Thirstland Trekkers. The fort has now been rebuilt into a tourist lodge.

LEFT: Entering the Khovarib Schlucht from the east in 1970. As one of the few government officials in the Kaokoveld I was able to explore what was then known as Southern Africa's last wilderness.

BELOW: Sanitatas Spring, in the pre-Namib, which in the 1960s was one of the richest wildlife areas in the region. On a single night I counted 55 elephants and eight rhino coming to drink.

LEFT: Young Himba men on the well-wooded highlands in 1968. After Namibia's liberation war spread into the Kaokoveld, the spears they carried were replaced by rifles handed out by the South African Defence Force.

BELOW: Himba women build traditional dwellings from flexible mopane branches that are then plastered with a mix of cattle dung and river sand. Traditionally men are not allowed to handle cattle dung.

Hartmann's mountain zebra, closely related to the Cape mountain zebra, are endemic to the arid western parts of Namibia and Angola.

Big game against the backdrop of picturesque desert scenery had the potential to be a major tourist attraction. But in 1970 the Kaokoveld was de-proclaimed as a game reserve, which led to virtually all of its wildlife being wiped out.

Ruacana on the Kunene River, the second-largest waterfall in Southern Africa, was a spectacular sight before most of the water was diverted through underground turbines to generate electricity.

The author (GOS) canoeing on the palm-fringed Kunene River between Ruacana and Epupa Falls in 1969. At that time a small number of hippo still lurked in the channels between the islands.

The Kunene's gorge through the Otjihipa Mountains, which I traversed on foot in September 1969.

The main chasm of the Epupa Falls.

The tortuous course of the Kunene River east of the Marienfluss, photographed from the highest peak in the Otjihipa range when Hugh Goyns and I climbed it in July 1969.

Following the course of the seasonal Hoarusib River through the escarpment ranges in October 1970, the route used by the Himba when taking their livestock to Purros after good rain fell in the pre-Namib.

An elephant cow and her newborn calf on the desolate plains near Purros. Having got our scent, the rest of the herd came looking for us with 'murder on their minds'.

After walking through sand dunes in the heat of the afternoon, we were relieved to see the olive-green Kunene River winding through the Namib Desert.

The lower Kunene, with Angola's Iona National Park on the northern bank, photographed on our hike from the coastal dunes to the Marienfluss in 1970 when elephant, black rhino and lion still ocurred here.

At the end of two exhilarating wilderness walks down the Hoarusib and lower Kunene rivers in October 1970: *From left:* GOS, Willy Davy, Norman Owen-Smith, and Paul Schoorn. *(Willy Davy)*

Hugh and Dorothy Goyns at the exit of the Kunene gorge, at the start of our hike on the Angolan bank from there to its mouth in 1973.

A bull elephant shot from an SADF helicopter in Iona National Park, which we found on the second day of our walk. Its tusks and feet had been removed with a power saw.

LEFT: GOS and family on the front lawn of Makukwe homestead on Liebig's Ranch in Rhodesia's lowveld in 1977. At the foot of the mountain in the background a security force patrol blundered into a guerrilla hideout and three young soldiers were killed.

ABOVE: The armoured landmine-proofed Land Rover I used while working on the ranch.

BELOW: In 1979 I returned to South West Africa to work as a regional nature conservator based in Keetmanshoop. The area of responsibility included Diamond Area No.1 in the southern Namib.

LEFT: The grave near Lüderitz of a 'wanderer' who never came home. The inscription reads: 'Here lies the body of George Pound of London. Died of hunger and thirst 1906.' Two years after his death, diamonds were discovered only 20 km away.

BELOW: Sand dunes in the Diamond Area. If the grass is green the large population of gemsbok inhabiting the southern Namib do not need to drink water.

LEFT AND ABOVE: In low-rainfall periods the gemsbok migrate eastwards to find grazing, but in the 1979 drought they were prevented from doing so by the border farm fences and many hundreds died of starvation. The inset photo shows the paths worn along the fence-line as they tried to find a way through it.

BELOW: The Fish River Canyon, at the bottom of which my five-year-old son Tuareg had a deep cut in his lip stitched by one of South Africa's top plastic surgeons.

After good winter rains wild flowers grow prolifically in the south-west of Namibia.

Dinteranthus wilmotianus, one of the endemic succulents growing here that are much sought after by ornamental plant collectors, feeding a lucrative illegal trade in them.

In 1980 I was transferred to Okaukuejo in the Etosha National Park. A major dilemma facing the park managers was the increasing elephant numbers, which was good for tourists, but led to all the trees around the water-points being killed. Watching a herd drink are my sons Tuareg and Kyle.

Veld fires, one of the most controversial aspects of range management. Although much time and money was spent in Etosha every year trying to put them out, the majority were caused by lightning and were, therefore, a part of the natural ecosystem.

ABOVE: The northern boundary of Etosha in 1980 showing the regularly burned open savannah in Ovamboland, while on the right is the dense scrubland that developed as a result of the park's fire prevention and suppression policy.

CENTRE: A close-up of the Ovamboland side, where the perennial grass tufts are healthy and the habitat is very suitable for grazing game such as wildebeest and zebra, which in the past migrated here during the rainy season to feed on the new growth after the veld had been burned.

LEFT: A close-up within Etosha: although the erecting of a fence along the Ovamboland border was blamed for stopping the annual wildebeest and zebra migration around the pan – and for the major decrease in both species' populations – without regular fires to rejuvenate the perennial grasses they had been smothered by their dead leaves and were now inedible. The thick bush would also make wildebeest more vulnerable to predation by lions.

I learned the most 'on the job' from three visionary men; Nolly Zaloumis, Neil Alcock and Allan Savory.

I had returned to South West Africa intending to use my 'experiential education' to conserve the Kaokoveld's wildlife and improve the range management. But much had changed in the 1970s. The ending of 500 years of Portuguese colonialism had tipped the military balance in favour of the region's liberation forces. In Zimbabwe, Ian Smith had finally renounced 14 years of UDI, and the country's war-weary people were preparing for British-supervised elections. Within a few months, Robert Mugabe would inherit the country Tanzania's President Julius Nyerere called 'the gem of Africa'.

The coming to power of the MPLA in Luanda had also enabled SWAPO to move its bases from Zambia to Angola, making it easier to infiltrate Ovamboland, where their greatest support lay. For the first time they now posed a real threat to South Africa's security forces, and the SADF had responded by launching cross-border raids on their bases, including Cassinga, where over 600 people died in May 1978. SWAPO claimed most of the casualties were non-combatant refugees, and the international journalists who visited the site shortly afterwards came to the same conclusion. In an attempt to contain the situation South Africa was forced to commit more conscripted soldiers to a war that now extended far beyond its own borders.

On the political front, the situation was also not as positive as it had seemed during my October visit. Because they were boycotted by SWAPO, the Pretoria-organised elections in 1978 had been rejected by the international community. Nevertheless, the new multiracial Constituent Assembly started dismantling the legislative pillars of apartheid, with stubborn opposition from conservative whites. No lessons had been learned from Rhodesia, and under the new South African Prime Minister, PW Botha, the battle lines had been drawn and the gloves taken off. Both north and south of the Orange River, the liberation struggle was entering its final and most brutal phase.

It was not just Southern Africa's human inhabitants that were paying the price of Pretoria's efforts to uphold white rule. At his home one evening Robbie told me that elephants were being killed on a massive scale in Angola and that those involved included senior government officials. One of his main informants was Jan Muller, a senior nature conservator based in Grootfontein. A few months later Muller was killed in a road accident while travelling back from Rundu, on the border with Angola. A grader had pulled onto the road in front of him and his vehicle ploughed into it. 'They got him,' was Robbie's bitter comment.

Robbie also told me of a case that had occurred the year before in the un-inhabited north-east corner of Damaraland, just outside Etosha. The tracks of a large number of men had been discovered, and suspecting that they were SWAPO guerrillas the security forces had been called in to set up an ambush. But when they opened fire, killing one man and injuring a number of others, it was found they were 'just a gang of poachers'. Among the men arrested were a number of white Angolan refugees, but although a large amount of ivory and rhino horn was recovered, they never appeared in court. 'They couldn't be charged because they knew too much,' Robbie told me.

*   *   *

I started the 1980s by applying for leave, and we spent three weeks in Cape Town and its environs, our first real holiday as a family. On our return Robbie told me my request for an aerial census of the Diamond Areas had been approved, and early in April Matt de Jager arrived in the DNC's Piper Super Cub to carry it out. In spite of it being only a two-seater, the 'Kriek' had a slow stalling speed and was highly manoeuvrable, both considerable advantages when counting game. Its disadvantage was being so light that the strong desert winds often tossed it around in the air, and we had a few rather hairy takeoffs and landings on makeshift runways. Matt, who clearly loved this type of flying, made light of his unintentional acrobatics, but on two occasions he became very quiet and I noticed beads of perspiration on his forehead.

Eugene and Johan joined me on the census, which included the whole Sperrgebiet from the Orange River to Sossusvlei. With only six days' flying to cover such a large area, we relied on our preliminary ground surveys to es-tablish where rain had fallen, and concentrated our efforts there. This meant missing some animals, but I was confident the great majority of gemsbok would be where there was green grass.

To confirm this, in the corner opposite the farms Tsirub, Nieu Tsaus and Paddaput, where the heaviest storms had occurred, we counted over 2 600 gemsbok. Further south, two more concentrations of about 1 200 and 300 were found near the eastern border, where lighter showers had also fallen. Together with 440 gemsbok in the Koichab Pan and the few stragglers we did see, the total count for Diamond Area No 1 and the adjoining State land was 4 700 gemsbok, nearly 1 000 springbok and 650 ostrich. Only 450 gemsbok were recorded on the border farms, but with rain having now fallen in the Sperrgebiet many of the animals that had not been captured or shot by the landowners might have returned to the desert.

In Diamond Area No 2 Eugene counted 5 020 gemsbok, giving a grand total of just over 10 000 for the entire southern Namib. Two previous aerial censuses had been carried out in the Sperrgebiet: one in May 1976, when 3 700 gemsbok were recorded, and the other a year earlier, in which a total of 2 600 had been counted. Together they showed a considerable increase in gemsbok numbers, in spite of the large-scale harvesting on border farms that had taken place in recent years.

Before writing up my report I spoke to the control warden for the south, Giel Visser, who had been stationed in the area during the early 1970s, when farmers were granted emergency grazing in the Sperrgebiet. Because of the prevailing drought and the competition with large numbers of sheep, he believed that there had then been only about 1 000 gemsbok in the whole southern Namib. If so, they had made a remarkable recovery, showing how well they were adapted to living in a region with virtually no surface water – as long as some rain fell there. But this did not happen in 1978, and the winter rain in 1979 only temporarily relieved the situation. Although scattered summer downpours occurred in March 1980, I predicted that if the winter rains failed the gemsbok would again be forced to migrate eastwards – where the guns and capture vehicles of the border farmers were waiting.

* * *

In March Peter Lind was transferred to the DNC's game capture unit and Pieter Mostert replaced him as the senior nature conservator in Keetmanshoop. Although a dedicated conservationist, Pieter was also a stubborn advocate of fair play, and had recently made an official complaint against one of his colleagues for physically abusing a black labourer. I knew this had not gone down too well with some of our more conservative bosses in Windhoek, and suspected that his posting to the least popular station in the country was punishment for this. Needless to say, I was very happy to be working under my old friend, but our time together would be short.

Soon after the aerial census, Robbie mentioned that there was talk of my being transferred. As one of the few conservators who enjoyed working in the

south, this made no sense to me. But as the rumour persisted I asked Robbie
to drop the word in Windhoek that if my transfer was inevitable, I would like
to be sent to either Naukluft in the Namib Park or the Waterberg Plateau –
two remote outstations with vacant posts. There was a third unfilled position
in Okaukuejo that I told Robbie I did not want. On my previous visits to
Etosha's headquarters I had found it to be a place of gossip and backbiting,
where senior officials jockeyed for position and their wives could make life
very difficult for those who did not fit into their conventional mould. In June
I was officially informed of my transfer to Okaukuejo!

During my last month in Keetmanshoop I wrote up my project on the
southern Namib gemsbok, which included recommendations for their future management. I concluded that their physiological and behavioural
adaptations to this unique desert ecosystem enabled them to drink very
infrequently. However, during extended dry periods they needed to migrate
inland to find grazing. From the time the border farms had been fenced this
seasonal movement was restricted to within the Diamond Area, and when
sheep farmers were granted emergency grazing in the Sperrgebiet during
the late 1960s and early 1970s their numbers had crashed. Nevertheless,
when the drought broke and the sheep moved out, the gemsbok population
had rapidly increased.

Prior to 1975 the farmers along the Diamond Area would have kept their
boundary fences in good order, to prevent gemsbok coming onto their land
and competing with their livestock. But the situation changed when the new
nature conservation ordinance was introduced. With the karakul pelt industry in decline and a high demand for game in other parts of the country,
gemsbok were now a valuable resource, and many of the farmers made open-
ings in their fence-lines to allow them onto their land. Although it was techni-
cally illegal, once they were on a farm and the 'gates' closed they belonged to
the landowner. We could deny the farmer a permit to utilise them, but as they
were now prejudicing the survival of his sheep, if taken to court it was a case
that the State would be unlikely to win.

In early 1979, when gemsbok were dying of starvation on the Diamond
Area side of the fence, I had asked one of the country's reputable game dealers, Willie Delfs, if he was willing to capture and sell the animals that had
come onto the farms. This would be done on behalf of the State, but with
some of the income going to the landowner on whose property they had been
caught. If his capture costs were covered he was happy to do so, but Head
Office had turned this proposal down.

An alternative solution was proposed by Robbie: equipping the boreholes that were drilled in the 1960s for the sheep farmers who had been granted emergency grazing. Around them there were still some old and blackened tufts of grass, and although they now had very little nutritional value, with water nearby they might have enabled some of the gemsbok to survive until rain once more fell in the desert. His suggestion was also not acted on, and as there were no further attempts to resolve the issue I proposed a solution that would legitimise the situation along the Diamond Area border, as well as benefiting both the State and the gemsbok.

With gemsbok movement inland now restricted, I believed their present numbers were too high to be sustained in a low-rainfall period. But even if a population crash did not occur, the vegetation surveys I had carried out showed that serious damage had already been done to the desert's perennial plants. If this was allowed to continue it would negatively affect the future survival of all the wildlife in the southern Namib. Consequently, to prevent further degradation of the habitat here I proposed that the total gemsbok population be reduced, and maintained at about 6 000.

The first option for removing the excess animals was for the DNC to capture and supply farmers wishing to re-stock with gemsbok. Thereafter they should be put on tender to recognised game dealers, while any remaining animals could be harvested for their meat. I also pointed out that the Diamond Areas were very well placed for the marketing of chilled game meat, because in Lüderitz there were already large freezing facilities that had been set up for its crayfish exporting industry. As they only operated from November to May, the legal crayfish catching season, while the best time for game cropping was from June to September, the two activities actually complemented each other.

However, the best long-term solution was for the gemsbok to be given access to the higher rainfall areas further inland. This could be achieved by the State purchasing unviable sheep farms along the Diamond Area border. That the gemsbok could make a strong economic claim to this marginal farmland was well illustrated by their remarkable performance during the 1970s, a time when very few of the border farms were able to support a permanent population of karakul sheep, the most drought-adapted of all domestic livestock. I ended by saying that if the funds were not available on the national budget, I believed the gemsbok could 'buy' the farms with the income they earned from being harvested.

Nothing came of the proposal, but after extensive coverage in the media on how the Sperrgebiet gemsbok were being exploited by the border farmers,

CDM erected a game-proof fence along the boundary of the Diamond Area, thereby effectively stopping any migration inland. A decade later a group of Windhoek businessmen saw the economic potential of the southern Namib's dramatic scenery and desert-adapted wildlife, and bought up the farms along the border of Diamond Area No 2, to create the 200 000 ha Namib Rand Resort.

CHAPTER SIXTEEN

ETOSHA: THE BURNING QUESTION

Driving through the gates of Okaukuejo I felt a twinge of nostalgia. I had visited Etosha since the 1960s, at first while working in Tsumeb and then with Burger Baard, when we stayed with its legendary warden, Peter Stark. At the time I was a novice, eager to learn from the pioneer wildlife managers who nurtured the Park through its early years. They had all moved on, replaced by a new generation of biologists, veterinarians and nature conservators, who were all now my contemporaries.

Our immediate neighbours were Hennie Theron, the Park warden, and Piet de Villiers, the man BAD had appointed in 1975 as nature conservator for Kaokoland, but stationed in Windhoek. Frustrated by only being able to make periodic visits to the area he was responsible for, Piet had resigned and was now carrying out research on Etosha's elephants. Across the road was the Park's veterinarian, Dr Ian Hofmeyr, while down a perpendicular street lived Hu Berry, a biologist who had just completed his doctoral thesis on the behaviour and ecology of Etosha's wildebeest population. I soon learned that Ian and Hu clashed professionally and were not on speaking terms.

The other houses accommodated married nature conservators, senior tourist officers, the head of the Park's road maintenance section and Major

Rheeder, who commanded a company of conscripted South African soldiers based in Etosha. Although we were just 12 families and a few bachelors, the white residents of Okaukuejo were firmly divided between Ian Hofmeyr's progressives, Hu Berry's conservatives and the ultra-rightwingers who rallied around Piet 'Olifant' de Villiers and the Major. June and I naturally gravitated towards Ian's side, but were determined to remain neutral and be friends with everyone in the camp. Now that I was so close to getting back to the Kaokoveld I did not want a repetition of my Cwaka College experience.

Apart from politics and personal conflicts there were many ecological issues to keep the Park's senior staff sparring. One of the most contentious was the considerable increase in elephant numbers, from only a few hundred around the Etosha Pan in the 1950s, to about 1 500 now concentrated there in the dry season, and a total Park population estimated to be over 3 000. They could not be accurately counted because many of the herds migrated seasonally into the homelands to the north and west. And as they could be outside of Etosha for many months, whose elephants were they?

Within a week of arriving I learned that the question was not just academic. One of my first tasks was to relieve a Pretoria Technical College student supervising a gang of labourers who were replacing fencing wire stolen by the Park's neighbours along its northern boundary. When I arrived at his makeshift camp he reported having seen many vultures circling a short distance over the boundary, and the next morning I took some of the workers with me and we drove into Ovamboland to investigate.

It did not take long to discover what had attracted the vultures. Within a few kilometres of the boundary we found five dead elephants and picked up 60-plus 7.62 'long' cartridge cases – the calibre of ammunition used by the South African security forces. The tusks had been hacked from each carcass and the tracks of the vehicle used in the killing and to carry away the ivory were still clearly visible. We followed them to a small village where an open Willy's Jeep was parked. On the loading box were more expended cartridge cases and plenty of blood. The people we questioned claimed not to know who the vehicle's owner was, but had no explanation for why it was standing in their village. As we were outside the Park, and within a military operational zone, I just wrote down its registration number, collected blood samples and a few of the cartridge cases, and then drove straight back to Okaukuejo.

On arrival I reported what we had found to Hennie Theron, but he told me that, as the elephants had been killed north of the border, we had no authority to follow up the case. Surely, I argued, no matter which side of the fence the carcasses were, they were obviously Etosha's elephants. But I was wrong. As Hennie pointed out, wild animals could not be owned, and he reminded me that the game on farms could only be utilised by the landowner while it was on his property. Although all elephants belonged to the State, if they were poached in Etosha then SWA's Nature Conservation Ordinance No 4 of 1975 applied, but it did not apply in the homelands. Therefore, as soon they crossed the Park boundary they fell under the conservation regulations of the relevant second-tier government, and we had no authority to implement it.

To make matters worse, he told me that there were no nature conservators stationed in Ovamboland, and the only option was to report the matter to the police in the homeland's capital, Ondangua. To my surprise, when I did so the officer on duty immediately agreed to meet me on the Etosha border the next morning.

When sergeants Du Plessis and Rust arrived we inspected the carcasses and then drove to the village where we found the vehicle still parked. After I had given them a sworn statement I handed the case over to them, not expecting to hear anything more about it. But a few weeks later I received a telephone call from Sergeant Du Plessis telling me that Martin Ndjoba, the son of Ovamboland's then Prime Minister, Pastor Cornelius Ndjoba, had been charged with illegally killing the elephants. I was even more surprised when in March the following year I was subpoenaed as a witness to a court hearing of the case in Tsumeb.

In fact, my evidence was not required because Ndjoba, who had not obtained the services of a lawyer, did not dispute killing the elephants, saying he had done so on his father's permit. However, as he could not produce it for the court to see, this defence was rejected. He and a State witness, Festus Ipinge, then claimed to have been forced into making statements 'under duress', but this was also not accepted by Magistrate Bouwer, who found Ndjoba guilty of illegally killing one or more elephants, as well as being in possession of ivory without a permit. On the first charge he was fined R100, and on the second R50! From his pocket he produced the cash, and I watched incredulously as he walked out of the court laughing and joking with his companions. He had every reason to take his sentence lightly. The total fine was less than the value of just one large elephant tusk!

As I watched the men climb into an expensive vehicle and drive away, I wondered how many more elephants this privileged son of one of the country's most prominent internal black politicians had killed. Would such a ridiculously low fine be a deterrent to him or other residents of the homeland in the future? Because of the high price of ivory the SWA Nature Conservation Ordinance now had maximum sentences for killing elephants, or being in illegal possession of their tusks, of R6 000 or six years in jail. But in the home-lands there had been no changes to the old BAD legislation, which still pre-scribed a maximum sentence of only R250. If Robbie Hawthorne was right about high-ranking government officials being involved in the illegal ivory trade, it would certainly not have been in their interest to update the home-land laws. This discrepancy was one of the main reasons why Bernabe de la Bat wanted nature conservation to be a first-tier government function, but until this happened, what hope was there of stopping commercial poaching?

The persecution of elephants in Ovaboland and Kaokoland had also led to many of them seeking sanctuary in Etosha, thus contributing to the increas-ing numbers within the Park. It was a boon for the tourists, but their impact on the woody vegetation around water-points was becoming a matter of ma-jor concern. The Okaukuejo waterhole was a prime case. In the 1960s it had been a secluded pool surrounded by leadwood and acacia trees. But by 1980 most of the larger trees were ring-barked or pushed over, and like the other waterholes in Etosha, only their fallen trunks remained as testimony to a time when shady groves grew around all of its natural springs, and elephant were rarely seen by visitors to the Park.

Many of the DNC's senior staff were now recommending that some elephants be culled in Etosha, using the events in Kenya's Tsavo National Park as an example of what could happen if this were not done. Of similar size to Etosha, and also a semi-arid ecosystem, Tsavo had large numbers of elephants compressed into it by human pressure on its borders, which in combination with frequent fires changed the vegetation from woodland to open savanna and grassland. When a severe drought hit eastern Kenya in the early 1970s many thousands of elephants and large numbers of rhino died of starvation. It was certainly a lesson for Etosha's managers, but at the start of the drought Tsavo had supported an estimated 40 000 elephants, not 3 000. The cropping of elephants for management purposes was also not just an ecological issue. They were highly intelligent animals, and the question of whether it was ethi-cal to do so had now entered the discussion.

The man in the hot seat was Piet de Villiers, whose research was meant to determine the maximum number of elephants that Etosha could carry, and – if the population exceeded that number – what should be done. Were trees more valuable than the great pachyderms that attracted thousands of tourists to the country every year? Scientists in Kruger National Park had decided on an optimal population of 8 000 and used helicopters and the paralysing drug scoline to kill hundreds of elephants every year. Culling could be rationalised by biologists, but with ivory poaching now taking place just outside the Park, what message would it send to the man in the street, or the many armed villagers living in Namibia's northern homelands?

In 1983 the DNC did decide to reduce the elephant numbers in Etosha, and a total of 525 were killed over two years. Since then no further culling has taken place, and in 2008 the population in the Park was still around 3 000.

* * *

For management purposes Etosha had been divided into eight sections. I was given responsibility for Area 4, which extended from Ombika Gate in the south to the northern border with Ovamboland. In the east it followed the rim of the huge salt pan that had given the 22 000 km² national park its name, while in the west my direct responsibilities extended to Ozonjuitji mbari borehole, where the tourist area of the Park ended.

The south and central parts of Area 4 consisted of broad treeless plains or open tree savanna, both growing on fine alkaline clay underlain by calcrete. As the soil was rich in calcium and other mineral salts it was sweetveld of the highest order, and in the past tens of thousands of wildebeest, zebra and springbok gathered here at the end of each wet season, drinking from many depressions that were briefly filled by the rain. When they dried up the great herds moved east to the permanent springs along the southern edge of the Pan, as part of their annual anti-clockwise migration around it.

In the north the vegetation was scrub savanna, with a few taller trees growing on termitaria and other fire refuge sites. Apart from along the edge of the Etosha Pan and a number of smaller salt pans, Kalahari sand covered the finer sediments laid down by the lake that once covered the whole of northern and eastern Namibia. Over the millions of years since then the minerals in the deeper sands had been leached out, causing the perennial grasses growing here to lose much of their nutritional value when dormant, only providing good grazing while still green.

Although Area 4 had three permanent springs, Ombika, Okaukuejo and Okondeka, a number of boreholes had also been drilled in an attempt to more evenly disperse the game throughout the Park. However, when overgrazing occurred around the artificial water-points in the sweetveld, some of them were closed down. The last two here, Adamax and Leeubron, were also de-commissioned in 1981, leaving only Pan Point in the sourveld part of Area 4, because it and Naravandu borehole in Area 5 provided water for elephants that inhabited the scrub savanna north-west of the Etosha Pan.

As its name implied, before it was closed the borehole at Leeubron was one of the best places around Okaukuejo to see lions. In the 1950s and 1960s the Park's nature conservators had once a week shot a zebra and off-loaded it near the water-point to provide a lion 'dinner party' for the tourists to watch. Up to 30 of the big cats had turned up for the feast, which became one of Etosha's major attractions at that time.

In the mid-1970s, when Rudi Loutit was responsible for Area 4, he nearly provided an unscheduled meal for the Leeubron lions. While on a horse patrol with Tobias Dougab, his Hei//om Bushman assistant, they had come across a pride of lions lying in a wooded grove near the water-point. Skirting around them, Rudi rode into a lioness lying in ambush away from the others, which chased after him. They galloped away, but when his horse passed under a tree the rifle slung over his shoulder caught on a branch, wrenching him out of the saddle. Although he landed right in front of the lioness, Rudi was able to get his wits together and fire into the air while she was still working out how – after chasing a horse – she had caught a man. When Tobias heard the shot he came back and together they were able to drive the other lions off.

Tobias, who became my assistant, was born in the Park and as a young man had hunted with a bow and arrow the game he now helped to protect. At the time the Hei//om were the only inhabitants of the area around the Pan, and when the German colonial administration proclaimed it as a game reserve in 1907, their hunting and gathering activities were seen as just part of the natural ecosystem. However, this policy changed in the mid-1950s, when the South African authorities recognised Etosha's tourist potential. All hunting was prohibited and the Hei//om were ordered to leave and seek work on farms in the Police Zone, or move into Ovamboland. Only men already employed as trackers or labourers were allowed to stay in the Park, confined with their families in compounds at Okaukuejo and Namutoni rest camps.

The result was that the next generation of Hei//om grew up in a world not of their choosing, where they had few skills to offer, and soon sank to the bottom of the social hierarchy. Within Etosha the sons of the employees were not allowed to go with their fathers into the field, as they would have done in the past. Instead they half-heartedly attended school, where they learned little that would be of value to life in the Park. When they were old enough, many were employed as labourers, but the exceptional bushcraft skills of the people who had once been masters of Etosha's plains were being lost.

*   *   *

Although I had not wanted a transfer to Okaukuejo, it was still a privilege to work in one of Africa's greatest national parks. My duties included horse and vehicle patrols to monitor game movements and record mortalities, as well as ensuring that tourists adhered to the many rules and regulations. I was also responsible for maintaining Area 4's water pumps and repairing the northern boundary fence, and all of these activities gave me plenty of time to study how the Etosha ecosystem functioned.

Many of the Park's species also occurred in the Kaokoveld, but here they paid little attention to vehicles and I could observe their behaviour at much closer range. This was particularly true of the predators, which – because they were persecuted by the local people – were seldom encountered in the home-lands. However, on horseback or foot it was a different matter, and whenever we came across lions always kept our distance.

At night they were even more dangerous, and Tobias told me one of my predecessors had been bitten on the leg by a lion when sleeping next to his vehicle. In the ensuing struggle it grabbed hold of his mattress and carried it off – hopefully coming to the conclusion that humans were tasteless and not worth eating. Consequently, while we were camping out Tobias always stuck a spade in the ground next to the fire, and after threading a stick through its handle hung his jacket and hat on it, assuring me that lions would not come close as long as it looked like someone was still awake.

The most infamous incident involving Area 4's lions occurred in 1950, when four contract workers decided to follow the shortest route back to Ovamboland – along the western edge of the Etosha Pan. At sunset they camped under an acacia tree a few hundred metres from Okondeka spring, and during the night a pride of lions found the sleeping men, killing and eating one of them while the others watched from the tree they had hurriedly climbed up. After the lions had devoured their first victim they then dragged two more of the men down from the branches and ate them too. Only one man, too high up in the tree for the lions to reach, was left alive in the morning when the lions departed.

On one of my tourist patrols to Okondeka I found a group of six young lions lying up under a spreading acacia, about 100 metres from the spring, and noticed that they were all looking intently at the only car in the parking area. Attracting their attention was a couple in the process of setting up a table and chairs for an early morning cup of tea. Next to them was their just-walking child. Pulling up alongside I politely told the man that in Etosha people were not allowed to get out of their vehicles.

'That's the trouble with this Park,' he replied angrily. 'The whole back page of our permit is filled with rules and regulations. From here we can see for miles around. Why shouldn't we get out and stretch our legs?'

I then asked him if he had seen the lions watching them, and suggested that he climb on the back of my truck from where they would be more visible under the bush I pointed out. After doing so, he jumped off and scooped their toddler back into the car. His wife also leapt into the passenger seat and immediately launched into a tirade about him having put their child's life in danger. While the man fumbled with the cups and thermos I folded up the table and put it in the vehicle's boot. Although I could have given them a fine, he was unlikely to get out of the car in the Park again, and as I suspected his wife would remind him of his irresponsible behaviour quite often in the future, I decided that no further punishment was needed.

* * *

When we arrived in Okaukuejo the Park's veterinarian, Ian Hofmeyr, was in the middle of a black rhino census. We had first met in 1973, when I was working for the State Museum and Ian was in charge of the game capture unit. At the time he was involved in relocating nuclear populations of the rarer species to Etosha and the Waterberg Plateau Park. During these operations Ian pioneered research into blood chemistry changes that occurred in wild animals under stress, and by 1980 had received international acclaim for his part in developing an antidote to white muscle disease, then the leading cause of game capture mortalities.

The most endangered species was the black rhino, and 42 were translocated from Damaraland, and 10 from around Purros in Kaokoland. When Ian became Etosha's veterinarian he focused much of his attention on monitoring their performance. To find out how many there were in the Park, over the full moon period all the available staff sat for 48 hours at every waterhole in one part of the Park. Apart from counting the rhino coming to drink, they also noted the animal's sex, age and horn shape, to ensure that the same animal was not recorded twice. The following month this was repeated in another area, until the whole of Etosha was covered.

As the census had begun a few months before my arrival I only participated in the last two waterhole counts. The first was at Okavao, a weak spring on the road to Otjovasandu, where only a single rhino came to drink on one of the two nights. Before the next count I told Ian that on similar moonlit counts I carried out in the Kaokoveld, I had found rhino sometimes only drank once in three days, and suggested the period be extended to 72 hours. This was done when the far west of the Park was covered in September.

This time I was allocated the well-used Otjovasandu spring. Over three nights 23 rhino came to the water, of which 17 were different animals. When all the data had been collected and analysed, Ian concluded that there could not be fewer than 180 rhino west of the power-lines from Ruacana, and that the total population was at least 350. As just 10 years earlier Eugene Joubert had estimated there were only 35 rhino in the west of Etosha and another 20 in the rest of the Park, even with the 52 animals that were translocated from Damaraland and Kaokoland they could not have increased by so much in such a short time. When I discussed this with Ian he told me that he had captured 30 rhino on the farms expropriated under the Odendaal Commission Plan to create Damaraland – where Eugene thought there were only seven!

This information was very interesting, because in his master's thesis Eugene had claimed that there were only 25 rhino in the Kaokoveld north of the Hoanib, whereas I had estimated the number to be 150. At the time it was believed that black rhino drank once a day, and Eugene had based his figure on the number of individual tracks seen at the known waterholes in the region. I had also found there were many more springs in the Kaokoveld than were recorded on our maps and that rhino often drank from very small pools of water. As a young researcher just out of Pretoria University it was not surprising that Eugene had grossly underestimated their numbers, and the 1980 Etosha rhino census gave my population estimate much greater credibility.

Although both elephant and rhino were doing well, this was not the case for all the game species. In the 1960s the then unfenced Etosha ecosystem had supported about 30 000 wildebeest and 25 000 zebra, whose annual anti-clockwise migration around the Pan was recorded by Ken Tinley and others. It began at the start of the wet season, when most of the large grazing ungulates that had gathered in the north-east of the Park dispersed into the sandveld north of the Pan, drinking from rain-filled pools in this otherwise waterless area. As these dried up they moved onto the open plains west of Okaukuejo, and during the dry months migrated back along the southern edge of the Pan, where there were many permanent springs, congregating in the north-east of the Park again at the start of the next rainy season.

For Etosha's grasslands it was a perfect system. The perennial tufts growing on the leached sandy soils to the north of the Pan would only be grazed for a brief period as the wildebeest and zebra migrated westwards in the wet season. Although the sweet grass on the southern plains was more heavily utilised, it was in the dry months when the tufts were dormant and thus could not be overgrazed. Furthermore, the hooves of large numbers of migrating game would have loosened the surface of the clay soils south of the Pan, enabling more rainwater to infiltrate and facilitating the germination of grass seeds. That the Etosha ecosystem was then highly productive was confirmed by the very high biomass of grazing ungulates it supported.

But this was no longer the situation. After most of the sandveld north of the Pan was de-proclaimed and added to the Ovambo homeland by the Odendaal Commission, the populations of plains game had crashed. To find out the reason for this Hu Berry had been appointed to study the behaviour and ecology of Etosha's wildebeest, and when I arrived he was writing up his research findings. His main conclusion was that when the Park's northern border was fenced, large numbers of plains game had been in Ovamboland, where they were exterminated by a combination of hunting and competition with the expanding human and livestock population there. Anthrax and high levels of predation by lions had then reduced the numbers within Etosha to their present totals of about 3 000 wildebeest and 9 000 zebra.

Hu believed a factor contributing to the many anthrax deaths was the gravel pits that had been dug to upgrade the Park's roads, into which spores of this deadly bacterial disease washed and were then taken in by animals drinking from them. Because they held water for longer than natural pans, he also saw them and the boreholes that were drilled on the plains being the cause of the overgrazing, and had recommended that Leeubron and Adamax windmills be decommissioned and the gravel pits filled in. As the soil was very shallow this could not be done by bulldozer so Alan Cillier, my counterpart in Area 5, and I covered the larger gravel pits with brushwood to stop animals drinking from them, and also to stop the silt carried into them by rainwater run-off being blown away by the wind.

According to Hu the heavy predation on wildebeest was because of the Park's high lion population, estimated to be about 500. Working together with a Windhoek gynaecologist, Jock Orford, he carried out the first contraception experiments on wild predators. It was a high-profile project, but ended when further research showed that so many of Etosha's lions were shot every year on the neighbouring white farms that their numbers were now also decreasing.

Although the mortality records kept by the Park's management staff confirmed that large numbers of wildebeest and zebra were killed by predators or died of anthrax every year, I was not convinced they were the underlying cause of the population declines. Both species had evolved with lions, and anthrax occurred throughout Southern Africa, so to me it seemed more likely that they were just symptoms indicating that the Park's grazing ungulates were now under nutritional stress, and therefore more vulnerable to predation and disease.

The reason for my thinking this was that the vegetation in Etosha had changed since my visits in the 1960s. Then the plains around Okaukuejo had been golden grasslands that at the end of the rainy season were dotted with thousands of wildebeest and zebra. Little more than a decade later they had become a dustbowl, and over large tracts of them the only plants were dwarf shrubs. Although Hu agreed that the plains were overgrazed, he assured me that when the Park received good rains they would look very different. But even if the grasslands appeared to recover after a favourable wet season, they now consisted mainly of annual species, and I did not believe that this was their natural state.

In our discussions Hu pointed out that there was still enough grazing off the plains to support the present wildebeest numbers, even in low rainfall years. This might be so, but they were adapted to live in open grasslands, and if forced to enter tree and shrub savanna would more easily fall prey to lions. Most of the grass there had also become rank and moribund from under-use, and wildebeest were short-grass feeders.

Another change in the vegetation around Okaukuejo was the dense stands of *Acacia nebrownii* and *Catophractes alexandri* shrubs that were encroaching onto the plains. Although they created a favourable habitat for browsers such as black rhino, giraffe and kudu, the numbers of which had all increased in recent years, it had considerably reduced the area of open grassland. This would have contributed to the overgrazing, in spite of there now being much fewer wildebeest and zebra, but could it alone have caused the major degradation of the sweetveld that they depended on in the dry season?

*   *   *

In late 1980 nature conservation was made a first-tier government function, and in November Bernabe de la Bat instructed me to discuss my transfer to Kaokoland with Ben van Zyl, who had returned to the homeland as its senior administrative officer. June and I left the next day, following the new gravel road to Opuwo. The previous year's rains had been very poor, and as none had yet fallen this season, along the way we passed herds of gaunt cattle wandering through veld that appeared to be completely devoid of grass cover.

Opuwo had also changed a great deal. Kaokoland was now a war zone, and military vehicles and men in uniform were to be seen everywhere in the town, which was now dominated by a large SADF barracks on the ridge above the new white residential area. We were greeted cordially by Ben van Zyl, who briefed me on the current situation in the homeland. It was worse than I expected. As there was a real danger of landmines and ambushes, government officials were only allowed to travel in convoy. Before going into the field they also had to get approval from the police, and make radio contact twice a day to report their whereabouts. He also told me that, because of the influx of security force personnel, there was no housing available in Opuwo.

The next day we accompanied Van Zyl to Okanguati, now a fortified military base, travelling in an armoured Casspir – the troop carrier used by police 'anti-terrorist' units. On the way we passed the burned-out hulks of a number of civilian vehicles. I also noted that instead of a spear, virtually every Himba man we saw now carried a rifle. The view from the small bullet-proof windows of the Casspir was not the best way to get an impression of the area, but I saw no grass at all along the whole way to Okanguati.

Under the prevailing security situation, with my every move monitored, there seemed little point in being transferred to Opuwo. Consequently, on our return to Okaukuejo I asked for permission to visit the Skeleton Coast Park to look for an alternative base. The arid country to the west of the escarpment was the most valuable from a nature conservation perspective, and was less likely to have been infiltrated by guerrillas. In December I wrote a report recommending Moewe Bay as the most suitable place for me to be stationed, with other options being Sesfontein and Otjovasandu. Although housing was a problem in all of them, we were prepared to live in a caravan until more permanent accommodation became available.

As I was again due for leave, while waiting for a response from Head Office we visited Zimbabwe to see how our friends and family were faring under the new government. After a week spent in Harare we drove down to Liebig's Ranch, staying with Arthur and Anzie Swales on Jopempi Section. From them we learned that three more of the white field staff had been killed before the ceasefire came into effect, including Max Stockhill, who drove over an anti-tank mine and died of his injuries while being airlifted to hospital. Many of the black workers had also been killed, among them my Lutope foreman, Chilongo, thus fulfilling the Shangane belief that seeing an aardvark in broad daylight meant death. But I could not find out anything about Eliot Thoma.

To add to the toll, Bruce Cook had died in a motorcar accident, in which Mike Gawler was also seriously injured. Richard Stringfield had taken over as the overall Ranch manager, and he told us that in spite of many suspected stock thieves having been shot, at least 27 000 cattle had been stolen during the war. If Zimbabwe's TTL residents were prepared to die for the few dollars they were paid for each head of cattle they stole, would the poachers in Namibia's homelands be deterred by a minor fine or a jail sentence when the reward for killing rhino and elephants was so much higher?

On our return from leave I was informed that my proposal for an alternative base station to operate from had been turned down. The decision had not been taken by De la Bat, who had just been promoted to the most senior post in the new SWA/Namibia civil service, but by Stoffel Rocher. As a last resort I accepted Opuwo as a base, but this was now also unacceptable. The reason Rocher gave me was that 'he would not be able to look himself in the mirror if anything happened to me'. As there was no love lost between us, and many other civil servants were working in Kaokoland, I took his concern for my safety with a pinch of salt.

With no hope of being transferred to Kaokoland before the security situation there improved, I settled back into my duties in Area 4. The 1981 wet season was even poorer than that of the previous year, and with very little new grass growth a severe drought now prevailed in Etosha. By June long lines of thirsty animals trekked daily to the Park's waterholes, raising clouds of fine dust that hung like a shroud over the plains. From the reports I received, the situation in the north-western homelands was even worse.

Our most important task was to keep all the boreholes functioning, so that the drought-stressed wildlife would at least have a reliable supply of water. The largest number was along the 19th latitude road to Otjovasandu – elephant country – and if a pump broke or ran out of diesel there would soon be many thirsty pachyderms standing nearby, waiting for someone to come and fix it. The older bulls seemed to understand what was going on, and at the sound of a vehicle often came right up to the trough and waited for the water to start flowing again.

As the Park's early conservators built robust structures for game to drink from, too wide for an elephant to step over, after starting the pump I would sometimes sit on the edge of the trough while a group of bulls put their trunks into the water just a few metres away. If I did not make any sudden movement they just quietly watched me with their hazel, worldly-wise eyes and continued drinking, close enough for us to have had a conversation – if only we shared a common language. Because they raided crops and we made billiard balls, piano keys and ornamental carvings from their tusks, humans and elephants had been deadly enemies for centuries, but did it have to be so? At least in Etosha a truce now reigned, but was it still possible for the residents of Kaokoland to share their land with these giants that could wreak havoc on a maize field, destroy windmills or kill a person with a single blow of their trunk?

That elephant are intelligent animals is indisputable, but do they also have a sense of humour? An incident that occurred while we were repairing a pump on Etosha's 19th latitude made me think that perhaps they did. On this occasion three bulls came to drink as soon as we finished working, and after putting our equipment away I carefully returned to the trough to clean my hands, with the elephants placidly watching me.

When I got back to the truck one of my young Hei//um workers decided his hands also needed washing. But whereas I had walked slowly, watching the elephants' reaction, he swaggered towards the trough, more aware of his human audience than the three bulls, which still seemed quite relaxed. Upon reaching the trough he made a great show of standing in front of the closest elephant, towering nearly two metres above him. However, just as he bent down to wet his hands it raised its trunk and sprayed the contents over him. In his haste to get away the young man tripped and sprawled in the sand, but hurriedly scrambled to his feet and sprinted back to the truck. The other workers roared with laughter and I was sure the old bull was also smiling.

Although we could provide water for Etosha's elephants and other game, what they really needed in a drought was food, and it was not within our power to do anything about this. The degraded state of the plains did not help the situation, but was it possible to reverse the overgrazing that I believed was still taking place? By using short-duration grazing Allan Savory had re-established perennial grasses on Liebig's Ranch and many others in Zimbabwe, but here we were dealing with wild animals in a natural ecosystem.

With its borders fenced and many artificial water-points, could Etosha still be regarded as a natural ecosystem? The great wildebeest and zebra migration around the Pan that had in the past maintained the productivity of its grasslands also no longer occurred. Instead, the herds of plains game now followed the rains westward along the Pan's southern edge, which meant that the sweet alkaline grasslands here were being grazed while they were actively growing. This would certainly have put the perennial grasses on the plains under pressure, even if no boreholes had been drilled there. So de-commissioning them alone would not solve the problem.

The solution lay in getting the grazing ungulates off the plains during the wet season, but was this possible now that the northern boundary had been fenced? Although it was just a standard cattle fence in Area 4, which was regularly broken by elephants, the section north of Namutoni was game-proofed and would prevent the wildebeest and zebra from migrating into southern Ovamboland. Nevertheless, there was quite a lot of sandveld north of the Pan inside the Park that was still available to them. But there was a good reason why they did not go there: The perennial grasses growing on the leached soils here had turned grey, and were now completely unpalatable.

In contrast, the grassland on the other side of the graded road separating the Park from Ovamboland was still healthy, and would provide good grazing in the wet season. An even more striking difference between the two sides was the state of the mopane shrubs that dominated the woody vegetation here. In Etosha they were mostly over a metre tall and were now shading out the grass, while in the homeland they were all less than half a metre high, and hardly visible under the perennial grasses. The reason for this was that this part of Ovamboland still regularly burned, whereas the Park's policy was to prevent any veld fires from coming in, and put out any that might start within it. Although they were never completely successful in achieving this, Giel Visser, who was based at Okaukuejo during the 1960s, told me that they spent much of every dry season fighting fires, most of which 'came in from Ovamboland'.

To stop Etosha from burning it had also been crisscrossed with firebreaks, which together with the road network confined any fires that did still occur to a small part of the Park. But was the previous high fire regime really man-made, or was it natural? Fortunately, good records were kept of all fires large enough to need putting out, and Prof Roy Siegfried, Hu Berry's supervisor, had analysed them and published a short paper on those occurring between 1970 and 1979. In it he stated that of the 56 fires during this period: 'At least 54%, and more probably 73% of them were caused by lightning.' Thus most of the fires Giel Visser and his colleagues had fought were natural, and before the grading of roads and firebreaks would have annually burned out much of the Park.

Most Europeans regard fires as dangerous and destructive, but in tropical savannah ecosystems they are the primary factor that maintains the dynamic balance between woody plants and perennial grasses. This is because trees and shrubs have their stem and leaf buds on their branches, where they will be killed by fires until they are high enough to escape the extreme heat zone. To counter this, woody species that evolved in regions with a naturally high fire regime have a band of secondary growth points at ground level, from which they will coppice if their aerial parts die. In spite of this, frequent burning controls bush encroachment by both killing new seedlings and retarding the growth of any that are able to become established.

In contrast, tufted perennial grasses have their main growth points at ground level, and because heat rises they are not damaged by veldfires. In fact, as their leaves die at the end of each growing season, burning revitalises them by removing dead material that would otherwise have built up on top of the tuft and prevented sunlight from reaching their leaf buds. If this 'top hamper' is not periodically removed perennial grasses will lose vigour and eventually die.

On nutrient-depleted soils, burning is the fastest way of recycling essential elements locked up in dead plant material, thereby making them more fertile. As long as there is moisture in the ground, fires stimulate a flush of highly nutritious new growth for both grazing and browsing ungulates to feed on. And as they occur in the dry season, when herbivores suffer the greatest nutritional stress, regular burning enables savannah ecosystems to support a higher biomass of large mammals.

Although the sweet grasslands south of the Etosha Pan would have been sensitive to continuous defoliation after being burnt, under the old migration system most of the plains game moved off them in the main growing period. However, on the Kalahari sands north of the Pan, fires were essential to make the sourveld palatable and thereby attract grazing animals onto it in the wet season. Now, with the much lower burning regime in the Park, the southern plains were being severely overgrazed while the perennial grasses on the northern savannas had become smothered with top hamper, and were dying from being under-utilised.

To confirm that the plains of Etosha had been degraded I needed evidence that they previously supported perennial grasslands. The only early botanical reference I found stated that Grootvlakte, a large treeless area west of Okaukuejo, had then been dominated by *Aristida* grass. As this genus now consisted mainly of annuals I was at first disappointed, but then remembered that all the present species of *Stipagrostis* had previously been included under the *Aristida* genus. In an old animal exclusion plot set up on Grootvlakte in the early 1970s, a few tufts of *Stipagrostis hochstetterana* and *S. uniplumis* – both of them strong perennials – also still survived. The reason for there not being more was easy to see; the fine clay soil had formed a hard cap, making it almost impossible for anything but pioneer grass seeds to germinate here. But in the past the hooves of the large migrating herds of zebra and wildebeest would have loosened the surface and made it a more favourable habitat.

I then questioned Tobias Dougab about the state of the plains around Okaukuejo when he was young. He told me that they had been 'much stronger' then, and that the Hei//om had burned the grasslands every year, as soon as the tufts dried out. As they were unlikely to have done so if the plains were covered by annuals, which would have left the ground bare until the next rainy season, it was further evidence that the sweetveld plains had previously been dominated by perennial grass.

If I was correct it also explained some of the other changes that had occurred in the Park since the 1960s. Regular burning would have prevented the plains from being invaded by shrubs, which together with the lower productivity of annual grass had forced the wildebeest and zebra to graze in areas where they were more vulnerable to predation by lions. Because anthrax spores are killed by extreme heat, the reduced frequency of veldfires would have increased the prevalence of the disease, explaining why many more of the Park's large mammals were succumbing to it than in the past.

The changed migration pattern of the plains game would not only have affected Etosha's vegetation, but also the dynamics of its predator population. Because lion prides are territorial, large numbers of wildebeest and zebra remaining on the southern plains throughout the year would have favoured them but not cheetah and wild dogs, both of which are well adapted to following migrating ungulates. This could explain why the numbers of lions increased during the 1970s, whereas the cheetah that were often seen on my early visits to Etosha were now scarce. In a 1950s report by the magistrate in Outjo, whose area of jurisdiction included the Park, he estimated the number of wild dogs in the district to be over 2 000. By 1980 there were none left. Their extermination on the farms was easy to explain, but one of the reasons why they died out inside a wildlife sanctuary could have been competition with resident lion prides.

I believed there was enough evidence to show that both man-made and lightning fires had been a key component of the Etosha ecosystem in the past, and that the only way to reverse the degradation of the plains was to restore the old burning regime. But as most of the senior DNC officials now in Windhoek would previously have worked in the Park, and spent much of their time fighting fires, they were unlikely to change the existing policy because a junior member of staff said that it was wrong.

Fortunately, Prof Siegfried was on my side. In his paper on the incidence of fires in Etosha he concluded that: 'Since veld-fire is a long standing factor in the evolution of southern African ecosystems, it follows that their biotas are adapted selectively to burning regimes. Therefore, a corner-stone of a policy for the management of nature reserves in these ecosystems should be the acceptance of naturally caused fires, and where necessary supplemented and complemented by artificial burning.'

I also had an ally in Trygve Cooper, the senior nature conservator in Namutoni, who had been a ranger in the Mkhuzi Game Reserve when June and I were running the ACE Project. As controlled burning was an accepted practice in the areas that fell under Natal Parks Board's control, Tryg had considerable experience of its impact on savanna ecosystems – but more importantly, what happened if you did not burn them.

The sweet grasslands north of Namutoni were generally in better condition than those around Halali and Okaukuejo, probably because large numbers of zebra and wildebeest only congregated here in the late dry season, moving off as soon as the rains set in. Nevertheless, Tryg was concerned about the invasion of woody plants, particularly onto the large Andoni plain, which had been cut in half by the Park's new northern border. With this in mind, he invited Jan van Niekerk, a pasture scientist with the Department of Agriculture, to come and look at the area and advise him on what should be done.

During his visit Jan told Tryg and me that in northern Namibia the productivity of over six million hectares of commercial farmland had been halved by bush encroachment, and that the primary cause was the removal of fire from the ecosystem. After spending a week in Etosha he wrote a report in which he concluded that a controlled burning programme was urgently needed.

A few weeks after Van Niekerk's report was sent to head office, Giel Visser called a meeting in Okaukuejo to discuss the burning issue. Hennie Theron and the Park's three resident scientists, as well as Tryg and I, were invited to participate, while all the other area conservators were given permission to attend as observers. At the end of it we unanimously recommended that controlled burning should take place in Etosha for the following reasons:

- Fire is part of the ecosystem.

- Fire promotes healthy vegetation and influences the migration routes of game, which in turn benefits the grazing.
- Fire controls harvester termite activity.
- Fire controls bush encroachment.
- Fires will to some extent keep game within the Park.
- Fire can be used as a management practice to create migration routes.
- Fire at the right time can control certain animal diseases.

Although final approval from Head Office was still needed, it was a major breakthrough. But there was one big problem: north-west Namibia, including Etosha, was in the grip of the worst drought in living memory. It was certainly not the best time to start burning the Park, but if given the go-ahead, Tryg and I felt that we could not let the opportunity slip through our fingers.

At the end of the meeting each area conservator had been asked to submit a list of the management blocks he wished to burn. Whereas Jan van Niekerk and Tryg focused on controlling bush encroachment, my main rationale for burning was to rehabilitate the southern plains by getting the grazing game off them during the wet season. In Area 4 the only northern block that still carried enough grass to sustain a reasonable fire was west of the Ekuma, one of the seasonal rivers that periodically flowed into the north of the Etosha Pan.

With more grass around Namutoni, Tryg chose a number of blocks to the east and south of the tourist camp, as well as the Andoni plain. In the past it was renowned as the gathering place for thousands of wildebeest and zebra at the start of each rainy season, from where they set off for the sandveld north of the Pan. The Park records showed it had not burned for 13 years and its eastern side was now being invaded by sicklebush. As important to me was that the coarse, salt-tolerant perennial grasses growing on it were now moribund and completely inedible, making the burning of Andoni a crucial first step towards re-establishing the old migration route.

In early September Hennie Theron informed us that Head Office had given permission to burn all the requested blocks – except Andoni! The DNC's old guard had a sentimental attachment to it, and could not bear the thought of this once splendid grassland being deliberately desecrated by a fire. From their Windhoek perspective they could not see that in Andoni's present state there was now virtually nothing on it for a wildebeest or zebra to eat.

The historic first controlled burn in Etosha took place outside the tourist area, south of Halali Camp. Although this part of the Park had no water and carried little game, we soon found that lighting a fire during a drought was not easy. Most of the perennial tufts had died from under-grazing, and after a frustrating day we gave up with much of the block still unburned – as was the case with most of the other areas that were recommended. Even in the Ekuma block the burn was disappointing. We had learned the hard way why Roy Siegfried's paper also stated that most of Etosha's fires occurred after high-rainfall seasons.

The poor results gave free rein to the critics of controlled burning, and even I was prepared to write the whole exercise off as a failure. However, in early December Tryg radioed me to say that a fire in Ovamboland had jumped the northern boundary firebreak and burned a large part of the Andoni plain. He invited me to come and have a look, and a few days later I went with him to the area. The first rains had just fallen and new green shoots were sprouting from the fire-blackened tufts. Grazing on them were at least 800 wildebeest, over 1 500 zebra, numerous springbok and about 60 eland, a species once common in the Namutoni area, but now rarely seen.

Driving to the border, Tryg showed me where the fire had come into the Park. The distance it had jumped was considerable, which hardly seemed possible considering the poor grass cover on the Ovamboland side of the firebreak. Seeing the puzzled look on my face, Tryg grinned and said: 'It did get a little bit of help.'

We then drove a short distance along the northern boundary, finding a break in the fence where at least another 150 wildebeest and many springbok were grazing on a burnt area inside Ovamboland. We had no way of knowing how many more might have moved deeper into the homeland, or what percentage of Etosha's zebra and wildebeest population were attracted onto Andoni. But just revitalising the perennial grasses here and setting back the encroaching sicklebush ensured that our 1981 fires did achieve some positive results. The big question now was: where would the zebra and wildebeest on Andoni go as the rains moved westwards?

*   *   *

In Kaokoland the drought was having an even greater impact than in Etosha. A few months earlier Nat Gibson, a journalist from United Press International, had visited me in Okaukuejo after a fact-finding trip to Opuwo. His description of the situation there was grim. Tens of thousands of cattle, goats and sheep had already died of starvation, with many households having lost all the livestock they owned. A major famine had only been averted by emergency feeding centres being set up by the South African Defence Force. The collapse of the homeland's rangeland that Nico Smit had predicted in 1968, which was the rationale for our failed livestock marketing project, had finally occurred.

To save what remained of their herds, the Herero living on Etosha's western boundary had cut sections of fence-line so that their cattle could graze inside the Park. Initially, the senior nature conservator at Otjovasandu, Chris Eyre, negotiated with the local traditional leadership to keep some control over the situation. But he had now been transferred to Damaraland, one of the first DNC officers to be stationed in a homeland. As the drought worsened his young and inexperienced replacement, Marcellus Loots, was fighting a losing battle against the stockowners, and in this part of Etosha cattle had become almost as numerous as wild animals.

The two Herero headmen nearest to Otjovasandu were Keefas Muzuma and Joel Tjiahura, whom I had developed a good relationship with while working for BAD. But getting involved in the struggle to secure the Park's western border would put me in a Catch-22 situation. If I was sympathetic to the stockowners it was likely to prejudice my chances of being transferred to Kaokoland, while if I did one day get back to the homeland, the support of these two powerful traditional leaders would be crucial to stopping the poaching. Fortunately, I was never asked to assist.

The news from Damaraland was equally bad. In late 1980 a *Sunday Times* article by Peter Kenny had reported that large numbers of wild animals were dying in what had previously been the western part of Etosha. In 1978 the area was leased out for trophy hunting to ANVO Safaris and the concessionaire, Volker Grellmann, imported bales of lucerne in an attempt to prevent more game from dying of starvation. But in such a large tract of land feeding wildlife was a hopeless task. When the 1981 rains brought little relief there was nothing that he or anyone else could do to save the situation.

Although working in Etosha meant I was just a stone's throw from the Kaokoveld, as Bernabe de la Bat was no longer DNC's director it now seemed unlikely my transfer there would happen soon, or at all. However, in late 1981 Blythe Loutit made me an intriguing offer. She and Ina Britz, the wife of CDM's prospecting team leader in Damaraland, were planning to form an NGO that would support Chris Eyre's efforts to bring the poaching under control. Was I interested in heading its field operations?

Their idea had been sparked by the shooting of a bull elephant in the Hoanib River by one of Volker Grellman's clients a few months earlier. Known as 'Skeuroor' because of a large tear in his left ear, he was the dominant bull in the only viable population of elephants left in western Kaokoland, which was at the time being studied by a Pretoria University researcher, Slang Viljoen. Although the hunt had been legal, because the bull was regarded as a 'desert elephant' it caused a major outcry amongst Southern African conservationists, which was aggravated by the professional hunter's unrepentant attitude to the killing.

Skeuroor's death was, in fact, the result of a miscommunication between two strong-willed men, Chris Eyre and Volker Grellman. Up until then ANVO Safari's trophy hunting had been restricted to the higher-rainfall eastern parts of their concession, as well as any problem animals that threatened either the lives or livelihoods of the local farmers living south of the Red Line. However, when Chris became responsible for nature conservation in Damaraland he believed that his BAD predecessor had been too liberal with the issuing of hunting permits, including those for problem elephants, and was determined to rectify this.

When Grellmann requested his annual problem elephant quota, Chris told him that from now on each case would be investigated before a permit was issued. This did not suit the professional hunter, who had got used to knowing at the beginning of the year how many elephants he could hunt south of the Red Line, which enabled him to book clients accordingly. When Chris dug his heels in, Grellmann decided to do what his contract had always allowed but he had never done – shoot an elephant in the desert.

A few days after Skeuroor was killed, Ina and Colin Britz visited Grellmann's hunting camp and reported it to the Namibian press. Blythe then took the matter a step further, flying to Cape Town where Tony Heard, the editor of the *Cape Times*, and freelance journalist Margaret Jacobsohn used their political contacts to get her an interview with John Wiley, the United Party's shadow Minister for the Environment. He tabled a motion in parliament condemning the killing of a desert elephant, and recommended a ban on all hunting in Namibia's homelands. When the furore died down and no action resulted from it, Blythe decided to do something about the situation herself. As a government official, Rudi could not get directly involved, so she teamed up with Ina Britz to start the Namibia Wildlife Trust.

June had reservations about my accepting Blythe's offer. We had worked for an NGO before and she knew the drawbacks: I would once again be leaving a secure job and a comfortable home for a life of insecurity with no fixed abode. She had also just been appointed as the Park's nursing sister and was looking forward to taking up the post. But I had not come back to Namibia to work in Etosha, and the DNC's new conservative hierarchy meant that joining the NWT was now my best chance of getting into the Kaokoveld. Nevertheless, before I would consider joining Blythe and Ina I set three conditions: their NGO had to have a board of trustees, I would need my salary guaranteed for two years, and the second-tier authority in Damaraland had to approve the project.

In February 1982 Ina Britz flew to Okaukuejo with Clive Walker, the director of the Endangered Wildlife Trust, whose report on his 1977 trip to the Kaokoveld had alerted me to the serious poaching taking place there. Clive told me the EWT was prepared to pay my salary for at least two years. To this Ina added that a number of the country's most prominent businessmen had agreed to become trustees of their NGO. She had also made an appointment for us all to see the Executive Committee of the Damara Representative Authority (DRA) that afternoon. We took off for Khorixas straight after lunch.

At the meeting Clive gave an explanation of the EWT's present activities, after which Ina spoke about the formation of the NWT, and how she saw it assisting Chris Eyre's work. The Damara leaders listened carefully before the chairman of the Executive Committee, Chief Justice //Garoeb, gave his response. He first thanked Clive for the support the EWT was giving to Slang Viljoen's elephant research and their offer of help for Ina and Blythe's planned project, assuring him that both had the DRA's full blessing. His only question was – when could the Namibia Wildlife Trust start operating?

*   *   *

Although I had joined the DNC with the aim of getting back to the Kaokoveld, my decision to leave Etosha was not made easier by recent developments in the burning programme. Shortly after New Year, Tryg told me that all the zebra and wildebeest had moved off the Andoni plain. By then the wet season had started in earnest and good rainfalls were being recorded in the central parts of the Park. Hoping that at least some of them had followed their old migration route, in late January I drove along the northern border to Poachers Point, a peninsula that jutted into the Pan just west of Andoni. On it I found a large number of wildebeest, zebra and springbok, but I was unable to count them because the very wet conditions made driving off the track hazardous.

By February the heavy rains had made the road along the border impassable, and because of the military activities in Ovamboland, flying over the area was not permitted. Horseback was the only other way of getting there, so I loaded the gelding I used for patrol work into a horsebox, and drove up to the now flowing Ekuma River. No wildebeest or zebra were on the block we had burnt to the west of it, so I crossed the causeway and made camp.

Early the next morning I saddled up and headed south-east across the scrub-covered plains towards the Oshingambo River, which also flowed seasonally into the Pan. Before reaching it I met a long column of zebra, amongst them groups of 20 to 30 wildebeest, walking steadily towards the Ekuma. As they showed no fear of me on horseback I followed the swelling throng, which did not stop to eat or rest. In the background was a vast sea of salt stretching uninterrupted to a horizon made invisible by the dust and haze.

When the migrating herds reached the mouth of the Ekuma they stopped on the bank of the broad stream that was flowing slowly into the Pan. Only after many hundreds of animals had gathered there did the first zebra wade into the muddy shallows, and then swim for about 30 metres through the deeper water in the middle. As I watched, about 600 zebra and 170 wildebeest crossed the Ekuma and then walked down the Pan's western shores towards Okondeka. Although they missed the block we burned, thanks to Tryg having helped the fire onto Andoni at least some of Etosha's grazers did not utilise the southern plains during the wet season. I also believed that if the perennial grasslands north of Namutoni were burned every year, many more of them would follow the same route to the plains west of Okaukuejo, thus re-establishing the annual anti-clockwise migration around the Pan.

The next morning I again rode towards the Oshingambo but saw no sign of any more zebra or wildebeest. Where were the rest of the animals that had been on the Andoni plain in December? Were they still grazing north of the Pan in Etosha, or had they crossed the fence into Ovamboland? If so, would they return to the Park, or had they walked into the rifles that so many of the homeland's residents now owned?

That afternoon I packed up and returned to Okaukuejo, hoping to get one of the other conservators to accompany me back to the area. Even if we saw no more migrating wildebeest and zebra, I could at least show them the tracks of those that had crossed the Ekuma. But when I arrived back in camp I found it to be a hive of activity. Apparently 'terrorists' were heading towards Etosha, and all available field staff were required to assist in the follow-up operation.

Early the following morning Hennie Theron briefed us on the situation. About 20 SWAPO guerrillas had taken advantage of the good rains to infiltrate deep into the commercial farmland south of the Park. However, before they carried out any attacks their presence was reported by a farm worker and the Outjo Commando, together with the police counter-insurgency unit, Koevoet, were on their spoor. Realising they were being followed, the guerrillas had split up, with one group heading west towards Otjovasandu, and the other back to Ovamboland by the shortest route – through the middle of the Park.

By nine o'clock there were two military helicopters and eleven 'Buffel' troop carriers parked outside Okaukuejo gate – more soldiers than I had ever seen in one place during the Rhodesian war. Because they did not know their way around the Park, or how to react should they encounter dangerous animals, our role was to accompany each section to ensure their safety – and that of Etosha's wildlife. My charges were to set up an ambush around Okavao, in case the guerrillas tried to get water there during the night.

We finally left Okaukuejo after lunch and moved into our position a few hours before sunset. The young men with me were all South Africans doing their compulsory military service, 19- or 20-year-old city boys who knew very little about wild animals. They had even less experience of real warfare and were nervously excited on the surface, but underneath most of them were clearly terrified by the possibility of a shootout. Who could blame them? They had no cause to die for in Namibia.

Apart from lions roaring nearby, nothing happened during the night and late the next afternoon we were all called back to Okaukuejo. Koevoet had caught up with the guerrillas and killed all nine of them just inside Etosha's southern border. That night in the staff clubhouse I heard that two of them had been driven over by Casspirs and the others shot down 'like rabbits'. However, the police officers sitting at the bar admitted that they had all died bravely, with some of them standing up and firing at the huge armoured vehicles until they were killed. I could only wonder at the courage of these young men who were on foot taking on the might of the South African Defence Force.

After the excitement of the previous two days no one was interested in coming with me to see if any more wildebeest and zebra had migrated around the Pan. With the deterioration in the security situation my colleagues also now believed that attracting game to the Park's northern border was not a good idea. Even on horseback, patrolling the area was dangerous, which would make it difficult to protect the migrating herds from poachers. It was another conservation quandary. The primary role of the Park's nature conservators was to stop its wild animals from being illegally hunted – not to manage the habitat they depended on for their wellbeing. That responsibility lay with the research section, but there had not been a botanist in Etosha for five years.

A few months later this would be rectified by the appointment of Trevor and Karen Nott, Natal University graduates who had majored in pasture science and botany. After assessing the situation Trevor also recognised the key role that fire had played in the Park and drew up a controlled burning policy that was implemented for the next 15 years. But he had not known Etosha's alkaline plains in the 1960s, and motivated it on the grounds of revitalising the Park's un-grazed and moribund grasslands, not to re-establish the migration route of wildebeest and zebra around the Pan.

In the mid-1980s Malan Lindeque, who replaced Piet de Villiers as Etosha's biologist, recommended that the Park should be managed with the aim of one day removing the northern boundary fence, thereby allowing the plains game to again move freely into southern Ovamboland. It was a bold proposal that to be successful would have first required a major change in the DNC's attitude towards the residents of the homeland. But with the liberation war still raging, it was not given serious consideration.

I did not have the chance to discuss my range management theories with either Trevor or Malan. In March I resigned from my post with DNC and accepted Ina and Blythe's offer to join the Namibia Wildlife Trust. June was given permission to stay on in our Okaukuejo house and continue working as Etosha's resident nursing sister.

CHAPTER SEVENTEEN

THE END OF THE WORLD

On 2 April 1982 Ina Britz picked me up in Okaukuejo and we drove to Wêreldsend, the CDM prospecting camp that would be the Namibia Wildlife Trust's field base. It was a five-hour journey that bridged two different worlds – from the flat, dusty plains of Etosha to the rugged basalt ranges of western Damaraland. I would also be exchanging the comfortable life of a civil servant for the insecurity of once more working for an NGO – and a brand new one at that. Could Ina and Blythe raise the funds to keep it going? As importantly, would they and the businessmen who had agreed to serve as the NWT's trustees accept the unorthodox approach I planned to use for stopping poaching in the region? And if we failed, what would happen when the two years that the EWT had committed to paying my salary ended? I had changed jobs many times in the past, but now I had three children to support.

In spite of these uncertainties, for me it was the end of a long, hard road back to Namibia's north-west. I would not be living in the Kaokoveld I had known in the 1960s, which was now a conservation disaster and wracked by warfare, but as we drove into the valley of the Huab River the rugged scenery around us was equally impressive. By all accounts, there was also still enough wildlife left in Damaraland to justify a last-ditch effort to save it.

When we crossed the Huab and entered the basalt ranges the sun was already low on the horizon and the stone-strewn slopes of the mountains glowed red in the evening light. Here were only widely scattered homesteads, with small flocks of karakul sheep and goats nearby; in between, the rugged landscape was bare apart from a few shrubs and gnarled mopane trees along the water-courses. Before the drought, Ina told me, the area had supported large numbers of springbok, gemsbok and mountain zebra, but we saw no wildlife at all.

One hundred and twenty kilometres west of Khorixas, the last place where petrol was available, we turned left towards Torra Bay on the Skeleton Coast, and 25 km further on met the veterinary cordon fence that formed the new 'Red Line'. Here we left the graded road, and after passing through a double gate drove into a grove of euclea trees where CDM's exploration staff lived. In the fading light the country around us was starkly beautiful, dominated by an imposing round-topped mountain that towered over the surrounding rocky desert.

Wêreldsend was the last farm before the rainfall became too low even for karakul sheep. Because of its isolation it had been called World's End, one of many ironic names given by white farmers to the huge tracts of semi-desert they obtained for virtually nothing in the 1950s. But although their land was acquired cheaply, and generous subsidies were granted by a government that saw its votes coming mainly from the rural areas, the southern Kaokoveld had not been an easy place to farm in. Droughts were frequent, lions and other predators plentiful, and only rudimentary tracks linked the remote homesteads to Khorixas and Kamanjab, the two nearest towns. It was pioneer country that had to be tamed by individual ingenuity and endurance in the face of considerable adversity. However, in spite of the lack of infrastructure and services, the tough men and their hardy womenfolk had toiled through the good and bad times to make a living in this inhospitable part of South West Africa.

When in 1970 the government expropriated over 200 farms here to create a homeland for the Damara people, there was an outcry from the country's Afrikaner community. At the time I was living in Opuwo and listened as my BAD colleagues debated the issue. Although all of them were staunch National Party supporters, they saw it as a betrayal of the people who had voted them into power! The landowners were well compensated for the farms they lost, as well as for any real or claimed improvements made on them. To sweeten the pill, they were also paid *verdrietgeld* – an extra amount for the grief of being uprooted from their homes and having to leave behind the graves of the family members who had died during their brief stay in the Kaokoveld.

When the exodus finally took place many of the farmers broke down their houses to ensure that no blacks could move into them, while other homesteads had their doors, window frames and roofing material ransacked by the new residents of the region. On Wêreldsend the crumbling walls of a simple brick house still stood on a low ridge overlooking the camp – all that remained of the hopes and dreams of a family that had once lived 'at the end of the world'.

When we stopped, Ina's husband, Colin, produced a cold beer and welcomed me to Damaraland. Although the CDM camp was very basic, they had made their lives quite comfortable, as I found when I was ushered into a tin shack for an excellent meal prepared by their cook. After dinner we sat around the campfire and talked about the poaching situation in the region for a few hours, before I was led along a path through the trees to my room for the night – one of two guest huts at the back of the camp.

I soon fell asleep but in the early hours of the morning a great commotion from where Ina and Colin lived woke me. It sounded like a pig being slaughtered, and between the squeals I could also hear Ina shouting hysterically. After a few seconds I realised that she was calling for me to bring a light quickly, as there were lions in the camp! Next to my bed was a small torch which faintly illuminated the shadows as I carefully found my way to the camp's main hut, where Colin explained what had happened.

It being a warm night they had decided to put their double bed outside under the trees, and when he got undressed Colin had dropped his overall on the ground next to the bed for their bullterrier to lie on. He was fast asleep when a lion sprang over him onto the dog – the cause of the pig-like squealing I had heard. Scrambling out of bed, Colin, with Ina just behind him, had run to the tin hut we now stood in to get a .375 rifle he kept in a gun safe there. But they had left their only torch next to the bed, and in the darkness had been unable to find the key to the safe.

By now the squealing had stopped, and we did not know if the lion was still there. I stepped outside the hut and shone my little torch towards the bed. In its faint light I could just see what appeared to be a lion's head visible behind it. It looked like 'Bully' was still in its mouth!

After finding the safe key Colin took out his rifle and loaded it, but as the penlight torch was of little use I slipped into a vehicle that Ina had parked nearby, switched on the headlights and turned it towards the bed. The lion glared back into the beam and did not move, enabling Colin to kill it with a single shot in the brain. After making sure that it was dead, I knelt down next to Bully and instinctively put my hand on his chest. I had already said to Ina, 'I'm afraid he's dead,' when I felt his heart beat once, then again, and a few seconds later he took a large gulp of air. Amazingly, in spite of the deep holes in his shoulder, chest and neck, he was soon limping around, looking rather sorry for himself, but very much alive!

While Ina put the kettle on, Colin and I drove down to the staff quarters at the south end of the camp to tell them what had happened, and advise them to stay indoors. As they gathered around the vehicle one of the men told us that something had scratched on the door of his hut during the night. Thinking it was a dog he had just kicked the door and told it to *voetsek*! In the car's headlights, the tracks around the hut confirmed that his 'visitor' had indeed been a lion.

Colin and I then drove around the camp, finding another six lions and a hyena in the thick sedges less than 100 metres away. Using the vehicle, we chased them for some distance into the desert, and once we were satisfied that they had got the message they were not welcome, joined Ina for a much-needed cup of tea. Over it I complimented my hosts for laying on such an exciting introduction to Wêreldsend.

On closer examination we found that the young male lion that had caught Bully was extremely thin, no doubt the reason why he had been so bold as to come right into camp. During the two years of drought the region's game had been concentrated around the springs, thus providing easy meals for the lions. However, when good rains fell the previous month, the surviving game dispersed into the desert, making it very difficult for them to find prey. The balance between the hunters and hunted had now swung the other way and 'lion problems' would become a common occurrence over the next few months.

In the morning I radioed Chris Eyre and informed him of the night's events. He promised to be at Wêreldsend that afternoon, to see for himself what had happened. As I had not seen Chris since his transfer to Khorixas, his visit would also give me the opportunity of explaining to him what we were planning to do in the area.

The Namibia Wildlife Trust was not the first non-governmental organisation to raise funds for stopping the poaching in the Kaokoveld. In 1981 the United Kingdom-based People's Trust for Endangered Species, through its South African representative, Nick Carter, had donated R5 000 to Blythe

Loutit, who used most of it to employ Peter Erb, the son of a Swakopmund friend, who had just returned from university. What remained put fuel into her private vehicle for patrols in the Uchab River area.

While waiting for Chris to arrive I walked around Wêreldsend and noted a grass hut that had recently been built just to the south of the camp. I asked Colin and Ina what it was for and they explained that it was to be the set for a scene in a film Nick Carter and Blythe were planning to make. Intrigued, I asked Ina for more details and she told me local actors would be filmed sitting around it when a nature conservation official drove up, and after searching the hut and finding a rhino horn, arrested them. The aim was to dramatise the poaching crisis in the region, and hopefully loosen the purse strings of potential donors.

Fundraising would be essential to maintain our operations, but I was uncomfortable with the theme of the film. It would portray conventional anti-poaching activities that were failing throughout most of Africa, and just entrench the current stereotype of black Africans being the criminals, when it was the buyers, most of whom were white, that were the real villains in the illegal ivory and rhino horn trade. I also felt that any publicity we produced should not further alienate the local people, or their leaders, whose support would be critical to the success of our efforts to stop the poaching. Before leaving Etosha I had drawn up a set of objectives that I believed should be the main focus of the NWT's Damaraland/Kaokoland Project. They were:

1. **To create an awareness of the need for good conservation among all the residents of Kaokoland and Damaraland.** Particular emphasis would be put on the arid western parts of the region – a unique national asset with exceptional tourist potential. Our priority target groups here would be the political and traditional leaders, farmers and other rural residents, teachers and students.

2. **To train suitable inhabitants of Kaokoland and Damaraland in nature conservation so that in future they might play an active professional role in the conservation of the region.** Young, suitably qualified Damara and Herero men would be employed to work and train under me in conjunction with other competent persons working in the region. After some years of practical experience, suitable trainees would be offered bursaries to follow nature conservation diploma courses at Cwaka College in KwaZulu.

3. **To assist the nature conservation officers in controlling illegal hunting in the region.** This would be done by conservation extension and education amongst the local population, and also by the regular patrolling of sensitive areas by Trust personnel. Because the NWT staff did not have legal powers of arrest, all information and evidence obtained would be handed over to the nature conservation authorities for further investigation and/or prosecution.

4. **To promote a better understanding of the ecology of this unique region.** During the course of our other activities and as part of the training programme, Trust staff would gather information on game numbers, distribution and movements. Plant and other surveys would also be conducted.

When Chris arrived and had heard our account of the lion saga, I gave him a copy of our proposed objectives to read, and watched as he paced back and forth puffing large clouds of smoke from the battered pipe he smoked. Finally he gave his opinion: 'You must remember that you're not wearing a uniform now, Garth. I'm in charge of conservation in Damaraland and you can't just do what you like around here. You and Colin had the right to shoot this lion to protect the lives of the people living in the camp, but I don't want to find myself having to come down here one day to arrest someone for breaking a regulation in the ordinance. I'm not so worried about you – you know the law – but we can't have Ina and Blythe thinking they own the wild animals in this part of the world. Women shouldn't get involved in conservation. You know what they're like. They get bloody emotional about things. I can see them just causing me problems in the future.'

Now nearing 40 and still a confirmed bachelor, Chris was widely recognised as one of the best field conservators in the country, who put his heart and soul into whatever task he was given. However, he was of Irish stock, which together with his Virgo star sign meant that arguing the negative side of any issue was his automatic starting point. But I knew that his BAD predecessor in Khorixas had left a legacy of corruption and dereliction of duty regarding hunting by the white officials working for the second-tier government. Consequently, he saw his first priority as being to stamp his authority on conservation in the homeland and 'get some order and control back into the system'.

I assured Chris that I would be in charge of the NWT's field operations, not

Ina and Blythe, and would keep him well informed of our activities. I was also well aware that I no longer had the legal rights of a nature conservator, and it was for this reason that my main focus would be on conservation education and extension work, while any information we did get about poaching would be brought straight to him.

In spite of his concerns regarding an NGO working in the area and his reservations about 'women in conservation', Chris was broadly in agreement with our planned objectives. He had himself recognised that working through the local leaders was critical, and had already got the Damara Representative Authority to ban all hunting in the Homeland – including 'pot licences'. This had not made him popular with the other government officials. It was also his policy not to charge local people for poaching ordinary game in the first year after his arrival in Khorixas: 'These people have been hunting all their lives,' he told me. 'I can't just come in here and start arresting every Damara farmer that kills a springbok for the pot. Many of them lost all of their livestock in the drought and they're now hungry. I'd poach the odd animal myself if I was in their position.'

Chris believed that his pragmatic approach was paying off. He had developed a very good relationship with Chief Justice //Garoeb and the other members of the Damara Executive Committee. His leniency with regard to minor hunting offences by local people also meant that he had been well received by most of the black farmers in the homeland. However, the year was almost up and he planned to take a much harder line in the future.

That Chris wanted to establish his authority in the region was understandable, but I was surprised by the level of hostility my erstwhile superiors in the DNC felt towards the NWT. They saw nature conservation as being solely a government function, and whereas the SWA Wildlife Society was tolerated, even useful at times, because it did little more than protest about environmental issues, we were planning to undertake fieldwork. At first they just mocked Ina and Blythe's initiative: what could two women do to stop the illegal hunting of rhino and elephant? However, when I resigned and joined the Trust their attitude hardened, and they claimed that it was illegal for us to do anything at all related to conservation in the homelands. I knew that there was no law to stop us, however. We just had to be careful.

They had also misjudged the two women who had started the NWT. When Ina set her mind to do something she let no one stand in her way, no matter how high his rank in government or status in society. Blythe was equally determined, although she operated in a less up-front manner. Both were deeply committed to saving the wildlife in Damaraland, and they were a formidable combination.

*   *   *

A few days after my arrival at Wêreldsend, Colin, Ina and I drove to the Achab River, a tributary of the Uniab – the dry watercourse that drained most of the area north of the camp. In March, soaking rains had broken the drought and short emerald-green grass now covered the stony flats between the ranges. Grazing on it were a few small herds of springbok, gemsbok and mountain zebra that had survived the two previous years when virtually no effective rain had fallen. If we could stop the local people's hunting, there was still a chance of saving the common game species in this part of Damaraland – but what hope did we have of stopping the elephant and rhino poaching?

We followed the Achab to its junction with the Uniab and stopped on a promontory overlooking the beds of the two seasonal rivers, which were covered with large shrubs and scattered trees. We had been there just long enough for Colin to crack open a can of beer when we heard a loud roar and then squealing about 100 metres up the Achab. A few seconds later a back-pedalling rhino bull and a very angry cow – apparently fending off his attentions – emerged from the bushes. Behind the cow came a half-grown calf. The bull was clearly intent on doing his bit to boost the Damaraland rhino population, but she was not having any of it, while the calf seemed rather mystified by all the attention its mother was getting.

Excited by my first rhino sighting in Damaraland, I tried to get closer, but the trio got my wind and ran off, climbing out of the riverbed and keeping up a steady trot until they had disappeared from view up a side-valley. It was an auspicious start to my stay at Wêreldsend, and as we drove back to camp I hoped the cow would be less obstinate in the days ahead. Didn't she know that the Kaokoveld rhinos were in danger of becoming extinct?

In the afternoon great cumulus clouds built up, and as we drove into Wêreldsend the heavens opened up and lashed the desert with blinding rain. When the storm ended we heard a rumbling sound coming from the direction of the rocky riverbed just behind the camp. Walking to its bank Colin, Ina and I watched as it was transformed into a raging red torrent, in places nearly a metre deep. The next morning we measured 26 mm in the camp's rain gauge, and with the heavy storms that had occurred in March, the drought in this part of Damaraland was now definitely broken.

Over the Easter weekend June and the boys drove from Okaukuejo to join me. As I still did not have a project vehicle, Colin used one of CDM's Land Rovers to take us into the north-east of the homeland. To get there we drove up the now gravel road towards Sesfontein, crossing the veterinary cordon fence at Palmwag, ANVO Safaris' hunting camp, and then turning onto a rough track about 50 km beyond. Until 1970 this area had been part of Etosha, and was still mostly uninhabited. At a small spring a few kilometres from the main road Colin stopped to show us the carcass of a rhino with its horns cut off – one of many dead rhino and elephants that he and Slang Viljoen had seen in February while conducting an aerial survey. Chris Eyre was following up the case, but by the time the carcasses were discovered they were months old and there seemed to be little chance of arrests being made.

We drove on through lightly wooded hills, passing an older rhino carcass, again with only the horns cut off. Beyond it was a strong spring that formed a series of pools down the side of a deep valley. Here Colin led us to the carcasses of three elephant cows and a large sub-adult. They had all died within a few metres of each other, apparently having bunched up for protection when the bullets started flying. A fifth carcass was lying about 50 metres away. Nearer to the spring were the older remains of another four elephants that had also been poached for their ivory. I took photographs before leaving this valley of death – all of us quite sickened by the carnage that had taken place in it.

We camped in a tributary of the Ombonde River that ran down the edge of a broad plain known locally as the 'Serengeti'. This was the country I had travelled through during the 1970 drought, when looking for cattle that had illegally entered the game reserve. Then it had been full of game, but on this trip, apart from four giraffe and two springbok, we had seen only carcasses. Although it was good to finally have my family with me in the Kaokoveld, as we sat around the fire that evening I found it hard to be cheerful. I had come back too late. What big game still survived was clearly under siege, and unless we stopped the slaughter soon their populations would be unviable.

June picked up my depression, perhaps thinking that I blamed her and the boys for holding me back when the region's wildlife desperately needed someone to blow the whistle on what was happening. But I could only blame myself for having been misled by John Vorster and Anton Rupert's public announcement that a game reserve would soon be established in the Kaokoveld. Why were these plans not implemented? Had the cabinet deliberately held back in order to keep their homeland hunting grounds open for a few more years?

The next morning we came across the fresh tracks of a large herd of elephants – possibly as many as 20 – that had crossed the riverbed where we slept the day before. Cheered by the thought that at least some elephants survived in the area, we drove south to a second spring in the upper reaches of the 'Serengeti' river. Here we found the carcasses of another eight elephants and two rhino. Some of the elephant carcasses were quite old, and their tusks had clearly been removed with a power saw. This was not the work of local people, but were their killers also still operating in the area?

Later that morning we saw four elephant bulls on the Serengeti and a cow herd of 18 up another valley – probably the same herd whose tracks we found earlier. The next day we found six more, bringing the total of living elephants seen to 28, but there were no calves amongst them. While sitting on a ridge watching the last group I wondered what these highly intelligent animals thought when they visited the springs where so many of them had been killed. Man had hunted elephants for centuries, but in their lifetime had never done so here on this scale. And with the de-proclaimed western part of Etosha no longer a sanctuary, was there any safe place left for them?

During the three days with Colin we also saw 21 giraffe, one kudu, two springbok, a cheetah and the carcass of a gemsbok that had been killed by hyenas. As this was meant to be the area where the most game survived in the Kaokoveld, it was hardly an impressive tally. Of even greater concern was that we found no recent sign of rhino, although Colin said they had previously been quite common here. Had they all been poached?

On Easter Monday June and the boys drove back to Okaukeujo. We had seen too many carcasses for it to have been an enjoyable trip. But the scenery had impressed her and the few sightings of wild animals we did have were especially memorable against the backdrop of rugged mountains, and all the more precious because of their precarious future.

*   *   *

In mid-April Peter Erb, who had been working with Blythe in the Uchab River area, joined me at Wêreldsend. As the promised Endangered Wildlife Trust vehicle had not yet arrived, Colin got permission to loan us the oldest Land Rover in CDM's fleet and suggested we patrol up towards the Aub and

Barab – two large northern tributaries of the Uniab River. This was one of the remotest parts of Damaraland, and he knew that some rhino still occurred there. After three days in the field we had seen 16 zebra, 5 gemsbok and a herd of 18 springbok. But we did find a large bull rhino and were able to get close enough to take good photos of it for an identification file I intended starting.

Because of the very low game numbers Peter and I also recorded any spoor or fresh dung seen, which at least showed us that some game still survived. On the positive side, we only found the remains of two dead elephants and no rhino, but the area was vast and we had just covered a tiny part of it. There were many zebra, gemsbok and kudu carcasses that appeared, as they were still intact, to have died of starvation during the drought. The dead and dying animals would have been a boon for the predators, which was confirmed by our finding lion and leopard spoor in a number of places, as well as plenty of hyena tracks.

Spending time in the field with Peter gave me a chance to access my young colleague. Just 20 years old, thin and bespectacled, he was more academic than athletic, and my first impression was that he would not be able to cope with the tough task that lay ahead of us. Perhaps for this reason Ina had taken an instant dislike to Peter, and had Blythe not fiercely supported her friend's son, she would undoubtedly have sacked him. However, as Peter was prepared to work for a very low salary, I felt he should at least be given a chance to prove himself, and suggested he work with me for another three months. During this time I found his enthusiasm and willingness to do anything I asked more than made up for any physical shortcomings, and at the end of the period recommended we keep him on. I did not regret this decision.

In late April three Pretoria university professors, Fritz Eloff, Guillaume Theron and Koos Bothma, arrived at Wêreldsend. In 1975 they had been commissioned by the SA Nature Foundation to draw up master-plans for conservation and tourism in Namibia's two north-western homelands. Willem van Riet had coordinated the field work and Slang Viljoen, then a master's student, had carried out a survey of the large mammals in the Kaokoveld. Although their recommendations had not been implemented, the professors had maintained a foothold in the region through their supervision of Viljoen's later PhD research on the elephants in the arid west of the region.

The next morning our three guests, Colin and Ina, Slang and his two local assistants, Peter Erb and I set off for the Hoanib River on the western route via Hunkab, a spring deep in the desert. At the time the only track into this seldom-visited part of Damaraland was from inside the Skeleton Coast Park, across the lower Uniab River and then up its tributary, the Samanab, onto the basalt plains in the north-west of the homeland. It was through true Namib, but storms a few weeks before had produced a shimmer of green and a few pools of water still stood against the sand dunes here. Along the way we saw a herd of about 100 springbok, as well as a few gemsbok and ostrich that had followed the rain into the desert.

We continued northwards, with Slang following a virtually invisible track across the barren gravel flats to Hunkab, where we stopped briefly to look for elephant tracks. We found none, but some old dung near the water confirmed that the pachyderms had visited the area in the recent past. There were also the clear footprints of at least one rhino.

Since leaving Wêreldsend we had been driving almost non-stop for eight hours, but the professors had little time and lots of ground to cover. After sandwiches handed round by Ina, we all piled back into the trucks and drove on, leaving the basalt plains and following the course of the Mudorib River through desolate schist and gneiss ranges to where it joined the lower reaches of the Hoanib. About 10 km from the junction we had a brief sighting of a rhino bull that stared vacantly in the direction of our vehicles before running off. Slang recognised it as one of at least three rhino that he knew inhabited this remote and inhospitable place.

We camped for the night on the banks of the Mudorib, within sight of the Hoanib River, which here formed the boundary between Damaraland and Kaokoland. In 10 hours of driving we had covered nearly 200 km, seeing just one rhino, four mountain zebra, 18 gemsbok, about 120 springbok and eight ostrich. I had been hoping that most of the region's migratory game had moved west to take advantage of the brief availability of green grass in the Namib. But we had covered enough ground to show me that this was not the reason for the very low numbers further inland.

The next day we drove up the Hoanib for about 10 km, again finding only old signs of elephants, and then up the Obias, a northern tributary we followed onto the Giribes plain. Here green perennial grass stretched to the distant hills, but we counted only nine ostrich feeding on it. This was country I had known in the 1960s, and I told my companions that after good rains I had once seen over 100 gemsbok as well as large herds of springbok and many flocks of ostrich on these plains. They said nothing, but the grim look on their faces showed that they shared my disappointment at how little game we had encountered on the trip.

Before crossing the Giribes we stopped on its south-western edge to visit the site of an experiment that Prof Theron had previously set up to solve one of the region's mysteries. Like many before him, he had been intrigued by the evenly spaced 'fairy circles' on this and other sandy plains on the edge of the Namib. His theory was that the toxic succulent, *Euphorbia damarana*, had once grown in them and poisoned the soil around its roots, thus preventing grass from growing there. As there were now no euphorbias growing on the Giribes plain itself, where most fairy circles occurred, if this was the cause, the toxins they released would have to be very persistent.

Consequently, to see if the size and shape of the bare circles remained constant, on a previous trip a number of them had been measured and photographed. But to his disappointment Prof Theron found that grass was starting to cover one of them, and a new bare patch seemed to be opening up nearby – where no euphorbia had grown. Nevertheless, to finally prove or disprove his theory we collected soil from the centre of the circles for experimental purposes back in Pretoria. Although none of the grass seeds planted in it germinated in the first year, suggesting that the soil was indeed toxic, when the pots were watered again the following year they produced a good crop of grass. Another theory was that there were termite nests in the middle of each circle, but as there was little sign of their activity on the Giribes, and they are capable of foraging much further, this was also unlikely. To date, no one has conclusively solved the mystery.

That afternoon we drove via Sesfontein and the Khovarib Schlucht to the 'Serengeti', where we camped, and the following morning visited some of the elephant and rhino carcasses Colin had shown June and me a few weeks before. This time we saw only two small herds and a single bull elephant, one zebra and nine ostrich in this part of Damaraland, and by the time we got back to Wêreldsend the three professors were deeply distressed. They too had known the Kaokoveld in better times, and although they were appalled by the poaching in the 1970s, had still believed the situation could be turned around. They now thought it was too late to stop Damaraland's wildlife from being exterminated, as had already happened in Kaokoland.

At Ina's table that night I said nothing. I had joined the NWT believing that if we got the local communities' support the poaching could be brought under control, but I had been naive to think it would be that simple. Why should Himba, Herero and Damara people care about the disappearance of wild animals that brought them no benefits apart from what they could illegally sell or eat? Were the professors right that it was too late to do anything?

Was the sight of elephants, rhino and giraffe against a backdrop of desert mountains now destined to become just a fading memory in the minds of the few of us who were privileged to have known the Kaokoveld before the killing started?

My sombre mood was deepened a few days later when I heard over the Wêreldsend radio that Bernabe de la Bat had suffered a series of heart attacks and died. His new position had included re-organising the South West African administration under a multiracial government. Coercing his more right-wing colleagues into accepting the inevitable political changes could not have been easy and probably contributed to his untimely death at just 53 years of age.

*   *   *

That living with large predators could be dangerous and costly for local communities was brought home soon after my arrival in Damaraland. In the first week we received a radio call from Mike Booysens, the headmaster of the primary school at Bergsig, a small village 25 km east of Wêreldsend. He told us that a lioness had come into the school grounds the previous evening, and although she only tried to catch some fowls, he was concerned about the safety of the children if she returned. As no one there owned a firearm he asked if we could come to their assistance.

Just before sunset Colin, Ina and I drove to Bergsig, and after speaking to Mike decided to camp at a reservoir between the hostel and the makeshift houses where most of the residents lived. If anything happened at either place we would hear the commotion and be close enough to respond. After lying awake until about 11 o'clock we laid out our bedrolls and went to sleep. All was quiet during the night, but when we got up the following morning we discovered that the lioness had come back, and her tracks came to within 10 metres of where we had been lying!

As no livestock or people had been attacked, we could at least claim credit for having frightened her away. But before driving back to Wêreldsend we were confronted by a very irate Volker Grellmann, the professional hunter based at Palmwag, who had also heard about the lioness at the school. He told us that he had carefully planned a more permanent solution to the problem, and had brought two of his clients with him to execute it. For bait they had slaughtered a goat and hung it in a tree near the village, next to which they had sat up all night. Unfortunately he had not informed Mike Booysens of his plan to bait the lion, and because of our late arrival we had not told any of the villagers about our presence at the reservoir. His relationship with Ina had already been strained by the bad publicity she and Blythe generated after the killing of Skeuroor, so Volker was not amused by our intervention, and told me out of the others' hearing that he was sorry the lioness had not taken 'a small bite out of Ina's very ample bottom'.

Over the next few months, lion, cheetah and leopard problems became the order of the day in western Damaraland and southern Kaokoland. With virtually no game left, the starving predators turned their attention to the only remaining prey – the local people's cattle, goats and sheep. From their side the stockowners used whatever means they had available to kill as many predators as possible. In Kaokoland, where the pastoralists were armed and used to dealing with stock-raiders, the battle was usually one-sided, although a few of the more wily animals were able to live on beef and mutton for some months before being shot, trapped or poisoned. However in Damaraland, where firearms were scarce, some farmers lost considerable numbers of their livestock.

At Palm Pos, north of Bergsig, a pride of 14 lions jumped over the kraal fence and killed 96 sheep and 17 goats, half the farmer's remaining flock, in a single night! Gys Simon, the family head here, told me that he threw burning sticks at them, but they paid little attention to this and just became aggressive if he ventured too close. The following evening Volker Grellmann, this time without clients, waited for the lions to come back and shot 11 of them, leaving only one adult male and two females to ensure that there would still be some lions to trophy hunt in the future.

The only human fatality occurred in Sesfontein. Late one night a Damara man was woken by the restlessness of his goats and went out to investigate. In the moonlight he saw an animal slinking away, and taking it to be a large dog, went back to bed. A few minutes later, a lion entered the hut and grabbed hold of his wife. Using a hearthstone, the only weapon available, he hit it on the head and managed to pull it off her. Then, telling her to pick up their three-year-old child and run away, he also escaped from the hut. But once outside he found that in her terror and confusion his wife had not taken the child with her.

Afraid to go back into the hut, the man ran to the Sesfontein army base, where the young officer in charge, Tom Prinsloo, drove a military vehicle back to the scene. At first he shone the truck's headlights through the door, but could only make out the shape of the lion. However, when he went around the back of the hut and looked through one of the small windows, the half-eaten remains of the child were clearly visible. He shot the lion.

Although predator problems were widespread, our neighbouring community on the 'Odendaal' farms around Bergsig suffered the most. To make matters worse, they had only recently been moved here. Prior to 1974 their homes had been in the vicinity of Riemvasmaak, a Catholic Mission near the Orange River in the north-western Cape, from which they had taken their group name. The reason for their removal by the South African government was the increasing pressure being applied by the UN to grant Namibia independence, and Pretoria's need to have a military presence on what might soon become the country's new front line. It was their land that was the most suitable and expedient to build a base on.

To give the expropriation of their land a semblance of legitimacy, an ethnologist was appointed to find out where the people living around Riemvasmaak 'really belonged'. Although they were of mixed descent, and Afrikaans was their home language, most of them could speak Nama – which was also spoken by the Damara people in Namibia. The fact that many of the 'Odendaal' farms in the newly created Damaraland had not yet been settled no doubt also played a role in his conclusion that this was where they should be moved to.

One of the Riemvasmaker headmen, Jacob Basson, was invited to visit the area with a delegation of elders. They were well treated along the way, and as the white farmers had left three years before and it had received good rain, they found the rocky landscape covered in grass, with many springs and boreholes sunk by the previous owners. When Basson returned with a favourable report, about half the Riemvasmaak community agreed to make the 1 500 km trek to Damaraland, but as one of them told a newspaper reporter at the time: 'We knew that the government wanted our land and that remaining on it was no longer an option.'

The area they were resettled in was similar in climate to the north-western Cape, and the hard-working Riemvasmakers made the best out of their new situation. However, they soon learned that the land was not as productive as it seemed when Jacob Basson's delegation visited it, and the drought in the early 1980s dealt the community a devastating blow. For some of them the lion problems they were now experiencing was the final straw.

*   *   *

My first chance to see Damaraland from the air came in late April. In order to keep track of the widely dispersed and very mobile surviving elephants, the EWT funded a bi-monthly aerial survey to assist Slang Viljoen's research. The pilot was Marten Bertens, a Swakopmund resident who made his Piper Cherokee aircraft available for little more than the cost of the fuel – his personal contribution to conservation in the north-west of Namibia.

Because the survey entailed flying low over mountainous terrain, Marten flew with only two passengers, and Colin accompanied Slang on the first morning. The area they covered was east of the road to Sesfontein, and they counted a total of 76 elephants, most of them in the vicinity of the Serengeti. During the afternoon I flew with Slang over the Barab, Aub and Uniab rivers, as well as the western basalt plains, but we saw no elephants. However, we did count 17 giraffe, 154 mountain zebra, 21 gemsbok, two springbok, two ostrich and four black rhino. The next morning another 20 elephants were found in the lower Hoanib River, while three sub-adults were seen in the Hoarusib, inside the Skeleton Coast Park.

Having so recently visited the sites where 17 elephant and four rhino had been gunned down, this was not encouraging. On their first morning flight Slang and Colin had also flown over a group of armed men riding donkeys south of Sesfontein, heading straight towards the headwaters of the Aub and Barab rivers, where the most rhino were known to occur. On the second day we saw another party of eight armed men on donkeys in the hills between the Giribes Plain and Purros – where I had seen rhino in the 1960s. In frustration Marten dived low over this group, but they knew there was nothing to fear from an aircraft and just continued on their way.

Flying over this part of Damaraland brought home to me the vast size and ruggedness of the area where the majority of wildlife now survived. Back at the camp, Slang told me that most of it had no vehicle access tracks, and the only way to get there was by driving up the rocky riverbeds, which was very slow going. As the aerial survey had clearly shown me the futility of trying to carry out anti-poaching activities from the air, if we were to have any hope of catching the poachers we would have to cover the area on foot. But they would be on home ground in a game they had been playing unopposed for many years.

In late April the NWT's Damaraland/Kaokoland Project finally got 'on the road' with the donation of a Datsun 4x4 Tracker by the Endangered Wildlife Trust. With the loaned CDM Land Rover, Peter Erb and I were now able to work independently, and I divided the area of our operations along the veterinary fence. Peter would patrol the lower Huab and Uchab rivers while I covered ANVO's hunting concession and southern Kaokoland. The parts of

Damaraland further inland were left in the capable hands of Chris Eyre and the assistant he had brought with him from Etosha, Lucas Mbomboro.

Before giving Peter responsibility for the area south of the fence, I undertook two reconnaissance patrols there: the first from the pass over the Grootberg range down the Klip River into the Huab valley, and the second from Wêreldsend southwards across the lower Huab to the Uchab. In six days the only wild animals seen were two herds of five zebra each, but I did find scattered spoor of elephant, rhino, lion, kudu, gemsbok and springbok, as well as the tracks of three giraffe near the junction of the Klip and Huab rivers. The wildlife situation in this part of Damaraland was grim, but the spectacular mountain scenery gave it undoubted tourist potential, and made our efforts to save what little remained well worthwhile.

In mid-May, a few days before the first meeting of the NWT's Board of Trustees, Slang Viljoen came to Wêreldsend and put a proposal to Ina Britz, in her capacity as its executive director. If we were really serious about trying to stop the poaching we first needed to know what, how much and where game still occurred in the north-west – and the only way to do so would be to carry out a proper aerial census of the whole area, from the Uchab to the Kunene River. In such a vast tract of land it would be impossible to get accurate numbers, but flying systematically over the parts of Damaraland and Kaokoland where his groundwork showed that wildlife still occurred would give us a good estimate of the important species' populations. It would also enable us to establish priority areas for our vehicle and foot patrols.

Ina asked how many flying hours would be needed to do the job. Before he answered, Slang sucked for a while on his bent-stemmed pipe. As part of his master's degree, he had done three aerial censuses in the Kaokoveld, and from this experience reckoned that, even if we just counted the area from the escarpment westwards, a minimum of 30 hours would be needed to cover Kaokoland properly. Northern Damaraland, where the largest numbers of game survived, would need to be flown more intensively. It would make sense to do the Skeleton Coast Park as well, he added apologetically.

'So it's 100 hours,' Ina said.

'Yes, if we want to make our results credible,' Slang replied, 'but we could reduce the flying hours if ...'

Ina cut him short. If he needed 100 flying hours then that was what he would get. Raising sponsorship for the census would be her responsibility. Slang and I should just make sure that the job was done well: 'No corners must be cut. I want our census to be even better than the one the

Department is doing in Etosha,' were her final words on the subject.

Slang and I just looked at each other. We had to admit that Ina's attitude was right, but convincing the Trust's management committee and getting sponsorship would take more than just positive thinking.

Putting together the NWT's Board of Trustees had been a major achievement. The chairman, Peter Böttger, was the managing director of SWACO, one of the country's oldest companies. The Vice-Chairman, Hennie van der Westhuizen, was CDM's head of exploration and had made Wêreldsend available for our operations. Also enticed or cajoled by Ina and Blythe into becoming trustees were Doug Hoffe, CDM's managing director, Barry Clements, the PRO for Rössing Uranium Mine and a previous director of the Wilderness Leadership School, Allan Walkden-Davis, the PRO for Shell, John Kirkpatrick, a respected Windhoek advocate, Jock Orford, the gynaecologist who put Etosha's lions on the pill, and Walter Böttger, also with SWACO and a leading member of the Wildlife Society. Colin, Blythe and Slang were also trustees, while the irrepressible Ina had appointed herself its executive director.

Although the NWT's board comprised some of the country's leading businessmen and environmentalists, there were no black faces on it. But this could not be blamed on Ina and Blythe. In 1982, wildlife conservation was still the exclusive preserve of pale-skinned Namibians. At the time there were no blacks employed by the DNC above the rank of labourer, and the members of the Wildlife Society, the only other conservation NGO, were also all white. However, if there were no appropriate candidates from the country's non-white communities to make the NWT board more representative of Namibian society, at least the four objectives I had drawn up would focus on involving the local people and their leaders.

At the Trust's first meeting I said little about the aerial census, except that it would be very beneficial to our work. Ina did the rest. The farm-girl from Kamanjab had the bit firmly between her teeth and the captains of commerce and industry appointed to oversee the NWT's activities were not going to hold her back. By the time wine and snacks were served, all the trustees had agreed to Slang's proposal. As long as Ina could raise the funds the census was on. The only issue left was – when? The good rains had brought the game down onto the western plains where they would be easier to count, so the best time was right away.

'By July at the latest,' said Slang. Ina looked hard at him for a few seconds and then said: 'Then we'd better get moving on it.' Nobody else said a word. The Executive Director had spoken.

With Ina and Blythe's support, my four objectives had also been approved by the trustees. The only issue that caused some dissent was what to do about the region's starving predators. A recent press report had stated that lions were in danger of dying out in Damaraland, and in response the chairman proposed that the NWT buy donkeys with which to feed them. Having the previous week seen four lions too weak from hunger to stand up, I did not dispute the fact that they were in trouble, but I strongly opposed interfering in nature's way of reducing their numbers. I believed that if the local people knew we were feeding lions, they would be seen as 'belonging to us' and any future livestock killed, or any attack on humans, would be regarded as our responsibility. In spite of the present low game numbers, I was also confident that a few would survive, and even if none did, when their prey populations increased some lions were sure to come into the homeland from the neighbouring Etosha National Park.

Although the trustees accepted my position on not feeding lions, many of them were very concerned when, at the end of 1982, Chris Eyre reported that a total of 76 lions, 33 cheetah and 9 leopards had been killed by the Damaraland farmers and Volker Grellmann. An unknown number had also died of starvation, and for many years the lion population in the north-west would remain critically low.

After the board meeting Ina stayed on in Windhoek. When I next saw her, Shell Petroleum had agreed to donate 30 drums of aviation fuel, Westair, a local aircraft hire company, would provide a Cessna 210 Centurion at reduced rates, and Marten Bertens and Hans Kriess junior would pilot the plane in shifts, free of charge. Only the actual cost of the aircraft hire was still outstanding, but Ina was confident that she would have that too before July. At Wêreldsend, we held a meeting in which it was decided that Slang would plan and lead the census, Colin and Ina would be in charge of logistics and catering, while I, as the new boy on the block, would be the general assistant. It was a good team. Marten and Hans knew the difficult terrain we would be flying over; the high-wing, high-powered aircraft was ideal for the job, and nobody had more up-to-date knowledge of the area than Slang and Colin.

*   *   *

Although the NWT was in charge of implementing the Damaraland/ Kaokoland Project, it worked closely with three partner NGOs: the EWT in South Africa covered my salary and gave support to Slang's research; the UK-based People's Trust for Endangered Species paid Peter; and the Swakopmund Centre of the Wildlife Society helped Blythe with her monitoring of the rhino in the Uchab River valley. From the DNC side, Chris Eyre and Lucas Mbomboro were responsible for law enforcement in Damaraland and Kaokoland, while the Skeleton Coast Park staff – Ernst Karlova, Rudi Loutit, Peter Tarr, Steve Braine and Jaap Meyer – carried out periodic patrols into the far west of the two homelands. What we did not have was support from the DNC's senior staff in Windhoek, who were hostile to me personally, no doubt for political reasons, and to Ina and Blythe because they had the audacity to start an NGO that was operating on their turf.

Nevertheless, I hoped that in time they would see our work as complementary, and not in competition with their efforts to bring poaching in the region under control. Until then, to make sure that there was good communication between all of us based in the north-west I suggested that a co-ordination committee be set up, which was agreed to by all the local parties.

Our first meeting was held at Wêreldsend, in early June. It was an important step towards better co-operation, but that we still had some way to go was emphasised by a radio message we received a few days later from the nature conservator based at Otjovasandu: a truck-load of mountain zebra were already on their way from Etosha to be released at Wêreldsend. Our only previous information on the translocation had been a report in the press stating that the DNC was planning to take zebra back to Damaraland, without any mention of when or where they would be released.

I was well aware of the reason for their being removed from western Etosha. At the height of the drought large numbers of mountain zebra had migrated into the Park from southern Kaokoland and northern Damaraland, with some of them moving as far east as Okaukeujo, and a few even being seen around Halali camp. When the first good rains had fallen in February 1982, they headed west again and soon more than a thousand zebra were concentrated along the border fence around Otjovasandu. Ian Hoffmeyr had recommended the obvious course of action: open the fence and allow them to 'go back home'. This simple solution was turned down by Head Office, but when they threatened to overgraze this part of Etosha, the Park's management committee had recommended that the unnaturally high number of zebra here be reduced by either translocation or culling.

The first load of 34 zebra arrived late that evening, and were released on the flats just north of the CDM camp. From the nature conservator accompany-

ing them we learned that hundreds more had been caught and were standing in holding pens. However, as the game capture unit had only one vehicle
to transport them, just a single load per day was possible. To make matters
worse, the truck broke down and the second load of zebra did not arrive until
a week later. By now the penned animals were under considerable stress and
their condition was deteriorating. It was just the sort of situation that Ina
excelled in. Decisive action was called for and she immediately radioed the
DNC director, Polla Swart, offering to pay for the hiring of commercial cattle
trucks to transport the zebra. But they were not yet prepared to accept help
from an NGO, and her offer was turned down.

Five days later the next 30 zebra were loaded at Otjovasandu, but this
time two of the truck's tyres burst on the way to Wêreldsend, and the driver
had no option but to release them – south of the veterinary fence! We were
then informed that no more zebra could be moved until new tyres had been
purchased in Windhoek and taken to Otjovasandu. This time Ina was not
prepared to take no for an answer. Negotiating a good deal with a transport
contractor she grew up with in Kamanjab, Karel Kruger, she arranged for him
to bring the rest of the captured zebra to Wêreldsend at NWT's cost. Within
a week all of them had arrived. Apart from the 30 released south of the fence
and seven that died in transit, a total of 253 mountain zebra were offloaded.

* * *

Ten days before the start of the census, my mother and a family friend, Fiona
MacKenzie, came to visit. As the school holidays had just started, June and
the boys were also able to join us on a patrol through ANVO's concession to
Purros. In the 1960s the lower Hoarusib River had been the dry-season gathering area for large numbers of the Kaokoveld's western elephant population,
and when my brother, friends and I had hiked from Omutati to Purros in
1970 we had seen over 80 of the desert giants along the way. The tall riparian
woodlands, broad plains and arid mountains here also epitomised the spectacular scenery in the far northwest of Namibia, making it the place I had
most wanted to show June.

The day after my visitors arrived at Wêreldsend, we all piled into the
CDM Land Rover and headed north, first spending a few days in the Uniab
catchment. Although we saw little game, the season's good rains had caused
every river to come down in flood, leaving standing water along their rocky

courses that provided swimming pools for our eight- and six-year-old sons. To add to the fun, the dry elephant droppings made great 'Namibian snow-balls' for Tuareg and Kyle to throw at each other. It was the holiday I had waited many years to take my family on.

From the Uniab we cut across the basalt plains to Hunkab, now a flow-ing spring where both elephant and rhino had recently drunk. We camped near the junction of the Mudorib and Hoanib rivers, sleeping on a tarpaulin next to the Land Rover. In the early hours of the morning I awoke to find an elephant bull standing less than 20 metres from us. For a few moments it just stood there, perhaps contemplating our intrusion into one of the last safe refuges of the Kaokoveld's wildlife, and then turned and walked silently away. My mother and June awoke just in time to see its shadowy form disappearing into the vast silvery moonscape around us.

We saw no elephants in the Hoanib, and followed the Obias to the Giribes plain before joining the main track along the Gomatum River to Purros – the route I had travelled with Jod van der Merwe almost 15 years before. But this time there were no pronking springbok or herds of gemsbok along the way, and although the sandy flats flanking the Hoarusib had more grass than I had ever seen before, there was no game or livestock on them. Nostalgically I stopped under the large camel thorn tree where I had camped in the 1960s. But this time there were no elephant droppings littering the ground around it, and although the landscape was even more spectacular than I remembered, it was now lifeless.

After making a fire for tea I walked away from my family, hoping to find some evidence that a few elephants still came to Purros, but all I found was a piece of dried dung that was many years old and barely recognisable. When I tried to pick it up it just crumbled – like my dream of the western Kaokoveld one day becoming a sanctuary for its unique desert wildlife. I sat for some time on the river bank thinking about what could have been. When the red-ness had gone from my eyes I went back to my family.

Next day we drove downstream, into the bare rock ranges the Hoarusib had cut through on its way to the Skeleton Coast. About 5 km into the gorge we came across a few Himba and Herero tending small gardens of maize and veg-etables they were irrigating from the strong stream of water here. Among them was Isak Uararavi, a man I had met in the 1960s. He remembered me and we talked briefly about the old times, before the big drought, when he had been a wealthy cattle owner. They had all died, he told me, and among all the families living at Purros there were now only seven head of cattle and a few goats left.

While the rest of the party paddled or played in the clear water, Isak told me about the terrible years when no rain at all had fallen at Purros. As a last resort they had taken their cattle into the Skeleton Coast Park, but the nature conservators based here had driven them out, threatening to shoot any livestock they found within it. One by one, they had watched each animal get too weak to stand. His family would have starved too, if whites had not come from Windhoek and brought them food. They also taught his people how to irrigate crops on the banks of the river. But when the rains came again the food aid stopped. Now there was lots of grass, but no cattle left to eat it, and the people at Purros were surviving on the few cobs they harvested from their gardens.

Before leaving I asked Isak about the elephants that had been so plentiful around Purros. He confirmed that there were no longer any in the area, but could not say what had happened to them. Perhaps they had moved away, he said, or died in the drought like everything else. But I knew that was not so. A few kilometres upriver was a rudimentary camp set up by the police, and I wondered how many Purros elephants had been killed by the well-armed men who had come to this remote place to 'rest and recreate'.

The following day we headed back towards Wêreldsend. On the return journey I was very poor company. In spite of what Slang and Colin had told me I had clung to the hope that the situation in western Kaokoland was not all bad. But if there was as little wildlife further north as there was in the Hoarusib valley, then it was even worse than they said. The only way to find out for sure was to fly over the area.

*   *   *

Slang had decided to start the census along the Kunene River. Our base camp would be on the 'Red Flats' near Onyuva, 20 km north of Orupembe, where he and Colin had marked out a makeshift landing strip. I knew the area well and needed no directions to get there. In April 1969 I had seen over 600 Burchell's zebra on these plains, as well as many Hartmann's mountain zebra, gemsbok and springbok.

Because of my family's visit I only left for Onyuva on the day that the census began, reaching the Red Flats just as the sun was setting. I found Marten, Colin and Peter busy refuelling the plane, while Slang sat next to the fire going through his notes, and Ina was in her makeshift kitchen preparing our evening meal. Also in camp were Peter Tarr and his wife, Jacqui, from Möwe

Bay in the Skeleton Coast Park, who had come to show a DNC presence on the census. As I went around introducing Fiona, who had decided to stay for another week, I could see by the grim look on everyone's face that it had not been a great day's flying.

When the aircraft had been refuelled and Colin had handed around beers, Slang briefed us on what they had seen: six live elephants and two carcasses on the Kunene, but nothing else apart from 20 crocodiles in the river. On the entire Marienfluss they had recorded only 10 zebra, four gemsbok and 17 springbok. The Hartmann valley was a little better: here they saw six giraffe, nearly 80 zebra and 23 gemsbok, but only a few scattered springbok. They also counted 50 ostrich on the Marienfluss and another 24 in the Hartmann valley, as well as seeing plenty of bustards and korhaans. But all told, it wasn't much for more than six hours of flying.

To add to the sombre atmosphere, Slang said that on an aerial census in 1977 he had counted over 2 000 springbok on the Marienfluss, and the Hartmann valley had been full of zebra, gemsbok and springbok. I told the group that on our walk along this part of the Kunene in 1970, we had seen 26 elephant, heard lions on both nights and found rhino dung heaps all along the river's banks. But that was before the ivory poaching and the drought. Now there were just six elephants and very little other wildlife surviving in the far north-west. Worse, Slang also told us that all the elephants they had seen were cows, and that from his previous aerial surveys and groundwork, he was sure there were no bulls left here. Unless a way could be found to artificially inseminate the cows, the lower Kunene elephant population was on a dead-end road.

By this time Ina had joined us and she immediately took Slang's pessimism as a challenge: 'If it can be done with cattle, then why not with elephants?'

'Who's going to get the sperm from an elephant?' Slang replied. 'The way you do it with cattle is to stick an electric prodder up a bull's arse and shock his prostate until he ejaculates. That could be a little tricky with an elephant.'

This at least brought some laughter to relieve an otherwise gloomy evening. With Chris Eyre and the rest of the Skeleton Coast Park staff, our little group sitting around the fire represented the last chance of turning the situation around. If we failed, the Kaokoveld's wildlife would share the fate of big game over most of Africa. But how many people would mourn its demise? The region's remoteness and the previous restrictions on access meant that only a handful of whites had ever visited Namibia's north-west. The local people would certainly not shed any tears if there were no more large predators left, and could we expect them to be sorry if the last elephant and rhino also died? Now that they had lost most of their livestock in the drought, they would surely see the ordinary game as just an alternative source of meat – for as long as it lasted. Considering the example set by the white government officials in the homelands, could we blame them?

As Ina was not pleased about my arriving a day late, I was excluded from the next day's flying team. The area covered was from Orupembe south and westwards to the Skeleton Coast Park boundary. Here six giraffe, 55 zebra, 22 gemsbok, two kudu and 178 springbok were counted. While I was in Etosha, Tryg Cooper had assured me when he left Möwe Bay in early 1981 there had still been at least five rhino here, but no sign of them had been seen from the air.

On the third day Slang covered the hill country along the eastern edge of the pre-Namib, including Sanitatas, which in the 1960s had been the best game area in the Kaokoveld. As I was again not asked to be one of the observers on the plane, the Tarrs, Fiona and I drove to the Kunene River at the north end of the Marienfluss. It too had received good rain, but we saw no wildlife apart from a few ostrich.

We got back to camp well after dark and found only Slang and Colin sitting quietly at the fire. They had flown for another six hours – covering the area from Otjiha along the escarpment to Sanitatas, and then down the Khumib and Hoarusib rivers to Purros – and had counted only 14 zebra and a jackal. They had also seen 13 elephant and two rhino carcasses. 'Killed a long time ago,' Slang said, while he was carrying out his early research in Kaokoland during the late 1970s. The drought wasn't the cause of all the zebra and other game dying around Sanitatas either, he added: most of it had been poached long before 1980. The army, under Captain Jurie Lombaard, and the police were the main culprits, but everyone had joined in the slaughter, even the local *dominee*.

Having now paid for my sin of arriving late, I was assigned a seat on the plane for the next two days' flying. We flew the south of Kaokoland, but here game numbers were just as low until we reached the Hoanib River, where we counted 25 elephants along its lower reaches, and another five on the Beesvlakte, giving a total of 36 for the west and south of the homeland. However, we also recorded another 21 dead elephants, which together with those near Sanitatas and on the Kunene meant that we had seen 35 carcasses, just one less than the number of living elephants.

With the aircraft now due for a service, and Marten also needing a break from flying, he returned to Swakopmund. When Hans Kriess came back with the plane, we based the team at Wêreldsend, and started counting the areas of Damaraland where game was known to still survive. As expected, in the

ANVO hunting concession, which had until 1970 been part of Etosha, the game numbers were significantly higher. By the end of the census we had recorded a total of 184 elephants and 23 rhino south of the Hoanib, but had also seen another 85 elephant and 19 rhino carcasses. Although the ratio between live and dead animals was better than in Kaokoland, the killing grounds had now moved south, and neither species was capable of breeding at anywhere near the rate that they were being poached.

As elephants are easy to see from the air, and the total for both homelands of 220 closely matched Slang's ground research, he was confident that we had recorded all of the resident herds in the census area. Before the liberation war extended into Kaokoland, preventing him from working on the border with Ovamboland, he knew of another 80 elephants there. But from the Martin Ndjoba case I knew that large-scale poaching was taking place north of the Park, and I wondered how many of them were still alive.

Because of the size of the area covered, even 85 hours of actual census time only provided us with the minimum population for each species. Because they favoured bushy habitats, black rhino and kudu were especially difficult to see from the air and their numbers recorded were of little value. However, the recent good rains in the west had attracted the zebra, gemsbok and springbok out onto the open pre-Namib plains, where they were much more visible, and this greatly improved the accuracy of the total numbers counted. As giraffe are also easy to see, even in woody areas, their total population count could be regarded as reasonably accurate.

In spite of these shortcomings, a comparison of the 1982 census figures with those of previous aerial counts carried out in Kaokoland and Damaraland did provide population trends for most of the larger species. For the former, Slang used the two counts of slightly shorter duration that he did in 1977, a year when good rain also fell in the west:

Species	1977 May (25 hrs)	1977 August (25 hrs)	1982 July (35 hrs)
Elephant	41	34	36
Giraffe	32	52	45
Burchell's zebra	667	55	0
Hartmann's zebra	1 199	492	193
Gemsbok	1 191	1 182	164
Springbok	4 859	2 526	217

Finding comparable earlier counts for Damaraland was more difficult. Although aerial surveys had been carried out by Piet de Villiers in 1975 and GP Visagie in 1977, there was no record of the area covered, the time of the year, or in the case of Visagie, even the number of hours flown. Only one aerial count, undertaken by J le Roux in October 1978 'over the uninhabited area north of the Uchab River, including the north eastern corner' could be compared to the NWT census, but it had only been of 10 hours' duration. Nevertheless, by extrapolating the numbers of animals seen to match the increased counting time (shown in brackets) it did give an indication of the population decline for each species between 1978 and 1982. As Le Roux was likely to have focused his flying time in the larger river valleys, the preferred habitat of elephants and giraffe, his figures for them have only been multiplied by three times.

Species	Le Roux October 1978 (10 hrs)	Viljoen July 1982 (50 hrs)
Elephant	135 (337)	184
Giraffe	94 (470)	232
Kudu	202 (1 010)	41
Hartmann's zebra	1 544 (7 720)	563
Gemsbok	825 (4 125)	404
Springbok	875 (4 325)	309

Predictably, the NWT's census method was criticised by the DNC's researchers, who believed that only they were capable of carrying out such an exercise. But as Slang had more experience in counting game from the air than any of them, we paid little attention to this. At the very least, the census had given us an overview of what and where wildlife still occurred, as well as providing a baseline for future aerial counts. It also gave us some idea of how many animals had died in the drought. But in the case of elephants, although our seeing very few calves of less than five years old showed their breeding rate was depressed during the dry years, there was no doubt that poaching had been the major cause of their declining numbers.

CHAPTER EIGHTEEN

'DESERT ELEPHANTS'

It was not the first time the Kaokoveld elephants had been killed for their ivory. At the end of the nineteenth century the Thirstland Trekkers slaughtered even greater numbers, selling their tusks to buy the basic necessities they could not grow or make for themselves. On their way through South West Africa the mounted Boer hunters established a formidable reputation, including the record for the most elephants killed in a single day. This occurred while hunting south of the Okavango River, where Hendrik van Zyl and five companions drove a large herd into a swampy pan in which they became bogged. They then surrounded them and shot every one, a total of 103. In the following two weeks Van Zyl's party brought down another 75 elephants, collecting over five tons of ivory which was sold in Cape Town for £4 200.

After settling in southern Angola some of the Thirstland Trekkers returned every year to hunt in the Kaokoveld, killing mainly elephants, but also hippo and rhino for their skins, which were cut into strips and sold as sjamboks. In the 1930s Von Moltke interviewed some of the men who had taken part in these expeditions for his book, *Jagkonings*. In it he stated that the most successful of them, Jan Robbertse, with his team of hunters, had shot 180 elephants in the Kaokoveld and southern Angola in just one year, and that they killed over 2 000 between 1892 and 1908, when the German *Schutztruppe* based at Sesfontein finally made their forays across the Kunene too dangerous. From the profits Robbertse was able to purchase farms in the Transvaal for each of his five sons and four sons-in-law.

The Thirstland Trekkers were not the only exterminators of big game in south-western Africa during the nineteenth century. Whites of many different nationalities did their share of the killing for food, sport, science – and when it came to elephants, the commercial value of their tusks. The result was that by 1890 wildlife numbers, and particularly those of elephants, had crashed throughout the region.

Eight years after the German flag was raised on the south-west African coast, the first wildlife conservation regulations were introduced by the colonial authorities in Windhoek. All hunters were required to obtain permission from the local governor, cow elephants could not be killed and a closed season was laid down for ostrich, which were then much sought after for their feathers. Fifteen years later Governor von Lindequist proclaimed the first four game reserves where all hunting was prohibited, including the Kaokoveld and the area around the Etosha Pan.

Soon after the surrender of the German colonial forces in 1915, rumours of gun-running across the Kunene River and a resurgence of elephant poaching in the Kaokoveld led to the South African military administration dispatching Major CL Manning to the area to get first-hand information on the situation. Accompanied by a detachment of police, Manning set off by ox-wagon from Kamanjab, trekking through the Khovarib Schlucht to the German Fort at Sesfontein, where he outspanned for a week.

While at Sesfontein Manning was visited by Vita Thom, the Herero leader who had recently come into South West Africa from Angola. Oorlog, as he was known to the whites, invited him to visit Otjijanjasemu, the hot springs in the northern Kaokoveld where he and his followers had settled. In his diary Manning wrote that 'a strange force' which comprised himself and a police contingent on horseback, Oorlog's men riding on oxen, and a group of 'wild Tjimba' accompanying them on foot, headed northwards and reached Otjijanjasemu in late August 1917.

Along the way, Vita related his life story and requested permission to remain in South West Africa. He assured the South African officer that his wish to return was because of his 'great love for the British' – conveniently forgetting to mention that the Portuguese authorities were planning his arrest and imprisonment for raiding neighbouring tribes and plundering their livestock.

However, Manning was impressed by Oorlog's demeanour and wrote: 'My experience is that he is a peaceful law abiding chief, always anxious to do anything required of him by the government.'

From Otjijanjasemo, with only Sergeant PJ Botha for company, Manning rode on to the Kunene, where they met and discussed the border situation with local Portuguese officials and Jacob Ericksson, a son of the Swedish hunter Axil Ericksson and the daughter of the prominent Herero chief, Kambazembi. On their return he wrote in his diary: 'I have now decided to trek west over the mountains and reach Ombepera if possible, to get guides from Chief Kasupi to the softer veld towards the sea and work down to Zessfontein by that long way round. I will thus be able to get my footsore horses through, I hope, and obtain meat, besides seeing a vast tract of unknown country.' Manning also noted that: 'The only inhabitants of the Kaokoveld appear to be Oorlog's followers (sixty-nine adult men) and his Tjimba (one hundred and fifty men), Katiti's one hundred and twenty adult Himba men and Kasupi's fifty adult men, besides the nomadic Tjimba.'

From Ombepera they proceeded via Sanitatas down the Khumib River, where they were able to get water on their way through the Namib Desert to the sea. Manning wrote that along the coast: 'We marched on foot without boots to save our leather, worn-out after some hundreds of miles of mountains and stones.' At the Hoarusib mouth they turned inland, walking to Purros and then on to Sesfontein. He had covered 650 miles in two months, and in his diary concluded: 'We have seen most of the Kaokoveld and I am glad to say that we have brought back every horse and all government equipment.'

By the end of his trip Manning was of the opinion that not more than 250 elephants still survived in the region north of Sesfontein. A decade later, Vita Thom told Captain Guy Shortridge, during his expedition to the Kaokoveld, that there were only two or three large herds, totalling about 500. After spending many weeks in the Territory, Shortridge estimated their population to be about 600.

In Lawrence Green's *Lords of the Last Frontier*, on the 1951 Bernard Carp expedition to the Kaokoveld, he states that SWA's first two game wardens, 'Sangiro' Pienaar and PJ Schoeman, both estimated elephant numbers in the Kaokoveld to be between 1 200 and 1 500. Their figures were based on water-hole counts, and as they had access to the whole region, would have also included the western Etosha Game Park between the Hoanib and Uchab rivers.

The Carp expedition's guide, Dennis Woods, a surveyor and mountaineer who had made five previous trips to the Kaokoveld, told Green that on a walk down the Hoarusib River valley, 'days had past when he was seldom out of sight of elephants'. He also claimed to have once met 'a column of more than a hundred elephants ... a tremendous phalanx of great bulls in the lead, then the main mass of the herd, younger bulls, cows with calves and elder bulls bringing up the rear'. He added that: 'Not one of them loitered to tear down branches, not one broke the silence ... They were travelling hard, their minds on some distant water-hole or favoured grazing ground.'

Woods, who took a keen interest in the Kaokoveld elephants, believed that he had seen a meeting of most of the 'Namib elephants' that day – made up of nearly all of the herds that lived on the edge of the desert. It was a season of intense drought, he told Green, 'when for some mysterious reason the elephants travel in company and gather in large numbers round their traditional pools'. His estimate for the elephant population in the Kaokoveld was 600, but he was referring only to the area north of the Hoanib.

During my residence in the Kaokoveld, I had also found the Hoarusib River and its many tributaries to be the heart of the Territory's elephant country. I also noted that in the dry season, because of the many springs along the lower Hoarusib, and the acacia pods that fell at this time of the year, large numbers concentrated here. When the rains started, however, the elephants dispersed into the neighbouring mountains, drinking from pans and pools that remained along watercourses that had come down in flood.

My estimate of the number of elephants in the pre-Namib and escarpment ranges between the Hoanib and Kunene rivers was 200 to 300. I found the second largest sub-population, comprising at least 200 elephants, occurred in the eastern sandveld between the Joubertberge and Ovamboland border. A third important sub-population ranged over the less inhabited parts of the northern highlands, while in the south elephants were common in the dolomite hills, moving in and out of western Etosha across the Ombonde River. After two years of hiking off the beaten track and moonlit waterhole counts, I put the total population in the then Kaokoveld at between 700 and 800. But this did not include the lower Hoanib River and the western Etosha Game Park, which together probably supported at least another 400 elephants.

These estimates from diverse sources suggested that, from a low point of just a few hundred after the Thirstland Trekker hunting, the elephant population in the north-west had increased to at least 1 200 by 1970. Five years later, when Slang Viljoen began his master's research on Kaokoland's wildlife, he took my estimates of the various sub-populations as his baseline, but found that illegal hunting had already taken a heavy toll. Only a few herds

still survived north of Opuwo, and numbers throughout the rest of the homeland were in steep decline. By the time he returned to university in 1978, the
only viable elephant populations on the highlands were on the Ovamboland
border and along the Ombonde River. In the pre-Namib, the desert-living
elephants had been reduced to a few harassed herds and scattered individuals
along the lower Kunene, Hoarusib and Hoanib rivers.

When entry restrictions into the homelands were removed in 1978, Clive
Walker accompanied Professor Eloff on a fact-finding mission to Kaokoland.
After coming across four elephant carcasses with their tusks removed, he
wrote the report that brought me back to Namibia. The only outcome was
Slang Viljoen's return to the area in 1980, to do research on the Kaokoveld
elephants. By then the poaching had moved south into Damaraland, and in
the first two years he and Colin Britz found over 100 carcasses, including 25 in
the Hoanib valley west of Sesfontein. In just twelve years the elephant population in the north-west had been reduced from over 1 200 to less than 300.
Although hunting pressure may have caused some of them to migrate into
Etosha, the great majority had been killed for their ivory.

*   *   *

The situation in the Kaokoveld broadly mirrored what was then happening to the elephants across most of Africa. From a low point at the end of
the nineteenth century, colonial restrictions on hunting and the creation of
wildlife sanctuaries had resulted in a steady increase in their numbers until
1970, at which time there were estimated to be between two and three million elephants on the continent. However, during the next decade commercial ivory poaching escalated, decimating the populations in East, West and
Central Africa.

The turning point was a severe drought that hit north-eastern Africa in the
early 1970s. By then most of the previously free-ranging elephants had been
compressed into protected areas by the region's rapidly increasing human
population. In the Tsavo National Park, the very high density of elephants, in
combination with bushfires, had devastated its arid woodlands, and at least
10 000 had died of starvation. This would not have affected the overall picture
if large amounts of ivory from the dead elephants had not been collected by
people living around the park, and sold to businessmen on the Somali and
Kenya coastlines. The flood of tusks into this ancient Arab trade-route had re-

vitalised the ivory market, which now included fashion jewellery and *hanko*, the personal seals of wealthy Japanese family heads.

By the time the supply of tusks from drought-killed elephants dried up a few years later, Middle Eastern oil wealth and Japan's booming economy had pushed the price of ivory so high that the trade was too lucrative to abandon. Using automatic firearms now freely available from the many civil wars in the region, local people and gangs of Somali *shifta* began killing live elephants to meet the demand of an insatiable black market. The result was that the elephant population in Tsavo was reduced from an estimated 44 000 before the drought to only 6 000 a decade later.

Ivory poaching also spread to other wildlife sanctuaries in Kenya, as well as to neighbouring countries. By the early 1980s it had moved across West Africa and south through Tanzania into Zambia, bringing the Luangwa Valley's huge elephant population under siege. But apart from sharing the bonanza of higher ivory prices, we had no reason to believe there was a direct link between the killing of elephants in the Kaokoveld and the illegal trade over the rest of the continent. So who was behind it?

From the hunting by helicopter on the Kunene in 1974 and the Marten Ndjoba case north of Etosha, I knew that people in very high places, both white and black, were involved. Further evidence of this had come from Dr Dan Craven, who I got to know while based in Okaukuejo, and who would later become an NWT trustee. In the 1970s Dan had practised in Ovamboland, where he and his botanist wife, Pat, were appalled by the hunting excesses of the local government officials and visiting politicians. Dan had exposed some of the worst cases to a Cape Town journalist, Graham Ferreira, and he gave me the press cuttings that he kept at the time. They made very interesting reading.

The earliest was a front-page lead in the *Windhoek Advertiser* of 29 July 1977, under the headline: 'Sixty-page Poaching Report Frozen by Pretoria's SWA Ban'. The paper's unnamed correspondent then went on to say:

> Potgieter Street moved yesterday with a far-reaching request to all newspaper editors to keep certain reports from their columns because a massive propaganda onslaught against the Defence Force and Government institutions in South West Africa was expected. So sweeping is the request that it has virtually terminated any reference to any irregularity, however innocuous. The request also froze a 16 000-word report by the *Windhoek Advertiser* which dealt with poaching.

Speaking yesterday was Major-General Wally Black, Director of General Operations, who said that this campaign was aimed at driving a wedge between the Government and the inhabitants of South West Africa... The more publicity given to this, deliberately or unwittingly, would lend more support to the enemy propaganda campaign. Consequently the SADF urgently appeals to the press and the public to take no notice of such allegations, but rather to report them to the SADF with the minimum of delay... Where previously the South African Defence Force was the only target for smear tactics, it can now be expected that other government institutions which play an important role in the maintenance of law and order and the peaceful development of SWA will now also become propaganda targets.

In a column alongside the lead article, the *Windhoek Advertiser's* editor had given his comments:

In recent weeks a special investigative reporting team, of which this newspaper was part, launched a substantial investigation, not to uncover scandals or corruption, but to find evidence to support certain poaching allegations made by us and which led to the subsequent imprisonment of one of our newsmen (for refusing to disclose the source of his information). In this investigation we were aided by numerous civil servants and other people. They stepped forward, many of their own initiative, and to us it was heartening to realise that public service has such men...

As a result of the investigation we prepared a 16 000 word report which would have been published in four consecutive issues starting today. It was tremendous copy. It was also chilling copy. Not as some of our enemies would suggest of South African soldiers raping black girls... No, a calm cool factual story of game dying and the eyes peering over the muzzles were in most cases not those of men in uniform... In their four point request Pretoria has asked us not to say anything about the destruction of game. We have no choice but to oblige. We do so with a heavy heart because our report would have assisted defence headquarters, and in fact the government to rid itself of certain most undesirable characters who in the long run are going to smear South Africa's name...

So what was it all about? Fortunately the *Cape Times* in South Africa was not intimidated by the government's 'request' not to publish any accounts of misconduct by the SADF or senior government officials. On 4 August it printed the information Graham Ferreira had gathered during his two-week investigation, in which he travelled 5 000 km and spoke to many leading conservationists. He had found that there were widespread fears about the fate of wildlife in northern SWA.

One of the people he interviewed was Bernabe de la Bat, who confirmed that hunting in parts of the country not under his jurisdiction was becoming worse, but said there was 'nothing he could do about it'. De la Bat was not sure who issued the permits for hunting in these areas, but a spokesman for BAD in Pretoria told Ferreira that in Ovambo, Kavango and Caprivi this was done by their own legislative councils. In Kaokoland, Damaraland, Hereroland and Bushmanland, hunting permits were still issued by the Secretary for Bantu Administration in Pretoria.

On 19 August the *Cape Times* published an article about an experienced BAD game ranger in Ovamboland, Henry Markram, having been transferred out of the homeland after questioning Jannie de Wet's killing of an elephant in late 1976. According to the report, the Commissioner General had shot two bull elephants from a Defence Force helicopter at Onaiso, near Omutambo Mauwe quarantine camp, on the border of Etosha. De Wet had claimed the elephants were damaging windmills in the area, but Markram told Ferriera there were no windmills near Onaiso, and that the local people told him they knew of no problems caused by elephants anywhere in the vicinity.

However, before Markram had been able to complete his investigations he was transferred to the Ciskei homeland in South Africa. The *Cape Times* correspondent also established that De Wet had bought the tusks of both elephants from the State for a total of R110 – the price of about two kilograms of ivory on the international market at that time.

Ferriera further revealed that permits for this and other elephant hunts in SWA's homelands had been issued in Pretoria, and signed by Mr IP van Onselen, the Secretary for Bantu Affairs – who himself admitted shooting a number of problem elephants. When contacted he informed the reporter that De Wet simply told him elephants were causing problems at a waterhole and he issued a permit on the strength of his word. But Markram countered this by saying he saw no point in having a nature conservation section in BAD 'if the secretary is going to write out permits for De Wet without consulting his conservation officer. And why did he do the shooting?'

Ferreira's most sensational disclosure was a first-hand account of black-faced impala hanging from an SADF helicopter at Epupa Falls in 1974. The witnesses were a CDM geological exploration team comprising Lee Harrison, Chris Boshoff, Noel Eason and Colin Britz – Ina's husband.

'We were all pretty upset because the black-faced impala is an endangered species,' one of them told Ferreira. 'Two of our party jumped into a Land Rover and raced down to the camp where the helicopter was landing to get a better look at the buck and the people in the helicopter... The people I recognised were Mr Jannie de Wet and Ben van Zyl, whom I had met before.'

Van Zyl assured them that they had permits to hunt the impala, but the following day John Kirkpatrick, a prominent Windhoek lawyer and NWT Trustee, arrived at Epupa. After hearing the geologists' story he visited the government officials' now abandoned camp.

'It looked as if they had taken a lot of trouble to conceal all traces of the campsite,' Kirkpatrick told Ferreira, but he scratched around and unearthed a buried piece of paper and an empty cartridge box. On the paper was a list of names and their sleeping arrangements in the tents. One of them was PW Botha, then Minister of Defence, who four years later would become President. Confirmation that it was the cabinet minister came from an 8 mm film that Lee Harrison took of the helicopter landing, in which PW Botha's characteristic bald head was clearly visible at one of the windows!

When the security police heard about the very incriminating film they severely harassed Harrison, but he refused to hand it over. However, a few months later he committed suicide, apparently because of personal problems, and the film then fell into the hands of his boss, Hennie van der Westhuizen, the head of CDM's geological exploration unit. As he was also the vice-chairman of the Namibia Wildlife Trust, I asked Hennie about Harrison's film and he told me it was in the company safe, where it would be 'secure until some future date when it might be needed'.

Although the story Ferriera got from the CDM field staff and John Kirkpatrick was three years old, it was still a political bombshell, so before publishing the *Cape Times*, editor Tony Heard first submitted it to Defence Headquarters, giving them a week to respond before they went to print. But there was one critical flaw in the story. Either the reporter or the CDM field staff had got the date of the incident wrong by one day, and Tony Heard was informed by the SADF that they could prove PW Botha was not at Epupa on the day stated in the report. The following day General Black circulated his 'request' to newspaper editors not to publish allegations incriminating the

SADF or senior government officials in northern Namibia. In spite of this, the *Cape Times* did publish the story, but they deleted any reference to the Minister of Defence.

As a result of these media accusations, the officer commanding all SADF operations in Namibia, Major General Jannie Geldenhuys, announced that a Board of Enquiry had been appointed to investigate and report on allegations of misconduct in the Defence Force. Persons or organisations wishing to submit written or oral evidence had to do so by 16 September, three weeks from the day Geldenhuys made the announcement. Eighteen months later the Deputy Minister of Defence, Kobie Coetzee, announced the findings of the Board. It was admitted that SADF helicopters had been used to hunt in the homelands, but the Air Force was simply responding to requests by local Bantu Affairs Commissioners to provide assistance in dealing with elephants that were causing damage to water installations.

At the time a Windhoek businessman, Eric Lang, offered a reward of R5 000 to anyone supplying information leading to a conviction for illegal hunting by government officials. But no one came forward and the Board of Enquiry ended in a whitewash. It would have given me great pleasure to present my evidence of an elephant being shot from an SADF helicopter on the lower Kunene in 1974, inside a neighbouring country's national park. But when the enquiry took place we were living in Rhodesia and I was unaware of it.

Dan Craven told me other stories of politicians and government officials hunting in Ovamboland and Kaokoland, including an account of Prime Minister John Vorster shooting an elephant in the Ombonde River in 1973. At the time a picture of Vorster standing next to a dead elephant appeared in the popular Afrikaans magazine *Die Huisgenoot*. The caption under the photo stated that it was shot in Rhodesia, but the background looked exactly like the limestone mountains at the entrance to the Khovareb Schlucht.

It was clear that many of those responsible for safeguarding the homelands' natural heritage had played a major role in squandering it. But what we knew was only the tip of the iceberg; it was unlikely they had killed up to 1 000 elephants in Namibia's north-west. Nevertheless, they had set an example to lower ranking civil servants and the local people in the region, and made it very difficult for anyone to be prosecuted for hunting illegally.

Of the 128 elephant carcasses Slang Viljoen found between 1980 and 1982, all but 22 of them showed clear signs of having been poached. Although some of them had their tusks removed with a power saw, in the majority of cases they were cut out with an axe, suggesting that local people were now doing most of the actual killing. There seemed to be no shortage of firearms in the Kaokoveld, but who supplied the ammunition, and most importantly, who was buying the ivory?

When the followers of Vita Thom and Muhona Katiti came back from Angola after 1915 they brought their weapons with them. These old guns, many of them museum pieces that were handed down from father to son, had probably been used for many years to supply Portuguese traders along the Kunene with small amounts of ivory, rhino horn and game skins. Although ammunition for them was difficult to obtain, from the 1950s the government also issued rifles to recognised headmen in the Kaokoveld so that they could deal with predators that killed their livestock.

As these weapons were relatively few in number, the scale of the recent hunting suggested that they were not the only ones being used. The answer came on a visit to Opuwo later in the year. Sergeant Webster, the senior police officer there, told me that when the liberation war spread westward, the military authorities gave out .303 rifles to every adult male resident who asked for one 'to protect his family from SWAPO insurgents'. They were not licensed and no records were kept of how many were handed out, but he estimated the number to have been between 1 500 and 3 000 – each with 100 rounds of ammunition. Even taking the low figure, this meant that a minimum of 150 000 cartridges were in circulation among the local people, more than enough to kill all the remaining big game in the region.

The various arms of the security forces would also have had a virtually unlimited supply of ammunition available to them, but whereas they probably hunted any game they encountered out of boredom, the Himba and Herero had a much more pressing need to do so. With most of their livestock having died in the drought, providing their families with meat was obviously the primary one, but the cash obtained from selling ivory and rhino horn could also be used to purchase cattle in the commercial farming area to rebuild their herds.

The local people had the means and motivation to poach, and with game numbers now at critically low levels, I knew that just carrying out conservation education and extension work would not save what little remained. A vigorous anti-poaching campaign was also needed, but if heavy-handed methods were used the chances of our getting their support for conservation would be compromised.

* * *

Compared to the scale of elephant poaching taking place over the rest of the continent, the numbers being killed in the Kaokoveld would have been seen as insignificant if it were not for the habitat that some of them lived in. The African elephant is one of the most adaptable of large mammals, being equally at home in rain forests, woodlands and savanna. But there were only two places left where they lived in an area receiving less than 150 mm of rainfall: in the north-west of Namibia, and in the Gourma Reserve in Mali, where about 200 elephants were also threatened by illegal hunting. In recognition of their precarious status, at the 1981 meeting of the IUCN's African Elephant and Rhino Specialist Group both populations were accorded the highest priority for conservation.

How the biggest land mammal on earth was able to sustain itself in a desert was a major focus of Slang's PhD research. However, studying these very mobile elephants in some of the most rugged country in Southern Africa was not an easy task. A decade of persecution had so traumatised them that on becoming aware of humans or a vehicle their immediate response was to bunch up and set off at a fast shuffle out of the danger zone. If surprised or approached too closely they also often charged, and we had no reason to doubt that their intentions were homicidal.

But Phillip Viljoen was not a typical scientist. Nicknamed Slang because of his snake-catching exploits as a schoolboy, he was an introverted outdoorsman whose trademark was walking barefoot on even the roughest terrain. As he freely admitted, his early academic achievements had not been of the highest order, but when the Pretoria University professors looked for a postgraduate student to take on the task of studying the large mammals in the Kaokoveld, he had been their first choice.

In the two years he was based in Opuwo, Slang had observed the uncontrolled hunting then taking place in the homeland, and saw the only hope of saving the region's big game as being to proclaim a game reserve in the arid west. When this did not happen he returned to the region in 1980 with a mission – to use the precarious status of the few remaining desert-living elephants as a flagship for the conservation of all the other desert-adapted species.

Although the DNC took over responsibility for nature conservation in SWA's homelands the following year, he found there was still a surprising reluctance on the part of many of its senior officials to recognise what a priceless asset the Kaokoveld elephants were. His main opponent was Eugene Joubert, now the Assistant Director for Research, who believed that the herds in the west had been forced there by the poaching and were, therefore, not special at all. Slang countered this by pointing out that in 1895 Georg Hartmann had reported elephants in the northern Namib – a time when the Kaokoveld was virtually uninhabited and poaching by the Thirstland Trekkers had only just started.

However, what annoyed Slang most was Eugene's claim that there were, in fact, too many elephants in the lower Hoanib, his main study area, and that they were killing the winter thorn trees along the riverbed. He could not deny that many of them had been severely debarked, but by counting their numbers on aerial photographs taken of the Hoanib valley in 1963 and again in 1982, he was able to show that the difference was negligible. He also found that winter thorns are able to survive being virtually ring-barked, and that the main cause of mortality was changes in the river's channels that deprived them of the underground water they depended on.

Slang's research on the Kaokoveld's elephants was given a great deal of publicity by the EWT and SA Nature Foundation, with the emotion generated by their threatened status leading to their 'uniqueness' often being overstated. Claims not backed by credible evidence were made that they had longer legs or bigger feet, and even that they were a separate sub-species. Although Slang did not support these, he believed the elephants had made behavioural adaptations to their arid environment that, combined with their intimate knowledge of the area, made them ecologically unique and, therefore, irreplaceable.

By following individual bulls Slang found that they were capable of going for up to four days without drinking. But was this because they were forced into an 'unnatural' habitat by poaching, or had the elephants in the west now also become physiologically adapted to living in a desert? If so, then they had to have been living in the western Kaokoveld for thousands of years – enough time for their kidneys to have become more efficient. To find out if they did need less water passing through their kidneys to keep them functioning effectively, Slang's university supervisors decided to inject a Hoanib elephant with a radioactive tracer, and then monitor how long it remained in the bloodstream. The results would then be compared to a similar exercise carried out on a Kruger National Park elephant, to see if there was, in fact, a significant difference in the water retention period.

In May I joined Slang and the vet who would administer the tracer, Dr Zen Fourie, on the edge of the Hoanib floodplain, inside the Skeleton Coast Park. As the experiment was paid for by the EWT, Clive Walker also flew up with Dr Anthony Hall-Martin, an elephant researcher based in Kruger Park, Chloe

Rolfes of the Nasionale Pers group of newspapers, and their pilot, Peter Joffe. From the NWT were Colin, Ina, Hennie van der Westhuizen and myself. The DNC was represented by Chris Eyre and Dr Theuns van Wyk, a veterinarian who would assist and monitor the operation.

By the time everyone had arrived a cold wind was blowing from the west, and as we huddled around the fire Slang talked to us about his research and recent events in this part of the Kaokoveld. Having come a day earlier, I had established that there were three bull elephants, 18 cows and six sub-adults on the floodplain, which together with three more adult males were, according to Slang, all that now remained of the Hoanib sub-population. When he started his research there were many more, but in the bushes along the river's banks and on the plains west of Sesfontein were 25 carcasses, most of them bulls, clearly showing the poachers' preference for the bigger tuskers. Because of the stress the Hoanib elephants had been put under there were also no calves under the age of seven years.

Although the elephants now preferred to stay in the lower reaches of the Hoanib River and its tributaries, away from human settlements, in the drought one of them had been shot in an irrigated garden by a local man at Otjindakue, near Sesfontein. However, as the tusks had not been removed and the people living there had made many complaints about crop-raiding elephants, Chris Eyre had gone against the orders of his superiors in Windhoek and not prosecuted the man responsible for killing it. Since then Slang had not known them to move east of Sesfontein, and after the good 1982 rains they spent most of their time on the floodplain, grazing on the lush annual grass growing there and drinking from a deep pool that was formed by the Hoanib's floodwaters damming up against the dunes.

Slang believed the sub-population had included the elephants inhabiting the lower Hoarusib River, and on a number of occasions recorded them crossing the desert to its lower reaches. Once there, they stayed within the Skeleton Coast Park, where a stream of water flowed to within a few kilometres of the coast. After Skeuroor was shot by Volker Grellman's client in 1981, the only adult elephant to survive the poaching in the Hoarusib had also moved to the Hoanib and became the dominant bull there. He was accompanied by three surviving sub-adults, but they had not been fully accepted by the resident matriarchs and always stayed on the fringes of the herd.

For the water retention experiment Slang had chosen the second largest bull on the floodplain because it had one of its tusks broken off at the lip and would therefore be easy to recognise in the future. The next morning it was immobilised and injected with a radioactive tracer, but from then on things did not go so smoothly. To record the level of the tracer in its bloodstream after it had dispersed, a second blood sample was needed 24 hours later, but for the whole of the next day the bull stayed in dense *Sueda* shrubs, making it too dangerous to try and dart it. However, this was done the following morning, and again on the fourth day, to measure how much of the tracer still remained.

But it was all for nothing. No similar experiment was carried out in Kruger National Park, which meant that no conclusions could be drawn about the kidney efficiency of the Hoanib elephants and, thereby, whether they had become physiologically adapted to living in very arid conditions. But whether they were 'desert elephants' or just part of a much larger population that was now living on the margin of the species' habitat did not change their threatened status. And if the DNC hierarchy in Windhoek saw no reason to regard their conservation as a high priority, we in the field certainly did – not least because elephants in such a spectacular environment had the potential to one day become a major tourist attraction.

* * *

When the researchers, vets, project visitors and the press had flown or driven back to their workplaces, we were left to find a way of stopping the poaching. Chris Eyre had followed up the ban on hunting in Damaraland by getting Kaokoland's Herero Administration – still made up mostly of white officials – to stop issuing pot licences. As SWA's Nature Conservation ordinance was now also applicable in the homelands, the only legal killing of wildlife that could take place was that done by the clients of ANVO Safaris in their concession area. And as it would be difficult to convince the local people that they should put their rifles away while wealthy foreigners were still hunting, Chris was able to reduce their quota to just a few mountain zebra, as well as any elephants or predators causing major problems to the farmers in Damaraland.

Chris and Lucas were also following up on the elephant and rhino carcasses seen during Slang's February aerial survey, but as they were at least two months old it seemed unlikely that any arrests would be made. However, I underestimated my colleague's determination and Lucas's investigative skills. From an informant they obtained the name of a young Herero man, Benjamin Batjiya, who had accompanied the hunters. The teenager was taken into custody, and under interrogation gave them the names of the other five men involved.

Two of them were from Warmquelle, including Piet Hizeraku, who had been part of the gang of poachers apprehended by the security forces near Otjovasandu in 1978. The other three were residents of Kaoko Otavi, including two Humu brothers, from the same family as the man who had offered to sell me a rhino horn in 1968! It was a major breakthrough, but they all denied being involved in the case and Chris needed some hard evidence before he could be sure of getting them convicted.

Our first successful illegal hunting case came during the July aerial census. Early one morning, while flying up a tributary of the Aub River, we saw a thin wisp of smoke from a fireplace. When Marten Bertens flew low over it we could see no people, but three donkeys were tied to a nearby tree. As there was nothing we could do about it from the air, after noting the place on my map I asked Marten to fly back to camp, and from there I radioed Chris Eyre in Khorixas. He agreed to come out that afternoon.

When Chris and Lucas arrived I explained the situation and then we set off. At the time the only track into the area was the graded line along the old Etosha boundary, which ended at the Aub canyon. From there we drove up the riverbed until it got too dark to continue. By then I estimated we were within 5 km of the suspected poachers' campsite, and hoping that they had not heard the sound of our vehicle, we stopped for the night.

At first light Chris, Lucas, Peter and I started walking, reaching the place we had seen from the air just as the sun rose over the mountains. But the embers in the fireplace were cold, showing that the men who camped there had left the previous day, probably soon after we had flown over them. From the many cooked bones we found lying around it was clear that they had been eating a lot of meat, and Lucas confirmed that it was not from a goat. As we were now sure that they had been hunting, Chris and Lucas decided to follow the donkey tracks that headed north towards Khovarib village on foot, while Peter and I returned to Wêreldsend to call in air support.

We were back in camp by midday and soon had a plan of action. Presuming that the poachers were heading for home, Marten and Slang would fly over the plains on the direct route from the Aub headwaters to Khovarib. Steve Braine, a nature conservator from Mowe Bay who had come to observe the census, would drive with me along the main road to the village. If likely suspects were spotted from the air Marten would land the plane on a straight section of the road and inform us.

At about four o›clock the aircraft located three men on donkeys heading straight for Khovarib. After landing and giving us their approximate position Marten then took off again and flew in circles above them. The ground was not too rocky here, so it was relatively easy for Steve and me to drive across-country and intercept them.

The middle-aged Damara men we apprehended were certainly poachers – the bulging bags of dried meat they were carrying confirmed that – but they were not what I had expected. Joel Hoeb, Ferdinand Aviseb and Reuben Stander were all old residents of the area who had no doubt been hunters all of their adult lives. However, the dilapidated state of their clothing made it unlikely that they had been involved in poaching elephants or rhino. When they recovered from the shock of being caught they also politely answered all our questions in broken Afrikaans, admitting that they had killed a number of Hartmann's zebra.

Late that afternoon we found Chris and Lucas on the side of the main road. They had walked nearly 30 km over extremely rough terrain and were not in a good humour. After returning to Khovarib to formally arrest the three men, we all drove back to Wêreldsend where we celebrated our first poaching case in an appropriate manner. A few weeks later Chris informed me that they had all pleaded guilty and been given six-month prison sentences.

Although sending the three old men to jail had given me no pleasure, it did at least send a message to the local people that hunting would no longer be tolerated. Together with the elephant and rhino carcasses Slang and Colin had seen from the air it had also shown the poachers that they could still be detected and arrested in the most inaccessible parts of the region. But I knew that regular flying over the whole area would be too costly, and with so few of us on the ground the chances of catching people in the act of hunting were very slim indeed.

In spite of the odds against us, our second poaching case occurred less than a month later. This time Peter and I were on a foot patrol east of the Sesfontein road, near to where Colin had shown June and me so many elephant and rhino carcasses. We followed a blood trail to a place where the feet of a mountain zebra had been buried. Leading away from it were fresh donkey tracks, so Peter and I drove to Khorixas to inform Chris.

We arrived late in the afternoon and found him going over the statements of the five men he had arrested from Warmquelle and Kaoko Otavi, looking for contradictions to use in evidence against them, and he was not at all pleased to hear our story. 'The last thing I need now is another bloody poaching case. Are you sure the zebra was not killed weeks ago? I'm not walking another 30 km over Damaraland rocks following donkey tracks if they are more than a day old.'

Fortunately, I had brought two of the zebra feet with me, and after he had carefully examined them Chris agreed to come with us to the site, which we reached late that night. The next morning we followed the donkey tracks deep into the hills until, two hours and about 10 km later, we walked into a makeshift camp. Three very surprised Herero men were sitting around a fire, and while Chris interrogated them Peter and I followed a well-used path leading out of the camp to where we found strips of meat that had been draped over bushes to dry. As there was such a large amount of it I suspected that it was not just for home consumption.

When I got back the men had told Chris that they and their wives lived at a nearby stock-post, and were employed by the local ambulance driver, Moses Ganuseb, to herd his cattle and goats. As they admitted to having killed three zebra and a kudu it seemed like an open-and-shut case of illegal hunting, but Chris was clearly not very happy. After we had drunk a cup of tea with the poachers he called me aside.

'If I put all three of these men in jail, who is going to look after the livestock? There are lions around here, so I can't leave their wives to do it alone. I'll only arrest two of them, but they must decide amongst themselves which one stays with the women.'

I did not think it would be an easy decision to make, but after a short discussion they informed us that they had made their choice. The other two men were taken back to Khorixas where, a few weeks later, they were both found guilty and sentenced to eight months in prison. After this case I knew that Chris and I were going to work well together.

*   *   *

In October, I could report to the Trustees that in the second three months of NWT operations our activities had led to the arrest and conviction of five poachers and the confiscation of three .303 rifles. Chris had also investigated two cases in the south of the homeland, resulting in the conviction of one Damara man, who was sentenced to six months in prison, while the other case had not yet gone to court. It was a good start, which certainly justified our presence in the area. But we had only caught a few minnows. It would be a lot more difficult to catch and convict the big fishes.

Patrolling the area was only one of the NWT's objectives. We also planned to employ and train local young men who wanted a career in nature conservation, and I hoped to get the most promising of them accepted for the diploma course at Cwaka College. As they would need to have at least a Standard 8 school certificate, in June I held a meeting with the Damara Executive Committee, at which I informed them of my intentions and asked for their assistance. The response from the MEC for Education and Culture, Simson Tjongarero, was positive and he made two broadcasts over Radio Damara, asking for interested candidates to apply to his office.

Sixteen young men applied, but only four met the education qualifications and gave good reasons why they wanted to work in nature conservation. When they were interviewed two of them were found to be totally unsuitable, and a third took a job with the railways before we could inform him of his selection. This left us with only one candidate, Levi Richter, a farm boy from near Khorixas, so we appointed him to start in August. However, it soon emerged that his family were very unhappy about him becoming a 'wildlife policeman' and at the end of his first month Levi decided to resign 'for personal reasons'.

As nature conservation was a new profession for blacks in Southern Africa our difficulty in finding suitable applicants was not unexpected. In the past Damara people had lived from hunting, and now that it was illegal, being employed to protect wild animals would make a young man very unpopular at home and amongst his peers. For this reason another of my objectives was to start an environmental awareness programme in the local schools, which I hoped would help attract better candidates in the future. However, it was even more important for us to carry out extension work among the homeland's farmers, and as I needed a translator for this I asked Lucas Mbomboro for his advice. He knew just the right man for me.

Elias Hambo's mother was the daughter of Kapuhe Mbomboro, the Herero lineage head whose grave was a mandatory stop for everyone visiting Purros. His father was a Damara man who herded Kapuhe's cattle, so he was fluent in both languages, and as he had been adopted and raised by Jaap Meyer, the veterinary official and later nature conservator based at Otjovasandu, he also spoke excellent Afrikaans. In his late teens he had got a job in Etosha's road maintenance team, where he stayed for 15 years before going farming south of Khorixas. But he had lost all his cattle in the drought and was now looking for work.

In spite of never having spent a day in school, Elias had taught himself to read and write in Otjiherero, but more importantly I found him to be practically minded and happy to spend long periods in the field. However, what I appreciated most was his great sense of humour and an infectious belly-laugh that would lighten many of our difficult times during the early years of the Project. Elias turned out to be the ideal assistant for me, and we got on well from the start.

With a full-time translator I was now able to start on our most difficult challenge – trying to convince the residents of the region that they should stop hunting. But if I wanted them to pay any attention to what I said, I would first have to win their trust, which meant listening to the very real problems they were facing after the drought, and providing whatever assistance I could. Consequently, much of the remainder of 1982 was spent visiting the farmers in areas where significant numbers of big game still occurred. As some of them got to know me better we were able to discuss the wildlife around them, and whether they saw it as having any value.

The almost universal response was that living with wild animals brought only costs. Predators were killing the few livestock they had left, elephants damaged their water installations, and now that people were being jailed for just trying to add a little meat to their families' diet, even the edible game no longer had a value. I sympathised with these problems, but pointed out that if the wildlife was conserved it could one day attract tourists to the region, creating jobs and bringing money into the area. When the numbers increased they might also be allowed to start hunting again.

The Damara and Riemvasmaker farmers were the most sceptical. Tourism was not something they had heard of blacks benefiting from, and they had no faith in the law ever allowing them to kill wild animals legally. The game belonged to the whites, and only they would be given permits to hunt. Many of the farmers I spoke to saw nature conservation as just another trick played on blacks by the government in Windhoek.

Predators were the biggest problem to the Riemvasmaker community, and a rumour even spread that the DNC had brought lions from Etosha and released them on their farms 'to drive them off their land so that it could be proclaimed as a game reserve'. Because he was initially unwilling to shoot lions and had told some local farmers that they also needed to be conserved, Chris Eyre took the brunt of their anger.

Where elephants still occurred, the stockowners complained about their damaging windmills, reservoirs and water-pipes, and the whole community was intimidated by living in close proximity to such large and potentially dangerous animals. What made it worse was the helplessness the local people felt when they came to drink from their household water-points. And because elephants were specially protected by the nature conservation ordinance, it led to many community members believing that their lives were put above those of human beings.

One of the farms that I regularly stopped at was Palm, where an elderly Damara man known only as 'Old Kaokoveld' was living with the wife of a prominent Khorixas businessman, Andries Avarab. Although there was a strong natural spring nearby, a few elephant bulls regularly drank from a reservoir next to the house and broke the branches off the fig and *Prosopis* trees that had been planted there.

On every visit he complained bitterly about the damage they caused and the danger they posed to the people living there. Eventually, tired of hearing the same story each time we met, I told him that the only solution was for them to be shot. He took a few seconds to digest what I said, and then replied: '*Niemand moet een van* my *olifante skiet nie.*' (No one must shoot one of *my* elephants.) At the time I had started to think that getting the local communities' support for stopping the poaching was a hopeless task, but Old Kaokoveld's response made me believe that it was possible. The key was – whose wild animals were they?

* * *

Although no elephants had been seen in the basalt ranges on the April aerial survey, or during our early patrols there, by July the sub-population of 30 elephants that Slang also regarded as 'desert living' were back in the Uniab basin. But they were not alone. When Colin and Ina took the chairman of the EWT's Board of Trustees, Ken Whyte, through the area they saw a total of 55 elephants – hardly giving him the impression that they were endangered.

The publicity that had been given to the shooting of Skeuroor and reports of hunting by government officials in the Kaokoveld also resulted in a number of high-profile media personalities visiting Wêreldsend in the second half of 1982. The first was Max du Preez, the Windhoek representative of the Nasionale Pers Unie, who later founded the liberal Afrikaans newspaper *Vrye Weekblad*. He was followed in November by Tony Heard, editor of the *Cape Times*, accompanied by Margie Jacobsohn, a free-lance journalist who had opened political and media doors for Blythe Loutit when she visited Cape

Town to drum up support for conservation in the region.

Ina also took the well-known Namibian radio personality and author, Olga Levinson, into the Uniab basin, where they saw the first 'desert elephant' calf to be born since the drought. As we knew of no more elephants having been poached we were able to end the year on a cautiously optimistic note. However, a week before Christmas I was again reminded of the size of the challenge we faced in changing attitudes to nature conservation – and not just of the region's black communities.

Since the 1950s Torra Bay had been a popular fishing spot on the Skeleton Coast, where white farmers from inland took their families on annual summer holidays. In the early days the rudimentary roads through the basalt ranges had tested the skills of the drivers, with the last difficult pass to be negotiated situated 10 km to the east of Wêreldsend. From here on it was downhill virtually all of the way to the coast, and over the years it had become mandatory to stop at the top of this last obstacle and *steek 'n dop* (have a drink).

Although the road to the coast had now been upgraded and 'Dopsteekhoogte' could be climbed with ease, most families on their way to Torra Bay continued the tradition. The result was that the hilltop was littered with shattered glass and beer cans, so in early December we decided to clean up the mess, and also put a 200 litre drum on the side of the road. To get a little publicity for our conservation activities Peter painted the NWT's logo – the silhouette of a rhino encircled by the outline of its spoor – on our improvised litterbin. A week later I drove over Dopsteekhoogte, but found the drum empty and broken glass and cans once more scattered around. To add insult to injury our rhino logo had been shot full of holes!

CHAPTER NINETEEN

RHINOS ON THE BRINK

In the early 1980s rhino numbers were in steep decline throughout Africa and Asia, threatening the survival of a taxonomic family that had been on earth for more than 40 million years. During that time many genera evolved, with over 30 species, including the largest land mammal ever to have existed – *Baluchitherium grangeri,* which stood six metres at the shoulder and weighed 20 tons. Prehistoric rhinos once occurred on every continent except Australia.

All but five species – three in Asia and two in Africa – are now extinct. The largest of them is *Ceratotherium simum,* the white or square-lipped rhino, which can weigh over two and a half tons and have a shoulder height of up to 1.8 metres. As it is a grazer it inhabits open woodlands and savannas. The other African species is *Diceros bicornis,* the black or hook-lipped rhino, which weighs only 1 500 kilograms and is less than 1.6 metres at the shoulder. It is a browser and can live in most habitats, from desert to dense forest.

Rhino experts believe that before the large-scale introduction of firearms into Africa there were estimated to have been at least half a million black, and over 100 000 white rhino on the continent. The famous nineteenth-century explorer, Richard Burton, noted that in what is today Tanzania 'the black rhinoceros with a double horn is as common as the elephant', while in 1828 Dr Andrew Smith, the founder of the South African Museum in Grahamstown, saw between 100 and 150 rhino on a single day's journey through the north-west Cape. However, once firearms became available both African rhinos proved easy to hunt. At the start of the twentieth century Frederick Courtenay Selous wrote that 'thousands upon thousands of these huge creatures were killed by white hunters and natives armed with the white man's weapons'.

The first European explorer in what is now Namibia was Willem van Reenen, who in 1785 undertook an expedition across the Orange River, reaching the vicinity of present-day Keetmanshoop. By the time he returned to the Cape nine months later he had killed 65 rhino, six giraffe and many other animals. As Europeans started moving inland from Walvis Bay they also took a heavy toll on the wildlife. In his 1856 book on travel through south-western Africa, *Lake Ngami*, Charles John Andersson wrote that a fellow Swede, Hans Larsen, 'was an excellent and indefatigable sportsman, so successful that, though on his first arrival the country had literally teemed with rhinoceroses, lions, giraffes, zebras, gnoos, gemsboks &c., he had all but exterminated them'. He added that: 'To give the reader some idea of the abundance of the game and wild beasts then existing in this part of Africa, I may mention that Hans once shot, with his own hand, no less than nine rhinoceroses in the course of a single day.'

Andersson was no slouch with a firearm either, claiming to have shot 'upwards of one hundred' rhino in the five years after his arrival. But what made this slaughter all the more senseless was that he makes no mention in his book of rhino horns being sold, and wrote that Larsen was 'virtually a vegetarian'. The first European explorers in what became South West Africa had found themselves in a veritable zoological garden and appear to have killed wild animals simply because they were there, and they had the weapons to do so.

Of course, most of the early hunters did eat meat and so did their employees, as well as the many camp followers they collected along the way. Andersson's companion on his first expedition, the English sportsman Francis Galton, wrote in his book: 'I like rhinoceros flesh more than any other wild animal. A young calf rolled up in a piece of spare hide and baked in the earth is excellent. I hardly knew which of the little animal is best, the skin or the flesh.'

During the colonial era in other parts of Africa rhino were also exterminated to open up land for agricultural projects. In the 1940s AJ Hunter, working for the Kenya Game Department, shot 996 black rhino in one district so that cash crops could be grown by the local people of the area. The scheme failed and Hunter later wrote: 'Is it worth killing off these strange and marvellous animals just to clear a few more acres for people that are ever on the increase?'

When Kenya gained its independence there were still plenty of black rhino in its game sanctuaries and remoter areas, the largest number being in Tsavo National Park, where there were an estimated 3 000 in 1970. At the time the Park's 40 000 elephants were literally eating themselves and the rhinos out of house and home. In the 1970–72 drought more than 1 000 rhino died of starvation, and as was the case with ivory, their horns were sold to Arab traders plying the East African coast. Initially they were just another commercially valuable wildlife product, but within a few years the value of the glutinous hairy protuberances on a rhino's nose increased ten-fold – from US$50 to US$500 a kilogram – making them the most prized target of the continent's poachers.

In spite of Kenya banning hunting in 1977, and all trade in wildlife products a year later, the poaching of rhino continued in all its parks and game reserves. Bureaucratic rivalry, corruption at the highest levels and a lack of resources prevented the dedicated conservation officials on the ground from stopping the slaughter, and in a few years Kenya's rhino population declined by 50 per cent. Spearheaded by well-armed Somali *shifta*, the poaching epidemic spread to neighbouring countries, and soon nowhere were rhino safe from the voracious trade. One of the continent's priceless natural assets was being decimated, and when scientists calculated the losses per country, it became clear that if the rate of decline continued, black rhino would become extinct in less than two decades!

While the end destinations and uses of ivory were well known, the ancient trade in rhino horn was shrouded in myth and mystery. Consequently, in 1979 the World Wildlife Fund commissioned Dr Esmond Bradley Martin, a lanky Kenya-born Englishman with a shock of white hair, to find out who was buying the horn, for what purpose, and why its value had risen so rapidly. With his wife Chryssee he travelled to many parts of the world, visiting countries where rhinos still lived and where their illegally acquired horns were transported to, as well as the places where the products they were made into were sold. What he found changed the conventional thinking about virtually everything to do with the rhino horn trade.

Until then people believed rhino horn was used mainly as an aphrodisiac, but the Bradley Martins found that this was only true for the people of Gujarat and their neighbours in the far north of India and Nepal, and accounted for just one per cent of all the rhino horn being sold. For the rest of Asia, by far the greatest use of rhino horn was as an analgesic, to treat headache, fever and a wide range of other ailments. But as this trade dated back thousands of years, it could not have suddenly pushed the black-market price so high.

One of the countries visited was North Yemen, where they noted that it annually imported huge amounts of rhino horn. Once in the country it was carved into the handles of traditional daggers called *djambias* that were worn as a status symbol by wealthy Yemeni men. Over the next few years the Bradley Martins pieced together how the oil-boom in the Middle East had contributed to the slaughter of Africa's black rhinos, and the crucial part that was being played by this little Arab State of less than six million people.

In the 1960s North Yemen was one of the poorest countries in the world, with no modern schools, local doctors, paved roads or any form of industry. But the 1970s brought a spectacular change to the people's fortunes. Although no oil was found in North Yemen, it neighboured Saudi Arabia and money soon started pouring into the country as direct aid, as well as the wages of migrant workers on the richest oilfield in the world. By the end of the decade the per capita income of Yemenis had increased seven-fold, and they had become affluent consumers importing luxury items from around the world – and one of them was rhino horn.

Previously only sheiks and other wealthy tribal leaders could afford to buy a *djambia* made from rhino horn, but now every man returning from the oilfields of Saudi Arabia wanted to own one. Bradley Martin also found that the best *djambias* were being sold for up to U$12 000 in Sanaa, the capital of North Yemen. This was what had caused the sudden increase in price – and rhinos throughout Africa were paying with their lives for it.

Although North Yemen was taking an abnormally large share of the horn that came onto the black-market, the Far Eastern medicinal trade, because of its sheer size, was still the biggest consumer. Between 1979 and 1981, Bradley Martin visited Hong Kong, Singapore, Macao and many other cities in Taiwan, Indonesia, Malaysia and Burma. Of the 152 traditional pharmacies he went into, 99 had rhino products for sale. In most cases the shop owners were not aware of the plight of rhinos in Africa, and spoke freely to him about how the horn was sold. Because it could easily be faked the pharmacists first showed their clients the intact horn, before scrapings were taken from it. Back at home the buyer put a few of the shavings in boiling water and drank it as an infusion.

Thanks to Esmond and Chryssee Bradley Martin, we knew where the contraband rhino horn went and what it was used for. But it was a long road from the basalt hills of Damaraland to North Yemen, Hong Kong or Taiwan, and virtually nothing was known about the route Namibia's rhino horns followed, or the middlemen who bought and sold them along the way.

The first conviction of a buyer was in early 1983, when the owner of Central Garage in Outjo, Ziggi Goetz, was found guilty of being in possession of uncut diamonds as well as 68 rhino horns and 17 elephant tusks. He was caught in a police trap for diamond smuggling, but before his arrest he had also offered the undercover agent the ivory and rhino horn. The only information we got from the investigating officer was that they had been bought from residents of Kaokoland, and smuggled through the veterinary gate in gas cylinders that had their tops cut off and were then welded closed again.

Goetz was sentenced to two years' imprisonment for the uncut diamonds, but just one year, all of it suspended, and a fine of R2 000 for illegally possessing controlled game products. Considering that the maximum sentence for the latter offence was now six years' imprisonment, a fine of R6 000 or both, the magistrate had clearly seen diamond smuggling as the more serious offence. But to us, dealing in an indestructible gemstone could not be equated with the killing of 34 rhino – nearly three-quarters of the number that we believed still survived in Namibia's north-western homelands. It was time for magistrates and police to be included in our conservation extension activities, which Chris Eyre set about doing.

He and Lucas had also made good progress in the case against the men from Kaoko Otavi and Warmquelle, and they had been charged with killing 11 elephants and two rhino south-east of Sesfontein. Late in 1982 the teenager, Benjamine Batjiya, had pleaded guilty and been sentenced to six months in jail. However, the big breakthrough came when the two men from Warmquelle admitted their part in the killing, and agreed to be State witnesses against the three remaining members of the gang.

Our activities had also exposed more poaching cases, but without positive results. In October 1982, while patrolling on the Odendaal farms northeast of Wêreldsend, Peter Erb and I found the carcass of a three-quarter-grown rhino that was being fed on by a very thin lion. There were plenty of spotted hyena tracks nearby, but I did not believe that a rhino that size could have been killed by them or the lion, unless it was already injured. As neither Chris nor Rudi was available, we called in Peter Bridgeford from Moewe Bay in the Skeleton Coast Park, but our investigations proved fruitless.

Acting on my suspicion that the young rhino had been wounded Peter and

I concentrated our patrols in the area, and three weeks later another fresh rhino carcass was found near a spring 10 km further east. Although the bones had been scattered by hyena, the shape of the pelvic girdle showed clearly that it was a cow, possibly the mother of the large calf found earlier. This time Chris came with us to the scene, where we found two cartridge cases and a clear firing point near the spring, confirming that the cow had been poached, but there were no other leads to work on.

Our foot patrols uncovered another dead rhino in a well. Although there was no evidence of it having been shot, both horns had been cut off. Over the next few months seven more carcasses of rhino that had died before the drought ended were found. Five of them had definitely been poached, while the cause of death of the other two could not be established. Altogether it showed that in the last two years at least 10 rhino had died on the Odendaal farms west of the Grootberg mountain range. Our patrol work in the area also indicated that less than that number of rhino still survived there.

To keep track of the rhino carcasses we were finding and to ensure that none of them were counted twice, the skulls were brought to Wêreldsend. In the case of dead elephants we just carried back the lower jaws and hung them from the branches of the ebony trees at the southern end of the camp. With those already recovered by Slang Viljoen and kept at Moewe Bay, the total number of carcasses found was now 138 elephants and 52 rhino.

*   *   *

In February, after spending most of the previous eight years in the Kaokoveld, Slang Viljoen returned to Pretoria to write up his doctoral thesis. In this time his name had become synonymous with its 'desert elephants', and for many years he had kept the illegal hunting in this remote corner of Southern Africa in the public eye. To us in the NWT his knowledge of the area and its big game would be sorely missed.

When Slang left I took over one of his research assistants, Filimon Nuab, to be a translator for Peter Erb. As they were much the same age I saw Peter's theoretical knowledge of wildlife being complemented by the practical skills and experience of a young Damara man, who grew up herding goats and sheep around Khovarib. With Filimon working for him, Peter would also be more effective in his extension work with the farmers in southern Damaraland.

As the elephants in the Huab valley seldom moved further west than the

Riemvasmaker settlement at Die Riet, Peter and Filimon's work focused mainly on keeping track of the rhino we knew still occurred there. It was not easy, as the vast sweep of arid mountains and river valleys between the southern edge of the basalts and the Brandberg included some of the harshest habitat, most of it waterless, in the north-west. Because of its spectacular scenery, just seeing a few springbok, gemsbok or zebra there was a special experience. Finding a rhino in this barren landscape was an event to be remembered on the bad days when no wildlife at all was seen.

Although the number of rhino north of the veterinary fence was higher, we still had great difficulty finding them. After almost a year of patrolling I had actually seen one on less than 20 occasions. Apart from the census, when 23 were recorded, they were equally unlikely to be seen from the air, because unless caught out in the open their response to any sign of danger was to stand still, and in spite of their size they would become almost invisible. On a number of occasions after a rhino had been spotted from the air, when the plane turned around and flew low over the same place again, we saw no sign of it.

With such a high price now on their heads we needed to develop an effective way of monitoring the population. As rhino tracks were frequently seen, Blythe had started measuring the size of the hind footprint as a means of identifying individual animals. It worked reasonably well with the very small numbers inhabiting the dry washes and canyons along the Uchab River, but in the basalt ranges it proved less effective. I also found that the width of a rhino's track could vary considerably, depending on whether it was measured on hard or soft ground. Nevertheless, keeping a record of spoor sizes was useful, and together with the occasional sightings we were able to build up a file on each known rhino in Damaraland.

By early 1983 we had established that the area in which a viable population still occurred was from the Uchab to the Hoarusib, a distance of over 400 km from north to south, while the furthest east was in the Klip River, which dissected the Grootberg range. There were also at least two rhino left north-west of Orupembe, between the Nadas and Munutum rivers. Nowhere within this area did the average annual rainfall exceed 150 mm, below which was the international classification of a desert.

By far the highest density was in the basalt area, where the numerous springs and fertile volcanic soils created good habitat for black rhino. With very few access roads, this rugged region would in the past have provided a measure of protection to all the wild animals there, but our having found 10 carcasses on the Odendaal farms east of the Grootberg showed us that poachers had now started coming into this last refuge. To counter this Peter and I started carrying out regular foot patrols here, walking up to 20 km a day and sleeping under the stars next to our vehicles each night. It was tough going, but on each trip we learned more about the Kaokoveld's 'desert rhino'.

Unlike their 'white' cousins, which are regarded as relatively docile, black rhino are often portrayed as mean-tempered and prone to unprovoked attacks on people. In fact, for very good reasons, they are terrified of humans, and whenever they got our scent always ran away and did not stop for at least 5 km. Nevertheless, every rhino we encountered was treated with great respect and we always made sure there was a safe place nearby while approaching them.

In spite of our limited sightings, we were able to establish the habitats they preferred from their tracks and dung, as well as very visible urinations. Whereas the western population of elephants was dependent on the riparian vegetation along the largest seasonal watercourses in the dry season, rhino spoor was seldom seen here. Instead, those that inhabited the far west mainly browsed on the sparse shrubs and forbs growing in the smaller drainage lines and on the rocky hill-slopes. Their ability to utilise a range of succulents that were toxic to other species also made them much better adapted to living in a desert than the Kaokoveld elephants.

Although they are solitary animals, cows keep their calves with them until the next one is born, and female sub-adults often stay in close proximity to their mothers for a few years before finally drifting away. Dominant bulls also follow and try to stay with females that are in oestrus, but apart from these temporary liaisons, black rhino lead lonely lives – or so it seems to us. However, olfactory communication is continuously taking place between all the rhino in the area.

To facilitate this they have glands situated in the anus that make their faeces individually recognisable, and after defecating, the adults of both sexes scrape their back feet in the dung so that a scent trail is laid down as they walk. The dominant bulls also shuffle their hind legs around water-holes, 'ploughing' a double furrow in the ground that may stretch for 10 metres or more. This very conspicuous way of marking their territories often enabled us to identify the spoor of the alpha male.

Adult bulls also advertise their presence by curling their penises backwards and sending a fine spray of urine onto rocks or bushes along the paths they use, while cows use theirs to communicate information about their hormonal status. As rhino urine leaves a conspicuous white stain when it dries, noting if it was in a concentrated splash or in small widespread droplets enabled us to sex the individuals whose tracks we found without actually seeing them.

As Blythe knew most of the rhinos in the small Uchab population and had accumulated an extensive knowledge of the region's vegetation while working as a botanical artist, in early 1983 she started a more intensive study of the main plants that they fed on. More technical support and advice for her project was provided by a Cape Town University professor, Gideon Louw, while the dung samples she collected were sent to Dr Riena Biggs in Windhoek for laboratory analysis.

Initially, in addition to the People's Trust for Endangered Species grant she received via Nick Carter, Blythe covered the costs of her field work by selling her watercolour paintings of the desert. But when this proved insufficient she started a 'Save the Rhino' section within the Wildlife Society's Swakopmund Centre. Apart from fundraising, the more adventurous members went on weekend trips to southern Damaraland and provided us with many useful game sightings. To thank the Centre, Blythe and I gave a number of slide shows and talks at their monthly meetings.

In the difficult early years many other 'Swakopmunders' assisted those of us working in the field in a variety of ways, not least by their hospitality whenever we made town trips to get fuel and provisions. At the forefront were Dan and Pat Craven, Dave and Lorna Sandy, Barry and Judy Clements, Len and Karen le Roux, Kuki Kuhhirt, the owner of Kuki's Pub, and Werner Liescher, who made us honorary members of the First National Bank Club. When June left Etosha and joined me at Wêreldsend, we were also especially grateful to Andrew and Sue O'Shann for providing a home away from home for Tuareg and Kyle when they started school in the little desert town.

*   *   *

In March our many days spent on foot in the basalt ranges finally paid off. Acting on a local farmer's report of suspicious human tracks on the farm Palm, just south of the veterinary fence, Peter and I again patrolled this area. On our third day we almost fell over a three-month-old rhino calf, and as there was no sign of its mother in the vicinity I drew the obvious conclusion that she must have been killed. Sending Peter to inform Chris Eyre and get help to catch the calf, I stayed with it until he got back.

For most of the day the calf just lay in the shade, while I sat nearby keeping the jackals away. At about four o'clock it started walking again, and soon found some damp earth in a small watercourse. Obviously thirsty, it scraped the ground with its front feet, trying to expose enough liquid to drink. Although I knew that elephant and mountain zebra dug holes to get water, I had not seen rhino doing so. So to see how successful it was I moved in closer and sat on a rock bank 20 metres away. However, I had forgotten that young rhinos have better eyesight than adults, and after a few minutes it looked up and saw me. Although I froze it walked inquisitively towards me, and at about 10 metres charged, knocking the camera out of my hands before running off. Over the rocky ground I was unable to keep up and it soon disappeared from sight.

Luckily Peter returned about half an hour later with Filimon Nuab and Titus Mbura, a local man we had hired as caretaker at Wêreldsend camp. Together we followed the calf's tracks to where it was lying asleep in the shade of a large *Euphorbia damarana*. We all crept up behind it, and I signalled to Peter and Filimon that they should go round one side, while Titus and I went around the other. Before the calf could get up I dived onto it, expecting my colleagues to come to my assistance. But they had not played rugby, and while I struggled to hold down the squealing, kicking and butting little animal, they just looked on like spectators at a wrestling match. Only when I used industrial language implying that their jobs were at stake did they rather tentatively join in the fray. Between the four of us we were able to hog-tie the calf's feet and load it onto the Land Rover. It was a female, and although quite badly lacerated by jackals, was otherwise in good shape.

By the time we reached Wêreldsend it was dark, so while Peter, Filimon and Titus prepared an old stone enclosure as the calf's accommodation for the night, I contacted June, who was in Swakopmund visiting our two sons at their new school. Not wanting to disclose more information than necessary over the radio, I simply told her we had acquired a new baby and that she should come back as soon as possible, bringing antibiotics and lots of powdered milk.

The next priority was to give the calf something to drink, so after cutting a small hole in the cap of a litre Coke bottle and putting a cut-off section of Tuareg's bicycle tube over the neck, I filled it with a weak milk solution and went to see how thirsty our 90 kg baby girl was. In the dark she showed much less fear of me, and when I offered my two fingers to her she immediately started to suck on them, enabling me to slip the bicycle tube into her mouth. Apart from a blackened fingernail from a set of molars I did not think a rhino her age should have had, all went smoothly and she drank nearly two litres.

With nothing more that could be done that night I went to bed. It had been a long day.

As Chris was in the field, Peter had informed Rudi Loutit instead, and the next morning he arrived with Jaap Meyer, from the Park's Springbokwasser Gate. I had known Oom Jaap since my early days in the Kaokoveld, when he was stationed at Otjovasandu. According to Elias, in his younger days he had been renowned for his prodigious strength and fondness for bar room brawls, but he was now nearing 60 and was regarded as an elder statesman by all of us working in the area. Over a cup of tea I briefed them on the previous day's events, and as June had not yet returned from Swakopmund, I sent Peter and Filimon to show them where the calf had been found.

In the afternoon June arrived with the powdered milk and antibiotics. By now the calf was freely drinking from a bottle, and soon started following us around like a puppy. When her wounds had been disinfected all that our new baby still needed was a name. As June had obtained the drugs from Sue O'Shann, who worked as nursing sister for the Rössing Uranium Mine, we called her Sue.

Early the next morning I drove to Palm, where the carcass of a rhino cow had been found with its horns cut off, less than a kilometre from where Peter and I first saw the calf. When I arrived, Rudi and Jaap were following the tracks of what they thought were the donkeys used by the poachers. The very rocky ground made it difficult to find clear spoor, but I could see no sign of the characteristic frog that is in a donkey's hoof print, and was sure they were just mountain zebra tracks. Out of earshot, I asked Filimon for his opinion and he agreed with me, but had been afraid to contradict Rudi because of his volatile temper when things did not go according to plan. Also not wanting to provoke one of his outbursts, I decided to walk in a circle around the place where the rhino had been killed – the normal procedure after an incident in Zimbabwe's liberation war.

We soon found what we were looking for. Crossing a farm road to the north of the carcass were the tracks of two men walking away from it. Filimon and I followed them for about 8 km until we came to the veterinary fence. By then it was clear that they were heading towards ANVO Safaris' no-longer-used base at Palmwag, and as it was getting late we went back to where Rudi, Jaap and Peter were camping. During the day they had been joined by Senior Nature Conservator Alisdair McDonald, who the DNC Head Office had sent to take over the investigation. With him was a young game ranger from Rehoboth, Johan Wolher.

As the group was now so large, and I knew the NWT's executive director would not take kindly to being left in the dark about important events, I returned to Wêreldsend, and the next morning drove to Windhoek. There I briefed Ina on what had happened, and after clearing it with the DNC gave a statement to the local media. When I got back to Damaraland, Alisdair had arrested the eldest son of Goliat Kasaona, the Herero headman at Otjindakue village, just outside of Sesfontein.

From Filimon I learned that on the morning after I left they followed the tracks to Palmwag, where they found another of Goliat's sons, Phineas Kasaona, taking care of the camp. However, as none of his shoes matched the footprints leaving the site where the rhino was killed there was no direct evidence linking him to it. For a while it seemed like the trail had gone cold, but a breakthrough came when the veterinary staff at the gate told Filimon that Phineas' brother had recently visited him.

Johannes Kasaona's shoe print did match those leaving the scene, and under interrogation he eventually confessed to poaching the rhino cow. A second suspect, Tjozongoro, was also interrogated, but he steadfastly denied being involved, and with no evidence against him was released. Johannes Kasaona appeared in the Khorixas regional court a few days later. He was found guilty and sentenced to 18 months in prison. His accomplice was never identified.

Although we all complimented Alisdair and Rudi on a successful conviction, Chris was disappointed that the case had been rushed through court without first trying to find out from Johannes Kasaona who he was planning to sell the horns to. Filimon also told me that both Johannes and Tjozongoro were beaten and not given any water to drink for long periods. I understood the pressure that Alisdair and Rudi were under, but if we hoped to get the support of the local people we needed to interrogate the suspects in a less heavy-handed way.

There was also the fate of the rhino calf to be resolved. As it was illegal to keep a wild animal in captivity without a permit, I had reported her presence in our camp to the DNC's head office. Stoffel Rocher's initial response was that she should be put down, but I refused to allow this. When the Damara Representative Authority heard about the calf they claimed she belonged to them, and wanted her to remain at Wêreldsend. But 10 days later Ian Hofmeyr was instructed to take her to Okaukuejo, where in his expert hands she would have the best chance of surviving.

The calf soon settled down in her new home, shuffling behind Ian's wife,

Rea, wherever she went, which earned her the new name of Suzy Slippers, and jogging around the camp with Ian. But when she was two years old and weighed over 400 kilograms, Ian was killed in a vehicle accident and Rea left the Park. As the calf was now old enough to fend for herself she was put in the 500 hectare Kaobendes quarantine camp at Otjovasandu, and six months later moved to the 15 000 ha Karros Camp, where there was a population of about 20 rhino. So that she could grow up wild, instructions were given to the DNC staff not to have any contact with her.

Three years later Rea Hofmeyr came back to Etosha and went to see Suzy Slippers in Karros. When they found her Rea called the now five-year-old rhino and she immediately came up and nuzzled against her. On Rea's next visit four years later, by which time Suzy was a full-grown cow, she again responded to Rea's call and this time even lay down next to the surrogate mother she had only seen twice in seven years. Now 27 years old, Suzy Slippers has raised six calves.

*   *   *

A few days after Johannes Kasaona was convicted, the long-awaited trial of the men accused of poaching 11 elephants and two rhino, and suspected of killing many more, finally began in the Khorixas regional court. As it was on the day that Ian Hofmeyr collected the rhino calf from Wêreldsend I did not attend, but Chris informed me that the State witnesses had all given credible evidence and stood up well to cross-examination by the defence lawyer. The proceedings had gone slowly, however, and after two days in court the hearing was adjourned.

When it resumed in May, the Humu brothers were found guilty and sentenced to three years in prison, 18 months of which was suspended, as well as fines of R3 000. The other three men were given shorter terms in prison and lower fines. It was an improvement on the sentence handed down to Ziggie Goetz six months earlier in Outjo, but still far from the maximum of six years in jail, or R6 000, that had been introduced the year before.

Chris's greatest disappointment was not being able to charge the man who had bought the tusks and rhino horn from them. Under interrogation the Humu brothers had given him the buyer's name, but in spite of being offered a reduction in their sentence they had not been willing to stand up in court and be a witness against him. With no other evidence linking him to the case he could not be charged. A few months later, Chris met the man in a Windhoek pub, and they had a drink together. He did not deny being a 'smuggler', but told Chris he would have to 'prove it in court'. Some years later he was convicted of being in illegal possession of uncut diamonds and given a six-year jail sentence.

In March the police arrested a Damara man for poaching a kudu south of the veterinary fence. He was immediately brought to court, found guilty and fined R300. As others were known to have been involved, the case was then handed over to Chris, who with Lucas continued the investigation and had two more suspects arrested. The most pleasing aspect of this case was the co-operation given by the police, who in the past had a reputation for being major poachers in the homelands. Chris had worked hard at getting their support, and his efforts were now paying off.

A month later Chris found a local man on a donkey near Khovarib carrying seven elephant tusks in a sack. He was charged with illegal possession of controlled game products and sentenced to a fine of R2 000, or 12 months in prison. In May a white official living in Khorixas, Marius Visser, was convicted of killing an ostrich and fined R250, but in another case a Damara businessman accused of shooting a kudu in Damaraland was acquitted when in court the State's witnesses denied the statements they had previously made under oath. After dismissing the charges against the main accused, magistrate Tas Bonzaaier convicted both witnesses of perjury and sentenced them to prison terms of eight months each.

Thanks to Chris's policy of keeping the magistrates well informed of the conservation situation in the homeland, they too were now taking poaching cases more seriously. Together with the support of the police and the Damara Representative Authority, we had all the important government players on our side, but it was only half the picture. We first had to know when and where poaching occurred, and with so few of us in the field we were relying largely on luck to bring cases to court.

The poachers were also becoming more careful. The Humu gang had made no attempt to hide the carcasses of the animals they killed, but the rhino cow poached by Johannes Kasaona and his accomplice had been covered with branches to prevent it from being seen from the air. The stakes were also getting higher. When I informed Clive Walker about the Palm case, he told me that in North Yemen rhino horn was now retailing for up to US$3 000 a kilogram! As some of Damaraland's adult bulls were carrying over six kilograms of horn on their heads, even the small percentage of this that the local hunters received was still a great deal of money to the drought-impoverished people living in the homelands.

We also did not have many rhinos left to play with. In April Rudi combined all of our sightings in an internal memo to his superiors. In it he stated that 47 rhino had been identified in Damaraland, five of which were known to have been poached or died of natural causes since October 1982. In Kaokoland the situation was much worse, with very small numbers still surviving in only two areas – south of Purros and north-west of Orupembe. He concluded that there were a minimum of 44 rhino in the whole of the north-west, and 'possibly as many as 51'.

In 1970 I had estimated the number of rhino in what was now Kaokoland to be about 160, but in just over a decade all but a handful had been killed. Although there was no reliable estimate of how many inhabited the de-proclaimed western parts of Etosha, it was likely to have been at least 100. We now knew that none survived east of the basalt ranges, where over 30 carcasses had been found south of the Ombonde River. If only about 50 were now left in the whole north-west it meant that their numbers had declined by 80 per cent.

Catching poachers was also a losing game, since at least one rhino was lost for every arrest made. My experience of stock-theft in the Rhodesian lowveld had shown me that if there was sufficient incentive, there would always be young men willing to take major risks. And with the potential rewards from poaching rhino much higher than from stealing cattle, just patrolling the area would not be enough.

*   *   *

In November 1982 Elias and I undertook a trip through south-eastern Kaokoland, along the way visiting the Herero headmen I had got to know in the 1960s. My first stop was at Otjokavare, a strong spring around which Eugene Joubert had found the highest density of rhino before western Etosha was de-proclaimed. Since then a large settlement had developed around it, which was the home of Headman Keefas Muzuma.

Now in his early seventies, Keefas immediately recognised me, and after our formal greetings told me that he and his people were very grateful for my having allowed them to return to the place where they had lived before being moved to Ombombo in 1928. Having just been a junior agricultural official at the time, who had simply written a report to my superiors on their illegal entry into the Park, this was an exaggeration of my role. But I was the one they had dealt with, not the politicians in Pretoria who decreed that Otjokavare and the area west of it should become part of Kaokoland. And as Keefas Muzuma was one of the most influential traditional leaders in the homeland – whose help in stopping the poaching would be crucial – I did not argue the point.

We went on to discuss the recent drought, which Keefas said had made his people *ovaTjimba*, just like they were when the Nama stole their cattle. Having seen numerous dehydrated carcasses lying around most of the villages we had driven past, I knew he was not exaggerating. Later I would learn from the State Veterinarian in Outjo that of the 160 000 head of cattle in Kaokoland in the late 1970s, when the drought ended in early 1982 only 15 000 had survived. The numbers of goats and sheep had also decreased by over 50 per cent.

After sympathising with their plight I asked Keefas about the wildlife around Otjokavare. He confirmed that there were no more rhino and only a few elephants left, and admitted that drought was not the only cause of their disappearance. White people had offered money to his followers for tusks and rhino horn. He was not happy about this, but with everyone hungry it was difficult to stop them from hunting. Nevertheless, he promised his support for our efforts to protect the few wild animals that had survived.

From Otjokavare we drove on to Otuzemba, where I had spent many moonlit nights counting the game coming to drink from its double springs. At the time, the headman there, Werimba Rutjani, did not allow any hunting in his area, and in the dry season it had one of the largest populations of elephant and Burchell's zebra in the Kaokoveld. If any game was left on the highlands this was the most likely place to find it. Around the springs I saw a fair amount of elephant dung, as well as zebra, kudu and impala spoor, but their numbers were clearly far below what they had been in the 1960s.

When I went to see him Werimba also recognised me, and after a discussion on the impact of the drought I reminded him of the time he had told me about a white official who had hunted six kudu in his area. It was man's duty to look after God's creatures and not waste them, the elderly headman told me, adding that there would be more wild animals around Otuzemba if they did not move away from his area during the rainy season to places where he could not protect them.

Before leaving I told Werimba that I would ask the NWT to buy him a heifer as a reward for his exceptional contribution to conservation. At the next board meeting I did so, but the majority of trustees had written off Kaokoland as a lost cause, and my proposal was turned down. Fortunately, Ina supported me and she was eventually able to find a sponsor. However, as Otuzemba was in a war zone the logistics of getting the heifer there proved difficult, and by the time we had organised transport the project was overtaken by events that made it impossible. In the years ahead I was reminded of my 'broken promise' every time I visited Otuzemba.

It was too dangerous to go north of Opuwo, but I discussed the wildlife situation with a few of the people I still knew in the town. From them I learned that, apart from around Otuzemba, a few elephants also occurred along the border with Ovamboland, ranging as far as Ehomba, the home of the 'black Van der Merwe' family. Over the rest of the highlands there was no big game left, confirming what Ben van Zyl had told me in November 1980. As the drought had then only just started, the demise of the wildlife in this part of Kaokoland could not be blamed on it.

Most of the Herero and Himba we spoke to expressed regret at the loss of the wild animals they had grown up with, but their primary concern was how to make a living without cattle. In the aftermath of such a catastrophic event there was little point in questioning them about their role in the killing. It would also be unfair to blame the pastoralists for what had been started by men who earned salaries, and, unlike the early European hunters in Namibia, could not use the excuse of thinking that Africa's wildlife was inexhaustible.

We heard many heartbreaking stories on the trip, and there was little doubt that without the food aid provided by the International Red Cross and distributed by the South African Defence Force, many people would have died of starvation. But to the Himba and Herero, cattle were not just a source of milk and meat. Their whole culture was woven around livestock, and each family head's status and self-esteem were tied to him being able to carry out many social and religious obligations that required cattle. Faced with the humiliation of living without their beloved long-horned and multi-coloured herds, I was told that quite a few men had committed suicide.

The demoralising effect of having to stand in line for food handouts was also clearly illustrated by the numerous empty bottles of cheap alcohol now littering the squatter camps that had grown up around Opuwo. But the drought was not the only event that had disrupted the lives of the Kaokoveld Herero and Himba. The region was now also embroiled in a guerrilla war that had forced the pastoralists to choose sides between a government in Windhoek they saw no need for, and SWAPO, which was dominated by their eastern neighbours for whom they had no love.

The situation was exacerbated by an attack on the home of Johannes Ruyter, in which the much-respected headman was wounded in the knee. In another fire-fight between the DTA-supporting community at Ehomba and SWAPO guerrillas, both Frederik and Tom van der Merwe, who had worked for Tom Sopper and me, were also killed. As a result many young Himba and Herero were recruited into the SWA Territorial Force, where they earned high wages fighting on the side of South Africa. According to the members of the security forces I spoke to they made excellent soldiers, but it would put them in an invidious position if Namibia gained its independence and SWAPO came to power.

However, there was a silver lining. The huge die-off of livestock had at least reduced the grazing pressure on the degraded plateau rangelands and after the very good 1982 rainy season tall grass now grew where just a few months before there had been bare ground. Although it still consisted almost entirely of annual species, time would tell whether perennials could also re-establish themselves on the capped and eroded soils that covered much of the highlands.

Until cattle numbers increased there was little chance of my being able to convince the pastoralists that there was a need to introduce any form of range management, and for the immediate future our priority was to stop the poaching. But with so few of us on the ground, we needed more than just the passive support of the region's political and traditional leaders.

CHAPTER TWENTY

INVOLVING THE LOCAL PEOPLE

When I proposed the objectives of the NWT Damaraland/Kaokoland Project, our highest priority was to break the prevailing paradigm of nature conservation being a 'whites only' profession. My plan was to employ and train educated young blacks in the hope that it would encourage the Department of Nature Conservation to do the same. However, our first attempt to recruit school leavers was unsuccessful.

I made no further attempt because shortly thereafter the DNC did start appointing blacks above the level of labourer, although only in the ethnic homelands. They would also not be called nature conservators, as whites were, but game rangers, with a lower rank and salary structure. Nor would they have the same uniform, with Stoffel Rocher apparently having insisted that no blacks would ever wear the green bush jackets that had become the trademark of the DNC field staff. Nevertheless, as it was a step forward I saw no point in the NWT competing in the same small pool of suitably qualified candidates.

In late 1982 Chris Eyre was informed that game ranger posts in Damaraland had been advertised, and a few months later he received a batch of applications. Most came from youngsters hoping to find any kind of work, he told me, but there were some he thought showed promise. The best was a young man from Khorixas, Nahor Howaseb, whom he appointed early in 1983. Although he did not find the job easy, and in the first few years was often threatened by members of his community, Nahor stuck it out and when all racial barriers were finally removed became one of the government's most dedicated nature conservation officers.

Now that the DNC was employing black game rangers, I focused most of my attention on extension work amongst the local farmers. With Elias as my full-time assistant and translator I was now much more effective, but after the Palm rhino case Rudi offered Filimon Nuab a labourer's post at Uchabmond, which he accepted. I filled his position with another man who was more practical than academic.

Hendrik Roman, one of the Riemvasmakers I had got to know well, had a number of sons, the two eldest of whom had completed their schooling and entered respectable professions. The third had dropped out early and was married with two children, but still unemployed, and according to his father was 'getting up to no good in Khorixas'. However, he assured me that this rebellious son enjoyed the outdoors and just needed to find his direction in life. As there was a familiar ring to Bennie Roman's story, I appointed him to work with Peter.

When Chris employed a second Damara-speaking game ranger our combined field staff was increased to eight, but we still had only three vehicles between us to cover an area over four times the size of the Etosha National Park. In the Skeleton Coast Park there were a further five nature conservation officers with three vehicles, but they had been instructed to patrol only within the borders of the Park. As there was little game and no poaching there, this restriction put a question mark over the DNC's commitment to bringing illegal hunting in the north-western homelands under control.

The senior officials in Windhoek had also maintained their pressure on the NWT trustees to stop our fieldwork, and it was now starting to get through to some of them. At the latest board meeting I had been asked to move away from anti-poaching patrols and concentrate on environmental education in the schools, which was apparently more acceptable to the DNC. Since this was also one of our objectives I agreed to do so, but reminded the trustees that the threat facing the rhino and elephant had only marginally decreased, and with the government's lack of manpower and vehicles on the ground there was no room for complacency.

Working in Damaraland's schools was also not as politically benign as it seemed. Namibia's liberation struggle was moving into its final phase, and many of the rural education facilities had become hotbeds of anti-South African politics. With my reputation as a 'liberal' I knew that anything we did in schools was likely to arouse the suspicion of the security police, so from the start I kept them informed about our activities. Fortunately, the officer in charge in Khorixas, Warrant Officer Liebenberg, was also concerned about the poaching situation and supported our work.

My plan to show wildlife films and take groups of students on weekend excursions to Wêreldsend was also discussed with Simson Tjongarero, who sent a circular to all the headmasters informing them that we had the Damara Representative Authority's permission to carry out conservation-related activities at their schools. The Director of Education, Naas Maritz, who was known to be one of the region's leading big game hunters, also gave us his support, though his motives might not have been exactly the same as ours.

Initially we had only one 16 mm film: *Etosha: Place of Dry Water* by David and Carol Hughes, who after visiting us in February had donated a copy to the project. It had won a number of international awards for the conservation message it portrayed, but our young audiences' most audible response was to its many gory scenes of nature 'red in tooth and claw'. Nevertheless, at the end of each show we were inundated with questions about wild animals that also occurred in Damaraland, but which most of the homeland's school-going generation had never seen.

The weekend excursions to Wêreldsend were aimed at rectifying this, and just as I had found in KwaZulu, camping out in a wild environment and seeing big game was an exciting experience for children who now spent much of their life in a classroom. Although the numbers we could take on each trip were low, by focusing on first-year matrics we were at least reaching the privileged few that had received a secondary education and were, therefore, most likely to play leading roles in their communities.

But as rewarding as our film shows and field courses were, I had not resigned from my post in Etosha to work with schoolchildren. Poaching in the homeland was still far from being under control, and until it was I believed my time could be much more valuably spent talking to the region's farmers. Fortunately, the problem was solved in April, when Johan le Roux arrived at Wêreldsend looking for a job.

I had last seen Johan in the East Caprivi, where he was transferred to from Keetmanshoop. In early 1982 he resigned from the DNC to go crocodile catching with Mike Slogrove, one of the wild white men living in northern Botswana, but left after six months and then wandered around Southern

Africa looking for something worthwhile to do. When he heard I was working in Damaraland he decided to visit me and offer his services.

Johan's nature conservation experience and willingness to live in a tent and
work for a low salary made him the ideal person to take on our environmental awareness courses. But Ina was in a mood to show me who was the boss,
and opposed his appointment. Because of the pressure being put on them by
the DNC, the NWT's trustees were also reluctant to take on the responsibility
of another member of staff, and they sided with Ina. Fortunately, Blythe came
to the rescue by raising money from the Wildlife Society in Swakopmund to
pay Johan until the end of the year.

My conflict with the NWT's flamboyant executive director had not just
been over Johan's appointment. Although I recognised Ina as a remarkable
woman, without whose drive and determination the NWT would not have
got off the ground, she had become fiercely possessive and accepted no criticism of the way she ran its affairs. Even the board members, who collectively
controlled a significant part of Namibia's national economy, were unwilling to
stand up to her. In fact we were all intimidated by Ina's towering temper tan-
trums – but we also knew she was suffering from an incurable kidney disease,
which a few years later would cause her death at the age of just 38.

Ina, her three sisters and a younger brother had been raised on a farm in
the Kamanjab district. When she was a teenager her father was killed in a
borehole drilling accident, but her mother coped without a husband in an
area that was then on the frontier of white settlement. Ina had inherited her
mother's indomitable will to succeed, but as her kidney condition was diag-
nosed at an early age I suspected that sympathetic family and friends had
always allowed her to get her own way. As a result, if Ina was on your side you
could not ask for a better champion, but if for whatever reason she was not, it
was impossible to discuss anything with her.

Soon after I joined the NWT we clashed over a number of key policy issues, the most important being my firm belief that the Trust should be apo-
litical. Ina, on the other hand, saw the visits I organised for local community
members to Wêreldsend as an opportunity to promote the DTA, the political
party she strongly supported. Another bone of contention between us was
the use of the camp, which got worse when June and the boys left Etosha and
joined me in Damaraland. We also had many disagreements over how field
activities should be run – but in this I stood firm. In spite of my respect for
Ina's commitment to conservation in the region, I did not accept that she
knew better than me how to work with the local people.

My personal life was also in crisis. June had left a good job and a lifestyle she loved in Etosha to come and live with me in a caravan at Wêreldsend. It meant that Tuareg and Kyle had to become full-time boarders in Swakopmund, nearly 400 km away. As I was spending most of my time in the field, she believed I was neglecting my family for a cause that was already lost. I knew that I had become obsessed with stopping the poaching, but after everything that had happened, now that I had finally come back I could not just walk away from the Kaokoveld.

The ongoing conflict with Ina, opposition to our field activities from the DNC's head office, and now the NWT's Board of Trustees, were also all adding to the pressure I was under. So when June returned from visiting our sons and told me that they were being victimised and were very unhappy, it was the last straw. I saw only one solution: she had to live in Swakopmund, where she could get a job and be close to them. I gave her no option and she gave me no comeback. We did not live together again and were legally divorced five years later.

*   *   *

After a year at Wêreldsend we had made progress, and the publicity generated by our few successes was starting to produce some direct benefits for the project. The most valuable was a US$5 000 grant the EWT received from the Foundation to Save African Endangered Wildlife (SAVE), an American-based organisation run by Ingrid Schroeder and Babette Alfieri. It was used to buy a Land Rover truck to replace the Datsun Tracker. While in Windhoek to collect my new vehicle I also picked up Mitch Reardon, a friend from my days in Etosha.

At that time Mitch and his wife, Margot, had been based at Halali camp, from where they used their free time to photograph the Park's wildlife and produce a coffee-table book, *Etosha: Life and Death on an African Plain*. Impressed by Mitch's grasp of the conservation issues and his artistic skills, Bernabe de la Bat had appointed him as the DNC's publicity officer. It was the perfect position for him, and when he visited us in Okaukuejo he was full of ideas on how to promote Namibia's national parks and recreational resorts. However, when De la Bat left, the new Director saw Mitch as too outspoken and too liberal for such a key position. To get him to resign the DNC made his working conditions intolerable, and he eventually obliged them by leaving to write another book, *Zululand: A Wildlife Heritage.*

I met Mitch again while attending an EWT function in Johannesburg, where I brought him up to date on events in Namibia's north-west. By then he and Margot were separated, and with their second book already at the publishers, he was looking for a new project. As I could think of no one better able to capture the situation in the Kaokoveld, I invited him to spend some time with Chris Eyre and me in the hope that he would find inspiration for a third book.

Mitch and I spent a day at Wêreldsend before heading into the field with the new SAVE Land Rover. The first place we visited was the north-eastern corner of Damaraland, then known as the 'Five Farms', between the western border of Etosha and the Red Line fence. As these Odendaal-expropriated properties had not yet been settled by communal farmers the Damara Administration's Director of Agriculture, Johan Oosthuizen, had recommended that they be set aside as a wildlife sanctuary. Chris Eyre and the Damara Executive Committee had supported the proposal, and at the time the remaining border was being game-proof fenced.

I had previously recorded a fair amount of wildlife here, but on this trip we saw only a small herd of springbok and five mountain zebra, as well as the spoor of kudu, gemsbok and two male lions. Although the Five Farms had only one small spring and two weak boreholes that were maintained by the Damara Administration, the attractive koppies and sandy riverbeds gave it considerable tourism potential. All that the proposed sanctuary needed was protection from trigger-happy officials and the hungry local people. But as it was 160 km from where Chris was based in Khorixas and over 200 km from Wêreldsend, this was easier said than done.

Disappointed by how little game we had seen, we left the Five Farms and drove through the Red Line gate at Kamdecha into ANVO Safaris' concession area, and then down the Otjovasandu River to its junction with the Ombonde River. However, we saw no game here, and suspecting that poaching could be the reason, I stopped under a winter thorn tree so that we could do some walking. While Elias fetched firewood and laid out camp, Mitch and I climbed one of the nearby hills to scan the surrounding area with binoculars.

The area we were in was the wildlife migration corridor between Etosha and the western Kaokoveld that in 1971 Ken Tinley had proposed as an alternative to the Odendaal Commision Plan. It was magnificent country, with steep-sided hills separated by broad yellow grass plains through which the dark green course of the Ombonde and its tributaries meandered. It was the classic Kaokoveld that I had told Mitch about when we first met, but it now seemed to be completely devoid of wildlife.

As there was still an hour of sunlight left, I decided to walk in a wide arc back to our camp. We had not gone far before coming across the dehydrated carcass of an elephant cow. The tusks had been cut out with an axe, a sure sign that it had been poached. Depressed by this reminder of the slaughter that had taken place in this beautiful place, we walked on in silence, each to our own thoughts. After about 20 minutes I noticed vultures in the mopane trees about a kilometre from us. As there had to be another dead animal we went to see what it was, this time finding the sprawling remains of a large male giraffe.

A quick examination of the carcass showed that some meat and a strip of skin had been cut from the neck, no doubt to make sandals. Where the vultures had not landed there were human footprints and the tracks of a horse and a number of donkeys. With the sun now close to the horizon, there was little we could do but return to the vehicle, where Mitch and Elias prepared dinner while I called Chris Eyre on my mobile radio to brief him on what we had found. Chris promised to come right away, and by following our vehicle tracks down the riverbed he and Lucas arrived at our campsite just after midnight.

Early the next morning we all returned to the giraffe carcass, where Elias and Lucas gave their interpretation of what had happened. As we were in Herero country, not far from where they had both been born, they quickly summed up the situation. The horse would have been ridden by the hunter, and the donkeys just used to carry the meat back to their village.

So as not to warn the poachers of our approach, we followed the clear donkey tracks on foot. They led straight to Otokotorue, a small village on the road from Kamdescha Gate to Sesfontein. Initially the inhabitants claimed to have no knowledge of the dead giraffe, but when bags of dried game meat were found in one of the huts, there was little point in any further denials. However, they told us that the men who killed the giraffe were not in the village, having gone out early that morning on another hunt. While we waited for them to return, Chris and Lucas took statements from the men who carried the meat – itself an offence – establishing that a second giraffe and a gemsbok had also been poached.

Around midday two men, one carrying a .303 rifle, rode into the village. Their latest hunt had been unsuccessful, but Chris had already gathered more than enough evidence to convict them of illegally killing the giraffe. The older of the two, Adam Tjikwara, took full responsibility for planning the hunt, claiming that he had asked his accomplice, Chris Kangombe, to accompany him. With both men having admitted guilt, we all sat down to have a cup of tea and hear their story of what had happened.

Adam told us that he had borrowed the horse from a neighbouring village with the aim of hunting giraffe, and had sent Chris out on it to run one down. Chris then gave his side of events: 'I chased the giraffe until it got too tired to run anymore. I didn't have a rifle so I tried to kill it by throwing rocks at it. I hit it here and here,' he said, patting himself on the chest and biceps, 'and a rock also knocked out its right eye. But it still wouldn't fall down so I had to come back here and get a rifle to finish it off.'

It was not a pretty story, but Elias reminded us that the people in the area had lost most of their cattle in the drought and their main concern was for their families, not the giraffe. From his perspective, the two hunters had merely been thrifty, getting the maximum benefit with the minimum expenditure of their ammunition.

While Chris took the two accused to Khorixas, where they would be formally charged, Mitch, Elias and I went to inform their headman, Keefas Muzuma, a policy we had agreed to after our first poaching case. We also believed it was important for the traditional leaders of any men caught hunting illegally to attend their trials, so that they would hear the evidence against them and report back to their families that they had been fairly convicted, as well as what sentence they were given.

After listening to our explanation of the events at Otokotorue, Keefas expressed his regret for what had happened. He knew both the arrested men well and was surprised to hear that they were still hunting, even though he had asked his people to stop. Choosing his words carefully, he then told the group of men sitting around us that Chris Eyre had acted correctly, and that the two poachers would now have to bear the consequences of their actions. Before leaving I promised to inform the headman of the trial date, and arrange for a vehicle to take him and any of his councillors to Khorixas.

As the younger accused was the patrilineal nephew of Joshua Kangombe, Keefas Muzuma's sub-headman in Warmquelle, I next went to inform him of the case. I had got to know Joshua in the 1960s, when he was in charge of the cattle trespassing in the western part of Etosha, and he was one of the first traditional leaders I went to see upon my return. I had then reminded him of his promise to stop his followers from hunting while they were in the game reserve, and he assured me he had done his best, but that 'when a man has no cattle left, his stomach is the only thing he listens to.'

Joshua thanked me for bringing him the news about his nephew and Adam being arrested, and that evening called his councillors together to tell them what had happened. Elias attended the meeting, and the following morning he told me that Joshua had emphasised that the law against killing game did not come from the whites, but from their own headmen. I was very gratified by this. He and Keefas were key Herero leaders and their support was crucial to stopping the poaching.

At their trial the two men from Otokotorue both pleaded guilty, but in mitigation Adam claimed to have killed the giraffe to feed his six children. However, as they had left so much meat on the carcass the magistrate was unmoved, and sentenced them both to a fine of R1 200, or 12 months in jail, as well as confiscating the rifle they had used. They were given six weeks to raise the money. As Adam left the courtroom he walked past Mitch, and with a sad smile said: '*Muhona,* that was a very expensive giraffe.'

The NWT could chalk up another two convictions, but once again we were just lucky to be in the right place at the right time. We had also lost two giraffe and probably a lot more game killed by Adam and his accomplice before that. On the positive side, Chris and I were working well together, and by keeping the local traditional leaders informed of our activities, had started to develop a good relationship with them. But I wanted more than just their passive support. There had to be a way of getting them actively involving in stopping the poaching.

*   *   *

After the final hearing of the Humu brothers' case I brought Joshua Kangombe back from Khorixas, and as it was late in the evening we spent the night at Wêreldsend. Over dinner he and I again discussed the situation in the region. Although there was now plenty of grazing, with so few cattle left his people still had very little milk to live on. At Warmquelle the irrigated gardens were also giving poor yields, and as a result everybody was hungry. 'It is easy for us who have full stomachs to talk about protecting wild animals,' Joshua said, 'but it is hard for a man to put his firearm away if his children are hungry.'

When the Namas in Sesfontein had plundered their livestock, those who did not seek refuge in Angola survived by hunting, and since then the Kaokovelders had always been allowed to kill wild animals for food or to protect their livestock. But now men were being sent to jail for something they

had always done in times of need. Although Joshua told me he understood
the reason for this, most of his followers did not. If he called his councillors
together when we got back to Warmquelle, would I explain the new conservation laws to them, and tell them why it was now necessary to stop hunting?

The meeting, held under a tree at Joshua's *onganda,* was attended by about
20 senior men, many of whom were the stockowners who had taken their
cattle into western Etosha during the 1970 drought. At that time they had
threatened to go to war if the government tried to move them out again. The
problem had been solved by the west of the Park being de-proclaimed, and
like Keefas's followers they had not forgotten my sympathetic handling of the
situation. I hung my case for conservation on this.

After recognising the hardship the drought had brought, I reminded them
that when their cattle needed grazing they were given it on land that had been
set aside for the wild animals. Now the wildlife needed their help. People
were killing it for food and money, and if this continued soon there would
be nothing left for their children to see or live from. Therefore, they had two
choices: to carry on hunting until it was finished or 'tighten their belts' and
allow wildlife numbers to increase, so that in the future it could be used again,
but this time in a sustainable way.

I went on to say that the old laws on hunting in the homelands were made
by people in South Africa, who did not see the value of wild animals. These
laws were weak and many people had abused them, including government officials who hunted wastefully. However, the game laws for the white farms had
been written in Windhoek and were much better, and there was still plenty
of game on them. Because of this their owners were allowed to hunt kudu,
gemsbok, springbok and warthog for meat, as well as to sell them for money.

After the 1978 elections the new government had decided that there should
only be one nature conservation law for the whole country, but as the game
numbers were so low in the homelands the people there had not been given
the right to use it. However, it did allow the Director of Nature Conservation
to issue hunting permits in the places where the wildlife was well protected,
and if they now helped us stop the poaching, when the game numbers had
increased Chris Eyre and I would request permission for them to be allowed
to hunt again.

In the discussion that followed all the men who spoke agreed that there
was a need for conservation. They and their ancestors had always lived with
wild animals and they would be sorry if they disappeared for ever. However,
this did not include the species 'with claws' that preyed on their livestock,

which they should still be allowed to kill. Although they were sceptical about the government allowing them to hunt in future, by the end of the meeting there was consensus that the poaching must stop.

After the meeting Joshua's wife brought Elias and me a cup of sweet tea and we carried on talking about the wildlife situation. I told Joshua I was very encouraged by the words of his councillors, but would everyone in the community listen to them? Many would, Joshua replied, but not all of them. He believed that the hunting could only be stopped if the government stationed many more people in the Kaokoveld. This was very unlikely to happen, I replied, and even if they did the poachers knew the bush much better than the school-educated men the DNC employed.

Joshua agreed: 'The nature conservation officials are always in a hurry, and they just drive on the main roads. Everybody knows when they come here, so the poachers stay at home. When they go back to Khorixas they start hunting again.'

'So we both know the government cannot stop the poaching on their own,' I said. 'We need your help.'

'What can I do?' Joshua replied. 'I have no vehicle so it is not possible for me to see what my people are doing behind the mountains.'

When June and the boys left Wêreldsend I had bought myself a pipe. Slang, Chris, Lucas and Elias all sucked on theirs when the going got tough or they had to consider a serious problem. As Joshua also smoked a pipe I passed my tobacco to him and we all puffed silently for a while, thinking about what could be done.

The tracking skills and local knowledge of his people would be invaluable to us, while they in turn needed food to feed their families. I asked Joshua if he would be willing to select some reliable men from amongst his followers to patrol the areas where wildlife still occurred. In return for this service I would request the NWT Board to give them a monthly ration of maize meal and other basic supplies.

After thinking about it for a while, Joshua reminded me that not everyone in Warmquelle was a poacher, and if those that were had enough food for their children to eat, they would also stop hunting. Before we needed to refill our pipes, we had come up with a simple solution that would change the face of nature conservation in Namibia's communal areas, and have an impact far beyond their borders.

There were still details to be worked out. Most importantly, I did not want the men to work for us or the DNC. The traditional leaders should be responsible for conserving the wildlife in the areas under their jurisdiction, and this would only happen if they had the authority to supervise, and if necessary reprimand or replace a man who did not perform well. As they knew their people much better than we did, they were also more likely to choose the right people. If Chris or I selected them, and they failed to carry out their duties, the responsibility would be ours for having appointed an unsuitable person.

As game guards appointed by a traditional leader would not have any legal authority, Joshua and I agreed that their primary role was to carry the conservation message to the people living around them. For this reason I recommended that he choose mature men who were well respected in their local communities. Nevertheless, they would be required to undertake regular patrols, on foot or on donkeys, to record where and what wildlife still occurred in their areas.

Apart from keeping their headmen informed, 'community game guards' would be required to give a monthly report to the NWT staff member delivering their rations. These should include the game or spoor seen, carcasses found and the cause of death, as well as any suspicious human activities. Where and when they patrolled would be left for them to decide, as they knew the ways of local poachers better than we did.

At the NWT trustees meeting in June, I presented our plan to create a system of community game guards chosen by and working for their own traditional leaders. Most of the board members did not believe local people would ever give us information about illegal hunting, and at first it was turned down. But this time Ina gave me her full support, and as none of the trustees were prepared to oppose her, it was agreed that I could give a maximum of R50-worth of rations to six game guards for a trial period of one year.

With approval to appoint so few men, I decided that the priority was to protect the Uniab and Hoanib catchments, where the most elephant and rhino still occurred. At our next meeting, Joshua and I decided to place four of them to the north and east of this critical area, the direction from which all of the commercial poachers arrested up till then had come. The other two would be selected from communities in western Kaokoland, to monitor the few rhino and giraffe that still survived there. No community game guards would be appointed south of the veterinary fence, as this part of Damaraland could be patrolled by the DNC staff in Khorixas and by Blythe, Peter and me from Uchabmond and Wêreldsend.

The men chosen by Joshua were his brother, Hosia Kangombe, at Otokotorue, the home of the Ombonde giraffe poachers, and Elias Mosia at

Okomimunu, where many elephant and rhino had been killed in late 1981. To select the community game guards around Sesfontein, Joshua recommended that we approach his counterpart there, Headman Goliat Kasaona, whose eldest son had been convicted of poaching the rhino cow on Palm. After listening to our plan to appoint local people as guardians of the wildlife, and how they would operate, Goliat and his councillors also gave it their full support. To cover the lower Hoanib River they chose Sakeus Kasaona at Otjindakue and Abraham Tjavara at Ganumub, on the south-eastern edge of the Giribis Plain.

Appointing community game guards in western Kaokoland was more difficult. Vetamuna Tjambiru was the headman of the area around Orupembe, where at least two rhino still survived, but a recent upsurge in guerrilla activity around his home at Etanga prevented me from visiting him. Instead I made contact with the local sub-headman, Heova Tjiningire, who chose Tjahorerua Tjisuta from Orupembe on his behalf.

At Ina's request, the remaining post was given to Kamasitu Tjipombo, who had previously worked for Colin. At the time he was living with his wife and stepson at Ochams, a salty spring deep in the desert south of Orupembe, which apart from their small flock of goats was used by a few gemsbok, springbok and ostrich. I supported his appointment because Ina had been crucial to my getting the trustees' approval, and also because from Ochams he could cover the lower Khumib River, where most giraffe north of the Hoanib occurred. A few months later I was able to visit Etanga, where after listening to my explanation of the role that the community game guards would play, Headman Vetamuna approved the selection of both Kamasitu and Tjahorerua.

None of the community game guards chosen were literate, but to me this was an advantage as it meant they had not spent their youth in a classroom. Peter, Bennie or I could record their verbal reports when delivering their monthly rations, but we could not replace the bushcraft skills they had learned while growing up herding livestock. Because they were from the local community I also had no doubt that if any poaching took place near to where they lived they would know about it – but would they inform us? It was not long before we got the answer.

On my September ration run Kamasitu reported that a giraffe had been killed near the Nadas River. He had heard about it from the grandchild of his sister, who had found a piece of giraffe skin hidden under a stone near Orupembe. On his donkey he had followed the tracks of the poachers back to where it was killed. When he took Elias and me there all that was visible was a large pile of ash on the open plains, but from them Kamasitu scratched out a large molar tooth, the only identifiable part of the carcass left after the inedible remains had been burned.

He then took us along the trail of the meat carriers to where they had stopped in a riverbed to cook a meal on their way back to Orupembe. Near this fireplace Kamasitu had also found a small sliver of what was clearly giraffe skin on the ground. Together with the burnt tooth, it was the only evidence we had that an animal weighing a ton and a half had been poached!

It was not enough to build a case on, but the game guard also knew who killed the giraffe; a renowned local hunter named Twetjavi Tjambiru. Not wanting to implicate Kamasitu any further I took him back to Ochams and returned a week later with Chris and Lucas. By then the suspect had got wind of our investigation and left the area, but Lucas and Elias soon learned that he was now living in the rugged mountains at the southern end of the Marienfluss – where the people of Orupembe assured us we would never be able to find him.

Although it had not been easy to get Chris to come so far for just a piece of skin and a tooth, he now saw the arrest of Twetjavi as a personal challenge. After getting all the information we could about his whereabouts, we drove to Okatapati, the closest place that could be reached by vehicle, and then set off on foot into the steep-sided granite ranges.

Four hours of hard walking later we had followed livestock paths to a small *onganda,* where a young girl told us that Twetjavi was asleep in one of the huts. When he was ordered to come out at first he refused, threatening to shoot anyone who tried to arrest him. Eventually he did emerge, pointing his rifle menacingly at Chris, who as always was armed only with his pipe. But Lucas and I had him covered, and realising that he was outgunned, he handed over his weapon and accompanied us to Opuwo, where he was formally charged with poaching the giraffe.

When Twetjavi's case came to court he was found guilty and sentenced to a fine of R1 000 or one year in prison. However, on Chris's request all of it was conditionally suspended for five years. It had not been our intention to put a Himba in jail, only to make the point that hunting would no longer be tolerated by the government or their traditional leaders.

*   *   *

By late 1983, with the support of the Damara Representative Authority as well as the key Herero and Himba traditional leaders, we were in a much stronger position to stop the local people from poaching. And with so little game left in the region I hoped the white officials would also put their rifles away. Many did, at least temporarily, but a few of them still openly boasted that Chris would never catch them. One of the most brazen was Flip Els, a senior health inspector who had grown up on Marienphil, a farm that was expropriated under the Odendaal Plan and became part of the 'Five Farms'. As his job required him to make frequent trips into the field, I had no reason to doubt that his claim to be still hunting was true.

On a visit to Elias Mosia, the community game guard at Okumimunu, he told me that Flip Els had camped nearby and only left that morning. As I did not have the authority to search a vehicle I immediately returned to Wêreldsend and radioed Rudi, who sent John Knowles, a recently appointed nature conservator, and Filimon Nuab to accompany Elias and me on a follow-up.

At the Palmwag gate we learned that Els had made camp at the abandoned ANVO Safari base, within a kilometre of the veterinary fence. As he could not legally take raw meat across the Red Line, I suspected that one of his assistants might carry it over the fence, while he drove through the checkpoint and then picked the man up on the other side. Hoping to intercept the meat carrier, John and I spent the night on the bank of the Uniab River, the most likely place to cross the fence, while Elias and Filimon were sent to observe his camp from a nearby hill.

Early the next morning we heard Els's vehicle drive to the check-point, and a few minutes later two rifle shots echoed across the valley over our heads. The veterinary staff there must have tipped him off about our presence, and he was telling us that he knew where we were. By the time John and I got to the gate there was only a trail of dust on the road to Khorixas. He had won that round, and clearly shown us that whoever had the local people on their side would win the game. We were never able to catch Flip Els poaching, but one of his colleagues was caught twice – and the second case resulted from information provided by a community game guard.

Marius Visser, a junior health official under Els, lived next door to Chris Eyre in the Khorixas single quarters, and one Sunday afternoon Chris heard a series of clicks and tinkling noises coming from the other side of the thin wall dividing the two flats. Suspecting that it was the sound of someone cutting pieces of wire, the usual reason for which was to make hooks for hanging biltong, he invited himself into his neighbour's room and found a dead ostrich on the kitchen table. For this Visser was fined R500.

At the time we hoped that it would serve as a lesson to him, but in August the community game guard at Ganumub, Abraham Tjavara, showed me the tracks of a vehicle that had left the road and driven at high speed through the bush. The driver was Marius Visser, and it was clear he had been chasing a small herd of springbok. As we could find no evidence of him having killed anything I just asked the game guard to follow his vehicle tracks whenever he came back into the area.

A few weeks later, when Chris and I were on our way to Orupembe, Abraham showed us where Visser's truck had again left the road and travelled for seven kilometres across the Giribis plain. This time the spoor of a single springbok was visible running in front of the vehicle. At the point where he turned around the tracks ended, and although there was no sign of any blood, only some human footprints and a scuff mark in the sand, we were sure that the springbok had been killed. While Chris drove to Khorixas to question Visser's two assistants, I stayed to see what other evidence I could find.

From Abraham I learned that Visser had passed by Ganumub on his return trip late the same afternoon, and suspecting that he would have camped near Sesfontein, I went to see the community game guard there, Sakeus Kasaona. He showed me where Visser had slept that night, and on a nearby mopane tree we found marks where wire had been used to hang meat from. On the ground were drops of blood and a few long white hairs that could only have come from the back of a springbok.

I then returned to the Giribes plain and followed Visser's vehicle tracks from where they turned back onto the road and headed north towards Purros. After about 30 km they again turned off the road, this time into a rocky riverbed, where a little way downstream we found the remains of a fireplace. It looked like Visser had just stopped to make coffee or cook some food, but as we again found wire marks on an overhanging branch Sakeus dug beneath the ashes and uncovered the head, skin and feet of a female springbok, as well as a nearly full-term foetus. We now had hard evidence to base a case on, but Visser could still argue in court that the vehicle tracks we followed were not his.

That afternoon Chris returned with the two assistants, who were initially confident that we had no evidence against them. However, they became a little nervous when I said that someone had been watching them chasing the springbok from a nearby hill. To convince them we then followed their tracks across the Giribes to where the springbok had been loaded onto the truck and then on to where its remains were buried. Thanks to Abraham and Sakeus, the only thing we did not know was how it had been killed. But by now Visser's assistants believed our story and filled in this final detail for us. After being chased for such a long way the heavily pregnant female had died of exhaustion.

As it was Visser's second offence within six months, which meant that if found guilty he faced a possible jail sentence without the option of a fine, he hired Hennie Barnard, a lawyer with a formidable reputation of getting poachers off, to defend him. From his side, Chris knew that this was a case we could not afford to lose. Since 1982 he had brought a total of 12 illegal hunting or related cases to court, and 27 men had been found guilty. But apart from Visser, all of them had been black. If a white man was found not guilty in such a clear-cut case our credibility in the eyes of the local community would be seriously undermined.

Although the two assistants agreed to be State witnesses, I was concerned that they might be unnerved by Barnard's ruthless cross-examination tactics. However, when I met Chris in Khorixas on the evening before the trial I found that something else was worrying him. As was often the case in the circuit courts, the public prosecutor was a recent law graduate, with virtually no previous experience. But what made matters worse in his eyes was that the person whose competence would determine whether Visser was found guilty or not was a young woman.

On the evening before a trial it had become a habit for us to join the magistrate for a game of darts and dinner at the Khorixas Restcamp. Nothing directly relating to the case could be mentioned, but the general poaching situation in the area was often discussed, which gave some background to the evidence he would hear in court. On this occasion we also had the pleasure of Hennie Barnard's company, and although the young lady on whose shoulders Chris Eyre's reputation rested was not a darts player, she gamely joined in the fun.

However, it was soon apparent that the young prosecutor was very much in awe of the prestigious legal eagle she would be opposing in court the next day, which did not impress my confirmed bachelor colleague – but worse was to come. After dinner Hennie invited her to his bungalow on the pretext of showing her some 'legal precedents'. By now Chris was beside himself with fury, and when she finally headed for her own room he was waiting for her. From a distance I watched as he waved his old pipe in her face and gave her a stern lecture on the correct relationship between a prosecutor and defence lawyer on the night before a trial.

But Chris needn't have worried. His investigation was too thorough and the witnesses too reliable for Barnard to get his client off. Visser was found guilty of poaching the springbok, as well as hunting it by illegal means, and fined a total of R1 500. Together with the very high legal fees he would have had to pay, it was undoubtedly the most expensive springbok he had ever eaten – but Hennie Barnard had saved him from going to jail.

The Visser case was a major breakthrough, and sent a clear message to the old guard in Khorixas that hunting in the homelands was now a risky sport. It was also the first time in Damaraland that a local resident had brought about the arrest and conviction of a white government official for poaching. Remembering my days in the Kaokoveld under Commissioner Beesie Jooste, this gave me considerable satisfaction.

It had not taken long for the community game guards to prove their value, but equally important was the support given to us by their traditional leaders. An example of this was another giraffe poaching case uncovered by Kamasitu Tjipombo, this time in the Khumib River. The trail of our main suspect led us to Etanga, but as we entered the village we had to stop for a puncture, which alerted him to our arrival and gave him time to take off into the surrounding mountains. Instead of trying to track him down I just reported the case to Headman Vetamuna Tjambiru, who after conferring with his councillors assured us that the man we were looking for would be at our camp by early the next morning. In fact, shortly after sunset he was brought to us by a tribal policeman and readily admitted his guilt.

On this occasion I was again accompanied by Sakeus Kasaona, who had become my right-hand man after Elias decided to return to the family farm. Sakeus's place as a community game guard was taken by Salmon Karutjaiva, who lived at Otjatjondjira on the eastern edge of the rugged ranges through which the Hoanib River had cut its spectacular gorge west of Sesfontein.

*   *   *

In late 1983 Chris appointed another game ranger in Damaraland, Duncan Gilchrist, who with his wife Ruth arrived on a motor-scooter carrying with them just about everything they owned. A Namibian of Scots decent, Duncan was a stocky, hard-drinking and smoking man, with an 'in your face' attitude that would not have been out of place in a Glasgow pub. Swiss-born Ruth was soft-spoken and gentle, but had a passionate love of wild Africa.

As Duncan had previously worked for ANVO Safaris and been based at Palmwag, he was given responsibility for patrolling the concession area from Sesfontein with a young Damara game ranger, Augustinus Ochams. In early 1984 the first nature conservator to actually live in Kaokoland, Arno van Niekerk, was appointed in Opuwo. Less than two years earlier the DNC presence in the north-west, outside of the Skeleton Coast Park, had consisted of just Chris and Lucas. Now there were two senior nature conservators, three game rangers and two labourers.

Although Peter Erb went back to university at the end of 1983, Bennie and Sakeus were still with me. But most importantly, we now had the active support of the main Herero traditional leaders in the south and west of Kaokoland, as well as the six game guards they had selected. With their local knowledge and permanent presence on the ground in the key wildlife areas, we were now able to get convictions virtually every time a carcass was found – in some cases long after the animal was killed.

At the end of the community game guard system's first year I wrote a report to the Endangered Wildlife Trust on its achievements. In it I stated:

1. Between July 1983 and September 1984 a total of fourteen cases of suspected illegal hunting were reported in Kaokoland and Damaraland. Eight of these cases were picked up by the community game guards [CGGs], two by Peter Erb, one by Arno van Niekerk and one by game ranger Duncan Gilchrist.

2. The majority of the cases uncovered by the CGGs would almost certainly not have been found by conventional anti-poaching patrols. It was only because the CGGs lived in the area that they were tipped off by the local people.

3. During the follow-up investigations of a number of these cases the CGGs played a valuable role in the interrogation of witnesses and suspects, while their thorough knowledge of the area and people has enabled us to quickly track down persons wanted for questioning.

4. Apart from actual poaching cases picked up, the CGGs have also kept us informed of vehicle traffic in their areas, visiting parties on donkeys, game movements, the state of waters (including a considerable number of natural water-points not previously on our maps) and a variety of other information that has indirectly assisted with our anti-poaching work.

5. To date the CGGs have handed in five rhino horns and six

elephant tusks that were either picked up by themselves during foot patrols or were found by other local residents and reported to them. All horns and ivory have been handed in to DNC staff. A number of other previously unknown rhino and elephant carcasses from which the horns had been removed were also found by the CGGs and shown to myself or DNC staff.

6. Probably the most important role of the CGGs in anti-poaching is, however, their acting as a deterrent both to the local population, who know they are being closely watched by people who have a sound knowledge of the area, and also to non-resident government officials etc, who are aware that the CGGs exist but are not sure of their whereabouts. The fact that one of 'the locals' standing casually on the side of the road or herding his goats in the bush might be reporting their movements to us and the DNC makes illegal hunting a decidedly more risky occupation.

But the community game guard system should not just be seen as an anti-poaching force. By its active involvement of the rural population of western Kaokoland and NW Damaraland it can make an even greater contribution to the cause of nature conservation in the area. … Furthermore, by always working closely with the headmen, and insisting that all investigations in which we are involved are carried out with respect for human dignity (even the actual poacher's) we have reduced the possibility of local antagonisms developing… Over the past year we have, in fact, been able to create an environment of general trust and respect so that in all our contacts with the local population the D/K Project staff's words and deeds are judged rationally and not with the prejudice we would have been accorded if we had worked in isolation from the people, and therefore been regarded as outsiders. In short, we have now created a sound environment in which meaningful extension work can now be carried out.

I concluded the report with a breakdown of how much the CGGs cost in their first year of operation: R5 085 in rations and R760 for cash allowances, as well as jackets, boots, water bags and four donkeys donated by Rössing Uranium, Swakopmund Tannery, and a private individual. There were also the indirect costs of visiting the game guards to deliver rations and collect their reports. All told, operating expenses were under R10 000.

CHAPTER TWENTY-ONE

CONSERVATION AND POLITICS

In February 1984 I attended a workshop on rhino conservation that was organised by the Endangered Wildlife Trust in the Pilanesberg National Park. On my
way back through Windhoek, Peter Böttger, Chairman of the NWT's Board of
Trustees, asked me to come to his office. After thanking me for my hard work and
complimenting all of the staff on the successes that had been achieved, he told
me that the Damaraland/Kaokoland Project would be closing down on 31 March,
exactly two years after we had started operations. Bennie, Sakeus and I would be
given a month's notice, and we should all take whatever leave was due to us in
the next six weeks. He also asked me to inform Joshua Kangombe and the other
headmen who had appointed community game guards that the NWT would stop
supplying them with rations and cash allowances at the end of March.

As we were getting on top of the poaching, and with the support of the
local traditional leaders now had a chance of stopping it altogether, I was
more than a little disappointed. But the news was not entirely unexpected.
Nearly a year earlier the Director of Nature Conservation had announced
that they were negotiating with the Damara Representative Authority with
the aim of re-proclaiming ANVO Safaris' hunting concession, and thereby
linking Etosha with the Skeleton Coast Park.

It was an exciting prospect, and all of us in the field had wished the two parties success in their discussions, but I did not see it as a reason to relax our anti-poaching efforts. In fact, my concluding paragraph in the next quarterly report had warned: 'Because elephant and rhino populations in Damaraland are so low, it is critical that our control over poaching be maintained. A mere decade ago we heard about the proclamation of a great new game reserve in Kaokoland, when the numbers of these two species were still very healthy. But today their populations have been decimated, and we do not want the same thing to happen again.'

Working on the assumption that the negotiations would be successful, the NWT's sub-committee appointed to oversee the Damaraland/Kaokoland Project had come up with two alternatives for our future operations: a continuation of present activities, but focusing on Kaokoland, or carrying out a conservation education programme in the region. I had then drawn up a proposal for the former option, as well as a motivation for all of our field staff to remain in Damaraland until the proclamation actually took place and the new game reserve was adequately staffed by government nature conservators. But I had not taken into account the continuous pressure being put on the NWT trustees by the DNC, and in spite of the best efforts of Barry Clements and Dan Craven, the decision had been taken to cease operations and move out of Wêreldsend.

After their first public announcement the DNC had remained confident that the western part of the old Etosha would be re-proclaimed, but locally we knew that the discussions were not going so well. In fact, within a week of my meeting with Peter Böttger, the new DNC director, Polla Swart, gave a press interview in which he admitted that the negotiations 'had broken down and that the concession zone would thus not be proclaimed in the near future'.

Clearly scapegoats were needed, and in early March Chris Eyre was informed that he was transferred to Keetmanshoop. The NWT chairman was also told that our activities in the region had 'complicated the sensitive situation', and as the government had appointed more officers in both homelands our presence was no longer needed. But what were the real reasons for the failure of the negotiations? To find out, we must go back to before the ANVO hunting concession was granted, and also delve into political events at the time.

In 1970, when the Odendaal Commission recommendations were implemented, the newly created homelands of Damaraland and Kaokoland became a hunter's paradise for the resident government officials, visiting cabinet ministers and SADF soldiers. Together with the local people they had virtually wiped out the wildlife north of the Hoanib River, but north-western Damaraland, which had previously been part of Etosha, remained well stocked with big game deep into the 1970s.

At the time, South West Africa was taking its first tentative steps towards independence, albeit in the framework of Pretoria's internal settlement plan. In 1976 the constitutional conference held in the old Windhoek Turnhalle reached an agreement that was a compromise between the unitary state de-manded by the outside world, and the 'independent' homelands envisaged by the Odendaal Commission.

In July the following year Jannie de Wet, acting in his capacity as Commissioner General of the country's indigenous people, had established the Damara Representative Authority (DRA). Although this happened after the Turnhalle Conference agreed that nature conservation should be a first-tier government function, the new ethnic authority was given responsibil-ity for wildlife in the homeland. The significance of this became apparent in April 1978, when the DTA-supporting chairman of the DRA granted a 10-year trophy hunting concession to Damaraland Safaris Ltd. The full share capital of the new company was held by Otjiwa Game Reserve, a subsidiary of the General Development Company of Namibia – in which Jannie de Wet was one of the directors.

When journalists uncovered the link between the Damaraland hunting concession and De Wet a media storm broke out, in which both the Damara traditional leadership under Chief Justice //Garoeb and the South African parliamentary opposition demanded that it be cancelled. It was also found out that the General Development Company was owned by a South African tycoon, AP du Preez, who was known as the 'fish king' because of the fortune he had made from grossly over-exploiting SWA's marine resources. What would prevent the same thing from happening to Damaraland's wildlife?

Du Preez defended having obtained the concession in a press release, stat-ing that the numbers of animals hunted or caught would be subject to an annual quota established in consultation with the DNC, and that the Damara Representative Authority would receive 50 per cent of the annual profits. A condition of the concession was that intensive patrolling of the area would be undertaken to safeguard the area from poaching, and Damaraland Safaris would make a financial contribution to these security measures, and the peo-ple of Damaraland would be trained to fulfil these duties.

Nevertheless, because of the controversy, Damaraland Safaris was forced to sub-contract the hunting concession to ANVO Safaris, owned by Volker Grellmann, who assured the public that there would be no culling of game in the homeland. He also stated that no endangered species would be hunted unless the particular animal posed a threat to people or property, and added that ANVO's aim was to leave the area as unspoiled as possible. His main role would be to protect the game and to combat poaching, and an extensive survey would be conducted in Damaraland before any safari hunting took place.

Grellmann's known commitment to conservation, as well as the fact that he was a member of the International Association of Professional Hunters, the World Wildlife Fund and a founder member of the SWA Professional Hunters and Guides Association, placated most of the critics of hunting in the homeland. But not everyone: Dan Craven obtained a copy of an advert for ANVO's Damara Big Game Trails in *Hubertus: Internationale Jagd, Fischerei und Touristik Reisen,* in which cheetah, leopard, lion, elephant and black rhino – all of them regarded as locally endangered species – were offered as trophies. The cost to hunt them: US$700, $700, $1 180, $1 690 and $3 950, respectively.

In 1980 second-tier government elections were held for the first time in Damaraland, and won by the Damara Council led by Chief Justice //Garoeb. Within his political party he had gathered together a group of traditional leaders and prominent local businessmen who were all staunchly opposed to Pretoria's policies in Namibia. In response, the DTA-dominated central government in Windhoek disputed the election results and called for a re-run, which finally took place in 1982. However, in spite of a vicious smear campaign against the Damara Council, it won by an increased margin.

Justice //Garoeb studied law at the University of Zululand and returned to Damaraland in 1968 to complete his articles under the Bantu Affairs Commissioner. He would later write that: 'Because the policy which I was to pursue was not compatible with my own philosophy on human development I resigned and become a traditional leader.' This in turn led him to a career in politics under the banner of the Damara Council, which was established in 1972 as an autonomous body. After the 1980 election it would remain in power in the homeland until Namibia's independence.

From the 1970s the Damara Council had discouraged settlement in the old western Etosha, believing it to be unsuitable for agriculture and marginal for animal husbandry. However, as elephants and predators caused problems for the farmers in Khovarib and Sesfontein, they sought other ways in which the local people could benefit from the area. Initially they asked the government to establish a 'private people's park' in the ANVO concession, but as there was no legislation to support this, their request was turned down. The DNC then came up with a counter-proposal to proclaim the area as a national park, and to share the revenue with the second-tier authority, which led to the negotiations in 1983.

The DNC's negotiating team consisted of Stoffel Rocher, Dr Peet van der Walt, recently appointed Director of Research, and Danie Grobler, who was in charge of all the northern homelands. Although Chris Eyre was not part of the negotiations, he took them very seriously, and insisted that the NWT must 'keep its nose out.' Not wanting to jeopardise the outcome, I promised not to meet with members of the Damara Executive Committee until after the discussions were concluded. As they dragged on for more than six months, this negatively affected my relationship with them, because I focused all my attention on the community game guards and they concluded I was favouring the region's Hereros.

At the first round of talks the DNC representatives made it clear that as conservation was a first-tier government function, the Park would have to be under their control. However, they were prepared to give 25 per cent of the gate fees to the second-tier authority. This was not acceptable to the Damara Executive Committee, as it would mean giving up nearly a third of the land allocated to their people by the Odendaal Commission, for a relatively small financial return. Nevertheless, Chief //Garoeb agreed to take the DNC's proposal back to the other traditional leaders before a second meeting, at which the benefit issue and how the area might be jointly managed would be discussed.

After the first meeting both parties stated that the discussions had been positive, although no agreement had yet been reached. Unfortunately, this led some people in the DNC to become over-confident, and on 10 April the influential Afrikaans Sunday newspaper, *Rapport*, ran a front-page article heralding an 'awesome game park for Southwest' that would link the Skeleton Coast Park with Etosha, making it one of the biggest game reserves in the world. When contacted by their reporter, Chief //Garoeb had stated that the area allocated would not include the 'Five Farms', which the DRA wanted to develop as its own game reserve.

The DNC's next step was to negotiate with Volker Grellmann to cancel the remaining five years of his trophy hunting concession in Damaraland. These discussions were held behind closed doors, and on 17 June the *Windhoek Advertiser* carried a front-page report by Jean Fischer under the

headline: 'Blanket of silence over ANVO negotiations'. But she did find out
that Grellmann claimed to have invested between R250 000 and R350 000
in the area 'for game control, feeding and other aid projects for the benefit of
the people and wildlife of Damaraland'. He also told the reporter that he had
stopped all hunting in his concession since August 1981, apart from assisting
local farmers by killing problem lions.

Eventually, 'in the interests of the area being given better protection',
Grellmann agreed to an amount of R50 000 being paid as compensation for
the five remaining years of his concession, and R13 000 for his hunting camp
at Palmwag. As the DNC had no budget to cover the cost of buying ANVO
Safaris out, they approached the SA Nature Foundation, which agreed to give
them the R63 000 needed 'on condition that they could guarantee the concession area would be proclaimed in the near future'. Confident they had got over
the most difficult part of the negotiations – with Volker Grellmann – they
assured SANF Chairman Dr Anton Rupert that this would happen, and Peet
van der Walt even stated on the local TV station that the Park would soon be
proclaimed.

On 12 November, *The Star* also carried an article stating that: 'Two major
new game reserves in South Africa and Namibia – both potential national
parks – have been proclaimed in the last four weeks with surprisingly little
fanfare.' But the Namibian game reserve had not been proclaimed. In fact, after a second meeting between the two parties they were still far from reaching
an agreement. To the Damara Council the DNC's proposal of a national park
would result in their losing control over a renewable natural resource that
could in the future be of benefit to the inhabitants of the area. Consequently,
they asked the central government to either provide replacement land,
or agree to a joint venture whereby they would share the revenue 'as equal
partners'.

I knew that the DRA representatives were angered by the press and TV coverage, which presumed that because ANVO Safaris had been bought out the
proclamation of a national park could now go ahead. To keep the talks from
breaking down completely, the Administrator General, Dr Willie van Niekerk,
was called in to mediate, but in February 1984 his office issued a press release
stating: 'The Executive Committee of the Damara Representative Authority
has turned down an offer by the AG to develop 950 000 ha of Damaraland
as a conservation area.' In the *Windhoek Advertiser* the following day, Polla
Swart was quoted as saying he was very disappointed, but that all was not lost,
as a joint planning committee composed of Damara Administration leaders

and the Directorate of Nature Conservation was preparing projects for developing key tourist attractions in Damaraland.

As the Damara Administration comprised the mainly white civil servants in Khorixas, Swart's comments gave the impression that in future the DNC would not be working with the homeland's elected black leaders. In a subsequent edition of the *Windhoek Advertiser*, Chief //Garoeb also took exception to the suggestion that any offer had been made to 'buy the land'. He then told the reporter that serious differences of opinion existed between his Representative Authority and the Directorate of Nature Conservation, and that 'parting with the traditional land of his people would have far reaching political implications'.

When the DNC finally admitted that their plans to proclaim the concession area had been shelved, they were faced with having to explain what had gone wrong to Dr Rupert, as well as paying back the R63 000 the SA Nature Foundation had given them. Someone had to be blamed for the breakdown of the negotiations with the Damara Executive Council, and as both Chris and I had a good relationship with them we were the obvious candidates.

*   *   *

Although the NWT had bowed to the pressure exerted on them by the DNC, they did not pay my salary, so in early April Clive Walker and a high-level EWT delegation flew in to Wêreldsend to discuss the situation with me. By then it was unlikely that the concession area would be proclaimed in the near future, and recognising the danger of prematurely withdrawing from the region, they agreed to take over the running costs of the Project, including the community game guard rations and cash allowances, until the end of 1984. Further support would be reviewed in the light of how effectively the newly appointed DNC staff were able to keep the poaching under control.

Bennie, Sakeus and I had been given a temporary reprieve, but Chris was not so lucky. Although he was able to get a few weeks' postponement of his transfer, in mid-April he left for Keetmanshoop. It was a bitter reward for his outstanding service to conservation in Damaraland. In my last NWT quarterly report I paid tribute to the work that he had done in the three years he was based in Khorixas:

Prior to his arrival, poaching in the region was totally out of control and the surviving herds of big game were being exterminated at an alarming rate by both licensed and illegal hunters. At that time, it seemed inevitable that the once abundant wildlife of Damaraland would soon be wiped out – as had happened in the adjoining territory of Kaokoland.

After carefully assessing the situation, Chris and his able assistant, Lucas Mbomboro, set about turning it around. That they eventually achieved this was due primarily to Chris' quiet but relentless determination in following up poaching cases, as well as his likable personality which won him the loyalty and support of all other persons concerned about nature conservation in Damaraland, and even in some cases made reformed converts out of old poachers.

Chris would be the first to agree that he had received help from many quarters, but all of us involved in conservation in this region know that without Chris our task would have been hopeless. In fact, because of his remarkable succession of convictions, most of us in the field came to take it for granted that when a poaching case was discovered Chris would apprehend the person, or persons responsible. This is of course not the normal state of affairs for, finding a case is only the first stage, from there simply getting an accused to court requires painstaking investigation and even then, convictions are by no means a formality. Chris' personal record of sixteen major poaching cases taken to court with nearly forty persons convicted and only one main accused having ever been acquitted, speaks for itself.

Another major achievement of SNC Eyre was his convincing the authorities in Damaraland that no hunting should take place in 1982 and 1983. This total ban on all hunting was essential for effective law enforcement to be carried out. Finally, the fact that in spite of the many prosecutions he has made, Chris is still a respected and well-liked member of the community is an indisputable tribute to the way in which he has carried out his investigations and to the success of his conservation extension work.

The complete breakdown of negotiations between the DNC and the Damara Authorities regarding the proclamation of the concession zone is a severe blow to nature conservation in the region. However, all is obviously not lost, for as the past few years have shown, with dedication a relatively small group of people can control if not completely eradicate illegal hunting. In fact, our past successes have now ironically created the situation where there is some complacency about the actual state of affairs, with some influential persons apparently believing that we can now relax our vigilance. Without exception, however, every one of us directly involved in the area is well aware that our control of the poaching here is very tenuous indeed. For this reason we find the transferring of an exceptionally capable and experienced senior nature conservator out of the area at this critical time totally beyond our comprehension.

Chris's position in Khorixas was filled by Marcellus Loots, a much younger man with considerably less experience, and none at all in a homeland. This meant that, in spite of there being more DNC staff in the region, apart from Lucas Mbomboro, all of them had either recently been appointed or were new in the area. But whether it was by conviction, persuasion or expediency, the majority of NWT trustees now believed that the fate of wildlife in the northwest should be the sole responsibility of the government. All the structures and equipment at Wêreldsend were donated to the DNC, and it was only with difficulty that the EWT was able to negotiate the continued use of the three 'shacks' that Bennie, Sakeus and the camp caretaker, Daniel Haraeb, lived in. Fortunately, I had bought my caravan from CDM, but the tin hut and roof extension that served as my living area, kitchen and office now belonged to the government.

* * *

Although the DNC considered the poaching in Damaraland and Kaokoland to be under control, it was certainly not the case in the rest of Africa. At the Pilanesberg workshop I attended in February 1984, Esmond Bradley Martin told the gathering that over two tons of rhino horn was leaving the continent annually, in spite of a CITES ban on cross-border trade. On the positive side, it was down from eight tons in the 1970s, but it still translated into at least 1 000 black rhino being killed every year – out of a total population that numbered just 13 500. He believed one of the reasons for the decline in illegal exports was that the species had now become scarce north of the Zambezi River, and warned us Southern Africans not to be complacent.

Bradley Martin also stated that the DNC in South West Africa was the only government agency still selling rhino horn, with 73 kg having been auctioned in 1982 and a further 99 kg in 1983. Eugene Joubert, who also attended the workshop, told us that the horn had come from natural mortalities and those confiscated in Damaraland after rhino poaching cases. He added that SWA was not a signatory to CITES, because it was not recognised by the international community as an independent country. Nevertheless, Eugene assured the meeting that no sales would take place in 1984 or thereafter. At the meeting it also came to light that the Natal Parks Board was still selling rhino horn, even though South Africa was a member of CITES.

There were many other disturbing anomalies regarding rhino conservation in Southern Africa. Major Dan Mathee of the South African Police told the meeting that a dangerous loophole had been created by the fact that each province, together with SWA, had its own legislation on specially protected game. As an example, because the Natal and Transvaal authorities did not believe they had a commercial poaching problem, the maximum sentence for killing a rhino or being in possession of rhino horn was very light, while in the Cape there was no legislation at all regarding the species. This meant that a person found there with a sack full of rhino horns could not be prosecuted, and as there were no border posts between South Africa and SWA, this made a mockery of the very high sentences recently introduced by Windhoek.

That evening Major Mathee told me that a few months previously Robbie Hawthorne in Keetmanshoop had been tipped off about a consignment of rhino horns from northern SWA that was being taken to South Africa by a Mr Lofty-Eaton. Robbie arranged for his truck to be stopped and searched, but nothing was found by the inexperienced nature conservator who had manned the road block. However, when Lofty-Eaton reached his destination in Natal, Major Mathee had set a trap for him that led to his arrest for illegally having nine rhino horns in his possession. Because the maximum sentence under the Natal provincial legislation was a fine of R500, which could be paid as an admission of guilt, Mathee had tried to get the case moved to SWA, where the horns had come from and the maximum sentence was six years in jail, or a fine of R6 000.

Faced with a heavy fine and the possibility of going to jail, Lofty-Eaton might have revealed where he had got the horns from in exchange for a lighter sentence. But because of the high cost of transporting witnesses to Windhoek, Mathee's request was turned down and the case heard in Natal. Lofty-Eaton pleaded guilty and paid a fine that bore no relationship to the black market value of the horns.

Peter Hitchins, a rhino specialist from Natal, told me of a case involving a Mr Pong, who was known to be a major buyer of rhino horns, which were then exported to Taipei in diplomatic bags through the Taiwanese embassy in Pretoria. When they were finally able to arrest him he was given a fine of less than R1 000. At the workshop, the national and provincial Parks Boards in South Africa assured the participants that they did not have a rhino poaching problem. So where did the horns come from?

At the time, large numbers of elephants and rhino were being killed in Zambia, and there were rumours that many of the tusks and horns were going via South African airports and harbours to Taiwan, the only eastern country with diplomatic and trade relations with the 'Apartheid State'. They were also able to enter the Republic undetected because the Southern African Customs Union allowed sealed containers to pass through the member countries and be transported unopened to the port of exit.

To my surprise, at the Pilanesberg workshop Eugene Joubert stated that 'there was no longer a poaching problem in South West Africa', and that the DNC's 'biggest headache was what to do with the Damaraland and Kaokoland black rhinos'. There was a need to disperse them, he said, and asked whether any could go to arid national parks in South Africa. I argued against this, saying that conserving them *in situ* should take precedence over translocation. I added that although rhinos belonged to the State, they were living on communal land and for this reason the Damara authorities should be included in any discussions about their future. I also disputed Eugene's assertion that the rhino population in Etosha was safe.

This last point was based on information I had received from Ian Hofmeyr, who told me that in late 1983, while on a helicopter survey of the north-west of the Park, he had found three poached rhino carcasses. A few months after the workshop, Ian arranged to meet Johan le Roux and me at Pieter Mostert's house in Windhoek, where he told us he had evidence of at least 12, and possibly as many as 17 rhino having been killed near Otjovasandu in the previous year. He also said his superiors had instructed him not to say anything about the situation – but most disturbing was that no special measures had been taken to stop the poaching!

In November 1984 Ian Hofmeyr was killed in a vehicle accident, and shortly thereafter the information he had collected on poaching in Etosha was released to the press. In reply the DNC only confirmed that four rhino had been killed and their horns removed. To Brian Jones, a reporter for the *Windhoek Advertiser*, Stoffel Rocher said the dead animals had been found near the western boundary, which runs close to the Kamanjab–Ruacana road, and that the persons responsible were probably 'incidental hunters who did not specifically aim to kill rhino'. Rocher added that Etosha's nature conservators had many other jobs to do and 'unless they are expecting trouble, they cannot concentrate on anti-poaching measures'. He also told Jones that allegations that 12 rhino had been poached were 'nonsense' and that someone had 'spent a lot of time sucking their thumb'.

In September 1986, nearly two years later, a limping rhino bull was seen from the air in western Etosha. When the animal was darted it was found to have five bullets in it. After the wounds had been treated an intensive aerial search of the area was carried out and the carcasses of another four rhino were found – all had their horns removed. Further investigations led to the arrest of five Herero-speaking residents of south-western Kaokoland. Two whites were also later charged for being in possession of rhino horns. How many more rhino had been killed in Etosha between 1983 and 1986? But more importantly, would they have been poached if Ian Hofmeyr's warnings had not been so arrogantly dismissed by his superiors?

By the mid-1980s conservation decisions were so intertwined with National Party policies that the DNC hierarchy's response to any report depended less on its contents than the politics of the person who made it. And just how right-wing they were at the time was shown by a case made against my old friend and colleague, Pieter Mostert. It stemmed from his not being prepared to take the minutes at the research section's annual professional officers meeting.

The reason he refused to do so was that it would take place at the Windhoek Teacher Training College, which still fell under the Administration for Whites and was the only tertiary education institution in the country that did not allow blacks onto its campus. This meant that only the DNC's white staff could attend the meeting, and although there were then no black researchers, Pieter was standing on principle. The matter could have been resolved internally, but his superiors were so incensed by his insubordination that they charged him in a court with 'dereliction of duty'.

In his defence, Pieter claimed that the venue for the professional officers' meeting was deliberately chosen 'to exclude blacks from attending' and that he regarded this as 'blatant racism and an insult to my black colleagues'. He also stated that the conference organisers had turned down the request of a University of Zululand lecturer to attend because of the Training College's policy. In his judgement Magistrate DF Small found him guilty, not of dereliction of duty, but of the lesser offence of misconduct. Nevertheless, Pieter knew that it was the end of his career in nature conservation, and when he was offered a transfer to veterinary services he took it.

* * *

In mid-1984 the EWT sent Dr Peter Mundy to evaluate our activities, and after spending two weeks in the field with us he wrote a very favourable report on our work. Over the next few months we were visited by members of the Damara Executive Committee, as well as the Directors of Agriculture and Education, and a week later by Nolly Zaloumis, now the President of the SA Wildlife Society, who was accompanied by its director of Conservation, Keith Cooper, and the chairman of the Wildlife Society's Namib Centre, Werner Liescher. As promised, in October Clive Walker flew in to assess the situation in Damaraland, this time accompanied by Anthony Hall-Martin, the National Parks Board elephant biologist, and Peter Hitchins, the Natal Parks Board black rhino specialist. It would have been hard to find better qualified people to decide on our future.

After I had taken them through the area they were all very complimentary about what had been achieved in combating poaching, and they saw no reason why the project should not continue. But when the EWT delegation paid a courtesy call on the DNC in Windhoek, they were told that the funding for Bennie, Sakeus and me was expected to stop at the end of the year. It was made clear to them that the matter was not negotiable, and that if their support for us was not withdrawn it would jeopardise any future co-operation with the DNC in SWA, as well as the National Parks Board in South Africa.

A few weeks later Clive regretfully informed me that his board had decided to stop supporting us at the end of December 1984. They would, however, continue to pay for the rations and cash allowances of the community game guards, but the funds would be channelled through Marcellus Loots in Khorixas, and Hilmar van Alphen, who had replaced Arno van Niekerk as the senior nature conservator in Kaokoland.

We had one last chance to 'postpone our execution'. As the DNC would be taking over our role of supporting the community game guards, it was crucial that the new situation be explained to them and their traditional leaders, while Van Alphen also needed to be formally introduced to the men he would now be working with in Kaokoland. Because of the long distances involved this would take some time, so Blythe approached the Wildlife Society's Namib Centre and asked them to pay Bennie, Sakeus and my salaries, as well as vehicle running costs for a further three months, which they agreed to do.

The value of our staying in the area became apparent even before the EWT's funding ended. In November, while Sakeus and I were on a ration delivery run, community game guard Kamasitu Tjipombo told us he was being harassed by Twetjavi Tjambiru, the man convicted of killing a giraffe northwest of Orupembe. As it was by now well known who had given us the information that led to his arrest, Twetjavi had resurrected an old debt Kamasitu's family owed him. But although it had originally been just a single heifer, he now claimed seven head of cattle, the number of calves the heifer could have produced since the debt was incurred. He also claimed ten goats from the grandfather of the young boy who found the giraffe's skin – because he had cooked and eaten a piece of it!

If Twetjavi were allowed to get away with this intimidation it could discourage other game guards from reporting hunting by local people in the future, so we set off to find him. This time it was not difficult, as he was visiting Sanitatas, but when I confronted him he was only prepared to reduce his claim against Kamasitu by two head of cattle. This was still not acceptable, so we decided to take the matter up with sub-headman Tjurungaha, who lived in the mountains near Okatapati. After getting directions to his *onganda* from some local men, Sakeus insisted on going alone to fetch him. A few hours later he returned with the sub-headman and five of his councillors, but they sided with Twetjavi and also refused to accompany us to the area's overall headman, Vetamuna Tjambiru.

When he had listened to the case Vetamuna apologised for his people's bad behaviour, and again assured us of his support for our efforts. He then promised to summon the troublemakers to his court in order to sort the problem out. On our next trip to northern Kaokoland we heard that he had fined all seven family heads in the Okatapati area two goats each for 'inconveniencing the people from nature conservation, who were acting on his behalf'. Twetjavi had also dropped his claims against Kamasitu and the young boy's grandfather.

In spite of the increased DNC staff in the north-west, the poaching had not stopped. In January Elias Mosia, one of the game guards appointed by Joshua Kangombe, found a local man behaving suspiciously near Okamborombonga spring in the eastern concession area. As he refused to say what he was doing in this still-uninhabited part of Damaraland, Elias followed him home and slept outside his hut that night. Realising the game guard was not going to leave him alone, the man eventually admitted to killing a zebra. Marcellus and Lucas were called in to investigate, and when they interrogated him established that he had also taken part in the hunting of a number of giraffe and a rhino! He claimed that the man behind the poaching was Moses Ganuseb, the ambulance driver at Sesfontein, but when Moses was taken to the carcass he denied any knowledge of it.

At this point I joined the investigation, and found that the original man arrested was one of the three men whose hunting camp we found near Otjondumbu in September 1982. As they had at the time told us they were working for Moses Ganuseb, I suggested that we fetch the other two men and question them all together. When confronted with all three of his workers insisting that he was the one who had organised the hunts – and kept most of the proceeds – Moses finally admitted guilt. He was convicted of poaching a rhino and three giraffe, and sentenced to three years and three months in prison or a fine of R3 500, the highest so far achieved in Damaraland. As two of his accomplices were second offenders they were sentenced to 18 months in jail or R1 500, and the third to six months or R500. Moses Ganuseb paid his fine and also kept his job as ambulance driver, a post that fell under Flip Els. It was a very large amount for a local person to pay, and I wondered where the money had come from.

In March a resident of Khovarib, Meesig Taniseb, informed Lucas that a steenbok had been shot in the irrigated gardens the government had set up for the local people. Meesig was himself a well-known poacher, but had stopped hunting because the game numbers were now so low. For this reason he was angry about the steenbok that everyone knew having been killed. Lucas, whose interrogation skills had by now earned him the nickname 007, followed up the case and established that the man had hunted many other animals, including a rhino more than a year before. By then I was without a job and had no vehicle, so played no part in the investigation, but it once again showed that with the local people's support, convictions for poaching were possible even long after the event.

*   *   *

Under the agreement Clive Walker had reached with the DNC hierarchy in Windhoek, the community game guard system would be maintained under the supervision of Marcellus in Damaraland and Hilmar van Alphen in Kaokoland, but no arrangement was made for Bennie and Sakeus. As they had both proved to be excellent field workers, in December I met with Polla Swart and Stoffel Rocher to discuss their positions. They assured me that posts would be found for them within the DNC. When this had not happened by April, I asked for another meeting. This time they denied having made any promises. Fortunately, the Damara Executive Committee also brought the matter up with the DNC, which resulted in Rudi creating a position for Sakeus at Sesfontein, and one for Bennie at Moewe Bay, in the Skeleton Coast Park.

In May I was offered a post in the Damara Administration by Martiens Boshoff, who had taken over from Johan Oosthuizen as head of the agriculture section. It would mean moving to Khorixas and becoming a civil servant again, but the main reason I turned it down was because it would restrict me to working in Damaraland, where Marcellus's team had developed a good relationship with the community game guards. In contrast, during my brief contact with Hilmar van Alphen he had shown no interest in working with the local people. Moreover, soon after arriving in Opuwo he shot an elephant accused of damaging fences in the unused Omatambo Mauwe quarantine camp. In my report to the Wildlife Society I wrote: 'It is sincerely hoped that SNC van Alphen is as quick to react to a poaching case as he has been to this elephant "problem".'

Without the protection of the EWT or Wildlife Society I had now become fair game for my enemies in the DNC. In June Marcellus arrived at Wêreldsend with a letter signed by Danie Grobler, demanding that I remove all my possessions from the camp infrastructure, which now belonged to the government. Although my caravan was not included, the tin hut attached to it was. As the camp had nine huts, and only two of them were used by DNC staff from Khorixas when they patrolled in the area, the letter was clearly aimed at getting me to leave. But did I have any options?

From a lawyer friend I ascertained that although I had used the structures for over three years there was no legal basis on which to fight the order. In desperation I decided to ask the advice of Simson Tjongarero. He was sympathetic, and a few days later came to see the layout of the camp. He briefed Chief //Garoeb, and the matter was tabled at the next Executive Committee meeting, where it was decided to come to my assistance. A letter was written to the DNC stating that if they so badly needed my hut, the DRA would purchase another one and erect it wherever they wanted. Coming after the acrimonious negotiations between the two parties over the proclamation of the concession area, the letter's ironic tone must have annoyed Van der Walt and Rocher, but no further attempt was made to remove me from Wêreldsend.

The DNC hierarchy was not the only enemy I had made. On the January ration trip to north-west Kaokoland the people at Orupembe told us that Twetjavi Tjambiru had put a spell on me that would prevent me from working in the area. However, when I spoke to him he was very friendly and said he wanted to give me a sheep as a present, but that I would have to fetch it at Okatapati on our next bi-monthly ration trip. Sakeus, for whom witchcraft was a part of everyday life, insisted that I should not take the spell lightly and recommended that I see an *onganga* to get it removed. As doing so would have acknowledged Twetjavi's power to intimidate us, I just shrugged it off.

Because of the Moses Ganuseb rhino poaching case I did not go on the March ration delivery run to north-west Kaokoland, and in April the SAVE Land Rover was given to Blythe for her use, leaving me without a 4x4 vehicle – fulfilling Twetjavi's spell. However, in May Angela Fisher, author of the classic book on African jewellery and decoration, *Africa Adorned*, and renowned photographer, David Coulson, visited me at Wêreldsend. As they were looking for a guide to take them to see the Himba, I jumped at the opportunity of going with them in their vehicle.

Along the way we met Kamasitu and Tjahorerua, who both complained that Van Alphen had just dumped their rations and driven away, without even getting a report from them. His lack of interest in the community game guards was disappointing, but even more disturbing was finding parts of a wheel, brake drum and battery belonging to a Buffel troop carrier that had detonated a land-mine on the road into the Marienfluss. As it was just before the turnoff to Okatapati, if I had done a ration run in March and gone to collect the sheep Twetjavi had promised me, it could have been pieces of my Land Rover lying next to the road – and it was not mine-proofed!

In 1982 a tourist guide, Norbert Magura, had driven his Land Cruiser over a mine at the rapids in the Marienfluss. Although the vehicle was badly damaged, he and his clients only received minor injuries and walked to the military base at Otjinungua. Here they received little sympathy, no doubt because Magura had repeatedly been warned not to bring foreign clients into the area. At the time it seemed unlikely that SWAPO guerrillas were operating so far west, and as he had driven along the same track a few hours before, I suspected that he had detonated an explosive device laid for him by the SADF. If so, their deterrent was effective, for from then on I was virtually the only civilian who went north of Orupembe. As I was also not wanted there could I have been the target, and the troops in the Buffel just happened to make an unauthorised trip to see this spectacular part of the region?

Sakeus had another theory, and told me that the reason he had insisted on my not going with him to fetch sub-headman Tjurungaha in November was because the local guide had warned him of the possibility that SWAPO guerrillas were at his village, and a white man going there would inevitably have provoked a shootout. As the Okatapati people 'had friends with landmines' Sakeus was convinced it was their revenge for the humiliation we had caused them. It would certainly have been a practical way for Twetjavi to ensure that the spell he put on me was permanent.

After the good 1984 rains there was a general deterioration of the security situation in northern Kaokoland. The rugged Baynes and Otjihipa mountains were an obvious infiltration route from south-western Angola, and local rumour had it that there was an almost permanent presence of PLAN fighters there. In their remote villages and cattle posts the pastoralists were in the middle of a war they had not started or fully understood, and were vulnerable to indoctrination and intimidation from both sides. If they gave food or shelter to the guerrillas they ran the risk of being beaten up by army or police counter-insurgency forces, while providing information to the SADF often provoked retribution from SWAPO. One of the worst cases of this was the brutal killing of Vetamuna's eldest son – presumably because the Himba headman was a strong supporter of the DTA, but I hoped it was not also because of the help he had been giving us to stop the poaching.

Extra-judicial executions were not restricted to the liberation forces. In spite of the difficulty of getting uncensored news out of Namibia's operational areas, in the mid-1980s the *Windhoek Advertiser*, under its iconoclastic editor Hannes Smith, published a series of eye-witness accounts of SADF and police prisoners being tortured to death. By the mid-1980s the liberal English-language media had become the only reliable source of information about what was really happening in Namibia and South Africa, but even they would soon be muzzled by draconian press censorship legislation.

In late 1984 I was visited by one of a new generation of journalists, who were breaking the law to keep the world informed about events in South Africa's urban townships. Tony Weaver and his soon-to-be wife, Liz Fish, spent ten days with me in the field, and on his return wrote two balanced and insightful articles on the role that local communities were now playing to conserve wildlife in Namibia's north-west. When I saw him a year later in

Cape Town, Tony had been charged under the suppression of terrorism act for reporting on the summary execution of seven alleged ANC guerrillas in Gugulethu, near Cape Town. Just as in Rhodesia during the later stages of the war, the South African security forces had taken the gloves off, and were now being allowed to do just about anything to protect the country from a 'total onslaught by the forces of communism' – which included plundering neighbouring countries' natural resources.

By the mid-1980s strong rumours were surfacing of elephants and other wildlife being decimated in south-east Angola, where South African forces were operating in support of UNITA. A few years later these allegations were given international credibility when Monitor, a consortium of environmental and animal welfare NGOs, made a statement to a US Congressional sub-committee claiming South Africa was a major transit route for ivory and rhino horn from Angola, Zaïre, Zambia, Mozambique and Tanzania, and that it was occurring 'with the complicity of South African officials at the highest levels of government and the military'. According to the author, Craig van Noot, over 100 tons of ivory came into South Africa annually 'by road, sealed rail boxcars and on military and civilian transport planes that fly dozens of times a week delivering arms, medicine, food, machinery and other supplies throughout central and southern Africa'. He added that it 'was shipped out on aircraft or boats to Taiwan, a non-CITES nation that is rapidly replacing Singapore as the Far Eastern outpost for wildlife smuggling'.

The country most affected was Angola, the report said, where UNITA had killed up to 100 000 elephants to help finance its war against the MPLA, adding that 'South African four-wheel-drive trucks that carry war materials and other supplies across the Caprivi Strip to Savimbi's forces return laden with ivory and valuable tropical hardwood'. In Mozambique, the South African-supported RENAMO forces were also reported to have killed tens of thousands of elephants to help finance their insurrection. Pretoria rejected the accusations, but in its final years of rule the National Party was used to covering up its covert activities. And as was the case with many State-sanctioned murders of political opponents, it was only after the country's first democratic elections that the extent of its involvement in the ivory and rhino horn trade would finally be exposed.

* * *

Sitting alone at Wêreldsend, without a salary and only an aging saloon car Dan Craven had given me for transport, I received very little information about what was happening in the outside world. However, in Damaraland things were looking up for the first time in many years. Although a young elephant cow had died after falling over a cliff in the Hoanib in 1982, three calves had since been born there and survived. In the Uniab catchment a bull had also died of a severe leg injury, but here too there were at least three new calves. But most importantly, we knew of no more elephants having been poached.

There had also been no fewer than 12 rhino calves born since 1982, and their present breeding rate augured well for the future. With the good rains the populations of all the ungulates were also rapidly increasing, and even though the numbers of large predators were still very low, I was sure they would bounce back once their prey species recovered. Perhaps it was not too late to save the Kaokoveld's wildlife, but the responsibility for keeping the poaching under control was now solely in the hands of the DNC, and in July an incident occurred that again raised doubts about their commitment.

When Marcellus had delivered my Wêreldsend eviction letter, he told me that Jan Oelofse, a game rancher and renowned capture expert, had been given a permit to 'catch and release' two elephant calves in Damaraland. Although the operation was meant to take place in the east of the homeland, a few weeks later I heard a helicopter flying back and forth to the north of Wêreldsend. By chance Duncan and Ruth Gilchrist visited me that afternoon, so we set off in Duncan's vehicle to see what was happening.

On the bank of the Achab there were clear signs of where a herd of elephant had been chased across the rocky plains. In their panic they had kicked football-sized stones out of the ground, but that was not all. Hidden in a clump of euphorbia bushes was a dead baby elephant, with a broken leg and a bullet wound in the head. Further on we found three more places where other herds had been chased by vehicles, and no doubt the helicopter. It did not take a tracking expert to work out what had taken place, so we drove on to Palmwag, where the Oelofse party had made their camp.

As Jan knew us, we were surprised when he assured us that all had gone well with the capture of the baby elephants, and because there was a film crew present I did not discuss the matter further until we were alone together. When I told him that we had found the dead calf he said they had shot it because it had broken its leg in an accident, something that could happen in any game capture operation – which was true.

We camped that night at Palmwag, and early the next morning I found Jim

Fowler, the anchorman of the film, sitting by himself next to the fire. He told me they had been making a documentary on the six orphan elephant calves that Jan had acquired from the cropping operation in Etosha the previous year. As the film was part of an American TV series, *Wild Kingdom*, a few facts had been changed to make it more palatable to an audience that was against the culling of elephants. The new storyline was that the calves came from 'problem elephants' in Damaraland, and as the show needed to have plenty of action, Jan's role had been to drive into a herd, separate a baby from its mother and catch it by hand. Unfortunately the elephants had not been co-operative, and they had to shoot the scene four times. On their fourth filming attempt a young calf was stood on by one of the adults and its leg was broken.

Jim told us that he and the *Wild Kingdom* team were devastated by what had happened, and were planning to buy another calf to replace it! When I told him that this would not be possible he asked me not to say anything about the incident, and offered to make a large donation to our project, which I politely turned down. Clearly the film crew knew very little about wild elephants and could not be held responsible, but why had the DNC given permission for the still-threatened Damaraland elephants to be harassed in this way? At the very least Oelofse's permit should have stipulated that a DNC official had to be present during the capture operation.

By this time Jan had joined us and he was furious. So were we, not just because every calf was precious, but also because the elephants here had already been traumatised by poaching, and we never approached close to them in a vehicle. A week later Jan told the *Windhoek Advertiser* that the death of the calf was a 'freak accident' and that their aim had not been to capture it, only to drive the herd towards the television cameras with the helicopter. He also claimed the calf that died 'was probably a migrant from Etosha and could not have been one of the renowned desert dwelling elephants'. When the reporter contacted me for my comments I pointed out that the filming took place just north of Wêreldsend, which was well into the desert, and therefore it was certainly not an Etosha elephant.

A month later I had even more reason to be concerned about leaving the future of the Kaokoveld's wildlife solely in the hands of the DNC. While delivering rations Hilmar van Alphen, together with a stock inspector from Opuwo, Malcome van Reenen, arrived at Kamasitu's home at Ochams just before dark. After off-loading his maize-meal and other items they left immediately and drove across open plains towards Orupembe. From the ridge on which he lived the game guard watched their headlights get fainter, until about 25 km away they turned at right-angles to the road and headed for a short distance across the desert. After stopping for a while the vehicle returned to the road and then drove on. The next morning Kamasitu saddled up his donkey and went to see why they had stopped the previous night, and following the vehicle's tracks found the entrails, skin, head and hooves of a springbok and two gemsbok.

The next day he got on his donkey again and rode 30 km to the Skeleton Coast Fly-in Safari camp at Sarusas in the lower Khumib River. From there he radioed Steve Braine at Moewe Bay, who went with Kamasitu to the site where the animals had been killed. As Steve had no experience investigating poaching cases he handed it over to Marcellus Loots, who visited Van Alphen in his Opuwo home. In his deep freeze was meat neatly labelled gemsbok and springbok, and Marcellus also took blood samples from the back of his official truck. After impounding his rifle, he then took Van Alphen back to the site near Orupembe, where they picked up cartridge cases that matched the calibre of his rifle, and also his wedding ring! As Van Alphen made a written statement admitting that he and Van Reenen had killed the three animals, Marcellus gave his ring back to him.

It seemed to be an open and shut case, but when Van Alphen took the stand in the Opuwo regional court a week later he pleaded not guilty, and asked for time to get a lawyer. This was granted and the hearing remanded. As Van Reenen indicated he was no longer prepared to give evidence for the state, he was also charged and the two men hired Hennie Barnard to defend them. As a delaying tactic he got the case moved to the Windhoek High Court and postponed until April the following year. But what concerned me most was that Van Alphen was not suspended, and as he continued with his normal duties, to the local people it must have looked like he had got off the charge.

*　*　*

In October Angela Fisher came for a longer visit, and this time Chris Eyre took leave and joined us, as did Petra Mengel, Clive Walker's personal assistant, who had done much for the Kaokoveld behind the scenes, but had never actually been there. Luckily, by then the Oelofse and Van Alphen escapades had convinced Ingrid Schroeder that the SAVE Land Rover should come back to me, and we were able to use it to show Petra three herds of elephant, a rhino, and quite a few zebra, gemsbok and springbok before she returned to Johannesburg, a small reward for all the hard work she had put into the project.

Angela, Chris and I then drove to Purros, and from there up the Hoarusib River to Omutati, reversing the route I had walked with my brother and friends in 1970. This time, the only signs of wildlife were a few mountain zebra tracks. As Angela had come to take photographs of the Himba, the one group of traditional people she had not included in *Africa Adorned,* we continued along the road to Otjiu, then followed the Hoarusib via Ongango to the road from Opuwo to Etanga – the furthest north we could go in safety. Along the way we came across scattered villages and cattle posts where Himba families had returned to their pastoralist way of life and were slowly rebuilding their drought-depleted herds and flocks. But on the highlands there was no sign of any wildlife at all.

With no schedule the trip was very relaxed, with gin and tonics around the campfire each evening. It was the perfect holiday, but unlike my companions I had no work to go back to. The late payout of my government pension and a small royalty I had received for writing the text of a coffee table book by photographer Gerald Cubitt on Namibia's untamed places had almost run out. Fortunately, June had been able to get a job as a nurse on the Rössing uranium mine and rent a small house in Swakopmund. My family was surviving, but how much longer could I stay at Wêreldsend without a salary?

On the trip we all got on extremely well, and travelling to places I had known in the 1960s made it easy to forget that, in the eyes of the DNC hierarchy, Chris and I were the troublemakers who had subverted their authority over nature conservation by working with, and not against, the local people. However, on our way back through Sesfontein I was brought down to earth again. The officer in charge of the army platoon based there told me that he had been given instructions to find and arrest us for 'illegally entering an operational area'. As I had a good relationship with the young soldiers in this remote outpost, and we had reported in to him on our way north, the lieutenant had told his superior officers that he was unable to find us.

When Angela and Chris left, I went to see the head of the security police in Damaraland, Warrant Officer Liebenberg, who had in the past supported our conservation activities. He assured me that the order for our arrest had not gone through him, and said he would take the matter up 'at a high level'. A few weeks later he told me that, although the instruction came directly from army HQ, he suspected 'my old bosses in the DNC had played a role in it'. But he had sorted everything out and it would not happen again.

*   *   *

By late 1985 my finances were in dire straits. Thanks to a few good friends who secretly put money into my bank account, I could survive, but it was not enough to contribute anything towards the upkeep of our children. On Dan Craven's advice I had submitted the community game guard project to the Rolex Awards, and although it was featured in their annual publication it did not win any of the cash prizes. As a last resort I decided to write a book on the Kaokoveld and our unorthodox approach to stopping the poaching, so with my last few rand I flew to the UK to see Angela and discuss it with her publishers. But their response was lukewarm, and as she had started working on a second book in Ethiopia, a country that I as a South African could not go to, we drifted apart.

However, the trip was not totally in vain. While in London I visited the Environmental Investigation Agency (EIA), an NGO affiliated to Greenpeace that had done a great deal to expose the key players involved in the illegal trade in wildlife products. Its director, Alan Thornton, and his assistant, Suzie Watts, had heard of our work in the Kaokoveld from Nick Carter, and were pleased to get a first-hand account of the poaching situation in Namibia. In turn, they provided me with much information on where contraband ivory and rhino horns were going, and who the 'rogue States' were that facilitated it. As Craig van Noot of Monitor would later make public, South Africa was high on the list.

The EIA had just launched a campaign to stop all legal trade in ivory, making Alan very unpopular with the conservation authorities in Southern Africa, who saw 'sustainable use' as the best policy to conserve elephants. As I shared this viewpoint, Alan, Suzie and I had a long discussion on the subject. Although I recognised the present poaching problems faced by many African countries, I believed that in the long term elephants would not need protection, but land to live on. With the continent's rapidly growing human population it was unlikely that any more large game sanctuaries would be created; elephants would have to have a monetary as well as aesthetic value if we wanted the continent's rural people to live with them.

This could be done by trophy hunting where their numbers justified it, but the sale of tusks from elephants that had died naturally was also an important source of revenue. The real challenge was to find ways for local communities to get tangible benefits from them. Alan and Suzie believed that any legal trade in ivory would be opening a Pandora's Box that most African countries did not have the resources to cope with. In the end we agreed to disagree on the subject, but I respected the sincerity of their efforts to stop the present

Bethanis, one of the white-owned farms expropriated by the South African government in 1969 to create a homeland for the Damara people.

Wêreldsend, an abandoned farm in the pre-Namib from where Namibia Wildlife Trust staff operated in the 1980s. It is now a community meeting and training centre, as well as the base camp of Integrated Rural Development and Nature Conservation.

LEFT: Colin and Ina Britz with the starving young lion that caught their bull terrier while it was sleeping on Colin's overall next to their bed, on my first night at Wêreldsend.

BELOW: On my first trip back to the Marienfluss in July 1982, the scenery was as spectacular as I remembered it to be, but the only game seen was a few ostriches.

LEFT: During the 1980/81 drought 90 per cent of the cattle in Kaokoland had died of starvation, and their carcasses were still visible around every Himba and Herero *onganda*.

BELOW: A typical gang of mounted poachers in the early 1980s. Having lost their livelihood, and with rifles supplied by the SADF, the pastoralists followed the example of government officials and hunted what little game still survived.

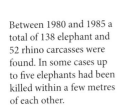

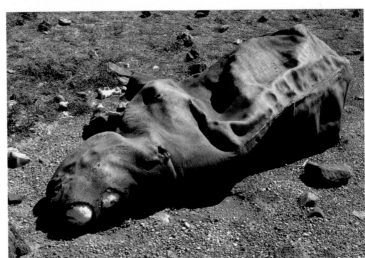

Between 1980 and 1985 a total of 138 elephant and 52 rhino carcasses were found. In some cases up to five elephants had been killed within a few metres of each other.

OPPOSITE: The giraffe poached near the Ombonde River in May 1983. From left: Chris Eyre, GOS, Elias Hambo and Lukas Mbomboro.
(Mitch Reardon)

ABOVE LEFT: The poachers; Adam Tjikwara (*left*) and Chris Kangombe (*right*) returning from another hunting expedition. (*Mitch Reardon*)

ABOVE RIGHT: Twetjavi Tjambiru (*right*), the renowned Himba hunter who was convicted of poaching a giraffe west of Orupembe in 1983 – the first case initiated by a community game guard. (*Mitch Reardon*)

BELOW: Herero headmen Goliat Kasaona and Joshua Kangombe (*seated*) with the community game guards they appointed in 1983. Standing, left to right: Abraham Tjavara, Hosia Kangombe, Sakeus Kasaona, Lukas Mbomboro (Chris Eyre's field assistant), Salmon Karutjaiva and Elias Mosia.

ABOVE: Chief Vetamuna Tjambiru at his holy fireplace. In the 1980s he played a crucial role in stopping the local people from hunting in western Kaokoland.

BELOW LEFT: Community game guard Tjahorerua Tjisutha, who covered the area around Orupembe.

BELOW RIGHT: Community game guard Ngevi Tjihaku on his donkey.

GOS with high school students from Khorixas. Enabling the younger generation in Damaraland to see big game was an important objective of the Namibia Wildlife Trust.

A more urgent objective – aimed at stopping poaching and not merely catching poachers – was getting the support of the broader community and their traditional leaders to conserve what wildlife remained. *(Mitch Reardon)*

Ochams spring, where community game guard Kamasitu Tjipombo lived at the end of the drought.

The plains around Purros after good rain. In the past the pre-Namib grasslands were only utilised by the pastoralists at these times, but in the 1980s a permanent community of Himba and Herero became established along the lower Hoarusib River.

ABOVE LEFT: GOS with
Margie Jacobsohn, who
came to Purros in 1985
to do post-graduate
research, standing in
front of the traditional
hut that the local women
built for her to live in.

ABOVE RIGHT: Margie
with Vengapi Tjiningiri,
one of her 'age mates'
in Purros. Vengapi
and her older sister,
Kata, both made major
contributions to her
research and became life-
long friends.

LEFT: Another of
Margie's age mates,
community game guard
Kamasitu Tjipombo's
wife, Kavetjikoterue,
collecting ochre at Otjize
– a three-day journey on
a donkey from Purros.
(Margie Jacobsohn)

The Hoarusib bull who survived the poaching around Purros by moving to the lower Hoanib River. When 'Skeuroor' was shot in 1981 he became the dominant bull here.

A small herd of elephants near Hunkab spring in the far west of Damaraland. The only other population of 'desert elephants' occurs in the Gourma Reserve on the edge of the Sahara in Mali.

LEFT: Black rhino are also well adapted to living in the Namib, where they feed on a range of dwarf shrubs and succulents, some of which have very poisonous sap.

BELOW: A lioness and cubs in the dunes near the Hoanib River mouth. During the 1980s a few small prides still inhabited the Skeleton Coast, but they were all killed when they went up the seasonal riverbeds and attacked livestock. In 2005 the first lion was seen back on the beach.

LEFT: When tourists started coming into Damaraland the game numbers were still low, but the background of rugged mountains made each sighting precious. Here giraffe are dwarfed by the Grootberg range.

BELOW: As wildlife numbers increased visitors had to be reminded that the area was not a national park, but a place where people, their livestock and big game lived together.
(Vincent Guillemin)

The Baynes Mountains east of Epupa Falls. In the German colonial times they were just a blank space on the map, and are still a virtually unexplored wilderness where new plant species have recently been discovered.

The arid savannah on the Kaokoveld highlands was once dominated by perennial grasses, but the breakdown of the pastoralists' traditional livestock management system has led to them being eliminated and replaced by annual species.

LEFT AND ABOVE: In an attempt to re-establish perennial grasses large numbers of cattle are herded together, using the impact of their hooves (*above*) to loosen the soil surface and create a more favourable habitat for seed germination. *(Colin Nott)*

TOP: Where there is no permanent grass cover the topsoil is lost to wind and water erosion and the exposed ground baked hard by the sun, creating an environment in which perennial grass seeds can no longer germinate.

The 1997 recipients of Golden Ark Awards from Prince Bernard of the Netherlands. On the right next to GOS and Margie Jacobsohn is John Newby of WWF International. The WWF family has given steadfast support to the Namibian programme since 1990.

East Caprivi: a very different environment to the Kaokoveld with a much higher density of people living from agriculture and fishing. In 1990 IRDNC started a community-based conservation project here to show that it can also work in many other parts of Africa.

slaughter. Alan in turn promised to see what he could do to 'keep me in the field'.

In January Blythe Loutit brought me visitors who would have made Warrant Officer Liebenberg's hair stand on end. Tony Heard, Margie Jacobsohn and Molly Green had all been to Wêreldsend before, but then Tony was just the editor of the *Cape Times*. Now he was the best known newsman in South Africa, who had made headlines across the world by publishing an interview with Oliver Tambo, the president of the African National Congress – an offence that under the country's security legislation carried a mandatory three-year jail sentence!

Tony published Tambo's views because he believed them to be 'a matter of overwhelming public interest'. Unlike the 1977 story on PW Botha hunting at Epupa, this time he did not submit it to the government for comment, or even inform his own staff – which could have made them also liable for prosecution. When the story appeared in print the security apparatus was caught flat-footed and initially thought he must have been given permission to do so. By the time they realised he had not, and had sent someone to arrest him three days later, the international press had picked up the story: there were placard-waving journalists standing outside the *Cape Times* building and a TV crew waiting to film him being taken away by the police. Not sure how to handle the case now that it was under the media spotlight, they simply charged Tony and released him a few hours later. He was eventually convicted and given a suspended sentence.

Margie Jacobsohn would have had the local security police worried too. Apart from having been married to Graham Ferreira when he exposed the hunting exploits of senior government officials and politicians in Namibia's homelands, she had helped Tony Heard publish the Oliver Tambo interview. She and Tony were also close friends of Winnie Mandela, the wife of the world's most famous political prisoner. But the reason for their visit was not journalism; Margie was looking for a suitable study site for the archaeology honours degree she was doing part-time through Cape Town University. On a previous visit she had been fascinated by the Himba, and Blythe had told her that I was the best person to get advice on where to carry out her research.

With the far north of Kaokoland too dangerous to work in I suggested Purros, where Heova Tjiningiri, the sub-headman of the Orupembe area, had moved to get away from the war. He had many wives, sisters and sisters-in-law, who – together with Kamasitu's wife, Kavetjikoterua, and his older sister's two daughters, Vengapi and Kata, all of them about Margie's age – would provide plenty of female company. The Purros community was also ideal for her proposed study of the changes in material culture that were taking place in Himba society, because it included the Uararavi and Karutjaiva patrilineages, which had recently adopted Herero dress and architecture.

Another advantage of Purros was its abundant permanent water and the shady trees growing along the banks of the Hoarusib River, making it the most practical place for her to be based. She was immediately struck by the stark desert scenery of the area and the friendliness of the Himba families I introduced her to. On the trip we also had a remarkable meeting of minds on a wide range of subjects, and I looked forward to her returning in July to start her research. Last but not least, on a recent visit to London she and Tony had met Alan Thornton, who asked them to pass on the donation he had promised me from the EIA.

*   *   *

In April 1986, eight months after they had shot two gemsbok and a springbok near Orupembe, the trial of Hilmar van Alphen and Malcome van Reenen finally began. By then the DNC hierarchy had decided that John Patterson, who had never even been inside a courtroom before, should be the senior investigating officer, and Marcellus Loots just a state witness. John was the first to give evidence, and described the events that led up to the arrest of the two accused. However, when the cross-examination started Hennie Barnard soon had him flustered, and after an hour of hard questioning played the card that would change the course of the trial. Handing John the police docket, he asked him whether it was complete. After paging through the many documents in the folder, John replied in the affirmative. But it was not.

When Marcellus had collected the docket from the police station in Opuwo, and taken it back to Khorixas to hand over to John, he had not checked its contents. Only three days later did he realise that the statement Van Alphen had made admitting his guilt was not there. It must have been removed by someone, but as he had already signed for the docket, it was too late to do anything about it. Embarrassed by his carelessness, Marcellus knew that unless a confession had been made in front of a magistrate it could not be used in court, so he had not told John about the missing document.

It was the opening Barnard wanted and had undoubtedly planned for. He then told the court that on the day they visited the site where the animals had been killed, his client had made a statement, and asked John if it was in the docket. John admitted that it was not, and that he had no idea where it was. To a defence lawyer of Barnard's calibre such a mistake was all that was needed to intimidate an inexperienced witness. During further cross-examining – which stretched into the following morning session – he was able to get John to agree that Marcellus had told Van Reenen that if he was prepared to implicate Van Alphen he would not be prosecuted, and also that 'Loots was obsessed with getting a conviction against his colleague in the DNC'.

When Marcellus finally took the stand, Barnard noted that in his initial evidence he had said that he had asked Van Alphen to be present when Van Reenen pointed out certain sites in the veld, but when cross-examined he had said that Van Alphen himself showed him the sites. It was a very minor contradiction, but Barnard was able to use it to make Marcellus admit that he had thus 'lied to the court'. He also suggested that the cartridge cases found at the site where the gemsbok and springbok were killed had been planted there by him because of his 'obsession' with getting Van Alphen convicted. It was a masterly performance by one of the best defence lawyers in the country, and as only two days had been set aside for the hearing it was then adjourned until July.

When the trial resumed three months later, Barnard opened by asking for the case against his clients to be dismissed on the grounds that two of the three State witnesses had proved to be unreliable, and therefore there was no legally admissible evidence linking them to the crime. Although Magistrate Christie Liebenberg stated that he was reluctant to do so, he had no option but to agree to the request, and Van Alphen and Van Reenen walked out of the court 'innocent men'. The third state witness, Kamasitu Tjipombo, had not even been called to give his evidence, and was incredulous when the outcome was explained to him. Margie, who was by then living in Purros and had brought him to Windhoek for the trial, tried to console him by saying that hiring Barnard cost them a lot of money, more than they were likely to have been fined. But the white man's justice system had lost all credibility in Kamasitu's eyes, and I knew that other homeland residents would come to the same conclusion.

Outside the courtroom Margie and I joined Hennie Barnard for a cup of coffee in a nearby café, and I asked him how he felt about getting a man off who was so obviously guilty. He smiled and told us that he would continue to defend poachers until the DNC learned that their officers were not well enough trained in investigation procedures to handle serious cases. It was the work of the police, he told us, but he did concede that Chris Eyre, who had won convictions both times he had come up against him, was the exception to this rule.

At about the same time as the final hearing of the Van Alphen case, Mitch Reardon's book, *The Besieged Desert,* was published to generally good reviews in the South African media. Apart from colourful descriptions of Chris and me, it was a lively account of the key ecological, social and political issues that made Namibia's north-west so fascinating. But the events he described occurred in 1983, and as a great deal had happened since then, I decided to write an updated article on the situation, which was published in the October 1986 issue of *African Wildlife*. It ended by saying:

> Over the past fifteen years the once magnificent wildlife of the Kaokoveld has been plundered and abused to the point where its survival now hangs in the balance. Since 1982, however, good rains have fallen over most of the region and, if poaching can be kept under control, the game herds will bounce back. Even the elephants and rhino can still recover if given a chance.
>
> But during the 1970s the general public was misled by official statements that all was well in the Kaokoveld. The government has now taken over total responsibility for conservation in north-western South West Africa/Namibia. We must not allow history to repeat itself in the late 1980s.

CHAPTER TWENTY-TWO

A DEGRADED ECOSYSTEM

When the NWT's Damaraland/Kaokoland Project began, our fourth objective was to: 'Promote a better understanding of the ecology of this unique region.' I justified this on the grounds that, apart from Slang Viljoen's doctoral and earlier master's research, and my 1971 manuscript on the Kaokoveld, the restrictions on access and present insecurity meant little was known about this remote part of Namibia. My interest was in more than just its wildlife; I also wanted to learn about the region's rocks and rainfall, its plants and people; not as separate subjects, but as an integrated and interacting whole. Seen together they might explain *why* the early 1980s drought had resulted in such a high mortality of livestock and wildlife, and *how* the recent human interventions contributed to this.

Nineteen eighty-two was an excellent year for getting information on the Kaokoveld's vegetation and smaller creatures. After the drought the good rains that fell deep into the desert resulted in a proliferation of annual grasses and forbs, including many species I had not seen before. Feeding on this sudden bounty was a frenzy of rapidly breeding seed-eating birds and rodents, as well as a vast array of creeping, crawling, flying and biting insects that had hatched from eggs laid many years before.

Mike Griffen, one of the DNC's biologists, saw our presence in the region as a good opportunity to learn more about the smaller vertebrate animals occurring there, and had provided us with sample bottles, as well as a large jar of formalin. Peter started collecting geckos, skinks and even toads that appeared in some of the ephemeral pools, while I focused on pressing plant specimens and finding out where and what large mammals still survived. With game numbers so low actual sightings were rare, and even for springbok, gemsbok and zebra we relied mostly on tracks or dung to establish their distribution.

The rains were poor the next year, but 1984 was another bumper season, with lush grasslands again stretching across the pre-Namib, allowing birds and rodents to multiply into their millions. Many migratory raptors also moved in to feed on them, while bustards, storks and korhaans grew fat on the locusts and caterpillars that threatened to reach plague proportions. However, it was not predation that brought insect and small mammal populations under control, but a succession of low rainfall years that followed. Soon the northwest was again in the grip of a drought, and as the food-chains collapsed the desert once more reclaimed the land it had lost. Here there was no 'balance of nature', just a boom and bust economy in which the species that could breed the fastest or migrate the furthest were the most successful.

Although severe droughts probably only occur a few times each century, in the Kaokoveld years of below-average rainfall are the rule rather than the exception. Their impact on individual species also depends on their numbers at the time. But was the very high livestock population in the late 1970s the primary cause of the massive mortalities that had taken place? To find out, I needed to understand how the key physical and biotic components of the ecosystem influenced the productivity of its rangelands – when they supported only wild grazers, and also after nomadic pastoralists entered the region. But most importantly, I needed to understand why the drilling of boreholes and the changed cattle management practices after the reduction of large predators caused the perennial grasses to die out.

On the plateau the first convectional storms occur as early as September, but these localised rainfalls usually bring little relief to the region's parched rangelands. The main wet season begins in late November or December, with the highest precipitation recorded in February and March. West of the escarpment effective rain seldom falls before the new year, but can continue into May. As there are very few weather stations in the Kaokoveld the only available figures are for Opuwo and Sesfontein which have an annual average of 340 mm and 100 mm respectively. At Wêreldsend in the pre-Namib,

28 years of rainfall records show the mean to be 75 mm per year, with a variation of 17–256 mm, while near the coast the average is less than 25 mm, and in most years no rain falls at all.

Although rain plays the greatest role in rangeland productivity, it is not just the total precipitation in a year that counts. When it falls, as well as how much and how rapidly it falls during each downpour, will influence the amount that actually sinks into the ground and becomes available to plant roots, before evaporating or infiltrating deep underground. As important is the slope and the substrate it falls on, which is primarily determined by the rock formations that underlie the area.

The major geological event that created the Kaokoveld's landscape is the breakup of Gondwanaland, the super-continent that once comprised Africa, South America, India, Australia and Antarctica. When Africa and South America separated, approximately 130 million years ago, the stretching apart of their tectonic plates generated enormous heat, which resulted in massive volcanic activity along the rift. Over millions of years multiple eruptions of liquid lava flowed over the surface, covering it to depths of up to 600 metres and solidifying into the basalt rocks that still cover much of the high ground between the larger river valleys in the west. Dominating the scene at the time was a free-standing volcano that is estimated to have been higher than Kilimanjaro. The remnants of its core still exist as the Brandberg, which at 2 570 metres is Namibia's highest mountain.

As seawater filled the gap between the two continents, land that was at the centre of Gondwanaland became part of Africa's south-western coastline. Here new river systems developed, gradually eroding valleys inland until one of them 'captured' the course of the Kunene, diverting it away from the vast lake that once covered the Kalahari, and causing what is now the Etosha Pan to dry up. However, the reason for the Kaokoveld's rugged topography is not because it is now on the coast, or even the massive outpourings of lava, but the relatively rapid rate at which Southern Africa has risen above sea level since the break-up of Gondwanaland. Although this has averaged only about one millimetre per century, over 130 million years this adds up to over a kilometre.

With the rise in elevation came erosion by the numerous watercourses that drain the highlands, reducing the Gondwana landscape into a matrix of plains, hills and mountains that attain an altitude of just over 2 000 metres on the northern plateau. In the west, once the Kunene and larger seasonal rivers removed the overlying basalt, they quickly eroded the softer rock formations beneath it, carving out impressive valleys and canyons through the escarpment ranges, where the Kaokveld's most dramatic scenery is now found.

To many people it might seem strange that in a region with a very low rainfall, water erosion has played such a major role in shaping the landscape. This is simply because the sparse plant cover is unable to prevent the soil from being washed away when storms do occur. Where the relief is steep the watercourses are also faster flowing, which increases the amount of sand and silt they can carry when they come down in flood. Consequently, in the west most of the soil on the hill and mountain slopes has been removed, exposing the earth's skeleton and creating an open air textbook on some of the major geological events in the planet's history.

The oldest rocks in the Kaokoveld are granite and granitic gneiss that formed when molten magma deep beneath the surface slowly cooled and solidified. Where the magma was forced upwards, but did not reach the surface, it created dykes and sills of dolerite that intrude into the overlying formations. The region also has the largest known deposit of anorthosite, an intrusive igneous rock that forms the strangely striped Zebra Mountains near the Kunene River between Swartbooisdrift and the Epupa Falls.

Above the basement granites are highly metamorphosed and folded marine sediments that were laid down in a primordial ocean that pre-dates Gondwanaland. These schist and gneiss formations are overlain in places by unfolded quartzite, the remains of which form the Baynes, Omuhonga and Ehomba ranges on the northern plateau. From about Opuwo southwards to the Hoanib valley the area is dominated by dolomite and limestone – rocks that were derived from coral and other primitive calcium-secreting organisms that lived in the warm ocean that once covered the whole region.

Adding to the complexity of the Kaokoveld's geological history are deposits of tillite, derived from glacial moraine, while immediately below the basalt in the west is a layer of windblown sandstone, indicating that before the breakaway of South America the climate was hot and dry. Finally, along the region's north-eastern border the dolomite is overlain by unconsolidated sediments deposited by the Kunene and Cuvelai systems when this part of the Kalahari was still a freshwater lake.

To complicate the landscape further, in places the chronological sequence of events is disrupted by major fault-lines in the earth's crust. The most obvious are the Marienfluss, between the Baynes and Otjihipa ranges and the Hoarusib valley upriver of Purros, where rocks of a different age and type are found at the same elevation. The granites around the Brandberg and dolerite intrusions along the lower Huab and Uniab also add variety to the spectacular scenery there, while the courses of all the major rivers have cut down through different rock formations, giving each of them their own unique character.

From an ecological perspective, the Kaokoveld's rugged topography and very varied geology have created an exceptionally wide range of macro- and micro-habitats for plants to grow in, from sheer cliff faces to stony pediments and broad valleys where the alluvial sediments may be many metres deep. Because the soil's texture and chemical composition, as well as how easily it erodes, are dictated by the rock it is derived from, there are also a diversity of substrates, each of which has its own biodiversity and production potential.

Granite that cooled slowly deep beneath the earth's surface will weather into coarse gravel, while the faster-cooling dolerite soils are much smaller grained. Basalt solidified even more rapidly when the lava came into contact with the air, and it breaks down into very fine clay. Soil from limestone, which is composed of pure calcium carbonate, has a texture like talcum powder. So too does dolomite, but as it is often mixed with particles of the substrate the marine organisms grew on, it frequently forms a sandy-clay or clay-loam. Sedimentary formations, whether metamorphosed or not, weather into grains that vary in size from coarse to fine, depending on their parent rock.

Although soil depth is the primary factor that determines how much groundwater is available for plant growth, texture also plays a role. Fine-grained substrates can hold less water, but in arid regions where the rate of evaporation exceeds the rainfall, the dissolved chemical salts are brought up to the surface by capillary action and deposited there when the water evapo-rates. The large space between the particles inhibits capillary action in the coarse-grained substrates, which results in most soluble nutrients being transported below the reach of shallow-rooted plants. Therefore, deep sandy soils have a higher production potential, but are less fertile than loam or clay substrates. To counter this, at the end of each growing season the perennial grasses on 'leached' soils withdraw the vital nutrients from their leaves and store them in their roots for use at the start of the next rains – the origin of the term sourveld.

Because they have deeper roots, a shortage of chemical salts is seldom lim-iting for woody plants, but the pH of the soil will influence the distribution of species. In general substrates derived from granite are acidic, while those that contain a high level of calcium are basic. In the Hoanib valley, which is flanked by limestone ranges, the deep very fine clay soils can have a pH of over 11, exceeding the range of tolerance of all but a few trees and shrubs, such as *Acacia tortilis*, *Colophospermum mopane* and *Salvadora persica*.

In the Kaokoveld virtually all of the soils are alkaline, and the arid savan-
nahs on the plateau are dominated by *Colophospermum mopane*. A common
associated tree species is *Terminalia prunioides*, but as neither of them grows
on deep sandy substrates or in places where frost regularly occurs, in these
areas they are replaced by *Acacia* spp. On the rocky hill slopes other conspicuous trees are *Sterculia quinqueloba*, *Kirkia acuminata* and *Adansonia digitata*,
with the genus *Commiphora* also being well represented. Along the larger
seasonal rivers the riparian vegetation is characterised by *Faedherbia albida*,
Acacia erioloba and *Combretum imberbe*.

Where the highlands have not been continuously grazed, the herbaceous
layer is still dominated by perennial grass, with some of the most common
species being *Stipagrostis uniplumis, S. hochstetterana, Heteropogon contortis,
Antephora pubescens, Cenchrus ciliaris* and *Urochloa mosambicensis*, while
Aristida meridionalis is prominent on deep sandy soils on the highlands.
However, over most of the plateau these perennials have been replaced by
annual grasses and forbs

West of the escarpment soil depth and, thereby, its water storage capacity, is the key factor that determines plant productivity and the distribution
of species. Although annuals will germinate wherever effective rain falls, because perennial grasses have to keep their organs alive throughout the year,
they can only survive on substrates that do not dry out for long periods.
Nevertheless, the deep sands in the pre-Namib support a good stand of perennial grasses, and they even grow on rocky substrates where the soil is more
than a few centimetres in depth – in spite of the average annual rainfall being
below 100 mm.

The combination of the Kaokoveld's low rainfall, rugged topography and
very diverse geology has also created a number of unique habitats, which have
made it one of the major centres of floral endemism on the continent. The
rarest tree in Southern Africa, *Kirkia dewinteri*, is only found on the slopes of
the limestone ranges flanking the Hoanib valley, while other prominent en-
demics include *Acacia montis-usti* on coarse granite substrates, *Acacia robin-
siana* in the basalt ranges and *Combretum wattii* in the rocky riverbeds in the
west. Together with the adjoining, ecologically similar parts of south-western
Angola, the region has the largest number of *Commiphora* species, as well as
numerous succulents and semi-succulents that occur here and nowhere else.

The rainfall, topography and geology also play a role in where and how
much surface water is available in the Kaokoveld. Apart from the Kunene
River, permanent springs are found along the courses of all the major sea-

sonal watercourses, wherever a rock bank has obstructed their underground flow. Some of these 'seeps' run for considerable distances, and as they are charged by the accumulation of rain falling in their large catchments, they maintain a more or less constant stream throughout the year.

In the basalt ranges springs are particularly common, and can occur in relatively minor watercourses. This is because the lava flows have different densities, causing infiltrating rainwater to collect and flow in underground aquifers over the less permeable strata, and wherever the overlying rock has been removed by erosion they run out onto the surface. As these 'contact springs' are recharged by local rain, the amount of water they produce fluctuates seasonally, as well as year by year, and some may dry up completely after a prolonged period of low rainfall.

In the limestone and dolomite areas there are also numerous springs, but they are not affected by the vagaries of the weather. As both rock types are soluble, rainwater soaking into the ground over millions of years has dissolved large subterranean caverns that form natural reservoirs. If geological forces exert pressure on them, their highly mineralised water is pushed upwards along fissures to the surface. Around some 'artesian springs' are grotesque formations of tufa that were created from the chemical salts deposited during evaporation – a testimony to how long they have been in existence.

Not all of the region is well endowed with permanent surface water. Large tracts are underlain by more porous rock formations where springs are scarce. But whenever heavy rain falls here it fills many pans and rock pools, some of which can last for many months. These temporary sources of drinking water enable the grazing ungulates to move away from the permanent springs in the wet season, thereby preventing the perennial grasses around them from being defoliated during the critical growing period.

In his 1971 report to the Wildlife Society, Tinley suggested that the Kaokoveld's wild herbivores were opportunistic and migrated to take advantage of changing conditions in their habitat. He concluded by saying: 'In this way the sensitive substrate is maintained in a good state, but movement is the key factor for the survival of the animal, as well as the substrate it depends on.' Although there is no record of wildebeest having occurred in the Kaokoveld west of the sandveld along the Ovamboland border, in the late 1960s I found Burchell's zebra to be widespread on the highlands. In my 1971 manuscript I wrote:

During the rainy season Kaokoveld zebra do a considerable amount of moving around, and large congregations frequently collect in the vicinity of rain filled pans in usually waterless areas. For example, over 500 Burchell zebra were seen on the grassy semi-desert plains between Orupembe and Onjombo (Onjuva) after good rains here in 1969. When the pans dried up the concentrations disappeared almost overnight, but as there are at least 4 000 Burchell's zebra permanently resident in the Kaokoveld, and very few are encountered at winter drinking places during the rains, there is no evidence to support the theory of a regular migration from the Etosha Game Park.

Slang Viljoen's 1977 report on the status and trends of the mammals and habitat in Kaokoland also records that 'Burchell zebra are spread out over the whole of Kaokoland apart from the Namib. Their presence is especially remarkable in the Baynes and Otjihipa mountains where they have apparently taken the place of Hartmann zebra. They show a prominent migration pattern in that during the rainy season they move deep into the western parts and in the dry season move great distances to the east.'

According to local informants in the 1960s, Hartmann's mountain zebra were previously more widespread and plentiful on the interior plateau, which was substantiated by them being very common in the area west of Otjovasandu before it was de-proclaimed. Their ability to dig holes in riverbeds and agility in climbing to small rock pools also enables them to graze in places that are inaccessible to both Burchell's zebra and livestock. In my survey of the larger mammals in the Kaokoveld I wrote that: 'In the harsh environment of the western regions, Hartmann zebra were found to range considerable distances, congregating in large numbers should any particular vicinity receive rain. At this time there is probably much movement between the sub-desert and the western plateau.'

In the past gemsbok undoubtedly occurred throughout the Kaokoveld, apart from the northern ranges. Like zebra they follow the rain westward, penetrating far into the Namib to wherever desert storms enable the perennial grasses to grow new shoots and the seeds of annual species to germinate. As long as there is still some green growth they do not need to drink, but as conditions dry out they move off the plains closer to the permanent springs, or congregate along the larger riverbeds, where the higher water table allows the perennial vegetation to retain moisture longer.

Although gemsbok are grazers by choice, when there is no grass available they will browse on a wide range of shrubs and forbs. Together with their low water requirements, this makes them exceptionally well adapted to surviving in the western Kaokoveld. They were also found to be equally at home in all habitats, with their broad hooves enabling them to venture deep into dune fields, while in droughts they can climb high up rugged mountain slopes in search of suitable forage.

In the 1960s springbok were still plentiful in the dolomite hills of southern Kaokoland and in the pre-Namib, but because of their narrow hooves avoided soft sandy substrates.

Like gemsbok and zebra, in the wet season springbok migrate westward and come together in very large numbers wherever rain has recently fallen. However, as they only eat grass when it is short and still growing, as soon as it matures the congregations break up and disperse to feed along the watercourses and on the lower hill slopes in the desert, where many of their favoured browse species occur. On the plateau the leaves of dwarf shrubs growing on the highly alkaline clay soils in limestone and dolomite areas form a major part of their diet during the dry season.

Because springbok prefer open areas where their vision is unrestricted, they were not found in the well-wooded northern highlands. In this habitat, wherever surface water was available, impala were still common in the 1960s, particularly along the Kunene and the larger seasonal rivers. Like springbok they only graze grass while it is still green, and for most of the year browse on the leaves, flowers and fruits of woody plants. Impala do not migrate, but when rain fills the pans and rock pools they move away from the springs and exploit areas that were not accessible to them in the dry season.

Before livestock were introduced into the region the wild grazing ungulates would undoubtedly have occurred on the highlands in much greater numbers. However, because they all moved away from the springs in the wet season, either by migrating westwards or by dispersing into normally waterless areas, their impact on the perennial grasses during the critical growing period would have been minimal. Therefore, although high rainfall periods and then droughts was the normal cycle in the Kaokoveld, it was the climate and grazing system that its rangelands had evolved with and were adapted to.

Initially the Herero-speaking pastoralists in the region followed a similar movement pattern to the wild grazers, taking the majority of their livestock away from springs in the wet season and only bringing them back when all the temporary waters dried up. In poor rainfall years, families living on the western plateau also took their cattle herds down the escarpment into the pre-Namib, where they grazed on the arid grasslands there until they were depleted or effective rain again fell on the highlands.

Apart from the losses due to disease and predation, the livestock population was limited by the amount of grass and browse available around the permanent waters during the dry season. As importantly, because lions were then plentiful, young men would have accompanied their cattle while out grazing, keeping them together for safety and taking them to different places according to where the best forage was to be found. As this was similar to the way wild grazers utilised the rangelands, the perennial grasses should not have been detrimentally affected.

However, by the 1960s the pastoralists' livestock management practices were already changing. The issuing of strychnine and .303 rifles to headmen had resulted in predators becoming scarce on the highlands, and because it was not necessary to herd their cattle, many stockowners left them to find their own favoured grazing. Increased contact with the outside world also led the Herero in the south to adopt many aspects of European culture, including the acquisition of material possessions that made it difficult to seasonally move to remote wet-season grazing grounds. With most of their livestock now staying close to the permanent water-points throughout the year, the perennial grasses around them were being continuously defoliated in the growing season.

To disperse the livestock more evenly across the Kaokoveld, a programme of creating artificial water-points was begun in the 1950s. By the time I left Opuwo a total of over 60 boreholes had been drilled, and a number of dams constructed across riverbeds. This considerably increased the area of dry season grazing available, which enabled livestock numbers to reach unprecedented levels, further extending the area of degradation. As the BAD agricultural officials believed it was too many cattle that caused overgrazing, an attempt was made to get the pastoralists to market some of their livestock, but when this failed they reverted to drilling more boreholes. It was the way white farmers opened up Namibia's central highlands for cattle ranching, but they fenced their land into paddocks through which their animals were rotated, which was not possible on communal land.

By the end of the 1970s over 180 boreholes had been drilled in Kaokoland, and cattle numbers had increased to around 160 000 and small-stock to about 125 000. As the new water-points were in areas previously used for wet season grazing, it meant there were few places left for the pastoralists to take their herds when it rained, and even the Himba were becoming more sedentary.

In the past there had always been uneaten grass far from the springs that livestock could walk long distances to in times of drought. But as many of the boreholes were only 10 km apart, over most of the highlands there were no ungrazed areas left when the rains failed for two consecutive years in 1980 and 1981. However, the major reason for the early 1980s drought having such a catastrophic impact was that the perennial grasses had been eliminated.

Before discussing why the change from perennial to annual-dominated grasslands caused 90 per cent of the pastoralists' cattle to die it is important to recognise that it was not thirst, but starvation that killed them. Therefore, as both cattle and sheep are primarily grazers, a reduction in the rangeland's productivity will become the limiting factor that determines their survival rate during low rainfall periods. With this established, we now need to look at some of the key characteristics of grass, as well as the vital role it plays in tropical savannas – and in all of our lives.

Most terrestrial ecosystems are characterised by trees and shrubs, but it is the lower stratum of herbaceous species that has the greatest production potential. This is because much of the energy and nutrients in woody plants are locked in their indigestible trunks and branches, while the majority of their edible leaves and twigs grow high above the ground, where only climbing animals, birds or insects can reach them. Dicotyledonous plants have also developed protective measures to discourage browsing, such as thorns, tannins and alkaloids in the leaves, poisonous sap, and in the case of some succulents, even cryptic coloration.

In contrast, perennial grasses are designed to be defoliated. Their leaves and culms are accessible and easy to digest, and because their meristems (growing points) are situated at the base of the tuft, if they are not grazed or periodically burnt, the dead material that accumulates over them will eventually smother the plant. When they are actively growing their leaves are also very rich in energy and protein, the reason why grasslands and open savannas are able to support the greatest biomass of large mammals on the planet.

But grass is not just good for animals. Without it humans would still be hunters and gatherers, because all of the staple grain crops we depend on have been selectively bred from native grasses, and most of the domestic animals that we get meat from are grazers. Until quite recently, thatching grass was also our most widely used protection against the elements, while the first paper was made from papyrus, which although a sedge, belongs to the same plant family. In spite of the major role that grass plays in our lives, how many people, including professional biologists, can name more than a few common species, or know much about its ecology and how best to manage it?

Ecologically, grass does much more than feed animals and support humans. A healthy sward of perennials slows down rainwater runoff, which increases the amount infiltrating into the ground. It also provides the soil surface with the most effective protection from the direct rays of the sun, thereby keeping it cool and reducing the rate of evaporation back into the atmosphere. In this way perennials considerably improve the water balance that in arid and semi-arid areas is the primary factor influencing plant productivity.

Among the many other ecological services provided by perennial grass is creating a favourable habitat for small animals, which are in turn a source of prey for species higher up the food chain. When grass litter is trampled into the ground it improves the structure of the soil, as well as feeding micro-organisms that break down organic matter, thereby promoting a rapid recycling of nitrates and other key nutrients. But the most valuable role played by perennial grass is to stop the loss of topsoil to water and wind erosion, which their well-developed root systems do more effectively than any other plant. For all these reasons, where they have been eliminated a spiral of degradation is set in motion that considerably reduces both rangeland productivity and biodiversity.

The main role in the ecosystem of the annual species is to invade bare ground, and thereby improve the micro-environment so that higher succession plants can colonise the area. Because they must germinate from seed at the start of each wet season, their initial growth is also much less than perennial species that already have established root systems – a crucial factor if there are long dry periods between rainfall events. On top of this, as most of their energy and nutrients are put into reproduction, their leaves are usually small in comparison to their inflorescences, making them less palatable to large grazing mammals. But most importantly, they have a much sparser basal cover to shade the soil and reduce rainwater runoff, while their small roots provide little protection against erosion and none during droughts, when no germination may take place at all.

By 1986, even though the drought had ended four years earlier and the numbers of livestock in the Kaokoveld were still very low, there was little sign of perennial grasses becoming re-established. The reason for this was not difficult to find. Wind and water erosion, exposure to the sun and the compacting effect of raindrops on all but the sandy substrates, had severely capped the soil over much of the highlands, making it almost impossible for perennial grass seeds to germinate. However, any attempt to reverse the rangeland degradation by introducing better livestock management would have to wait until the security situation improved.

*   *   *

The widespread loss of the perennial grass cover on the plateau was undoubtedly the underlying reason why the early 1980s drought resulted in such a high mortality of cattle, and with it the collapse of the Herero and Himba's pastoralist economy. But what caused the wild ungulates, which would have experienced prolonged dry periods in the past, to also die in such large numbers?

In the 1960s there were so many zebra in the Kaokoveld that some of my colleagues recommended they be culled because of their competition with the livestock for grazing. I opposed this and in my 1971 manuscript stated: 'There are over 100 000 head of cattle alone in the territory, and consequently the relative amount of grass consumed by five or six thousand zebra is not significant. Zebra are also able to graze greater distances from waterholes and, in fact, seldom compete directly with the native livestock.'

However, just six years later, in his 1977 report, Slang wrote: 'Although it is clear that the Burchell zebra numbers are declining there are still about 1 000 left in Kaokoland. They are being intensively hunted, especially in the inhabited areas and in the north-eastern parts, where they have been virtually exterminated.' As this major population decline occurred before the drought began, it must have been caused by uncontrolled hunting after the Kaokoveld was de-proclaimed as a game reserve – in spite of BAD's 1971 press statement that 'the conservation of fauna and flora will be carried out in accordance with existing SWA legislation and, if necessary, special steps will also be taken'.

In my 1971 manuscript I conservatively estimated Hartmann's zebra numbers to be between 1 200 and 2 000, adding that: 'The apparent trend of moving away from heavily populated areas will probably continue in the years to come, but the natural hardiness of this species, coupled with their largely inaccessible environment, should ensure their survival even if all the other larger game animals were exterminated.' Slang estimated that between 2 000 and 2 500 occurred in Kaokoland, mainly in the escarpment ranges and between Sesfontein and Otjovasandu. But in his report he stated: 'The population is well established although they are also being hunted for their skins.'

The high value of zebra skins was no doubt the major reason for the demise of the Burchell's zebra, but why did not more Hartmann's zebra survive the drought? A clue was provided on the trip Chris Eyre, Mitch Reardon and I took through Kaokoland in 1983. At remote springs deep in the escarpment mountains we found sacks and plastic hung from poles to stop game from drinking. Denied access to water and with the highlands devastated by overgrazing, as well as being hunted for their meat and skins, it is perhaps not surprising that so few survived north of the Hoanib River. In the ANVO concession, although many died of starvation along the north–south section of the veterinary fence, large numbers of Hartmann's zebra were able to migrate into the west of Etosha, some of which were later translocated back into Damaraland.

In a drought gemsbok also move east, where in the past there would have been large tracts of the highlands that were beyond the reach of livestock and more water-dependent wildlife. However, by the early 1980s the many artificial water-points had enabled cattle, goats and sheep to utilise almost all of the plateau, and as no effective rain fell in the west there would have been virtually no grazing or browse left anywhere for them to feed on. South of the Hoanib the large number of gemsbok carcasses found along the vet fence in the ANVO concession showed that they had tried to migrate inland, and some may have found their way into Etosha, but no gemsbok were translocated back into Damaraland.

In spite of the uncontrolled hunting, above-average rainfall in the 1970s enabled the springbok population to remain stable, and in his 1977 report Slang estimated there were between 6 000 and 6 500 in Kaokoland. However, on the 1982 NWT aerial census only 217 were seen. Although competition with goats and sheep would have contributed to the high mortality rate – as it would also have done for impala and kudu on the highlands – the ongoing hunting by both white and black residents of the region undoubtedly played a major role, particularly after the SADF gave out .303 rifles to the local people.

Of all the large ungulates, giraffe were able to survive the drought best, with their numbers in Kaokoland staying more or less the same between Slang's 1977 aerial survey and the 1982 census. But as he pointed out in his report, in the 1930s Shortridge found them to be widespread on the highlands, where apart from a small population along the Ombonde River they now no longer occurred. Because giraffe are highly prized for their meat, as well as their skins to make sandals, they were still a target for Himba and Herero hunters, who before the appointment of community game guards had threatened their survival north of the Hoanib River.

When Slang left in early 1983, the EWT continued flying 10-hour aerial surveys to monitor elephant and other game distribution and movements, although instead of every two months they only took place three times a year: In the wet season (February–April), the cold dry season (June–August) and the hot dry season (October–December). When the EWT withdrew its support for the project the surveys ended, but by then they had given us a good idea of where most of the larger mammals in Damaraland occurred at different times of the year.

As was the case north of the Hoanib, when it rained in the pre-Namib the Hartmann's zebra, gemsbok and springbok migrated west to exploit the new green growth there, and in dry periods moved inland. However, the opposite happened with giraffe, which in the wet season went east to browse on the new leaves of the deciduous tree species there. In the winter months they moved west, following the riverbeds or crossing the barren plains deep into the desert, providing one of the many remarkable sights the region has to offer.

Although both Slang and I disagreed with Ken Tinley's theory of an annual elephant migration between Etosha and the western Kaokoveld, the herds inhabiting the Uniab and its tributaries did go east in the rainy season. But their destination was only the valley of the Ombonde River, where the green tufts of perennial grasses that still grew on its deep sandy soils were a major part of their diet. When these dried out and their protein content dropped, the herds returned to the rock-strewn basalt ranges, finding sufficient browse along the mopane-dominated dry watercourses that traversed this part of Damaraland.

The reason for elephants going east in the wet season was easy to explain, but their spending the driest time of the year in the desert was more difficult. According to Eugene Joubert it was poaching that had driven them into the northern Namib and the behaviour of the Uniab elephants certainly suggested that they felt threatened when moving to the Ombonde. One day Blythe and I watched five herds near the Achab River, totalling over 50 bulls, cows and calves, walking in parallel towards the eastern horizon. Fifty years earlier Dennis Woods had witnessed a similar event in the lower Hoarusib, and believed that the 'great phalanx' of elephants he had seen moving up the riverbed knew that going east was dangerous.

A possible reason for them choosing to be in the west during the late dry season was because at this time of the year the prevailing wind is from the coast, which keeps the day temperatures there relatively cool – a critical factor for animals with a large body mass compared to the surface area of their skin. But whatever the reason may have been, once the poaching stopped and large tracts of more favourable habitat inland became safe, the number of elephants spending the period from around July to when the rains started in the Uniab and its northern tributaries steadily decreased.

During the early 1980s the approximately 80 elephants inhabiting the valley of the Huab River also seasonally moved from east to west, but did not go beyond the Riemvasmaker settlement at De Riet. However, a decade later, when the village was abandoned and only a few Damara families remained, some of them started following the riverbed deep into this spectacular part of the pre-Namib. A few breeding herds also moved south to the Ugab River, where the last elephants had been shot out over 40 years before.

As the sub-population in the lower Hoanib did not venture past Sesfontein, no one disputed their credentials as 'desert elephants'. Their usual movement was up and down the main riverbed and its larger tributaries, but in years when the floodwaters reached the dunes, they spent most of their time feeding on the lush annual grasses that grew on the floodplain's deep alluvial silts. They also sometimes crossed the desert to the Hoarusib River, but when there they always stayed within the Skeleton Coast Park. Once five of the Hoanib elephants walked along the sea shore past the DNC base at Moewe Bay – an amazing sight if anyone had seen them, but it was at night and only their tracks were visible on the beach.

In 1985 world-renowned wildlife film makers Des and Jen Bartlett made the Hoanib elephants into international celebrities when their television documentary, *Giants of the Skeleton Coast,* was shown by National Geographic. In one of its many memorable sequences they used two micro-lights to follow 29 Hoanib elephants, including three small calves, as they crossed the barren plains and sand dunes on their way back from the Hoarusib – a distance of 70 km as the crow flies and 120 km between water-points.

*   *   *

Thanks to the active support we were getting from the local community and their traditional leaders, and because their carcasses were hard to hide, we were confident that no elephants had been poached since 1982. But I was less sure about the rhino situation. The last one known to have been killed in Damaraland was by Moses Ganuseb just a year before, and with the NWT project having now been disbanded only Duncan Gilchrist and Augustinus Ochams were regularly patrolling north of the veterinary fence. Although the community game guards were still in place, because we wanted to keep live-stock out of the concession area they were all living around, and not within the main rhino range.

After the arrest of the Humu gang the poachers were also taking much more care in covering their tracks. In October 1985, while driving to Sesfontein I noticed some white objects lying about 100 metres from the road. They turned out to be the carcass of a rhino that had been partially buried and covered with brush. The bones were oily, which meant it was killed after the drought ended, but what concerned me the most was that we had all driven past it many times. If we did not see a dead rhino next to a main road, what chance was there of our finding any other carcasses in a million hectares of rugged mountains?

In February 1986, David Cummings, chairman of the IUCN's African Elephant and Rhino Specialist Group (AERSG), visited Wêreldsend, bringing news of the catastrophic poaching that was now taking place across Africa. Over half a million elephants had been killed for their ivory in the past 15 years, he told me, but because the rhino numbers were much lower their situation was even worse. In Tanzania, where there had been over 8 000 black rhino in the giant Selous Game Reserve, just a handful survived, and both the North and South Luangwa National Parks in Zambia were under siege. With gangs of poachers now crossing into Zimbabwe, game rangers along the Zambezi River had been given the right to shoot any person found unlawfully inside the parks.

Although the scale of the slaughter over the rest of Africa made our problems seem insignificant, Namibia's black rhino were the subspecies *Diceros bicornis bicornis* that had once inhabited the whole of south-western Africa, from the Cape to Angola, but now only occurred in Etosha and the Kaokoveld. The few that were left in the north-west were also valuable because they were the only viable population of rhino that lived in a desert. I had hoped to show David at least one of them, but in four days of driving through all the most likely places we saw none, and very little spoor. When we got back to camp I was worried. Were rhinos being poached right under our noses – as Ian Hofmeyr had found was happening in Etosha?

On the last night I expressed my fears to David, telling him that of the 27 adult rhino already identified north of the veterinary fence, 18 had not been seen for a year or more. In 1981 the AERSG had designated the 'desert elephants' as being the highest priority for conservation in Africa, so surely the Kaokoveld rhino – which did not depend on the large riverbeds and were thus better adapted to living in hyper-arid conditions – also deserved the same status? Before returning to Harare David asked me if I would be prepared to undertake a census of the rhinos north of the fence. A month later he informed me that the New York Zoological Society had agreed to donate R6 000 to cover the costs.

The main objective of the census would be to try and locate all the rhino that were already on file, but had not been seen lately, as well as adding any new ones found. From the updated version we could then work out the sex and age structure of the population, as well as its present distribution across the range. I also hoped to test different ways of finding rhino, so that a cost-effective method of monitoring them could be set up in the future. I estimated that the census would take me six months to complete, and although the money had not yet arrived from New York, decided to start immediately.

During the remainder of March I spent eight days in the field, covering 240 km in the survey area by vehicle and walking over 100 km, but did not find a single rhino. In April I was committed to attending the first hearing of the Van Alphen court case in Windhoek, and spent most of the rest of the month getting the support of Duncan and Ruth Gilchrist, Blythe and Rudi, as well as his Skeleton Coast staff, for the census. I also spoke to the Bartletts, who were based at Moewe Bay, and Des offered me the back seat of his microlight to see if it was more successful than larger fixed-wing aircraft in finding rhino.

This left five days for fieldwork, in which I found one rhino, an improvement on my efforts in March, but hardly an impressive achievement. In a preliminary report to David I stated that a major reason for my lack of success was that it was the height of the rainy season, when rhino were not dependent on permanent springs and dispersed across the vast area that made up their present range. I added that working on my own also made it both difficult and potentially dangerous to follow their tracks. To rectify this, in April I approached the Swakopmund Centre of the Wildlife Society and they agreed to pay the salary of a local tracker. The man I chose was my previous assistant, Sakeus Kasaona, who had not been happy living at Moewe Bay and had resigned from his DNC post.

Once Sakeus joined me our success rate improved considerably. During 20 days of fieldwork in May we successfully tracked six rhino, including two bulls not previously recorded. On a trip with Blythe into the hills east of Palmwag we also found a new cow. As it was her first time looking for rhino north of the vet fence I gave Blythe the honour of naming her, something she had done for all the known individuals in the Ugab valley. With Cindy added to the file, the average time taken to find a rhino had been cut down to just over three days. The census was on its way.

Giving wild animals names was then a controversial issue among scientists. Jane Goodall and Diane Fossey had started the trend by naming the chimpanzees and mountain gorillas they studied, which made them more endearing to the general public, but it was not quite the same with a ton and a half of antisocial pachyderm. Nevertheless, a name was easier to remember than series of code letters, and a few of the rhino in Damaraland, especially the mature bulls, did show signs of having their own individual character. One of them was Caesar, the dominant male in the upper Aub River.

His claim to fame was chasing Johan le Roux up a tree, and keeping him there for an hour, but Caesar had not been seen since then. In June, when Sakeus had taken some days off to see his wife, and I was working with Edward Eiseb and another DNC game ranger, we found a large spoor in the Aub that I was sure belonged to the elusive bull. However, Caesar had a big territory to patrol, and no doubt a number of cows to check up on, so he had walked a long way during the previous night. After three hours of tracking my two companions started flagging, but as he was a rhino I particularly wanted to find, while they took a rest I walked on, easily following his spoor along the bank of a watercourse.

About 20 minutes later I came to where the imprint of his huge body on the ground showed that he had lain down under a small tree. The shade had now moved, and so had Caesar, but I could not see where his spoor went on from this resting place. Then I heard something behind me, and turned to see the bull getting up from under a bush less than 15 metres away. I had walked past him without either of us becoming aware of the other. We were now, and like a sprinter out of the starting blocks I took off for a rocky ridge about 50 metres away – the loud snorting and breaking of branches behind me confirming that Caesar was in hot pursuit. Thanks only to my short start I was able to scramble up the slope just ahead of him, and watch as he swung away and trotted off up the valley, clearly very annoyed at having had his siesta interrupted. I had taken no photographs and did not even note his ear-marks, but there was no doubt in my mind who I had found.

Another bull with character was Stumpie, whose short tail was probably bitten off by a hyena when he was a calf. His territory stretched over a huge tract of the concession area around Urunendis Spring, from where Sakeus and I once tracked him for 22 km across the sparsely covered basalt plains. Stumpie also had a reputation of being 'bad tempered' after Duncan and Ruth had a close shave with him. To get a better look at the bull, they left their Land Cruiser, but he became aware of them and charged. They both ran back to the vehicle, with Duncan arriving first and jumping into the driver's seat. Thinking that Ruth was going around the other side, he closed the door behind him. She wasn't, but managed to squeeze through his open window just as Stumpie skidded to a halt, so close that the stones he kicked up hit the side of the truck. Needless to say, Ruth found the incident less amusing than Duncan.

My close encounter with Caesar had taught me to never track alone again. A second person was needed to keep checking ahead, so that the person following the spoor did not 'fall over' a sleeping rhino. After a few other lessons on how not to end up on the sharp end of a rhino horn, Sakeus and I formed an efficient team, finding 10 rhino in June, 11 in July, and 14 in August, in this case with the help of Des Bartlett and his micro-light. In September we found five rhino in a single day, and identified 19 different individuals in a nine-day stretch of fieldwork, an average of just over two a day.

In six months a total of 73 rhino were found, many more than all my sightings in the previous four years. The credit belonged to Sakeus, who quickly 'converted' his livestock tracking skills and had even begun to think like a rhino, often predicting where they were likely to go rather than bothering to follow their spoor. It was also sobering to realise how easy it would be for a home-grown poacher to find and kill them.

In spite of the hostility I still faced from the DNC's Head Office, the rhino census in Damaraland was a team effort, with the Gilchrists contributing many valuable sightings, and even Steve Braine at Moewe Bay adding two good records from the far west, one of them a bull not previously known. The critical task of keeping the rhino file up to date was given to Ruth, and her meticulous Swiss attention to detail ensured that no animals were double counted or different individuals recorded as the same rhino.

By the end of September we had collectively identified a total of 16 adult bulls and 18 adult cows, all of the latter with a calf at foot. The biggest problem was with sub-adults that had left their mothers, but did not yet have a characteristic horn shape or ear marks. I solved this by comparing the number of random sightings we had of this age category to those of adult animals, giving us an estimate of between 10 and 13 sub-adults, and a total of at least 62 rhino in Damaraland north of the vet fence. Only three previously known individuals were not found during the census, and 23 new rhino, mostly calves and sub-adults, were recorded.

Over the next two months I extended the census to the area between the vet fence and Huab River, finding a further four adult bulls and six cows, five of which had calves, and a minimum of three sub-adults. With the nine rhino Blythe knew in the Uchab area it gave us an estimated population of not less than 89 in Damaraland. In early 1987 Sakeus and I also confirmed that at least seven rhino survived in Kaokoland between the Hoanib and Hoarusib rivers, but we found no sign of any west of Orupembe. In 1985 community game guard Tjahorerua Tjisuta had found the carcass of a bull here, and as its horns were still in place it was presumed to have died of natural causes.

By excluding all calves under four years old, and adding those known to have been poached or died, the census enabled us to conclude that there had been approximately 75 rhino in the north-west when the NWT started operations. It was much higher than Slang estimated and more than any of us previously thought, but most importantly it showed that despite the losses the population had grown by 30 per cent since 1982.

However, the census was not just about numbers. In a paper I presented at the DNC professional officers' meeting in October 1986 I could show that, although using a micro-light was the quickest way of finding rhino, especially on the open plains in the west, by far the most cost-effective method was on foot with a good tracker. This had the added advantage of it being much easier to identify each animal found, which was critical to any rhino monitoring system set up in the future.

When Duncan was transferred to Namutoni in Etosha the following year, all the records that Ruth had kept were handed over to Blythe for her to maintain. Because of the increased responsibility of keeping track of the whole Damaraland population, not just the Uchab rhino, in 1987 she started the Save the Rhino Trust, which was independent of the Wildlife Society in Swakopmund. After the census Sakeus also joined Blythe to train the local young men she employed as rhino trackers.

To give an estimate of increases in the other game populations since 1982, during the rhino census I also recorded their numbers seen while driving or walking, which was then compared to Peter's and my 1983 vehicle and foot patrol reports. Although elephant and giraffe were encountered too seldom for a useful comparison to be made, the number of mountain zebra, gemsbok and springbok seen per 100 km travelled was found to be up by 60 per cent, 140 per cent and 180 per cent respectively.

In July 1986 the DNC had also conducted an aerial game census of the north-west. Although initially planned by Etosha's wildlife biologists as a strip count, the pilot and observers soon realised that it was impossible to fly transects in the mountains, and they adopted a method similar to that used by Slang in 1982. Over the intervening four years – one more than my comparative ground survey figures – the two aerial census results showed an increase of 90 per cent for mountain zebra, 180 per cent for gemsbok and nearly 300 per cent for springbok. With the drought broken and poaching under control, the populations of desert-adapted ungulates were all well on their way to recovering.

*   *   *

When Margie Jacobsohn came back in July to carry out her honours field-work, this time with her friend Dennie Smith, we met at a wildlife symposium in Swakopmund and again found we had much to talk about. While married to Graham Ferreira and on visits to Rudi and Blythe, she had gained an in-sight into the region's complex conservation issues, and was the first person I had met who immediately recognised the value of involving local people to stop the poaching, instead of just enforcing our Eurocentric legislation. But her background was also very different to that of any other woman I had known.

After matriculating Margie started as a cub reporter on the *Pretoria News*, rising up through the ranks to be the environment correspondent and later the first female features editor on the *Cape Times*. After she and Graham Ferreira divorced and a relationship began between her and the paper's edi-tor, Tony Heard, she resigned to follow her interest in archaeology at Cape Town University, while at the same time freelancing as Southern African cor-respondent for a consortium of 14 Dutch newspapers. On completing her degree, during which she had done fieldwork on early pastoralist sites on the west coast of South Africa, she decided to do her honours on modern-day herders, the Himba, a decision that would change her life, and mine.

Through her work as a journalist on a liberal English language newspaper, Margie got to know many young leaders in the ANC and its internal front, the UDF, and from them she learned how negative most black people's perception of nature conservation was. When she had tried to discuss environmental issues with them, their response was invariably to dismiss wildlife as irrel-evant and game reserves as just a waste of land that was needed by poor rural people. Although she believed their attitude was short-sighted, she knew of no examples of conservation having benefited black South Africans, and under apartheid it had more often disadvantaged them. What we were doing in the Kaokoveld had clearly demonstrated that the local people did care about wildlife, but she challenged me to take the next step and show how it could tangibly improve their lives.

Margie believed that just bringing the poaching under control was not enough. Our success had depended on the older men in the community, who still regarded wildlife as part of their cultural heritage. They wanted game back because they had grown up with it, and believed they had an ethical responsibility to conserve it, but did their children share these values? Most of them had gone to school, and their aspirations were to get a job and join the consumer society. With our history of excluding blacks from nature conservation, would the future politicians and bureaucrats in an independent Namibia care if the rhinos and elephants disappeared? There was also a cost to living with wild animals, which we could not realistically expect local people to bear if they received no benefit from it.

On her next field trip in September Margie came alone. She had just returned from Holland, where she had been to see her Dutch newspaper editors. This time I decided to show her more of the region's spectacular scenery and wildlife, including a trip down the Hoanib River – to see the elephants that local people were now protecting. At the mouth of the Mudorib we met Duncan and Ruth, whose sister and brother-in-law were visiting from Switzerland. As they had made their camp in a narrow drainage line I parked a few metres away, but put our bedrolls on top of a bank, from where there was a view across a sandy plain to the tree-lined course of the Hoanib, and the desert mountains beyond it.

In the early hours of the morning I heard a lion roaring; the sound made more awe-inspiring because it echoed off the bare rock faces of the ranges that formed a backdrop to the bright moonlit scene around us. After waking Margie I walked over to the Gilchrist party and woke them too, on the way back taking my shotgun from behind the seat of the Land Rover and putting it beside me. I then got back into my sleeping bag and waited for the lion to roar again. But there was only silence.

I had just started drifting back to sleep when my foot was given a hard yank. Instantly realising what it was, and knowing from previous encounters with lions in Etosha that I had to go on the offensive, I jumped up and waving my arms took a few steps towards the magnificent creature that was crouching five metres in front of me. I tried to shout, but on my first attempt could only manage a rather feeble squeak. Although the lion had initially got a fright and backed off, it was not going away.

By now Margie was standing alongside me, in a tremulous voice also trying to tell our uninvited 'dinner guest' he was not welcome. But the lion, its golden mane erect to make it look bigger, just flicked its tail and gave us a deep throaty growl. As it was clearly not intending to leave, my mind flashed to the shotgun that lay next to my bed, a few metres behind me. Signalling to Margie that she must stay where she was, I turned around and picking it up fired one barrel over the lion's head – keeping the second in reserve in case it still hadn't got the message. In the few seconds it took me to do so she was sure it had flexed its muscles to spring on her, but the sound of the first shot was enough. It walked off, stopping only once to look back and give us another Harley Davidson growl, before disappearing into the silvery distance.

After having disinfected a surprisingly minor wound on my heel we all went to bed, squeezed up like sardines next to Duncan's truck. The next morning when we examined the tracks left by the night's events, they showed that the lion had not gone far before it turned around and came back to the top of the bank, less than 15 metres from where we were. There was no way of knowing if it did so before or after we went to sleep.

Margie could not have asked for a more exciting start to her trip, and from there we followed a roundabout route to Purros, visiting community game guards Elias Mosia and Salmon Karutjaiva along the way. Both of them assured me that there was no longer any poaching taking place in their areas, and their only complaint was that they seldom saw Marcellus, who was responsible for delivering their rations and receiving their monthly reports. But when we drove on into Kaokoland both Abraham and Kamasitu had nothing good to say about Van Alphen, who was meant to visit them every month. According to the two CGGs this was not happening, and when he did bring their maize meal it was mouldy and full of worms.

Margie took notes of what they told us, and together with her experiences in Purros concluded that, whether by default or design, under the DNC the community game guard system was breaking down. As the EWT was paying for the rations and cash allowances, when she visited Johannesburg the following month she invited its new director, Dr John Ledger, to have lunch with her. There she briefed him on the situation, telling him that as things were now, she believed his organisation's money was being wasted. Margie then suggested that he come and see for himself, adding that if he could fly to Windhoek she would take him into the area with her own 4x4 vehicle.

In November John took her up on her offer, but the trip got off to a bad start. After a hot eight-hour drive they arrived at Wêreldsend to find the gate through the vet fence locked. Although the distance they had to walk to the camp was only a kilometre, it was not the best way to receive the guest on whose shoulders the community game guards, and my future depended. Worse was to come. Before they left town Margie had asked John what alcohol he drank. Only beer, he replied, so she bought a six-pack of Windhoek Lager and put it in a coolbox when we set off for the field. On the first day John drank five of them and was reaching for another when she told him that it was the last one – and there was no place to buy more where we were going. John was appalled, and so were we. Six beers a day was his normal consumption, and we would be away for four days!

Apart from the EWT Director's severe case of hops deprivation the trip went off well, with John being impressed by the desert scenery and its recovering wildlife populations. He also had the chance to meet Marcellus and Blythe, as well as Steve Braine and John Patterson from the Skeleton Coast Park, all of whom gave their views on the conservation situation in the region. As importantly, our visit to Sesfontein coincided with a meeting at which headmen Joshua Kangombe, Goliat Kasaona and Theophilas Havachab as well as four community game guards were present, while at Purros he met Kamasitu Tjipombo, who had played a major role in a number of crucial poaching cases.

When I took him back to Windhoek we stopped in Khorixas to meet with the Damara Executive Committee. John told them that he had heard all the problems, but also the many positive things that were taking place in the two homelands, and he pledged his support for future collaborative efforts with all the interested parties concerned about the people and wildlife in the Kaokoveld.

Privately, John told us he had seen and heard enough to convince him that, in spite of what the senior DNC officials were saying, they had not done a good job of maintaining the support of the local people. Before leaving he promised to brief the EWT Board at their next meeting, but added that it would not be easy to reverse a decision taken by his predecessor, who was still a trustee. Nevertheless, Margie and I had been impressed by John's quick understanding of the key issues. He was clearly an independent thinker – but would he have the courage to stand up against the South African government?

In early 1987 John told me that the EWT Board had agreed to start funding me again from 1 April. The total amount would be only R1 800 per month, half of which would be my salary and the remainder to cover vehicle running costs and employ a local assistant to act as my translator. However, the community game guards would continue being paid through the DNC officials based in Khorixas and Opuwo.

By then Van Alphen had been transferred to Keetmanshoop and Chris Eyre sent to Opuwo to take over responsibility for Kaokoland. In April 1987, Rudi Loutit was also promoted to the rank of principal nature conservator in charge of both Damaraland and the Skeleton Coast Park, while in Khorixas Tommy Hall had replaced Marcellus Loots. Although inexperienced in law enforcement when he arrived, with Lucas Mbomboro's help Marcellus had achieved an excellent success rate. Fourteen people had now been found guilty of poaching elephant or rhino in the north-west and the total number of convictions for all species was over 70. As there had only been one prosecution prior to 1982 it was an outstanding achievement, but without effective ground surveillance most of the cases would not have been detected.

After two years I was once again earning a salary. But with a strong team of DNC officials in the two homelands to support the community game guards, I was faced with the dilemma of finding a new role for myself. To coincide with the re-starting of an NGO project in the Kaokoveld and with Margie's help, I wrote an article for the EWT's quarterly magazine, *Quagga*, entitled: 'Wildlife conservation in Africa: there is another way.' It began by saying:

> Throughout Africa wildlife is in trouble. With a few notable exceptions, the situation north of the Zambezi and Kunene rivers could be described as desperate. Even in Southern Africa population growth, pollution and politics are having an unprecedented impact on natural resources. On the continent that was endowed with the greatest array of large mammals on earth, nature conservation has become a grim struggle to save what is left. There have been some outstanding successes; battles have been won; but seen as a whole who can deny that we are losing ground at a steadily increasing rate?
>
> Is wildlife conservation then a lost cause in most of Africa? Should we now 'cut our losses' and make a stand along borders that can be defended by megabucks and firepower? But in the long term, are there any 'safe' borders that can be protected by these means alone when population and political pressures really build up? Are we merely fighting to stave off the inevitable, for as long as possible? Or is there another way?

I then went on to describe some of the cultural practices employed by the continent's indigenous people to conserve wild animals by social sanction, taboo or decree by their traditional leaders. However, they had been undermined by the colonial governments' concept of 'royal' or State-owned game and the creation of wildlife preserves. At the same time the new authorities had taken measures to protect the settlers' livestock from diseases that resulted in huge numbers of wild animals being exterminated. From the local communities' perspective it would have seemed as if 'whites could with impunity slaughter and waste as much game as they wished, but a black man would be jailed for just trying to feed his family'.

In the late 1960s and 1970s legislation was passed allowing landowners in Namibia, Zimbabwe and South Africa to get conditional ownership over certain game species, thereby 'bringing wildlife down from its exalted pedestal and putting it in the market place'. This had initiated a thriving game farming industry in these countries that was based on sport hunting, meat production and tourism, but no equivalent rights were ever given to black communal area farmers, reinforcing the belief that 'wildlife belonged to the whites and therefore had little relevance and no value to them'. I then listed why this was not surprising:

1. With a few isolated exceptions, no attempt has yet been made to promote wildlife utilisation to the material benefit of African subsistence farmers.
2. Far too many game rangers/nature conservators still carry out their duties with an arrogance that implies little sympathy or concern for rural blacks and their legitimate endeavours in overgrazed and overcrowded 'homelands'.
3. Blacks have rarely been encouraged to visit national parks or game reserves.
4. In many areas wild animals still prey on black subsistence farmers' livestock and damage crops.
5. Virtually no attempt has yet been made to explain to rural blacks why antelope, elephants and even predators are valuable, and worth conserving.

Whether one's political views are liberal or conservative, who can deny that today the rural black man is the trump card of nature conservation in Africa? Now that firearms are freely available to him, it is *his* uncontrolled subsistence hunting that is having a devastating effect on large mammal populations throughout the continent. With a few exceptions *he* is doing the killing of Africa's threatened elephants and rhino populations, albeit for European or Eastern markets. It is also *his* assistance or lack of it, that frequently determines whether poachers are apprehended or not. Furthermore, it is *his* livestock that is now moving into many of the continent's last remaining wildernesses, and it is *his* ever-increasing numbers that are building up ominously around nearly all proclaimed game parks . . .

But with the rural black man on our side, wildlife could once more take its rightful place as one of Africa's greatest resources. With him against us, little of what conservationists hold dear is likely to survive into the twenty-first century. How can the rural black man's present, generally negative attitude to wildlife be changed? Simply by making wildlife in fact valuable to him. This could be done through:

1. *Conservation education*, particularly in rural black schools.
2. *Conservation extension* among the adults in rural areas, whose support is crucial now.
3. *New wildlife policies* that take into account the concerns of rural blacks and which facilitate wildlife becoming a tangibly valuable long-term resource to them.

In conclusion I stated that:

Only the government has the authority to change legislation, and in the long-term only it has the financial and staff resources to undertake effective conservation education and extension programs. However, the restrictive bureaucracy inherent in government agencies, accountable as they are to the tax-payer, makes it extremely difficult for them to be innovative, or venture into untested waters. But the wildlife crisis in Africa demands that someone take the plunge . . .

Non-Government Conservation Organisations can and must accept this challenge. Their role is not to usurp the legitimate functions of government, but to act as a pathfinder and catalyst. Once a new way has been tried and proved the NGO should withdraw, leaving it to the government agency to entrench and extend those projects that were successful.

CHAPTER TWENTY-THREE

THE PURROS PROJECT
AND MORE POACHING

With the populations of all the large mammals recovering it was time to honour the promise I had made to the local people that it would be them, and not white government officials, who would be the first to legally eat game meat again. In February, just before Marcellus left Khorixas, we jointly wrote a letter to his head office proposing that small numbers of zebra, gemsbok and springbok be cropped and their meat distributed to the communities that had shown their commitment to conservation. Our proposal received the support of the Damara Executive Committee and the white administration officials in Khorixas, who offered their services to do the actual hunting. The last hurdle was to get DNC approval, and this was also given a month later.

When Rudi took up his post one of his first responsibilities was to organise the game harvest. The animals hunted north of the Red Line were delivered to traditional leaders in Sesfontein, Warmquelle and Khovarib, while the meat of those shot south of it was sold to local people there at subsidised prices. In 1988 Rudi requested that another 50 zebra, 20 gemsbok and 70 springbok be cropped around Bergsig and in the concession area, but this time he insisted that only DNC staff do the hunting. Although the number of animals harvested was not enough for everyone to taste the 'fruits' of their conservation efforts, two important principles were established: that local communities could benefit from the wildlife in Namibia's homelands, and that it should be sustainably utilised to prevent another die-off from taking place in the next major drought.

The game harvest helped to win over sceptics in the community, but as they were not beneficiaries it did not go down as well with the white officials, and a few of them took the opportunity to also make a little biltong. A tip-off from a Riemvasmaker farmer near Bergsig led to Naas Maritz being charged with hunting a springbok for his own use. This was rather embarrassing for the homeland's Director of Education, so on the day of the hearing he slipped into the courtroom, pleaded guilty and paid a R500 fine, before going straight back to his office. But there were too many local people in court for the case to be covered up, and word soon spread that one of the old-guard white hunters had actually been convicted of poaching.

He was not the only one. Shortly thereafter Colin's brother, Martin Britz, who had been appointed as the nature conservator in southern Damaraland, charged two white residents of Uis for killing a gemsbok, and a year later the headmaster of the little mining town's high school, David Augustyne, was also found guilty of shooting a springbok and fined. Seven more cases of poaching south of the veterinary fence were taken to court during this period, as against only two in the areas where community game guards now operated, providing further evidence of how effective they had been in stopping the hunting.

The situation was not as good in Kaokoland, where the different arms of the security forces had become a law unto themselves, and they did not take kindly to the arrival of Chris Eyre in Opuwo. On his first visit to the local 'whites only' club, a senior officer in Koevoet, the notorious police 'anti-ter-rorist' unit, threatened to beat him up. Although Chris fancied his chances against the man on his own, he noticed that a number of other burly military types were appraising him from the bar, and suspected that if he stepped out-side he would not just be facing one opponent.

Margie Jacobsohn's presence in Purros was also not welcomed, and her first two applications for a research permit had been mysteriously lost. It was finally granted after she received the help of a Progressive Party member of parliament she knew, but when the local security police became aware of her previous political affiliations she was summoned to Opuwo. There she was told by Lt Henk Botha that they would be keeping a close watch on her. In fact, they did more than this.

A few weeks later she flew to Cape Town for a month, leaving her 4x4 vehicle at the Khorixas Rest Camp. On the way back to her study area she helped a Himba lineage head move his kid goats from a broken windmill to an alternative water-point, and when they reached Purros she asked her assistant, Shorty Kasaona, to wash out the back of her truck. Under the rubber mat he found a stack of SWAPO propaganda pamphlets that could only have been put there while her truck was parked in Khorixas. Margie hid a few of them in a tree in case they might one day be needed as evidence and then burnt the rest.

Within a few days the security police called in at her camp, and after the white officer had drunk a cup of tea, he asked if he could look inside the dung hut the women of Purros made for her to sleep in. While he did so, the two black constables wandered off to where her vehicle was parked and opened the back. When they found nothing there they looked around the rest of the area, at one point standing right under the tree where the remaining pamphlets were hidden. Clearly disappointed, the men left, but a few months later the tables were turned.

While visiting Margie I noticed the dust of a vehicle approaching Purros along the Orupembe road. As very few other people came into the west of Kaokoland at that time we both stood out of sight until it was only a few metres away, and then stepped into the track in front of it, forcing it to stop. The driver turned out to be Henk Botha, and with him was Kaokoland's head of military intelligence and Ian Patton-Ash, an ex-colleague from Etosha who had since resigned and was now living in Opuwo. On the back of the truck was a single black policeman.

When Henk got out it was obvious that he had been drinking, and as his legs were covered in blood Margie asked him who he had just killed. Ignoring her sarcasm, but clearly still surprised by our sudden appearance, he ushered me aside and said the blood was from a springbok he had shot, adding that the police were allowed to do so when on patrol. That may be so, I replied, but I would still be reporting it to Chris Eyre. He then changed his story and said he had 'only meant to shoot near the springbok and hit it by mistake'. As this was very far-fetched I told him to tell his story to Chris; perhaps he would believe it.

The next morning Margie and I set off to find Chris, who we eventually found on the Beesvlakte investigating a problem hyena case. As he had been very uncomplimentary about a woman researcher staying alone at Purros, and had told Margie that he would not come to her assistance if she got into trouble, she looked forward to showing him that her presence in the area could be of some value. However, Chris was not at all pleased with the news we brought him.

'I don't need this in my life,' he growled when I had given him all the details. 'These bastards can make things bloody difficult for us, and you now catch them poaching.' But after a second cup of tea he calmed down and said: 'I guess we better go back to the site and see if we can find some hard evidence that I can use in court.' We left immediately.

As Kamasitu had moved to Purros, we picked him up and drove back along the road towards Orupembe, soon finding where Henk's vehicle had stopped and they all got out. About 100 metres from the track there was dried blood on the ground that showed where the springbok had been shot, but it was still not enough to get a conviction. But in spite of it being hard gravel, Kamasitu saw that one set of footprints left the truck in the opposite direction, which we followed to a nearby kopje. There we found the head and skin of the springbok hidden in a crevice. It was the evidence Chris needed to open a case.

Charging the local heads of both the security police and military intelligence was not going to be easy. When Chris submitted the docket to the Attorney General he refused to prosecute on the grounds that Margie and I were known troublemakers 'who were trying to put the government in a bad light'. However, Chris stuck to his guns and Henk Botha did eventually appear in court, but by then he had come up with a third account of what happened. He now claimed to have only stopped near the springbok to photograph it, and was about to do so when the black security policeman on the back of the truck had shot it. Needless to say the latter admitted guilt and was fined R500, which was no doubt paid by his commanding officer. It was the second case where a white official had been charged with poaching and got off, but this time a black man who every local person knew was innocent had been convicted of the offence.

Subsistence hunting in the west of Kaokoland had also not stopped. In October Abraham Tjavara reported the killing of a zebra by two men from Otjikondavirongo. The case was followed up by John Patterson, Augustinus Ochams and Lucas Mbomboro, and both men were found guilty and given fines of R400 and R150. A few months later the Orupembe community game guard, Tjahorerua Tjisuta, told Chris that Kamasitu's stepson had shot a gemsbok and a springbok in the Khumib River. When I questioned him about it Kamasitu admitted covering up for his stepson, but denied any further involvement. Because of the key role he had played in both the Van Alphen and Botha cases, I wondered if his failure to report the case was due to family loyalty or to his disillusionment with the white man's system of justice.

In spite of this setback, John Ledger remained steadfast in his support for the community game guards, and on his second visit in February 1988 he committed the EWT to funding another six men. At the same time the Wildlife Society's Namib Centre agreed to pay for two more, enabling the shield around the rhino range to be reinforced and the network to be extended further north to the Marienfluss. More importantly, it allowed us to bring the local Damara traditional leadership into the project.

At Khovarib, Headman Gabriel Taniseb appointed Joel Hoeb, one of the three men convicted of poaching in July 1982, and Meesig Taniseb, who had reported the killing of a steenbok in the gardens that later led to Marcellus Loots' last rhino poaching case. As Theophilas Havachab had recently stood down as chief in Sesfontein, and the elections for his successor were about to take place, his senior councillor, Otto Ganuseb, chose Naftali Taurob to be the community game guard. This appointment was later confirmed by the new traditional leader there, Jeremiah Gaobaeb.

In Kaokoland, Vetamuna Tjambiru chose Karunganga at the Red Drum and Ngevi Tjihaku in the Okondjombo area, while Kahoravi Tjingee of Otjitanda chose Langman, one of his councillors. Chris also replaced Abraham Tjavara at Ganumub with Japi Uararavi, who lived at Tomakas. In the concession zone Goliat Kasaona chose Andreas Uaropatjike to work with Salmon Karutjaiva, and Joshua Kangombe retired his brother Hosia at Otokotorue and chose Masiare Tjindundumba to be responsible for the area around Palmfontein spring, where a number of Herero families had now moved.

All of the new community game guards were middle-aged men, who were no doubt hunters in the past, but Rudi and I were taken aback by Joshua's selection for the key rhino range west of the Sesfontein road near the watershed of the Aub and Barab rivers. Piet Hizeraku had been part of the gang ambushed west of Otjovasandu in 1978, and was also convicted with the Humu brothers four years later for killing eleven elephants and two rhino. But as Joshua pointed out, Piet knew the ways of poachers better than anybody else and was 'a man of the bush'. If we paid him to look after the wild animals he was sure he would stop hunting. As we could not expect Joshua or any of the other traditional leaders to take responsibility for the community game guard system if we did not respect their decisions, Piet was duly appointed.

Unlike many of the other community game guards, who relied heavily on information provided by the people living around them to keep track of what was happening in their areas, Piet spent most of his time in the field. Although he never caught any poachers, every local person knew it would be foolhardy to hunt in the vicinity of his home. Many years later when he was interviewed by a BBC film crew, Piet told them that he had only killed seven rhino, but could not remember the number of elephants. As he had always operated as part of a gang I wondered how many they had jointly accounted for.

*   *   *

No poaching of elephant or rhino had occurred for three years, and the traditional leaders were justifiably proud of the role that they and their game guards had played. But with the price of ivory and rhino horn now so high and the illegal trade flourishing in the rest of Africa, we could not depend on their efforts alone to ensure the survival of the still critically low big game populations in the region. To also gain the support of its younger residents, whose aspirations went beyond subsistence farming, direct economic benefits were needed, and the few tourists who had started visiting the region offered the best way of providing them.

Although the tourism potential of the western Kaokoveld had been recognised in the 1960s, the entry restrictions and then the security situation made its attractions virtually unknown to the general public. When the NWT project started, the only people visiting the region for recreational purposes were fishermen going to Torra Bay, and the few international clients flown into the Skeleton Coast Park by Louw Schoeman.

Trained as a lawyer, Louw first came to the Kaokoveld as the legal representative of a South African consortium with the prospecting rights on South West Africa's northern shoreline. In the 1960s he formed a company to mine amethysts at Sarusas spring near the Khumib River mouth, and was later involved in the government's plan – abandoned in the early 1970s – to build a harbour at Moewe Bay. By then the beauty of the desert had so impressed him that when part of the Skeleton Coast Park was put out on tender for low-impact tourism in 1977, he applied for and was granted the concession. Operating under the name Skeleton Coast Fly-in Safaris, Louw offered a unique experience, which would put the northern Namib Desert on the map as a world-class tourist destination.

By the mid-1980s two other tour operators had started taking clients into Damaraland: Gernot Senterfol of Southern Cross Safaris and Karl-Heinz

Grutemeyer, under the name of Desert Adventure Safaris. Both went as far north as the Hoanib River, but the local people got no benefits from them apart from handouts of food or tobacco. Nevertheless, the Damara Executive Commitee still regarded wildlife as a valuable asset, and even after the breakdown of negotiations with the DNC over the ANVO concession proclamation Chief //Garoeb told Brian Jones, a reporter for the *Windhoek Advertiser*, that the future economic development of the homeland was 'dependent on mining and tourism'.

A few self-drive tourists also came to see the 'White Lady' rock painting in the Brandberg and the prehistoric engravings at Twyfelfontein, but both of them fell under the National Monuments Council. To make matters worse the only accommodation then available in the homeland was the Khorixas Restcamp, which belonged to the parastatal First National Development Corporation. Travellers going anywhere else in Damaraland had to camp out, which provided no jobs and brought no revenue into the DRA's coffers. To rectify the situation, in 1985 the Damara Executive Committee decided to convert the now abandoned ANVO hunting camp at Palmwag into a rustic tourist lodge.

Although they had no budget to do this, building material was obtained from the Departments of Agriculture and Works, who also supplied construction staff. However, before the six bungalows and a dining area were completed they were informed by the DNC that, because tourism was a central government responsibility, it was illegal for the DRA to operate the lodge. But as there was no legislation stopping a second-tier authority from leasing out land it was the custodian of, or any infrastructure on it, the conversion of Grellmann's old hunting camp into a tourist facility went ahead.

The man put in charge of the project was Martiens Boshoff. Having only recently arrived in Damaraland, he asked my advice on how the vast ANVO concession should be managed. I recommended that the area around Palmwag, as far as the Grootberg Range in the east and the Aub River in the west, be kept open for the Lodge guests, while the rest should be divided along the Sesfontein road into two tourism concessions. A third could be created in the unsettled land south of the Red Line to the Uchab River. Martiens also asked me if I knew anyone who might be interested in leasing them. As I had previously met Louw Schoeman and Karl-Heinz Grutemeyer I suggested that he contact them.

In 1986 Desert Adventure Safaris leased the western concession, as well as Palmwag Lodge, and two years later Skeleton Coast Fly-in Safaris started operating south of the Red Line. The concession east of the Sesfontein road was only leased out in early 1990, by which time the Damara Representative Authority no longer existed. Initially this lease was granted to Wilderness Safaris in partnership with Afro-ventures, but after a few years Dennis Liebenberg, who had managed their operations, took over the area south of the Grootberg Range in his own name and developed Etendeka Mountain Camp.

Although the DRA leasing land for tourism was legitimate, because the area was not proclaimed there was no legal way of making people pay to enter the concessions. This problem was solved by a 1959 regulation stating it was illegal to drive off a proclaimed road on State Land without a permit, which had not been repealed when the homeland was created. Although contravening it carried a maximum fine of only R50, we believed that the majority of visitors to the area would be prepared to pay a small entry fee.

Palmwag Lodge opened in mid-1986, and soon became a popular destination for Namibians wishing to see the elephants, rhino and other big game that occurred in the basalt ranges. As the region's attractions were then little known in South Africa, and not at all further afield, John Ledger came up with the idea of my guiding high-paying guests through the area under the banner of the EWT. I would receive a daily rate to boost my salary, and as only one eight-day trip a month was envisaged, there would still be time to carry out conservation work between them. They would also promote tourism to the Kaokoveld, and thereby make more people aware of its still vulnerable wildlife.

With Desert Adventure Safaris providing the vehicles and catering, over the next five years 30 EWT tours were held, each comprising between five and ten guests. Although I followed a basic route to Purros and back via the western concession, there were no fixed overnight stops. Instead we just made camp wherever the setting sun found us, knowing that in the Kaokoveld attractive places to spend a night were not hard to find. Thanks to the DAS team of Andries Ferreira, Jurgen Broodman and sometimes Karl-Heinz himself, we provided our guests with a high standard of camp cuisine and comforts that included wine glasses at dinner and a bush toilet with a seat!

Initially Sakeus accompanied me, but after he joined the Save the Rhino Trust, Elias Hambo took his place. With their local knowledge and tracking skills we always found elephants, and on most trips saw at least one rhino, often at very close range. Although game sightings were infrequent, the backdrop of rugged mountains made up in quality for their lack of quantity, while our morning walks 'to read the local newspaper' added a new dimension to the bush experience of our mostly city-dwelling guests. As the majority of them were successful professionals in their fields, who had previously visited many other parks, our campfire discussions were informative and insightful – broadening both their knowledge and mine about happenings within and beyond the borders of the Kaokoveld.

As the main reason for coming on our tours was to see big game, I had to remind them that the area we travelled through had no conservation status. Here people shared the land and its resources with wild animals, the way they had done for countless millennia in the past – and I believed, could still do in the future. But this would only be possible if local communities were given the authority to manage and benefit from them. The EWT tours were not cheap, and as many of the guests were or had been hard-headed businessmen, it was not difficult to convince them that outside of national parks conservation had to be run on sound economic principles.

When Margie was in Purros we always called in to see her, so that she could tell our guests about her research. A visit to an *onganda* would also be arranged, where they were introduced to the senior family members and then taken on a guided tour. For wealthy whites whose everyday lives were cluttered with possessions, and who could buy all their basic requirements from a nearby supermarket, going into the home of skin-clad nomads was an unforgettable experience. Margie's knowledge of their customs and etiquette also ensured that our guests were not just seen as camera-wielding tourists, but as welcome visitors who came infrequently enough not to disrupt their daily lives.

To make our village visits less voyeuristic and more interactive, after they had been shown how ochre body lotion was prepared, and the different perfumes used by Himba women, one of the ladies in our party would be asked to empty out her handbag so that the merits of natural as against shop-bought cosmetics could be discussed. If our arrival in Purros coincided with a ceremony or social gathering, we would be invited to a night of Himba dancing, with Margie coercing the visitors into taking an active part.

One of our first guests was Stanislau Nevo, an Italian journalist, who wrote an article about the EWT tours in a major travel magazine, and from then on every August we ran at least one 'Italian tour'. The majority of its participants were fit young professionals so I usually took them up *Ombanga yazongombo* (the gorge of the goats), which led to a small spring high in the mountains where the Hoanib elephants sometimes drank. As reaching it entailed a hard

40 minute walk up a steep boulder-strewn watercourse, near the top of which was a rock face that needed the use of both hands and feet to climb up, it seemed impossible for elephants to negotiate. But the dung littering the route all the way to the water confirmed that they were capable of doing so.

After we returned to the vehicles on one Italian tour I noticed a geography professor sitting away from the group, and thinking that he may have over-exerted himself, I asked if anything was wrong. On the contrary, he replied, and told me he had just solved one of his country's greatest mysteries: 'For centuries we Italians have been looking for the pass that Hannibal used to take his elephants over the Alps, but we always thought that such huge animals needed an easy route. Today I saw that this is not so, and that they can climb up mountains just as well as goats!'

* * *

With Palmwag Lodge and concession operating successfully, the DRA decided to develop the Five Farms in the northeast of Damaraland, which Chief //Garoeb had named Hobatere. This time they entered into a 50/50 profit-sharing agreement with Jan Oelofse, who planned to use it for his hunting safaris. When a rumour spread that the Kaokoveld elephants would again be shot as trophies, the DRA and the DNC issued a joint press statement assuring the public that: 'No trophy hunting of desert dwelling elephant and black rhino in Damaraland will be allowed unless their numbers justify it.'

A month later the Secretary of the Damara Administration told Brian Jones of the *Windhoek Advertiser* that the DRA was planning to allocate individually owned farms in the Huab Valley and 'when they had to start paying for damage caused by the elephants living there they would begin shooting them'. Malan predicted that 'about 70 elephants will be shot out in the next two years', but added 'if the DNC allowed one elephant a year to be shot by a trophy hunter at the going rate of R20 000, there would be enough money to pay for the damage'. A few months later Jan Oelofse was given a quota for two trophy elephants a year in Damaraland.

I had no problem with a few bulls being hunted by high-paying foreign guests to recompense the DRA for the costs of repairing windmills and reservoirs – as long as it did not happen in the pre-Namib. Here the elephants caused no damage, and if they were killed for sport it would send the wrong message out to the local people. Consequently, when I met Steve Tors, one of

Jan Oelofse's professional hunters with an American client at Palmwag Lodge, I asked him if he was planning to hunt in the area. He said he was, so I asked him to pass a message on to Jan that if a single elephant was shot in the west I would ensure that it appeared in international media. None were.

At the time elephants were not the only wildlife causing the local farmers economic losses. Although very few lions had survived in the north-west, with the recovery of their prey populations their numbers were increasing, and so were incidents of livestock being killed. However, one of the lions in the Skeleton Coast caused a different problem, when it wandered south of the Uchab River and gave a family on the beach a fishing story their friends at home were unlikely to believe. At a distance they thought the lion was a large dog, but when it got closer and they saw what it was they abandoned their rods and picnic baskets and ran for their lives, with a hungry lion in hot pursuit – only just making it to their vehicle. As the annual influx of fishermen to Namibia's beaches was an important part of the national tourism industry, Tommy Hall was instructed to shoot the lion.

The other coastal lions did not remain inside the Skeleton Coast Park either. In low rainfall years, when there was no grass in the pre-Namib, many gemsbok and springbok gathered in the lower reaches of the dry riverbeds, and they moved inland to hunt them instead of seals. As the pastoralists also relied on the riparian vegetation at these times, their free-ranging donkeys and cattle added variety to the lions' diet. In April 1987 Louw Schoeman's chief of staff, Peter Uararavi, took his cattle into the Hoanib River and left them in the care of his wife and two young children. Seeing lion spoor nearby, when he returned to work he contacted Steve Braine at Moewe Bay, and asked the DNC to move them back into the Park. But as no cattle had been killed this was not done.

On Peter's next visit to his wife, she showed him the fresh tracks of a lion that had walked around the cattle kraal and right up to the half-finished hut where she and their children slept. He followed the spoor and shot a male lion, and also wounded a pregnant lioness, which was later killed by Steve. When I saw the skin it was clearly recognisable as the lion that had bitten me on the foot six months earlier.

Soon after this the pair of lions inhabiting the lower Uchab went upriver and killed a Brahman bull belonging to Andries Avarab, a Khorixas businessman. Flip Stander, a lion researcher from Etosha, and Martin Britz were sent to move them back into the Park, but they were only able to immobilise the female. Although their plan had been to take her to Cape Fria, where a seal colony had recently become established, on the way there she developed respiratory problems and was released at the mouth of the Hoarusib. Within a few days she had walked upriver to Purros, causing consternation in the community and bringing Margie's wrath down on the DNC officers 'for not having the courtesy to inform the local people there was a lion in their area'.

Without his mate the male wandered south, killing livestock in both the Omaruru and Swakop rivers before turning around near Sandwich Harbour, 20 km beyond Walvis Bay. After each of his meals a posse of farmers bent on retribution took up his spoor, while the DNC team tried desperately to find and capture him first. Eventually Flip was able to dart the lion and release him in the lower Hoanib River, where the lioness also moved after leaving Purros. Des and Jen Bartlett filmed the re-united pair engaged in 'paw play' and a few months later cubs were born. But their addiction to beef proved to be their downfall. On a foray upriver to near Sesfontein they were shot by local farmers, assisted by Lucas Mbomboro and Sakeus Kasaona.

The loss of these last coastal lions was a tragedy, but we had never asked Lucas and Sakeus, or any of the local people not to kill lions that preyed on cattle. The law gave all farmers the right to destroy predators that 'threatened their livestock' and one of the main responsibilities of the community game guards was to assist stockowners in serious cases of human wildlife conflict. During the year Tommy Hall also shot three problem lions in Damaraland, and the white farmers along Etosha's southern border killed an average of 40 lions a year that had come onto their farms from the Park.

*   *   *

In November 1987 Margie and I were invited to an IUCN conference in Harare on 'Sustainable economic benefits from wildlife and its contribution to rural development'. Although the organisers asked us to keep a low profile at the meeting – because some of the delegates from north of the Zambezi might boycott it if they knew that South Africans were attending – we jumped at the opportunity of hearing about conservation in countries that were not dominated by racial politics.

The conference was opened by the Minister of Wildlife and Tourism in Zimbabwe, Victoria Chitepo, who stated that natural resources were the real basis of human welfare, because they were our life support system. Unfortunately, she added, Africa was caught in a downward spiral of environmental degradation that was leading to abject poverty, and which could only be avoided by rational conservation and land use planning. She then asked conservationists and politicians to reflect on the question: are environmental problems really ecological, or are they socio-political and economic?

Thereafter speaker after speaker, including some of the continent's most eminent conservationists, stressed the importance and urgency of involving local communities in wildlife management and ensuring that they too bene-fited from it. One of the highlights was a case study on a new conservation initiative in Zambia's Luangwa Valley presented by Gilson Kaweche. There 114 members of the local community were trained as informal game scouts and given the same powers as national parks staff. This had led to villagers voluntarily supplying information on poachers' movements, which in turn reduced illegal elephant hunting by 80 per cent. In its first year ADMADE (Administrative Management Design) generated 144 000 kwacha, which had risen to 240 000 kwacha the following year, from legal wildlife utilisa-tion in the Lupande area alone – 40 per cent of which had gone to the local community.

The Zambian Director of National Parks, Dr H Chabwela, then gave his paper on the Kafue Wetland Project, in which he said that rural communi-ties acted the way they did because of the limited options available to them. Although they had to be included in the conservation of natural resources, we could not expect them to sacrifice what they needed now in return for prom-ises in the future. He concluded by saying: 'At this conference we have talked a lot about giving local people this and giving them that, but what has been forgotten is that they also want power. They want a say over the resources that affect their lives. This is more important than money.'

After these two stimulating presentations the paper on Zimbabwe's much talked about CAMPFIRE Programme (from Communal Area Management Programme for Indigenous Resources) was disappointing. The rationale be-hind it could not be faulted, but it had not yet got off the ground, although this was expected to happen in the near future. In his talk Dr Rowan Martin stressed CAMPFIRE was not an attempt to sell conservation to rural com-munities, but rather a new form of land use in communal areas that was com-pletely voluntary. However, permission from the government was needed before responsibility for wildlife management could be handed over to local people. This created a 'Catch-22' situation, because it could not be done until the community was ready, but they would not be able to get ready until they had authority.

One of the last papers was presented by Dr Perez Olindo, the Director of Kenya's national parks. He told us that after 1977, when the country had banned all hunting, the outfitters switched to photographic safaris and built a number of camps on communal land around Masai Mara National Park. The concessionaires paid a rental directly to the community councils, who were now earning millions of Kenya shillings annually, and it had resulted in them now regarding the wildlife as belonging to them and protecting it.

In his summing-up of the conference Gilson Kaweche stated that: 'we almost forgot the potential of using the local human resources'. Margie and I could not help thinking that if the policies recently initiated in the Luangwa Valley had been applied sooner they might not have lost tens of thousands of elephants, and virtually all of its 3 000 black rhino. We also wished that the Namibian and South African conservation authorities, who were so hostile to our community-based approach, could have attended the conference.

With the poaching of elephant and rhino having moved across the Zambezi into Zimbabwe, before going back to Namibia we visited Mana Pools, where I had hoped to meet Glen Tatham, the man in charge of the country's anti-poaching operations. As he was visiting Harare, Clive Swanepoel showed us around the Park's headquarters and he briefed us on the situation they faced. The men doing the hunting came from Zambia, he told us, and returned there to sell the horns and ivory. This made it impossible for them to be followed up, and because of the scale of the illegal hunting the anti-poaching units now opened fire on any unauthorised person found within the wildlife reserves along the Zambezi. More than 90 poachers had been killed, but coloured pins were also stuck into map on the wall marking where over 400 dead rhino had been found. In the dense valley bushveld and rugged escarpment ranges, I wondered how many carcasses had *not* been found.

They were grim statistics, but the young white Zimbabweans we met in Mana Pools seemed unwilling to think beyond the macho methods being used to fight their 'Rhino War'. An aircraft had recently been acquired and fitted with a machine gun to carry out 'search and kill' operations, which included randomly strafing the ground in a Vietnam style attempt to frighten the poachers. I also noted that in the ops room the Park's staff used the same jargon as during Zimbabwe's liberation war a decade earlier, when body counts were seen as the measure of success – and that war had been lost.

To obtain a balanced picture of conservation in the Zambezi valley, we then visited Russell and Lynne Taylor at their home in Matusadona National Park, on the banks of Lake Kariba. Russell had been a pioneer of the CAMPFIRE approach, and although he admitted not much had yet been done to implement the programme nationally, he was optimistic about what had been achieved in the neighbouring communal areas, which were still well stocked with big game. But would the new policies that he and Rowan Martin talked about come into effect in time to save the Zimbabwe's black rhino?

On our way back Margie and I were excited. If other countries were starting to return direct financial benefits from wildlife to their rural communities, then surely there was a way for us to do so too – even if it was only a small amount. And what better place was there to start than at Purros? Although game numbers there were still very low, the local people had shown they were committed to protecting them. In recognition of this Chris had arranged for the translocation of 12 giraffe from Etosha. Some months earlier a bull elephant had also drunk from the Purros spring – the first time in nearly 10 years. I also knew that if elephants were going to re-colonise the west of Kaokoland, then the lower Hoarusib, with its abundant water and broad riparian woodlands, would be the key.

Situated just 55 km from the coast, Purros had only been periodically occupied by pastoralists before 1970. However, a decade later the food delivered there by a Rotary Club in Windhoek had attracted many families that had lost their cattle during the drought. When it broke and the aid handouts ended, they were left in dire straits, as Mitch Reardon had graphically described in his book, *The Besieged Desert*:

An air of apathy and helplessness pervaded the camp; poverty and dependence on charity had leached the proud herdsmen's self respect and they had become neglectful, dirty and uncaring. Women begged listlessly, hissing 'present, present' while squatting vulture-like in the dust. A naked child stared in numb silence, picking idly at the sores that freckled his thin body. A coronet of flies fed undisturbed on the infected eyes of a baby, asleep on its mother's back. Overcrowding, flies, mosquitoes, disease and grinding poverty; the families that had come to Purros to collect emergency rations had simply stayed on, and had become reliant on an aid program funded by private donations that ceased once the drought broke. The impoverished Hereros would discover (if they did not already know) that Purros is too arid to support permanent settlement, and their future threatens to be as bleak as the past. (p. 150)

Four years later the situation had not improved much. Although the numbers of their goats and sheep had increased, and Skeleton Coast Fly-in Safaris employed a few local men, the community was still dependent on the maize gardens they irrigated downriver from Purros. Because of the need to keep the furrows clean, as well as weed and protect their crops from birds, they were no longer able to move their small-stock away from the spring in the wet season, which was having a negative impact on the vegetation along the banks of the Hoarusib.

On our return from Zimbabwe Margie and I drove straight to Purros, stopping only at Warmquelle to pick up Goliat Kasaona, the headman under whose jurisdiction the area fell. We needed him to call the community together for a meeting, so that I could ask them if they were happy about the way the EWT tours had been run, and whether they still wanted my guests to visit their homes. When they all agreed they should continue, I brought up a more sensitive subject; the elephant that had drunk from the Purros spring some months earlier, and this time their response was very different:

'Shoot the elephants. Or tell nature conservation to take them away. This is a place for people; we don't want them here.'

'Since the drought we have become poor, and because we have no milk we must grow crops to feed our children. We don't want elephants breaking into our gardens.'

'Why doesn't nature conservation keep its elephants away from Purros? Tell the rangers they must keep them in the Park. That is their place.'

Instead of responding to what was clearly a very emotional issue, we adjourned the meeting until the following morning and returned to our campsite. Nick Carter had joined us on the trip, and around the fire we talked about how the community's negative attitude to elephants could be changed. The problem was clearly the maize gardens, but even they could see that their being tied to them had resulted in their goats degrading the vegetation around Purros. The crops were also being plagued by mice, and what they harvested was no longer sufficient to meet their needs. If they had not been dependent on the gardens, Margie and I were sure that most of the community would have abandoned them and gone back to their previous nomadic way of life.

The next morning when we reconvened I told the gathering that next year I would give them R25 for every guest I brought to Purros. I emphasised that it was not a payment for visiting their homes, which they told us they had no problem with, but because the whole community was now looking after the wildlife my guests came to see. Everyone thought this was a good idea, and the elephant issue was not brought up again. The 'Purros Pilot Project' had begun.

The 1988 rains were poor throughout the northwest, and the R250 they received from every EWT tour provided each of the seven lineages at Purros with a 25 kg bag of maize meal, as well as some tea and sugar. Although it was not much, within a year they lost interest in the gardens, which were later washed away when the Hoarusib came down in flood. By then more elephants were drinking at the spring, but the local people were now only worried about the danger this posed to women and children when they went to fetch water. The following year Louw Schoeman, who took a lot more clients to Purros, also started paying a 'conservation levy' to the community.

The second part of the pilot project began after Margie expressed her concern about Himba women selling items of their apparel, some of them family heirlooms, to tourists that passed through Purros. Instead she suggested they make baskets and other traditional crafts for sale. At first they did not believe that whites would want to buy anything they had made, when they could purchase plastic or metal equivalents from a shop. However, Louw Schoeman's international guests soon taught the local women the value of a hand-woven basket, and as he did not allow them to bargain over the price, they also quickly learned how to exploit their market exclusivity.

Apart from bringing cash into the community and making them more tolerant of the elephants, there were also indirect spin-offs from the Purros project. The regular income from the EWT and Schoeman tours stopped local people from standing next to the road and begging for handouts from passing vehicles, creating a more dignified relationship between them and the increasing number of self-drive tourists that were visiting the area. Because older women were earning money from weaving baskets, it encouraged young girls to do so as well, revitalising a traditional skill that was in danger of being lost. But most importantly it had made wild animals into a valuable resource again.

Tangible evidence of this came soon after the first levy was paid. On my next visit to Purros the Himba sub-headman, Heova Tjiningiri, told me that one of his sons had killed a zebra in the mountains to the east of the village. As there were no roads into the area we could not have found out about it, but the old man said he had given his word that they would stop hunting, and as it was a member of his own family, he was willing to sell one of his cattle to pay the fine. I reported the case to Chris, but we agreed that just a warning was appropriate.

Not everyone was pleased about what we were doing at Purros. A few months later Margie and I were summoned to Okahandja by Ben van Zyl, who was now Permanent Secretary of the Herero Representative Authority. With him was Mr Nicklaus, the senior administrative officer in Kaokoland, who told us we had no right to pay local people for taking tourists to Purros. After we explained the reasons for our doing so Ben van Zyl said no more, but Mr Nicklaus still had reservations and warned us that 'if we gave the local people a finger, they will expect an arm in the future'. He was also unhappy about the selling of crafts, and told us that in the past when he wanted a basket from one of the women in Purros she gave it to him as a present, but now he was expected to pay for it!

In October 1988 we were invited to give a paper on the Purros Project at an EWT symposium on 'National parks, game reserves and their neigh- bours'. It was a subject that had become very relevant in Southern Africa, and the audience comprised a cross-section of government, NGO and ama- teur conservationists, as well as a sprinkling of black faces representing the ethnic homelands. Among the presentations were some on the pioneering new initiatives in Boputhatswana, under its conservation director, Roger Collinson. A low light was the paper by Salmon Joubert of the Kruger National Park. In it he stated that they had a strong fence between them and their neighbours, and their only concern about what was happening on the other side was the land degradation in the catchments of rivers flowing into the Park.

As the Purros Project had been running for less than a year, we just outlined the principles behind it and our other extension activities in the Kaokoveld, as well as the results we had observed to date. Nevertheless, from the enthu- siastic applause our paper received it was clear that actively involving rural black communities in conservation, and enabling them to benefit from wild- life, was an approach whose time had come.

*   *   *

Six months before the EWT symposium John Ledger had asked us to visit Eastern Caprivi, and give him a report on the wildlife situation there. His request was prompted by an article by Brian Jones in a recent edition of *African Wildlife* entitled 'The challenge of Caprivi', in which he claimed that major poaching was taking place there. In an earlier report for the *Windhoek*

Advertiser newspaper Jones had been even blunter about events in the north-eastern corner of Namibia. It was headlined: 'Caprivi's wildlife being shot to extinction'.

I had first visited East Caprivi in 1981, when I was asked to write the text of Gerald Cubitt's coffee-table book, *Namibia: The Untamed Land,* and at that time I regarded it as one of the country's natural gems. Although it was in-habited by more than 50 000 people, a DNC census carried out the previous year counted 1 696 elephants, 1 071 buffalo, 695 hippo, 287 zebra, 253 roan, 142 eland, 137 sable, 116 tsessebe, 270 sitatunga, and almost 13 000 lechwe. But a similar game count undertaken six years later found that elephant and zebra numbers were down by 50 per cent, buffalo, lechwe and sitatunga by over 80 per cent, while only 14 roan, 14 sable, one tsessebe and no eland were seen. By any standards it was a catastrophic decline, and John wanted us to find out who was responsible for the slaughter, and if we thought anything could be done about it.

Although the successes achieved in the Kaokoveld had started to be rec-ognised, many people were opposed to community-based conservation on the grounds that it could only work where there was a low population of pas-toralists. To counter this I had been looking for another place to test our ap-proach and Eastern Caprivi, which from a socio-economic perspective was very similar to much of central Africa, seemed like a good place to do so. In June 1988 Margie and I spent two weeks there, accompanied by Johan le Roux, who had been the nature conservator in charge of the homeland after he left Keetmanshoop.

After a long and dusty drive from Wêreldsend to Katima Mulilo, the heav-ily fortified administrative centre of the homeland, our first stop was the DNC office. Here I hoped to see Alisdair McDonald, who had led the investigation into the poaching of the Palm rhino cow, and was now the principal nature conservator for Caprivi. As he was in Windhoek, we spoke to Marnie Grobler, the resident biologist. I had previously met Marnie at the DNC professional officers' meetings and knew he was politically very conservative. But the lec-ture he gave us on the homeland's history, ethnic conflicts, and why conser-vation had failed, was so blatantly racist that when we left his office Margie thought he had been sending us up.

According to Marnie the Caprivians had no interest in wildlife, and the only way to prevent the last animal from being killed was for the DNC to proclaim game sanctuaries in the homeland. Discussions were already tak-ing place with the MaFwe Tribal Authority about two parks in their area, he said, and as the matter was very sensitive warned us that any contact we had with people in this part of Caprivi could undermine the negotiations. I did not want to be in a position where the DNC used us as scapegoats if the parks were not proclaimed, so we agreed to confine our visit to the east, which was under the BaSubiya Tribal Authority.

Hoping to get a more balanced view from Alisdair McDonald, we decided to wait in Katima for him to return and while there to get as much information as possible from the white residents of the town. From them we heard of large amounts of ivory being offered for sale in the region, as well as the smuggling of ivory and rhino horn from Zambia and Angola through Caprivi. One of our informants was a local policeman who confidentially told us this was done in container trucks passing through Katima on their way to Walvis Bay, or via Botswana to South Africa, which even the police were not allowed to inspect.

When Alisdair got back we went to his office, but were told that he was 'too busy to speak to us'. As we had been colleagues I was not going to be put off so easily, so at five o'clock we went to his home where I demanded that he at least offer us a cup of tea. Once we were inside and out of sight he sheepishly told us that after our meeting, Marnie had phoned their Head Office to inform Stoffel Rocher that we were in Katima, and he had given instructions that none of the Caprivi staff were allowed to speak to us.

Over tea Alisdair said their biggest problem was operating under the old homeland legislation, which had very low fines for illegal hunting or possession of ivory. However, in 1987 the SWA Ordinance was made applicable in Caprivi, and in that year alone 34 cases that involved 74 people were brought to court. Four Caprivians had also just been convicted of being in possession of four tusks and two rhino horns, and given fines that totalled R13 000, or 12 years in jail. With these much heavier sentences he was confident that they would soon get on top of the situation. We wished him luck, but if shooting the poachers did not stop the killing of rhino in Zimbabwe, could convictions alone bring the illegal hunting and trade in game products under control in the Caprivi?

The next morning we drove to Bukalo, the headquarters of the BaSubiya Traditional Authority. There we hoped to get a Caprivian perspective on the poaching, and what they thought should be done about it. We also needed to get permission to talk to people in the villages, and hire a translator, which had to be obtained at the senior *khuta*. After stating the reason for our visit the *Ngambela* told us: 'We are not against nature conservation; only the way it is being enforced. We are like a lion and a cow; there is no co-operation between us.'

Although the tribal councillors were initially suspicious of our motive for wanting to speak their people, after we told them about our project in the Kaokoveld we were given a letter authorising us to do so. Over the next week we held informal meetings at Kabe and Kapalota villages in the woodlands, Ihaha on the Chobe floodplain, and Muyako on the edge of Lake Liambezi, which still contained a considerable amount of water.

From the discussions at these villages it was clear that the Subiya put the blame for exterminating the wildlife on government officials and the SADF – who they said hunted for sport and not because they needed the meat. Nevertheless, some of them did admit that local people were also involved, and a man at Kapalota village told us: 'The whites no longer come here to hunt because there are so few wild animals left. Now it is the Caprivian workers who have rifles and go to the villages and ask if we want meat. They use spotlights at night, and some of them just leave the bad meat for the vultures. These people are stealing from Caprivi.'

At the start of the meetings many of the villagers said that they no longer wanted any wildlife in their areas 'because it now belongs to the government'. One woman told us nature conservation 'should take everything away, even the birds'. But as the discussions progressed, this attitude was usually replaced by concern for what was happening. A man from Kabe expressed this quite movingly: 'We did not believe that all the game could be killed, but now we have seen this with our own eyes. What will we tell our children when they ask us about wild animals? How can we say to them that the animals they see in books were once plentiful here?'

However, there was no disagreement about their dislike for the way conservation was being practised, and the biggest issue was over elephants that raided their crops: 'When whites come here they only talk about wildlife. But when we tell them of our problems they do nothing to help us. In Caprivi a man will get a heavier fine for killing an elephant than for killing a man. Before nature conservation came to Caprivi, the Khuta ruled all the game. When animals were a problem in the fields they appointed a hunter to kill them. In this way there was no over-shooting.'

On our return to Katima we obtained a copy of a talk that was given by businessman Chris Jarret to the local Chamber of Commerce, in which he said of the Caprivi situation: 'The local Tribal Authorities have not given their support in matters of nature conservation. This is understandable when one realizes that from the sixties onwards there has been a race between colonizer and colonized to see who can butcher the game first. But nobody slaughters their own valuable livestock for fun. Get the message home – and make the benefits of wildlife obvious – and a different attitude will prevail.'

Margie and I were prepared to take up the challenge. The population density of the Caprivi was nearly 10 times that of the Kaokoveld, and although large numbers of cattle were kept, the people here lived mainly from their crops – much like the rest of tropical Africa. In our report to John Ledger we recommended that the EWT start a project in East Caprivi before it was too late to save its wildlife. John was supportive, but his board felt that their limited financial resources could be better spent on conservation priorities within South Africa. However, a year later another source of funds was found, and in 1990 we started a second project in the Caprivi.

*   *   *

When we got back to the Kaokoveld it was again facing a drought. At Wêreldsend only 17 mm of rain had fallen in 1988, following 25 mm the previous season. Further inland the rainfall was also very poor, with the gaps between downpours too long to have any effect on the annual-dominated rangelands. What little grass did grow was soon eaten by the pastoralists' rapidly recovering herds, which were now being taken to wherever any old grazing still remained. In southern Kaokoland Headman Josef Japuhua requested and was given permission by the DRA to take cattle into the eastern concession around the Palmfontein and Okamborombonga springs, both important wildlife areas.

The lack of grazing was more acute west of the escarpment, and in July the Herero leaders in Warmquelle invited me to a meeting to discuss the situation. First they told me how much their cattle were suffering and that many would die unless new places for them to graze were found. Joshua Kangombe then said that because I had helped them before in a drought, they wanted to tell me that some people would soon be taking their cattle over the watershed to springs in the Aub and Barab river valleys.

Prior to 1970 domestic animals were not allowed to cross the Hoanib, but after the western parts of Etosha had been de-proclaimed Herero stockowners moved across it, and in the 1980/81 drought a few of them had even set up stock posts in the Uniab catchment. Although the area had been leased to

Desert Adventure Safaris as a tourism concession, it had no legal status and there was nothing to stop the Herero from taking their cattle there again. But it was also where the largest number of rhino survived, and if they moved in, would they ever move out again?

Was there no alternative? I asked, and added that although they had not received any benefits from Palmwag Lodge, the Purros community was now getting money from the tourists visiting their area. This they knew, and they supported the idea of wild animals having a place where there were no people, but they lived from their livestock and in a drought their needs had to be put first. A long debate followed before Stefanus Uakazapi gave me their decision. No one would move into the tourism concession until they had sent young men out to look for other possible grazing areas.

In fact, no Herero took their livestock over the watershed, although two residents of Sesfontein, one of them convicted rhino poacher, Moses Ganuseb, set up stock posts next to the main road inside Palmwag concession. Simson Tjongarero and Rudi Loutit gave them permission to remain there until the drought broke, but in spite of unusually heavy rainfall in October they did not move out, and their stock posts are still there today. Perhaps because of this, in the mid-1990s two Herero stockowners, Botes Kasaona and John Kasupi, also began seasonally using Dennis Liebenberg's Etendeka concession.

* * *

With the good rains in October the first drought since 1981 ended, and with both livestock and wild ungulate numbers increasing, the year ended on a high note. However, our complacency was shattered in February 1989, when on the way back from a trip with an old friend from my forestry days, Malcome Impey, we stopped at Palmwag Lodge and found it full of nature conservation officials. At the bar I learned that at least four rhino and an elephant had been poached. From Sakeus Kasaona I heard the full story of what had happened.

While he and Blythe were tracking a rhino on Otjihavera, an Odendaal farm east of Palmwag, they had found the fresh footprints of a man who appeared to be following the same animal. As they were unarmed and Sakeus was convinced that the person was up to no good, they returned to the lodge and radioed for help. The next morning Rudi called in an aircraft to fly over the area, and although no dead rhino were seen, an elephant carcass was found in the Klip River, near the road to Kamanjab. On the ground it was confirmed that it had been shot and one of its tusks removed. Whoever was responsible had not been able to lift the bull's head to remove the other tusk.

Having achieved little by flying over the area, Sakeus had taken the DNC officials back to the place where he first saw footprints, and this time followed them to the carcass of a rhino bull. They then tracked the poacher across the veterinary fence and the Kamanjab road to an abandoned house in the Klip River, where there were signs of people having recently camped. When they questioned the farmers living nearby they were given the names of two local youngsters that had stayed there with a 'Baster' from Rehoboth, who had arrived on a motorcycle. Under interrogation the young men admitted acting as his guides, and told them that a second rhino had been killed on Otjihavera, as well as a cow and calf on the farm Palm the previous month. A fifth rhino was wounded, which Sakeus and I later followed up and found dead at a nearby spring.

By the time we arrived at Palmwag the Police Diamond and Narcotics Squad, led by Inspector Hennie Brink, had taken over the investigation, and a few days later a 25-year-old Baster man, Pierre Jankowski, was arrested and charged with killing five rhino, three elephants and two mountain zebra, all of which were specially protected game. Although Hennie Barnard defended him the case was watertight, and in June he was convicted on all counts and sentenced to a total fine of R15 000 or nine years in jail, plus a further six years in jail without the option of a fine, but conditionally suspended for five years.

It seemed like heavy sentence, but if the R15 000 fine was paid Jankowski would not have to spend any time in prison. This was a great disappointment to us, especially as the suspension conditions were negotiated in camera by his lawyer. All that we knew was that he was required to do 'unpaid community service' for either the DNC or the police. In fact, the 'community service' deal that Hennie Barnard had struck would result in the most convictions for rhino poaching and illegal trading in controlled game products ever to be handed down by the country's courts.

A few weeks after the Jankowski case Adjutant Officer Eugene Barnes, acting on a tipoff from an informant, trapped Jasuva Kuvare trying to sell a rhino horn in Windhoek. But as Barnes was calling in a colleague to assist him, Kuvare managed to escape. However, the story behind this botched arrest began five months earlier in Opuwo, and thanks to the detailed statements taken later by Hennie Brink and Chris Eyre, the sequence of events leading up to it can be followed.

In January 1989 Rupuree Koviti, a member of Koevoet and the owner of a shop in Okangwati, asked Jackson Maharukua to go into Etosha and shoot a rhino. He offered to pay R1 000 for its horns and provided him with a .303 rifle and ammunition. Having just been discharged from the army for being absent without leave Jackson agreed to do it, and chose an unemployed friend, Ngaahua Tjiyombo, to go with him. Koviti took them both to where the Kamanjab to Ruacana road ran alongside Etosha's western boundary fence and dropped them off, giving each R10 to pay for a lift back to Opuwo when they had accomplished their mission.

After climbing over the fence they tracked and shot a rhino, and returned to the road where they buried the horns and the rifle before getting a lift back to Opuwo. There they found Koviti at his house with a grey-haired Baster man, Piet Jankowski, and his son, Pierre, who took them back to collect the horns. Jankowski agreed to buy them, but as he did not have enough cash with him he gave Jackson and Ngaahua R70 each, and took the horns with him to sell in Windhoek. When he had sold them he would give the balance of the money to Koviti to pay them.

In Opuwo Jackson stayed with an army friend, David Tjimuhiva, who when he heard of their exploits asked them to also hunt rhinos for him and Andreas Levi. They would pay the same amount as Koviti for the horns and also provide a rifle and ammunition. Jackson and Ngaahua returned to Etosha, where they shot a cow and calf. Levi paid them R500 immediately, and Tjimuhiva gave them the rest some time later.

In March they went to see Koviti and requested their money for the first rhino, but he told them that Jankowski had not yet paid him, and they would have to wait for it. However, a friend of his, Jasuva Kuvare, had money and agreed to pay them if they shot a rhino for him. This they did but were only given R350 each for the horns. Two months later they killed another rhino for Andreas Levi and were given R250 each, with the balance to be paid when the horns were sold.

In June they shot a second rhino for Jasuva, but when he picked them up on the Etosha boundary he only gave Ngaahua R80, saying that he was planning to get married and did not have enough money. Jackson became angry and told him 'it was easy to take them to the game reserve to shoot rhino, but when it came to paying it seemed to be difficult'. Jasuva then gave Jackson R100 and said he would pay the rest when he returned from Windhoek, where he was going to sell the horns. Under pressure to find a buyer before his wedding, he spoke to Piet Jankowski's son, who told him he knew of a man who paid very good prices for rhino horns, and arranged to introduce them.

Back in Opuwo, Jackson was also approached by Reuben Ipinge, who asked them to hunt for him, saying he would pay a higher amount than Koviti for a pair of horns, and added that they should stay in Etosha longer and shoot more than one rhino. A few days later they killed a cow and a large calf, but when Ipinge did not come and pick them up they buried the horns next to the road and got a lift to Opuwo.

Here they went to Ipinge's home, where they heard that Jasuva had been trapped by the police, but had managed to escape. Because of this Ipinge decided not to fetch the horns immediately, but to wait until things 'cooled down'. Jackson and Ngaahua then went to see Koviti to ask for the money he still owed them, but he only gave them R100 each, saying it was all he would pay them, adding that if they were unhappy 'they could go to the police and complain'. They then went back to Ipinge's house, but he only gave them a bottle of brandy.

In frustration Jackson decided to sell the horns of the last two rhino himself, and the next morning offered them to the owner of a shop in Opuwo, Jakob Kuvare. He agreed to buy them and took Jackson in his vehicle to fetch them. When they got back the shopkeeper gave him R50 and said he should come the next day for the rest. However, a week before Frans Petrus, a senior game ranger in Opuwo, had asked Jakob Kuvare to keep his eyes and ears open for people trying to smuggle rhino horn. That night he told Frans what had happened, who in turn informed Chris Eyre.

When Chris found Jackson he was very drunk, and under interrogation told him who his accomplice was. After arresting Ngaahua, Chris and John Patterson then took both of them to Etosha to point out the places where they had killed rhinos. On the way Jackson asked why they were only charging them and not the men who had bought the horns from them. Chris was happy to rectify this, and over the next few days Reuben Ipinge, Rupuree Koviti, Andreas Levi and David Tjimuhiva were all arrested by Inspector Hennie Brink.

However, the case did not end there. Under interrogation Koviti admitted killing another three rhino himself in Etosha, and it also came to light that two more had been poached in north-eastern Damaraland. By early August 15 people were in custody, including Piet Jankowski and Jeremiah Gaobaeb, the new Damara chief in Sesfontein, although he was later discharged. Among them was Ulrich Neberle, a hide and skin dealer in Windhoek who had paid

R13 800 for the horns of the three rhino Koviti shot in Etosha.

As the net spread wider, the two biggest fish caught were Dannie Coertzee, a Windhoek car salesman, and Jakobus 'Koos' Muller, an Okahandja businessman. Coertzee was the man Piet Jankowski had previously sold his rhino horns and elephant tusks to, and he had then sold them to Muller, who paid him R3 000 per kg for rhino horn and R120 per kg for high quality ivory. Hennie Brink's investigation also brought to light the reason why Piet Jankowski had not been able to get the money for the first horns Koviti had given him. At the time Koos Muller was in Taiwan, and as the price there had fallen, on his return he told Coertzee that he had decided not to sell any more horns until it went up again.

Although the nature conservators at Otjovasandu, under Russell Vinjevold, were well aware that rhinos were being killed inside the Park, and had found 22 carcasses, as the tracks of the poachers stopped at the main road they were unable to successfully follow up the cases. The same applied to the two rhino that came out of Etosha and were shot in north-eastern Damaraland. As no community game guards had been appointed in any of the villages neighbouring Etosha, they also had no source of information about suspicious movements there. In contrast, because of the regular monitoring of the rhino by the SRT, and the support of the local community, the second time that Pierre Jankowski came into the Palmwag area he was arrested.

The ease with which poaching could take place from a main road taught us a hard lesson, and as this situation also applied in much of the rhino range south of the vet fence, something needed to be done to provide them with better protection. In May Rudi Loutit decided to do what many conservationists had talked about, but no one had ever tried – cut the rhino's horns off so that there would no longer be a reason to kill them.

It was a solution that would affect more than just their looks. Rhino have horns for a reason; the bulls to establish territorial dominance and the cows to defend their calves from predators. But as their horns are just compacted hair, equivalent to our fingernails, they would grow back again. In an *African Wildlife* article, Sharon Montgomery wrote: 'Operation Bicornis can be seen as a desperate last-ditch attempt to conserve the unique Damaraland population of the black rhinoceros. It can also be seen as a positive exercise in the long-term conservation of a highly endangered species. Many questions need to be answered, but the only way these answers will be reached is by monitoring the effects of de-horning in the field.'

All the rhino south of the veterinary fence were dehorned, and 10 animals from the Springbok River and Otjihavera were translocated to the Waterberg Plateau Park, where they and another 20 from Etosha became the nucleus of a new black rhino population in Namibia. Thanks to the veterinary skills of Dr Peter Morkel and the professionalism of the game capture team there were no losses during the operation, but unfamiliarity with their new habitat led to three of the rhino taken to Waterberg dying after their release.

Over the next few years rhino were dehorned in parks and game farms in many other Southern African countries, undoubtedly stopping hundreds of both black and white rhino from being killed. Wherever it happened, de-horning was controversial, but among all of us working in Damaraland only ex-journalist Margie Jacobsohn predicted what a media sensation it would be. As soon as the news got out, foreign correspondents from around the world badgered an unprepared DNC public relations section for more details, and a few of them even turned up at Wêreldsend. Most of them were already in the country, having come to witness another, much bigger event unfolding in Namibia.

CHAPTER TWENTY-FOUR

INDEPENDENCE

Because the DTA government in Windhoek was not recognised by the international community, a number of high-level delegations had been sent to Namibia in an attempt to solve the political impasse and bring the country to independence. All of them failed, and by the late 1980s the counter-insurgency operations on the northern border had escalated into a full-scale war inside Angola. The turning point had come in January 1988, after the largest ever battle on the sub-continent – involving tanks, aircraft and artillery, as well as 6 000 troops on the South African side, and many more Cubans and Angolans – was fought around the strategic town of Cuito Cuanavale.

Militarily it was a stalemate. Although SADF frogmen floated down the Lomba River and blew up the bridge over it, thereby halting the FAPLA and Cuban advance on Jonas Savimbi's headquarters in Jamba, they were unable to dislodge the Angolan forces. With 60 000 Cuban troops supporting the MPLA government in Luanda, and Russian-supplied MIG-23 fighter jets having ended South Africa's air superiority, any more major battles would result in many South African soldiers coming home in body bags. Politically, this was something the National Party government in Pretoria could not afford.

Over the following six months, talks between South Africa, Cuba and

Angola were arranged in different international venues. They resulted in the withdrawal of all SADF forces from Angola and in August the signing of the 'Geneva Protocol' in which South Africa agreed to facilitate the implementation of the UN Security Council's Resolution 435, granting independence to Namibia. Cuba also signed a bilateral accord with Angola, by which it too would withdraw its troops from the country. The proxy Cold War conflict between UNITA, supported by South Africa and the United States, and the Cuban- and Russian-backed MPLA had ended.

Within Namibia there were also some moves towards reconciliation. In June 1988 a delegation of progressive whites met members of the SWAPO leadership in Stockholm, followed in October by a 'Consultative Conference' in Zambia that was attended by Sam Nujoma, Hage Giengob and Theo-Ben Gurirab, all of whom were destined to play major roles in the country's post-independence government. Finally, in December, under the auspices of the UN Secretary General, the date was set for a ceasefire between South Africa and SWAPO: 1 April 1989.

The end of such a long and bitter struggle did not go smoothly. On the day the ceasefire came into effect the two armies were meant to be confined to their bases, but on the night before over 1 000 PLAN combatants crossed the border from Angola, and were attacked by three South African battalions. As the UN Transitional Assistance Group (UNTAG) still had very few of its peace-keepers deployed, it made no attempt to stop the fighting, and over 300 SWAPO and 27 security force soldiers were killed.

Initially South Africa's Foreign Minister, Pik Botha, had suspended the peace process, but by then only a few white hardliners did not accept that after 70 years of being under the thumb of Pretoria, independence was now inevitable. The last battle would be fought in the ballot box against the political wing of SWAPO, which for most Namibians was an unknown entity, and which the South African government had for decades portrayed as communists and terrorists.

The election was close, with SWAPO and the DTA running neck-and-neck before the votes in Ovamboland were counted. However, the legacy of strictly enforced segregation and the brutal activities of Koevoet had ensured that the people living on the palm-dotted floodplains in the north voted overwhelmingly for the party that brought them liberation. The final tally was 57 per cent of the votes for SWAPO, and in Ovamboland it was nearly 90 per cent. On 21 March 1990, after 30 years in exile, Sam Nujoma became the first president of the Republic of Namibia.

The period after the ceasefire did not only result in a tragic loss of human lives, it also cost the Kaokoveld one of its priceless future tourist attractions. The six cows that Slang believed were the only elephants to survive on lower Kunene had produced three calves, proving that there was at least one bull in the area. Seven years later 14 elephants were known to range along the thin ribbon of riparian vegetation that bisected the sand dunes and lunar mountains here, and the population was on its way to recovery. But when the SADF pulled back from the border in April, Angolan forces were for the first time able to patrol along the river – and like their South African counterparts during the 1970s – they could not resist the temptation to boost their salaries by selling ivory.

In June, while flying along the lower Kunene, André Schoeman, Louw's eldest son, found the carcasses of three elephants on the northern bank, inside Iona National Park. Their tusks had been removed and the tracks of a large vehicle, undoubtedly belonging to the military, were seen nearby. After informing Steve Braine at Mowe Bay, permission was requested from the new Angolan Embassy in Windhoek to look for carcasses further away from the river. It was refused and André was told that if he crossed the border his plane would be shot down. By the time I heard about it, there were no elephants left in the most spectacular of all the places they had previously inhabited in the Kaokoveld.

Although it was a great loss to us, the elephants killed on the lower Kunene represented only one per cent of the average number being poached every week throughout the rest of Africa. And with the total elephant population on the continent now believed to be only 600 000 – down from at least one and a half million a decade earlier – conservationists throughout the world were calling for drastic measures to stop the slaughter. To most of them this meant banning all ivory sales.

Until then the Convention on International Trade in Endangered Species (CITES) had listed the African elephant on their Appendix Two, which only required that the trade in ivory be regulated. However, in the late 1980s many international NGOs, including the Environmental Investigation Agency under Alan Thornton, campaigned for it to be raised to Appendix One, under which all trade in its tusks or other body parts was prohibited. This would be a major blow to Zimbabwe's CAMPFIRE Programme, which needed the income from ivory to balance the costs of people living with elephants outside of national parks. Their opposition to the ivory trade ban was supported by other Southern African countries, but at the 1989 CITES Conference in Switzerland, the majority of its members voted for a three-year moratorium on the sale of ivory. By then the issue had divided conservationists like no other before it, and the battle between sustainable use advocates and the hard-line protectionists would not end there.

A major argument against the ban was that prohibiting the trade in rhino horn had not stopped the killing of this even more endangered species, but as John Ledger had pointed out at a Wildlife Society meeting in Windhoek, there was a difference between the two markets. Whereas rhino horn was a traditional medicine used in the Far East, most ivory was sold to the Japanese and wealthy Europeans, whose minds could be changed. Once again John had shown he was prepared to take an unpopular stand, at least in the Southern African context, but he did not support a permanent ban, just a moratorium to allow east and central African countries time to get the poaching of their elephants under control. In the meantime he suggested that the Purros Project example of making tourism contribute to rural economies be followed, thereby 'turning poachers into partners'.

The EWT's support for the community game guards and John's commitment to Margie's and my work at Purros had been crucial, but with Southern African countries now paying the price for failed conservation over the rest of the continent, the time was right to seek funding from the international donor organisations. In late 1989 we wrote to the World Wide Fund for Nature in Switzerland, where Dr John Hanks – who I got to know while running the ACE Project in KwaZulu – was the Conservation Director for Africa.

Their response was positive and in 1990 WWF joined the EWT in supporting the community game guards in the Kaokoveld, as well as a new project in Eastern Caprivi. For the first time we had sufficient funding to really put our community-based approach into practice, but without the support of the government our initiatives would remain as just 'pilot projects'. Therefore, on the day before the final election results were published, Margie and I wrote a guest article in *The Namibian* newspaper entitled 'Nature conservation is a political issue.' We started by asking the question:

Why is nature conservation a big turn-off to the majority of Namibians? Mention the subject to a resident of Katatura, Oshakati or Okakarara and the response is likely to be glazed eyes, dismissal or even open hostility. To this section of our population conservation is generally regarded as boring, elitist and irrelevant, and the typical conservationist is seen as a white, economically secure capitalist who cares more about wild animals than people. This was confirmed during the election campaign when not one party had conservation or Namibia's environment on their agenda.

In contrast, environmental issues are a major concern in most developed countries, and in Europe Green political parties have become a powerful force with links to both the left and the right. Here in Namibia, however, conservation seems to be a topic that only interests the wealthy. Yet, surely the wise use of our natural resources is the key to the country's future prosperity – and should it not, therefore, be of crucial interest to every one of our citizens?

We ended by saying:

The challenge now facing wildlife conservationists is to reconcile conservation priorities with the needs and aspirations of people – particularly those communities that are living in, or around our wildlife areas. The concept that conservation should involve and benefit local people is not new and over the last few years has become part of mainstream conservation philosophy. But in most areas, when it comes to actually implementing these strategies, theory has yet to be put into practice …

All too often colonial conservation policies have been perpetuated by post independence governments. Such policies have fostered alienation and apathy among the rural people, and the lack of support from this vital sector of the population has contributed to the steady destruction and/or degradation of the continent's natural resources. Hopefully the new government will break this pattern and seek ways to weave a conservation ethic into the social fabric of our country. Political ideologies may determine how the Namibian economic pie is divided, but it is our conservation policies that will determine the size of the pie.

A few weeks later we got a phone call from Brian Jones, who had resigned from the *Windhoek Advertiser* and taken a post with the public relations section of the DNC. We had known Brian for some time, and he had joined us on a number of trips in Damaraland – but that was before he joined the government. He asked us to meet with him and Dr Chris Brown, one of the country's dynamic young scientists and a leading progressive in the DNC. However, our meeting could not take place in Windhoek, where they might be seen talking to us. Instead we met at a café in Swakopmund, and both of them arrived out of uniform.

Chris told us that although West Caprivi was a proclaimed game reserve, during the liberation war it had been used by the SADF as a base for the irregular forces fighting in Angola. With Namibia on the brink of having a SWAPO government they would soon be evacuating the area, and it would revert back under the DNC. As it had been a military zone for so many years they did not know what wildlife occurred there, or anything about the people living within it. To find out they had been given approval for a multi-disciplinary team of biologists to survey West Caprivi's fauna and flora, but they needed people with social skills to interview the local communities. As the 'socio-ecological survey' would take place after Namibia's independence in March, Chris was confident that he could get permission for Margie and me to participate in it.

On 1 April we joined all the other participants at Buffalo Base on the banks of the Okavango River. A few months before it had been occupied by 32 Battalion, the former FNLA soldiers and their South African officers who had supported UNITA against the MPLA. Their first commander was the enigmatic Colonel Jan Breytenbach, who in 1975 led a flying column that advanced to within 40 km of Luanda, as well as the parachute battalion that attacked Cassinga three years later. Nearby was a graveyard of numbered headstones, the lonely final resting place of over 200 young men who had fought and died far from their homes near the Congo border.

After a briefing session we all went off to fulfil our respective tasks. As Brian, Margie and I formed the social team we visited places where people lived, to hear their concerns about the present situation and aspirations for the future. Our combined findings would enable the new Ministry of Wildlife, Conservation and Tourism (MWCT) to plan how West Caprivi game reserve's wild and human inhabitants could harmoniously share the land and its resources. As the Khoe and Vasekele Bushmen residents of the area had for 15 years been confined to military barracks, from where the younger men were employed as trackers in the SADF, this would not be easy. For Margie and me it was also the first time that we had been invited to join a team of government conservationists.

In ten days we held meetings with over 700 community members, out of the more than 6 000 people that lived in West Caprivi. Apart from being apprehensive about their future under a government they had fought against, most of them were happy about living with wild animals, which they had

done in the past. However, they were concerned about their land being designated as a game reserve, and what their rights would be within it.

'The army's nature conservation people shot many of our donkeys. What
will happen when the new conservation people come to live with us? How
many of our animals will they shoot? – Nature conservation never came here
to ask us what we think, like today, they just came to search our houses and
look into our cooking pots. – We don't know about this game reserve; we were
not consulted about it. – How could the government make this a game reserve
if it saw people living there? – How will this game reserve be organised? Will
nature conservation run it alone or with the people?'

This last question was at the heart of what the socio-ecological survey was
for, and around the campfire we described our community-based approach in
the Kaokoveld to the other participants. Some of them clearly felt threatened
by it. Marnie Grobler thought we wanted all of Namibia's national parks to be
run by local people. In fact we regarded the existing wildlife sanctuaries as
priceless examples of natural ecosystems that as far as possible should be kept
in a pristine state, and only the government had the authority and financial
resources to do this. But we did believe that a forum should be set up of park
officials and representatives from the neighbouring communities, to address
cross-border issues such as poaching, problem animals and fire management.

Marnie still saw this as 'experimenting with the future of the country's
wildlife, which could fail'. We argued that, as big game numbers were declining in all the homelands in Namibia the present policies had already failed,
and unless a new approach was found a potentially valuable resource for their
residents, and the country as a whole, would be lost. Because of my poor relationship with the DNC I was reluctant to get into a conflict with the officials,
but Margie had no inhibitions, and when Chris Brown passed a disparaging
remark about social scientists she took him on. In the heated debate that followed the rest of us watched in silence as the formidably articulate Dr Brown
met his match.

During the two weeks we spent in West Caprivi there were many robust
discussions about how the game reserve should be managed, and the role that
the people living within it should play. Not everyone on the team agreed with
our community-based approach, but Chris and Brian supported us and in the
years ahead we formed a partnership that would have a major impact on the
way conservation was practised in the communal areas.

*   *   *

A few weeks after the survey we got a message from the new Minister of Wildlife, Conservation and Tourism, Nico Bessinger, asking us to come and see him on our next visit to Windhoek. No reason was given and based on the problems we had experienced with the previous government we expected the worst. But we were given a very friendly reception. He then explained that as a member of SWAPO's internal wing he knew about our work in the north-west, and wanted us to help him implement his plans to make nature conservation relevant to all Namibians.

The first step was for us to attend a workshop of MWCT staff that he planned to hold, which would include representatives of all ranks and from across the whole country. The purpose was to use a consultative process to draw up a list of new conservation priorities. Twenty minutes later we walked out of his office feeling light-headed – after so many years of being in opposition to the government, we were at last on the same side.

When the workshop took place we were the only non-government staff that had been invited, and as we entered the hall it went quiet, and I felt the hostility towards us from most of the senior officials present. Before it started we had asked the Minister to explain why we were there, but he just brushed our request aside. As he would not be introducing anyone else he saw no reason to make an exception of Margie and me.

In his opening address Mr Bessinger said that during the workshop everyone had the same rank, and could say what they thought without fear of recriminations. It was very different to the way things had been done in the past, and as it sank in that the Minister meant what he said, the debate became lively and acrimonious, led by the two most fiery young Turks, Chris Brown and Malan Lindeque. Although Mr Bessinger said nothing all morning, when the meeting started getting out of hand in the afternoon he stood up.

'Although I asked you to all speak your minds, it now seems like we have two choices. We can have blood on the walls, or do what we in SWAPO did when drawing up a new constitution for Namibia. In the room with us were the same people we fought a bitter war with, and in my case who ordered my detention without trial. But we put all thoughts of revenge aside and used our anger to draw up the best constitution in the world. I would like us to do the same for nature conservation in this country.'

There was silence for a few seconds, and then the whole room, including the DNC old guard, burst into applause. It was a masterly performance that united friend and foe, black and white, to follow the process through until we had agreed on a new set of conservation priorities. One of the top five was involving local communities, but what it meant to each one of us at the workshop was probably very different, and putting policy into practice would be the hard part.

With a mandate from the Minister, Chris and Brian decided to carry out more socio-ecological surveys in other communal areas where significant populations of wildlife still survived, and we were again invited to join the team. The first was in East Bushmanland, followed by Eastern Caprivi, and then the Huab catchment and the Sesfontein District in Damaraland, both of which were now part of the new Kunene Region. The last was in the lower Kuiseb River in the Namib Desert Park. Wherever there was a strong traditional authority the surveys were conducted in partnership with it, which gave the process more legitimacy in the eyes of the community, while local government officials and any private sector operators were also invited to take part.

As we did in West Caprivi, Brian, Margie and I held meetings in a cross-section of villages to ask the residents what their development needs were, whether they still wanted to live with wildlife, and if so what problems they faced and how they wanted them to be addressed. On the last two days we came together with the appointed community leaders to present our findings, identify where they and the MWCT shared a common vision, and discuss ways of solving the remaining areas of conflict.

For most local people it was the first time they had formally sat down with government officials, and they used this opportunity to express many long-standing grievances about the way nature conservation was practised. Consequently, both in the villages and at the report-back sessions we had to facilitate frequent misunderstandings and sometimes bitter disagreements over what had happened in the past. But in spite of this, by the end of each survey it was surprising how much the government and community leaders' aspirations regarding wildlife coincided. And once this had been established, mutually acceptable solutions were found for many seemingly intractable problems.

Although the MWCT staff who participated frequently found the process traumatic, Margie and I had faced many hostile communities in the past and for us facilitating the social part and reducing the tension between the parties was a stimulating experience. It was ground-breaking and long overdue, and the moments of drama, despair, frustration and even black humour just added spice to Chris and Brian's recipe for taking up Nico Bessinger's challenge of making conservation relevant to all Namibians. And in all but one of the socio-ecological surveys a mutually agreed way forward was found.

The exception was the Huab catchment, where the Save the Rhino Trust had obtained funds from the European Union to start a conservation and rural development project. As it was on the SRT's turf, their staff and the government officials in Khorixas were tasked with informing the local communities beforehand, so that they would be prepared for our village and farm meetings. This was not done, and both Rudi and Blythe arrived late for the initial briefing. During the survey they also showed little interest in the process, with the result that we held few meaningful discussions on the future of wildlife in this very important part of Kunene Region.

Although each area we surveyed had its own issues and challenges, depending on what species occurred there, and in what quantities, as well as the community's social structure and dynamics, there were a number of common themes. Once the complaints about crop damage and livestock losses, and the way nature conservation officials operated had been aired, the great majority of local people interviewed still wanted wildlife to be conserved. The big issue was – who did it belong to? Most of their leaders knew that freehold farmers had been given conditional ownership over the huntable game on their properties, and they wanted to have the same rights on communal land. If there were tourist lodges in their areas they also wanted to benefit from them.

Most of their requests were very reasonable, but to accommodate them would require major changes in the policies under which nature conservation and tourism were carried out in communal areas. Having a new government in Windhoek would provide a golden opportunity, particularly as a SWAPO Cabinet resolution in 1991 had asked the MWCT and the Ministry of Finance to investigate how this could be done.

As Chris Brown had just been appointed head of the newly created Directorate of Environmental Affairs (DEA), and had played a major role in getting an environmental clause included in the Namibian constitution – the first country to have one – he was the ideal person to spearhead a campaign to implement the necessary changes. Brian Jones's deep understanding of the social issues involved made him the best man in the MWCT to work alongside him.

* * *

In between the socio-ecological surveys Margie and I still had our own projects to run. During John Ledger's visit to Namibia in 1989 he had formed a valuable partnership with Rössing Uranium's public relations officer, Clive Algar, and they jointly donated R18 000 to build an environmental education centre at Wêreldsend. The Save the Rhino Trust and the MWCT in Khorixas provided materials and vehicle support, while Pieter Mostert led a team of local artisans, David /Hovaseb, Elias Xuagub and Markus Roman, to carry out the actual construction. To run our field excursions for neighbouring schools the EWT had employed Charles Cadman, a young man from Natal, who left us in 1991 and was replaced by a British couple, Tim and Rosie Holmes. They were assisted by Sakeus Kasaona's son, John, who had recently matriculated at a Windhoek high school.

The Wêreldsend Environmental Centre was not just used for school courses. It also became a venue for training and planning workshops that we and other NGOs gave for local community members. From 1988, when the Windhoek Technical College started a diploma course in nature conservation, its organiser, Eckhardt Klingenhoffer, brought his students to us every year for practical exercises, and to learn about the community-based approach to conserving wildlife. When he left, Ibo Zimmermann, Willie Adunk and Peter Cunningham continued to bring their first- and later second-year classes to Wêreldsend; these, together with courses for students from other poly-tech faculties and the University of Namibia, are the backbone of the centre's education activities.

With the funding we now received from WWF and the ongoing support of the EWT, more community game guards were appointed, increasing their coverage of the key areas where wildlife still occurred. However, running projects in two regions more than 1 000 km apart, as well as taking part in the socio-ecological surveys, soon became too much for Margie and me to handle. In December 1990 we employed Mathew Rice to manage our East Caprivi project, and a year later hired Colin Nott, an MSc graduate in grassland science, to supervise our activities in the north-west.

After independence the funding that the SRT obtained from the EU also enabled it to appoint more local men as trackers to monitor the rhino population in the north-west, as well as focus on preventing and mitigating the damage elephants were causing farmers in the Huab valley. To co-ordinate the project they employed Dudu Murorua, a rising young star in Chief Justice //Garoeb's new political party, the United Democratic Front.

Although the Riemvasmaker community around Bergsig and De Riet were within the Huab catchment, on the socio-ecological survey we were told that they no longer wanted to be part of the SRT Project. The reasons they gave us were that Wêreldsend was much closer to them than Khorixas, and that they had a long association with Margie and me. After we had discussed it with Blythe we included them in our activities and asked them to select someone to act as their liaison officer. The man they chose was Bennie Roman, who had worked with Peter Erb and me in the early 1980s.

For our growing number of staff to function effectively we needed more vehicles. In 1988 the renowned wildlife artist, David Shepherd, had visited us and donated a painting of the desert elephants to the EWT, from which 350 copies were printed and sold. The proceeds were then used to buy and recondition an old Land Rover for the Wêreldsend Environmental Centre. John Ledger also convinced the Mazda Wildlife Fund to loan us a 4x4 Drifter truck that was ideal for our work in Caprivi, but was not suitable for the very rocky terrain in the basalt ranges.

This problem was solved when the British High Commissioner, Francis Richards, donated us a new Land Rover after we had taken him and his wife, Gill, through the north-west. However, before it could be handed over Francis told us there was a minor issue that had to be sorted out. The High Commission could not give a vehicle to 'Margie and Garth' – it had to have the name of an organisation. As we had never bothered about this before, we could not come up with one. 'Well, what do you do?' he asked, and Margie replied that we were trying to integrate rural development and nature conservation, instead of them being seen in opposition to each other. It was good enough for Francis and we got both a vehicle and a name: Integrated Rural Development and Nature Conservation. Although the acronym IRDNC was not easy to pronounce, it stuck – but we nearly lost the Land Rover on the same day it was given to us.

Straight after the handover, which was done in front of the press and TV cameras in Windhoek, we set off for Wêreldsend on a stormy March afternoon. With us were Tim and Rosie Holmes, who had flown in from the UK to replace Charles Cadman. About three-quarters of the way home we were stopped by the Goantagab River, which was flowing too deep to cross. Also waiting for the water to subside were a Swakopmund shopkeeper, Poofy Hofmeister, and his old father, in a Land Rover that was taking supplies to Palmwag Lodge.

After an hour the river had subsided enough for us to drive across, but Poofy took a slightly different route to me and got stuck in a hole. As neither of us had a towrope we cut wire off a nearby fence, and to make it stronger doubled it over twice. This made it quite short, which meant that I had to reverse back into the river in order to attach it to both vehicles. But when I tried to pull Poofy's Land Rover out my wheels just dug into the watery mud. By now we had an audience of local people, and while I was unhitching my vehicle they shouted that the river was coming down again!

As the water was rising fast, getting Poofy's father to the bank was our first priority. After Tim and I carried him there it was too late to do anything about the vehicles, and we watched Poofy's Land Rover float downriver until it hit a tree and turned onto its side. Because mine was on slightly higher ground we got all but Margie's archaeological samples off it, and I climbed onto the roof of the cab, hoping that my extra weight would stop it from being carried away. Although the water reached window height and for the next half hour it rocked and shuddered, my Land Rover stayed upright until the flood finally subsided, by which time it was dark and raining softly.

After a miserable night sleeping under a tarpaulin I had the embarrassing job of telling the High Commissioner I had drowned the vehicle that he donated us the previous day. Francis took it in good humour, and subsequently he and Gill became good friends who joined us on a number of other trips in the Kaokoveld. We also got the Land Rover back on the road, and it was finally scrapped after having done over 400 000 km.

* * *

In 1992 the MWCT asked IRDNC to also fund community game guards in the West Caprivi, which together with our Kunene and East Caprivi projects further stretched the financial resources of the EWT and WWF-International. Fortunately, a few months before we had been visited by two American consultants, Kate Newman and Barbara Wyckoff-Baird, and Kate told us that they had 'pots of money' for conservation in Namibia. The United States Agency for International Development (USAID) had commissioned them to find suitable projects in Namibia for it to invest in, and having heard of our work through the WWF network they had come to learn more about it. A year later a contract between the governments of Namibia and the USA was signed and the Living in a Finite Environment (LIFE) programme started. It would fund both of IRDNC's Caprivi Projects up to 1998, when WWF in the United Kingdom became our major donor.

Although USAID provided most of its operating funds, the LIFE programme was implemented by WWF-US and its in-country partners, the Rossing Foundation and the Namibia Nature Foundation. The person appointed to be the Chief of Party was Chris Weaver, a Colorado outdoorsman who had 11 years' experience on a rural development project in Lesotho. Chris's technical and fund-raising skills and his low-key leadership style would add immeasurable value to Namibia's fledgling community-based natural resource management (CBNRM) programme. As Barbara Wyckoff-Baird also joined LIFE, they both become outstanding ambassadors for a country whose efforts in the field of international aid had not always been successful.

The support we received from LIFE provided more than just financial security; it also linked us with other CBNRM programmes in Southern Africa. In late 1992 Chris Brown, Brian Jones, Margie and I were invited to a workshop in Hwange National Park, giving us an opportunity to meet many of the main role-players in Zimbabwe's CAMPFIRE Programme. As most of the participants were practising CBNRM and not just preaching it, we all had a lot to learn from each other's experiences. The workshop culminated in the drawing up of 11 key principles for working in rural communities that wanted to conserve their wildlife.

A few months later Margie and Brian visited the Muhenye CAMPFIRE Programme adjoining the Gonarezhou National Park, where income from trophy hunting was being distributed to individual members of the community. Although Margie got malaria that landed her at death's door in a Cape Town hospital, the trip enabled them to see firsthand how Zimbabwe's CBNRM programme was being implemented on the ground, and also get to know its facilitators there, Clive Stockhill, Ivan Bond and Brian Child.

As Margie and I became Namibian citizens after independence, and were no longer *persona non grata* in other African states, I was invited to give a paper on the evolution of CBNRM in Namibia at a symposium on Community-based Conservation in Tanzania, organised by the IUCN. Most of the presentations were on the background and policy framework for community-based initiatives in the host country, but there were also case studies from Zimbabwe, Zambia, Kenya and Uganda to learn from, as well as many opportunities to meet people involved in this rapidly growing field.

Although our work was becoming known outside of Namibia, Margie was taken by surprise when Douglas Reisner, the Director of the Namibia Nature Foundation, told her that a man in America was trying to contact us 'because we had won some sort of prize'. At first she presumed it was a hoax, but the next day he phoned and informed her that we had been chosen as joint winners of the Goldman Environmental Prize for Africa. If we accepted we would have to go to San Francisco in April for the ceremony. Still not sure that it was genuine, she asked for time to speak to me first.

I wanted no part in it. Even if it was not a scam, we had started getting onto a better footing with nature conservation's old guard, and an award was the last thing we needed. When I was profiled by *Time* Magazine in 1990 even some of the local DNC staff took exception to what they saw as my claiming the credit for the successes achieved in the north-west. The year before, I was given the 'conservationist of the year' award by the Rhino and Elephant Foundation in South Africa, and although it was a great honour I did not attend the ceremony to avoid the publicity. Lastly, I had set aside the April school holidays as time to spend with my sons. But eventually Margie got me to see reason. The award *was* genuine and included a prize of US$60 000 that was not easy to turn down.

At the presentation ceremony we were required to give a speech in front of a thousand San Francisco citizens. This was daunting enough, but how did we describe our work to wealthy Americans whose lives could not be more different to those of the communities in our project areas? Fortunately Margie came up with a theme, telling them how it felt to live in a dung hut with dangerous wildlife around you, as she had done when elephants returned to Purros. From this perspective they were not the wonderful animals portrayed in wildlife documentaries, or seen from a safari vehicle, but terrifying creatures that made fetching water from a spring and collecting firewood a hazardous occupation.

For millions of rural Africans this was a part of everyday life, but in spite of this we had found that most of the people in our project areas wanted to live with wildlife for cultural, ethical and aesthetic reasons. As an example of this I quoted community game guard Japi Uararavi, who had told me that in the past he enjoyed walking the 100 km from Purros to Sesfontein, because along the way he would see springbok, gemsbok and giraffe. But after the drought he saw no game 'and it was a very long distance to walk'. Nevertheless, the problems caused by wild animals needed to be addressed, and the cost of living with them balanced by real benefits going back to the local people. If ways could be found to provide these, we believed vast tracts of land outside of protected areas would become available for conservation and tourism.

Margie and I were not the first to have our work in the north-west internationally recognised. In 1988 Blythe had won the IUCN Species Survival Commission Peter Scott Merit Award for her efforts to protect the rhino in

Damaraland. After independence the world's conservation community also started paying much more attention to what was happening to the country's wildlife and wild areas. In 1994 Margie and I were recipients of the United Nations Global 500 Award, and three years later we were made 'Knights of the Golden Ark' by Prince Bernard of the Netherlands – no doubt to the chagrin of those who had in the past been opposed to our community-based approach.

Although each award was a great honour and helped us to raise funds, they did not change the situation inside the country. Once the DNC's old guard realised they were not going to lose their jobs under a SWAPO government, they settled back into their seats of power and most of them just paid lip service to the new direction that their minister, Nico Bessinger, planned to take. As a result there was a deep divide between the small group who believed in giving rights and responsibilities to communal area residents, and those who wanted to keep all decision making in the hands of professionally trained officials.

Among the latter were Rudi and Blythe, and our previous good relationship had deteriorated. The first crack appeared when the EWT stopped sending the money for the community game guard rations and cash allowances through the MWCT in Khorixas. John Ledger did this because we had expressed concern that under Rudi they were being used as an additional source of manpower for the government, which was undermining the main reason why the system had been successful – by making the traditional leaders who appointed them share responsibility for stopping the poaching in their areas.

As a Trustee of the SRT, I had also clashed with Blythe over the late submission of its annual financial statements. I knew this was just due to her artistic temperament, but with the Trust now receiving a major grant from the EU it had moved into the big league, and was legally bound to ensure they were produced on time. After a year of verbal attempts to rectify the situation I circulated a letter to the other Trustees about the matter. Blythe took exception to this and sacked the whole board, then invited only those of us that she wanted back onto it. Needless to say I was not one of them.

A more serious issue began with the poaching of a rhino in the Palmwag concession by Archie //Gawusab, the SRT's main tracker, and Ronnie Heigan, a local shopkeeper's son, in late 1989. Tommy Hall investigated the case and both men were found guilty, with Heigan being sentenced to four years in prison. As Archie had grown up in the Loutit home, Blythe made a plea to the magistrate for him not to be imprisoned. I supported her in court and he was given a suspended sentence, but when I reported another suspected rhino poaching case involving an SRT employee to Rudi in 1992, our friendship finally ended. As no investigation was carried out, Sakeus Kasaona, who had provided the initial information, resigned from the SRT and came to work for IRDNC.

By then the situation had become acrimonious, and I was excluded from all of the MWCT's activities, including the investigation of a rhino that was killed in the Palmwag concession in 1993. Although no one was charged, a year later one of Tommy Hall's informants told him that another rhino had been shot there by members of the MWCT's Anti-Poaching Unit.

I was also not consulted when the tourism concessions the Damara Representative Authority had created in 1985 were restructured. As the homeland administrations were disbanded after independence, the new government had at first not known what do with the annual fees paid by the concessionaires. However, a 1993 Cabinet decision put them under the authority of the MWCT and Rudi was tasked with defining their borders. He divided the two north of the veterinary fence along the Sesfontein road, and extended the Palmwag concession from the middle of the Hoanib River to its northern bank. Because the north of the Etendeka concession had been settled by Herero stockowners from over the Ombonde River, it was reduced to the area from the Grootberg range southwards.

Could we have avoided the breakdown in our relationship with Rudi and Blythe? Probably not, once they had moved to Khorixas, because the underlying conflict between us was the very different ways we believed nature conservation should be implemented in the north-west. Fortunately, most of the IRDNC and SRT employees remained on good terms, and just got on with their jobs.

*　*　*

After the game harvests for the local communities in 1987 and 1988, Rudi decided not to do so in 1989 because of the imminent national elections and the political uncertainty at the time. The next year it was again postponed because he first wanted an aerial census to be carried out, so that the present numbers and trends of the species to be hunted could be determined. When it showed they had all considerably increased since the previous count in 1986, with springbok numbers now exceeding 7 500 and those of gemsbok and zebra over 2 000, a third game harvest took place in 1991, with a total of 300 animals cropped, including four giraffe.

As the numbers hunted was more than double that of 1988, additional manpower was called in to assist from the MWCT's Head Office and Etosha, making the operation very expensive, while the rugged terrain took a heavy toll on the government vehicles. In his report Rudi estimated the cost to the government was at least N$60 000, or about N$200 per animal killed. The following year various options were investigated to reduce the costs, but none were acceptable and no harvest took place.

This meant game meat had been distributed only once in the previous four years, and with the Purros community now the only one receiving any benefits from their wildlife, I was worried about some people starting to poach again. By chance, at a workshop in the Waterberg Plateau Park in April 1993, I shared a room with Danie Grobler, which gave me an opportunity to discuss my concerns with him. Although he was sympathetic, Danie told me that his hands were tied by their very low budget – but I had a plan. What if the local people harvested the game themselves? Although Danie was hesitant at first, before we went to bed he had agreed to give it a trial for one year.

Once the quota had been approved, each headman would appoint men from his community to do the actual hunting. As the .303 rifles handed out by the army had not been taken back, and many of the old poachers had acquired heavier calibre rifles, the hunters could provide their own weapons. To ensure that the quotas were adhered to and any wounded animals followed up, a member of the MWCT's staff would be allocated to each harvesting camp. IRDNC's role was to make vehicles available to transport the meat to the villages, as well as to buy the ammunition needed, the costs of which would be refunded from the sale of the game skins.

The three communities that took part in the harvest were Sesfontein, Warmquelle and Bergsig. The quota approved was for 500 animals, comprising 81 Hartmann's zebra, 170 gemsbok, 181 springbok, 20 kudu, 4 giraffe and 44 ostrich, of which a total of 484 were actually killed. The value of the meat distributed was estimated to be N$146 800, while the skins were sold for N$18 250. The fuel and maintenance costs of the IRDNC vehicles used was N$10 600, and the ammunition purchased another N$6 300. This meant that the total cost per animal cropped, excluding the salaries and vehicles of the MWCT staff, was approximately N$34.

As the rangers monitoring the harvest had only minor complaints about the way it was carried out, the first community hunt was regarded as a great

farmers, a decade after the drought ended and the illegal hunting stopped, it supported a high density of game, including black rhino and elephant. With Caroline Ashley, a British sociologist working for the MET, providing technical assistance, Colin Nott and Bennie Roman were given the task of facilitating negotiations with the local people.

Our recommendation was for Trevor Duncan to go into a joint venture with the community, in which he brought in the investment capital, and they would provide the land and wildlife, as well as having the responsibility of protecting it. The management and marketing of the lodge would be in the investors' hands, but for their contribution to the success of the enterprise the local people would get a percentage of the income. As Trevor had no previous tourism experience, to ensure that this very high-value site was used to its full potential, we also recommended that a minimum rental fee be paid.

To negotiate the contract, six representatives were chosen by the community, but at the first on-site meeting they behaved atrociously. Trevor had brought meat and drinks for a relaxing evening around the campfire after their discussions, but not having previously been hosted by a wealthy white man, the Riemvasmakers could not resist the temptation to drink as much as possible and were soon inebriated. To make matters worse, without asking, the next morning they took the leftover food and drink home with them. Needless to say their prospective business partner was not impressed.

The next hurdle was to obtain a 'Permission to Occupy' certificate from the Ministry of Lands and Resettlement, a requirement of all commercial enterprises on communal land. However, this was blocked by Rudi on the grounds that the proposed place for the lodge was too close to a spring, and would prevent rhino from drinking. Although a second site was proposed and approved, by then Trevor was losing interest, and when negotiations stalled over the amount the community should get from the enterprise he decided to build his lodge on private land. IRDNC's first attempt to facilitate a joint venture had failed, but we had learned a lot from it – not least that rural communities needed training before they were ready to go into negotiations with the private sector.

In 1995 the largest tourism company in Southern Africa, Wilderness Safaris, asked us to help them negotiate a joint-venture lodge with the Riemvasmaker community. The site chosen by their operations manager, Peter Ward, was on the farm Fonteine, overlooking the spectacular lower Huab valley, which now had a resident population of elephants in the dry season. This time, to avoid any future complications about who represented the community, we contacted the Legal Assistance Centre's director, Andrew Corbett, who recommended that a Resident Trust be formed and registered with the High Court. Once this was done, any contract signed by the elected trustees would be legally binding.

When the community selected its representatives they were invited to Wêreldsend for a tourism orientation workshop, which started with a roleplay in which Margie and I took the part of the prospective investors. After greeting them and explaining our intentions, I offered the community N$25 000 for the right to build a lodge on Fonteine, and without hesitating their spokesman, Jantjie Rhyn, accepted. Although he did not even ask if it was a once-off payment or an annual rent, all the other participants supported him.

By the end of the workshop they had a much better understanding of the real value of their land and its wildlife, not as a marginal area for livestock farming, but as a top-class destination for eco-tourism. They were also ready to face Wilderness Safaris with a list of hard questions about income sharing, employment opportunities for their community and the training of local staff. However, Peter Ward soon showed himself to be committed to a fair deal for both the Resident Trust and the company he represented.

Knowing that profits can be fudged by increasing the capital investment and running costs, or by moving revenue between different business operations, we recommended that they ask for a percentage of the lodge's total income. It would also give the community a stake in the success of the venture and encourage all of its members, especially the local staff, to give it their full support. Peter agreed to this, and as the guests would pay an all-inclusive daily rate, the Resident Trust's share would be 10 per cent of that amount, minus the fees charged by external booking agents.

In April 1996 a joint venture contract to build and operate 'Damaraland Camp' was signed by Dennis Rundle, the director of Wilderness Safaris Namibia, and Bennie Roman in his capacity as chairman of the Ward 11 Residents' Trust. Apart from the more than 20 permanent jobs it created for local people, within a few years it was annually earning the community well over ten times the amount we had offered their representatives in our roleplay at Wêreldsend.

In fact, Damaraland Camp proved to be a winner right from the start. The spectacular scenery, big game, and the marketing skills of Wilderness Safaris all contributed to this, as did the high standards set by the first managers, Louis Noortje and Hoens Potgieter. But what made it stand out most was the warm welcome guests received from the local staff and any local people that they met on their field excursions. The whole community regarded it as their lodge, and were determined to make it a success. Because of this, and the fact that it was the first joint venture between a private sector tourism operator and communal area residents, in 1998 it was nominated by the prestigious British Guild of Travel Writers as one of the top three eco-tourism destinations in the world.

* * *

The 1994 elections were again won by SWAPO, this time with a two-thirds majority. The next year Gert Hannekom replaced Nico Bessinger as the Minister of a renamed Ministry of Environment and Tourism. We would miss Nico's visionary leadership, but by then IRDNC's honeymoon with the government had ended, and some of our staff had found themselves being labelled unpatriotic. At a meeting in West Caprivi Andrew Corbett and I were also singled out for a tongue lashing by President Sam Nujoma. On that occasion it was because the LAC and IRDNC were in a legal battle to stop the Ministry of Home Affairs expropriating a community-owned campsite on the banks of the Okavango River for staff housing. But the underlying reason for our being so unpopular was the role we were playing in the environmental impact assessment for the Epupa Dam.

Because of its rapid fall in elevation the Kunene River had long been regarded as very suitable for the generation of hydro-power, and a series of dams had been planned by the South African government along its course. In the mid-1970s the turbines had been installed at Ruacana in a tunnel that bypassed the 80 metre high waterfall, and a large storage dam was under construction at Calueque in Angola when it was damaged by rockets fired from MIG fighters during the liberation war. In spite of this, with a barrage across the river just above the falls it still had an operating capacity of 250 megawatts, enough to supply the country's needs at the time of independence.

Anticipating that the demand for electricity would increase, Namibia and Angola had agreed to jointly develop a second hydro-power scheme downriver 'in the Epupa area or other location'. The project was overseen by a Permanent Joint Technical Committee, and a smaller Steering Committee for the Feasibility Study to supervise the consultants and review their report on behalf of both governments. The dam site Namibia preferred was 10 km below Epupa Falls, which would inundate an area of 270 km^2 and stretch 60 km upstream, while Angola wanted the dam built 30 km downstream in the Baynes Mountains, which when full would just reach to the foot of the falls. Both sites were investigated by the consultants, as well as a third, 10 km upstream from Epupa.

Margie and I, as well as Chris Tapscott from the Namibian Institute for Social and Economic Research, were appointed to carry out the social side of the pre-feasibility study. On our initial visit to the area in July 1992, we took Elias Hambo and Shorty Kasaona with us as translators, and before our community meeting stopped on a ridge overlooking the Epupa Falls and explained to them what was being planned by the engineers. After sitting for a while looking at the narrow 40 metre deep chasm the Kunene plunged into, the numerous smaller cascades and baobabs clinging to bare rock above the falls, and the backdrop of palms that contrasted with surrounding arid mountains, Elias turned to us and said: 'Muhona, we Herero know that white people are very clever and can do many wonderful things, but can they make a tree?'

In his characteristically insightful way my colleague had got to the heart of what was really at stake. We could no more make a tree than re-create this beautiful waterfall once it had been inundated by the dam. But Namibia needed electricity to light the homes and power the TV sets of the people who had been neglected during the apartheid era. The Epupa scheme would produce 600 MW, much more than both countries required for many years into the future. Fortunately, it was not up to us to decide which was more important. Our task was to interview the affected people and find out what they thought.

Our first meeting was at Omuhonga, where many of the local Himba elders had come together for a funeral. The two most important leaders present were Hikominue Kapika, the son of Munimuhoro and now the chief of the Epupa area, and his senior councillor Katjira Muniombara, who had walked with me in the Baynes Mountains 25 years earlier and was almost blind. Chris Tapscott led the discussion.

A delegation from Nampower had already visited the area and informed them of the proposed dam and the benefits it would bring them, and they had accepted it. But after we had talked for a while I realised they seemed to have no idea of its size, so I asked them about this. It would be very big, one man said, and he pointed out an outstanding leadwood about 400 metres away, and told us it would stretch from where we sat to the tree. With their only reference being a dam built near Otjitanda many years before, which was about half that size, to them anything bigger than it was 'very big'.

When I told them the whole Kunene valley would be under water as far upstream as Enyandi, 50 km east of Epupa, there was deathly silence for a few seconds, and then a few of the old men started to wail. The other elders also began chanting, an eerie sound that Margie and I had only previously heard at funerals. Through Elias, Katjira told us that such a dam 'would be the death of the Himba people'.

Although they were not prepared to continue the discussion, we did learn that the Nampower delegation had given Chief Kapika a letter, but because he could not read he never opened it, and had left it with his wife at Ombuku. As it would be useful for us to know what it said, Elias and I drove to Ombuku, where a young girl fetched the plastic wrapped letter from the fork of a tree inside the cattle kraal. On our return the chief gave us permission to open it. Nowhere did it state how big the dam would be, and although there was a map attached, it was a smudged photo-copy on which even we were unable to read the place names.

The actual feasibility study and EIA was carried out by a consortium of Scandinavian, Namibian and Angolan consultants, and began in August 1995. Namibia's social impact team consisted of just Margie and Dr Michael Bollig from the University of Cologne, who had done fieldwork among the Himba after independence. As we had been so busy working with Chris and Brian on the socio-ecological surveys and starting our Caprivi project, Margie had not yet written up her doctoral thesis. This was not an issue until the Epupa pre-feasibility study, when she felt the Swedish team leader had patronised her and Dr Mary Sealy, after they had asked to see the final version of the report before it was published. To prevent this from happening again she took eight weeks off and finished her thesis, graduating in November 1995.

When she was approached to be on the social team Margie had to think hard about whether to accept. We both believed it would be a tragedy to inundate the Epupa Falls, one of the region's major tourist attractions, and if she took part in the feasibility study we would have to remain neutral in the brewing controversy over the dam. What made her accept was that it was the first major environmental impact assessment to be carried out in Namibia, and would set a precedent for all future large-scale developments in our young country. Therefore, it was imperative that it conformed to internationally accepted standards, which included the full participation of the affected people. With their many years of research among the Himba, she and Michael Bollig were the best persons to ensure that this happened.

Before the EIA started we asked the community leaders in the Epupa area what they needed to become actively involved in the process. They told us that not having a vehicle was their main problem, because their dispersed settlements made it difficult for them to communicate with their followers. It also meant they were dependent on the government for transport to meetings. To rectify this we obtained a grant from a Dutch NGO, Wilde Gansen, and bought an old Toyota Land Cruiser, which was put under the authority of Katjira Muniombara, the highly respected councillor of Chief Kapika.

On her first field trip Margie was assisted by Tina Coombs, a university friend, Lina Kaisuma, a young woman from Warmquelle whom IRDNC had recently employed, and Shorty Kasaona. In each area they were also accompanied by a man chosen by the local headman to introduce them and report back to the broader community on their activities and results. During her second phase of interviews Karine Rousset, a postgraduate intern, took Tina's place and Mutjimbike Mutambo became Chief Kapika's permanent representative on the team.

The questions asked covered a wide range of issues, including household composition, socio-economy, water and health problems, and the aspirations of the people living in and around the inundation area. To get to the remote villages a helicopter was made available to them, and as Margie did not go anywhere without taking our two Staffordshire terriers, she convinced the pilot they were perfectly trained and should come with her on these trips. Two dogs arriving by helicopter were a great icebreaker at her meetings.

Although her group mostly camped out, when they returned from the field to re-supply, clean up, fix punctures and relax for a day or two, they all trooped into the base camp to make themselves tea or stay for a meal. As they were often accompanied by community members, and the dining area was where the consultants' laptops were connected, this meant the project's planners had to meet on social terms the local people whose homes and family graves they would submerge if the dam was built.

Remaining neutral over the Epupa Dam was not easy. While Margie tried hard to be professional, some of her part-time helpers could not hide their feelings. One of them was Chris Bakkes, who we had employed to train the community game guards. Before joining IRDNC he had been a wilderness trails officer in the Kruger National Park, but resigned after losing an arm in a crocodile attack. Understandably, Chris was quite subdued during the first few months he worked for us, but when he visited the feasibility study camp his fighting spirit returned, and he took great pleasure in annoying the consultants by singing uncomplimentary songs about engineers late into the night.

The SWAPO party faithful felt no need to stay impartial over a project that in its construction phase would create many jobs and commercial opportunities. As the Himba were uneducated and had no appropriate skills, most of the jobs would go to people from outside the affected area. However, those who saw themselves as the first in line for this economic windfall regarded anyone who did not support the building of the dam as being against the region's development and disloyal to the government. Once it became known that IRDNC had given the 'blue Toyota' to the community leaders, our staff became a target for their anger and abuse.

A major reason for the Himba opposing the dam was that their many graves along the Kunene would be submerged, preventing lineage heads from visiting them to pay homage and pray for guidance from the spirits of their forefathers. The riparian vegetation also provided crucial forage for their livestock in the dry season, while the fruits of the vegetable ivory palms were an important source of food for the people. They were also concerned about large numbers of people coming into the area to seek work, which would cause social strife and crime, especially stock-theft, and if they did not leave after the construction phase their leaders believed they would lose control over the area.

As the EIA progressed, the controversy over the Epupa dam spread throughout the Kunene Region, causing the re-emergence of the old divide between the Big Group and Small Group that had begun in the 1960s. Chief Paulus Tjavara, the leader of the former, supported the Himba's stand against it, while Chief Johannes Thom and Titus Muhenye, a civil servant and shop owner in Okanguati, were strong proponents of the dam. Outside the region, conservationists and international NGOs also voiced their opposition to the project, antagonising the government and setting the stage for the bitterest environmental battle our newly independent country had experienced.

In October 1996 the feasibility study team's first report-back meeting took place in Windhoek. As no transport was provided for representatives of the affected communities to attend, IRDNC made one of its vehicles available, which together with the infamous 'blue Toyota' brought 22 Himba representatives to the conference centre. As they were wearing traditional dress this caused quite a stir amongst the international delegates and the government officials present, but they sat quietly while the engineering consultants gave a series of very technical presentations. However, just before lunch Chief Kapika stood up and insisted on being given a chance to speak.

He was told they could put their case in a separate room over the lunch break, but he objected to this and the IUCN-appointed chairman, Raul du

Toit, eventually agreed to the chief being given a slot in the afternoon session. When his turn came he began by asking: 'If a dam was going to be built in Windhoek, would a meeting about it be held at Epupa?'

He went on to speak for 20 minutes, covering in detail the reasons why his people opposed the project. If Raul thought he had fulfilled his obligation to give the affected community a fair hearing, the delegation from Epupa thought otherwise. When the chief sat down one of his councillors rose to present his objections to the dam, and after he had finished a third and fourth man stood up to have their say. An hour later, Raul finally got a chance to ask Chief Kapika how many more of his people wanted to speak. It was the Himba way to give everyone a chance to say something, he replied, including the five woman who had come with them! By now the precisely timed programme was in tatters, and before they had all spoken the meeting ended.

Chief Kapika's point had been taken, and the next report-back session took place in Opuwo, in March 1997. The Deputy Minister of Mines and Energy, Jasaya Nyamu, was the main speaker, and VIPs, including the Swedish Ambassador, were flown in to see how much support the dam had in the region. This time Nampower hired a band to sing songs about the dam after each speaker, ensuring that the audience was filled with young people who were hoping to benefit from the employment opportunities the project would bring. The report-back programme was also arranged to have the pro-dam speakers on the first day, while the affected community was only given time the next morning – after the VIPs had flown back to Windhoek!

In a carnival atmosphere a thousand people gathered in an open-air venue, where in disregard for the EIA process, Deputy Minister Nyamu said in his speech: 'It is not about whether the dam will be built, but only about where it will be built.' This was devastating news to the people living in the area and before lunch the Legal Assistance Centre lawyer representing them, Norman Tjombe, objected to his clients' not being given a chance to speak while the VIP guests were still there. With the Swedish Ambassador sitting next to him, the Deputy Minister could hardly refuse and one member of the affected community was allowed to speak on their behalf. This was done very eloquently by the chairman of the Epupa Development Committee, Vahenuna Tjitaura.

Another ploy that Nampower used to attract pro-dam supporters to the meeting was distributing free T-shirts with 'Viva Epupa' emblazoned across them. As we saw many Himba wearing them, when Margie visited their headmen the next morning she asked if they knew what the words on them said. They told her that as they could not read, how could they know? When she explained what the slogan meant, young men were sent out to collect every T-shirt worn by a Himba, and an hour later a large ochre-stained pile was put in front of her, which the headmen asked her to 'give back to the government'. This she refused to do. They had taken them, so they should return them.

It was the last straw. At a meeting called that afternoon, the community leaders told Margie that because the Himba were illiterate the government had deliberately humiliated them, and after thanking her team for what they had done, said they would no longer take part in the feasibility study. Everyone had heard the Deputy Minister say the dam would be built, so they would have to continue their opposition to it in other ways.

At the next consultants' meeting, Margie informed them of the community's decision, pointing out that without their participation she could not develop a mitigation strategy for the dam. The Scandinavians' response was that she knew the Himba well enough to do it on their behalf, and when she refused to do this the team leader accused her of being 'a militant'. However, the Namibian and South African consultants all supported her, and they recommended that the Steering Committee ask the government to publicly withdraw the Deputy Minister's statement. This would enable Margie to ask the community leaders to continue with the process. It was not done, and instead a group from the University of Namibia was sent to Epupa to produce a mitigation strategy. But even though Nampower gave Chief Kapika a new Toyota Hilux, he refused to co-operate with them and they went back empty-handed.

In July 1997 a German NGO sponsored Chief Kapika to tour Sweden, England and Germany, where he received considerable publicity for his stand against the Epupa dam. Because the Feasibility Study was incomplete without a mitigation strategy, and thus not 'bankable', the Joint Steering Committee was also unable to recommend that the project go ahead, and Norway and Sweden, which had hoped to get the contract to build the dam, withdrew their support. At the time of writing a new EIA had started for a hydroelectric dam at the Baynes site, 30 km downriver from Epupa.

CHAPTER TWENTY-FIVE

COMMUNAL CONSERVANCIES

By early 1993, Chris Brown and Brian Jones had drawn up a draft policy that gave the communal area residents rights over wildlife equivalent to the rights freehold farmers were granted in 1975. It was based on the aspirations voiced during the socio-ecological surveys, the Hwange principles, and the conceptual foundations for CBNRM that had been proposed by one of the founding fathers of the CAMPFIRE Programme, Prof Marshal Murphree of the Centre for Applied Social Sciences at the University of Zimbabwe. They were:

- economic benefits from the sustainable use of natural resources;
- devolution of authority over wildlife to the de facto land users;
- collective ownership of all common property resources;
- an adaptive policy framework and management strategies.

For economic benefits they looked at trophy hunting, which was already well established in Namibia and underpinned a dynamic game farming industry on freehold land. Their objective was to allow local communities to enter this lucrative market. Although hunting concessions had in the past been granted to private sector operators in the communal areas, because the land was under the jurisdiction of the State, the fees they paid had all gone to the national treasury.

Initially they considered sharing the income from hunting between the government and local people, as was the case in Zambia's ADMADE programme. However, during a visit to Namibia by a delegation from CAMPFIRE in July 1993, Brian Child and Ivan Bond argued that this put wildlife utilisation at a competitive disadvantage to livestock farming. And where land was at a premium it would result in there being little incentive to conserve big game, especially species that caused economic losses to the people living with them.

They also told us that one of the main flaws in Zimbabwe's CBNRM programme was that it devolved the rights over natural resources to Rural District Councils, a government structure that was both bureaucratic and politicised. A further drawback of RDCs was that they had authority over large geographic areas that included many diverse communities, some of which had a high human density and little or no wildlife, while others had few people and still supported good big game populations. This had led to the question of how the income from natural resources should be equitably distributed, an issue that many Councils had not yet been able to resolve.

Brian and Ivan, who were both resource economists, recommended that Namibia go below district to local community level. From a social perspective, the smaller the management unit the more cohesive it would be. Other advantages were that structures made up of the people who lived with the wildlife would better understand its conservation needs, and were less likely to be influenced by external events. On the negative side, in arid areas many species were migratory and best managed on large units of land. On freehold land the movement of game across farm boundaries was the major cause of conflict between landowners. However, pioneering work had been done there by Mick de Jager, who encouraged them to remove their external fences and jointly manage and utilise their wildlife in 'conservancies' – a name he had taken from a similar programme being promoted by the Natal Parks Board.

Because wild animals, unlike livestock, only belonged to a farmer while they were on his property, the 1975 Ordinance had made appropriate fencing a legal requirement before use rights could be granted. On communal land there were no fences – and without defined borders, which community should be allowed to benefit from migratory game? For this reason, the boundaries of 'communal area conservancies' would have to be negotiated between neighbours, but instead of fences a GPS could be used to record the agreed reference points on a map.

Another problem was that the 1975 Ordinance granted utilisation rights to a single landowner, which could not be done in communal areas because the wild animals were a common property resource. To resolve this, a representative committee would be needed to take responsibility for the management of the conservancy, ensure that its natural resources were sustainably utilised, and equitably distribute any benefits coming from them. This opened up two further issues: how would its members be chosen, and what role should the traditional leaders play?

A characteristic of Namibia's communal areas was their great diversity, both ecologically and ethnically, which resulted in them supporting a wide range of subsistence economies and social systems. Consequently, to create a national policy for conservancies that would be appropriate to hunter-gatherers, nomadic pastoralists, crop farmers and fishermen was not possible. There was also a big difference in the way customary governance functioned, and how much authority their chiefs and headmen had over their followers. The only way to overcome this would be to make the legislation flexible enough for communities to adapt its basic principles to match their own needs and aspirations.

After Chris and Brian had drawn up their proposed policy it was given to Minister Bessinger, who called a meeting of traditional and other leaders in the communal areas, to hear their views and get further input. Brian then accompanied Deputy Minister Ben Ulenga and the Permanent Secretary, Hanno Rumpf, on a trip to Opuwo and towns in the former Ovamboland to promote the Ministry's new community-based approach. They found there was general support for it, and the 'Policy on Wildlife Management, Utilisation and Tourism in Communal Areas' was passed by the SWAPO cabinet in March 1995.

To ensure that the new policy was actually implemented, and could not be blocked by officials who felt threatened by it, Chris and Brian included a statement that the 1975 Ordinance should be amended to entrench the local communities' rights in legislation, which would also prevent those rights from being arbitrarily retracted in the future. The downside to this was that any change to existing laws had first to be approved by the Ministry of Justice and then passed by the national parliament. As the senior MET staff – including those against the community-based approach – would be responsible for implementing the new legislation, their support was also needed.

To obtain this, Chris and Brian discussed the proposed amendment with MET Director Polla Swart and Leon van Rooyen, who agreed that communal area residents should benefit from wildlife utilisation, but not just the communities where it occurred. For this to happen, they proposed the setting up of wildlife councils comprising MET officials, traditional leaders and a member of the Regional Council, to manage natural resources and decide on how the income from trophy hunting and tourism should be used. However, Chris and Brian argued that if everyone received benefits there would be no incentive for the people who were actually living with the wildlife to become actively involved in its conservation.

As they were unable to resolve this issue, when they sat down with Leon and Danie Grobler to write the final draft of the legislation, it was a compromise that included provisions for the creation of both conservancies and wildlife councils. The local communities would be left to decide for themselves what type of natural resource governance they wanted, but it was agreed that conservancies would take precedence and could still be formed – even in areas where a wildlife council had already been established.

In 1996 the *Nature Conservation Amendment Act* was approved by cabinet and then passed by the National Assembly and National Council without any changes. However, it soon became as controversial as the 1975 Ordinance had been – only this time the battle lines were different. Although no one disagreed with local communities getting benefits from wildlife, a hard core in the MET and some NGOs was opposed to subsistence farmers being given authority to manage natural resources. It was not only whites that felt this way. During a workshop at Wêreldsend, one of the new black nature conservators said bitterly that he had spent twelve years in school and another three years studying for his diploma, and now we were telling him that he should listen to his illiterate grandfather!

Margie and I were also no longer the only ones being maligned by conservative officials in the MET. Colleagues of Chris and Brian started calling them the 'dream team' – not as a compliment, but in reference to the unrealistic ideas they had come up with. In spite of this, by the mid-1990s we had made some converts. At a conference organised to discuss the conflict between humans and wildlife in communal areas, some old guard officials proposed that local communities be given total responsibility to deal with problem animals. Although it was to some extent just passing the buck for this thorny issue, their suggesting that black farmers be given any authority at all would not have happened in the past.

However, when it came to conservancies, nothing that the MET field staff heard from Chris and Brian would allay their concerns. And as the only people they trusted were their superiors in the Ministry's Parks and Wildlife Management section, Danie Grobler, Leon van Rooyen and Chris Grobler visited all the MET's northern regional offices and Etosha to show that they supported the new communal area policy and legislation. This was a turning point: although not everyone was convinced, at least the top government officials were now behind Namibia's CBNRM programme.

*   *   *

Having a legal framework to operate in was a big step forward, but converting legislation into practice was not a simple matter. For a conservancy to be registered, the community first needed to meet a number of conditions: its borders had to be defined, a representative committee elected, its members registered and a constitution written. They also had to draw up wildlife management and equitable benefit distribution plans before their application could be submitted to the local MET office, and a copy given to the regional governor for his comments. If all the requirements were completed the application was then sent to the MET head office for their approval and the signature of the Minister, before its details were published in the *Government Gazette*.

Once gazetted, the conservancy became a legal community-based organisation with both consumptive and non-consumptive utilisation rights over the wildlife and other natural resources within its borders, as well as the responsibility to manage them sustainably. But if the elected committee failed to fulfil these prescribed obligations the Minister of Environment and Tourism could, after giving due warning, de-gazette the conservancy.

For many communities the most time-consuming part of the registration process was negotiating their borders, and as the MET required them to have signed agreements with all their neighbours, this could take years to finalise. Nevertheless, it was an important exercise because it ensured that a conservancy's boundaries were established by its members, in contrast to the CAMPFIRE Programme, where they were the pre-defined wards within a district. By persevering with the long and often difficult border negotiations, the community also showed that they were serious about wanting to manage their own natural resources.

It was not only disagreements with neighbours that held up the establishment of a conservancy. Around the Palmwag and Etendeka tourism concessions, the most important wildlife area in the Kunene Region, it was internal conflicts that caused a delay. Here the community was divided ethnically between Damara and Herero, as well as by allegiance to different traditional leaders. Even though these disputes pre-dated the CBNRM legislation, having to decide whether to form one or two conservancies, where the borders would be, and who should sit on the management committee, just added fuel to the flames.

Herero traditional leaders Keefas Muzuma and Joshua Kangombe wanted one conservancy stretching from Etosha's western border to the Skeleton Coast Park, but the old Big and Small group division raised its head again and Goliat Kasaona and Josef Yapuwa, who between them claimed a large part of the area, rejected this. Opposition to the CBNRM policy by many local MET officials and the Damara Kings Council created further confusion, which would delay the development of conservancies in southern Kunene Region for many years.

Although the residents of Purros initially planned to form a single conservancy with Sesfontein, because of the conflicts there they decided to go it alone. But by then the dispute over ownership of the campsite had split the community, leading to Peter Uararavi's group boycotting all further meetings. Nevertheless, with IRDNC support the majority of people here went ahead with the registration process, alienating Margie and me from Peter and his brother Japi, who was one of the early community game guards and had been a good friend of ours.

Encouraged by Koos Vervey, an ex-commandant in the SADF who had built a rustic lodge at Otjinungua, the small Himba community in the Marienfluss and Hartmann valleys also decided to form a conservancy. To reduce the potential for conflict they made their eastern border the foot of the Otjihipa range, which excluded their headman, Kahoravi Tjingee, and the much larger number of people around Otjitanda above the escarpment. However, as the stockowners living on the plateau bring their cattle down into the Marienfluss when good rains fall there, this meant that they would have no economic incentive to support conservation or grazing management there.

Because of our agreement with the SRT, IRDNC restricted its activities south of the veterinary fence to Ward 11, where the local people had already registered a Residents Trust for their joint venture with Wilderness Safaris. However, in 1996 the ANC government in South Africa offered the Riemvasmakers in Namibia the opportunity to go back to their old homes along the Orange River, and more than half of them did so. This left large tracts of land in the basalt ranges unoccupied, which were then settled by Damara and Herero farmers, splitting this once tightly-knit community along ethnic lines.

To add to the turmoil, Regional Governors in Kunene and Caprivi were initially unwilling to endorse any conservancy applications for registration, unless they were given a greater say in the process. This was resolved by the MET calling a meeting of all 14 governors to explain why the authority over wildlife utilisation had been devolved down to the community level. The Damara traditional leadership in southern Kunene Region, supported by the MET staff in Khorixas, also tried to install a wildlife council south of the veterinary fence, in spite of the existence of emerging conservancies there. But pressure from the local people themselves prevented it from happening.

One of the reasons for the high level of conflict in Kunene Region was because the wild animals here were no longer seen as just an extra source of meat. Thanks to the Damaraland Camp joint venture and the Purros community campsite, the local people had now learned that through tourism they could also earn money and get jobs, making gaining control over the areas where big game still occurred critical to the success of their conservancies. At a more personal level, getting onto a committee that was responsible for distributing the income could mean cash in their pockets.

The community game guards, whose role in stopping poaching had led the way for use rights over wildlife being devolved to communal area residents, at first just watched the scrambling for position and power from the sidelines. However, at a meeting to explain why they would in future fall under conservancy committees, and not their traditional leaders, one of them stood up and expressed his feelings about what was happening: 'The game that is now plentiful around our villages belongs to us, and if the youngsters who have done nothing to protect it also want to have wild animals they must go and get their own.'

I understood where he was coming from. Namibia's CBNRM programme was starting to attract major donor funding, and because the younger generation were better educated they were getting most of the new employment opportunities that became available. Over the next few years this would result in many of the illiterate older men in the community either withdrawing, or being pushed out of positions of influence in the emerging conservancies. Their wisdom and experience would be sorely missed.

Although any major economic changes in rural communities could be expected to upset the social equilibrium, these disputes reinforced the CBNRM detractors' case that communal area residents could not work together, and were thus not capable of managing their natural resources. To counter this we pointed out that there were also major disagreements between individual farm owners on the freehold conservancies, but this had not made them un-viable. It was also better for the issues causing the conflict to be brought out into the open and resolved before conservancies were registered, so that when their committees began operating they would be able to focus their attention on making them ecologically, socially and economically sustainable.

In June 1998, two years after the conservancy legislation was passed, Torra and /Hoadi //Hoas in the Kunene Region, together with Salambala in Caprivi and Nyae Nyae in Otjozondjupa Region were gazetted. Three months later, in recognition of Namibia's CBNRM Programme 'coming of age', President Sam Nujoma, who had been made patron of the communal area conservancies, was given WWF-US's prestigious Gift to the Earth Award. It was fitting that the head of the government should receive the public accolade for the country's pioneering conservation policy and legislation, but the real credit belonged to MET's visionary first Minister, Nico Bessinger, and the 'dream team' of Chris Brown and Brian Jones.

* * *

Once the first conservancies were gazetted the devolution of rights and responsibilities over wildlife to communal area residents faced its greatest test. Would they manage their natural resources sustainably, and could these new community-based institutions function effectively? Perhaps most important of all, would they be able to earn sufficient income to be weaned off donor funding and one day become financially independent?

The residents of Torra Conservancy had already shown their commitment to conserving their now plentiful wildlife, and with a lucrative joint venture with Wilderness Safaris and Bennie Roman as their first chairman, we were confident that they would be successful. However, the emerging conservancies north of the veterinary fence consisted mainly of subsistence pastoralists with a low level of education, and would need considerable support to enable them to fulfil their legal obligations and meet the expectations of their members.

With the increased funding we were now receiving from WWF-UK we were able to employ more qualified staff and divide them into three teams that were co-ordinated by Colin Nott. The first, under Anton Esterhuizen, who had been the MET's acting regional warden for the north-east of Namibia, would provide conservancies with technical advice and training in natural resource management. Anna Davis, an MA graduate who had grown up in Zimbabwe and Malawi, did the same for institutional issues, and Bennie Roman was given the responsibility of facilitating income-generating enterprises. After Tim and Rosie Holmes resigned, Ed Humphrey, an Australian who had previously worked for the Ministry of Youth and Sport, took over the running of Wêreldsend Environmental Education Centre.

When Colin was seconded to the LIFE Programme, and Anna joined the Namibia Nature Foundation, Bennie Roman took over as the co-ordinator of IRDNC's Kunene Project, and Ed Humphrey facilitated enterprise development. After completing a nature conservation diploma course at the Poly-Tech, John Kasaona was appointed to lead the institutional support team. By then we had opened an office in Windhoek that was run by Annetjie Bonthuis, and when she resigned to marry Pierre du Preez, who later became the MET's rhino management specialist, Karen Nott replaced her. As she had a master's degree and had previously worked in Etosha, Karen also organised our CBNRM courses for tertiary-educated students at Wêreldsend.

In addition to the technical advice and training provided by IRDNC, conservancies needed interim financial support to pay their game guards and other staff wages and running costs. This investment into these new community-based organisations was essential for them to fulfil their responsibilities as custodians of the wildlife within them. But unlike private sector businesses, it would be repaid by the increasing big game populations on communal land, thereby considerably extending the area of Namibia where trophy hunting and photographic tourism could take place. Because not all conservancies had the same potential to generate income, the amount of financial assistance they received was graded according to whether they were on a major tourist route, or if they included natural resources with a high national value.

As more communities asked IRDNC for support to form conservancies, the annual budgets we submitted to our donors also increased. Fortunately at WWF International, John Newby and later Tom McShane, who had himself implemented a CBNRM project in Gabon and written a book on the subject, understood that development projects in Africa required substantial assistance to be successful. With their ongoing support we were able to expand our activities in both Kunene and Caprivi, and as importantly could employ and train more local people, on whose shoulders the long-term sustainability of conservation in communal areas ultimately depended.

When WWF-UK took over as our major donors we were again lucky to have as our link person Peggy Alcock, who was so enthusiastic about the

Namibia programme that she brought us into their People and Planet campaign, so that other countries and WWF staff in Godalming could learn about a people-centred way of conserving endangered species. Over the next few years a number of IRDNC and conservancy workers visited WWF projects in Scotland, where crofter communities faced similar issues of governance over natural resources. For Bennie Roman, John Kasaona, Lina Kaisuma and the Torra Conservancy's field officer, Vitalis Flory, it was their first trip overseas and although they felt like country bumpkins in the big cities, they found they were able to teach their UK counterparts a few lessons on how to devolve authority to local people.

In 2002 Peggy also arranged for Margie to present a paper at the 'Rio plus Ten' Conference in London, which she gave jointly with John Kasaona. Speaking just after Tony Blair and Clare Short, the Secretary for International Development, they did their best to outline the essence of CBNRM in the 20 minutes allowed. To such a high-powered audience this was not easy, but Margie was fascinated to hear the same basic principles that were used in Namibia's programme being articulated by the environmental officer of a large 'Do it Yourself' company, who had been hired to clean up the appalling conditions in the developing country factories that they outsourced work to.

When Margie asked John what had impressed him most on their trip, he told her it was the low-key security around Tony Blair and the informal way he was treated by the conference delegates. Hearing the Prime Minister being called by his Christian name was amazing – something that would never happen in Namibia. He was also surprised by how hard white people, who were obviously well off, worked in England, and after seeing buildings that were 800 years old, how long the country's history was. For a young man who grew up in Sesfontein it was an invaluable experience, which stood him in good stead as he rose up through the ranks in IRDNC. In the years ahead, John would be invited to the United States on a number of occasions, and in 2010 gave a very well-received talk on Namibia's CBNRM programme at the prestigious Technology, Entertainment and Design (TED) Conference in Los Angeles.

With reliable donor partners IRDNC was able to support many more conservancies, but the demand for our services seemed never-ending. The residents of the communal areas had waited a long time to be given the legal authority to manage and benefit from their natural resources, and communities across the whole country were soon working on the requirements for registration. In parts of Kunene Region where virtually all wildlife had been shot out in the 1970s and early 1980s, game guards were appointed to protect the few kudu and impala that still survived, or the springbok and mountain zebra that had migrated inland from the pre-Namib. Although many of the emerging conservancies were off the main tourist routes, they still wanted wildlife back for their children to see, and to hunt in the future when their numbers had built up again.

As the CBNRM programme grew and expanded to other regions, more organisations began providing support. From 1993 the LIFE Programme gave financial grants to the MET, emerging conservancies and local NGOs, as well as employing a team of technical experts who were based in Windhoek. Together with the Rössing Foundation under Len le Roux, they also assisted King Taapopi of Uukwaluudhi to establish the first conservancy in the politically important Omusati Region. When the SRT's Huab Valley project ended, the Directorate of Environmental Affairs was able to access funds to support the community living east of the Grootberg range, where six local people were appointed as 'environmental shepherds'. Two American Fulbright scholars were based there to monitor the increasing wildlife populations and find ways of reducing the damage caused by elephants to the farmers' water-points and fences.

In southern Kunene and Erongo regions the Rural Institute for Social Empowerment (RISE), directed by Pintile Davids, helped local communities to conserve their wildlife and fulfil their registration requirements, while the Ju/'hoa community was given ongoing support by the Nyae Nyae Development Foundation (NNDF) and LIFE. Even though there was very little wildlife on communal land in the south of the country, the local communities there also wanted the right to manage and benefit from the natural resources they did have, and they were supported to form conservancies by the Namibia Development Trust (NDT), directed by Ronnie Dempers.

In 1995 a meeting of IRDNC, Rössing Foundation and LIFE held at Wêreldsend led to the formation of the Namibian Community-Based Tourism Association (NACOBTA), an umbrella body for all income-generating activities in the communal areas that were dependent on natural resources. After receiving a grant from the LIFE programme, an office was opened in Windhoek and Maxi Louis appointed as its first director. NACOBTA's main function was to improve the standards of community-run and individually owned enterprises through training courses and by accessing donor funding. It would also provide a booking service for campsites and market its members to Namibian tourism associations and at international trade fairs.

Last but not least, the Legal Assistance Centre advised emerging conservancy committees on constitutional matters and reviewed joint venture contracts with the private sector. Directed by Andrew Corbett, it had started as a legal support NGO exposing abuses of the security forces in Namibia, and after independence expanded its activities to include land rights and assisting the CBNRM programme. When Andrew resigned he was replaced as director by Clement Daniels and then Norman Tjombe.

Because of the number and diversity of organisations involved, one of the most important early contributions of the LIFE programme was the steering committee that brought MET's Director of Parks and Wildlife, Maria Kapere, its Director of Environmental Affairs, Chris Brown, the heads of the NGOs, and a representative from USAID around the same table. It was the first time we had all planned together, and there was no shortage of robust discussion on the key principles of CBNRM, as well as what training and financial assistance each conservancy needed to become registered and ultimately self-sustainable.

In July 2000 the LIFE Steering Committee's coordinating role was taken over by the Namibia Association of CBNRM Support Organisations (NACSO). A small secretariat was created under Karl Aribeb, who was replaced two years later by Patricia Skyer. In addition to quarterly meetings to discuss the overall direction of the programme, working groups were established for natural resource management, business and enterprise development and institutional issues that would guide and coordinate the activities of the various implementing agencies.

By then Chris Brown had left the MET to become director of the Namibia Nature Foundation, and Brian Jones resigned soon afterwards to freelance as a consultant. Peter Tarr took over as the head of the Directorate of Environmental Affairs, followed a few years later by Theo Nghitila. Although the MET decided not to join NACSO, the 'dream team' that had played such a crucial role in getting the CBNRM policy and legislation passed stayed involved with the programme. While Margie was on NACSO's steering committee it meant she and Chris could also continue sparring, and at the same time ensure that the theory underpinning Namibia's community-based approach maintained its academic edge.

The Desert Research Foundation of Namibia (DRFN), the country's most important scientific NGO, did not become a member of NACSO. During the 1990s they had carried out a number of ecological studies in the north-west, but as they did not have the staff to implement their findings little of practi-

cal value resulted from them. Nevertheless, under Dr Mary Seely's director-
ship, they did not support the devolution of rights and responsibilities to local
communities, a common standpoint among the scientific fraternity.

Margie and I were less surprised that the SRT did not join NACSO. Whether
it was because of their conflict with us or conviction, Blythe and Rudi made it
very clear that they did not believe in conservancies. However, they did train
as rhino trackers many local young men who under Mannetjie Hoeb monitored the population, thereby reinforcing the local people's commitment to
conservation and their sense of pride in the successes that had been achieved
in protecting the region's rhinos. After Mike Hearn became the SRT's research
co-ordinator and Simson Uri //Gob took over as the director of field operations, their relationship with the CBNRM support NGOs also improved.

*   *   *

Five years after Torra and /Hoadi //Hoas were registered, another 14 conservancies had been gazetted in Kunene Region, and a total of 27 in the whole
country. However, becoming a legal community-based organisation was just
the first step. Like any other business, they would now have to manage their
assets, keep records of income and expenditure and provide feedback to their
members. For subsistence farmers who had previously only been responsible
for their own households and livestock, this required a steep learning curve.

To ensure that IRDNC's support staff and conservancy committees remained focused on the priority issues, quarterly planning meetings were introduced at Wêreldsend. There the NGO teams and community representatives first reported back on their progress over the previous three months, and
then planned their activities for the next quarter. As the local MET rangers
and biologists, other NGOs and private sector operators in the area were invited to attend, the holding of regular meetings provided a forum for sharing information between all the stakeholders. They also enabled the committees to hold IRDNC and MET accountable for our actions, or inaction, with
regard to conservancy registration or wildlife management. Initially, some
MET officials took exception to this and stopped participating, but over time
both parties recognised that they were now on the same side, and a spirit
of co-operation developed between community members and government
rangers – an uncommon situation over most of rural Africa.

When quarterly planning meetings began IRDNC staff led the process, but as the conservancy representatives became more confident they started advising each other on ways to overcome the many hurdles on the road to registration. At times this could be humorous, as when a large Herero man renowned for his chauvinism lectured a newly formed committee on its gender balance! Nevertheless, the point had been made, and it had more impact coming from a member of the community than in a lecture by one of IRDNC's staff.

In fact, because this was a sensitive subject in traditional societies, it was not our policy to promote quotas for the number of women on the committee. Instead we held courses in public speaking for local women, to help them become more assertive at decision-making meetings. With the role models provided by IRDNC's female members of staff, their participation in the CBNRM programme soon increased and many conservancies appointed women to key positions on their committees. In 2009 Anabeb became the first conservancy to choose a woman chairman.

Although most issues could be left for the communities to solve themselves, one that did need outside intervention was the conflict between the human residents of the region and wildlife. As they were no longer being poached for ivory, the elephant population increased from about 280 in 1982 to a total of 387 counted ten years later, and by the end of the millennium their numbers were estimated to be over 580 – some of which had undoubtedly come into the north-west from Etosha. Predators were also making a comeback, but whereas the law allowed farmers to kill them if they threatened their livestock, elephants could only be hunted by MET staff after they had raided crops or damaged water installations. The limited capacity of the regional offices to respond to such cases, and the lengthy process involved in getting offending individuals declared as 'problem animals' meant that this seldom happened.

In the early 1990s the SRT used their funding from the EU to build dry stone walls around the artificial water-points in the Huab catchment, which proved effective if there were alternative places for the elephants to drink. But in many parts of Kunene Region there were no springs, and as they became less afraid of people, groups of bulls and even some cow herds started walking between the houses to reach a reservoir. Apart from the threat they posed to human life and property the elephants also drank large quantities of water that under the Ministry of Agriculture, Water and Rural Development's new policy, farmers in the communal areas had to use their own money to pump.

Assisting communities north of the veterinary fence to address human–wildlife conflict fell on the shoulders of Anton Esterhuizen, who built alternative elephant drinking places away from the villages, and for crop damage experimented with simple electric fences. Although they proved successful if well maintained, this was often not the case, and there were just too many scattered villages and fields to be protected with the limited funds available.

To find out if technological solutions were cost effective we needed to know more about the extent of the problem, and where the most affected areas were. The community game guards, who were required to report serious cases of human–wildlife conflict, provided some information, but as many of them were illiterate it was not easily accessible. To make it more systematic for the MET and NGO support organisations, and user friendly for the conservancy committees, Dr Greg Stewart-Hill of the LIFE programme and Jo Tagg in the DEA developed punch-cards on which the game guards used icons and bar-charts to record all the 'events' that occurred in their areas. This data was then consolidated monthly and annually into box files that provided easy reference for a wide range of topics, including human–wildlife conflict and the species involved.

Field testing of the system was done by Dave Ward, a consultant working for LIFE, and Beaven Munali, the head of IRDNC's Natural Resource Management team in the Caprivi, with technical input from Richard Diggle, who had taken over from Mathew Rice as the project co-ordinator. The Caprivians took to the 'Event Book' like ducks to water, but it was not so readily accepted by Kunene conservancies. They had been conserving their wild animals for longer and had more big game than Caprivi, they told us, and saw no reason to change from their old way of recording information. However, it soon became apparent that the underlying reason was because they had not been involved in developing the new system – a good lesson for the Windhoek-based advocates of 'rolling out' the 'best practice' in other places.

Once the problem was recognised, sympathetic handling of the situation led to the Event Book being used by all the gazetted conservancies, and within a few years it had become the standard monitoring system in Namibia's communal areas. In fact, it has proved so successful that it was adapted and re-named as the 'Incident Book' by the MET field staff in national parks, as well as by government wildlife authorities in a number of other countries.

Although the Event Book gave us more accurate information on human–wildlife conflict in the conservancies, it just confirmed what we already knew: that with elephant and large predator numbers having increased in the communal areas, the damage they caused might be reduced by technological interventions, but could not be eliminated. The only long-term solution lay in the costs to local communities being balanced by their getting direct economic benefits from the problem-causing species. The best way to do this was by trophy hunting, and annual quotas were granted to gazetted conservancies, which could then be tendered out to a qualified professional hunter. Although many tourism operators opposed all forms of hunting, now that the poaching had stopped, if we wanted the residents of communal areas to share their land with wildlife, a few individuals would have to 'pay the rent'.

Initially the professional hunters were wary of going into a contract with a rural community. There were also high logistical costs in travelling to remote communal areas to hunt game that was available on the freehold farms. Consequently, when Savannah Safaris negotiated the first contract with Torra Conservancy, the prices they offered for the species on quota were quite low. As this was expected we kept the concession period short, so that both parties could get to know each other. By the time their contract was renewed their concerns had been dispelled, and they were prepared to pay substantially higher amounts in order to offer their clients the privilege of hunting on a large area of unfenced land that had excellent trophies on it.

As more conservancies were gazetted the MET allowed a few elephants and predators to be included on the quotas, to compensate for the economic losses they caused. This attracted more trophy hunting outfitters to the communal areas, enabling competitive market forces to dictate the prices received for the animals hunted. For the first time destructive and potentially dangerous species had been given a financial value, and although the individual farmers whose livelihoods they threatened still got no direct benefit, there was a noticeable change in the local communities' attitude to them.

To maintain a high standard of trophy quality animals, conservative quotas needed to be set, which required a credible, regularly repeated way of counting the game in each conservancy. In 1998 an aerial census had been carried out in Kunene Region – the first since 1990 – but it was at a low intensity and as only Torra and /Hoadi //Hoas were then registered, did not differentiate between individual conservancies. Greg and Jo also believed that flying would be too expensive in the long term, so instead they proposed an annual road count along the same routes and at the same time of the year. After being trained by MET and NGO staff, local community members were used to keep the costs down and ensure that each conservancy shared ownership over the process and its results.

The first road count was carried out in June 2001, and they have taken place every year since then. Although they only provided the minimum numbers and trends for species seen in high enough numbers to be reliable, even when conservatively extrapolated they showed that the wildlife in Kunene Region had made a remarkable recovery. From only 526 springbok actually seen during the NWT's 100-hour aerial census, their population was estimated to be 23 000 in the 1998 aerial count and a minimum of 72 000 from the 2007 road count. The low extrapolated estimates for other large ungulates was 15 800 gemsbok (from 568 in 1982), 11 800 mountain zebra (from 756), and 520 giraffe (from 277). The recovery of their prey species also allowed the large predators to increase, and in 2008 Dr Flip Stander's research showed that there were more than 100 lions in the north-west – mainly in the Palmwag concession. Flip also followed a small pride down the Hoarusib River to the coast – the first time lions had been seen on the beach since 1988.

By any standards it was a remarkable turnaround, and as the region's cattle, goats and sheep numbers had also risen to above those at the start of the 1980/81 drought, there was now a danger of another mass mortality of both domestic and wild ungulates occurring in the next low rainfall period. To address the situation, in 2006 the MET called a workshop at which it was agreed that to limit competition with the local people's livestock and lessen the impact of a future drought, ways of harvesting more wildlife from the conservancies should be found and encouraged.

As trophy hunting only removed a small number of animals, and relatively few were taken off for the communities' own use, between 2003 and 2009 Torra Conservancy was granted permits to capture a total of over 3 000 springbok, which were sold to freehold farmers and game dealers. Where the game populations justified it, the MET also approved 'shoot and sell' quotas to conservancies, giving them a further source of revenue from their excess wildlife. Because veterinary restrictions did not allow any products from cloven-hoofed species to cross the Red Line, those situated to the north of it sold the meat to butchers in Opuwo and Oshakati, as well as their local lodges.

For the remote north-western conservancies that were unable to attract commercial hunters, Anders Johansson, who with Staffan Entcrantz had been a long-term supporter of IRDNC, and was a keen hunter himself, came up with another way of earning income. Instead of local people shooting the animals on their 'own use' quota, he proposed offering non-trophy safaris in which paying clients would do the hunting for them. This would allow each guest to take a 'bigger bag' and as the law required a professional hunter to accompany them, it would be carried out more efficiently.

* * *

The live sale of game, trophy hunting and the commercial harvesting of meat all provided valuable income to Kunene Region conservancies, reducing their dependence on donor funding and in some cases enabling them to cover their staff wages and running costs. However, the low number or absence of high-value species such as elephants and buffalo meant the benefits from trophy hunting would always be limited. This was compensated for by the spectacular desert scenery in which the wildlife occurred, making photographic tourism their greatest potential sources of revenue.

The non-consumptive use rights granted to conservancies by the amendment to the Nature Conservation Ordinance gave them authority over any tourism activities within their borders, but this was not so easy to implement. The legislation had also stated that 'existing leases' could not be included within a conservancy, which meant any 'permission to occupy' (PTO) granted to a lodge before it was gazetted had to be excluded. Therefore, the committee had no say over what happened within the designated area of the PTO, nor could it legally demand payment for the clients it accommodated. As Namibia's constitution gave citizens the right to travel anywhere in the country and the transport ordinance did not allow gates to be put across proclaimed roads, the conservancy could also not charge self-drive tourists for entering them.

With the very successful Purros Campsite as an example, the frustration of watching tourist vehicles driving past and bringing no benefit to the community led to a number of budding local entrepreneurs seeing the chance to make a few dollars. Soon more campsites sprung up along the main tourist routes, but without the capital to provide water or build basic infrastructure, many of them just consisted of a signboard in a shady place. Nevertheless, if a visitor spent the night there a man would appear to claim payment for them having camped under 'his trees'. Although this did enable a few individuals to get some income from tourism, the rudimentary facilities they offered were giving community-run enterprises a bad reputation, which was not the image that the CBNRM programme wished to portray.

Instead of opposing these initiatives, the solution lay in creating more opportunities for the registered conservancies to get direct revenue from tourism. For this, NACOBTA and IRDNC obtained EU funding that enabled us to commission Trevor Nott, who had resigned from his post in Etosha and was now making artistic furniture from railway sleepers, to upgrade the Purros and Khovarib Schlucht campsites, as well as build new ones in the Doro /Navas and /Hoadi //Hoas conservancies. A second EU grant was later accessed for Trevor's team to extend the network of high-quality conservancy-owned campsites in the communal areas, as well as to complete the mid-market lodge that Peter Uararavi's group had started building on the Purros Campsite PTO, but which was stopped by the High Court decision against them.

Managing a campsite was a good way for local communities to enter the tourism industry, but the income they earned was small in comparison to that generated by the private sector operators catering for international visitors. Although existing lodges had no legal obligation to pay a bed-night levy, taking their guests outside of their PTO area did require them to go into a formal agreement with the conservancy. To facilitate this in the Marienfluss, NACOBTA and IRDNC invited the owners of the three lodges on the lower Kunene, the conservancy committee and their traditional leader, as well as the Regional Councillor, to a week-long process which we hoped would promote a more positive relationship between the private sector operators and their neighbouring community.

It began with all the participants visiting each of the lodges and the conservancy's campsite in the Marienfluss, where they heard about their operations, problems and what was required from the other parties for them to be successful. The next step was to develop a common vision, which was followed by a discussion on the main issues that were identified by the lodge owners and the conservancy. In many cases simple solutions could be found, while others would be included as contractual obligations in an agreement between them. Only on the last day did they address the matter of a financial payment to the conservancy for the use of their land and the conservation services that they provided. Their first offers were very disappointing, but after a number of further meetings joint-venture contracts were signed with all three operators.

Over the next few years IRDNC and the LAC facilitated income-sharing agreements with Skeleton Coast Fly-in Safaris for its other camps in Purros and Torra conservancies, as well as between the owners of a rustic lodge at Swartbooisdrift in Kunene River Conservancy. Because they were all preexisting enterprises, during the negotiations most of the cards were stacked in favour of the private sector operators, who were quick to plead poverty when it came to sharing income with their local communities. As a result the financial benefits from them were limited, and did not come close to covering any of these conservancies' management costs.

Hobatere, Etendeka and Palmwag concessions could also not be included in the neighbouring conservancies, but unlike PTOs that comprised just the area immediately around the lodge, they were 30 000 ha, 40 000 ha and 580 000 ha in size. Their concessionaires also had the exclusive right to take guests into them, and apart from the few families living on the road to Sesfontein, they were not permanently inhabited by people or livestock. With their wildlife populations having recovered they had become some of the most valuable tourism real estate in the country, and should have been the main source of revenue for their neighbouring conservancies.

In the early 2000s the Hobatere concessionaire, Steve Braine, started negotiations over income sharing with /Hoadi //Hoas, his southern neighbour. Although separated by the veterinary fence, when Ehirovipuka was gazetted in 2001 they also claimed benefits from Hobatere on the grounds that lions and other predators came out of it and killed large numbers of their livestock. But with time on his side, by 2008 – ten years after /Hoadi //Hoas was gazetted and 18 years since Steve took over the concession – the only financial benefit the two conservancies had received from it was compensation paid for livestock lost.

Although Dennis Liebenberg of Etendeka Mountain Camp had initiated a voluntary levy to the main villages closest to his concession in the mid-1990s, this had stopped when the local people decided to form conservancies. After the registration in 2003 of Omatendeka and Anabeb, the conservancies that shared a common boundary with Etendeka concession, Denis also began benefit-sharing negotiations with them, but by 2008 they too had not been concluded.

Palmwag concession and lodge were leased to Desert Adventure Safaris (DAS) by the Damara Representative Authority in 1986. However, 17 years later the neighbouring communities had still not received any financial benefit from this huge tract of land that they agreed to set aside for wildlife and tourism. Consequently, when in 2003 DAS sold the majority of shares in its Kunene Region operations to Wilderness Safaris Namibia (WSN) – the company that had a joint venture with Torra Conservancy – we hoped the local people would at last be rewarded for their major contribution to conservation in the north-west. But Peter Ward, who negotiated the Damaraland Camp contract, had since left and the company now had a new top management structure.

Under Dave van Schmeerdijk, who took over as CEO from Denis Rundle, WSN upgraded and extended Palmwag Lodge to 40 beds, and built a luxury tented camp south of the Uniab River, where SRT trackers were employed to find rhinos for their clients. In 2005 WSN opened a third camp at Amspoort in the lower Hoanib that could almost guarantee its guests good sightings of 'desert elephants'. Apart from this, they operated a very popular campsite with a bar and kiosk attached, ran guided game drives into the concession area, and collected fees from any self-drive tourists who used it. DAS had done well out of Palmwag, so with the increased number of beds and Wilderness Safaris' renowned marketing ability, we expected them to do even better.

Recognising the considerable investment costs WSN had incurred, no meetings were arranged with their three neighbouring conservancies, Sesfontein, Anabeb and Torra, until February 2006, when a memorandum of understanding was signed. Although the income-sharing deal that WSN offered them seemed to be the same as that for Damaraland Camp, there was a small but very important difference: whereas Torra received 10 per cent of the 'net to camp turnover', in this case it was 10% of the 'net accommodation turnover'. Just how much this affected the payment only became apparent when the amount each conservancy received did not even cover the wages of their game guards!

To WSN's credit this was a back payment from March 2005, but when the three conservancies earned only marginally more in the following year I asked Dave van Schmeerdijk for a meeting. At it he agreed to change 'net accommodation' to 'net to camp', which doubled the second annual payment, but Sesfontein and Anabeb conservancies' income was still substantially less than their basic running costs. And if the neighbouring communities received no financial benefit from the huge area they had set aside for wildlife and tourism two decades before, would they continue to support conservation in the future?

Although WSN had the tourism rights in Palmwag concession, the status of the land had not changed from that of a communal area, which meant the local people were still legally entitled to move into it with their livestock. As I did not want this to happen, and the concessionaire had no obligation to pay them anything at all, I did not pursue the matter any further. Nevertheless, I was disappointed that the company started in 1983 by Colin Bell and Chris McIntyre with high ideals and just two Land Rovers, and which now owned or operated more than 60 lodges in Southern Africa, could not see that the greatest threat to tourism in the communal areas was losing the local communities' commitment to conservation.

To promote more advantageous deals the EU gave the MET a grant to provide equity funding for conservancies going into new joint ventures with the private sector. The first to benefit from this was Doro /Navas, which went into partnership with Wilderness Safaris Namibia to build a lodge in the Aba-Huab valley. As the conservancy was now contributing the land and wildlife, the cost of protecting it, and also a large part of the infrastructure investment costs, the share of the 'net to camp income' it received was increased to 15 per cent.

The remaining N$4 million of the EU funds was used to build a mid-market lodge for /Hoadi //Hoas on top of the Grootberg range. In this case the conservancy is the owner of all of the fixed assets and has hired a management company to run and market the business. In spite of the guest occupancies being low in the first few years, thanks to its spectacular situation and the excellent game viewing, which includes elephants, rhino and lion, it has now become a popular destination – another step along the road to empowering the local communities and enabling them to get a fairer share of the income from the booming tourism in Kunene Region.

*   *   *

The enthusiasm with which communal land residents embraced CBNRM took us all by surprise. A major reason was the job opportunities and benefits it provided in the remote rural parts of the country, where very little development had previously taken place. Through the many NGOs supporting conservancies it also brought large amounts of donor funding into Namibia, which at a time when the MET budgets were being cut, raised concern among some of its senior officials. To them, uplifting the inhabitants of the communal areas was the sole responsibility of SWAPO, and they felt threatened by the leading role played by what they saw as white-run organisations. At the time, the Kenya and Zimbabwe governments were accusing NGOs of promoting opposition parties, and this contributed to their uneasiness about the situation.

For a while there were rumblings about not registering any more conservancies, and a few more politicised 'card carrying' senior officials even talked about stopping the CBNRM programme altogether. Fortunately, after Willem Konjore was appointed as the MET Minister and Dr Malan Lindeque became the Permanent Secretary, they both recognised that such a popular grassroots movement was unstoppable and decided instead to increase the government's involvement in it.

This was done by creating a CBNRM support unit within the Directorate of Parks and Wildlife that was headed by Tsukhoe //Garoes, the daughter of Justice /Garoeb, who was now a member of parliament. With the MET's full participation, a decade after the first conservancies had been gazetted there were a total of 53 in Namibia's communal areas, covering 122 900 square kilometres and with over 220 000 people living in them – 15 per cent of the country's land surface and over 12 per cent of its population. An additional 23 emerging conservancies were in the process of fulfilling the legal requirements to be registered.

Although there were still many conservationists who did not believe in the devolution of rights and responsibilities over natural resources to local communities, nobody could dispute that it had dramatically changed their attitude towards living with wildlife. In the former ethnic homelands, where in the 1980s the big game had seemed doomed, the numbers of all species were now increasing, and in recognition of the crucial role that the local people were playing, the MET embarked on a major re-introduction programme. Between 1999 and 2007, over 3 700 animals of 14 different species were captured in national parks, or bought from freehold farmers, and trans-located to 15 communal area conservancies. In Kunene Region this included returning black rhino to places where they had previously occurred, but had all been killed during the 1970s and early 1980s.

The information collected annually by NACSO also showed that the economic benefits the CBNRM programme generated for local communities had increased from N$600 000 in 1998 to nearly N$42 million in 2008, of which conservancies earned more than N$32 million in cash and kind. Of this, N$13.5 million was from all forms of hunting (N$8.6m in direct payments, N$4.5m as the value of meat distributed, and N$550 000 in wages), and joint-venture tourism contributed N$16.9 million (N$5.1m in direct payments, N$8.0m in wages, N$1.0m in payment for services and N$2.8m for 'in kind' benefits). Other revenue was N$880 000 earned by community campsites, N$2.1 million for the sale of veld products, and N$280 000 from the sale of crafts.

The ripple effect of opening up vast new tracts of land for tourism and trophy hunting in the communal areas was also estimated to have contributed approximately N$223 million to net national income in 2007, and a total of N$945 million from when the first conservancies were gazetted. Although the SWAPO government had not put nature conservation high on its political agenda when it first came to power, once the achievements and popular support of the CBNRM programme became more widely known, conservancies were included as part of the country's Vision 2030, Millennium Development Goals and Rural Poverty Reduction Strategy, as well as the shorter-term objectives of its National Development Plans.

As the benefits to conservancies increased and some of them became independent of donor funding, the support role played by MET and NGOs changed but did not end. They still needed training in managing their natural resources, accounting for income and expenses, assistance in negotiating contracts, and many other activities that were the responsibility of their committees. We were all on an untravelled road and mistakes were made; conservancies 'misappropriated' money – in some cases very large amounts, staff that had never worked before did not always perform to western standards, internal squabbles continued, and politics muddled matters even more. The private sector was often frustrated by these and other shortcomings, but cases of poaching were now rare and in all the communal areas wildlife numbers continued to increase.

In our modern world, where teaching the younger generation honesty and social responsibility seems to have fallen through the cracks, one of IRDNC's most difficult roles was giving training to conservancy committees in financial accountability. In Kunene Region this thankless task fell on Lucky Kasaona, the youngest son of Headman Goliat Kasaona, who had been a founder of the community game guard system. With technical support from Anna Davis and his team of John /Gabusab and Lina Kaisuma they gave workshops on basic bookkeeping and the use of computers, as well as assisting committees to organise annual general meetings at which the broader community membership approved their budgets and expenditures, and received feedback on the conservancies' progress during the previous year.

Apart from conserving the wildlife on which hunting and photographic tourism in Namibia's communal areas were built, another key role of conservancies was providing a local management structure to oversee the use of all natural resources. In the Kunene Region IRDNC investigated the commercial potential of the resin annually exuded from the stems of *Commiphora wildii*, an endemic dwarf tree in the pre-Namib, which was used as a perfume by Himba women. Margie had long believed that it could be a valuable source of household income in the far north-west, where they grew prolifically on the hill slopes, but without a representative and legally mandated institution to prevent it from being unsustainably exploited by non-local entrepreneurs she had not followed up on her idea.

When all the conservancies here had been gazetted Margie invited Tony Cunningham, who was world renowned for his pioneering work on the commercialisation of indigenous plant products, to visit the area. After getting his support Karen Nott was given responsibility for the project, and initially carried out ecological and social surveys to ensure harvesting would not be detrimental to the plants or the people who traditionally used them. Working with CRIAA, an international NGO, samples were then sent to Europe to determine its value as an essential oil. The results were promising and two cosmetic companies with good reputations for fair trade and recognising intellectual property rights were chosen to market the product. In 2007 the first four tons of resin from five conservancies were harvested and sold, and two years later 275 individual members earned over N$300 000 – providing the household income needed in these remote pastoralist communities to pay school and clinic fees, as well as buy basic commercial goods.

Based on the successful devolution of rights over wildlife, a similar policy was adopted by the Directorate of Forestry, which was supported by the German Development Service (DED) and their donors the German Development Bank (KfW). Most of the community forests established were in the higher-rainfall northern and eastern communal areas, where they opened up a range of new natural resources that local people could gain custodianship over and derive income from. In 2006 there were 13 gazetted community forests covering an area of 4 600 km^2, with 36 700 people living within them, and another 34 were emerging.

In a very successful HIV/AIDS awareness programme in the Caprivi, IRDNC's Janet Matota, working with Velia Kurz and John Odeke of NACSO, used the conservancies as a conduit to get information and assistance to the rural villages. All of their offices also displayed posters on the disease and its prevention, as well as making free condoms available, while the key to bringing the infection rate in antenatal women down from 43 per cent to 32 per cent was following the basic CBNRM principle of giving the responsibility for finding ways of reducing and mitigating the impact of the epidemic to the local communities themselves. During the 2008 outbreak of polio in Namibia, conservancies were also specially mentioned by the Ministry of Health for the very valuable role they played in making the national vaccination programme a success.

Once the boundary disputes were resolved, conservancies also often brought different ethnic groups and feuding factions together to discuss issues related to wildlife. In East Caprivi, where the four traditional chiefs were in bitter conflict over land rights, they found common ground in supporting conservation at international conferences, and their representatives sat amicably next to each other in quarterly planning meetings. Apart from elephants streaming in from Botswana now that they were not being poached, the recovery of big game in Caprivi was still far behind that in Kunene Region. But we had come a long way from the first village meetings Margie, Johan le Roux and I had held in 1988, when the local people shouted abuse at us for suggesting that wild animals should be protected. Through conservancies they were now no longer seen as belonging to the government, and virtually everyone wanted the wildlife back.

*   *   *

A major environmental problem not being addressed by the CBNRM programme was the deteriorating rangelands in the Kaokoveld. On my return to Namibia in 1979 I had been fired up by Allan Savory's high-density, short-duration grazing system, which I believed could reverse the widespread loss of perennial grasses if adapted to conditions in the communal areas. Because no fences were allowed in them, and many stockowners shared the same land, this would not be easy, but if nothing was done to improve the situation the future of both the pastoralists' way of life and the wildlife in the region would be compromised.

Two decades after the 1980/81 drought the livestock numbers in the northwest had recovered, and as more boreholes were drilled the area of degradation had been extended to cover virtually the entire highlands. To keep their herds alive in subsequent years of low rainfall some Himba moved west and south, seriously degrading large parts of the once lush perennial grasslands on the Marienfluss and virtually eliminating the perennial grasses on the 'Serengeti' plain south of the Ombonde River. As these and many other key wildlife areas were now supporting permanent populations of cattle, goats and sheep, much of the uninhabited wilderness I had known in the 1960s was being lost.

The only way to stop the degradation would be to implement a system of livestock management that rehabilitated the perennial grasslands, but this was not possible until we could find a suitable donor organisation to invest in such a project. The opportunity arose in 2002 when we were visited by Andrew Corbett and Michael Bollig, who had worked with Margie on the social team of the Epupa hydro-electric dam environmental impact assessment.

They had been asked by Edgar Brueser of the German Evangelical Development Services (EED), a long term supporter of the LAC, to find a suitable CBNRM activity for them to fund. I suggested that they become our partners in a holistic range-management project, but warned them that it could be many years before any significant results were achieved. A few months later Edgar informed us that as long as they were satisfied with the way their money was being spent they were 'prepared for a long haul.' Because he had a master's degree in pasture science, Colin Nott was the obvious choice to lead the project, so after sponsoring him on a course to learn Allan Savory's principles and implementation techniques of 'planned grazing' at his Africa Centre for Holistic Management near Victoria Falls, three pilot areas were chosen.

The initial objective of the project would be to test the impact of high-density, short-duration grazing on a number of different substrates, to see if loosening the soil by hoof action promoted the germination of perennial grass seeds. The pilot areas we chose were in the emerging Epupa Conservancy on the northern highlands, Okongoro on the edge of the Kalahari sandveld in the east, and Okangundumba in the dolomite hills south of Opuwo. Although conservancies did not have the rights over grazing, which fell under the Ministry of Agriculture, they did provide a defined area with a representative committee as an entry point to the local stockowners.

In all three conservancies the grasslands had been reduced to annual species for as far as their free-ranging cattle could reach from the existing permanent water-points. If there were still sufficient perennial grass seeds in the soil it would then be essential to ensure the seedlings were not continuously grazed, so that they could establish nutrient reserves in their roots. For this to happen, as well as to get maximum hoof impact, the cattle needed to be kept close together and not allowed to utilise the same place for more than a few days. On Liebig's Ranch this was done with fenced paddocks that the cattle rotated through, but on communal land the only way was by herding, with all of the stockowners in a given area combining their livestock while out grazing.

To start the project we selected a prominent person from each conservancy to act as the local facilitator. Together with members of IRDNC's senior staff, they were taken to two semi-arid regions in South Africa to meet commercial farmers who had re-established the perennial grasses on what they had photographs to show was previously just bare ground. The districts chosen were Vryburg and Graaff-Reinet, where in every case we found that the grazing systems they used were based on the principles advocated by Allan Savory. Colin then made a second trip, this time including traditional leaders and officials from the Ministry of Agriculture, who were also impressed by what they saw and heard from the landowners. Although they used fences to manage their livestock, in our discussions many of them told us that if labour was less expensive and problematic they would have preferred to herd their cattle, as it provided more flexibility.

The next trip we undertook was to the Africa Centre for Holistic Management in Zimbabwe, where 600 cattle, donkeys and a flock of goats were taken out to graze by just three herders. Up till then most of the group had been confused by what the term 'herding' meant, but after accompanying the livestock into the field for the day a few of the older men remembered when they had herded their families' cattle, to protect them from predators. That night they told us to stop talking about 'this new grazing system' as it was the way their fathers and grandfathers had managed livestock in the past. For us this was a turning point, but times had changed: would their children still be prepared to herd cattle?

Colin's first step was to divide the three conservancies into grazing areas, map the water-points and establish how many families used them. The three local facilitators we had appointed, Shake Matundu, Mutjimbike Mutambo and Tumbe Tjirora, were then tasked with finding out in which of them the stockowners were willing to put their cattle together. As this had not been done in the past it did not prove easy, but eventually two pilot sites were identified in each conservancy where herding could begin.

Before this happened there were more hurdles to be crossed. As predicted, among the Herero the younger generation were unwilling to become herders unless they were paid, which was only resolved by the stockowners agreeing to do so. In Epupa conservancy the Himba had no problem finding herders who did not need to be paid, but Chief Kapika, who had refused to come on the trip to Zimbabwe, would not give his support to the project. As a strong traditionalist he did not want his cattle mixed up with those from other holy fires, but in the end his opposition was overcome by an agreement whereby he would keep his livestock within a defined area, and the people implementing planned grazing would not allow theirs to enter it.

In the first few years Colin and his team, to which David Kangombe and Uhangatenua Kapi had been added, faced a number of other setbacks. With the considerably increased herd sizes many of the existing water-points proved inadequate, necessitating the upgrading of pumps and even the drilling of new boreholes in some places. In 2006 a large veld fire burnt most of the annual grasslands in one of the Okongoro pilot grazing areas, leaving only blackened earth until the first heavy rains, and causing the suspension of the project there. The following year Kunene Region suffered a severe drought, with many cattle dying before it was broken in early 2008. In spite of this, herding had continued through the dry season in all but the fire-affected area in Okongoro, and drought-related cattle deaths were found to be significantly lower than in the neighbouring parts of the three conservancies.

After the project began, a number of unpredicted benefits were also noted by the participating stockowners. The cattle's condition and milk production improved significantly, while losses due to theft and predators, both of which had increased in the north-west, were virtually eliminated. Another advantage of the livestock being herded during the day and kraaled at night, was that if elephants broke the fences around their fields cattle could not enter through the breaks, which often resulted in more damage to the crops than that caused by the elephants. Although it would be a long time before the perennial grasses were rehabilitated, the commitment to the planned grazing project was high, and many more conservancies wanted to be included in it.

CHAPTER TWENTY-SIX

LOOKING BACK AND FORWARD

Much has changed since I first visited Opuwo more than 40 years ago. The dusty little outpost that then consisted of eight houses and a few shacks for the black staff has become the bustling capital of Kunene Region, with government offices, a large hospital, schools, tourist lodges, supermarkets, and even internet cafes. Along its main streets visitors from around the globe now mix with traditionally dressed Himba, Hakaona and Zemba women, some of whom pose for photographs or sell poor-quality crafts. Just like most rural African towns, plastic bags and other refuse litter the vacant ground, but Opuwo has retained its mystique of being on the frontier – where the old continent and the new world meet.

In Sesfontein the old German fort has been rebuilt into a lodge, and where there were only date palms and wheat fields there is now a junior secondary school, a shop, adjoining bar and cement-block houses along the road through the village. Under the acacia and sycamore fig trees around the main spring are the conservancy's office and its campsite, which has proved popular with foreign visitors who want to experience 'a night in the community'. In spite of there being no municipal refuse removal, because its residents are within a conservancy and are now directly benefiting from tourism, it is kept remarkably clean.

Apart from a few government offices and a luxury tourist lodge, little development has taken place in Khorixas since independence, and the Damara Representative Authority's administration building overlooking the town now stands as a slightly dilapidated epitaph to the National Party policy of ethnic homelands. Although the town's inhabitants have used their ingenuity to find ways of making a living, until they receive a fair share of the income from tourism – which their leaders' foresight made possible – their lives are unlikely to significantly improve.

Away from the few towns and villages, where in the 1960s there were only two-spoor tracks through the rugged ranges, and there was no vehicle access at all over much of the Kaokoveld, a network of trunk roads has been graded. The route from Kamanjab to Opuwo has also been tarred, and today Sesfontein, Twyfelfontein and Torra Bay can be reached in a saloon car unless heavy rains have made the river crossings impassable to all but 4x4 vehicles. However, once one leaves the proclaimed roads there are still only two-spoor tracks, retaining the region's wild atmosphere.

The people of the Kaokoveld have also changed. The descendants of the Kubun Bushmen that Van Warmelo interviewed at Sesfontein in the 1940s have all been absorbed into the Damara community, and the hunter-gatherer Tjimba who inhabited the mountain ranges near the Kunene now keep livestock and dress like their neighbours. Only a few families remain of the Topnaar dynasty that ruled Sesfontein for 100 years, the rest having been moved to Namaland under the Odendaal Commission plan.

Apart from altering borders and relocating people, the developments brought about by the Odendaal Commission also brought the residents of the region into the modern world of consumerism and exchanging their time for money. While the older pastoralists still cling to their traditional beliefs and practices, most of the younger generation now put the acquisition of material possessions before herding cattle, and personal aspirations over obligations to the ancestral spirits or their responsibility to the broader community. As a result the Himba, whose isolation and livestock wealth once enabled them to remain aloof from events in the rest of the country, have become part of the new Namibia.

The physical appearance of the youth has also changed. Because they no longer spend their days herding cattle, and hitching a lift is the preferred way of visiting distant friends or family, many have become as soft-muscled as their European counterparts. Young Himba men have also taken to wearing brightly coloured loin-cloths and T-shirts, and very few of them now plait their hair into *ondatu* pigtails, while the older men no longer wear the large sheepskin *ondumbu* turbans that were put on after marriage. Most Himba women still dress traditionally, but zips, brass cartridge cases and safety pins have been incorporated into their apparel, with new 'fashions' appearing from time to time – such as black shop-bought tufts at the end of the lengthened braids worn on reaching puberty. Hakaona women have even added rolled-up Windhoek lager and Coke cans into their 'traditional' hairstyles.

However, these are just superficial signs of a society in transition. The deeper changes are psychological, brought about by three traumatic events, two of which – the loss of their cattle and the liberation war – occurred simultaneously in the 1980s. To pastoralists the loss of their livestock is the worst thing that can happen, for it does not only destroy their subsistence economy, but also breaks down the social fabric within the community. Lineage heads who have no cattle cannot exercise their religious authority, young men no longer have a role to play, and without milk to distribute women lose one of the main sources of their power in the family.

The negative impact of the liberation war was that it divided the residents of the region into those for and against SWAPO, with those who remained neutral finding themselves harassed by both sides. In the 1980s the mechanised South African security forces had seemed invincible to most Kaokovelders, and as a result many of them were shocked by their withdrawal in 1989, and by SWAPO winning the elections and becoming the new government in Windhoek.

The combined impact of these events caused the wealthy stockowners, who in the past needed little from the modern world and merely tolerated the presence of government officials, to lose confidence in their old ways and become open to anything it could offer them. In our travels through the Kaokoveld during the early 1990s we found that alcohol abuse and depression had become major problems, and whereas hospitals and schools were almost universally rejected by the Himba and Herero in the 1960s, the white man's medicine was now seen as superior to their own, and sending their children to school as a means of providing them with a better future.

The third disruptive change was the sharp increase in tourist numbers after independence. The traditional leaders, who expected all visitors to greet them, found the behaviour of people who just drove past their villages disrespectful – as if they were now the owners of the land. Even those who stopped to take pictures seldom asked permission to do so or spoke to the elders living there. By the mid-1990s there were cases of stones being thrown or abuse shouted at tourists, caused by the frustration the residents felt at the intrusion of so many strangers into their midst, and their lack of control over them. The situation could have escalated if it were not for CBNRM programme giving conservancies authority over tourism in their areas, which has now made the Kunene Region one of the safest and friendliest places to visit in Southern Africa.

*   *   *

When I left the Kaokoveld in 1970 I kept in contact with Hugh and Dorothy Goyns until our trip down the lower Kunene, but we drifted apart after I married June. I later read that Hugh became the oldest man to climb above 7 000 metres in the Himalayas, and we met again in 1991 after Dorothy had died. At the age of 83 he was still very fit and 'heading for a hundred'– which he always assured me he would make – when he was murdered in his Benoni home by intruders.

Johan Malan became professor of anthropology at the University of the North in South Africa, but later returned to his roots in missionary work. My brother Norman also followed an academic career, becoming Professor in African Ecology and head of the Centre for African Ecology at the University of the Witwatersrand. In 2000 he was internationally rated as one of the few A-grade scientists in Southern Africa and also became the first South African invited to be an Honorary Member of the Ecological Society of America.

Some of the first group of 17 Cwaka College nature conservation students later did exceptionally well in their careers. Phineas Nobela worked in Pilanesberg National Park under Roger Collinson, where he excelled in environmental education and extension work among the local community. He then joined SAN Parks and rose to the rank of chief warden Norman Mathebula was the first warden of Madikwe Game Reserve, and later became Regional Manager of Eastern Parks for the amalgamated Cape, Transvaal and Bophuthatswana Nature Conservation Administrations. Kulani Mkize took over as the director of the KwaZulu-Natal Parks Board when George Hughes retired.

Mlindile (Simeon) Gcumisa ran the Wildlife Society's in-service training courses on ecology and nature conservation for teachers and supported Wildlife Clubs in schools until 1979, when ACE was handed over to the KwaZulu Bureau of Natural Resources. He also produced a regular radio programme, *Ubuhle Bemvelo* (The Beauty of Nature). In 1981 the ACE Project was revived by the Wildlife Society under Jim Taylor and with the Umgeni Valley Project evolved into Share-Net, a resource materials development network and training centre. Umgeni Valley is now the headquarters of the Southern African Development Community's Regional Environmental Education Programme.

Nolly Zaloumis later became President of the Wildlife Society – now the Wildlife and Environment Society of Southern Africa (WESSA). In 1992 he received the Order for Meritorious Service (Gold), presented by then President FW de Klerk for his leading role in the promotion of environmental education. His younger son, Andrew, is the director of the Strategic Development Initiative for northern KwaZulu-Natal, which has pioneered the participation of local communities in conservation and tourism in South Africa.

Under pressure from the government Allan Savory left Rhodesia in 1979 and five years later opened the Centre for Holistic Management in Albuquerque, New Mexico, USA. There short-duration grazing evolved into 'holistic planned grazing', a more flexible way of managing rangelands, using the same basic principles. Operating under the registered trademark of Holistic Management, certified educators have been trained in 19 states of the USA and in 10 other countries, including Namibia, South Africa and Zimbabwe.

Liebig's Ranch was cut up and a part of it became communal land. The rest was sold to private investors and included the Bubye and Bubiana rhino sanctuaries. However, when there was a resurgence of commercial poaching in the lowveld in 2004, many of the rhino on Bubiana were killed and those that survived were moved to a safer place.

In 2009 the Sperrgebiet was proclaimed a national park that linked up with the Ai-Ais/Fish River Canyon National Park and the Richtersveld National Park across the Orange River in South Africa, forming the Ai-Ais/Richtersveld Transfrontier Conservation Area. The following year the entire Namibian coastline became the Namib-Skeleton Coast National Park, 107 500 km^2 in size and the eighth largest protected area in the world.

By 2010 two conservancies, King Nehale and Sheya Shuushona, had been established on Etosha's northern border. If the gap between them is also gazetted as a conservancy and the fence taken down, the Park's wildebeest and zebra populations will again be able to safely migrate around the Pan. However, for this to happen an appropriate burning policy will have to be introduced.

Elias Hambo, Sakeus Kasaona and Shorty Kasaona have now all died.

So too have the old traditional leaders Keefas Muzuma, Joshua Kangombe, Goliat Kasaona, Vetamuna Tjambiru, Otto Ganuseb and Gabriel Thaniseb, as well as the early community game guards, Salmon Karutjaiva, Johannes Kasaona, Abraham Tjavara, Meesig Taniseb and Naftali Taurob. In 2006 the promising young rhino researcher, Mike Hearne, tragically drowned while surfing, and two years later Blythe Loutit passed away. Without their commitment to conservation in the Kaokoveld, the success story it has become today would not have been possible. The present generation is now reaping the fruits of their efforts and what they did should not be forgotten.

In 2010, after a combined total of almost 60 years' experience of the Kaokoveld, Margie Jacobsohn and I stood down as directors of IRDNC. The new co-directors would be John Kasaona (Kunene), Karine Nuulimba (Caprivi) and Colin Nott (HRM).

*   *   *

Although the Kaokoveld's rugged mountain and desert scenery, Epupa Falls and the traditionally dressed Himba would have attracted visitors even without any wildlife, the chance of seeing big game against a background of spectacular landscapes has now made the region the third most popular tourist destination in Namibia. But the present situation could easily have been very different. The reasons why we succeeded in stopping the poaching, while other parts of Africa failed, are worth analysing.

After achieving independence the majority of countries on the continent retained the nature conservation legislation inherited from their colonial powers, but when the black market price of ivory and rhino horn soared in the mid-1970s, law enforcement on its own proved to be ineffective. A major factor contributing to this was the antagonism that local communities felt towards the wildlife authorities, which led to them actively or passively supporting the poachers. In some cases the involvement of civil servants and politicians supplementing their salaries or promoting power and patronage, made the illegal trade in ivory and rhino horn harder to control. The situation in SWA's homelands was similar, and in the early 1980s seemed hopeless to the senior DNC officials in Windhoek.

To counter the onslaught on their rhino and elephant populations, most government conservation agencies, assisted by foreign donor organisations, strengthened their anti-poaching activities along military lines. In Zimbabwe and Kenya this included giving park rangers the right to shoot suspected poachers, while Botswana deployed its defence force with the same mandate in its protected areas. But in spite of this the killing of elephants and rhinos continued until the early 1990s, when the CITES ban on all ivory trading came into effect, and there were fewer than 1 000 black rhino left in Africa north of the Kunene and Limpopo rivers.

When the DNC eventually realised that many rhinos had been killed in Etosha, they also set up an armed anti-poaching unit, which was trained by ex-SAS officers from the British-based Stirling Foundation. Even with them operating inside the Park major poaching continued until 1989, and it was only thanks to Sakeus Kasaona's tracking skills and the information provided by a local shopkeeper in Opuwo that most of those responsible were finally arrested.

At the time, conservation academics estimated that at least US$200 needed to be spent per square kilometre annually on law enforcement to successfully protect rhinos. And yet by actively involving the region's traditional leaders through their appointment of community game guards, we were able to virtually stop all illegal hunting in Damaraland at a tiny fraction of this cost. However, Chris Eyre and I were not the only ones to see the local people as our allies and not our enemies.

The first African government to involve local communities to stop commercial poaching was Zambia. In September 1983, after the country had lost most of its elephants and virtually all its rhinos, a workshop was held in the Lupande Game Management Area adjoining South Luangwa National Park. From it two pilot projects emerged that were aimed at giving local people economic benefits from trophy hunting. The first was ADMADE, the brainchild of Dale Lewis, an American working for the National Parks and Wildlife Service, and funded by USAID. The second was Luangwa Integrated Resource Development Project (LIRDP), which started five years later under the authority of President Kenneth Kaunda, and was sponsored by NORAD.

Clark Gibson's 1999 book on the political economy of wildlife policy in Africa, *Politicians and Poachers*, gives a description of the impact of the two projects on both the poaching and the local people. In it he states:

> To close what had become an open-access wildlife commons in Zambia, ADMADE and LIRDP each offered an array of benefits designed to encourage locals to protect rather than hunt animals. A number of rural residents gained employment as wildlife scouts and

general labourers. Certain traditional leaders also received control over the revenue that the programs apportioned to local communities. ADMADE and LIRDP revenue built schools, health clinics, bridges, and other community-level projects. And both programs intended to foster cooperation between scouts and residents.

Yet even with ADMADE and LIRDP in place, rural residents continued to kill, consume, and trade wild animals illegally. Although wildlife scouts made more arrests for poaching-related activities, and although both programs seemed to stem the killing of large mammals, locals kept hunting – at rates comparable to those of the days before ADMADE and LIRDP's operations. ADMADE and LIRDP also failed to defuse the long-standing hostility between scouts and residents (p. 119).

Gibson then went on to argue that their weak performance was primarily due to the type of costs and benefits they produced:

The programs augment conventional enforcement and provide community-level goods … Rather than convincing individuals to opt for conservation per se, the programs ultimately offer incentives quite similar to those of conventional policy, whereby locals do not own or control their wildlife resources and their use of wildlife remains illegal (p. 120).

Gibson based his findings on interviews that Stuart Marks, a researcher in Luangwa valley, carried out with five local hunters, which showed that their total off-take of game meat stayed more or less constant from 1988 to 1993. However, the number of arrests for poaching by the Zambian Wildlife Department's Luangwa Command increased from 112 in 1985 to 197 in 1990, while arrests by ADMADE wildlife scouts rose from four in 1988 to 19 in 1993 – confirming that hunting by local people did not stop after the programme started operating. The LIRDP wildlife scouts were more successful at arresting poachers (188 in 1988, to 417 in 1990) as well as confiscating firearms (from 82 in 1988 to 1 063 in 1990), but was this the primary objective of the project? And if communities continued to hunt in spite of the financial benefits they received from ADMADE and LIRDP, why did poaching virtually stop within a few years in north-west Namibia, without economic incentives?

Although the wildlife scouts appointed by ADMADE and LIRDP were all local people, as were the community game guards that the NWT and later the EWT supported in Kaokoland and Damaraland, there were some major differences between them:

- The wildlife scouts worked for the project but within the government structure, while the CGGs were responsible to their headmen and only paid by an NGO.
- To qualify as a wildlife scout the local people had to meet minimum education and physical standards, whereas most CGGs were illiterate and chosen for their maturity and experience.
- Wildlife scouts were given two years of formal training and then housed in camps, while the CGGs were encouraged to use their own initiative and operated from their homes.
- The main function of the wildlife scouts was anti-poaching and they had powers of arrest, whereas the CGGs were required to do extension work, game monitoring, and just report suspected illegal activities to their headmen, as well as to the NGO and nature conservation officials.

By not focusing on arresting poachers, but rather on getting the traditional leaders' active participation in conserving wildlife, we were more effective in stopping all forms of illegal hunting, in spite of the region's residents having just started to recover from a disastrous drought. This 'soft' approach also enabled us to develop a good relationship with the broader community, and as their eyes and ears were now on our side it became very difficult for any outsiders to poach undetected.

In Zimbabwe the shooting of over 120 suspected poachers did not stop the killing of rhinos in the Zambezi valley, and the last 250 had to be translocated to the commercial farming area, where specially protected 'rhino sanctuaries' were established. Although the CAMPFIRE programme only operated on communal land, when it finally began in late 1988, conservationists hoped it would offer an alternative way of ensuring the future of the country's big game outside of protected areas, or on private property. Furthermore, if local communities started seeing wildlife as a valuable resource it could also reduce the illegal hunting in adjoining national parks, thereby providing a safe area for elephants and other migratory animals to disperse into.

Compared to ADMADE and LIRDP, the devolution of rights and responsibilities was much greater under the CAMPFIRE legislation, but most rural district councils covered a considerable area, of which only a small part might contain sufficient wildlife for it to be sustainably utilised. Because of bureau-cratic mismanagement or political favouritism, the communities that suffered the cost of living with big game might not always receive their fair share of the income derived from it. The concentration of power at district level also did not encourage active participation in the programme at the local level.

In 1989 the first district council, Nyaminyami, bordering on Matusadona National Park, was granted 'appropriate authority' status, and in the first year it earned Z$272 000 from trophy hunting and Z$47 000 from a culling opera-tion. CAMPFIRE was finally on the road, and over the next decade would generate millions of US dollars for remote rural communities, some of them the most economically disadvantaged in Zimbabwe. In spite of its design shortcomings, it soon became the most successful and publicised CBNRM programme in Africa, carrying the flag for a new kind of conservation that benefited both wildlife and local people. Unfortunately, recent political events in the country have taken it out of the limelight and limited its income-gen-erating potential, but many CAMPFIRE areas are still functioning – a tribute to the principles on which it is based.

*　　*　　*

Both the Zambian and Zimbabwean models of CBNRM are primarily de-pendent on consumptive use of wildlife to generate economic benefits for rural communities, which it is presumed will provide an incentive for them to conserve it. But financial gain is not the only motivation for the actions of subsistence farmers, and seen from a household perspective, losing rights over natural resources will not necessarily be compensated for by communal projects, particularly if decisions about how the money is used are made by government officials, private sector operators, NGOs or even their traditional leaders. Recognising this, in the CAMPFIRE programme Brian Child and Ivan Bond promoted individual payouts, some of which could then be volun-tarily contributed towards locally chosen development projects that benefited the whole community.

Before the 1996 conservancy legislation in Namibia there was no legal framework for providing communal area residents with financial benefits from wildlife. Nevertheless, in a relatively short time we were able to change the local people's negative attitude towards nature conservation and get them on our side. This was done by involving the traditional leaders in decision making over the wildlife in their areas, and through their appointment of game guards that were accountable to them and not the government they also became responsible for its protection. In this way they regained some control over what had in the past been a valuable natural resource and once more felt ownership over it, while we got the local community's support in stopping the poaching.

In the western world, where benefits are defined by their monetary value, we often fail to see that ownership over an asset is an equally important human motivator for responsible behaviour. This is especially true in the case of wildlife, which rural communities believe was 'stolen' from them by colonial governments. But in the Kaokoveld during the 1980s the wildlife did still belong to the State, and fostering ownership was not simply a matter of appointing community game guards. As what we actually did has been covered in the preceding chapters, I will here just summarise what we found to be the key principles of a community-based project.

Building relationships. Before any new interventions are proposed time should be taken to learn what is happening on the ground and why, as well as the stakeholders for and against what you hope to achieve. More importantly, this will enable the local people to get to know you and your organisation, and why *you* think changes to the status quo are necessary. In our case, it was over a year before the first community game guards were appointed. Much of this time was spent travelling in the area where poaching was taking place and talking to the farmers and their traditional leaders, as well as keeping contact with the Damara Representative Authority, the DNC staff, police and magistrates.

It goes without saying that if you want to be listened to you have to respect the local people and their culture. You also cannot expect them to be interested in your problem if you do not care about theirs. Two of the major difficulties faced by subsistence farmers are transport and communication, and as the project had vehicles and radios, whenever possible we assisted with these. Because we were based in the area and not in the capital or regional centre, community members could easily visit us and were welcomed when they did so. We also employed local people, thereby providing them with an economic benefit, and giving us an insider's perspective of the social events and intrigues that are part of everyday life in rural Africa. In time all these factors led to our being regarded as part of the community, with shared interests and concerns – including the poaching.

Negotiation not consultation. All too often in what has become the highly specialised field of environmental conservation, policies and actions that will affect the lives of local people are drawn up by qualified professionals in comfortable city offices. At best a few prominent and well-spoken members of the community will be called to a workshop to get their input, before the final product is taken to meetings in the affected area to get approval from the people living there. Because the visiting delegation is much better educated than them they will often not oppose it, and the policy is adopted, or the actions implemented, in the belief that a full consultation process has been followed. But has the local community really bought into the plan, and will they give their active support to it? Or will they just passively watch to see what happens, and carry on as usual?

The community game guard system was not my idea. I had a problem with the poaching that was taking place, while Headman Joshua Kangombe was mainly concerned about the welfare of his followers after the drought. Together we found common ground that would address both issues, and because he had played a part in finding the solution Joshua was committed to its successful implementation. Conversely, most of the NWT trustees did not initially give their support to our plan because they were not part of the negotiations in Warmquelle that led up to it.

Another example is the process followed in the socio-ecological surveys that the MET carried out in the early 1990s. It started by holding village meetings and interviews with all the stakeholders to find out their attitudes to nature conservation, what the major issues were, as well as their aspirations regarding wildlife management and tourism in the future. Over the last two days the government officials, representatives of the traditional leadership and other interested groups agreed on a common vision, and then *negotiated* solutions to the problems that stood in the way of achieving it. The end result was that Namibia now has what is regarded as the best community-based conservation legislation in Africa. But even more importantly, because they participated in developing it, the rural communities have wholeheartedly bought into the CBNRM programme, and the wildlife populations in virtually all of the communal areas are increasing.

Partnerships. While most African countries have depended on an armed militaristic approach to commercial poaching, in Kunene Region a three-pronged strategy is used: management and law enforcement by the MET, regular monitoring by Save the Rhino Trust, and the vigilance of the people living in and around the rhino range. Since the mid-1980s this partnership has proved to be very successful, enabling Namibia's northwest to have the only thriving black rhino population in a communal area on the continent.

As important has been the excellent working relationship between field staff and the Windhoek-based technical experts, ensuring that modern science and local knowledge and skills are moulded together into effective solutions to problems encountered on the ground. The programme has also benefited from numerous exchange visits to or from similar projects in Africa, as well as from as far away as Cambodia, Jordan, Mongolia and Peru. Although they were for only a few days or weeks, they have linked Namibia into a network of people around the world who believe that the future of the our natural resources cannot be left to the politicians and technocrats, but must also actively involve the communities who live with them.

The value of partnerships does not only apply in the field. Without WWF's long-term support IRDNC could not have provided conservancies with the training and investment they needed in their early years. As the CBNRM programme has grown and expanded into other communal areas, the new partners joining NACSO have all brought their own expertise and experience to assist communities wishing to gain rights and responsibilities over their natural resources. However, at the root of Namibia's successes is the spirit of collaboration that has developed between the government, NGOs and their international donors – the key to all endeavours to conserve wildlife or uplift people.

This said there is still a role for 'lone rangers' who identify problems and stand up for issues that nobody else is prepared address, but they can only be catalysts. To bring about any meaningful and sustainable change to the status quo it will be necessary to involve all the stakeholders. Initially it may not be possible to get everyone on board, but paradigms only change when there is a critical mass of support for a new way of doing things.

Benefits. Just focusing on economic incentives, without granting local communities at least conditional ownership over valuable natural resources as well as rights to participate in management and decision-making, will only have limited success. This said, financial benefits are still essential to compensate for the costs of living with destructive and potentially dangerous big game. In the Kunene conservancies the value of the livestock killed by cheetah, leopard, hyena, and in some cases lions, adds up to many hundreds of thousands of Namibian dollars every year, which very few freehold farmers in Namibia, or anywhere else in the world, would accept. Elephants also break into maize fields, damage water installations, and by coming into villages to drink from reservoirs, pose a threat to human life.

As the legislation has made conservancies responsible for protecting their wildlife, this entails employing game guards and other staff to account for their finances, to keep the required records on all forms of hunting, and to do general administration work. Because Kunene conservancies are very large, their membership widely dispersed and the banks situated hundreds of kilometres away, those with high income-generating potential also run and maintain at least one 4x4 vehicle. Consequently, they need to earn considerable income just to cover their management expenses, let alone provide their members with tangible benefits from the wildlife they are now conserving.

In many cases parts of conservancies have also been zoned exclusively for tourism or trophy hunting. The best example is the huge Palmwag concession that the stockowners in Warmquelle, Sesfontein and Khovareb agreed not to utilise in the 1980s. As a reminder that they could still legally move into it and that the local communities had not yet received any direct benefits for their major contribution to conserving its wildlife, two farmers breached this agreement in 2003. John Kasupi and Botes Kasaona took their large herds to drink from the spring in front of Palmwag Lodge. Cattle walking between the bungalows caused consternation amongst the guests, until the then concessionaire, Jokkel Grutemeyer, provided an alternative source of water for their livestock.

*   *   *

Over and above the cost of living with wildlife and protecting it, now that tourism is booming in Namibia's north-west, conservancy members also deserve a fair share of the profits being made by lodge owners, mobile safaris or professional hunters. After all, it is their land and the wildlife they conserve that has made the Kaokoveld into such a popular destination for local and foreign visitors. In spite of this, most of the tourism operators were initially reluctant to pay a formal levy to communities, and some still regard such payments as a charitable gesture to their poor neighbours. As this legacy from the apartheid era is now the greatest overall threat to the CBNRM programme, possible reasons for their attitude will be discussed.

Before independence the DNC regarded nature conservation as solely its responsibility, and the costs of protecting wildlife throughout the country came from the government's budget. Consequently, any private sector tourism company operating in a national park or on State land paid an annual fee to the national treasury. The only exceptions to this were Palmwag, Etendeka and Hobatere concessions established by the Damara Representative Authority, but after 1990 they also fell under the MET.

When the liberation war ended a few private sector operators obtained PTOs to build lodges in the communal areas, for which they paid a nominal amount of N$480 a year. As a result they got used having the right to conduct their businesses for virtually nothing, leaving the conservation of the wildlife their guests came to see in the hands of the MET. Their only obligation to the local communities who lived around them was to provide a few employment opportunities.

However, with the devolution of the rights and responsibilities over wildlife and other natural resources to conservancies this situation changed. Although the MET retained its authority over specially protected game and is still responsible for enforcing the law, its limited capacity in communal areas meant that nature conservation is now de facto in the hands of the local people. In spite of conservancy committees still being inexperienced, with the support of the broader community poaching is rare and the populations of big game on State Land outside of national parks is increasing. In the west of Kunene Region some species are actually now more numerous than in the 1960s.

Because tourism in communal areas was previously subsidised by the government, the private sector operators there have not recognised that conserving elephants, rhino and other big game costs a great deal of money. To put this in perspective, what WWF-UK and IRDNC's other donors have invested to support conservation and tourism in Kunene Region over the past twelve years is in excess of N$60 million. But with conservancies now gazetted in all of the main wildlife areas in the north-west they have phased out their financial support, resulting in the situation where local communities are now subsidising the private sector operators!

Many lodge owners also still believe that the employment opportunities they provide are enough to maintain the local people's support for conservation. But paying for work is an agreement between the employer and his employees for the work they do, and who of us regards our salaries as a benefit? If they are well paid – and the wages in communal areas are generally very low – it will influence the communities' attitude to the lodge, but it does not cover a conservancy's costs for protecting the wildlife on which the success of the lodge's operations are based, or the losses conservancy members suffer from elephants and predators.

Although attempts have been made to explain the new situation to the lodge owners, many of them are still reluctant to pay a fair percentage of their income to their de facto landlords for the conservation services they provide. In East Caprivi this resulted in the ten lodges situated in gazetted conservancies paying a total of only N$716 000 in 2008, while four of them paid nothing at all! If it were not for the three professional hunting outfitters paying six of the conservancies over N$2.3 million for their concessions, and IRDNC and the ICEMA Project still providing some financial support, most of them would be unable to cover their costs, let alone provide any benefits to their members.

Another reason why many lodge owners fail to recognise that viable conservancies are crucial to sustainable tourism in the communal areas became apparent when Margie and I stayed in a Wilderness Safaris' lodge in Zambia's Kafue National Park. After it nearly burnt down because of the large fuel load of moribund grass around it, an experienced local guide told us that the concession manager had not taken his advice to implement a pre-emptive early burning policy. When we met him, he turned out to be a young white South African from Johannesburg, whose only qualification for making decisions on this contentious ecological issue was a master's degree in business administration.

In fact, very few lodge owners and guides, including the high-ranking staff of tourism companies, have had any actual experience in nature conservation. They may have spent many years observing wild animals, but being a 'Land Rover jockey' is very different to protecting endangered species, especially in communal areas. And as tourism has become big business, with large multinational corporations involved, having an MBA degree or a background in accounting is more likely to help you up the promotion ladder than field experience. The result is that most private sector operators do not see the link between a supportive local community and the long-term success of their enterprises.

Nevertheless, by 2010 most lodge owners in Kunene Region – willingly or after some coercion – had signed contracts or MOUs with their de facto landlords, and Wilderness Safaris' joint-ventures with Torra and Marienfluss and Country Lodges' with Uibasen, now earn good income for these conservancies. On top of this, the jobs and training they provide has enabled many local community members to become professionally involved in the hospitality industry, and some of them have started their own small-scale tourism enterprises, thereby joining the ranks of Namibia's new generation of entrepreneurs.

An underlying issue facing NGOs facilitating deals between conservancies and private sector companies, or individuals operating in communal areas, is the real value of the land and wildlife their businesses are based on. As a comparable example on private property, the owners of Namib Rand Nature Reserve, situated on the edge of the southern Namib, charge all visitors a daily fee of N$142 for the use of the land, over and above the cost of their accommodation. If the same had been done for the Palmwag tourism concession, which is still just communal land, the amount the 'landowners' would have received from Wilderness Safaris for the more than 20 000 bed nights sold there in 2008 would have been N$3 million – five times what the neighbouring conservancies were actually paid. And the wildlife on Namib Rand does not include elephants, black rhino and lions.

Accepting that security of tenure issues limit the private sector's ability to raise capital from the bank, as joint-venture contracts with gazetted conservancies are legally binding, does this justify the discrepancy in the value of communal land and its wildlife resources? Ideally competitive market forces should prevail, the way fair prices are now obtained for trophy hunting contracts, but this is not possible for the existing lodges. An example of the power of the free market is the MET's tourism concession inside the Skeleton Coast Park from Cape Frio and the Hoarusib mouth, where Wilderness Safaris operates a single luxury tented camp. In 2008 they paid the State N$1.5 million for the exclusive rights to bring tourists there, but when it was put out on tender two years later, the highest bids for a ten-year concession were over N$50 million – an average of N$5 million a year.

Although the lodge owners pay lip service to promoting nature conservation, in practice this also just seems to apply when their own interests are at stake. When the owners of Okahirongo Lodge at Purros wanted to build a tented camp on the Kunene River in the Marienfluss, they asked for IRDNC's support and were shown three sites that would not impact on the experience of the many tourists visiting this iconic part of Namibia. But instead of all the buildings being situated behind a ridge as had been agreed, five chalets were placed on top of it – right in front of a viewpoint used by thousands of other visitors to the Marienfluss. As their position negatively impacted on the 'sense of place' of this spectacular part of Kunene Region, I arranged a site visit with one of the shareholders, the architect and building contractor, who all agreed that the offending structures could be moved. However, the Italian investors were not willing to do this.

Eventually they were convinced that an EIA should be done, which made provision for opposing the five chalets. Although the Federation of Namibian Tourism Associations (FENATA) was informed of this, only Koos Vervey objected to their visual impact. The response of Wilderness Safaris, who also have a lodge inside Marienfluss Conservancy, summed up the general attitude of the private sector – they did not see a problem with the Okahirongo chalets because 'they did not frequent the view site'. Did this mean that if it did not disadvantage them, other lodges could do whatever they wanted to?

Most photographic tourism operators are against hunting and in the west of Kunene Region 'desert' elephants and lions should certainly be worth more alive than just a pair of tusks, or a skin on a wealthy client's wall. But to whom are they more valuable alive? Not the local communities who pay the costs of living with them. So until all of the non-hunting tourism operators pay a fair share of their profits to the conservancies they will continue to see consumptive use as the best form of compensation for their losses.

Although the trophy hunting outfitters pay market-related prices for the animals their clients hunt, their recognition of the local communities' contribution to conservation is no better than that of their non-consumptive counterparts. For too many late payments have been the order of the day, and in some cases legal action has been the only way to try and recover what conservancies are owed. Working with inexperienced rural communities is not without its problems, and cases of corruption and mismanagement have occurred, but it is incumbent on those of us who had a more privileged upbringing to set the example.

The conservation ethics of the professional hunters has also not always been as good as they claim them to be. When an elephant or lion has been declared a problem animal by the MET and a permit is issued to the local concessionaire to dispatch it, all too often the largest tusker or lion with the biggest mane is shot, whether it was the one causing the problems or not. An even worse case happened in Sesfontein Conservancy in 2010.

Five years earlier a small pride of lions took up residence in the lower Hoarusib, and although they killed donkeys and some cattle, including a bull belonging to the headman of Purros, Daniel Karutjaiva, the community decided to live with them. Since the drought their herds and flocks had recovered, and with two joint-venture lodges and a popular campsite the local people were doing very well from tourism. In time the lions became so habituated they sometimes spent the day resting in the shade a few hundred metres from the conservancy office, but they were now regarded as *their* lions – just another species that the government had given them the responsibility to conserve.

To enable the community to earn direct income from the lions, in 2009 Flip Stander trained three local men in the use of radio tracking equipment in order to monitor their movements and also find them for tourists. The project had just started when 'Leonardo', the adult male in the pride, wandered into the adjoining Sesfontein Conservancy and was shot by a client of Keith Wright, the trophy hunter who had the concession there and in Anabeb Conservancy. As Wright knew there were no lions on the quota for Sesfontein, and only a lioness on his Anabeb quota, the MET decided to charge him. But it will not replace Leonardo's value as a tourist attraction in this spectacular desert environment. His death is also a setback to the planned 'lion tours' that could be an example to other conservancies that there are non-consumptive ways of benefiting from predators.

It was time for a different kind of tourism in communal areas, and Anders Johansson came up with a concept: if the present operators did not recognise the local communities' contribution to their success, then conservancies should start their own safari company. He and his wife Agneta provided a loan to purchase vehicles and high-quality camping equipment, and as the five far north-western conservancies he chose were not able to run the tours, a top-class manager and host was employed. The man appointed was Russell Vinjevold, who had been a senior nature conservator in Etosha, before guiding walking trails in Kruger National Park and then operating mobile safaris in the Kaokoveld.

As Kunene Conservancy Safaris (KCS) supports the government's policy of sustainable use, and recognises the need to harvest wildlife to reduce the risk of a major die-off in a future drought, as well as generate income for local people, it also has a separate hunting arm. Conservancy Hunting Safaris (CHS) is managed by Tommy Hall, who was a senior nature conservator in Damaraland before he became a professional hunter. It specialises in ethical trophy and premium hunting in the vast unfenced areas of the five participating conservancies.

The goal of KCS and CHS is not just to give all of the profits to the local communities, but also to actively involve them, so that their clients can socially interact with the people who live in the area and are conserving its wildlife. In this way they will get an authentic experience, and not just the sightseeing trip offered by the present private sector tourism operators. As both companies are led by experienced conservationists they will also get an insider's perspective of Namibia's CBNRM programme.

*　*　*

A major challenge facing most conservancies is addressing the losses suffered by local farmers as a result of the increasing numbers of wildlife within them. In the Eastern Caprivi, where poaching by local people is now rare, large numbers of elephants have crossed the Chobe and Linyanti rivers from Botswana, and in low-rainfall years the damage caused to the maize and millet crops is considerable. At these times Beaven Munali's weekly radio programme on nature conservation is inundated by telephone calls from angry community members, and in 2009 it led to the local Farmer's Union petitioning the government against conservancies.

Although there are fewer problems caused by elephants in Kunene Region, on the highlands a few people have taken matters into their own hands and shot bulls that came too close to their homes, or broke into their maize fields. Here the greatest losses are from predators that annually kill hundreds of thousands of dollars' worth of livestock. One of the achievements of the CBNRM programme has been to stop the indiscriminate killing of lions, leopards and cheetah, but with their numbers increasing something needed to be done to prevent the situation from spiralling out of control. Fortunately, most of the problem-causing species have a high value to tourism operators and trophy hunters and, therefore, have the greatest potential to generate financial benefits. But the income they earn is shared between the whole community, whereas the costs are borne by individual households.

Direct compensation is a sensitive issue to governments, because it opens them up to liability for a wide range of public losses to wild animals. In most cases they also do not have the funds to pay out claims, or the manpower to verify and process them. The high annual premiums charged by insurance companies for numerous relatively minor claims made this route too expensive. However, many conservancies were earning good income, had game guards to ensure that their members did not fabricate claims, and the staff to do the paperwork involved. The solution was for them to start their own 'self-insurance scheme'. With start-up funding from the Goldman Foundation in

San Francisco, in 2003 IRDNC facilitated a pilot Human–Animal Conflict Conservancy Self-Insurance Scheme (HACCSIS) for livestock losses in three Kunene and two Caprivi conservancies.

The first step was to negotiate with conservancy representatives and the local traditional authority which predators should be included and which domestic animals farmers could claim for, and to put a value on them. Mutually agreed conditions were also laid down for when compensation would not be paid, which formed the basis of each conservancy's problem animal management strategy. The game guards were given responsibility for confirming that livestock deaths were actually caused by predators and a quarterly review panel was set up, comprising regional MET and NGO staff, as well as members from the traditional authority and conservancy committees. In the trial first year IRDNC covered all of the approved claims, but thereafter conservancies had to pay 50 per cent of them from their own income. This was crucial to ensure game guards and committees did not collude with claimants over natural mortalities.

Even though the amounts paid did not cover the full value of the livestock losses the response was positive, and by 2008 seven Caprivi and five Kunene conservancies were participating in HACCSIS for predators, and a comparable scheme for elephant damage to crops was being piloted in Caprivi. However, just before the 2009 national elections the MET introduced its own human–wildlife compensation plan for all residents of the communal areas, using N\$2.2 million from its Game Products Trust Fund. As it intends to cover the whole claim from government coffers the scheme will be open to abuse, and N\$2.2 million will not last very long.

Although human–wildlife conflict management and mitigation strategies can reduce the antagonism local farmers feel towards elephants and predators, the CBNRM Programme will not be secure until all the conservancies' members are in some way benefiting from them. And yet a decade after Torra and /Hoadi //Hoas were gazetted, less than 15 conservancies earned enough income to undertake community development projects or provide individual dividends, and Sesfontein was only just able to cover its management costs. As its members and those of Anabeb had 25 years earlier voluntarily not used the huge Palmwag concession for grazing, enabling it to become one of the most valuable wildlife areas in the country, this is morally unjustifiable and a blot on the record of the exclusive concession holder.

To rectify the situation, in 2008 the Namibian Cabinet passed the Policy on Tourism and Wildlife Concessions on State Land, under which neigh-

bouring conservancies would be granted the head concession and allowed
to choose their own partners to operate them. The same year /Hoadi //Hoas
and Ehirovipuka became joint concessionaires of Hobatere, and Omatendeka
and Anabeb were awarded the Etendeka concession in 2009. In 2010 the head
concession for Palmwag was granted to Sesfontein, Anabeb and Torra. If they
are all able to negotiate fair joint-venture contracts for the rights over these
prime tourism destinations, the wildlife heartland in Kunene Region – where
CBNRM in Namibia was born – will finally have achieved its full potential of
benefiting both wild animals and local people.

*   *   *

The active involvement of the rural communities proved the most successful
way of conserving rhino in the 1980s, but the recent resurgence of poaching
has shown that the demand for their horns in China and Vietnam is still there,
and the prices being offered on the black market are now much higher. In five
years since 2004 a total of 174 rhino were killed in Zimbabwe, and although
37 suspects were arrested only seven have been convicted. Returning to their
old ways, the wildlife authorities there also shot nine poachers, but the illegal hunting by highly mobile gangs has continued. In South Africa over 400
rhino were killed from 2006 to August 2010, with most of the poaching taking place on private land, but a significant number were killed in the Kruger
National Park.

The value of ivory has also tripled, and Kenya had at least 270 elephants
poached in 2009, while Zambia officially lost 135 elephants, although DNA
testing of confiscated ivory suggested the number is much higher. Caprivi
also had a spate of elephant poaching in 2009, but most of those involved
were convicted thanks to information provided by local people and the diligent follow-up by MET rangers and IRDNC staff. In two cases poachers from
Zambia were chased away by villagers living nearby before they were able to
remove the tusks.

Support for wildlife conservation within conservancies is still high, but the
stakes have been raised and it needs only a few local community members to
become disillusioned by the lack of financial benefits for commercial poaching to start again. The old men who cared about wild animals for altruistic
reasons only have passed away, and the younger generation is much more
materialistic. To succeed in this round the private sector must become real

partners, so that the whole community regards these iconic species as more valuable *to them* alive than dead.

By devolving the rights over consumptive and non-consumptive use of wildlife to the local communities, Namibia's CBNRM programme has kept the poaching of elephants and rhinos under control, but can it work in other countries? Although the situation on the ground will be different in each case, the basic principles, if not the actual method of implementing them, hold true wherever illegal hunting occurs. Even where the poachers come from across international borders, it will be difficult for them to operate undetected by the communities that live in or around the threatened species' range. And if they are working with the conservation authorities, the information they provide will be crucial for making arrests and getting convictions. Military tactics may contain the situation, but with so much money now involved will it alone *stop* the killing of elephants and rhino?

A harder question to answer is whether CBNRM principles are also valid for other criminal activities. However, it is worth remembering that in all communities the great majority of people are law-abiding citizens, and the primary focus should be on *them* and their needs, not on the less than 5 per cent who are the actual offenders. In the Kaokoveld during the 1980s we were losing the game until the local people joined our side, after which their support only needed to be activated. How it is done must be worked out *with* and not *for* them, and cannot be 'rolled out' in other communities or countries. This is a time- and resource-consuming process, but the rewards will more than repay the costs.

On a continent where conservation success stories are rare, the Namibian CBNRM programme is recognised as one of the few examples of combining modern science with local skills and knowledge that has been successfully put into practice. But conservancies have done more than just increase wildlife populations on communal land, thereby enabling subsistence farmers to diversify their economies. They have also addressed a major problem faced when managing common property resources, namely the lack of a legally mandated representative structure at the grassroots level. Without it, Garret Hardin's predicted 'tragedy of the commons' is inevitable. But through conservancy committees that are accountable to the broader community a range of previously intractable impediments to the sustainable management of natural resources and the equitable distribution of the benefits derived from them are removed.

In spite of their shortcomings conservancies can also be valuable in mediating labour disputes. Unfortunately, lodge operators usually try to resolve serious cases on their own, which often leads to fuel and not water being thrown onto the flames. However, where a good relationship has been established between the management and their conservancy even the most difficult issues can be amicably resolved. And if the committee is unable to help the traditional authority should be asked to step in – but they are more likely to do so if they have been kept regularly informed of the progress, and not just the problems, at the lodge.

As many tourism operators have found, even if a representative committee is in place, things do not always go smoothly. The income from hunting and photographic tourism has brought a new dynamic into previously subsistence farming communities and the introduction of western education has led to members of the 'me now' generation being elected to positions of power. But it is worth looking at what can happen where no conservancy exists. The situation around the Epupa Falls is a good example.

Because it is a prime tourism site, a privately owned tented camp and a campsite were established here after independence, and another rustic lodge was built at the time of the Epupa Dam EIA. As the community did not have any rights or responsibilities over their natural resources they initially received nothing at all from the operators, who still only pay a small amount to Chief Kapika. The frustration of the local people has resulted in a generally unfriendly attitude towards tourists, as well as the soliciting of money at the viewpoint, or for just walking on the path downriver. But worst of all is the unregulated development taking place at Epupa, which apart from the untidy village with bars and disco music now includes another lodge overlooking the falls that did not do an EIA, and will impact on the experience of other visitors to this major tourist attraction.

A recent trend has been the establishment of transfrontier conservation areas (TFCAs) spearheaded by South Africa's Peace Parks Foundation. However, a mistake made when creating the TFCA across the Kruger National Park's eastern border with Mozambique was not to involve the local people living along the Limpopo River before elephants were translocated onto their land. The hostility it caused towards the conservation authorities could have been avoided if there had been a local structure to communicate through and to jointly manage and mitigate the human–wildlife conflict that was bound to occur.

The Kavango-Zambezi (KAZA) TFCA, involving five countries – Namibia, Botswana, Zimbabwe, Zambia and Angola – and including over 20 national parks, game reserves and state forests, as well as many communal areas, will be the largest in the world. In fact, it is so big that no single institution will be able to manage it, unless it is broken up into smaller units, each with their own responsibilities and incentives to conserve the natural resources within them. The already active conservancies in the Caprivi put it ahead of the game, while Botswana has community trusts and Zimbabwe has its CAMPFIRE areas. In western Zambia the community resource boards and village action groups will need to be revived, and Angola has yet to establish a CBNRM programme. But if each component is given the support it needs, this huge complex will only require co-ordination between neighbours to make the future of Africa's largest population of elephants secure.

Where a socially cohesive unit is too small to be ecologically viable, the size of the area can be scaled up by a number of conservancies and any adjoining protected areas forming a joint management board. Along the Kwandu River in East Caprivi this has been done with the Mudumu North Complex, which comprises two national parks, a state forest and four conservancies, further cementing the relationship between the local communities and government officials. A similar structure is being established between Mudumu and the Mamili national parks, and in future they could be created along the borders of Etosha to jointly address issues such as poaching, human–wildlife conflict and fire management.

The CBNRM programme has improved wildlife conservation and built the capacity of local communities in many less obvious ways. These include an understanding of modern democratic processes at the local, regional and national levels, rural women becoming involved in the public arena, and the younger generation exercising their rights and responsibilities in a more accountable way, all of which are contributing to a stronger civil society. Together with the economic opportunities that tourism has brought, this has played a major role in transforming the communal areas from neglected backwaters into a dynamic part of independent Namibia.

What CBNRM cannot do alone is eliminate poverty, although this has been achieved in some conservancies that have high-value natural resources and very few members. As is the case over the rest of sub-Saharan Africa, population growth still outstrips economic development, and this goal will only be possible if both sides of the social equation are addressed. At the end of the Second World War Kenya's population was less than five million, but is now approaching 40 million. Namibia's wide-open spaces are deceptive. In 1970 the Kaokoveld was inhabited by 13 000 pastoralists, but this figure has more than doubled since then. Rangelands with decreased productivity that are supporting many more stockowners – with or without conservancies – are a no-win situation.

In the 1970s, when Dr John Hanks directed the Institute of Natural Resources at Natal University, he campaigned for family planning in Southern Africa. At the time it was a politically charged subject that was seen to be directed at the black population. But the apartheid era has ended and the liberation wars have been won. Although statistics show that when people's standard of living improves they have fewer children, Africa is in a Catch-22 dilemma: with more school leavers annually entering the marketplace than can find jobs, unemployment is increasing, which in turn enables fewer people to move into the middle class. In Namibia's communal areas hunting, tourism, irrigated agriculture or creating industries will not bring long-term prosperity unless reducing population growth is also put on the government's development agenda.

*   *   *

In Kunene Region wildlife has once more become part of the communities' economic and cultural future, but the underlying problem of rangeland degradation is still far from being solved. And if it is not reversed the Himba and Herero's pastoralist lifestyle will be undermined, and nature conservation in its true sense – the maintenance of biodiversity and ecosystem productivity – will be just an illusion.

The loss of perennial grasses impacts more than just livestock performance. Without a permanent cover for food and protection small ground-living species cannot survive, and if they die out, so do their predators. The once-common dwarf mongoose appears to now be extinct in the Kaokoveld, and although the disappearance of vultures, bateleurs and tawny eagles on the highlands is due to the indiscriminate use of strychnine, the demise of the non-carrion eating raptors has been caused by the lack of their prey.

Today very few hippos occur in the Kunene River, due to both hunting and competition with cattle for the sparse grass along its banks and on the islands. But the damage done to this previously pristine river is more than just the loss of grazing. Zemba farmers from around Ruacana have now moved downstream, and to cultivate their crops have cleared all the riparian vegetation right down to the low-water mark. This has resulted in large amounts of alluvial soil being washed away and the Kunene, once a clean river even in flood, is now as brown in the wet season as most other watercourses in Southern Africa.

The large seasonal rivers have also not escaped from the rangeland degradation on the plateau. The best example of this is the Hoarusib, which upstream from Purros spring used to be a winding river that supported many large winter thorn trees in its bed, with their pods providing an important source of protein for wildlife and livestock in the late dry season. However, recent exceptionally high floods have uprooted and swept away most of them, as well as straightened and widened the river's course so that much of it has become just a broad expanse of barren sand.

Before blaming this on climate change – a catch-all for most environmental problems today – let us first look at the effect that losing the perennial grass cover has on rainfall run-off. In my 1974 *Cimbebasia* ethno-botany paper I quoted an experiment conducted in the American state of Idaho, from the book *Before Nature Dies*, by Jean Dorst. He wrote: 'It has been found that annual pastures lost 60% of their water during violent storms, from rivulets which carried away 16 tons of soil per hectare. In neighbouring grassland, sheltered from overgrazing, where there was a predominance of perennials, only 0.5% of the water ran off and 15.4 lbs of soil were lost per hectare.' It does not take an Einstein to work out where the increased rainfall run-off goes, or why the larger rivers draining the Kaokoveld highlands now come down in such devastating floods.

Although the facts around overgrazing have been well known for many decades, the solutions have been stereotyped and the successes minimal. One reason for this is that most scientists advocate what they learnt at university, and many never move beyond this comfort zone. For them new ideas or ways of doing things are seen as a threat, not just to the existing theories, but also to the validity of their careers up until then. But science has been built on the shoulders of those who came before. The men who conserved nature in the 1970s were not wrong, but the problems now being faced have changed, and so must the ways we address them. In our dynamic modern world, the conventional wisdom can be a major obstacle to finding the solution to a problem.

A good example of this is the ongoing drilling of boreholes, now paid for by foreign donors, in spite of it having long been recognised that without reducing cattle numbers or implementing a grazing system around them, this just extends the area of degradation. In 2007 IRDNC was able to establish a partnership with the latest benefactors, the Icelandic International

Development Agency (ICEIDA), to introduce holistic range management at 22 new artificial water-points they were creating. Fortunately, by then many of the local stockowners had heard about the benefits of herding their cattle and most of them were prepared to do so. But we are playing catch-up in a game that started half a century ago, when the first boreholes were drilled in the Kaokoveld and the last lion was killed.

Another challenge faced by the IRDNC range management project was getting official recognition from the Ministry of Agriculture, at both national and regional levels. It was achieved by involving the government extension officers and rural water supply staff, and also because they did not have a better solution to the overgrazing problem. To publicise the advantages of holistic range management, in 2007 Colin Nott contracted Andy Botele to make a DVD, 'Herding the Future', in which local pastoralists talked about their own experiences of planned grazing. It was translated into five local languages and shown on Namibian TV, as well as in five other countries.

There are now 18 places in Kunene Region where stockowners are herding their livestock or have agreed to start doing so, and planned grazing has been introduced into IRDNC's Caprivi Project. Through the Millennium Challenge Account (MCA) – a multi-million dollar grant from the USA to the Namibian government for rural development – it will also be the central component of land-use management strategies in six other communal areas. For his tireless promotion of planned grazing Colin Nott has been appointed as the rangeland specialist for the national MCA programme.

*   *   *

In 2010 Namibia had been independent for two decades and Hifikepunye Pohamba had begun his second term as president. With peace restored considerable progress has been achieved, and although the gap between rich and poor is wider, at least it is no longer on racial lines. From a conservation perspective wildlife numbers have increased, with 90 per cent now occurring outside of national parks. Tourism has also overtaken agriculture to be the country's third-largest foreign exchange earner, and is running neck-and-neck with offshore fishing for second place.

Recognising the contribution tourism is making to the national economy, the parastatal Namibia Wildlife Resorts was created, which has upgraded the accommodation in Etosha and other parks, making them into world-class tourist destinations. Apart from a brief period when a few officials felt threatened by the role of NGOs, SWAPO's Ministers of Environment and Tourism, from Nico Bessinger to Netumbo Nandi-Ndaitwah, have also provided the strong leadership that Namibia's CBNRM programme needed. It may have been funded by foreign donors, but it is a home-grown initiative that has evolved from the grass roots of our society, and for this reason alone should be able to withstand the challenges of the future.

In 2010, using a grant from the Millennium Challenge Account, the MET carried out their first rhino translocation operation to the northern Kunene, where they had all been killed in the 1970s. Most gratifying was the enthusiastic response of the recipient Himba community, with over 150 people coming to see and touch a tranquillised rhino when it was off-loaded from the truck before being taken to the release site by helicopter. Even the older men, who had no love for rhinos in the past, recognised their tourism value and wanted their children to grow up with them – just as they had done 40 years earlier.

With many more local communities asking to get rhino back, Pierre du Preez, the MET official spearheading the re-introduction of wildlife back into conservancies, has plans to establish other populations in northern Kunene during 2011. Elephants are also returning to places where they occurred in the 1960s. A cow herd recently drank at Sanitatas for the first time in over 30 years, and two bulls followed the Kunene River from Swartbooisdrift to near Epupa Falls. After he retired from the MET Chris Eyre was employed to develop alternative drinking places for the growing elephant population on the plateau, to reduce the conflict with the communities there. The Kaokoveld has now come full circle, from having lost virtually all of its wildlife to once more being an example of how people and big game can live together.

The events described in this book, and what grew out of them, hopefully contain some lessons for changing our society and its values, which is so desperately needed today.

We cannot continue to despoil and overcrowd the wonderful planet that we live on. As Elias Hambo said to Margie and me when overlooking the Epupa Falls, in spite of our amazing technological inventions 'we cannot make a tree'. Nor can we make a blade of grass or a rhinoceros. We need them all, some because they are our primary source of energy, but other living things because they enrich our lives just to know they are there, even if we personally never see them.

Humans have been around for a very short time, but in our greed, self-centredness and scientific arrogance we are now disregarding the ecological principles and processes that made life as we know it possible. Although the earth will survive, if future generations are also to have the privileges nature has bestowed on us – that we now take for granted – we must change our ways before it is too late.

My last words are to the younger readers, who can easily be overwhelmed by the magnitude and complexity of the problems the world is facing today. If you believe in a cause and are prepared to stand up for it with passion and perseverance, you can make a difference. Conserving our natural environment will not make you materially rich, but there is no greater satisfaction than having made our planet a better place to live on, even if it is just in a very small way.

BIBLIOGRAPHY

Adams, Jonathan S. and Thomas O. McShane. *The Myth of Wild Africa: Conservation without Illusion.* W.W. Norton & Company, New York, 1992.

Andersson, Charles John. *Lake Ngami.* Hurst and Blackett Publishers, London, 1856. Reprinted by C. Struik, Cape Town, 1967.

Andersson, Charles John. *Notes of Travel in South Africa.* Hurst and Blackett Publishers, London, 1875. Reprinted by C. Struik, Cape Town, 1969.

Andersson, Charles John. *The Okavango River.* Hurst and Blackett Publishers, London, 1861. Reprinted by C. Struik, Cape Town, 1968.

Bond, Creina. 'A stitch in time', *African Wildlife*, vol. 29, no.1, 1975.

Bond, Creina. 'When it is late afternoon', *African Wildlife*, vol. 30, no. 2, 1976.

Bond, Creina. 'A black man's view of game ranching', *African Wildlife*, vol. 30, no. 4, 1976.

Bonner, Raymond. *At the Hand of Man.* Alfred A. Knopf, New York and Random House, Toronto, 1993.

Bradley Martin, Esmond and Chryssee. *Run Rhino Run.* Chatto & Windus, London, 1982.

Buthelezi, Chief Gatsha. 'We will protect wildlife, but we need your help', *African Wildlife*, vol. 25, no. 3, 1971.

Cubitt, Gerald and Garth Owen-Smith. *Namibia the Untamed Land.* Don Nelson Publishers, Cape Town, 1981.

Dasman, R.F., J.P. Milton and P.M. Freeman. *Ecological Principles for Economic Development.* New York, Wiley, 1973.

Gibson, Clark C. *Politicians and Poachers: The Political Economy of Wildlife Policy in Africa.* Cambridge University Press, Cambridge, 1999.

Green, Lawrence G. *Lords of the Last Frontier.* Howard B. Timmins, Cape Town, 1952.

Hall-Martin, Anthony, Clive Walker and J. du P. Bothma. *Kaokoveld: The Last Wilderness.* Southern Book Publishers, Johannesburg, 1988.

Jacobsohn, Margaret. *Himba: Nomads of Namibia.* Struik Publishers, Cape Town, 1990.

Ledger, John. 'Wildlife conservation in Namibia for the 1990s', *Rössing*, May 1990.

Levinson, Olga. *Diamonds in the Desert.* Tafelberg Publishers, Cape Town, 1983.

Liebenberg, Louis. 'The tracker in wildlife management', *African Wildlife*, vol. 45, no. 4, 1991.

Loutit, Blythe and Malan Lindeque. 'A great step for the desert giants', *Quagga*, no. 17, 1988.

Malan, J.S. 'Double descent among the Himba of South West Africa', *Cimbebasia*, 1973.

Malan, J.S. 'The Herero-speaking peoples of Kaokoland', *Cimbebasia*, 1974.

Malan, J.S. *Peoples of Namibia.* Rhino Publishers, Wingate Park, 1995.

Malan, J.S. and G.L. Owen-Smith. 'The ethnobotany of Kaokoland', *Cimbebasia*, 1974.

Malthus, Thomas. *An Essay on the Principle of Population.* J. Johnson, London, 1798; Electronic Scholarly Publishing Project, 1998, sourced at http://www.esp.org.

Marks, Stuart A. *The Imperial Lion: Human Dimensions of Wildlife Management in Central Africa.* Westview Press, Boulder, Colorado, 1984.

Marsh, John H. *Skeleton Coast.* Kuiseb Verslag, Namibia, 2006.

McShane, Thomas O. and Michael P. Wells (eds). *Getting Biodiversity Projects to Work: Towards More Effective Conservation and Development.* Columbia University Press, New York. 2004.

'Milking the elephant, milking the rhino', *Insight Namibia*, June 2010.

Mokgoko, Kgosi E.M. 'Conservation and the black community', Wildlife Society Diamond Jubilee Issue, 1986.

Moltke, J von. *Jagkonings.* Protea Boekhuis, Pretoria, 1943, reprinted 2003.

Montgomery, Sharon. 'Operation Bicornis: a new initiative to save Damaraland's black rhino', *African Wildlife*, vol. 43, no. 5, 1989.

Owen-Smith, Garth. 'Through the Kunene Gorge on foot', *African Wildlife*, vol. 24, no. 2, 1970.

Owen-Smith, Garth. 'The Kaokoveld: last wilderness', *African Wildlife*, vol. 26, no. 2, 1972.

Owen-Smith, Garth. 'Proposal for a game reserve in the Western Kaokoveld', *South African Journal of Science*, vol. 68, no. 2, 1972.

Owen-Smith, Garth. 'The Kaokoveld, South West Africa/Namibia's threatened wilderness', *African Wildlife*, vol. 40, no. 3, 1986.

Owen-Smith, Garth. 'Wildlife conservation in Africa: there is another way', *Quagga*, no. 17, 1987.

Owen-Smith, Garth. 'Wildlife management in Sub-Saharan Africa', *Quagga*, no. 22, 1988.

Owen-Smith, Garth. 'The evolution of community-based natural resource management in Namibia', *Community-based Conservation in Tanzania*, IUCN Species Survival Commission, no. 15, 1996.

Owen-Smith, June. 'Zulu Safari', *African Wildlife*, vol. 29, no. 4, 1975.

Potgieter, De Wet. *Contraband: South Africa and the International Trade in Ivory and Rhino Horn.* Queillerie Publishers, Cape Town, 1995.

Prins, Herbert H.T., Jan Geu Groothuis and Thomas T. Dolan (eds). *Wildlife Conservation by Sustainable Use.* Kluwer Academic Publishers, Dordrecht, 2000.

Reardon, Mitch and Margot. *Etosha: Life and Death on an African Plain.* C. Struik, Cape Town, 1981.

Reardon, Mitch. *The Besieged Desert.* William Collins Sons and Co Ltd, Johannesburg,

1986.

Savory, Allan. *Holistic Resource Management*. Island Press, Washington, 1988.

Savory, Allan, with Jody Butterfield. *Holistic Management: A New Framework for Decision Making*. Island Press, Washington, 1999.

Schoeman, Amy. *Skeleton Coast*. Macmillan South Africa, Johannesburg, 1984; updated 1996.

Smith, Robert Leo. *Ecology and Field Biology*. West Virginia University, West Virginia, 1966.

Smith, Robert Leo (ed.). *The Ecology of Man: An Ecosystem Approach*. Harper & Row, New York, 1972.

Stals, E.L.P. *Die Van der Merwes van Ehomba*. Nationale Boekdrukkery, Goodwood, Cape, 1988.

Stals, E.L.P. and Antjie Otto-Reiner. *Oorlog en Vrede aan die Kunene: Die Verhaal van Kaptein Vita ('Oorlog') Tom of Herunga*. Capital Press, Windhoek, 1999.

Tinley, Ken. 'Etosha and the Kaokoveld', Supplement to *African Wildlife*, vol. 25, no. 1, 1971.

Van Riet, Willem. 'Canoeing the Kunene River', *African Wildlife*, vol. 19, no. 4, 1965.

Van Warmelo, N.J. *Notes on the Kaokoveld (South West Africa) and its People*. Government Printer, Pretoria, 1951 (republished 1962).

Vigne, Lucy and Esmond Bradley Martin. 'Kenya tries to save its rhinos', *Quagga*, no. 15, 1986.

Persons wishing to get further information on Namibia's Community-based Natural Resource Management Programme should obtain copies of:

Namibia's Communal Conservancies: A Review of Progress and Challenges in 2007 and the annual updates for 2008 and 2009 by NACSO (Namibian Association of CBNRM Support Organisations), P O Box 98353, Windhoek 2010 (Tel. +264-61-230888).

Namibia's Communal Conservancy Tourism Sector, Conservation and the Environment in Namibia, Venture Publications, P O Box 21593, Windhoek 2010.

INDEX